DICKENS STUDIES ANNUAL

Essays on Victorian Fiction

DICKENS STUDIES ANNUAL

Essays on Victorian Fiction

DICKENS STUDIES ANNUAL

Essays on Victorian Fiction

VOLUME
43

Edited by
Stanley Friedman, Edward Guiliano,
Anne Humpherys, Natalie McKnight, and Michael Timko

AMS PRESS, INC.
New York

Dickens Studies Annual
ISSN 0084-9812
e-ISSN 2167-8510

Dickens Studies Annual: Essays on Victorian Fiction welcomes essay- and monograph-length contributions on Dickens and other Victorian novelists and on the history of aesthetics of Victorian fiction. All manuscripts should be double-spaced and should follow the documentation format described in the most recent *MLA Style Manual.* The author's name should appear only on a cover-page, not elsewhere in the essay. An editorial decision can usually be reached more quickly if two copies of the article are submitted, since outside readers are asked to evaluate each submission. If a manuscript is accepted for publication, the author will be asked to provide a 100- to 200-word abstract and also a disk containing the final version of the essay. The preferred editions for citations from Dickens's works are the Clarendon and the Norton Critical when available, otherwise the Oxford Illustrated or the Penguin.

Please send submissions to The Editors, *Dickens Studies Annual*, Ph.D. Program in English, The Graduate Center, CUNY, 365 Fifth Avenue, New York, NY 10016-4309. Please send inquiries concerning subscriptions and/or availability of earlier volumes to AMS Press, Inc., Brooklyn Navy Yard, 63 Flushing Ave.–Unit #221, Brooklyn, NY 11205-1073.

Dickens Studies Annual: Essays on Victorian Fiction is published in cooperation with Queens College and the Graduate Center, CUNY.

International Standard Book Number
Series ISBN: 978-0-404-18520-6

Vol. 43 Cloth ISBN: 978-0-404-18943-3
Vol. 43 e-ISBN: 978-0-404-90043-4

All AMS books are printed on acid-free paper that meets the guidelines for performance and durability of the Committee on Production Guidelines for Book Longevity of the Council on Library Resources.

AMS PRESS, INC.
Brooklyn Navy Yard, 63 Flushing Avenue–Unit #221
Brooklyn, NY 11205-1073, USA
www.amspressinc.com

Manufactured in the United States of America

Contents

Preface

Although birthday observances commemorate the past, they customarily also include a wish for the future—for "many more" celebrations. For living persons, the desire is for sustained life; for Dickens, who died 142 years ago, our hope is for the continued survival of his writings. The remarkable way in which the popularity of his works has transcended boundaries of time, nationality, ethnicity, language, age, education, and socio-economic class seems attributable to the diverse appeals of his art: sentiment and satire, joy and pathos, the farcical and the moralistic, the topical and the universal, complicated large narrative structures and precise, meaningful details, evocative settings and startling events. Like Shakespeare, Dickens offers the realistic and the strange, characters both typical and unique, and feats of language that remain fascinating even after they have become familiar.

On April 15, 2011, *Dickens Studies Annual*, AMS Press, the CUNY Graduate Center, and New York Institute of Technology sponsored an un-birthday event, "Dickens on Broadway: A Pre-Bicentennial Celebration," featuring a panel discussion by Dickens scholars and a performance reading of Dickens selections by Michael Slater, the author of an acclaimed recent biography of the Inimitable. Our bicentennial volume opens with a transcript of this panel discussion, edited by Edward Guiliano, the President of NYIT, who served as host and moderator at NYIT's Auditorium on Broadway.

The eight scholarly studies appearing next, like the articles in previous issues of *DSA*, reveal extraordinary variety in subjects and approaches while exploring significant features in fiction by Dickens and his contemporaries.

Because Russia has long been one of the many non-English-speaking countries in which translations of Dickens have attracted a large following, we take pleasure in including two surveys: Julia Palievsky and Dmitry Urnov, who, before emigrating to the United States and becoming faculty members in American higher education, served for many years as academics in Russia, have discussed "A Kindred Writer: Dickens in Russia, 1840–1990," while Tatiana Boborykina, who teaches in The Department of Liberal Arts and Sciences of St. Petersburg State University, has considered "Dickens in Post-Soviet Russia." We thank all three for offering their valuable perspectives on Dickens's appeal in Russia.

We thank, too, Nancy Metz for her informative, judicious survey of Dickens studies published in 2010, and we are grateful to David Garlock for his stimulating examination of "Recent Studies in Literary Darwinism: 1990–2010."

Once again, we express deep appreciation to all who submit essays for our consideration and to the scholars who generously serve as outside readers and provide detailed reports that are extremely helpful to our contributors and to us.

We also thank various academic administrators for practical assistance: President William P. Kelly, Provost Chase Robinson, Ph.D. Program in English Executive Officer Mario DiGangi, and Nancy Silverman, Assistant Program Officer, Ph.D. Program in English, all of The Graduate Center, CUNY; and President James L. Muyskens, Acting Dean of Arts and Humanities William McClure, and Department of English Chair Glenn Burger, all of Queens College, CUNY.

In addition, we are indebted to John O. Jordan, Director of The Dickens Project at the University of California, Santa Cruz; JoAnna Rottke, Project Coordinator for The Dickens Project; and Jon Michael Varese, the Project's Research Assistant and Web Administrator, for placing on the Project's website the tables of contents for volumes 1–27 of *DSA*, as well as abstracts for subsequent volumes. (These items can be found on the Project's website: <http://dickens.ucsc.edu>. Click "Resources" to find the link, at the left, to *Dickens Studies Annual*.)

We are grateful to Gabriel Hornstein, President of AMS Press, for consistent encouragement and generous support; to Jack Hopper, retired Editor-in-Chief at AMS Press, for many kinds of important assistance; and to David Ramm, Editor-in-Chief at AMS Press, for innovative advice and valuable guidance. Finally, we thank our editorial assistant, Julia Fuller, a doctoral student at the Graduate Center, CUNY, for her reliable, efficient, and intelligent fulfillment of many necessary chores and also for skillfully preparing a transcript of the "Dickens on Broadway" panel discussion.

—The Editors

Notes on Contributors

TATIANA A. BOBORYKINA is Associate Professor of Literature at St. Petersburg State University in St. Petersburg, Russia. In addition to a book, *The Artistic World of Charles Dickens's Christmas Books* (in Russian and in English), she has published essays on Dickens, Oscar Wilde, Bernard Shaw, and Mark Twain, as well as essays on ballets based on literary works, including *The Karamazovs*, after Dostoevsky's novel; *Anna Karenina*, after Leo Tolstoy's novel; *Seagull*, after Chekhov's play; *Onegin*, after the novel in verse by Alexander Pushkin; and others. She is currently completing an English–Russian book "Another Realm for the Word" on the translation of literature into the language of choreography.

NILS CLAUSSON, after receiving his Ph.D. at Dalhousie University, spent two years as a research associate at the Disraeli Project, Queen's University at Kingston, before joining the English Department at the University of Regina in 1984. His annotated bibliography of Disraeli is forthcoming in Oxford University Press's Online Bibliographies. As well as articles on Disraeli, he has published on Charles Dickens, Elizabeth Gaskell, Oscar Wilde, Matthew Arnold, G. K. Chesterton, H. G. Wells, D. H. Lawrence, World War I poetry, Arthur Conan Doyle, and George Orwell. He is currently writing a book on Conan Doyle's fiction.

DAVID GARLOCK has taught English and comparative literature at Baruch College of the City University of New York and English as a second language at Norwalk Community College in Norwalk, Connecticut. Publications include articles on Darwin, Dickens, and Hardy. His primary areas of interest are gender studies and the impact of nineteenth-century science on Victorian literature and culture.

NANCY AYCOCK METZ is Professor of English at Virginia Tech. She is the author of the *Companion to Martin Chuzzlewit* (Greenwood, 2001) in the series edited by Susan Shatto and David Paroissien. Her articles about Dickens have been published in the *Dickensian*, *Dickens Studies Quarterly*, *Nineteenth-Century Fiction*, and *Victorian Studies*. Her recent work addresses the impact of his first American journey on Dickens's thinking about language, the urban landscape, history, memory, and travel.

CAROLYN W. DE LA L. OULTON is a Reader in Victorian Literature at Canterbury Christ Church University. She is the author of *Literature and Religion in Victorian England: From Dickens to Eliot* (Palgrave Macmillan, 2003), *Romantic Friendship in Victorian Literature* (Ashgate, 2007), *Let the Flowers Go: A Life of Mary Cholmondeley* (Pickering & Chatto, 2009), and *Below the Fairy City: A Life of Jerome K. Jerome* (Victorian Secrets, forthcoming 2012).

JULIA PALIEVSKY, graduate and Professor of English, Moscow State University; Fulbright Scholar, University of Virginia; Professor Emerita, Nassau Community College, State University of New York. She is the author of *William Faulkner* (Moscow, 1970) and has translated into Russian: Byron, C. P. Snow, Theodore Dreiser, Faulkner, and other English and American writers. She is currently working on "*Hamlet* in Russia" for The New Variorum Shakespeare (with Dmitry Urnov).

DAVID PARKER has taught for the University of Sheffield, the University of Malaya, and Britain's distance-learning Open University. For more than twenty years he was the Curator of London's Charles Dickens Museum. After his retirement from the Museum, he was made an Honorary Research Fellow at Kingston University, London. He is the author of many publications on Dickens and other literary topics. His most recent book was *Christmas and Charles Dickens* (AMS Press, 2005).

KATIE R. PEEL is an assistant professor of English at the University of North Carolina Wilmington. Her research and teaching interests include Victorian, queer, young adult, and children's literatures. Her recent work includes articles on Charlotte Brontë's *Villette* and *Jane Eyre*.

CLAYTON CARLYLE TARR is a Ph.D. candidate at the University of Georgia. He earned his B.A. from Indiana University and his M.A. from the University of South Carolina. He specializes in eighteenth- and nineteenth-century British Literature and is currently writing his dissertation on framing devices in Gothic novels. He has also written on nineteenth-century literary bog bodies and has a forthcoming essay on Christina Rossetti's "Goblin Market."

DMITRY URNOV, graduate of Moscow State University, Member of the A. M. Gorky Institute of World Literature, Soviet Academy of Sciences; John M. Olin Professor, Adelphi University, Garden City, New York. He has published extensively on English and American writers and has written prefaces to Russian editions of *Oliver Twist* (1980) and *The Old Curiosity Shop* (1982, 1986). The author of "Gogol and Dickens" in *Gogol i Mirovaya Literatura* (*Gogol and World Literature*, 1988), he is currently working on "*Hamlet* in Russia" for The New Variorum Shakespeare (with Julia Palievsky).

JENNIFER PRESTON WILSON is Associate Professor of English at Appalachian State University. She has published essays on Richardson's *Clarissa* and Austen's *Pride and Prejudice* and is currently working on an article on Dickens's *Bleak House*.

MADELEINE WOOD is a sessional lecturer in the Department of English and Comparative Literary Studies at the University of Warwick. She is also a member of the Oxford University Department of Continuing Education tutor panel. Her research and teaching interests include the nineteenth-century novel, comparative literature, psychoanalysis, and gender studies. She has published articles on Charlotte Brontë, Wilkie Collins, Charles Dickens, psychoanalysis, and gender theory.

JOLENE ZIGAROVICH is Research Assistant Professor in English at Claremont Graduate University. Her publications include *Writing Death and Absence in the Victorian Novel* (Palgrave MacMillan, 2012), and she has edited the collection *Sex and Death in Eighteenth-Century Literature* (Routledge, forthcoming 2012). Her work has been previously published in *Dickens Studies Annual*, *Studies in the Novel*, and *Eighteenth-Century Life*. She is also assisting with the second edition of *Great Expectations: A Norton Critical Edition* (forthcoming 2012) and contributing an essay on the novel's illustrations.

Dickens on Broadway:
Future Dickens, Digital Dickens,
Global Dickens—A Panel Discussion

Edited by Edward Guiliano

This event was part of Dickens on Broadway: A Pre-Bicentennial Cel-ebration, sponsored by Dickens Studies Annual, *AMS Press, The CUNY Graduate Center, and New York Institute of Technology, and held at the NYIT Auditorium on Broadway on April 15, 2011.*

Moderator
Edward Guiliano
President of New York Institute of Technology and Professor of English

Panelists
Duane DeVries
Associate Professor Emeritus of English at Polytechnic Institute of
New York University

Jonathan Grossman
Associate Professor of English at University of California, Los Angeles

Michael Hollington
Visiting Fellow at Clare Hall, Cambridge, and former Professor of English at the
University of Toulouse-Le Mirail and at the University of New South Wales

Shari Hodges Holt
Instructional Assistant Professor of English at the University of Mississippi

Natalie McKnight
Professor of Humanities and Associate Dean for Faculty Research and
Development at the College of General Studies, Boston University

Trey Philpotts
Professor and Chair of the English Department at the University of Arkansas,
Little Rock

Nathalie Vanfasse
Professor of English Literature at Aix-Marseille Université (France)

For further information, see Notes on the Speakers at the end of this transcript.

Edward Guiliano: Good afternoon and welcome to the NYIT auditorium on Broadway for a pre-bicentennial celebration of Dickens. That means we are here on the eve of the two hundredth anniversary of the birth of Charles Dickens in part wondering "why" and "will." *Why* are *we* so interested in Dickens when so many of his contemporary writers have faded from our consciousness, and will we still be interested in twenty-five, even one hundred years from now? We are here on Broadway, the great white way, for discussion touching Dickens global, Dickens digital, and future Dickens. *Dickens Studies Annual: Essays on Victorian Fiction* is a sponsor of today's event, along with the publisher AMS Press, the Graduate Center of the City University of New York, and the producer of my tie today, New York Institute of Technology.

Dickens on Broadway. It makes one pause. Dickens himself was, of course, on Broadway during his first visit to New York in 1842 during his trip across various cities in the U.S. "Was there ever such a sunny street as this Broadway," Dickens wrote in *American Notes*. "The great promenade and thoroughfare, as most people know, is Broadway; a wide and bustling street, which, from the Battery Gardens to its opposite termination in a country road, may be four miles long." While in New York, Dickens and his wife, Catherine, stayed at Carlton House on Broadway. But the phrase "on Broadway" does not bring to mind images of Catherine Dickens or even Ellen Ternan, but of the theater. In the past century and a half, more than forty major productions on Broadway have emerged from Dickens's writings. The earliest was a production of *Oliver Twist* on Broadway that opened on February 14, 1860. While my favorite Broadway Dickens thus far was the two-part *Nicholas Nickleby* production, arguably the most successful was the award-winning musical version *Oliver!*—so successful that it was made into a movie. Which brings us to another manifestation of the Dickens experience: film. Of course, many a Dickens film has been played on Broadway, maybe even in this auditorium. So successful was the movie *Oliver!* that it won an Academy Award for best picture in 1968. [A video clip is shown.]

I would like to introduce and invite our distinguished panel to the stage. [Lists panelists' names.] Before I turn to our formal topics—Future Dickens, Digital Dickens, and Global Dickens—I would like to go around the panel with a question or two as a means of introduction.

EG to Michael Hollington: Michael, since you are the only one here who is from England, what was it like experiencing Dickens as a child?

Michael Hollington: I didn't have a Dickensian childhood; I had a reasonably pleasant one. I was introduced to Dickens earlier than to any other classic writer and I first read him in the form of *Classics Illustrated*; maybe some of you will remember these too. I had a kind of haunting as a child by Monks as my nightmare character, in Oliver's half-brother, you remember. There was another means a bit later when my father worked as an estate agent. Sometimes people would die without a will and he would look over their house and he might put the odd book in his pocket, because nobody would know, and the books were invariably Dickens. He put them behind glass, these little, leather-bound versions of Dickens and I thought I would like to read those, they must be interesting. (He did not, by the way, but eventually I did.) Then, I used to go to the library and read *Oxford Illustrated* versions of Dickens. To this day, I find it really difficult to read Dickens without all of the great illustrations. Any Dickens text has to have those.

EG to Shari Hodges Holt: When I say the word "Dickens," what is the image that comes to your mind?

Shari Hodges Holt: I think of an old photograph of Dickens that helped me get through my senior honors thesis. I was writing about doppelgangers in *Great Expectations* and was writing day and night, struggling to meet my graduation deadline. A friend who knew I was having trouble sent me a postcard that was a photograph of Dickens sitting astride a chair, leaning forward with his arms crossed atop the chair, looking defiant, looking directly into the camera, looking at me. So I pinned it to a chair opposite to me across the desk and every time I got to a difficult spot I would look up, see him looking at me and I would throw things at him. As a scholar, I think that encapsulates my contentious relationship with Dickens. I am intimidated by him, but I adore him. The fact that it is a photograph also embodies what drew me to him, not just as an author, but in terms of his entire career as a popular figure, as one of the most photographed of Victorian novelists. His celebrity and his ability to combine that with artistic genius is just amazing to me and is part of what attracted me to his work. That old photograph, which acted as a doppelganger for me as I was working, helped me to get through that dark part of my honors thesis.

EG: If I was your adviser, I would have sent you a little statuette of dueling frogs. Because Dickens could not write without his bronze dueling frogs on his desk. You all remember the story when he went to off Switzerland and having writer's block until the frogs arrived. Deadlines didn't matter, frogs mattered.

EG to Nathalie Vanfasse: How is it that you became interested in Dickens, growing up in France?

Nathalie Vanfasse: I did not have the Dickensian background English people have, who grow up with *Oliver Twist* or *Great Expectations*. I came across Dickens's work quite by chance in a public library, and it was in French, I am afraid. I was fascinated with some of the characters in *Great Expectations*: Pip, Miss Havisham, Wemmick and his split personality—which I somehow identify with in many ways. I was also captivated by the way Dickens could see into people's souls.

Although there was nothing really Victorian about my first experience of Dickens, I did compare him with nineteenth-century French writers. I was struck by the parallel in *Great Expectations* between Magwitch and Jean Valjean, Victor Hugo's convict. From there, I continued to read Dickens and became even more aware of similarities between Hugo and Dickens, for instance the way they empathize with very ordinary people and are able to see both the humor and the tragedy these people experience in their daily lives. I also later, but only later, became aware of the similarities between grotesque characters in Dickens's work and Balzac's. In short, this is how I came to meet Dickens and to enjoy his work.

EG to Trey Philpotts: We are on a panel here with very distinguished scholars; Shari didn't have an adviser who gave her dueling frogs, but someone gave her a photograph. So, Trey, how about your influences as a scholar. Who were your mentors along the way that introduced you to Dickens?

Trey Philpotts: I would instance a couple of people, actually three or four very quickly, two of whom I have never met. But I think all of us have been influenced by the books and the academic criticism we've read. First of all, Richard Altick has done terrific work and has certainly influenced me in my own scholarship. If you have not read his work, it is very accessible and fascinating; I would strongly recommend that you read it. A more theoretical critic is Mary Poovey, who has done wonderful work. She is very informed about the period, about an incredible amount of Victorian minutiae and yet she is also very sophisticated and theoretically informed. On a personal basis, the two people who have served as mentors to me and have been absolutely wonderful are Susan Shatto, who lives in Edinburgh, and David Paroissien. I was just talking to Michael Slater a few minutes ago about David's influence. David is the general editor for *Dickens Quarterly*; he has done a number of things over the years for the Dickens Society. Both Susan and David have been shown by him [Michael] what being an editor means, what being a scholar means, and the hard work and labor that goes into both. They are incredibly meticulous and demanding people, and incredibly generous people.

EG to Natalie McKnight: Let me ask you the same question I asked Trey but with a slight push to it by saying that there are people who influenced you as a scholar, but did they influence you to be a Dickens scholar?

Natalie McKnight: There are two men I would really like to pay tribute to, so I am glad you asked me that question. David Paroissien obviously has been a big mentor for me as well, but the two I want to focus on were people I had met before I really decided to be a Dickens scholar.

One of them was John Carey at Oxford University. I attended many lectures at Oxford and they were all informative, but some of them were a struggle—that is, a struggle to stay awake. But not John Carey's. He was so funny and was very good at bringing out the absurd patterns that you see in Dickens. He was a great reader of Dickens too. He had a way of punching words that really brought out the humor and the rhythm in Dickens's language, so that his in lectures, as opposed to people nodding off, people would literally be falling out of their seats laughing—those who had seats because it was standing room only in his lectures. I remember he had this way of punching words, like, ***babies*** and his eyes would [McKnight makes an emphatic hand gesture around her eyes]. I can't say it. I say *babies* and a couple of you chuckle; he would say ***babies*** in a way and everyone would just crack up. Even to the point that years later when I was reading his book *Violent Effigy* and I was looking for a particular pattern in the index; I came across the entry in his index: babies, bottled. I started laughing. I thought now there's a brilliant man whose index makes me laugh. How often has an index made you laugh?

And Elliot Gilbert, who was a visiting professor at the University of Delaware when Trey and I were there, had the same capacity to bring out the humor in Dickens. But he also could bring out the pathos. He would take a little bit of each graduate seminar to read passages from Dickens and people would be literally weeping around the table. It is the only time I ever wept in a graduate seminar, except out of boredom. Those two experiences together, the comedy and the pathos of Dickens, I thought now this is a figure I could spend my life with. And so I have.

EG to Duane DeVries: Here's a choice: your favorite character or your favorite novel in Dickens?

Duane DeVries: I will start with my favorite novel, which is *Bleak House*, partly because I am very close to it. I did an edition of it for the Crowell Critical Library many years ago and in order to prepare the copy my wife and I read *Bleak House* to each other aloud. It is strange, I have another weeping story as a matter of fact. When we got to the part where Jo dies and we are reading it to each other with the punctuation, like, *Dead comma your Majesty period Dead comma my lords and gentlemen period Dead comma capital right capital reverends*, and so on until we got to the part, *And dying thus around us comma every day period* [ch. 47]. And my wife and I just had tears streaming down our faces. It may have been because of the punctuation, I don't know.

EG: And would you like to take a stab at the other question?

Duane DeVries: My favorite character . . . maybe the one I would most like to be is Trabb's boy in *Great Expectations*. We first meet him in his employer's tailor shop and Pip, on the way to London, is getting fitted for a new suit. Trabb's boy is sweeping the floor and he sweeps all of the scraps onto Pip's shoes. Pip develops a lasting dislike of him from that point. Trabb's boy is something of a prequel to Sam Weller. And then, Pip encounters him again many years later after he has been in London and, dressed very smartly, comes back to this little town in Kent where he was born and he meets Trabb's boy once again. I have a certain passage (the following quotations appear in *Great Expectations* vol. 2, ch. 11 [or ch. 30], unless otherwise indicated):

> Casting my eyes along the street at a certain point of my progress, I beheld Trabb's boy approaching, lashing himself with an empty blue bag. Deeming that a serene and unconscious contemplation of him would best beseem me, and would be most like to quell his evil mind, I advanced with that expression of countenance, and was rather congratulating myself on my success, when suddenly the knees of Trabb's boy smote together, his hair uprose, his cap fell off, he trembled violently in every limb, staggered out into the road, and crying to the populace, "Hold me! I'm so frightened!" feigned to be in a paroxysm of terror and contrition, occasioned by the dignity of my appearance.

Pip is wearing a great-coat here. But then, Trabb's boy disappears, runs around the block essentially, and shows up again. This time he has the bag over his shoulder, and

> honest industry beamed in his eyes, a determination to proceed to Trabb's with cheerful briskness was indicated in his gait. With a shock he became aware of me, and was severely visited as before; but this time his motion was rotatory, and he staggered round and round me with knees more afflicted, and with uplifted hands as if beseeching for mercy.

Trabb's boy runs around the block again, and this time he shows up with the bag, which is apparently empty, around his shoulders. Pip writes:

> He wore the blue bag in the manner of my great-coat, and was strutting along the pavement towards me on the opposite side of the street, attended by a company of delighted young friends, to whom he from time to time exclaimed, with a wave of his hand, "Don't know yah!' . . . Don't know yah!"

And they chase Pip essentially out of the town. But then Trabb's boy shows up later, again, after Pip has been attacked by Orlick, and helps to rescue Pip from the cellar or place where he is being held. Trabb's boy, now an "overgrown young man," saves Pip by being "true to his ancient habit of happening to be everywhere where he had no business" (vol. 3, ch. 14 [or ch. 53]). Pip concludes that Trabb's boy

> would have been affected by disappointment, if he had known that his intervention saved me from the limekiln [where, DeVries inserts, "presumably, Orlick would have disposed of the body"]. Not that Trabb's boy was of a malignant nature, but that he had too much spare vivacity, and that it was in his constitution to want variety and excitement at anybody's expense. When we parted, I presented him with two guineas (which seemed to meet his views), and told him that I was sorry ever to have had an ill opinion of him (which made no impression on him at all).

EG: I think the panel has established two facts. One is that Dickens makes us weep, so Michael [Slater], your job later on is to make us laugh. The other is that it is intimidating to talk about Dickens when you quote his words because he's more interesting than we are ever going to be.

EG to Jonathan Grossman: Jonathan, we are up to you by process of elimination, what character do you identify with, and identify with is, of course, often different than who do you like the most.

Jonathan Grossman: That is a tough question. I think for people who work on Dickens the idea of identifying with characters becomes, as you work on them, a tough one because you are supposed to analyze those characters as well. So you are sometimes mixing together two different aspects and that can be hard. I would like to say that I identify with the omniscient narrator, but I don't. In fact, I was thinking that the best thing to say as a response to that question is something like what is fascinating to me is the way in which, as I return and return to Dickens novels, I can find excitement comes from the multiplicity of ways I can identify with different characters and the discovery of new analyses of different characters. And as you age, the experience makes you all the more aware of how limited is your knowledge: so for me, today, I identify with Arthur Clennam, dizzy, lightheaded, unaware of what's going on around him, confused by the multi-plotted world in *Little Dorrit* that bewilders him with the close connections he has to strangers, all of which is very real, all the more real sitting up here with this audience of people I do not know. At the same time, Miss Wade's analysis is cutting and brilliant in *Little Dorrit*. One would like to identify with her too. But why choose? I think the thing that is extraordinary about Dickens is the continual discovery that each character you might have dismissed or thought was stupid returns with a worldview that you have suddenly come to a place where you can understand it much more.

EG: So we've met the panel. Now we are going to turn to each of our topics in sequential order, Dickens Global first, Dickens Digital second, and Dickens Future third.

Dickens Global

EG to Natalie McKnight: Let's start with Natalie, one of our coeditors of *Dickens Studies Annual*. What evidence do you see today around you that demonstrates the global impact of Dickens?

Natalie McKnight: I am just going to give a brief survey based on my experience as a member of the Boston Dickens Fellowship and as the archivist and subscriptions manager for *Dickens Quarterly* and a coeditor of *Dickens Studies Annual*. First of all, as the subscriptions manager for *Dickens Quarterly*, I know that we have subscribers from every continent on the planet except Antarctica, and I am working on that. It is perhaps a revelation of what a geek I am that one of my missions in life is to have somebody in Antarctica subscribe to *Dickens Quarterly*.

I thought I would start out by focusing on some of the Dickens fellowships. I believe we have one of the youngest members of the Dickens fellowship in the audience today, he is Jordan Cerbone and he is sixteen. Jordan is my encouragement that Dickens is continuing on into the next generation. And we have one of the oldest members of the fellowship here today, Rose Roberts, and she is ninety. Sixteen and ninety just in this one room, so that is pretty good. This is just a quick survey of some of the fellowships we have around the world, including Australia, Canada, Denmark, France, India, New Zealand, the Netherlands, the U.K., and the U.S., of course, none in South America yet, but we are working on that as well. I just wanted to pay tribute to some of the fellowships around the world, starting with the Japan Fellowship and the Christchurch Fellowship out of solidarity with their suffering in the wake of the recent quakes that they have experienced. And then the New York Fellowship, with Rose Roberts, who is the president, and we have quite a few members here, a thriving branch that I have the pleasure of being an honorary member of. The Chatham-Kent fellowship, which is joining with the Dickens Society for a major bicentennial conference.

Then there are the conferences that have been going on around the world recently, including a Dickens conference in Italy, which unfortunately I could not get to because I did not have enough money, but that is another story. A wonderful conference last year in Aix-en-Provence; there is one this summer coming up in Normandy at the Château Cerisy. There was the conference in Jerusalem, which was cosponsored by the Dickens Project, which also cosponsors the annual Dickens Universe at UC Santa Cruz. There is just a plethora of conferences that are coming up with this bicentennial.

EG: We are the first.

Natalie McKnight: And I love that. Ours is the first, we are trumping them all by starting a year early. So we will always have been the first. There is one in St. Anselm in New Hampshire in July; again, of course, the UC Santa Cruz conference in August, and the wonderful *A Tale of Two Cities* conference coming up in February that starts in Paris.

Michael Hollington: It is actually four cities.

Natalie McKnight: Yes, it starts in Paris and ends in London. What a wonderful gig, I am saving up for that. It also goes to Boulogne and Rochester.

Michael Hollington: It starts in Paris and goes to Condette [near Boulogne], the love nest, then to Chatham and Rochester, and it ends in London.

Natalie McKnight: And then not to be trumped there is one in Lowell, Massachusetts, which does not sound as glamorous as Paris and London, but after all, Lowell was Dickens's favorite city in America. (Of course, that was 170 years ago.)

But it is not just conferences—Dickens's presence is all over the world. There are Dickens stamps in Botswana, Antigua, Barbados, St. Vincent, and, of course, the U.K. and the U.S. The Dickens Institute in Uruguay, which is a language institute that they have chosen to name after Dickens. And, as you know, my desire is to have something in Antarctica, and I just found out that Jordan Dickens runs the power plant at McMurdo Station in Antarctica, so it managed to happen without me. I have tried e-mailing to see if he would subscribe.

Michael Hollington: Maybe he would hold a conference there.

Natalie McKnight: Imagine that, a Dickens conference in Antarctica. Sometimes, though, when you search the web for the presence of Dickens, what you find is that maybe he is being drunk more than read. There are a smattering of Dickens pubs around the world. To give a small sample of these pubs, in Portsmouth, Ohio, they have a Dickens quiz; there is one in Bordeaux, in St. Petersburg, Russia. Holland has a Dickens festival at a pub; there are Dickens pubs in Stockholm, London, Ontario, Worthing in Sussex. So, one has to think, maybe next the moon? Imagine a Dickens pub module moving in for its lunar landing.

My point is that Dickens seems to reach people around the world wherever they are on the planet. There is an essay in a recent *Dickens Quarterly* by Monica Latham in which she looks at the fairly recent book *Mr. Pip*, about a teacher who is teaching *Great Expectations* at a school in Papua New Guinea. One of the things Latham points out in this article is that Dickens can reach schoolchildren even in this island in Papua New Guinea for two reasons: it is because of what they can relate to in Dickens and what they cannot relate to in Dickens. So it is both poles, sameness and difference. In Dickens they see emotions that they can relate to, recognizable, powerful human emotions that transcend time, space, gender, race. But what they also love about Dickens is that delicious alienation you feel when you are immersed in a place that is nothing at all like where you are living at the moment. They love all of that quotidian detail of Victorian London, the speech patterns, the clothes, the food, and none of it is recognizable. That is part of the beauty of it because they are experiencing a lot of horrifying violence where they live. When they can go to Dickens, they can go someplace else and it saves them, it saves their sanity to be able to go to someplace other than where they are living. I think that most of us here, we are probably all Dickens lovers or we would not be here, can recognize the dual paradoxical pleasures in reading Dickens, that recognition of human emotions but also that enjoyment of being immersed in a place that is completely other than where we are.

EG: Yes, Natalie, you illustrated that Dickens survives two hundred years after he was born, including by citing the Dickens Fellowship, which was established in 1905, so something happened thirty-five years after his death that demonstrates renewed interest. But then you came around to children in Botswana and or in some places around the world explaining that part of his continuing appeal is that you can escape to Dickens in Papua New Guinea.

So, Michael, what can we do about rescuing the widespread belief in many countries that essentially Dickens is a writer for children?

Michael Hollington: That belief has been around for some time. In Germany in the 1920s, the great philosopher-critic Adorno gave a speech in which he is already rescuing *The Old Curiosity Shop* from the German view by then that

Dickens had become a writer for children. I have heard that said from a number of quarters. I asked a Russian person, not a Dickensian, but I asked her who I could get and I have never been able to get anyone in Russia. I have got one old lady, a ninety-three-year-old, Tatiana Diakonova, who wrote on Dickens in Russia, but that suggests that it is not easy to find because she said that Dickens is for children.

By the way, I am editing *Dickens in Europe*, so from Iceland to Armenia I have been in touch with people, and although there is not going to be a conference in Antarctica, there is going to be one in Iceland next year, so that is the nearest I can offer.

But yes, [Dickens is widely considered a writer for children,] and this is reflected I think in certain countries. Do you know that the least translated Dickens novel into the European languages is *Our Mutual Friend*, which is one of the greatest of the novels, I think. I would myself say it's *Little Dorrit* or *Our Mutual Friend*, rather than *Bleak House*. It is not translated into Czech; for instance, I have got a nice Czech person in Prague trying to get someone, well trying to get some money really, as usual, but no luck. It is not translated into Bulgarian while just about every other novel is, and particularly *Oliver Twist* is a favorite, and that is the focus of the child, I think, for many. Polanski's film— I am not wildly impressed with it—he said, "I made it for my children," which I think is not an adequate thing to do with *Oliver Twist*. It does not compare with the great David Lean film, which we are going to see a bit of. Grahame Smith, the president of the Dickens Fellowship, thinks that Lean's is the greatest film. [Clip of Oliver "asking for more" is shown.]

I will end by referring to a fine French writer, who writes for both children and adults, Michel Tourney. He says that the very greatest writers are those who appeal not only to children; in other words, they transcend these categories of children's literature and adult literature. We, of course, are seeing the rise of the study of children's literature, and I think rightly so, in universities. But that particular transcendence of the two—personally, I think that is what Dickens offers.

Then, just to add to Natalie's list of conferences, there are a lot of things in Europe next year. In addition, there is a wonderful thing in Istanbul next year. It's a Round Table: Charles Dickens, Past, Present, and Future—with myself, Victor Sage, Dominic Rainsford, and Jeremy Tambling. On October 19–20, there will also be a conference at Thessaloniki in Greece on Births, Marriages, and Deaths in Dickens, organized by Katerina Kitsi and Valerie Kennedy. There is one in Australia in April that David Ellison is organizing. Regenia Gagnier will be there, and myself. So Dickens is truly global in 2011.

Shari Hodges Holt: Can I respond just briefly to Michael's comment about the movie adaptations? It is interesting that you brought up the David Lean *Oliver Twist* because I think the cultural response to that particular adaptation is in part responsible for later film adaptations that tend to sanitize the text and make it more appropriate for children. That 1948 adaptation brought up accusations of anti-Semitism with the depiction of Fagin in that film and that led to productions like Polanski's *Oliver Twist*. With Polanski and his background, you would think that he would be one to capitalize on the darkness in Dickens's text, the subversive and the radical qualities of it; instead, he chose to do something that would particularly appeal to his children. So we get this whole plethora of adaptations geared toward children, like the Disney adaptation where Fagin is reformed in the end rather than captured and prosecuted.

But one thing I would like to point out, even with the children's adaptations, is if we look at the cultural environment in which they are produced, sometimes they actually highlight some of the more mature aspects of Dickens's fiction. For instance, if we look at the Saban cartoon production of *Oliver Twist*—Saban Entertainment's *Adventures of Oliver Twist* ran as an animated television series for children in 1996 just after the great orphanage debate, the controversy surrounding Newt Gingrich's Contract with America, in which he proposed welfare reform that involved removing the children of welfare mothers from their homes and placing them in orphanages. Of course, that provoked comparisons between his plan and the workhouse system in *Oliver Twist*. In this particular cartoon production, what is interesting is that it focuses on a plot of Oliver trying to find his mother, who is still alive. In a situation similar to that proposed for welfare children under the Contract with America, Oliver has been taken from his mother by the government and placed in an orphanage and then in a workhouse, from which he escapes at the beginning of the series and spends the entire series looking for his mother while evading government agents. So I think this production is very interesting for how it picked up on the attitude in Dickens's original novel; an attack on a culture that criminalizes poverty and that lacks compassion for the poor was something that they found was relevant at the time this cartoon was produced. So, sometimes even the children's adaptations can bring up more mature issues.

EG to Nathalie Vanfasse: So, Nathalie, let us use that as a segue. Is it that today Dickens's works are becoming global, as evidenced by our previous speakers, because they are giving us some new means of understanding some of the socioeconomic and political issues all around us? Is Dickens resonating in many countries in times of financial crisis? Is that what Shari was getting at in America, wedding Newt Gingrich and a cartoon rendition of *Oliver*?

Nathalie Vanfasse: I would like to build on what Shari has just been saying. I find it interesting that Dickens has sometimes been sanitized, and I would like to point out that he can in turn be used to sanitize other works. To demonstrate this I will use another film adaptation from his work. *Slumdog Millionaire* is an adaptation from an Indian novel by Vikas Swarup, marginally inspired by Dickens's *Oliver Twist*. It has been made into a worldwide movie by the British filmmaker Danny Boyle. The film adaptation draws more extensively from Dickens's novel and, in so doing, it somehow sanitizes the Indian novel by reducing its Indianness and making it more global. In this adaptation Dickensian references give Westerners a way of understanding what an Indian megalopolis is like today. Just try explaining to someone who's never been there what it's like to live in these cities. One way of doing so would be to say: "Think of the smells, think of the pollution, think of child labor, think of slums but also of immeasurable wealth—in other words, think of Dickens." Dickens is one way, not of reaching a complete understanding but at least of getting a feel of those cities. Conversely, try explaining to first-year or third-year students, especially in France, what Victorian London was like. They haven't the slightest idea and sometimes don't even care. But if you suddenly ask them if they have seen the movie *Slumdog Millionaire* and its depiction of resilient street kids struggling to survive in the slums of Mumbai and scavenging on garbage heaps, they will immediately become attentive. The film gives them an inkling of what Dickens's London was like, and Dickens in turn helps us understand today's globalized world.

Another interesting point about Dickens is that he gives us a sound lesson in economics, though it is couched in humor. Who would have thought economics could rhyme with laughter? Take Mr. Micawber, for instance, who just cannot manage his finances. He nonetheless tells David Copperfield, "[Young man,] annual income twenty pounds, annual expenditure nineteen six, result happiness. Annual income twenty pounds, annual expenditure twenty pounds ought and six, result misery" (ch. 12). Now let me show you that, in fact, Dickens is giving us a serious lesson in economics. Lately, economists have become very interested in psychology. The way the economy behaves is not just mathematical; it is linked to people's psychology. A number of important books have been published by Nobel Prize winners, in particular, a book by Robert Shiller based on remarks made by Allen Greenspan about "irrational exuberance." Now that's something you wouldn't expect in economics. Economics are thought to be rational and yet, suddenly, economists are becoming interested in their irrationality. A recent book entitled *Animal Spirits* has been written by George Akerlof and Robert Shiller. Now this is even more unexpected: to think of *animal spirits* shaping the laws of economics! And the subtitle of the book reads, "How Human Psychology Drives the Economy, and Why It Matters for Global Capitalism." Basically, this is what Dickens has been telling us all along. Akerlof and Shiller show us that until now economists have not sufficiently taken into consideration two essential elements: the first is that people have corrupt and anti-social behaviors and that this affects the economy—think of Mr. Merdle—and the second is that we all behave sometimes in totally incoherent and illogical ways, which brings us back to Mr. Micawber. Akerloff and Shiller also claim that economics are made of stories. Just imagine: literature intruding into the world of economics! And yet, according to Akerlof and Shiller, the stories of our lives dovetail with the lives of others and they all aggregate into a national or international story, which becomes global and plays an important role in the economy. So economics and literature may not be as divergent as we think.

This brings me to a French economist, Daniel Cohen, who has written a book on the prosperity of greed. Cohen says that human history can alter the iron laws of economics and that at a given moment, people pathologically and collectively choose to ignore the reality principle. Now, isn't this precisely what Mr. Micawber is doing? He's a pathological spendthrift—he just can't resist spending his money—just like Little Nell's grandfather, who gambles compulsively. Besides compulsion, two other reasons for ignoring the reality principle are people's egos and wish fulfillment. Now why do people let themselves be hoodwinked by Mr. Merdle in *Little Dorrit*? Because it flatters their egos to be among the happy few who get to invest in Merdle's "prestigious" projects (Mr. Dorrit is proud to entrust his money to the great Mr. Merdle) or because Merdle's promises seem to make their dreams come true (the inhabitants of Bleeding Heart Yard think Mr. Merdle will enable them to live the Victorian dream). All of this eerily reminds us of of the subprime mortgage crisis or of the Madoff affair and shows us how modern Dickens still is and how psychologically perceptive his novels are. In a light and humorous way, his fiction gives us an important lesson about today's global economics.

EG: Nathalie, you may be amused to know that every year I need to give a state-of-the-institution address to a large audience and I have repeatedly quoted Mr. Micawber's annual income message in that speech.

Let me ask a question of the panel about reverse globalism. We have established that there is a lot of interest in and correlatives with Dickens around the world, whether it is with children or adults. I am teaching a course in poetry, and I have five students from China in the class. They are very fine students, very diligent, and every time they need to pull from their literary experience or history to write or chat online with their classmates they often quote Wordsworth because, I suppose, they studied Wordsworth in the twelfth-grade equivalent in China so that he is part of their literary culture and experience. Similar to Dickens in the developing world or elsewhere where he has remained popular. I am thinking about reverse influence, the perspectives on Dickens in Russia, or China, or France, pick the country. Will they, could they, serve as a stimulus for interest here in the United States or in England? That is, the reverse flow of stimulus of ideas to keep Dickens alive globally by reigniting interest here. Honestly, I cannot imagine an American kid reading some of Dickens's novels, the vocabulary is completely lost, and it seems to me that we are moving back to the comic-book version. So does anyone on the panel want to comment on the reverse influence of globalism on the source?

Michael Hollington: I certainly want to say that we are impoverished by only reading English language writers on Dickens and that there are in Europe hosts of people who illuminate Dickens. Kafka would be one of them, for instance, who wrote about Dickens's heartlessness. And it is very paradoxical that beneath the sentimentality there was, for Kafka anyway, heartlessness. I do think that as someone who works quite a lot on Dickens in Europe, I find myself constantly illuminated by reading critics in other traditions rather than in English, and I certainly do think that [not doing] this is a gross error.

Jonathan Grossman: In *Little Dorrit*, I think Dickens addresses the issue directly because that is where he starts to write in faux-French and addresses the monoglot nature of the English novel. So *Little Dorrit* is the book to think about for that question because in it Dickens is specially interested in internationalism. It is the first novel that he doesn't open in England; he opens it in Marseilles, and it has that incredible opening, "Thirty years ago Marseilles lay burning in the sun, one day." By putting the "one day" at the end, what he is doing is creating a false "once upon a time." Then, however, instead of actually beginning, there is a long opening in Marseilles where nothing seems to be happening, and yet time seems to be passing. Then we dive into a chapter, rendered in English, but held, we understand, in French by the characters, only some of whom are French. By opening an English novel this way Dickens seems to be saying something about the monoglot nature of the English novel itself and pointing out that things happening abroad—including people's foreign talk—matters not just at some later time to what will go on in England, but rather matters simultaneously to what is happening inside of England. England was not just the seat of an empire but, especially in relation to Europe, acting a part of an ongoing global world, and I think *Little Dorrit* is the first attempt by Dickens to deal with this international synchronic activity And if you look at the great maps of Dickens's travels after the 1840s, you can really see, biographically, why he begins thinking about this.

Michael Hollington: And, of course, the second part of *Little Dorrit* takes place in Italy and has a crucial role in the development of those characters who do develop, although there are only a few of them. There used to be a view that Dickens was narrow and insular, but I think gradually that has changed.

Jonathan Grossman: Especially that is true in the later novels with *Great Expectations* and *A Tale of Two Cities*. A wonderful joke of *Little Dorrit* is that the English now can stroll over to Rome where once upon a time England was the far-flung colony of Rome.

EG: In *A Tale of Two Cities* it is easiest to see this intentional parallel. At this point, we are running a little slow on our progress, but there is time if anyone in the audience has a question.

Audience Question: I like editorial cartoons a lot and it seems to me that in Dickens the grotesques and the characterizations relate to the kind of impact that editorial cartoons have. That there is a pictorial aspect that advances their impact, and I wonder if one of you could comment on that.

EG: "What is the use of a book without pictures," to quote Alice. Dickens's novels were heavily illustrated and we do get caricature elements in the kind of illustrations that go with it for exactly the point that you are making. He does sometimes make very subtle points, but more often than not, through comedy he just hits you over the head and that is where the editorial vein of it comes in.

Natalie McKnight: Also, one of the things I love about the illustrations—and, like you, [Michael,] I can't read the novels without the original illustrations— is that, yes, they are depicting a scene that Dickens had described, but Phiz was such a great illustrator that there is much more going on there, so it really becomes this dialogue. Dickens would not work with an illustrator who was not pretty obedient, but, also, he would not work with somebody who was not pretty creative. When you look into those scenes, particularly Phiz's, you can see his own creative spin. I'm thinking of Edith, in *Dombey and Son*, pointing down at Carker and her arm is this wonderful, strong diagonal and behind it is this illustration of Judith and Holofernes, and it is not in Dickens's description at all. It is like a magic box: you open a box, and there is another box in it, and another box in it. So here, you open a text, and then you look at the illustration, and there is the scene, but then there is something else there, and it just pulls you. It has this dimensionality and this offers interdisciplinarity, too, that I think really enhances the experience.

Digital Dickens

EG: Let us move on to Digital Dickens. How do we study Dickens today, for example? Trey, how do the current digital technologies influence our own research and our work in the classroom?

Trey Philpotts: One thing I think that we are all realizing now and certainly will realize in the very near future is the influence of Google books. Keep in mind the very simple fact that Google has currently digitized over 15 million texts.

They estimate there are 130 million unique volumes in the world and they expect that by the end of the decade they will have digitized them all. There are parallel projects by other research institutions as well. It is dangerous to speculate about the future, because one will most certainly be wrong, but what seems very promising in the near future, because of all this information that is out there now, is something that Franco Moretti refers to as "distant reading," which is the opposite of close reading. That is where you collect enormous amounts of data, which computers now allow us to do, and you study the patterns or mine the data. This seems almost an anti-humanist approach, but it is quite possible, and there are already some interesting things being done in this vein. I think quantification will be the next big thing in literary studies and in particular in Dickens studies.

Let me just give you a couple of very quick examples. There is something called an Ngram viewer, which is produced by Google labs right now. This is basically a way to do searches in all of their volumes, their subset is 5.2 million volumes and tell us exactly the number of hits. So, for instance, you could search for Charles Dickens between 1860 and more or less the present. What you find is kind of heartening and kind of not. This just records the number of hits, but you will see that in the late nineteenth century and early twentieth century it rises to a peak and then there are some considerable valleys marking the First and Second World Wars and then there was a rise after World War II; however, the downside is a fairly long term and steep decline which would suggest at a very quick glance that Dickens is being mentioned less as the years and the decades go by. Obviously, we all value close reading, but here you are looking at information from a distance, looking at maps.

One of the sites I want to mention is Dickens Journals Online. The University of Buckingham in England, and John Drew in particular, are working to digitize all of *Household Words* and all of *All the Year Round*. In fact, if you go to the website and are interested, many of you being members of various Dickens societies and groups, they invite your participation to correct their work. They have digitized the texts and are now trying to work on transcriptions of the digitized photographic representations of the text, so they are looking for volunteers to help correct the transcripts. Again, this will produce an enormous amount of information. John Drew sent me an email the other day with an article he had just completed using this vast amount of information in trying to determine if Dickens wrote this anonymous text in *All the Year Round*, about which we are not certain. He sent that information to a team in Australia and they looked at particular word patterns that are more or less unique to Dickens, and John has written this article that makes a pretty persuasive case that a particular anonymous article is in fact written by Charles Dickens from 1863; I believe it is entitled "Temperate Temperance." John, as part of Dickens Journal Online, will be mapping the locations mentioned in the various Dickens journals in very precise ways. But there are many other innovative and interactive things going on. UCLA currently has a site Hyper-Cities, which is not particular to Dickens, but it will eventually be a wonderful site where you have a number of historical maps for major world cities that are laid over other earlier maps. Along with that, there are a bunch of primary and secondary texts that are grouped together at this site, related to those maps and related to those cities. New York City is particularly rich, Los Angeles is particularly rich; unfortunately, London at this point just has one city. There will be a lot of new things in the next few years almost certainly, if technology expands more rapidly as it has done.

I have to remind myself that it was in the mid-1990s when the Internet took off, and that is well within my professional lifetime. Looking at how much it has developed from then to now is just remarkable.

EG to Duane DeVries: How do we cope with all of this information that is forthcoming, or is actually current since we can't even sift through it? Trey raised the word Google more than once; if you Google Dickens nearly 11,000,800 items pop up today, or the number at least. I don't know how you would go through all of that. So how do we deal with such masses of information, how do we cope, and how do we navigate? Students of course don't navigate, they most often take the first five items that fit the bill. What do we do about that?

Duane DeVries: I suppose the answer is you do not cope, really; but, there are ways of approaching all this material. It happened in the 1990s when I was working on the first volume of my Dickens bibliography, which dealt with bibliographical material. I had to confront the problem of the Internet: how do you put this into a bibliography? Well, you start with websites that have links, and some of them have hundreds and hundreds of links to other websites that are relevant to the website you have tuned in to, so to speak. I think I got my first links from the bibliography in *Dickens Quarterly* and that went back to 1989. When I went to those websites, there were all these links, and I started going off in this direction and off in that direction; you get to a link and there would be more links, and eventually you began to see which of the links you were connecting to were useful to you. So that is one direction. I think these were like bibliographies because of the links. I don't know what the other 11,000,500 sites that I never looked at were about, but many of them pertain to very individual things like people named Charles Dickens who aren't Charles Dickens.

Then I began to explore other possibilities and suddenly realized that there were many books I could look at on the Internet. Google books is of course where you go now, but one of the main websites I used was Project Gutenberg, where you could go and read Dickens novels in a plain text version. Now, when you go to Project Gutenberg and a number of the other sites, you have a choice of how you want your Dickens work, in a facsimile version with all of the illustrations, or a plain text version which you can copy, in whole or in part, on to your computer and have it permanently. Besides reading Dickens novels, you can read a good number of books now about Dickens. John Forster's big biography is available on many websites, as well as a surprisingly large number of works that arc out of print and out of copyright.

EG: So, reading Dickens on our iPads, is that the same experience as reading in a first edition or in a paperback edition? We are an iPad university, so we are all up on that.

I have a confession. I asked Shari, if I say the word Dickens, what comes to mind; well, when we conjured up this conference and the phrase "digital Dickens" came up, I wasn't thinking of database searches and Google books. I thought about digitalized versions of texts, but I was really thinking digital means new media. As film and movie adaptations become more omnipresent, will they encourage people to read, the way Oprah does when she talks about a book, or a movie come out, and we do more? Or, are they going to completely distort who Charles Dickens is because we find him through these new media representations? So I will throw that out to the panel if anyone would like to comment on the impact of digital media on Dickens, media being what we are talking about with Digital Dickens.

Shari Hodges Holt: I would like to comment specifically, since you mentioned digital film, on the predominance of YouTube. If you think about what you can do if you search for Dickens on YouTube.

EG: Which students do in class and the next thing you know, you are talking about somebody reading Dickens or showing their third-grade class acting out Dickens . . .

Shari Hodges Holt: And I do think that may be a useful pedagogical tool depending on how you apply it. If you do a search on YouTube for Dickens, what often comes up are students' own video productions related to Dickens where, as you say, they have adapted a scene from a novel and made a little film of it. They may have made a documentary film about Dickens's life or some aspect of the novel they are studying, and they post it on YouTube to share with other people, from which you get the interactive element of other people commenting on their video. I have actually used YouTube in my own class when I have taught Dickens where I have had students looking for video clips and then responding to them back and forth comparing, when they find a clip that is an adaptation of a specific scene from a novel, the text in the novel to the scene that they see on YouTube. Anything that promotes that kind of interaction with the students, that gets them involved in going back to the text, I think can be helpful and useful.

For other types of digital adaptations, aside from video adaptations, I go back to references in comic books, which Michael brought up. During the past five years there has been a movement towards more pedagogical uses of comics and graphic novels in the classroom. Graphic novels are novel-length comic-book versions that are intended for more mature audiences. Just within the last few years, several new, really fine adaptations of *Great Expectations*, *A Christmas Carol*, and *Oliver Twist* have come out. There are several companies that produce these specifically for use in the classroom. One company called Classical Comics produces adaptations of canonical literature, including Dickens and Shakespeare, specifically for classroom use along with teaching aids and other things. But they also have a new digital media format where they have partnered with a computer software designer that created a software called Comic Life. They gave the Comic Life creators several images from their graphic novel versions of *Great Expectations* and *A Christmas Carol* and then Comic Life has provided this as part of a teaching package to those instructors who have assigned the novel in their courses. Teachers are able to allow their students to use this computer software with the images already in it so that they can digitally manipulate these illustrations of *Great Expectations* and *A Christmas Carol* and add images of their choice to create their own digital comic-book adaptation of the novel.

EG: So that is a digital media adaptation. Is it a translation or an interpretation, bringing us back into academic discourse?

Shari Hodges Holt: Yes.

Nathalie Vanfasse: To enter into the text, you have talked about using images and you also mentioned using YouTube clips that show people reading Dickens. It seems to me that in the very act of reading, something essentially Dickensian can be expressed, particularly through voices. Why not also use MP3s? This format is also digital, and it enables us to enjoy Dickens's text in all its purity and vitality. People are still very responsive to his words, in part because, as we will experience during Michael Slater's reading, Dickens's writing, when read out loud, is really enthralling. Couldn't we find ways of promoting Dickens's voice and text through digital devices centered on the ear rather than the eye?

EG: All we need is a fireplace, an MP3 player, and we move back in time. But you are absolutely right, when you have students hear fiction or poetry read aloud, especially when the authors mean to have it read aloud, it draws them in because they cannot read the text, but with drama you don't really need to understand every word or every allusion to be able to love and appreciate it.

Audience Question: This is a two-part question: (1) What would Dickens think if he came back in our own time? and (2) Is there a social imperative to scholarship on Dickens because of the way our society neglects its poor? [This question devolves into a political statement, and the speaker is diplomatically asked to sit down.]

Duane DeVries: Well, Dickens certainly would have found a lot of material in our everyday society.

Trey Philpotts: I do want to respond to that. Frankly, it is why I teach. I want these students to read Dickens, putting aside technology for a minute, because Dickens puts them in touch with the world, not just the Victorian world, but the world we live in.

Natalie McKnight: Same thing, I pick Dickens over Dryden because he addresses these issues (although I like Dryden too).

Audience Question: I want to ask the panel a question about technology. There are now online concordances to Dickens, so you can look up the occurrence of a word like *labyrinth* and find out that it appears more frequently in *Little Dorrit* than in any of the other novels. I wonder to what extent this convenience steers the direction of scholarship itself possibly in a specious sort of way, or allows a certain kind of academic work to be done more easily that isn't necessarily more creditable just because it's easier to do. For example, I am actually more familiar with Milton than I am with Dickens, but when I read Dickens I always hear echoes of Milton. I was reading *Oliver Twist* where the words *heat* and *dust* came up in very close combination to one another and anyone who knows Milton well thinks that this is a reference to *Areopagitica*. But what I do know of Dickens leads me to think that it is very unlikely that Dickens is quoting Milton or has embedded some covert allusion to Milton; as far as I know, Dickens did not study Milton closely. Yet, the availability in an electronic concordance allowed me to draw conclusions perhaps out of context about Dickens's familiarity with Milton that I think would not strike a person normally. So that is my example, but my question is: do the new technologies steer scholarship in a new direction?

EG: I would like a shot at that. First of all, it does steer scholarship, but that is not bad. If you were getting a Ph.D. in chemistry, you can get it in three or four years. All you need to do is go to the best university with the latest piece of equipment, and you can do an experiment that no one else has ever done. No doubt it was a valuable experiment; you had a mentor and an adviser; you did something, and it was published and accepted. But you could not do that today because it would be old science if it is from ten or twenty years ago. It is the exact same thing now. We have some tools we have not had before to data-mine Dickens, and we will find some lost or unattributed articles, we will find some references from literary works, and we will be making connections in content and/or in form that we were not able to make before. Editors of journals, like us, will either say, this is nonsense so who cares, or, this actually advances our thinking on Dickens. So when we advance knowledge it gets published and whatever the latest technology is, we will have a period of a few things that will come out, or maybe a lot of things for a while, and then we will move on to the next technology. You do not abandon the past, you just are building upon the past with new tools that make it easier to approach the text.

Trey Philpotts: I will just quickly add that what you have said is very relevant for me because of the work I have done on *The Companion to Dombey and Son*, which will be coming out next year. It is a heavily annotated gloss on the novel itself, part of The Companion series, but the editors and myself for the book had access to millions of books on Google, primary source documents from the nineteenth century. Forget concordances, they are instantly searchable in mass. There is a danger to that; say, you have this phrase you think is unique to Dickens and you want to see where did that come from, you type it in and what happens is that you get hundreds of them and you realize that it is a cultural cliché. It does not sound like a cliché to us today because we do not use it, it has died, but it was to Dickens. Does that mean that if you go back and find the very first place where the phrase was used, that Dickens knew the work? No. So you have to use your critical skills, as with any other thing.

Audience Comment: Just a comment on what Trey said earlier about quantification of literature. Although I have much admiration for Google and those technologies, I think it is a real challenge to try and quantify the cultural impact that Dickens had. It is obviously much more than searching for Charles Dickens, but it is all kinds of other works, like periodicals and newspapers. We see it every day, the word "pecksniffian" being used, or "Scrooge," or "humbug," or newspaper headlines with a variant on "great expectations" or "a tale of two cities." So I think it is a real challenge to quantify the cultural impact of Dickens.

Trey Philpotts: Absolutely, and again I think a lot of it is using your critical skills to not take arguments too far and to know what you are getting. One of the things I noted when I did use the Ngram viewer was that you type in Charles Dickens or George Eliot and you get these charts that show how often they are mentioned. Surprisingly, from the mid-1860s to the present, George Eliot shows up a lot more than the phrase Charles Dickens and you wonder why. That seems counter-intuitive in a way because Dickens was presumably the more popular writer over the last 150 years. Why? Well, perhaps because Dickens can show up in a book by himself, people know Dickens, but if you just say Eliot, it could refer to any number of things and so you are going to get more hits. So you have got to use your critical skills to be able to make distinctions in this.

Dickens Future

EG to Jonathan Grossman: We have segued into Dickens Future, and maybe the future we are talking about now is just a couple of years away or a couple of days away. But I would like to segue to Dickens's future as a general topic and stay with the same theme by asking Jonathan, what if anything does Dickens have to do with this future in the communications revolution raging on around us, with the smart phone and the web and all of the digitalization we have just been talking about?

Jonathan Grossman: I do not have much time and I have an agenda, so I am going to take you briefly through an argument. But, first, I want to make a point that was not quite said earlier. One of the things that the quantification discussion we just had involves—and Trey was really good about all of the amazing things that the digital revolution does—is that it puts a lot of pressure on scholarship to use arguments, and I think this needs to be said. People can solve questions much more quickly; that means the arguments and what they do with the contextualization offered by data really matter.

So, we have been talking a lot in here and it is incredible how much the digital has come up on the one hand, and, on the other hand, "Dickensian" or "Dickens" has been floating around in this room, very much attached to *Oliver Twist*, and attached to poverty and urban squalor. This is definitely an important popular culture attachment to Dickens. But we also use the term "Dickensian" about movies and stories that have coincidences in which characters crisscross or where, say, we see overlapping moments in which characters just miss each other. In this interweaving, interconnected sense of Dickensian, it would be a truly Dickensian moment if one of the people sitting way in the back here happens to be someone I knew ten years ago. I am interested in this facet of the Dickensian—and how such coincidences relate to the communication revolution we have been discussing. I want to talk to you about this other aspect of Dickensian, which is extremely important for Future Dickens: call it 'the network Dickens'—the Dickens that is about crisscrossing coincidences and the seemingly improbable interweavings of characters' lives. I think those aspects of Dickens we call coincidences are actually reflecting a small-world phenomenon, the phenomenon of a networked world. We have been talking in here about the communications network, and the fact that we are inside the communications revolution is very apparent. I want you to feel your historicity in that regard for just a moment, in our smartphones, and Google, all of what we have been going on and on about.

To return to Dickens's time, it was a combined revolution, a communications and a transportation revolution. I am interested in those two revolutions, and for a moment I want to divert you to thinking about the other half of the networking revolution, the one that got me here 2,741 miles, at 471 miles an hour, in five hours, on a plane. In Dickens's time he had two revolutions going on, and though I think Dickens was seriously interested in the communications revolution, I want to shift our thinking for a moment towards the passenger transport revolution and the importance of *that* network. Passenger transport has been in a bit of a lull, though maybe we have Google cars coming that will drive themselves, or a return to steam cars, which were around in Dickens's time—that is, as steam coaches. Dickens was interested in the technological advances—the stage coaches, the trains, the steam ships—but what I take to be one of Dickens's main achievements is to anatomize the public transport system as a system. We all understand that Dickens could anatomize bureaucratic systems and critique the institutions that sustained them separately from human purposes and that is why we look, for instance, at *Oliver Twist.* We look at it as a critique of an institution against an impoverished human individual caught in it. We tend to think of that as the dichotomy we have, the impoverished individual against the larger institutions, but Dickens was an expert at analyzing systems generally.

The case I want to make to you is that one of the systems he analyzed and did not critique as severely, although he did critique it, was the passenger transport system that created the live networking of people. In the history of criticism, Edmund Wilson says Dickens is anti-institutional; Amanda Anderson says he has a systems view that is harmful to individuals; George Orwell despaired about Dickens because he thought he had nothing to offer but a cri de coeur to be more humane and so on. I think actually Dickens was a little more canny than that; he was analyzing the communication and the transport revolutions that were going on around him. Those systems seemed to be bringing people together into a network, and we are full-on a part of that network transformation. And this is why "Future Dickens" seems a no-brainer to me. There is a little bit of defensiveness in the room, but I go to Dickens *because* he is one of the early analyzers of a system and a network society.

In terms of the passenger transport network, I will summarize two argumentative points. First, throughout Dickens criticism, people have thought of his continuing to write about stagecoaches as nostalgic. He kept going back to portray the stage coaches of the 1820s, we noticed, but he had railways that could take him fifty-five miles an hour. Little Nell walks to Birmingham, and that trip only took Dickens a few hours on the train. He does a story about walking the long-distance highways, and in that story, too, he writes about the stagecoaches. Why does he keep going back? The account has been that it is nostalgia for his childhood, but I do not think that is right. I think that Dickens went back in time because he was returning to the beginning of the passenger transport revolution. He is returning, biographically, to a time when he was a newspaper reporter zooming around. This was not ye olde England. What

Dickens saw, and we have not remembered adequately, is that the transport passenger revolution begins with the stagecoaches and the acceleration that the stagecoaches provided, and then what you got was a train of coaches, and, that was a link, not a divide, between an agrarian society and an industrial one. And the essential link was that the stagecoaches set up a system of passenger transport between 1784 and the 1820s (when the roads were being macadamized), doubling the speed of connection, and then the railways just carried this accelerating system on. So the first argumentative point is to shift our perspective on Dickens away from thinking he is nostalgic for stagecoaching, but rather to see him as someone who matters to our future because he looks back to the beginning of the networking that began for him both in the passenger transport networks and in the communication networks in the 1820s.

The second—and final—argumentative point I want to talk to you about is a more complicated aspect of that networking by passenger transport: this is, that the transport revolution brought along with it something that is on all of your watches today, standardized time. This standardized time was originally called "railway time"; it brought you here on time, and is keeping me on time as best I can right now. Standardized time arose from synchronizing the nineteenth-century clocks at a distance. The problem was that as the sun went across even the tiny island of England, time was not the same east to west; Bath was about fifteen minutes off. When people moved quickly between London and Bath their times were out of joint. This synchronization of time that came about because of the speeding of the railways was also a dimension of the future—our future—that Dickens grasped. It represents the imagining of ourselves as a network embedded all the way down into our very temporal notion of ourselves as being synchronously acting around the globe. And I do not think that sense of contemporaneous, synchronous, connected global existence existed as strongly in the eighteenth century. So the next time you pick up a Dickens novel, and you find yourself reading about the separate characters acting in the "meanwhile" and thinking about how "meanwhile" structures those big, multi-plotted novels such that we follow the characters crisscrossing and interweaving, think also about the way in which a passenger transport network lay behind that historically and enabled that networking of which we are now a complete part. That future seems to be unrolling extremely fast right now in the communication network, and my hope here today, having traveled all this way, is that it will someday again unroll equally as fast in terms of passenger transport network as it did in Dickens's time.

EG to Shari Hodges Holt: Shari, you get the honor of bringing us full-circle. In the digital network we live in, visual adaptations certainly have been what is promoting Dickens globally and locally. How is that going to impact the future reading of Dickens?

Shari Hodges Holt: We tend to be defensive about adaptations, particularly with the film adaptations leading to a distortion of Dickens. We talked about how film adaptations tend to encourage the idea that he is a writer for children, but Juliet John in her recent study of Dickens and mass culture, which I think was published just this past year, argued that the film adaptations in particular have made Dickens the international icon that he is today. That is, he has reached the level of international icon comparable to Shakespeare largely because he has permeated various cultures around the world, primarily through film. So, I think we need to think very carefully about the legacy of film adaptation and how that will impact the future of Dickens studies. And, of course, Dickens's works have inspired more film adaptations than any other author, except perhaps Mary Shelley or Bram Stoker.

Rather than viewing the liberties that film adaptations often take with the original text as a violation or distortion of the text that threatens the survival of the text in the future, what has happened in about the last decade is that film theorists have begun to examine film adaptations as one means by which societies engage in an ongoing critical response to literature, one means by which they re-envision the literary source from a variety of culturally relevant perspectives, keeping the source alive within that society. Film scholar Robert Stam is one of the central scholars working on the nature of adaptation now and has published several works over the last ten years, using the biological evolution metaphor to describe this process of how film adaptations can help texts survive. He says, "If mutation is the means by which the evolutionary process advances, then we can also see filmic adaptations as mutations that help their source novel survive. Do not adaptations adapt to changing environment and changing tastes as well as a new medium?"

I will be focusing again on some film adaptations of *Oliver Twist* as a case in point. Starting with the 1948 David Lean adaptation, I want to focus on the portrayal of Fagin, the Jewish leader of a gang of pickpockets in the novel. Of course, when the novel was first published it was greeted with accusations of anti-Semitism, and then the same thing happened with this famous production by David Lean, which was carefully based, in its costume and make-up design for Fagin, on Dickens's text and George Cruikshanks's original illustrations for the novel. When this film was released, it evoked negative Jewish stereotypes for post-Holocaust audiences. We have to think that adaptation is a matter of interpretation, and interpretation is time-bound. It is inevitably affected by the time period and the historical moment in which the interpretation was created. This film, as a result of the post-Holocaust sensitivity about negative Jewish stereotypes, resulted in riots at its premiere in Berlin; also, the film was banned in the United States for two years until an expurgated version was released with many of the close-ups of Fagin cut out. And it was largely because of this film, as we talked about before, that for several decades film adaptations began to de-emphasize Fagin's ethnicity and to sanitize him of his more villainous aspects.

I want to compare that to the most recent adaptation, the 2007 BBC television adaptation starring Timothy Spall as Fagin, which was produced in a post-colonial environment that has attempted to give a voice to people who have been marginalized because of race or ethnicity. This production deliberately accentuates Fagin's ethnicity far more than in Dickens's novel or in Lean's movie in order to rewrite him sympathetically as a victim of an anti-Semitic society. [An image from a different movie is shown.] This is one of the only film versions to include the scene of Fagin's trial, which is usually omitted from film adaptations, and in this case, it is written to incorporate an intertextual nod to Shakespeare's *The Merchant of Venice* when the judge gives Fagin the opportunity to receive a lighter sentence if he will agree to convert to Christianity and he refuses to do so and is hanged as a result. So this sympathetic portrayal, even though it is different from the source text, asks us to engage critically with the source text in terms of its depiction of Jewishness, its use of Jewish stereotypes, and this adaptation also, especially with its reference to *The Merchant of Venice*, places the novel in a broader context of representation.

EG: If you are working on Dickens Future and you are talking about a mutation, that is forcing us back to see the text in two different time periods, and it will morph and that is the future direction?

Shari Hodges Holt: What I want to argue is that adaptations like this prompt us to explore critical issues within a text and also to reveal how we have read those texts at different cultural and historical moments. Instead of distancing the original text from the film adaptations in an effort to protect Dickens from distortions, what I would argue is that, for the future, we take a more intertextual approach that incorporates the adaptations into the study of their original sources. I think that is a challenge for us as teachers because most of our students know Dickens primarily through the films, and many of them have not even encountered him through the novels until they get to our classroom. So I would argue that, as teachers of literature, we can use film adaptations in the future to promote a constructive dialogue between visual and verbal cultures in our classrooms, and this is going to be a key feature to Dickens's survival in a world saturated by visual media in the future. How rigorously we interrogate that legacy of visual adaptation is up to us as teachers and critics of literature.

Audience Comment: Are you familiar with Helene Hanff, who wrote *84 Charing Cross Road*? She came very late in life to liking Dickens. She had dismissed him because she just did not like him, but then she began to cherish him, I think.

Audience Comment: I am going to bring up audiobooks which for the aging baby-boomers is a great way to get Dickens and you mention, Professor

DeVries, about reading *Bleak House* with your wife, and that is a nice way to get to enter Dickens . . .

Duane DeVries: It is better without the punctuation.

Audience Comment continued: Yes, that is true. And also we are a multitasking society, and an audiobook can free us up to do other things.

Audience Question: I am a student at NYIT from Old Westbury; we drove all the way here. I want to ask the panel, as a representative of the younger populace and as someone who goes on YouTube and Facebook all of the time, why should we read Dickens? Why should we read about a man who lived long ago, who wrote long ago and whose works are gradually disappearing? Why should we care about this?

EG: That is one way of framing the theme of the conference, and we have been trying to answer that question. And it is the right question because we live in a thirty-second sound bite world, so what is the thirty-second answer to this student?

Trey Philpotts: One thing I always tell my students, and great writers do this generally, is that Dickens teaches you to pay attention. Ultimately, to me, that is what a lot of life is about, paying attention to the world around you. He clearly had this incredible visual memory that he could produce in his writing, and he could see the poverty around him, and he could reproduce it very viscerally. If my students have the imagination, or I can help them develop the imagination, or Dickens can help them develop this, it is relevant to them. Again, I think for some of the questions we have had about the world we live in, he is very relevant.

Natalie McKnight: I will go back to my theme of sameness and difference. I think that there is much in Dickens that can shed a light on things that are going on right now, as people have been showing; but also, we should never only care about what we know. We should never only be absorbed in our own lives. If you are going to be a growing, thriving individual, you have to be immersing yourself in things that you do not know, things that are alien to you. Otherwise, you just ossify. So it is because of the sameness and how it relates, but also because of the difference.

EG: I will give our oldest attendee the honor of the last question or comment, and not because she has a great Dickens T-shirt on.

Rose Roberts: I do not think that Charles Dickens will ever go out of style. In all of his fifteen novels, there are passages that affect every emotion, parts that make you cry, make you laugh, make you angry, make you curse him, but they cover all of the emotions that we feel *now*. And that is human nature, so I do not think that Dickens will ever go out of style. As long we are around and emote and have reactions that we do as human beings, Charles Dickens will fit the bill.

EG: Hear, hear! I think that is a fitting note to end this section. Thank you all.

Notes on the Speakers

Duane DeVries, Associate Professor Emeritus of English at Polytechnic Institute of New York University, served as general editor of The Garland Dickens Bibliographies and is general editor of The Dickens Bibliographies, published by AMS Press, in progress. In the latter series he published Volume One (*Bibliographies, Catalogues, Collections, and Bibliographical and Textual Studies of Dickens's Works*) of *General Writings of Charles Dickens and His Writings and Collected Editions of His Works: An Annotated Bibliography* in 2004. Volume Two (*Autobiographical Writings, Letters, Obituaries, Reminiscences, Biographies*) has recently been published. He is also author of *Dickens's Apprentice Years: The Making of a Novelist* and a number of articles and reviews. He is a former President of the Dickens Society.

Jonathan Grossman is Associate Professor of English at UCLA. His first scholarly article appeared in 1996 in *Dickens Studies Annual.* It looked at Dickens's representations of Jewish characters, especially in relation to the narrator. His book *The Art of Alibi: English Law Courts and the Novel* (Johns Hopkins UP, 2002) then offered two chapters discussing how Dickens dealt with trial scenes as a means to thinking about his own narrative strategies. Grossman has just completed his second book, *Charles Dickens's Networks: Public Transport and the Novel* (Oxford UP, 2012). It is all about the nineteenth-century revolution in public transportation and about that expert in all kinds of locomotion: Dickens.

Edward Guiliano is President and CEO of the New York Institute of Technology (NYIT) and recognized around the world as an eloquent spokesman and advocate for global higher education, sustainability, and emerging technologies. A professor of English and a widely published author on Victorian literature—especially the works of Lewis Carroll and Charles Dickens—he has coedited *Dickens Studies Annual* since 1978 and is the author or editor of numbers books, including, with Philip Collins, *The Annotated Dickens*.

Michael Hollington is Visiting Fellow at Clare Hall, Cambridge, and thus a life member of the college. He was Professor of English at the University of New South Wales in Australia until his retirement in 2002, and Professor of English at the University of Toulouse-Le Mirail until retirement in 2007. He is the author of *Dickens and the Grotesque* and has edited the four-volume anthology of Dickens criticism in the Critical Assessments series. He is currently at work editing the Continuum Press volume *Reception of Dickens in Europe.*

Shari Hodges Holt is Instructional Assistant Professor of English at the University of Mississippi. She is the coauthor of *Ouida the Phenomenon* (with Natalie Schroeder; U of Delaware P, 2008), as well as papers on Charles Dickens, Gothic fiction, and film adaptations of literature. Holt is currently completing a monograph that examines cinematic and television adaptations of Dickens's novels as examples of how Dickens is "read" in other media and under varying cultural and historical circumstances.

Natalie McKnight is Professor of Humanities and Associate Dean for Faculty Research and Development at the College of General Studies, Boston University. She has published *Idiots, Madmen and Other Prisoners in Dickens* (St. Martin's, 1992), *Suffering Mothers in Mid-Victorian Novels* (Palgrave Macmillan, 1996), and *Framing Films* (Kendall Hunt, 2009), and she has recently edited and contributed to *Fathers in Victorian Fiction* (Cambridge Scholars, 2011). She is delighted to be a coeditor of *Dickens Studies Annual* and the Archivist and Subscription Manager of *Dickens Quarterly*, as well as a member of the Boston branch of the Dickens Fellowship.

Trey Philpotts is Professor and Chair of the English Department at the University of Arkansas at Little Rock and the Review Editor for *Dickens Quarterly*. He has published *The Companion to Little Dorrit* (Helm, 2003) and is a contributor to *A Companion to Dickens* (Blackwell, 2008). He has also published articles in *Dickens Quarterly*, *Dickens Studies Annual*, and *The Dickensian*. His most recent book, *The Companion to Dombey and Son*, is scheduled to be published in 2012.

Nathalie Vanfasse is Professor of English Literature at the Université d'Aix-Marseille, France. Her research interests and publications focus on Dickens's novels and on his travel writing. She is the author of *Charles Dickens, Entre normes et déviance* (Presses Universitaires de Provence, 2007) and has coedited (with Anne-Marie Kilday) a volume of articles entitled *Social Deviance in England and in France c. 1830–1900* (*Cahiers Victoriens et Edouardiens* 61 [April 2005]). She has guest edited (with Marie-Amélie Coste and Christine Huguet) a selection of articles on "Dickens Matters" (September 2011) and "Dickens and History/His Stories" (December 2011) for the *Dickens Quarterly*. She has also guest edited (with Luc Bouvard, Marie-Amélie Coste, and Christine Huguet) a special bicentenary issue of the *Cahiers Victoriens et Edouardiens* on *Dickens in the New Millennium* (February 2012) and she is currently coediting (with Christine Huguet) a volume on *Dickens, Modernism and Modernity* (forthcoming, Editions du Sagittaire, 2012).

Knots in Glass: Dickens and Omniscience from Boz to Bucket

Clayton Carlyle Tarr

When Dickens's characters use vitreous objects to observe, they evidence the author's fluid conception of omniscience at the character level. Following the pedestrian reports of the physically limited Boz, Dickens increasingly endows select characters with extraordinary dexterities that make them powerful observers. These faculties Dickens first grants to his villains, whose methods of surveillance prove oppressive and dangerous. But in Mr. Bucket, the formally unique detective in Bleak House, *Dickens demonstrates that omniscience at the character level can benefit both narrative and social progress. Bucket achieves this omniscience through his tricks of the trade: looking down through skylights, he mimics Lesage's lame demon, Asmodeus, and navigating London's dark underworld with bull's-eye lanterns, he becomes a Virgil-figure. By exploiting glass objects to achieve narrator-like access to private spaces, Bucket negotiates and connects the novel's many oppositions—geographic, temporal, and formal—thereby demonstrating that omniscience is not an ethereal authority reserved only for narrators, but rather can be a real prospect for both characters and perhaps the author himself.*

> Rightly viewed no meanest object is insignificant; all objects are as windows, through which the philosophic eye looks into Infinitude itself.
>
> —Thomas Carlyle, *Sartor Resartus*

The house of fiction has in short not one window,
but a million. . . . [A]t each of them stands a figure
with a pair of eyes, or at least with a field-glass,
which forms, again and again, for observation, a
unique instrument, insuring to the person making
use of it an impression distinct from every other.

—Henry James, *The Portrait of a Lady*

Rather than words comes the thought of high
     windows:
The sun-comprehending glass,
And beyond it, the deep blue air, that shows
Nothing, and is nowhere, and is endless.

—Philip Larkin, "High Windows"

Dickens uses vitreous objects as mediums for observation to push the boundaries of character omniscience. These glass gazes act themselves as windows to reveal how he imagined, and his characters negotiated, his fictional world. In *Dombey and Son* (1846–47), Dickens expresses frustration over material barriers to domestic surveillance: "Oh for a good spirit who would take the housetops off, with a more potent and benignant hand than the lame demon in the tale" (702; ch. 47). While Lesage's demon, Asmodeus, may lift rooftops, for Dickens's physically limited characters to gaze into houses necessitates a more "benignant hand" that is capable of exploiting real architectural and visual accessories.[1] "Let us view the workroom of a large establishment," *Chambers's Journal* entreats readers in 1855, "Asmodeus-like, peeping through the sky-light" ("Industrial" 328). Anticipating this connection, Dickens drew on the ubiquitous presence of skylights in nineteenth-century London to provide his characters real-world access to Asmodean omniscience.[2]

This essay will follow Dickens's characters from the ground up, starting with *Sketches By Boz* (1836) and ending with *Bleak House* (1853). As the novels progress chronologically, their characters move with increasing vertical acumen, and become more and more capable of realizing Asmodean observation. First, it is pertinent to establish that, in the face of over a century of taxation, skylights became not just architectural showpieces, but living necessities, a social injustice Dickens excoriates as a journalist and exploits as a novelist. In tracing the function of skylights and their relationship to the progress of select characters, we are able to observe precisely how Dickens draws on the conditions of the real urban world to imagine his narratives. Second, I will trace the movement of Dickens's characters from an embodied flâneur who walks, observes, and can be observed, to the extraordinary, and formally distinctive, detective in *Bleak House*.[3] I hope to reconsider this novel, Dickens's most ambitious narrative experiment, quite literally through the lens of Mr. Bucket. It is through Bucket that Dickens most explicitly explores, in Richard Maxwell's words, "the interaction between the apparently limitless metropolis and the limited human mind" (290). Through his vitreous observations (using skylights at London's heights and bull's-eye lanterns at its depths), Bucket freely negotiates the inscrutable realms of *Bleak House*—geographic, temporal, and formal.[4]

Bucket is the perfect archetype for Audrey Jaffe's "semi-omniscient figures" who "disturb . . . the boundaries between first- and third-person narration" (17). Although Dickens's proposal for *Household Words*, "to suppose a certain SHADOW, . . . a kind of semi-omniscient, omnipresent, intangible creature" (*Letters* 5: 622–23), never came to fruition, he did employ this idea of semi-omniscience at the character level in his novels.[5] But this omniscience is no "fantasy" (6), as Jaffe conceives it, when it can be had in the real world; when "omniscience can be located" not just in meta or liminal sites of "tension" between narrators and characters (4), but instead through physical and geographic realities; when seeing what is meant to be unseen is a matter of exploiting objects of real availability that are not fictional constructs, but actual constructions. Before proceeding to Bucket's movement and glass-use, the faculties through which he achieves semi-omniscience, it is pertinent to elucidate the conditions that led to a proliferation of skylights in nineteenth-century London.

"The novel is founded on glass culture" (132), Isobel Armstrong asserts. But skylights rarely take center stage, and certainly are subordinate to the abundant lower windows, which routinely provide the means for both inward and outward surveillance. Still, the Brontës, for example, experimented with the architectural location of skylights: Bertha Mason escapes from one in her attic in *Jane Eyre* (1847); the ghostly nun, Alfred, enters through one, "day and night left half-open for air" in *Villette* (1853, 524; ch. 40); and Catherine climbs through skylights to get to Heathcliff in *Wuthering Heights* (1847). Yet none is probably more (in)famous than that built for Thomas Carlyle's sound-proof study, completed in 1853 in the attic space of his Chelsea home—a space George Eliot surely had in mind when she constructed Philip's "'sanctum'" painting room, complete with "'a capital light . . . from the roof'" (539; bk. 6, ch. 8), in *The Mill on the Floss* (1860).[6] Carlyle meant it to be a sanctuary from the "demon fowls" of the noisy and distracting outside world (*Reminiscences* 194). As John Picker argues, the sound-proof room with a prominent skylight represented "a newly masculinized space reserved for the sounding of [Carlyle's] own writerly voices" (55). It was in this "very light" room that Carlyle was able to produce his meticulous, six-volume biography of Frederick the Great (1858–64, *Collected* 28: 282). But, as Carlyle later reveals, the study was a "flattering delusion of an ingenious needy builder" (*Letters* 2: 21). The "spacious skylight," Reginald Blunt writes in 1895, "drove Carlyle to despair by besmutting his books and papers" (61).[7] In a 9 September 1853 letter to Ralph Waldo Emerson, Carlyle laments, "Alas, this is not the kind of *silence* I could have coveted, and could once get,—with green fields and clear skies to accompany it!" (*Collected* 28: 265). An integral component of the architect's "bad building," the leaky skylight might have been to blame for making the room "by far the noisiest in the house" (*Letters* 2: 21).[8]

In spite of (and perhaps because of) their permeability, skylights proved popular for myriad reasons: most obviously, they were an excellent source of light which shone down rather than across, like windows. The 1841 *Penny Cyclopædia* applauds "the picturesque effect produced in an interior where the light falls in from above" ("Skylight" 91). In 1860, S. C. Capes writes, "something should be given in favour of skylights, in consideration of the light falling at angles of incidence more favourable to the reflection and due diffusion of light in the apartment" (142). Skylights also became the preferred lighting method for museum designers. But even more important, skylights helped house-owners negotiate around the unpopular and expensive window tax. Even the staid *Athenæum* offered an opinion, proposing

> a method of economising our sky-lights which might have ingeniously baffled that minister of financial ingenuity, the window tax gatherer. The mode is quite simple by which the beam is imprisoned wherever we can catch it, and let out wherever we please. Under the title of the "Diurnal Reflector," French optician, M. Troupeau, has taken out a patent for a plate of metal silvered over so as to have highly reflective power. This plate is placed beneath any sky-light or window so as to receive on its face the natural light, and at such angles as will project that light forward into any particular corner or passage that may need it. The light thus obtained is, of course, not of that dazzling character which might be dangerous to tender eyes, but it will be found to serve for many useful purposes.
>
> (qtd. in "Prize" 11)

The notion of imprisoning light will be particularly applicable to my discussion of lanterns later, but for now it is important to consider that skylights were thought to be more effective than windows at diffusing light throughout a house. Perhaps even more significant, however, because skylights would have been more difficult for the tax gatherer to spot, they became a welcome alternative to windows, which were increasingly bricked up to save money.

The window tax was instituted in 1696 and required house-owners and landlords to pay a variable rate corresponding to the number of windows that exceeded an established maximum. In 1833, Parliament twice voted down measures to abolish the tax, resulting in significant protest that escalated into the Coldbath Riot, where a police officer was stabbed to death (Hepburn 542–43). By midcentury, disgust with the tax had reached a fever pitch, and, not surprisingly, Dickens voiced his opinion. In a 23 January 1851 letter to Henry Austin, Dickens writes in a postscript, "Have you any printed particulars in any Reports, concerning the more obvious absurdities & evils of the Window Tax? If you have, and can send them up to me . . . , I think I can do great service to the Repale [*sic*] cause" (*Letters* 6: 265).

Several contemporary texts railed against the inequity of the tax, but probably most widely disseminated was M. Humberstone's *The Absurdity and Injustice of the Window Tax* (1841), which argued that taxing the "light of heaven . . . is monstrous" (6).[9] Another pamphlet, "The Wonder of the Window-Tax" (1848), begins, "'What a dreadful shame to tax the Light from Heaven!'" (1).[10] The anonymous author suggests that the window tax compromises civic wellbeing and, as a result, the economy: "daylight is one of the means whereby *labour* is assisted, *health* promoted, and *wealth* obtained" (2). "It is a strange contradiction," the author continues, "that whilst we are improving our sewerage, our lighting and paving, and our street-ventilation, we are still compelled, or at least *induced*, to *darken* and deteriorate our dwelling-houses!" (18). In 1850, Eliza Cook observes, "Light for the dwelling, and light for the mind—healthy homes and healthy intellects—are alike imperatively called for; and legislators certainly could not more effectually supply those important requirements, than by abolishing the taxes on window light and the taxes on knowledge" (386). Dickens clearly received something on the issue from Austin because, just a month after his letter of request, he criticized the tax in a *Household Words* article, "Red Tape." Dickens supplements Humberstone's claim that the tax was "certainly an unaccountable favouring of the RICH which cannot be reconciled to reason or equity" (7) by lampooning:

> It is a beautiful feature in this tax (and a mighty convenient one for large country houses) that, after progressing in a gradually ascending scale or charge, from eight windows to seventy-nine, it then begins to descend again, and charges a house with five-hundred windows, just a farthing a window more, than a house with nine. This has been, for so many years, proved—by Red Tape—to be the perfection of human reason.
>
> (421)

Echoing over a century of complaints, Dickens criticizes the tax's class inequity and argues that it limits light and air, "the first essentials of our being" (421). After maintaining that light is essential to the human nervous system, and that those "bred in darkness droop, and become degenerate" (422), Dickens turns his attention to the unsanitary dwellings of the poor. To save money, landlords bricked up windows, which had "murderous effects of a prohibition of ventilation in the thickly-peopled habitations of the poor" (423). David Trotter argues that "the discursive economy to which Dickens gained access at this time began to shape his imagining of the disposition and regulation of society," which he could see as "a system of flows and stoppages" (104). Restricting light and air meant impeding the civic circulation needed for both sanitation and (most important for Dickens) reading.[11]

Other novelists criticized the window tax, but it was Dickens who most overtly condemned the injustice of taxed circulation.[12] Interestingly, skylights routinely serve to mitigate at least some of the harm: in *Nicholas Nickleby* (1839), the Mantalinis' shoddy, constrictive milliner shop is "a close room with a sky-light, and as dull and quiet as a room need be" (209; ch. 17); in *Barnaby Rudge* (1841), an "unglazed skylight" allows "for the admission of light and air into the lobby" (408; ch. 49); "an old, disjointed, rickety, ill-favored skylight," in *Martin Chuzzlewit* (1844), "which looked distrustfully down at everything that passed below" (126; ch. 8), may serve to ventilate Todgers's house, squeezed in as it is by "London," which "stood perpetually between it and the light" (128–29; ch. 9); and at the scene of Merdle's suicide in *Little Dorrit* (1857), "A skylight had been opened, to release the steam with which the room had been filled" (738; bk. 2, ch. 25).

In the Dickensian world, skylights promote the circulation of not only air and light, but also information. The secret knowledge awarded by glass gazes allows characters to serve as agents for civic progress and narrative flow. "From *Bleak House* on," Trotter argues, "Dickens began to introduce characters whose function was not simply to resolve mysteries, but to enact the resolution of mystery; not simply to interpret, but to embody . . . the hermeneutic activity on which social process depends" (112–13). While the "Red Tapist" will "wind," "bind," and create "imaginary obstacles" to restrict social progress ("Red Tape" 420), in *Bleak House* Mr. Bucket has "a duty to perform" (312; ch. 24)—which contrasts with the circular impotence of Chancery—to solve crime in order to resolve the narrative.[13] D. A. Miller calls this move from the stagnation of law courts to the action of criminal investigation a "curious formal torsion" (66). Arguing that Bucket influences the very structure of *Bleak House*, Miller also proposes that the "excruciating *longueurs* of Chancery existed mainly to create the market for Mr. Bucket's expeditious *coups*" (74). Before we arrive at Bucket's novel emergence, however, I would like to track the formal and geographic movements of select characters who precede him.

The roving reporter in *Sketches By Boz* is regulated by the physical limitations of embodied narration. Rambling about London's streets and peering in shop windows, Boz remains distant from, but not invisible to, the scenes he sketches. Because Boz never rises, as future characters so nimbly will, to a position suited for concealed observation, he warrants treatment as a character—perceptive and imaginative, but certainly never omniscient.[14] An interaction in "Meditations on Monmouth Street," which occurs after some of Boz's most exultant and imaginative contemplations of London life, best evidences his character limitations. Interrupting his story, an old woman yells, "'Hope you'll know me agin, imperence!'" (103). Her disgust at Boz's surveillance demonstrates the unavoidable voyeurism of street- and character-level observation. Boz is forced to conclude the scene: "as we were conscious that in the depth of our meditations we might have been rudely staring at the old lady for half an hour without knowing it, we took to flight too, and were soon immersed in the deepest obscurity of the adjacent 'Dials'" (104). Boz's "dream bursts of its own excess," J. Hillis Miller notes, and he "finds himself back to himself"

(128). Now conscious of his own material reality through the recognition of another, Boz flees. He achieves anonymity, moreover, not by disappearing like a shadow, but by mixing his body with the throng of humanity in the surrounding streets of the notorious Seven Dials. For Boz, skylight-peeping is unnecessary and perhaps inconceivable. When, in "The Hospital Patient," Boz is forced to "pause beneath the windows of some public hospital and picture . . . the gloomy and mournful scenes that are passing within" (277), he is stymied by high windows, a barrier that many subsequent characters overcome.

This limitation at the street-window level is also present in *The Old Curiosity Shop* (1841). In yet another direct reference to Asmodeus—"the historian takes the friendly reader by the hand, and springing with him into the air, and cleaving the same at a greater rate than ever Don Cleophas Leandro Perez Zambullo and his familiar travelled through that pleasant region in company, alights with him upon the pavement of Bevis Marks" (250; ch. 33)—the narrator is still rather Boz-like, and oddly pedestrian, as he continues the scene from ground-level:

> In the parlour window of this little habitation, which is so close upon the footway that the passenger who takes the wall brushes the dim glass[,] . . . hung, all awry and slack, and discoloured by the sun, a curtain of faded green, so threadbare from long service as by no means to intercept the view of the little dark room, but rather to afford a favourable medium through which to observe it accurately. There was not much to look at.
>
> (250; ch 33)

Had the Brasses invested in new drapery, the narrator's view would have been obscured, and his gaze from the street impeded. Luckily, the scene is uninhabited, a "mere still-life," and the narrator can rely on descriptions of its residents in the past tense: Mr. Brass "has already appeared in these pages," and "Such *was* Miss Brass in person" (250–51; ch. 33, emphasis mine).

Where the narrator demonstrates limitations, Quilp thrives on physical freedom. In a "secret survey" (384; ch. 51), in which the reader also participates, Quilp observes while avoiding observation. The "prime mover of the whole diabolical device" (497; ch. 66), Quilp represents an entirely new character-type in Dickens, obviously unable to achieve omniscience, but certainly an ancestor of semi-omniscient characters. Using Dickens's later terminology in his proposal for *Household Words*, Quilp is "omni-present," able to be anywhere so quickly and surreptitiously that he seems to be everywhere. Quilp continually enters unseen, hiding behind doors and looking through slits and keyholes, cowering in corners, and, most important, positioning himself at covert heights to peer downward.[15] Reveling in Quilp's supposed drowning, and "raising his eyes to the ceiling with a sigh," Mr. Brass opines, "'who knows but he may be looking down upon us now. Who knows but he may be surveying of us from—from somewheres or another, and contemplating us with a watchful eye!'" (370–72; ch. 49). Quilp often does survey from overhead: at the Brasses', "the window was suddenly darkened, as by some person standing close against it. . . . [T]he top sash was nimbly lowered from without, and Quilp thrust in his head . . . standing on tip-toe on the window-sill, and looking down into the room" (253; ch. 33). In a later scene, perched atop Kit's carriage, Quilp hangs "over the side of the coach at the risk of his life" (367; ch. 48), and leers down at Kit's mother seated below.

Because Quilp has the ingenuity and physical prowess to gaze from heights Boz cannot reach, he transcends the limits of character—but it is a status he cannot maintain. For when the light is shut out on him, he reverts to a character, a stumbling body, and finally a corpse to be mercilessly flung about and abandoned. Quilp descends from subject to object, from "he" to sharing a pronoun with the water that kills him:

> It toyed and sported with its ghastly freight, now bruising it against the slimy piles, now hiding it in mud or long rank grass, now dragging it heavily over rough stones and gravel, now feigning to yield it to its own element, and in the same action luring it away, until, tired of the ugly plaything, it flung it on a swamp . . . and left it there to bleach.
>
> (512; ch. 67)

Left in the darkness, Quilp's hue whitens, producing a horrifying chiaroscuro, blending into the white page and out of the black text, as he disappears from the narrative. With an ironic twist, Dickens begins the next chapter: "Lighted rooms, bright fires, cheerful faces, the music of glad voices, words of love and welcome, warm hearts, and tears of happiness—what a change is this!" (512; ch. 68). And what a change indeed from Quilp's violent demise after Nell dies, and "still her former self lay there, unaltered in this change" (540; ch. 71). Garrett Stewart argues that the death scene "polarization of Nell and Quilp" is evidence of the "major structural relationship of the novel" (98, 91).[16] While Quilp meets his fate in darkness, the light on Nell will never go out. Before dying, she requests, "'put near me something that has loved the light, and had the sky above it always'" (540; ch. 71). She is placed under a "coloured window" where the "changing light would fall upon her grave" (543; ch. 72), making her image, as Jane Eyre describes the imagination, an "ever-shifting kaleidoscope" (268; ch. 21), contrasted to Quilp's bleached (and beached) body, and suggestive of the "magic reel" that "has led the chronicler" through the narrative (548; ch. 73).[17]

Although characters in *The Old Curiosity Shop* primarily travel horizontally through geographic space, *Dombey and Son* in great part concerns the opposing vertical movement of its antagonists. Most notably, Mr. Dombey descends from a self-imposed status above his family, indeed above the world, into it, as a member of Florence Dombey's new family. Recalling his dying wife clutching his daughter, Dombey "could not forget that he had had no part in it. . . . [H]e stood on the bank above them, looking down a mere spectator—not a sharer with them—quite shut out" (42; ch. 3). However, as Dombey is increasingly humbled—by little Paul's death, business failures, and an unhappy marriage—Carker ascends. Sitting quite literally on his "high-horse," Carker increasingly looks down on other characters, his very image and status altering as the story proceeds: "There was a faint blur on the surface of the mirror in Mr. Carker's chamber, and its reflection was, perhaps, a false one. But it showed, that night, the image of a man, who saw, in his fancy, a crowd of people slumbering on the ground at his feet . . . looking down, maliciously enough: but trod upon no upturned face—as yet" (415; ch. 26). As with Quilp, characters begin to fear Carker's omni-presence and potential downward gaze:

> "Hush!" said Rob, glancing cautiously up at the packer's, and at the bottle-maker's, as if, from any one of the tiers of warehouses, Mr Carker might be looking down. "Softly."
> "Why, he ain't here!" cried Mrs Brown.
> "I don't know that," muttered Rob, whose glance even wandered to the church tower, as if he might be there, with a supernatural power of hearing.
>
> (691; ch. 46)

Carker's power is even more effective than his predecessors because his gaze often achieves disembodiment: he sees through Rob's surrogate eyes or spies from impossible distances. Quilp's gaze, on the other hand, remains material, his body hidden, his eyes peering through keyholes and crevices. But Carker's semi-omniscience is just as fleeting: "far from resuming the mastery of himself, he seemed . . . to lose it more and more as the night crept on" (841; ch. 55). Shut out of the light, and meeting a similar end as Quilp, Carker descends from disembodiment, and potential semi-omniscience, to physical and mental instability, finally slipping "on to the road below him," his body "beaten down, caught up, and whirled away," as the train "cast his mutilated fragments in the air" (842; ch. 55).

These violent, vindictive deaths suggest something at stake for Dickens—an anxiety over the ethics of narration. Quilp and Carker must be killed and ceremoniously taught a lesson. They function as Icarus figures, rising too high, too close to narrative omniscience, perhaps too close to the author.[18] For both, the sharp fall to death involves darkness and a loss of bodily control, an ironic punishment for characters who were so calculating and physically dexterous. While Quilp becomes a "ghastly freight" (512; ch. 67) in the thrashing current, Carker is dismantled by a train. Both corpses are passive parcels driven (and Carker riven) about by mediums for transporting information.[19] Dickens dispatched them invested with a message: going from dynamic character to flaccid object(s) requires just a moment of weakness, a stumble in the dark. What is left for Dickens after this interrogation and passionate erasure of his villains, then, is to empower a hero, to make a do-gooder better at doing good. By *Bleak House*, skylights provide positive access to omniscience for the altruistic Bucket, but they were anxiety-inducing objects in previous novels, chinks in the armor of domestic spaces, and transparent sites for oppressive and dangerous views.

In contrast to the naiveté of those under surveillance by Quilp in *The Old Curiosity Shop*, characters in *Dombey and Son* participate not only in looking down into private spaces, but also in looking up, wary of being watched from above. As Jaffe reminds us, *Dombey and Son* allows "readers to see through the rooftop, becoming . . . secret observers of family life" (79–80). Throughout the novel, skylights provide the means for inward and outward surveillance, which demonstrate respectively Asmodean omniscience and a fear of it. Rob the Grinder, employed as a proxy spy by Carker, takes the "freedom of peering in, and listening, through the skylight in the roof" at the group aboard Bunsby's boat negotiating Walter Gay's rescue (372; ch. 23). The scene, complete with Rob's confused stare down through the skylight, appears in a Phiz illustration (fig. 1). Florence employs the same method of surveillance before Rob, "glancing down the open skylight" at Captain Cuttle and the sage, Bunsby (368; ch. 23). More disturbing skylight surveillance, however, occurs during Edith's great alterations to the Dombey household. As the house is undergoing its transformation from both inside and out, Florence sees "a whole Olympus of plumbers and glaziers . . . reclining in various attitudes, on the skylight," and she also notices that "a dark giant of a man with a pipe in his mouth . . . was staring in at the window" (442; ch. 28). Once a sanctuary from the world's gaze, the Dombey house becomes subject to voyeuristic outside surveillance. This marks Dombey's pecuniary and personal fall as perhaps even more damaging than Carker's physical fragmentation, for the transparency of the Dombey house makes Asmodean observers out of anonymous, and potentially dangerous, spectators.[20]

By far the most communication through skylights in *Dombey and Son* occurs at Sol Gills's shop, The Wooden Midshipmen. Before Walter leaves for Barbados, Florence offers her friendship and service to Gills and proposes her eternal sisterhood to Walter. Not a part of these proceedings, Susan Nipper sits, engaged in her own exclusive conversation with a skylight: she "heaved a gentle sigh as she looked up at the skylight," "nodded at the skylight, in approval of the sentiment expressed," and "imparted a great deal of private emotion to the skylight, during this transaction" (293–94; ch. 19). That Susan engages in this unspoken discourse with a skylight suggests that she acknowledges, if not accepts, the inescapable reality of skylight observation. Mr. Dombey also looks up at skylights, always during moments of remorse: "he still stood gazing upwards, until the dull rays of the moon, glimmering in a melancholy manner through the dim skylight, sent him back to his room" (113; ch. 8); and, much later, using the same skylight to reminisce on his now empty and childless house, he "stopped, looking up towards the skylight; and a figure, childish itself, but carrying a child, and singing as it went, seemed to be there again" (907; ch. 59). Even Cuttle communicates in this manner: he looks "up at the stars at night, through the skylight . . . as if he had established a kind of property in them" (397; ch. 25); he looks "up at the skylight, until the day, by little and little, faded away, and the stars peeped down"; and after he learns of Florence and Walter's engagement he screams in delight, "tossing up his glazed hat into the skylight" (771; ch. 50), for a moment blocking the outside view of this private scene.

Techniques of surveillance through skylights peak in *Dombey and Son* not surprisingly during the height of furor over the window tax. However, just

Fig. 1. "Solemn reference is made to Mr. Bunsby."

following *David Copperfield* (1849–50), the tax was repealed, and Dickens's use of skylights as devices of narrative import wanes. But one crucial skylight gaze remains in *Bleak House*, a trade secret, it seems, of Mr. Bucket's detective practice.[21] Although Katherine Williams argues that "Bucket is wedded to the ground. He is terrestrial, looking up, around, in, and sometimes through" (77), and this is generally the case, his vertical movements establish his semi-omniscience as an Asmodean observer. Etymologically, "to detect" is derived from the Latin verb "detegere," which means "to take the roof off" (Schor 4; Cain 62). It is interesting, then, that Bucket begins his detective work as an Asmodean figure by observing through skylights.

We learn that Mr. George's Shooting Gallery is "a great brick building composed of bare walls, floors, roof-rafters, and skylights" (271; ch. 21), and, in the matter of a few pages (as the chapter-title reveals), we for the first time meet Bucket. He has a "ghostly manner of appearing" (275; ch. 22)—both in a room *and* in the narrative. Introducing his detective, Tulkinghorn portentously declares, "'This is only Mr. Bucket'" (275; ch. 22). Although Tulkinghorn is the "'master of mysteries of great houses'" (451; ch. 36), Bucket assumes this role during his detective work, recognizing that he has roof access for spying on Mr. George's Gallery. During a conversation with Esther concerning Bleak House, Mr. Jarndyce compares his dwelling to a family property in London, which resides in "'a street of perishing blind houses, with their eyes stoned out; without a pane of glass, without so much as a window-frame'" (89; ch. 8). Mr. George's Gallery seems to be one of these blind edifices, its windows long since bricked-up to avoid window taxes (a fitting condition of course for a shooting gallery).[22] When Bucket determines to look for Gridley at Mr. George's, then, he resourcefully does so from above. Although Mr. George looks "up at the moon now shining through the skylights" (272; ch. 21), he mistimes his glance, for Bucket proudly admits to him, "'I was on the roof last night, and saw [Gridley] through the skylight, and you along with him'" (312; ch. 24). Bucket then condemns Gridley for "'forcing me to climb the roof here like a Tom Cat'" (314; ch. 24).[23]

As further evidence of his unique vertical movement, Bucket not only scales rooftops to solve the novel's mysteries, but he must also plunge London's nebulous depths. To perform the latter, however, requires a special light. Once the first volume of *Household Words* was published on 30 March 1850, Dickens's narrative apparatus had become even more indistinct than the "shadow" he proposed to John Forster: a disembodied nothing that could invade the home and be part of "that light of Fancy" which "can never be extinguished" ("Preliminary" 1).[24] Bucket's journeys to London's underworld necessitate a similar narrative light, one that demonstrates, in Dorothy Van Ghent's words, the "demonic life of things" in Dickens (419). Although Dickens's early engagement with skylights as a means for a realistic domestic gaze seems divergent at best to Bucket's lantern-use, they are connected in many ways: the distorting, focusing eyes of crown glass, the ability to "imprison" and to manipulate light, and that in the very utility of distributing light to dark spaces both can be used to liberate *and* to oppress.[25] Isobel Armstrong observes, "the staring panoptical sockets of window go right the way through Dickens's *Bleak House*" (128). But Buckct's skylight-surveillance and the animate, ocular lanterns he employs both to negotiate darkness and to immobilize select characters have their nascence in the several "knots in glass" Dickens describes elsewhere in his novels.

In "Thoughts about People" in *Sketches By Boz*, Dickens details the monotonous day of the common London man: in the midst of his toils, he "looks up to the ceiling as if there were inspiration in the dusty skylight with a green knot in the centre of every pane of glass" (252). Dickens is referring here to crown glass, which is formed by blowing glass into a globe, transferring it to a pontil rod, and then flattening it through repeated heating and spinning. The point at which the rod enters creates what is known as a bull's eye.[26] By the mid-nineteenth century, glass was a mass-produced commodity, and advancing techniques in clear broad glass, best evidenced by Robert Lucas Chance at the Great Exhibition (Armstrong 37), made image-distorting crown glass decorative, but no longer practical for spaces requiring transparency. Mario Praz argues that Dickens observes "through a peculiar distorting lens, fantastically distorted" (172). In the 1840 preface to *Master Humphrey's Clock*, Dickens describes himself as "one whose vision is disordered, . . . conjuring up bright figures where there is nothing but empty space" (iii). Crown glass thus serves as an apt metaphor for how we see in Dickens's novels when we consider the glass, following Praz's observation, as deceptive and illusory to willing imaginations.[27] It is of interest, then, to observe the instances when crown glass produces this animation—and especially so when Bucket is around.

Bull's-eye glass was used prevalently in the eighteenth century, especially on ships. In *American Notes* (1842), Dickens describes aboard a ship "a large bull's-eye just over the looking-glass which would render shaving a perfectly easy and delightful process" (6; ch. 1). Of most interest, however, is when Dickens anthropomorphizes bull's-eye glass into staring eyes: in *Barnaby Rudge* (1841), the Vardens' locksmith shop is "a shy, blinking house, with a conical roof going up into a peak over its garret window of four small panes of glass, like a cocked hat on the head of an elderly gentleman with one eye" (38; ch. 4); in *Martin Chuzzlewit* (1844), the door at Todgers's "had two great glass eyes in its forehead, with an inquisitive green pupil in the middle of each" (145; ch. 9); in *Little Dorrit*, Mr. Sparkler, aboard a gondola, had "undeniably, a weak appearance; with his eye in the window like a knot in the glass" (520; bk. 2, ch. 6); and at the scene of Mr. Dolls's death in *Our Mutual Friend* (1865), "the window bec[ame] from within, a wall of faces, deformed into all kinds of shapes through the agency of globular red bottles, green bottles, blue bottles, and other coloured bottles" (713; bk. 4, ch. 9). But perhaps the most telling appearance of eyes in glass in Dickens comes again in *Barnaby Rudge*.

The eponymous character's argument with Mr. Chester concerning clothes, which "dance and leap," hanging to dry outside, is worth quoting in full:

> "Clothes!" echoed Barnaby, looking close into his face, and falling quickly back. "Ha ha! Why, how much better to be silly, than as wise as you! You don't see shadowy people there, like those that live in sleep—not you. Nor eyes in the knotted panes of glass, nor swift ghosts when it blows hard, nor do you hear voices in the air, nor see men stalking in the sky—not you! I lead a merrier life than you, with all your cleverness. You're the dull men. We're the bright ones."
>
> (94; ch. 10)

Here the idiot Barnaby groups himself with imaginative observers like Boz, especially the Boz of "Meditations on Monmouth Street," who fills hanging clothes with their original owners, and engages them, just like Barnaby, in a dance.[28] Barnaby's reference to glass knots points not only to his ability to imagine a gazing eye behind the glass, but also to the illusory properties of this manufactured distortion. Isobel Armstrong argues, "The window's changing perspectives create an uneven relation between the gazing subject and the world—what matters is how the *window* makes you see, not only how you *see* through it—and ensure that there is never a wholly protected one-way movement of vision" (115). Anticipating Henry James's "house of fiction" metaphor cited above, Barnaby's sight is manipulated by the window; he sees a "distinct" image inaccessible to Mr. Chester and to anyone else, a frustrating reality of the illusion of vision. Perhaps this is how his author felt, too.[29]

In 1905, the famed electrical engineer Silvanus P. Thompson described "old-fashioned windowpanes" that effect an optical illusion:

> the glass in the middle is sometimes made up into a lump of glass, a knot of glass. Now if you look through the window near one of those knots or lumps of glass, and watch some vertical object moving behind it, you see the object at first on one side of the knot slightly distorted; but as it moves on a little it seems suddenly to disappear, and then reappear at the other side of the knot, as though it snapped across.
>
> (40)

This illusion can serve as a useful metaphor for the instantaneous movement of many Dickens narrators and characters. Barnaby is himself an example, "'here one hour, and there the next'" (92; ch. 10). And Mrs. Sparsit comes to mind in *Hard Times*: she could "shoot with consummate velocity from the roof to the hall" and was never "seen by human vision to go at a great pace" (194; bk. 2, ch. 9).

Perhaps the best examples of instantaneous movement, however, are Dickens's detectives. Bucket's precursor, Mr. Nadgett of *Martin Chuzzlewit*, moves about London "stealthily," "so wrapped up in himself," "hovering," "slinking," and "winding" (587; ch. 38) and "always made his appearance as if he had that moment come up a trap" (588; ch. 38). In 1882, *Lippincott's Magazine* observes that Nadgett is as "watchful as fate itself, and as omnipresent" ("Types" 418). Most important, however, is Nadgett's method of investigation. Although "every button on his coat might have been an eye: he saw so much" (587; ch. 38), to watch Jonas Chuzzlewit "'almost without rest or relief'" (784; ch. 51), Nadgett anticipates Bucket's vertical surveillance methods: "'From that garret-widow,'" Nadgett shares, "'I have watched this house and him for days and nights. . . . I think I never closed my eyes'" (786; ch. 51). Thus, while Nadgett painstakingly watches Jonas from an attic window, and Carker in *Dombey and Son* ascends his "tower" (691; ch. 46) metaphorically, Bucket does both, for he traverses London's heights and depths with great physical prowess *and* "mounts a high tower in his mind, and looks out far and wide" (673; ch. 56).[30]

D. A. Miller argues that "Bucket himself is *not* contained in the way that characters ordinarily are" (79). Not contained, but certainly a container for and of secrets. As Mrs. Bagnet puns, "'Bucket is so deep'" (625; ch. 52). Like Snagsby, we are left "quite in the dark as to who Mr. Bucket may be," for, unlike the full names provided for James Carker and Daniel Quilp, "'This is only Mr. Bucket'" (275; ch. 22). Still, Dickens endows Bucket with a life Nadgett is denied. Nadgett's identity is "a complete absence of identity," John Bowen observes, "an abyss of meaning without intent" (195). Tigg Montague considers his detective "'a mere piece of furniture'" (591; ch. 38). In Phiz's illustrations, while Nadgett's face is partially obstructed as he leers over his shoulder at Jonas Chuzzlewit (fig. 2), Bucket gets full exposure (fig. 3) holding the Bagnet children, Quebec and Malta, on his knees, signifying that, at least at this moment, he is the center of Dickens's world.

In 1853, a reviewer for *Putnam's Monthly* observes, "Mr. Bucket . . . fills a very large space in Bleak House, and is one of the best characters in it; he is a higher order of Sam Weller, and we hope there are plenty of originals like him in London, for most valuable members of our social organizations are the Buckets" ("Characters" 560). The review is intriguing because it makes note of Bucket's scope in the territory of the novel, and because it characterizes Bucket as a metonym for a whole body of social do-gooders.[31] In "On Duty with Inspector Field" (1851), one of several features on London's police force in *Household Words*, the detectives use their lanterns, which Dickens calls "flaming eyes," to incapacitate targets for inspection: "O! If it's the accursed glaring eye that fixes me, go where I will, I am helpless" ("On Duty" 312). These mesmerizing, ocular lanterns become synecdochal for the whole body of detectives. Their "flaming eyes" penetrate darkness and see what normal eyes cannot, thus curbing delinquent activity though an oppressive, vitreous gaze.

Bucket discloses, "'I know so much about so many characters, high and low'" (638; ch. 54). Now traversing London's depths, Bucket manipulates bull's-eye lanterns, called such because, like the crown glass with knots in skylights, they work by using the bull's-eye as a focusing lens, shooting light out at specific targets much like a flashlight.[32] Searching for Jo in Tom-all-Alone's (like Diogenes "looking for an honest man" with his lamp), Bucket "takes a lighted bull's-eye from the constable on duty there, who accompanies him with his own particular bull's-eye at his waist" (277; ch. 22).[33] Bucket "turns his bull's eye on a line of stinking ruins" (278; ch. 22), while Mr. Snagsby follows his "two conductors" (aptly named both because the lanterns shoot out light and because Dickens had

Fig. 2. "Mr. Nadgett breathes, as usual, an atmosphere of mystery."

adopted the name Mr. Conductor for *Household Words* just two years prior). During their search for Jo, the party finds a "lair," and Bucket enters, "glaring in with his bull's-eye" (278; ch. 22). Bucket makes conversation with the patrons of the dark and dingy room, "offensive to every sense," and, "as he turns his light gently on the infant, Mr. Snagsby is strangely reminded of another infant, encircled with light that he has seen in pictures" (279; ch. 22). But after Bucket "throws his light into the doorway," it is Jo who "stands amazed in the disc of light, like a ragged figure in a magic-lanthorn" (280; ch. 22).[34]

Ronald R. Thomas reads Bucket's lantern use and image-capturing eye as evidence of the period's proliferation of photographic portraits, arguing that "the literary detective appears in the Victorian imagination looking and acting very much like a camera" (134). We might instead think of Bucket's bull's-eye lantern as a metaphor for the "light of Fancy" that Dickens's omniscient narrator effects in *Household Words* ("Preliminary" 1). Furthermore, in his earlier proposal to Forster, again using rhetoric that could describe a bull's-eye lantern, Dickens seeks to make a "Power . . . concentrate into one focus all that is done in the paper" (*Letters* 5: 623). However, Bucket's lantern-use is suggestive of not only Dickens's omniscient narrators, but also the author himself. As R. Shelton Mackenzie notes,

Fig. 3. "Friendly behaviour of Mr. Bucket."

The great power of Dickens, before years came on, was in his eye. When he was in Rome, he sat in the *halle de hôte*, opposite a somewhat vulgar woman, whose loudness of manners attracted his attention. Thenceforth, ever and anon he flashed upon her the "full blaze of his visual orb," which, as all who knew him must remember, was a very large one. At last, the lady cried out, in the unmistakable cockney vernacular: "Drat that man there—I wish he'd take his *heyes* (eyes) hoff my face. They're like a policeman's bull's eye!"—Such, also, was the searching glance he cast upon life.

(245)

It is fascinating to compare the scene to "Meditations on Monmouth Street" in *Sketches By Boz*, but most important is the woman's characterization of Dickens's powerful, oppressive eye as a bull's-eye lantern.[35] As Graham Storey observes, "it is surely possible to believe that . . . Dickens saw much in common between the omniscient author and the omniscient detective" (48). And like his detective, "Dickens's imagination," in John Rignall's words, "moves amidst darkness and mystery, exploring obscure corners, seizing on odd details, pursuing the grotesque and eccentric" (62).[36]

Later in *Bleak House*, Dickens continues the light and eye metaphor: "some dungeon lights burning, as the lamp of life hums in Tom-all-Alone's, heavily, heavily, in the nauseous air, and winking—as that lamp, too, winks in Tom-all-Alone's—at many horrible things" (551; ch. 46).[37] An Argus-figure, Bucket seems "to possess an unlimited number of eyes" (281; ch. 22).[38] Recall that Bucket's party enters Tom-all-Alone's with two bull's-eye lanterns, yet another set of eyes to survey the scene for the "sharp-eyed man in black" (275; ch. 22). Reversing the workings of real sight, in which light travels into the eyes and is projected as images onto the retina, Dickens projects his "mind's eye" image through bull's-eye lanterns and onto the page.[39]

During Bucket's search for Jo, Dickens crafts a terrifying canvas of Tom-all-Alone's and its Morlock-like inhabitants: "Whenever Mr. Snagsby and his conductors are stationary, the crowd flows round, and from its squalid depths obsequious advice heaves up to Mr. Bucket. Whenever they move, and the angry bull's-eyes glare, it fades away and flits about them up the alleys, and in the ruins, and behind the walls, as before" (278; ch. 22). And leaving "that pit" (echoing Byron's description of London in *Don Juan* as a "half-quenched volcano" and the "Devil's drawing-room" [*Major Works* 10: 642–43]), still followed by the mob, the "restoration of the bull's eyes" is made to the policeman, and the "concourse of imprisoned demons, turns back, yelling, and is seen no more" (281; ch. 22). In Dorothy Van Ghent's words, "This is Hell" (427). Dickens paints the squalor of Tom-all-Alone's as the gates of a Dantean underworld, all but saying, "Abandon all hope, ye who enter here" (Dante 3.9).[40] Here London's underbelly resembles Dante's third ring of gluttony, its inhabitants "Ceaseless, accursed, heavy and cold, unchanged / For ever, both in kind and in degree," where "Large hail, discolor'd water, sleety flaw / Through the dun midnight air stream'd down amain" (6.7–10). Dickens describes the space:

these tumbling tenements contain, by night, a swarm of misery. As, on the ruined human wretch, vermin parasites appear, so these ruined shelters have bred a crowd of foul existence that crawls in and out of gaps in walls and boards; and coils itself to sleep, in maggot numbers, where the rain drips in; and comes and goes, fetching and carrying fever, and sowing more evil.

(197; ch. 16)

Phiz's illustration of Tom-all-Alone's suggests an even deeper level of Hell, as supporting beams placed in the shape of a giant number seven figure prominently (fig. 4).

Fig. 4. "Tom-all-alone's."

In the seventh circle, the violent dwell, including those who did violence to their bodies in suicide. The doll hanging to the left is particularly suggestive of Esther's early burial of her "dear old doll" (24; ch. 3) or is perhaps a portent of Pip's vision of Miss Havisham hanging in the brewery in *Great Expectations*. Michael Patrick Hearn argues that *A Christmas Carol* (1843) was influenced by Dante's *Inferno*: among other parallels, Marley leads Scrooge just as Virgil leads Dante (102). We also cannot ignore the many corpses in the Thames as an eerie echo of the river Styx in *Our Mutual Friend* (1865), nor should we disregard the Dedlocks' servant, Mercury, who "conduct[s]" Tulkinghorn (who, like Jo, "has not yet died" [197; ch. 16]), like his namesake leading the dead into Hades (13; ch. 2). And, late in *Bleak House*, Bucket becomes a Virgil figure, leading Esther on a lengthy and terrifying search for Lady Dedlock throughout London's depths.[41]

Most important, however, whether Bucket ascends rooftops or descends into a Dantean London-Hell, he negotiates what is meant to block his vision (walls and darkness) by using glass. When Bucket looks through skylights, he achieves real-world Asmodean omniscience, and when he uses the illuminating and focusing power of lanterns he participates in observational disembodiment, manipulating light, like the omniscient narrator, to highlight his subjects while at the same time blinding them from any view of his corporeal presence.

Not only does Bucket shrewdly navigate the novel's vertical realms, but he also penetrates its narrative boundaries. In a famous passage early in *Bleak House*, the narrator posits,

> What connexion can there be, between the place in Lincolnshire, the house in town, the Mercury in powder, and the whereabout of Jo the outlaw with the broom, who had that distant ray of light upon him when he swept the churchyard-step? What connexion can there have been between many people in the innumerable histories of this world, who, from opposite sides of great gulfs, have, nevertheless, been very curiously brought together!
>
> (197; ch. 16)

It is up to Bucket to detect these "connexion[s]." The "distant ray" which shines on Jo appears meek when measured against the apotheosizing light of Bucket's lantern. In 1853, a reviewer for *Bentley's Miscellany* writes, "Mr. Bucket is a portrait that stands out from the canvas just like a bit of life" ("Gossip" 374). Granted semi-omniscience, Bucket gazes from rooftops, plumbs hellish depths, appears and disappears like an apparition, and uncovers innumerable connections between characters. As David Trotter puts it, Bucket "ensures the flow of information through his hieroglyphic powers, and the flow of compassion through his attentiveness to feeling under inauspicious circumstances" (117). Thus, Bucket also connects the novel's two narratives, so often opposed to one another in an endless series of binaries, by freely flowing between them.[42]

Bucket's appearance in chapter 57 marks the climactic convergence of the heretofore split narratives. Arriving at Bleak House in the previous chapter, he tells Mr. Jarndyce, "'Time flies'" (673), yet Dickens halts the progress of the novel for an installment break, leaving Bucket to wait on his transcendent move to Esther's narrative, when he "snaps" across a bull's-eye knot seven years into the future.[43] In 1866, Dickens inserted the appropriate running headline to accompany this section: "Time is everything to Mr. Bucket" (802). And in his working plans for these chapters, Dickens determined, "All Esther's Narrative? No" (795)—for it would be Bucket's, too.

Bucket's power only increases as the narrative proceeds: unlike Richard, who quickly fades and dies after his move from Esther's narrative into the omniscient narrator's, Bucket thrives in Esther's world; it is there that he "mounts a high tower in his mind" (673; ch. 56)—that moment when he is most narrator-like. It is no surprise that the arrival of the "person entrusted with the secret" that precipitates the novel's action, that "benignant hand," who transcends both narrative binaries and boundaries with his detective "connexion[s]," leaves Esther not in her "right mind until hours had passed" (674; ch. 57). Bucket's semi-omniscience puzzles Esther, as she reveals, "I wondered how he knew that" (679; ch. 57). Although Bucket is "no great scribe" (629; ch. 53), his words—his narrative of surveillance, connection, and pursuit—find their way to the page through Esther's fastidious pen. In a wonderful syntactic play, Bucket asks Esther, "'you know me, my dear; now, don't you?'" (689; ch. 57). After Esther's skirting response, Bucket inquires again, "'Now you know me, don't you?'" (690; ch. 57). What begins as harmless idiom Bucket transforms to profound statement of temporality. The question is, of course, when and what is now? For "time and place cannot bind Mr. Bucket. Like man in the abstract, he is here to-day and gone to-morrow" (626; ch. 53). So enigmatic are Bucket's movements that the narrator switches from his customary present-tense to future, several times noting what Bucket "will be" doing before he is actually doing it. We learn later that he has been almost everywhere and had his hands in everything. Closely guessing the ages of the Bagnets' children, Bucket ominously quips, "'I generally am near'" (593; ch. 49). When he wants to be, he is as invisible as the omniscient narrator, and both exert much influence with their forefingers.

To return to the beginning of this essay, when Dickens writes in *Dombey and Son*, "Oh for a good spirit who would take the house-tops off, with a more potent and benignant hand than the lame demon in the tale" (702; ch. 47), he seems rather directly to portend the necessity of designing a character like Bucket, whom he describes in *Bleak House* as a "benignant philosopher," whose "fat forefinger seems to rise, to the dignity of a familiar demon" as he "pervades a vast number of houses" (626; ch. 53).[44] Later, again referring to Asmodeus, Dickens writes in "A Tour in Bohemia" (1854), "If I could drive some hundreds of the well-dressed units of what is called society into the pens of Smithfield market, and then have some Asmodeus at my bidding to untile, not the roofs of the houses, but the heads of the assembly, and read their working brains, what a well-informed man I should be to be sure" (500). As Bucket gazes "up at the house windows" and "along the people's heads, nothing escapes him" (627; ch. 53). It requires just a "moment's hesitation" by Snagsby, and Bucket "dips down to the bottom of his mind" (275; ch. 22). In short, Bucket demonstrates that, at least in his fictional world, Dickens did "have some Asmodeus at [his] bidding" ("Tour" 500).

NOTES

1. Alain-René Lesage (1668–1747) wrote *Le Diable Boiteux* (1707). In the novel, which was translated in English to *The Devil upon Two Sticks*, the hero Cleophas frees the lame demon Asmodeus from a bottle. In return, Asmodeus takes flight with Cleophas, alights with him on rooftops, and lifts the roofs so Cleophas may see inside. The novel begins with Cleophas fleeing from assassins: he "suddenly emerged, by the skylight, from the house. . . . The bravos followed him for some time over the roofs of the neighbouring houses; but . . . he at length reached a garret, whence the welcome rays proceeded, and without ceremony entered by the window" (1–2). To say that nineteenth-century writers were obsessed with the figure of Asmodeus would be taking it lightly. Dickens's 7 October 1849 letter to John Forster concerning the narrative apparatus for *Household Words* implicitly refers to Asmodeus: "I want to suppose a certain SHADOW, which may . . . loom as a fanciful thing all over London" (*Letters* 5: 622). Referring to his own "lameness" in a 2 April 1823 letter to Thomas Moore, Byron writes, "I am *Le Diable Boiteux*,—a soubriquet, which I marvel that, amongst their various *nominis umbrae*, the Orthodox have not hit upon" (136). Byron's "Granta" (1806) begins,

> Oh! could Le Sage's demon's gift
> Be realized at my desire,
> This night my trembling form he'd lift
> To place it on St. Mary's spire.
> Then would, unroof'd, old Granta's halls
> Pedantic inmates full display.
>
> (1–6)

Works by two of Dickens's good friends—Edward Bulwer-Lytton's novel *Asmodeus at Large* (1833) and Augustus Leopold Egg's painting *The Devil upon Two Sticks* (1844)—further evidence its cultural pervasiveness. Critical attention to Asmodeus references in Dickens and their importance to his imagining narratives is equally voluminous; to name only a few: Jonathan Arc's *Commissioned Spirits: The Shaping of Social Motion in Dickens, Carlyle, Melville, and Hawthorne* (1979), Kate Flint's *Dickens* (1986), Katherine Waters's *Dickens and the Politics of the Family* (1997), Sharon Marcus's *Apartment Stories* (1999), Michelle Mancini's "Demons on the Rooftops, Gypsies in the Streets: The 'Secret Intelligence' of *Dombey and Son*" (*Dickens Studies Annual* 30, 2001), and Efraim Sicher's *Rereading the City/ Rereading Dickens: Representation, the Novel, and Urban Realism* (2003). Mancini argues, "the devil's differences from the flâneur—vertical elevation and satirical detachment, rather than horizontal penetration and at least intermittent if ironic sympathy—make the figure an ambiguous role model for Dickens's own artistic practice" (114). I will establish, however, that Dickens's omniscient figures after *Sketches By Boz* do move vertically and often mimic Asmodeus.

2. Dickens's friend and collaborator, Albert Richard Smith, also connects Asmodeus and skylights, describing in 1842 the wonderful sights afforded by a train ride: "the rapid dioramas of sectional habitations and domestic interiors . . . [were] exceedingly interesting. The engine became a locomotive Asmodeus, hurrying . . . from roof to roof in quick succession, . . . [and in] close intimacy with the garret-windows" (512).

   In her pioneering analysis of the Dickensian world, Dorothy Van Ghent argues that "environment constantly exceeds its material limitations. Its mode of existence is altered by the human purposes and deeds it describes" (424). If the "life absorbed by houses" (420) makes them function as semi-animate surrogates for their inhabitants' heads, then characters who scale rooftops and gaze down through skylights achieve the real-world Asmodean omniscience that Dickens desires. Probably the best examples of this come in *Bleak House*. Mr. Jarndyce describes the state of Bleak House when he first arrived: "'the brains seemed to me to have been blown out of the house too; it was so shattered and ruined'" (89; ch. 8). And Richard describes his pending case in Chancery to Esther as a house (clearly alluding to Asmodeus): "'If you were living in an unfinished house, liable to have the roof put on or taken off—to be from top to bottom pulled down or built up—to-morrow, next day, next week, next month, next year—you would find it hard to rest or settle'" (462; ch. 37).

3. For discussions on Dickens and the flâneur that are grounded in the work of Baudelaire and Benjamin, see Michael Hollington's "Dickens the Flâneur." *Dickensian* 77.2 (Summer 1981): 71–87; Jaffe's *Vanishing Points* (1991; ch. 1); and John Rignall's *Realist Fiction and the Strolling Spectator* (1992; ch. 5).

4. I am not the first to place such narrative onus on Bucket. Ian Ousby argues that Bucket "can transcend the partial viewpoint to which most of the characters are limited and see the world from a godlike eminence like that enjoyed by the third-person narrator" (392). Albert D. Hutter looks to analyze "Dickens' double narrative in *Bleak House* and his creation of a synthesizing detective figure" (298). While I agree that Bucket "moves between the two narrations and brings them together" (309–10), I argue Bucket is even more important to resolving issues of time, synchronizing the present and past through his physical and formal movements.

5. Bucket's shadow has similar powers. Sir Leicester "seems to shrink in the shadow of [Bucket's] figure," and, after he takes a seat, Bucket "diminishes his shadow" (638; ch. 54). Bucket nicely echoes Dickens's proposed apparatus for *Household Words* when he leads Hortense away from Chesney Wold: "It is impossible to describe how Mr. Bucket gets her out, but he accomplishes that feat in a manner so peculiar to

himself; enfolding and pervading her like a cloud, and hovering away with her as if he were a homely Jupiter, and she the object of his affections" (653; ch. 54).

6. Carlyle's sound-proof study presents an interesting parallel to the "private domicile" of Professor Teufelsdröckh in *Sartor Resartus*, published in serial from 1833–34. Teufelsdröckh boasts, "'I see it all; for, except the Schlosskirche weather cock, no biped stands so high'" (16; bk. 1, ch. 3). Teufelsdröckh's dwelling also anticipates Dickens's "observatory" at Todgers's in *Martin Chuzzlewit* (131; ch. 9) and, most important, demonstrates the possibility for real-world Asmodean omniscience:

> It was the attic floor of the highest house in the Wahngasse; and might truly be called the pinnacle of Weissnichtwo, for it rose sheer up above the contiguous roofs, themselves rising from elevated ground. Moreover, with its windows. . . . it was in fact the speculum or watch-tower of Teufelsdröckh; wherefrom, sitting at ease, he might see the whole life-circulation of that considerable City; the streets and lanes of which, with all their doing and driving . . . , were for most part visible there.
>
> (16; bk. 1, ch. 3)

7. Both Dickens and Carlyle refer to leaky skylights: at Chesney Wold in *Bleak House* (1853), melting snow falls "upon the roof, upon the skylight; even through the sky-light, and drip, drip, drip, with the regularity of Ghost's Walk, on the stone floor below" (701–02; ch. 58); and, as a result of "sudden cataracts of rain," Carlyle writes in a 29 March 1851 letter, "The 'Crystal Palace' is taking in floods of rain,—drip, drip in all corners" (*Collected* 26: 51–53). In *Miss Leslie's Lady's House-Book* (1850), Eliza Leslie recommends, "Care should be taken that all the wood-work of the sky-light (as well as the glass) fits tightly; otherwise it will not only leak from rain, but from the melting of the snow, when it thaws" (327).

8. Carlyle abandoned his study in 1865, converting it into maid's quarters, and thus back into a feminine space. For an interesting parallel, see C. Anita Tarr's "Getting To the Lighthouse," which discusses Carlyle's soundproof study and its influence on Woolf's *A Room of One's Own* (1929).

9. Dickens also mentions having read a lengthy piece on the subject from the 1844 *Westminster Review* (see "Postscript" 252–62).

10. The pamphlet includes a poem on the subject signed by "D. J."; the first stanza is worth quoting:

> "Examine well our tax on *Window Light*:
> Did ever a fool's blunder, or the pen
> Of 'moody madness' ever once indite
> A public Act more ruinous?—for when
> The people thus change sunlight into night,
> As, more or less, they do before all men,
> A lunatic would laugh, it looks so funny;
> The people *lose the light*, the Peers *the money*."
>
> (3)

11. Later in the same year (1833) that Parliament voted down measures to abolish the window tax, Dickens published his first essay, "A Dinner at Poplar Walk," in *The Monthly Magazine*. The 1851 Great Exhibition at the Crystal Palace ended just before the tax was repealed. Isobel Armstrong traces the developments of new glass-making techniques in the nineteenth century that "created a new glass consciousness and a language of transparency" (1).

12. In Charlotte Smith's *The Old Manor House* (1793), Orlando "found many of the windows bricked up, the economy of the present possessors not allowing them to pay so heavy a window tax" (503; vol. 4, ch. 12). In *The Professor*, which Charlotte Brontë wrote in 1846, Crimsworth relates, "light not being taxed in Belgium, the people never grudge its admission into their houses" (65; ch. 7). In Elizabeth Gaskell's *Wives and Daughters* (1865), "it was a tradition in the servants' hall that . . . the library windows had been boarded up to avoid paying the window-tax. And when the 'young gentlemen' were at home the housemaid, without a single direction to that effect, was regular in her charge of this room; opened the windows and lighted fires daily" (80; ch. 6). In Wilkie Collins's *The Woman in White* (1860), Walter Hartright explains, "The room had once been lighted by a small side window; but this had been bricked up, and a lantern skylight was now substituted for it" (488; ep. 3, ch. 9). Because the bricked-up windows (and broken door locks) trap Sir Percival inside the burning church, one could read the scene as Collins commenting on the window tax by making the money-hungry Sir Percival meet this fate. Worth further mention is Collins's novel *Heart and Science* (1883), which contains the following discussion: "'Has nobody peeped in at the windows?' she asked. 'There are no windows—only a skylight in the roof.' 'Can't somebody get up on the roof, and look in through the skylight?'" (160–61; vol. 1; ch. 12).

13. Armstrong reads Chancery as "a principle of exclusion, as its glass door becomes a barrier and the lantern admits no light" (247).

14. Boz for Jaffe "resembles" Dickens's proposal for *Household Words*, but he "points away from the identity of author and narrator toward that of character" (24). Julian W. Breslow argues that Dickens "develops the narrator as a consistent character who provides the reader with an authoritative perspective from which to view and judge the world of *Sketches*" (127).

15. Reading from a Lacanian perspective, Jaffe argues that "Quilp becomes both subject and object of the reader's gaze; seeing what he sees, we suddenly see him as well" (55). Quilp also monitors other characters using mirrors: "Mrs Jiniwin happening to be behind him, could not resist the inclination she felt to shake her fist at her tyrant son-in-law. It was the gesture of an instant, but as she did so and accompanied the action with a menacing look, she met [Quilp's] eye in the glass, catching her in the very act" (47; ch. 5).

16. In Phiz's illustration, Quilp's corpse faces up as he lies sprawled out on a sandbar after his fall. In George Cattermole's illustration, Nell ascends to heaven, as four angels transport her upwards toward rays of light.

17. This scene is also suggestive of Phillipe Jacques de Loutherbourg's late-eighteenth-century magic lantern shows. Loutherbourg "constantly experimented with the distribution and control of light" (Altick 120), placing "stained glass slips of yellow, red, green, purple, and blue" in front of lamps for effect (123). John Plunkett suggests the "magic reel" is a reference to the moving panorama, which makes Dickens a "lecturer-cum-showman, whose role is to explain the moving scene passing before his readers" (8). In *Barnaby Rudge* (1841), Dickens writes that "Chroniclers are privileged . . . to overcome . . . all obstacles of distance, time, and place" (80; ch. 9), suggesting an early conception of the transcendent power over material and temporal limitations that he wished his narrators to achieve.

18. "Carker," Jaffe notes, "with his powers of observation and ability to move between public and private life, is inescapably linked to the narrator" (88). And Garrett Stewart suggests, "Dickens throws a great deal of himself into Quilp" (97).

19. Still, Carker's death lacks the deliberate move to pronoun objectivity; his body, though in "fragments," maintains its subjectivity. After Carker is gathered up, however, Dombey sees "some*thing* covered" (842; ch. 55, emphasis mine), and both villains are early compared to animals: Quilp has "the aspect of a panting dog" (29; ch. 3) and Carker "the snarl of a cat" (195; ch. 13). George Eliot's *Romola* (1863) contains a similar punishment for a powerful antagonist. Romola feels that Tito Melema "had the power of seeing everything without seeming to see it" (349; bk. 3, ch. 43). But Tito is not "quite omniscient" (474; bk. 3, ch. 64) and nearly drowns attempting escape from an angry mob. He is ceremoniously finished off by Baldassarre after being, like Quilp, "cast violently on the grass" (498; bk. 3, ch. 67).

20. A similar anxiety infests Mr. Jaggers's office in *Great Expectations* (1861): it "was lighted by a skylight only, and was a most dismal place; the skylight, eccentrically pitched like a broken head, and the distorted adjoining houses looking as if they had twisted themselves to peep down . . . through it" (164; ch. 20). Making note of Dickens's desire for an Asmodean domestic view in *Dombey and Son*, Colette Colligan argues, "the secrets that the novel hopes to uncover . . . do not entirely dwell within the female characters, but most saliently within Dombey himself" (102).

21. In chapter 1 of *Bleak House*, echoing *Dombey and Son*, the Lord Chancellor sits, "outwardly directing his contemplation to the lantern in the roof" (6). The "lantern" here is a large, multi-paned skylight that resembles what Rob peers through (fig. 1). In *The Pickwick Papers* (1837), Sam Weller looks "right up into the lantern in the roof of the court" (483; ch. 34). I am purposefully omitting the first-person *David Copperfield* (1850), but it is worth noting that David observes like Florence, Rob, and later Mr. Bucket: "I must not forget that we went on board the yacht, where they all three descended into the cabin, and were busy with some papers. I saw them quite hard at work, when I looked down through the open skylight" (23; bk. 1, ch. 2). Worth further mention is the chapter's title: "I Observe."

22. In "Among Sharp's," a story that appears in Dickens's *All the Year Round* for 1868, the narrator describes a similar shooting gallery: "I looked in at that open door. I saw a strong room or cell, seven feet square, as near as I can judge—nothing but

bare brick walls, no window (it was lighted for the moment from the passage), and deep sawdust on the floor. Both the men were beside the door, standing half in light half in shadow" (252).

23. Bucket's comparison is apt, for the other cat in the novel, Krook's Lady Jane, also stalks her prey, Miss Flite's collection of birds. Lady Jane, Miss Flite explains, "'is greedy for their lives. She crouches on the parapet outside for hours and hours. I have discovered . . . that her natural cruelty is sharpened by a jealous fear of their regaining their liberty. . . . She is sly and full of malice. I half believe, sometimes, that she is no cat, but the wolf of the old saying'" (54; ch. 5). Lady Jane is also purported to "roam the house-tops" (493; ch. 39).

24. Elizabeth Deeds Ermarth argues that the narrator in a realist text is "'nobody'. . . . [It] is not individual, and it is not corporeal. . . . [I]t is a collective result, a specifier of consensus" (65).

25. Peter Thoms notes that Bucket's "powers" suggest "how particular acts of investigation may engender an oppressive sense of widespread surveillance" (159).

26. In a 1 February 1851 *Household Words* essay titled "Plate Glass," which appeared just days after his letter to Henry Austin concerning the window tax, and three months before the Great Exhibition, Dickens narrates a trip to the Thames Plate Glass Company to witness and exalt in the manufacturing process of plate glass.

27. Crown glass, flat on the sides, but bulging and thick in the middle, also presents an interesting parallel to E. M. Forster's definition of flat and round characters. Even more interesting, however, is Forster's short discussion of the first three chapters in *Bleak House*, during which he describes the narrator's omniscience: "his eyes . . . grow weak" before he "inhabits" Esther (78). In addition, Dickens does use crown glass as a metonym in *A Tale of Two Cities*: "soon the large-faced King and the fair-faced Queen came in their golden coach, attended by the shining Bull's Eye of their Court, a glittering multitude of laughing ladies and fine lords" (180; bk. 2, ch. 15). Several critics have noted this as a reference to Carlyle's "Oeil de Boeuf," the term he applies to the court at Versailles in *The French Revolution* (1837). Again, we return to the conflation between skylights and bull's-eye glass, as an Oeil de Boeuf is "an octagonal vestibule lighted by a small oval window" (*OED*), which typically was featured on roofs or above doors.

28. In *Sartor Resartus*, Teufelsdröckh notes, "With awe-struck heart I walk through that Monmouth Street, with its empty Suits, as through a Sanhedrim of stainless Ghosts. Silent are they, but expressive in their silence: the past witnesses and instruments of Woe and Joy, of Passions, Virtues, Crimes, and all the fathomless tumult of Good and Evil in 'the Prison men call Life'" (178; bk. 3, ch. 4). The influence on Dickens here is clear.

29. Thomas Hardy describes a similar experience in *Under the Greenwood Tree* (1872): "The window was set with thickly-leaded diamond glazing, formed, especially in the lower panes, of knotty glass of various shades of green. Nothing was better known to Fancy than the extravagant manner in which these circular knots or eyes distorted everything seen through them from the outside—lifting hats from

heads, shoulders from bodies; scattering the spokes of cart-wheels, and bending the straight fir-trunks into semicircles" (105; pt. 2, ch. 6). The fitting name of Hardy's heroine, Fancy, suggests the role the imagination plays in this vitreous illusion.

30. Much critical discourse has been levied concerning this passage. James Buzard argues that Bucket's "failure" to find Lady Dedlock in time "makes a mockery of an established ideal of knowledge which he appears to invoke" (20). Richard Maxwell observes that Lady Dedlock "can be tracked to the spot of her death only by a return to earth" ("Dickens's" 297) and then later argues, "Bucket is not infallible, certainly not capable in himself of healing the novel's various rifts—just as he is incapable of finding Lady Dedlock before she has died" (*Mysteries* 360; n. 32).

31. So, too, does Anthony Trollope in *The Warden* (1855): "Perhaps, however, Mr Sentiment's great attraction is in his second-rate characters. If his heroes and heroines walk upon stilts, as heroes and heroines, I fear, ever must, their attendant satellites are as natural as though one met them in the street: they walk and talk like men and women, and live among our friends a rattling, lively life; yes, live, and will live till the names of their calling shall be forgotten in their own, and Buckett and Mrs Gamp will be the only words left to us to signify a detective police officer or a monthly nurse" (126; ch. 15). The misspelling of Bucket's name here is oddly prevalent across of variety of works. Perhaps some have conflated Dickens's detectives, Bucket and Nadgett. Trollope incorrectly predicted Mrs. Gamp's semiotic history, as her name was instead adopted as slang for an umbrella.

32. In *The Pickwick Papers*, Mr. Pickwick uses "'the most extraordinary lantern'" which "threw a very brilliant little tunnel of light before them, about a foot in diameter. It was very pretty to look at, but seemed to have the effect of rendering surrounding objects rather darker than before" (553–54; ch. 39). In *Our Mutual Friend*, Mr. Inspector also uses a bull's-eye lantern.

33. Bucket also may remind us of Carlyle's Diogenes Teufelsdröckh.

34. The magic lantern "permeated all aspects of [Victorian] life" (23), Grahame Smith observes. Michael Slater notes that Dickens featured a magic lantern at his son's birthday party in 1843 (212). And probably most quoted is Dickens's frustration in a 30 August 1846 letter to Forster over trying to compose *Dombey and Son* while living in Switzerland: "a day in London sets me up again and starts me. But the toil and labour of writing day after day, without that magic lantern is IMMENSE!!" (*Letters* 4: 612). Joss Marsh notes that Dickens's childhood fascination with magic lanterns manifested itself into a prevailing metaphor in his adult writing. The invention and proliferation of dissolving-view technology during front-projection lantern shows made the magic lantern, Marsh argues, "a Victorian metaphor for transformation, truth-telling and spiritual regeneration" (3). For example, in *Bleak House*, Bucket "appeared to vanish by magic and to leave another and quite a different man in his place" (311; ch. 24). Maria Cristina Paganoni has recently used the magic lantern "as an apt image to emphasise the surrealistic qualities of Dickens's imagination" (3) in order to provide a conceptual framework for her greater project on doubles in Dickens. Francesca Orestano goes further: "Dick-

ens's experiments with description rely on the magic lantern technique because its heterogeneous images, dissolving and melting into each other, endow the written text with the paradigmatic cogency of visual forms in their mutually creative relationship" (264). I am less concerned, however, with understanding Dickens through the aesthetic product of the magic lantern (a painted or photographed image made large and manipulated on a canvas) than with how he gets there, how he imagines narrative through the effects of glass production and use that provided him a novel way of seeing, experiencing, and narrating the world.

35. Although Mackenzie does not acknowledge when this occurred, Dickens visited Rome in 1844 and 1853. During the first trip, he wrote *Pictures from Italy* (1846), which Kate Flint fittingly calls in her introduction to the text "a chaotic magic-lantern show, fascinated both by the spectacle it offers, and by himself as spectator" (vii). The second trip came on the heels of his arduous completion of *Bleak House*.

36. Rignall proceeds to argue that Dickens's novels "reveal not the loss of the flâneur's vision," evidenced in *Sketches by Boz*, but rather "its development" (64). While Bucket "gives physical form to the flâneur-like qualities of the anonymous narrator" (70), the reverse is also true: the narrator assigns Bucket qualities of omniscience.

37. Dickens's words, "lamp of life," may also refer to Ruskin's *Seven Lamps of Architecture* (1849), notable for the number seven (see fig. 4), and for its chapter, "The Lamp of Life," in which Ruskin argues that in "the highest order of creative life, . . . the mind of man," objects "become noble or ignoble in proportion to the amount of the energy of that mind which has visibly been employed upon them" (190).

38. In "Signs of the Times" (1829), Carlyle makes an interesting comparison between the police and Argus: "'superior morality' is properly rather an 'inferior criminality,' produced not by greater love of Virtue, but by greater perfection of Police; and of that far subtler and stronger Police, called Public Opinion. This last watches over us with its Argus eyes more keenly than ever; but the 'inward eye' seems heavy with sleep" (50).

39. Dickens may also be alluding to the illusion of binocular vision, the knowledge of which, evident through devices like the stereoscope, reflected "a radical abstraction and reconstruction of optical experience, thus demanding a reconsideration of what 'realism' means in the nineteenth century" (Crary 9). Binocular vision, the combination of the different images from two eyes, creates depth. With the two bull's-eye lanterns, then, Bucket creates visual depth in the "squalid depths" of Tom-all-Alone's (278; ch. 22). In *The Pickwick Papers* (1837), Sam Weller explains, "'Yes I have a pair of eyes . . . and that's just it. If they wos a pair o' patent double million magnifyin' gas microscopes of hextra power, p'raps I might be able to see through a flight o' stairs and a deal door; but bein' only eyes, you see, my wision's limited" (484; ch. 34). Later in the novel, Dickens sides with Sam's limitations: "Some men, like bats or owls, have better eyes for the darkness than for the light. We, who have no such optical powers, are better pleased to take our last parting look at the visionary companions of many solitary hours, when the brief sunshine of the world is blazing full upon them" (799; ch. 57).

40. In Charles Kingsley's *Alton Locke* (1850), a novel concerned with both Dickens and Carlyle, the eponymous narrator paints a similar portrait: "It was a dark, noisy, thunderous element, that London life; a troubled sea that cannot rest, casting up mire and dirt; resonant of the clanking of chains, the grinding of remorseless machinery, the wail of lost spirits from the pit. And it did its work upon me; it gave a gloomy colouring, a glare as of some Dantean 'Inferno,' to all my utterances" (94–95; ch. 9). Worth further mention is Elizabeth Barrett Browning's description in *Aurora Leigh* (1856) of the London poor who inundate the scene of Romney and Marian's marriage:

> Those, faces? 'twas as if you had stirred up hell
> To heave its lowest dreg-fiends uppermost
> In fiery swirls of slime,—such strangled fronts,
> Such obdurate jaws were thrown up constantly
> To twit you with your race, corrupt your blood,
> And grind to devilish colours all your dreams.
> (4.587–92)

41. During this journey, Esther envisions "a face, rising out of the dreaded water" (678; ch. 57).

42. These binaries are often also characters. See Dona Budd's "Language Couples in *Bleak House*." *Nineteenth-Century Literature* 49 (Sept. 1994): 196–220.

43. Bucket also speaks the last words in the present-tense, third-person chapter 56, and the first words as he invades Esther's past-tense, first-person chapter 57.

44. Bucket's forefinger is several times referred to as his "familiar demon" (626, 634; ch. 53; 636, 645; ch. 54). Dorothy Parker notes, "it is Bucket's hand rather than finger that is emphasized at the outset" (31).

WORKS CITED

Altick, Richard. *The Shows of London*. Cambridge: Harvard Belknap, 1978.

Armstrong, Isobel. *Victorian Glassworlds*. Oxford: Oxford UP, 2008.

Blunt, Reginald. *The Carlyles' Chelsea Home*. London: George Bell, 1895.

Bowen, James. *Other Dickens*. Oxford: Oxford UP, 2000.

Breslow, Julian W. "The Narrator in *Sketches By Boz*." *ELH* 44.1 (Spring 1977): 127–49.

Brontë, Charlotte. *Jane Eyre*. Ed. Stevie Davies. London: Penguin, 2006.

———. *The Professor*. Ed. Margaret Smith. Oxford: Clarendon, 1987.

———. *Villette*. Ed. Helen M. Cooper. London: Penguin, 2004.

Browning, Elizabeth Barrett. *Aurora Leigh*. Ed. Margaret Reynolds. New York: Norton, 1996.

Buzard, James. "'Anywhere's Nowhere': *Bleak House* as Autoethnography." *The Yale Journal of Criticism* 12.1 (1999): 7–39.

Byron, Lord. *Byron's Letters and Journals*. Vol. 10. Ed. Leslie A. Marchand. London: J. Murray, 1980.

———. "Granta." *The Complete Works*. Vol. 7. Paris: Baudrey, 1825. 175–79.

———. *The Major Works*. Ed. Jerome J. McGann. Oxford: Oxford UP, 2000.

Cain, Lynn. *Dickens, Family, Authorship: Psychoanalytic Perspectives on Kinship and Creativity*. Burlington, VT: Ashgate, 2008.

Capes, S. C. "On Light: Its Influence on the Proper Arrangement in the Plans of Buildings." *The Civil Engineer and Architects Journal* 23 (1860): 140–43.

Carlyle, Thomas. *The Collected Letters of Thomas and Jane Welsh Carlyle*. 35 Vols. Durham, NC: Duke UP, 1970–2010.

———. *Letters and Memorials of Jane Welsh Carlyle*. 2 Vols. New York: Charles Scribners, 1913.

———. *Reminiscences*. London: Macmillan, 1887.

———. *Sartor Resartus*. Ed. Rodger L. Tarr. Berkeley: U of California P, 2000.

———. "Signs of the Times." *A Carlyle Reader*. Ed. G. B. Tennyson. Cambridge: Cambridge UP, 1984. 31–54.

"Characters in *Bleak House*." *Putnam's Monthly* 2 (Nov. 1853): 558–62.

Colligan, Colette. "Raising the House Tops: Sexual Surveillance in Charles Dickens's *Dombey and Son* (1846–48)." *Dickens Studies Annual* 29 (2000): 99–144.

Collins, Wilkie. *Heart and Science*. Vol. 1. London: Chatto & Windus, 1883.

———. *The Woman in White*. Ed. Camille Cauti. New York: Barnes & Noble, 2005.

Cook, Eliza. "Light and Sunshine." *Eliza Cook's Journal* 2 (May 1850): 385–86.

Crary, Jonathan. *Techniques of the Observer*. Cambridge: MIT Press, 1996.

"Curiosities of Taxation." *All the Year Round* 36 (1885): 268–74.

Dante. *The Inferno*. Trans. H. F. Cary. London: Wordsworth Classics, 1998.

Dickens, Charles. *American Notes*. Ed. Patricia Ingham. London: Penguin, 1972.

———. "Among Sharps." *All the Year Round* 19 (1868): 250–53.

———. *Barnaby Rudge*. Ed. Gordon W. Spence. London: Penguin, 2003.

———. *Bleak House*. Ed. George Ford. New York: Norton, 1977.

———. *David Copperfield*. Ed. Nina Burgis. Oxford: Oxford UP, 2008.

———. *Dombey and Son*. Ed. Andrew Sanders. London: Penguin, 1995.

———. *Great Expectations*. Ed. Charlotte Mitchell. London: Penguin, 1996.

———. *Hard Times*. Ed. Kate Flint. London: Penguin, 1995.

———. *The Letters of Charles Dickens*. 12 vols. Eds. Madeleine House, Graham Storey, Kathleen Tillotson, Nina Burgis, et al. Oxford: Oxford UP, 1982–2002.

———. *Little Dorrit*. Eds. Stephen Wall and Helen Small. London: Penguin, 2003.

———. *Martin Chuzzlewit*. Ed. Margaret Cardwell. Oxford: Clarendon, 1982.

———. *Master Humphrey's Clock*. Vol. 1. Philadelphia: Jesper Harding, 1847.

———. *Nicholas Nickleby*. Ed. Paul Schlicke. Oxford: Oxford UP, 2008.

———. *The Old Curiosity Shop*. Ed. Norman Page. London: Penguin, 2000.

———. "On Duty with Inspector Field." *Selected Journalism 1850–1870*. Ed. David Pascoe. London: Penguin, 1997. 306–17.

———. *Our Mutual Friend*. Ed. Jennifer Mooney. New York: Modern Library, 2002.

————. *The Pickwick Papers*. Ed. James Kinsley. London: Oxford UP, 1948.

————. "Red Tape." *Selected Journalism 1850–1870*. Ed. David Pascoe. London: Penguin, 1997. 420–26.

————. *Sketches By Boz*. Ed. Dennis Walder. London: Penguin, 1995.

————. *A Tale of Two Cities*. Ed. Richard Maxwell. London: Penguin, 2000.

————. "A Tour in Bohemia." *Household Words* 9 (1854): 495–500.

Eliot, George. *The Mill on the Floss*. Ed. A. S. Byatt. London: Penguin, 1985.

————. *Romola*. New York: Thomas Crowell, 1891.

Ermarth, Elizabeth Deeds. *Realism and Consensus in the English Novel*. Princeton, NJ: Princeton UP, 1998.

Flint, Kate. Introduction. *Pictures from Italy*. By Charles Dickens. London: Penguin, 1998.

Forster, E. M. *Aspects of the Novel*. New York: Harcourt Brace, 1927.

Forster, John. *The Life of Charles Dickens*. Vol. 2. London: Chapman and Hall, 1890.

Gaskell, Elizabeth. *Wives and Daughters*. Ed. Margaret Lane. London: Dent, 1966.

"A Gossip About New Books." *Bentley's Miscellany* 34 (1853): 367–74.

Hardy, Thomas. *Under the Greenwood Tree*. Ed. Geoffrey Grigson. London: Macmillan, 1975.

Hearn, Michael Patrick. *The Annotated Christmas Carol*. New York: Norton, 2004.

Hepburn, James G. *A Book of Scattered Leaves: Poetry of Poverty in Broadside Ballads of Nineteenth-Century England*. Vol. 2. London: Associated University Presses, 2001.

Humberstone, M. *The Absurdity and Injustice of the Window Tax*. London: W. S. Orr, 1841.

Hutter, Albert D. "The High Tower of His Mind: Psychoanalysis and the Reader of 'Bleak House.'" *Criticism* 19.4 (1977): 296–316.

"Industrial History of a Straw-Bonnet." *Chambers's Journal* 3 (1855): 327–28.

Jaffe, Audrey. *Vanishing Points: Dickens, Narrative, and the Subject of Omniscience*. Berkeley: U of California P, 1991.

James, Henry. *The Portrait of a Lady*. Ed. Robert D. Bamberg. New York: Norton, 1975.

Kingsley, Charles. *Alton Locke: Tailor and Poet*. Ed. Elizabeth A. Cripps. Oxford: Oxford UP, 1983.

Larkin, Philip. *Collected Poems*. Ed. Anthony Thwaite. New York: Farrar, Straus and Giroux, 2003.

Lesage, Alain-René. *Asmodeus; or, The Devil on Two Sticks*. Trans. Joseph Thomas. London: Joseph Thomas, 1841.

Leslie, Eliza. *Miss Leslie's Lady's House-Book*. Philadelphia: A. Hart, 1850.

Mackenzie, R. Shelton. *Life of Charles Dickens*. Philadelphia: P. B. Peterson, 1870.

Mancini, Michelle. "Demons on the Rooftops, Gypsies in the Streets: The 'Secret Intelligence' of *Dombey and Son*." *Dickens Studies Annual* 30 (2001): 113–40.

Marsh, Joss. "Dickensian 'Dissolving Views': The Magic Lantern, Visual Story-Telling, and the Victorian Technological Imagination." *Comparative Critical Studies* 6.3 (2009): 333–46.

Maxwell, Richard. "Dickens's Omniscience." *ELH* 46.2 (Summer 1979): 290–313.

———. *The Mysteries of Paris and London.* Charlottesville: UP of Virginia, 1992.

Miller, D. A. *The Novel and the Police.* Berkeley: U of California P, 1988.

Miller, J. Hillis. *Victorian Subjects.* Durham, NC: Duke UP, 1991.

Orestano, Francesca. "The Magic Lantern and the Crystal Palace: Dickens and the Landscape of Fiction." *Dickens: The Craft of Fiction and the Challenges of Reading.* Ed. Rossana Bonadei. Milan: Edizioni Unicopli, 2000. 249–69.

Ousby, Ian. "The Broken Glass: Vision and Comprehension in *Bleak House.*" *Nineteenth-Century Fiction* 29 (1974–75): 381–92.

Paganoni, Maria Cristina. *The Magic Lantern: Representation of the Double in Dickens.* New York: Routledge, 2008.

Parker, Dorothy. "Allegory and the Extension of Mr. Bucket's Forefinger." *English Language Notes* 12 (1974): 31–35.

Picker, John M. *Victorian Soundscapes.* New York: Oxford UP, 2003.

"Plate Glass." *Household Words* 2 (1851): 433–37.

Plunkett, John. "Optical Recreations and Victorian Literature." *Literature and the Visual Media.* Ed. David Seed. Cambridge: D. S. Brewer, 2005. 1–28.

"Postscript." *Westminster Review* 41 (1844): 252–62.

"A Preliminary Word." *Household Words* 1 (1850): 1–2.

Praz, Mario. *The Hero in Eclipse in Victorian Fiction.* London: Oxford UP, 1956.

"Prize Essay." *The Gilbart Prize Essay.* Ed. Granville Sharp. London: Groombridge, 1854.

Rignall, John. *Realist Fiction and the Strolling Spectator.* London: Routledge, 1992.

Ruskin, John. *The Seven Lamps of Architecture.* London: George Allen, 1903.

Schor, Hilary M. *Dickens and the Daughter of the House.* Cambridge: Cambridge UP, 1999.

"Skylight." *The Penny Cyclopædia* 22 (1841): 91–93.

Slater, Michael. *Charles Dickens.* New Haven: Yale UP, 2009.

Smith, Albert Richard. "A Visit to Greenwich Fair." *Bentley's Miscellany* 11 (1842): 511–20.

Smith, Charlotte Turner. *The Old Manor House.* Ed. Jacqueline Labbe. New York: Pandora, 1987.

Smith, Grahame. *Dickens and the Dream of Cinema.* Manchester: Manchester UP, 2003.

Stewart, Garrett. *Dickens and the Trials of Imagination.* Cambridge: Harvard UP, 1974.

Storey, Graham. *Charles Dickens:* Bleak House. Cambridge: Cambridge UP, 1987.

Tarr, C. Anita. "Getting To the Lighthouse: Virginia Woolf and Thomas Carlyle." *Midwest Quarterly* 42.3 (Spring 2001): 257–70.

Thomas, Ronald. R. *Detective Fiction and the Rise of Forensic Science.* Cambridge: Cambridge UP, 1999.

Thompson, Silvanus P. Rev. of "Hydrodynamical and Electromagnetic Investigations Regarding the Magnetic-Flux Distribution in Toothedcore Armatures," by H. S.

Hele-Shaw, Alfred Hay, and P. H. Powell. *Proceedings of the Institution of Electrical Engineers* 34 (1905): 37–41.

Thoms, Peter. "'The Narrow Track of Blood': Detection and Storytelling in *Bleak House.*" *Nineteenth-Century Literature* 50.2 (Sep. 1995): 147–67.

Trollope, Anthony. *The Warden.* Ed. Owen Chadwick. London: The Trollope Society, 1995.

Trotter, David. *Circulation: Defoe, Dickens, and the Economies of the Novel.* New York: St. Martin's, 1988.

"Types of Faces." *Lippincott's Magazine* 30 (1882): 417–19.

Van Ghent, Dorothy. "The Dickens World: A View from Todgers's." *The Sewanee Review* 58 (1950): 419–38.

Williams, Katherine. "Glass Windows: The View from *Bleak House.*" *Dickens Studies Annual* 33 (2003): 55–85.

"The Wonder of the Window-Tax." Bridgewater, UK: J. Clarke, 1848.

The *Pickwick* Prefaces

David Parker

Dickens wrote or rewrote prefaces for the first edition of The Pickwick Papers *(1837), for the Cheap Edition (1847), for the Library Edition (1858), and for the Charles Dickens Edition (1867). In them the voice of the reformer is to be heard, the voice of the champion of those who found few champions. But at moments another voice displaces it—preening, prickly, and mendacious. Cavalier about facts, and adapting to circumstances as the years passed, it is a voice which insists that Dickens alone was responsible for making the book what it was, for realizing that the humble serial might be a suitable vehicle for durable fiction, for overcoming youthful limitations, for attracting publishers by remarkable early achievements, and for turning a sequestered country childhood to good account. Dismaying though it is to hear this voice, it leads us to the conclusion that Dickens could write about Mr. Pickwick because, in effect, he was Mr. Pickwick. Both were generous, chivalrous, and valiant when power was abused. Both looked for acclaim, resented their achievements being picked over, and bridled at the least slight. The prefaces are further proof of Dickens's talent for making enduring literature out of his own imperfections.*

Dickens either wrote or rewrote a preface to four editions of *The Pickwick Papers* published during his lifetime.[1] Individually, they are revealing. Studied as a series they are even more so, not least because we hear discordant voices in them. One of these does not represent Dickens at his best, but is instructive all the same.

Dickens Studies Annual, Volume 43, Copyright © 2012 by AMS Press, Inc. All rights reserved.

The preface to the first edition was probably written during October 1837, while he was working on the final double number of the novel. It was distributed with the number, and bound into the first volume edition.

The next preface was for the Cheap Edition of the works, launched by Chapman and Hall in 1847. At intervals between then and 1867, some years after the first volume edition had appeared, a Cheap Edition version of each book by Dickens was issued, in three formats affordable by all but the poorest of readers: in weekly parts at 1½d each, in monthly parts at 7d each, or complete in cloth-bound volumes at prices ranging between 2s 6d and 5s. *Pickwick* was the first book to appear in the edition. Bradbury and Evans took over production of the edition between 1858 and 1861. Chapman and Hall resumed in 1863.

Dickens wrote no more brand-new prefaces for *Pickwick*, but he revised the Cheap Edition preface for the Library Edition of his works, launched early in 1858. Not all the reviews of *Little Dorrit*, completed the previous year, had been enthusiastic. Relations between Dickens and his wife were deteriorating, and they were to separate in May. Dickens is likely to have been wondering about the effect such developments might have upon his reputation as a perennially popular family novelist. Seeking something more than public acclaim, he heeded a suggestion, made by Forster in the autumn of 1857, that an edition of his works be put on the market, appealing to better-off and more discriminating readers (*Letters* 8: 436). The judiciously named Library Edition, he was persuaded, would enhance the status of his works in a way the Cheap Edition never could. Chapman and Hall published the edition jointly with Bradbury and Evans. Volumes were elegantly bound, and the cramped double columns which had characterised the Cheap Edition were abandoned. There was a new vignette half-title for each volume, but no illustrations. The price was 6s per volume. Longer novels comprised two volumes. Once again, *Pickwick* was the first book to be issued in the edition.

The Library Edition did not sell as well as Dickens had hoped it would, so the project was revised. Between 1861 and 1874, Chapman and Hall issued 30 volumes of an Illustrated Library Edition, designed to have a broader appeal. Volumes were priced at 7s 6d each, all the original plates were included, new ones were provided for books that had originally appeared without illustrations, but no changes were made to the prefaces.

The Charles Dickens Edition was the last collected edition of Dickens's works to be launched during his lifetime. Some features suggest it was prompted by his growing sense of mortality. Each volume was bound in red cloth, with his monogram on the cover and a facsimile of his signature stamped in gold. The name chosen for it, "may suggest to the author's countrymen his present watchfulness over his own edition," the prospectus said, "and his hope that it may remain a favourite with them when he shall have left them for ever." Each book in the series was complete in a single volume. There were 21 in all, some priced at 3s 0d, some at 3s 6d. Books originally published with plentiful illustrations came with a selection of eight. Others came with only four. Prefaces were revised or rewritten (Schlicke 205). As ever, *Pickwick* was the first novel to appear in the edition, in 1867. Its preface was a very slightly revised version of the one for the Library Edition.

One thing that stands out in the prefaces is the way Dickens felt driven to protect his reputation against claims made on behalf of Robert Seymour, the illustrator whose proposal for a series of etchings led to the launching of *Pickwick*, and who committed suicide while working on illustrations for the second monthly number. To begin with, during a discussion with William Hall in the chambers where Dickens lived, he had been offered only the opportunity to supply text to accompany etchings devised by Seymour. He urged that the etchings should follow where the text led rather than the other way around, however, and his counter-proposal prevailed (*Pickwick* 885; Forster bk. 1, ch. 5).

The first-edition preface, though, reveals that there was a degree of compromise. "Deferring to the judgment of others in the outset of the undertaking," Dickens declares, he "adopted the machinery of the club." He is alluding to what lay at the heart of Seymour's original proposal—that the serial should feature a Nimrod Club of inept Cockney sportsmen. He "gradually abandoned" the business of the club, Dickens says, but his words indicate something less than outright rejection of Seymour's plan (*Pickwick* xcix).

In the 1847 preface, however, we see a shift of position. Dickens affects vagueness, pretending not to remember that the Nimrod Club had been Seymour's idea. It was "a notion," he says, "either on the part of that admirable humorous artist," or on the part of William Hall—"I forget which." Deference to the judgment of others is forgotten, too. "My views being deferred to," he declares, "I thought of Mr Pickwick, and wrote the first number." He manages to suggest that his own wish to be accommodating prompted such compromise as there was: "I connected Mr Pickwick with a club, because of the original suggestion, and I put in Mr Winkle expressly for the use of Mr Seymour."

The emphasis upon his own volition had evidently to do with Dickens's wish to reply to "various accounts of these Pickwick Papers; which have, at all events, possessed—for me—the charm of perfect novelty" (*Pickwick* 883–85). What he was alluding to became clearer not long after weekly parts of the Cheap Edition began to appear. An American newspaper published a report about the genesis of the book:

> It is now, we believe, generally known that the Pickwick Papers originated with the artist—poor Seymour who, having executed seven or eight etchings, sought a purchaser for them and sent forth his wife for the purpose of finding one. She entered by chance the shop of Chapman and Hall, Strand, and submitted the designs which were at once accepted; subsequently application was made to one Mr Charles Dickens to accompany them with letter-press, and the immortal Pickwick was the result.
>
> (*Republican Compiler*, 17 May 1847)

Pickwick did originate with Seymour, and the application to Dickens for the letterpress was made subsequently, but there are errors both of omission and commission in the report, which was evidently based on claims being made by Seymour's widow.

Left in poverty by her husband's death, she was talking down Dickens, and talking up her husband. Hall had doubtlessly confirmed Dickens's version of their negotiations, contradicting vexatious claims. Edward Chapman certainly did. In a letter to Dickens of 7 July 1849, he commended the account in the 1847 preface: "It is *so* correctly described," he said, "that I can throw but little additional light on it" (*Letters* 5: 575n). But Chapman had not been present during the initial interview. He was merely reiterating what his partner had told him, and Hall, alas, died the year the Cheap Edition was launched, so that public confirmation was no longer to be had from him. It must have been exasperating for Dickens, but he was scarcely going the right way about placating the widow, by pretending to forget her late husband's seminal role.

By 1858 he had even more reason to be exasperated. In the autumn of 1854, Mrs. Seymour had supplemented the story in the *Republican Compiler*, widely retold, with a privately printed pamphlet, *An Account of the Origin of the "Pickwick Papers."* This preposterously allocates Dickens an entirely subordinate role in the shaping of the book:

> Mr Dickens edited a work called "The Pickwick Papers," which was originated solely by my husband in the summer of 1835, and but for a cold (which brought on a severe illness) which he caught on Lord Mayor's Day, on taking his children to view the procession from the Star Chamber, would have been written, as well as embellished, by himself; this cause alone prevented him from doing so, as the numerous periodicals he was constantly engaged upon had greatly accumulated during his illness.
>
> (Kitton 42)

Perhaps Dickens could have stomached the *Republican Compiler*, but this was evidently too much. Mrs. Seymour manages to say that Dickens was only the editor of *Pickwick*, that her husband had been its sole originator, but that he did not write it. "Who did?" we might reasonably ask. Unsurprisingly, the "various accounts of the origin of these Pickwick Papers" of the 1847 preface is grimly emended in 1858 to "various accounts in print" (*Pickwick* 883n).

In 1866 Seymour's son abetted his mother's campaign with a letter to the *Athenæum*, repeating the claims she had made in her pamphlet, and promising further revelations (*Athenæum*, 24 Mar. 1866). Provoked by this, Dickens wrote to the *Athenæum* himself, giving his own account of the genesis of *Pickwick*—contriving to talk down Seymour's role, it has to be said, scarcely less than the widow had talked down his: "Mr Seymour the artist," he affirmed, "never originated, suggested, or in any way had to do with, save as illustrator of what I devised, an incident, a character (except the sporting tastes of Mr. Winkle), a name, a phrase, or a word, to be found in 'The Pickwick Papers'"

(*Athenæum*, 31 Mar. 1866). All true, of course, but it leaves Seymour's original idea out of the picture.

Dickens sent an account of the matter to his eldest son as well, and asked him to procure written confirmation of the way the interview with Hall had proceeded from his mother ("Letters. . . . Supplement V" 153). Catherine, Dickens's fiancée at the time, had been present during the discussion with Hall in 1836, but the couple had separated in 1858.

Wound up by all this, in the 1867 preface Dickens chooses to be precise rather than vague. He fulminates against what he not unreasonably calls "intangible and incoherent assertions," and his memory is miraculously restored. The agreement with Chapman and Hall was concluded, he says, "in the presence of two persons, both living, perfectly acquainted with all these facts, and whose written testimony to them I possess." The second witness was his brother Frederick, also present during the negotiations with Hall. Dickens invokes the testimony of Edward Chapman as well (*Pickwick* 886n).

Dickens's exasperation at the scheming of the Seymours is understandable. There were issues at stake more than mere reputation. Mrs. Seymour asked Dickens for assistance more than once, and in 1845 he subscribed to a fund for the education of her children (*Letters* 4: 418 and nn.). By 1866 he was convinced she was bent upon extortion ("Letters. . . . Supplement V" 153). But it is still fair to ask whether the prefaces do justice to the man whose proposal had triggered the *Pickwick* project, and whether Dickens had to be quite so ruthless in defending his own role. The 1867 preface derides the notion that the illustrator "had some share in the invention of this book" (*Pickwick* 886n). This goes beyond the forgetfulness affected in 1847, into positive misrepresentation. Mrs. Seymour and her son were shadowy figures with a grudge, whom the public might have been trusted to recognize as such. By 1867, few readers could have been in doubt that *Pickwick* was by Dickens. All the evidence supported his story, none of it the Seymours'. A quieter assertion of the facts, unmanipulated and undeviating, would have been more dignified—and kinder.

Another change we can see as we move from preface to preface is in Dickens's attitude towards the literary standing of *Pickwick*. In the 1847 preface, he declares that the book began life only as a "monthly something" to accompany "certain plates to be executed by Mr Seymour" (*Pickwick* 884). These words confirm what Dickens told Catherine in February 1836 about the upshot of the negotiations with Hall. He was being offered the opportunity, he said, "to write and edit a new publication they contemplate, entirely by myself; to be published monthly and each number to contain four woodcuts" (*Letters* 1: 128–29). To begin with, Dickens made no challenge to the common view that serialized fiction was not to be compared with three-decker novels. And it was only in November 1836, eight months after *Pickwick* had been launched, that he ventured to use the term "novel" (*Letters* 1: 189). Even then he did not insist on it. He continued to think *Barnaby Rudge* would be his "first Novel" (*Letters*

1: 165, 283). By the time he wrote the first-edition preface in the autumn of 1837, as the task of writing the book drew to a close, he was more confident about its value, but he did no more than remind readers that the objection to episodic fiction "has been made to the works of some of the greatest novelists in the English language" (*Pickwick* xcix).

The 1847 preface is bolder about the value of the book. It champions "Cheap Literature," which should not be "behind-hand with the Age." *Pickwick* relies for effect upon "diverting characters and incidents," he grants, at the expense of "ingenuity of plot," but he is unapologetic about having ignored warnings in 1836 against such "a low, cheap form of publication." His argument, though, is marred by forgetfulness, if not downright dishonesty. In a footnote he invites readers to compare the twenty monthly parts of *Pickwick*, costing a total of nineteen shillings, with "the then established price" of three-volume novels— "about four guineas and a half" (*Pickwick* 883–88). In fact the standard price for a three-volume novel in 1836 was one guinea and a half (Garside passim).

Come 1858, and Dickens wanted to impress readers, not with the cheapness of his books, but with their standing as works of narrative art. Come 1867, and he wanted to impress readers with the durability of his reputation. There is no more talk of cheapness in the prefaces.

Dickens's attitude to his first extended work of fiction also changed in step with the refinement of his art. In later life he told a friend "he did not much care for *Pickwick*" (Fielding 95), and Percy Fitzgerald testifies that he "never spoke of it himself, nor did he much care to hear it spoken of" (1: 5). He seems to have allowed himself to think of the book as an apprentice work. The prefaces record his growing determination to see it as such in a curious way. Dickens was twenty-four when he launched *Pickwick*, twenty-five when he brought it to a conclusion. The voice we hear in the first-edition preface, however, has the assurance of middle-age. It touches sagely upon technical problems and solutions. He strove to make each part complete in itself, he confides, as well as to produce a harmonious whole: "It is obvious that in a work published with a view to such considerations, no artfully interwoven or ingeniously compli-cated plot can be with reason expected. The author ventures to express a hope that he has successfully surmounted the difficulties of his undertaking." (*Pick-wick* xcix). No hint of youthful struggle is allowed in the 1837 preface.

Later prefaces, though, show the author of *Pickwick* getting younger, as the author of all of Dickens's other works got older. In 1847 and 1858 he declared himself to have been twenty-three. In 1867 he became younger still: "a young man of two or three-and-twenty" (*Pickwick* 882 and nn.). It is hard to believe he never did the arithmetic.

Yet, if he came to look upon *Pickwick* as an apprentice work, Dickens never stopped wanting to impress readers with the talent of the apprentice. Chapman and Hall, he remarks in the 1847 preface, were prompted to offer him the chance to write text to accompany Seymour's illustrations "by some pieces I was at that time writing in the Morning Chronicle newspaper" (*Pickwick* 884). He is alluding to pieces later collected in *Sketches by Boz*. The *Chronicle* was the leading Whig newspaper of its day and a prestigious vehicle for short fiction. Dickens worked for it as a journalist, and it did indeed publish a number of the *Sketches by Boz*. But publication history alone rules out the claim that Chapman and Hall were influenced by those sketches. Five of the sketches were published in the *Morning Chronicle* in late 1834, more than a year before the launch of *Pickwick*. Between January and August 1835 another 20 were published in its sister paper, the *Evening Chronicle*. All of these subsequently appeared in the *Morning Chronicle* too, but only one—"Our Parish," on 26 December 1835—during the period when Chapman and Hall were considering the proposal that led to *Pickwick*. The next to appear in the *Morning Chronicle* did so on 18 March 1836, after Dickens had started work on *Pickwick* (Newlin 1: 45).[2]

Dickens's claim, moreover, was eventually denied by the publishers of *Pickwick*. "I was not aware that you were writing in the *Chronicle*," Edward Chapman told him in 1849. His choice had been motivated by advice from Charles Whitehead, editor of Chapman and Hall's *Library of Fiction*, who had identified Dickens as the author of pieces published in the *Monthly Magazine*, a less prestigious publication (Forster bk. 1, ch. 5; *Letters* 5: 575n). If Chapman and Hall were at all influenced by works of Dickens actually appearing when they were putting the *Pickwick* project together, it would probably have been by sketches that appeared between September 1835 and January 1836 in the even more down-market *Bell's Life in London*.

Yet in the 1858 preface we find the same story: Chapman and Hall were "attracted by some pieces I was at that time writing in the Morning Chronicle newspaper." Dickens by then knew this to be untrue. Even in the 1867 preface he prevaricates. Chapman and Hall, he says, were "attracted by some pieces I was at the time writing in the Morning Chronicle newspaper, or had just written in the Old Monthly Magazine" (*Pickwick* 884n). No mention is made of *Bell's Life in London*, or of *The Library of Fiction*.

Dickens also suggests that Chapman and Hall might have been impressed by the collected *Sketches by Boz*. One series of the *Sketches*, he grandly remarks in the 1847 preface, "had lately been collected and published in two volumes, illustrated by my esteemed friend Mr George Cruikshank" (*Pickwick* 884). Lately is the word. The first collection of the *Sketches by Boz*, illustrated by Cruikshank, was published by Macrone on 8 February 1836, just two days before Chapman and Hall contacted Dickens about the project that became *Pickwick*. They might have heard the book was being published, but are unlikely to have read much of it. The same claim is to be found in the prefaces of 1858 and 1867.

The spin Dickens gave to his family background in 1847 and in subsequent prefaces has already attracted commentary—my own included (91–94)—but it cannot go unmentioned here. Dickens states he resisted full acceptance of

Seymour's proposal for a Nimrod Club because, "Although born and partly bred in the country I was no great sportsman, except in regard of all kinds of locomotion" (*Pickwick* 885). You can say he was born and partly bred in the country, only if you understand "country" to mean anywhere outside of London. He was born in the bustling dockyard town of Portsmouth, and, apart from a two-year interval in the capital, for the first ten years of his life his family lived in or near such dockyard towns: Portsmouth, Sheerness, Chatham. However close fields, woods, and streams might have been, moreover, they would have afforded few legitimate sporting opportunities to the small son of a middle-class clerk. Game laws effectively restricted most sporting activities to landowners. The repeal of the more stringent acts in 1827 and 1831 came after the Dickens family had moved to London. And in the mid-1830s Dickens was only just beginning to master kinds of locomotion other than walking. Catherine, his fiancée, worried about his horsemanship when he was sent by the *Morning Chronicle* to report on an election in Kettering in 1835. Dickens had to assuage her fears by joining other reporters in hiring a chaise (*Letters* 1: 109). During the 1835 general election, covering the contest in Chelmsford, he hired a gig: "and what is more," he comically boasted, "I actually did the four and twenty miles without upsetting it" (*Letters* 1: 53). Dickens was not the son of the manor he contrives to suggest, neglectful of gun and rod, but haunter of the stable from a tender age.

From his published works, from his letters and his speeches, from judgments made by his contemporaries, and from biographies, students of Dickens can gauge the man's character and know him to have been, for the most part, compassionate, magnanimous, and principled. He was no saint, certainly. He was troubled and morally complex, as prone to error as most, but for all that he was a striver after the good, a loather of the false, a staunch friend—with marked exceptions a conscientious family man—and a champion of the defenseless. The *Pickwick* prefaces themselves reveal a passion for justice, largely selfless. They show him to have been, in particular, an indefatigable campaigner for improvements in the lot of the least privileged and the least fortunate.

In the 1847 preface he lists social problems which *Pickwick* had highlighted, plus others that had subsequently engaged his attention. History proves the importance of most of the problems he identified. It is not difficult to detect his exact knowledge of the issues. Nothing is withdrawn from the list in the 1858 and 1867 prefaces.

One or two ills, he concedes in 1847, had been remedied in the previous ten years. Legal reforms, he observes, "have pared the claws of Messrs Dodson and Fogg" (*Pickwick* 887). Keenly alert to whatever might be actionable, readers will remember, attorneys Dodson and Fogg characteristically provoke Mr. Pickwick in front of witnesses: "You had better call us thieves, sir; or perhaps you would like to assault one of us. Pray do it, sir, if you would; we will not make the smallest resistance" (*Pickwick* 295). They are masters of legal process at the expense of justice. Measures brought in by the reforming Lord Chancellor, Lord Brougham, during the 1830s and 1840s, had rendered the law less susceptible to cunning manipulation. A start had been made on reforming Chancery, the Old Bailey had been reformed, and a royal commission was at work, digesting all criminal law into a single code. By 1845 Brougham was able to boast that, of the 62 defects in the legal system he had denounced in an 1828 speech, 56 had been remedied.

Dickens also took satisfaction, we can be sure, from changes that were made in "the laws relating to imprisonment for debt" (*Pickwick* 887). Pre-trial imprisonment for debt had been abolished in 1838, and the Fleet Prison had been demolished in 1846.

But it was an age of reform, and many more reforms were being sought. Dickens reminded his readers in 1847 of the way Bardell v. Pickwick drew attention to "The license of Counsel, and the degree to which Juries are ingeniously bewildered" (*Pickwick* 887). The "licence of counsel" signified the putative entitlement of a barrister to make any conjecture about matters of fact not strictly counter to evidence, so long as it served his client's interests— the means by which Serjeant Buzfuz ingeniously bewilders the jury (*Pickwick* 515–33). There was still vocal support for the license of counsel in 1847. A letter to the *Times* from a barrister argued that counsel's duty was simply "to frame the best defence in his power from the evidence given at the trial." "The principle of advocacy," it insisted, would be "abolished altogether," should the license of counsel be curbed (*Times*, 30 December 1847). This was in fact an abuse unremedied in Dickens's lifetime.

The 1847 and subsequent prefaces urged "an improvement in the mode of conducting Parliamentary Elections" (*Pickwick* 887), but it was only with the Ballot Act of 1872 that all Dickens sought was achieved. "Magistrates in town and country," the prefaces urged, "should be taught to shake hands every day with Common-sense and Justice." The Municipal Corporations Act of 1835 and the Summary Jurisdiction Act of 1848 improved the quality and performance of the magistracy, but its power, prestige, and high-handedness were not finally curbed until the Local Government Act of 1888 was passed.

The prefaces looked forward to a time when "Poor Laws may have mercy on the weak, the aged, and unfortunate." Poor relief only began to change during the early decades of the twentieth century. The prefaces also urged educational reform, but it was not until 1870, the very year of Dickens's death, that an Education Act opened the way to free and compulsory elementary schooling for all. They urged prison reform: it was not until the Prisons Act of 1877 that the penal system was put on a sensible footing. They urged sanitary reform. Some progress was achieved in Dickens's lifetime, an important Public Health Acts was passed in 1848, and government reports directed more and more attention to the issue, but the corner was not turned until further acts were passed in 1872 and 1875 (*Pickwick* 887).

The curious fact is, we hear two distinct voices in the prefaces. One is the voice of the selfless reformer, champion of good causes, champion of those who found few champions—the voice appropriate to the face of Dickens that George Orwell imagined in 1940:

> He is laughing, with a touch of anger in his laughter, but no triumph, no malignity. It is the face of a man who is always fighting against something, but who fights in the open and is not frightened, the face of a man who is *generously angry*—in other words, of a nineteenth-century liberal, a free intelligence.
>
> (104)

Yet this voice is displaced at moments by one that is preening, prickly and mendacious. Pettily so doubtless, forgivably so perhaps, but undeniably so. Nor is it just the voice of insecure youth. It is to be heard right through to 1867, when Dickens was 55. Rosemarie Bodenheimer has heard a similar voice, principally in Dickens's early letters—though "it never goes away entirely." It is "the voice of indignation and self-justification set off, apparently uncontrollably, by incidents in which Dickens feels slighted, misread, taken advantage of, or unjustly criticized" (Bodenheimer 23). In the *Pickwick* prefaces, fear that he might be exposed to such vexations is as instrumental as any exposure Dickens might have suffered but, given that, Bodenheimer's judgment stands. Dickens's own intentions and behavior, she observes, "are always exemplary, while others accuse him unjustly or take advantage of him without crediting his excellence. He is not angry or aggressive, only sometimes 'hurt'" (25).

Perhaps the first question to ask about the less estimable voice in the prefaces is, does it matter? The history of literature is packed with examples showing the writer to be wiser and better than the man (or indeed the woman). We accommodate the bad behavior of a Byron, a Gissing, or a Larkin. It is only the way that Dickens saw himself, and has been seen by so many, that makes it harder to do in his case. Should we not just swallow our disappointment, be realistic, and make little of this unedifying voice?

A conspicuous symmetry, however, and a conspicuous contrast caution us against neglecting it. *The Pickwick Papers* is a book about a man committed to a sense of what is due to him. Mr. Pickwick seeks to put behind him an early life devoted to gainful toil. He lays claim to wisdom, learning, and distinction. The merchants and shopkeepers of his circle make him happy by applauding these qualities in him. The less admirable of the two voices we hear in the prefaces is that of a man with a strong sense of what is due to him. He seeks to put early drudgery behind him. He believes himself to be to be exceptionally talented, and wants this to be recognized. He is unhappy with anything that threatens to dim the luster of his talents.

The symmetry is inexact, though, and we cannot help noticing contrasts. Mr. Pickwick is not as exceptional as he supposes. Dickens was every bit as exceptional as he supposed. Mr. Pickwick's delusions are redeemed by guile-lessness and an ability eventually to recognize them as such. Dickens's hunger for applause by no means excluded guile, and it never diminished.

We are embarrassed by the lesser voice of the prefaces because Dickens's undisputed defense of the good and the just encourages in us a sequential construction of his life and art. It is easy to think of his books as a distillation of the wisdom he acquired in life. But this construction is too simple. Sometimes the books distill wisdom he had acquired. Sometimes they are the culmination of his quest for wisdom. Sometimes the writer sees what the man has failed to see. Sometimes the books transcend the faults of the man.

The fact is, Dickens could write about Mr. Pickwick because he was Mr. Pickwick—or he at any rate contained within himself something profoundly Pickwickian. Like Mr. Pickwick, he could be selflessly generous, chivalrous when chivalry was called for, and indignant at the abuse of power. But he was also wont to look for acclaim, to resent his achievements being picked over, to bridle at the least slight. And it is the fictional character, in this case, who manifestly learns from his mistakes. Dickens learned from his more patchily, more slowly, more painfully. But, as Rosmarie Bodenheimer has shown, it is possible to know something without learning from it. "Pompous, hypocritical, and delusional language characterizes many of Dickens's characters," she points out: "Through these exaggerated fictional talkers, Dickens suggests his capacity to know with one part of his mind the rhetorical defences he mounts in his own dealings with others" (32).

Dickens was at times capable of contemplating his own endeavors with the ironic detachment he brought to those of his characters. This is something we can see in the one preface to *Pickwick* I have yet to mention—not written by Dickens as a preface, but used as such by Carey, Lea and Blanchard, who published *Pickwick* in Philadelphia, in five phased volumes, the first of which was issued in November 1836. I am speaking of the extended advertisement for *Pickwick* published on 26 March 1836 in the *Athenæum*, and scooped up by the publishers for the American edition, with no more authorization than they had for the text of the book itself.

With no great accuracy, the advertisement promises what Boz will extract from the papers of the Pickwick Club. More to the point, though, it is written entirely from within the ironic scheme of the book, giving prospective readers a tantalizing foretaste of it. Mr. Pickwick, for instance, is described as "the great traveller"

whose fondness for the useful arts prompted his celebrated journey to Birmingham in the depth of winter; and whose taste for the beauties of nature even led him to penetrate to the very borders of Wales in the height of summer.

This remarkable man would appear to have infused a considerable portion of his restless and inquiring spirit into the breast of other members of the Club, and to have awakened in their minds the same insatiable thirst for Travel which so eminently characterized his own. The whole surface of Middlesex, a part of Surrey, a portion of Essex, and several square miles of Kent, were in their turn examined, and reported on.

(*Pickwick* xx–xxi)

Nor is the irony relaxed when prospective readers are introduced to Dickens himself—or to a projection of Dickens himself with most of the customary disguises shed. It is not just the convenient narrative voice, Boz. It is "the author of 'Sketches Illustrative of Every Day Life and Every People.'" This is the "gentleman whom the publishers consider highly qualified for the task of arranging these important documents, and placing them before the public in an attractive form." This is the individual who, with Seymour we are told, will succeed Gibbon on the Roman Empire, Hume on the history of Great Britain, and Napier on the Peninsular War, in delineating "the deeds and actions of the gifted Pickwick" (*Pickwick* xx–xxi).

Strip away every vestige of literary disguise, though, let Dickens address his public in a voice undeniably his own, and the result is very different. To have *Pickwick* contaminated by quibbles was unendurable for him. It had been his escape capsule from the vicissitudes and traumas of his early life. It had been the project that launched him into fame, esteem, and prosperity. However he came to think of the book, he wanted his private narrative of its origins to be preserved. He wanted it to be understood that he and he alone was responsible for making it what it was, for realizing that the humble serial might be a suitable vehicle for durable fiction, for overcoming youthful limitations, for attracting publishers by remarkable early achievements, and for turning a sequestered country childhood to good account. Writing the prefaces for the British editions, he found these to be comforts he could not surrender.

Mr. Pickwick, it should be said, more than compensates for whatever is touchy and self-absorbed in the prefaces, but we must not overlook the man, however much we look to the writer. In *Pickwick*, a sense of what is right is reached by way of personal experience of self-righteousness. Here as elsewhere Dickens demonstrates a special condition of his genius, an extraordinary ability to make enduring literature.

NOTES

1. This paper is based upon one read at the Fourteenth Annual Dickens Society Symposium, at Providence College, Providence, RI, 6–9 August 2009.
2. Paul Schlicke has kindly supplied me with an account of the publication history of all the pieces eventually incorporated into *Sketches by Boz*, more detailed than Newlin's—which nevertheless remains a very useful guide to the subject.

WORKS CITED

Bodenheimer, Rosemarie. *Knowing Dickens*. Ithaca: Cornell UP, 2007.

Dickens, Charles. *The Letters of Charles Dickens*. Ed. Madeline House, Graham Storey, Kathleen Tillotson, et al. The Pilgrim/British Academy Edition. 12 vols. Oxford: Clarendon, 1965–2002.

———. "The Letters of Charles Dickens. Supplement V." Ed. Angus Easson and Margaret Brown. *Dickensian* 101 (2005): 134–58.

———. *The Pickwick Papers*. Ed. James Kinsley. Oxford: Clarendon, 1986.

Fielding, K. J. *Charles Dickens: A Critical Introduction*. London: Longman, 1960.

Fitzgerald, Percy. *The Life of Charles Dickens as Revealed in his Writings*. 2 vols. London: Chatto, 1905.

Forster, John. *The Life of Charles Dickens*. Ed. J. W. T. Ley. London: Palmer, 1928.

Garside, Peter, Anthony Mandal, Verena Ebbes, Angela Koch and Rainer Schöwerling. *The English Novel, 1830–1836: A Bibliographical Survey of Fiction Published in the British Isles*. <http://www.cardiff.ac.uk/encap/journals/corvey/1830s1836.html>.

Kitton, Frederic G. *Dickens and His Illustrators*. 2nd ed. London: Redway, 1899.

Newlin, George. *Everyone in Dickens*. 4 vols. Westport, CT: Greenwood, 1995.

Orwell, George. *A Collection of Essays*. New York: Harcourt Brace, 1946.

Parker, David. *The Doughty Street Novels*. New York: AMS, 2002.

Schlicke, Paul, ed. *Oxford Reader's Companion to Dickens*. Oxford: Oxford UP, 1999.

Whispers and Shadows: Traumatic Echoes in Paul Dombey's Life, Death, and Afterlife

Madeleine Wood

Dombey and Son *traces and retraces the influence of parent upon child with an almost obsessive compulsion; while other themes are undoubtedly present, they are consistently brought back within the confines of the familial narrative. The essay argues that trauma theory provides us with the necessary lens through which to examine* Dombey and Son. *Fanny Dombey's death in the first chapter of the novel inscribes parental loss as a primal moment that is subsequently constituted through a series of differential repetitions, with Paul's own death reinscribing the trauma. Paul himself, denied an identity of his own, becomes a talismanic narrative presence: a force through which other characters orientate themselves, both before and after his death. The "primal scene" represented by Fanny's death retrospectively reveals the fundamental problematic explored by Dickens: the irresolvable conflict between mother and father in which the child is implicated. Dombey's fantasies are an intrusive force, which, when coupled with the uncanny reemergence of the dead mother, propel Paul to a certain death. Paul Dombey is the direct point of intersection for the primal conflict between mother and father: Florence becoming the Echo who lives, potentially to tell and work through the trauma.*

81

Dombey and Son traces and retraces the influence of parent upon child with an almost obsessive compulsion; despite the sustained relationship Dickens creates between the colonial mercantile context and the Dombey family itself, ultimately the story of the firm's fall is brought back within the confines of the familial narrative, as becomes apparent when the firm's ship, the *Son and Heir*, disappears without a trace shortly after Paul Dombey's death. As numerous critics have noted, this was the first of Dickens's novels for which he made number plans; however, criticism of the novel has not adequately addressed the fact that Dickens self-consciously structures the novel via a trauma. Fanny Dombey's death in the first chapter of the novel inscribes parental loss as a primal moment that is subsequently constituted through a series of differential repetitions, with Paul's own death reinscribing the trauma.

Criticism of the novel's familial dynamics has often focused upon Florence and her father's neglect (Hilary Schor and Anny Sadrin take this approach), while Julian Moynahan and Lynn Cain emphasize instead Florence's victorious engulfment of those she loves. Paul himself tends to get lost in these critical strategies; however, on a psychosymbolic level he is at his father's mercy in a far more sinister way than Florence: death shadows him from birth. His very selfhood is crushed before it is begun: as we see in the opening scene he is only ever "Son." The critical neglect of Paul's story occludes the traumatic structuring of the novel; Paul himself, denied an identity of his own, becomes a talismanic narrative presence: a force through which other characters orientate themselves, both before and after his death. The novel's traumatic structure underlines the thematic centrality of the parent to child relation: the affect passed from parent to child emerges as a pervasive and encroaching power that transcends death itself; Dombey's fantasies are an intrusive force, which, when coupled with the uncanny reemergence of the dead mother, propel Paul to a certain death. This essay will argue that trauma theory provides us with the necessary lens through which to examine this, arguably the strangest of Dickens's novels.

Trauma

The model of trauma used for this reading is primarily based upon Sigmund Freud's, taken from his writings of the 1890s (notably *Studies on Hysteria*), which were published prior to *The Interpretation of Dreams* in 1900. These Freudian theories are combined with ideas proposed by French psychoanalyst, Jean Laplanche, who has reconceptualized Freud's early trauma theory in terms of his own "general theory of seduction." Laplanche's idea of seduction underpins my reading of *Dombey and Son*: Laplanche theorizes that the intrusive introduction of the unconscious parental "message" plays a formative role in both the normative and pathological development of the child. Contemporary trauma theories expounded by Dominick LaCapra, Cathy Caruth, and Ruth Leys are also important here, as is Judith Greenberg's idea of traumatic "echoes." The scope of this essay does not allow a full-scale critique of the theories at stake, nor do I attempt to resolve the tensions and inconsistencies between the various theorists; instead, the essay will draw out the relevant concepts and difficulties for a traumatic reading of *Dombey and Son*, before moving onto examine the novel in detail.

Freud formulated the "primal scene" in *Studies on Hysteria* as the originary moment in the trauma, which subsequently leads to a proliferation of auxiliary scenes; the temporal and symbolic relation between these "scenes" created the hysterical symptom. Importantly, for Freud, a trauma cannot exist as an isolated event: a trauma is always a *post*-traumatic disorder. The initial scene is rendered traumatic precisely because it is not felt as such at the time; it lacks affect, and it is only through the operation of *nachtraglichkeit* (translated by Laplanche as "afterwardsness" [Laplanche, "Afterwardsness" 260]) that the "event" can gain potency. Even in Freud's early neurological study, "A Project for a Scientific Pathology," we see this in Emma's history. Emma, a young woman with a phobia of going into shops alone, first presents Freud with a scene, from when she was twelve, in which she went into a shop and had to leave in a panic because she thought the shopkeepers were laughing at her clothes. Through analysis, the scene pointed back towards an earlier childhood moment when a shopkeeper groped the little girl under her dress; the symbolic relation between these two scenes retrospectively engendered Emma's adult phobia, Freud arguing that it was the sexual awareness of puberty (present in the second scene) that belatedly renders the first scene pathogenic (Freud, "Project" 354). This temporal relation implies that something more than the external event is at stake; as LaCapra argues "even an actual event must be the object of phantasmatic investment to become pathogenic" (LaCapra, *History and Psychoanalysis* 16). LaCapra's emphasis here is an important one; while some recent theories have tended to reduce the idea of trauma to the "event" (a problem Ruth Leys explores in *From Guilt to Shame* [9]), both LaCapra and Leys retain Freud's most radical insight: the potency of psychical reality; a reality that evades the simple dichotomy of true versus false: real or imagined. Dickens himself reveals a deep awareness of psychical reality in *Dombey*; dream-like sequences merge with the primary narrative, and Paul's life is characterized by a strange hallucinatory feel in the wake of his mother's death and the loss of his nurse.

Leys draws out the importance of Freud's mimetic theory of trauma; as she says, in a mimetic (or identificatory model) there is a "regressive identification with the original traumatogenic person, scene, or event," which leads to the compulsive repetition Freud identified throughout his case histories (8). This emphasis on mimesis or identification is crucial to an understanding of *Dombey* since the trauma of the mother's death cannot be separated from Paul's and Florence's subjectivities: Fanny's death is not simply an event that happens *to* them since it forms the crux of their selves. Paul identifies with the moment of loss itself: the repetitive refrain that he is "old fashioned" is finally translated on his sickbed, where the "old fashion" is neither more nor less than death itself. Florence, on the other hand, is closely identified with the dead mother herself; at times this association is so pronounced that Florence seems little more than a shadow or a ghost. The Dombey family as a whole can be analyzed in terms of its shifting identifications. Following Dombey's second marriage, Florence disastrously identifies with both her father and her stepmother Edith, and the ensuing conflict between the two identifications engenders the violence between father and daughter, as we shall see later in this essay.

The fact that for Freud the traumatic symptom is built up by a temporal sequence, characterized by *nachtraglichkeit*, is provocative for a narratological analysis; in *Dombey and Son* Dickens creates repetitive echoes that collectively point towards the fundamental familial conflicts. In her article "The Echo of Trauma and the Trauma of Echo," Greenberg persuasively argues that "translating the trauma into language or narration demands a negotiation of 'indirect feeling'—or . . . a reliance on echoes" (320). In this vein, Caruth, in line with Freud, argues that "trauma is not locatable in the simple or violent original event in an individual's past, but rather in the way that its very unassimilated nature—the way it was precisely *not known* in the first instance— returns to haunt the survivor later on" (4). For both Caruth and Greenberg, the ability (or inability) to bear witness or testimony becomes central to their analyses, although this happens in slightly different ways. Caruth uses the metaphor of a voice crying out from the wound to argue that trauma is always bound up with an encounter with the other: the story of the crying wound is "the story of the way in which one's own trauma is tied up with the trauma of another, the way in which trauma may lead, therefore, to the encounter with the other, through the very possibility and surprise of listening to another's wound" (8). This idea of attentiveness is intrinsically bound up with an ethical imperative throughout Caruth's analysis, and we can see a similar imperative enacted in the novel; after Paul's death the story of Dombey and Florence is figured in exactly these terms: Florence's voice, calling out from the wound of Paul's death, is not attended to by Dombey, and chaos ensues.

Greenberg's idea that the mythic figure of Echo can helpfully represent the disrupted and belated act of "telling" in a traumatic stress disorder also resonates with Dickens's technique in *Dombey*: through the echoing motif of the mother's song, sung by the grieving Florence both before and after Paul's death, Dickens beautifully implies Florence's inability to tell her *own* story, compounded, of course, by Dombey's narcissistic inability to listen to it. Florence is, instead, trapped by the maternal and fraternal loss; as Greenberg argues

Echo's story in particular frames a doubly frustrating condition of trauma: first the inability to originate or control speech (the inaccessibility of the original event and the impossibility to narrate it), and then, the isolation or rejection that occurs after the fragments Echo finally finds to utter go unattended.

(332)

Significantly, Florence's voice is not itself enough to enable a process of working through; it is only when the "sun/son" shines upon her that her voice achieves potency.

The exact nature of "working through" remains provocatively ambiguous throughout Freud's theorizations, but nevertheless relies upon the idea that the reintegration of traumatic material within conscious thought can lead to the cessation of unconscious compulsive repetitions. This was, for Freud, emphatically a dialogic process enabled by the therapeutic space and the transferential relation between analyst and analysand (Freud, "Remembering"). For the purposes of this essay, I follow LaCapra by suggesting that "working through" can be helpfully correlated with mourning, whereas "acting out" (or compulsive repetition) can be connected with melancholia. As LaCapra says, in mourning there is a "relation to the past which involves recognizing its difference from the present" (LaCapra, *Writing History* 70): drawing this out further, we can suggest that working through is inherently relational: it involves a negotiation that is both temporal and intersubjective. The acting out of trauma implies that the past possesses the present, just as the lost object possesses the ego in melancholic states.

Significantly, childhood was inextricably connected to both Freud's and Dickens's explorations of trauma. In their writings, they each privilege childhood as the locale for the most profound traumatic scenes: in differing ways, Freud and Dickens represent childhood memory as a normative form of hysterical symptom. For Freud himself there was no clear distinction between a traumatic forgetting and "normal" processes of memorization. In "Screen Memories" (1899) he argues that childhood "memories" operate as screen memories for psychological conflicts, which, for the most part, remain unconscious (Freud, "Screen" 307). Further, "memory is present not just once but several times over . . . it is laid down in various species of indications" (Freud, "Letter 52" 233). In *Great Expectations* Dickens likewise suggests the privileged relation between childhood memory and the development of a trauma; little Pip's terrifying encounter with Magwitch in the graveyard "stands in" for the horrific loss of his parents and siblings, which is never fully acknowledged by the narrator. It is a primal scene, inscribed in the novel as a precipitating force. As we see from the unfolding of events, the encounter continues to resonate—to echo; the meeting with Magwitch determines Pip's subsequent attitude to his "expectations" and to Miss Havisham and Estella. Pip's guilty identification with Magwitch renders him criminal in his own eyes, but likewise displaces the very real guilt he should feel for his snobbish behavior towards Joe.

There is a useful slippage in Freud's writings between the literal primal scene of trauma, seemingly abandoned by *The Interpretation of Dreams*, and the "primal scene of fantasy," first formulated as the imagined scene of parental sex in "A Case of Paranoia Running Counter to the Theory of the Disease" (1915). While this maneuver may at first seem to undermine Freud's trauma theory, I argue that this slippage can actually be a helpful one, potentially revealing more about the central role identification plays in trauma. This originary moment of fantasy does not rely upon a single participant, one lost mother, or one castrating father, as it can only be constructed in the real and imagined interplay of desires between the two parents and the listening or watching child: the scene presenting a signifying sequence or complex to the child. Significantly, this intimates a mode of psychical reality irreducible to a single consciousness or monolithic desire, despite Freud's inability to theorize fully the implications of his own concept. Ikonen and Reichardt reinforce this point of view in their discussion of the "primal scene of fantasy" through the notion of inclusion and exclusion. As they rightly point out, in order to come into being the subject must be both included and excluded from certain structures: to be "somebody" one must be included, but to avoid being turned into "somebody else" one must also be excluded (65). Paul Dombey's problem is that he is not excluded enough: Dombey's mercantile ideal embraces Paul, while rejecting his wife, Fanny, and daughter Florence: Paul's subjectivity is essentially prohibited as a consequence. He is, in Ikonen and Reichardt's terms, "somebody else": he is "Dombey and Son." The scene by Fanny's deathbed is an ode to paternal obsession, rather than a revelation of shared parental love or desire, and everything that happens in the novel subsequently speaks back to this primary problem.

If we lay aside the manifest sexual spectacle underpinning the "primal scene of fantasy" in "A Case of Paranoia," we can observe that this foundational moment involves a latent confrontation of desire between mother, father, and child: a confrontation that for Freud, crucially, has the ability to act as a trauma, but on the level of fantasy. Trauma changed status for Freud, but it was not simply abandoned, instead moving further from the literal into the realm of psychical reality. Despite this maneuver, the tension between the "real" and the "imagined" haunted Freud until his death, as his obsessive analysis of the Wolfman's primal scene reveals. As Laplanche and Jean Bertrand Pontalis point out in *The Language of Psychoanalysis*, Freud's conception of the "primal fantasy" is also problematized by his reliance on an idea of "phylogenesis" (or genetic, inherited, trace memory): an idea that makes an appeal to a distinct reality, albeit a distant and archaic one (331–33). However, we do not have to see Freud's uncertain maneuvers as entirely compromising the validity of the concept of "primal fantasy." The slippages between the known and the unknown, the apparent and the hidden, the imagined and the seen, are indeed crucial to the operation of trauma as later theorists have shown. In "The Primal Scene of Atrocity," Auerhahn and Laub argue that the parents' obsessive retellings are just as elliptical and effacing as speech, while silence is just as burdened as speech. Auerhahn and Laub further argue that the "black hole" of the parents' trauma becomes an alternative "primal scene," the crux for the children's developmental processes (360). In light of these ideas, I argue that Fanny Dombey's death in the opening chapter of *Dombey and Son* operates as a "primal scene" and becomes the crux for the text's development as a whole (as well as Paul's and Florence's processes of development specifically); further, that the scene retrospectively reveals the fundamental problematic explored by Dickens: the irresolvable conflict between mother and father in which the child is implicated. Paul Dombey is the direct point of intersection for these issues: Florence becoming the Echo who lives, potentially to tell and work through the trauma.

Dickens himself was well placed to understand the significance of childhood trauma, as numerous critics and biographers (beginning with John Forster) have noted. The exact sequence of these infamous events has been recently questioned;[1] Claire Tomalin writes "how long he remained pasting and labelling is unsure, not least because he could not remember himself. It seemed to have lasted from February 1824, when he was twelve, to March 1825, when he was thirteen" (Tomalin 28). Michael Slater largely supports this view, writing, "the exact date when Dickens began work at Warren's is unknown but seems likely to have been 9 February 1824" (Slater 20). Robert Douglas-Fairhurst's confident assertion that despite the "false trails and dead ends [supposedly presented in Dickens's autobiographical fragment], it is possible to reconstruct the true sequence of events with some accuracy" (Fairhurst 29) entirely misses the point of why we might wish to do so. The exact sequence of events can have no import outside of our consideration of Dickens's emotional and authorial investment in his own history. Regardless of the exact ordering of events, the autobiographical fragment contained in John Forster's first biography eloquently reveals Dickens's sense of humiliation, abandonment and despair. It is important to note that following his dismissal from the factory, Dickens's resentment became increasingly bound up with his mother, rather than his father:

> My mother set herself to accommodate the quarrel, and did so next day. She brought home a request for me to return next morning, and a high character of me, which I am very sure I deserved. My father said I should go back no more, and should go to school. I do not write resentfully or angrily; for I know how all these things have worked together to make me what I am; but I never afterwards forgot, I never shall forget, I never can forget, that my mother was warm for my being sent back.
>
> (Forster 49)

While it is not my intention to suggest that there is a straightforward relation between Dickens's life and the novels themselves, it is clear that Dickens's larger vision was undoubtedly precipitated, although not reducible to, his own experiences as a child. The combination of paternal failure and (perceived) maternal cruelty expressed in the fragment was reworked compulsively in various forms throughout the novels, most directly in *David Copperfield* and *Little Dorrit*. For Dickens, both as a subject and an author, the child's primal scene of fantasy or trauma was unavoidably bound up with forms of parental failure. Moreover, the irresolvable tension between the father's failure, and the mother's apparent cruelty is likewise played with consistently throughout his novels (although the parental roles are far from static). The childhood traumas are, over and over again, correlated with a primal conflict between the maternal and paternal; the feckless William Dorrit is set against the steely Mrs. Clennam; Magwitch symbolically opposes Miss Havisham; Mrs. Joe and Joe are set in comic conflict. In *Dombey* Dickens uses maternal death as the traumatic event that subsequently allows a thorough exposition of the problematized relationship between parent and child; however, further, as Fanny's death reveals, mothers and fathers operate in an unavoidably dialectical fashion: their children, whether in childhood or adulthood, form the point of intersection for a specifically gendered conflict. This conflict is perpetuated, rather than resolved, by the death of the mother. In *Dombey* the centrality of parental death or absence not only testifies to the psychological problems engendered by mourning (to which I shall return), but also implies a fault line in parenthood itself.

It is the notion of a parental fault line that Laplanche uses as the basis for his "general theory of seduction" (Fletcher 10). This theory lies outside of more traditional trauma studies, but nevertheless is inextricably tied into Freud's early theorizations, as well as later texts, such as the "Three Essays on Sexuality," that focus on infantile development. While it is obvious that the infant's encounter with the world is characterized by a cacophony of information provided by the surrounding adults, loaded with affect, ethics, and thought, Laplanche pushes this idea further by arguing that the other's unconscious unknowingly engenders our own. Laplanche's theory relies on the premise that unconscious parental desire is transmitted to the infant as a verbal, or non-verbal message. This "compromised message" operates as a "signifier to the subject," becoming the determinant force in the development of infantile subjectivity. Parental nurturance "maps" unconscious sexual signification onto the child's body. Once implanted this becomes libidinally invested and phantasmatic: this is a two-phased schema, involving implantation, followed by translation, binding and repression (Fletcher 31). The remainder left over after the infant's attempt at translation is the "source object of the drive," or the repressed (Fletcher 32). The child's reception of the compromised message becomes the first stage of an encounter with the other in a theory of subjectivity that is necessarily traumatic, in the sense that it precipitates a process of repetition, in which something that was lost is sought again (namely the parental "message"). This theory of subjective development resonates strongly with what we see in *Dombey*: the primal scene by Fanny's deathbed introduces a series of compromised parental messages which both Paul and Florence attempt to translate; Paul's ultimate failure to survive the process is indicative of the affective violence created by Dickens in this opening scene, a violence replayed and repeated throughout the novel.

Bad Blood

Dombey and Son falls naturally into well-defined narrative sections, the first dealing almost exclusively with the birth, education, and death of Paul Dombey. The question of parental influence predominates throughout this section, with a dialogue created between the maternal and paternal. As Denis Donoghue observes, an opposition is established between the "icy" Dombey and his children, who are associated with the sea, depth, and the flow of life (391); Auerbach supplements this with the claim that masculinity is associated with time, femininity with space (106). She correctly identifies gendered conflict as determining *Dombey and Son* as the "loss" at the center of the novel (97); but, in fact, this "loss" is far more specific than Auerbach implies. Indeed, the conflict is not solely between "man" and "woman," or indeed between masculinity and femininity, as Claire Senior suggests (112), but between motherhood and fatherhood. Maternal influence appears in this first part of the novel as a flux, represented in fluid form, and bearing the possibility of moral, social, and physical pollution. The search for an appropriate wet-nurse for Paul is, after all, a search for a worthy source of milk. Milk is not the only fluid correlated with maternal influence since it stands for that more primal presence: blood. In *The Child, the State and the Victorian Novel*, Laura Berry explores the contemporary discourses that surrounded breast-feeding: milk was deemed to be far more than food, since it also provided moral sustenance via the bond created between mother and child (66). Childhood was a time of danger, both physical and moral. As Melisa Klimaszewski further argues, milk was a commodity, capable of exposing the economic foundation of the family institution (139).

Fanny Dombey's failure to provide her husband with a boy for the first ten years of their marriage is perceived by Dombey and his sister, Mrs. Chick, as a sign of failure, even neglect of duty in the opening chapter: in Mrs. Chick's eyes, Fanny hasn't made enough "effort," and her death is likewise seen as a personal failing. But Fanny's death is undoubtedly presented as the novel's primal traumatic moment: the first chapter ends with her death, described by Dickens with portentous words, establishing for the first time the shadowy symbolic presence of the sea found persistently throughout *Dombey and Son*: "The mother drifted out upon the dark and unknown sea that rolls round all the world" (11). Death is a drowning: Fanny clinging to Florence as her "slight spar" (10). These first references ensure that the idea of maternal loss is insepa-rable from the recurring image of the sea. Despite the brief sense of grand tragedy, Fanny herself is largely obscured throughout the chapter; far more description is expended on Miss Tox and Doctor Peps. Dickens effectively holds back the pathos, creating it subtly through Fanny and Florence's final desperate embrace. Through the use of the free-indirect style, the chapter's dominant tone is Dombey's own, as the narrator looks over his shoulder to build the scene and the character's psychological condition: "But what was a girl to Dombey and Son! In the capital of the House's name and dignity, such a child was merely a piece of base coin that couldn't be invested—a bad Boy—nothing more" (3). The humorous second paragraph, in which Dickens com-pares the appearances of Dombey and "Son," establishes the pattern whereby Paul is subsumed into his father's identity:

> Dombey was about eight-and-forty years of age. Son about eight-and-forty minutes. Dombey was rather bald, rather red, and though a handsome well-made man, too stern and pompous in appearance, to be prepossessing. Son was very bald, and very red, and though (of course) an undeniably fine infant, somewhat crushed and spotty in his general effect, as yet.
>
> (1)

The repetition of the family name emphasizes its various resonances: with its hints of "dominating," "dominial" (the latter meaning "of or pertaining to own-ership" in the *OED*), and even "domesticate." By naming the family "Dom-*be*," Dickens hints at the overriding passion for control which is Dombey's raison d'être, and that becomes increasingly apparent as the story progresses. If we interpret Fanny's death as a primal loss, as indeed Dickens encourages us to do in the chapter's final words, it is significant that the source of loss is simultaneously obscured: the mother's suppression in this scene provokes her uncanny return. Maternity in *Dombey and Son* is both too absent, and all-too present; maternal loss is placed at the heart of the narrative, but can only be conceived of via the paternal fantasy that dominates the first chapter. Maternal ideals are, in fact, curiously lacking from *Dombey and Son*. Fanny Dombey's death paves the way for a plethora of figures to perform the maternal function for little Paul: Polly, Mrs. Chick, Miss Tox, Mrs. Pipchin, Susan Nipper and ultimately Florence herself; but at no point in the novel does Dickens present such a eulogy on motherhood as he does later in his career through the "little mother," Amy Dorrit. The death of the primal mother leads not to a clear nar-rative ideal, but to a split and fragmented representation of motherhood.

If we consider this opening scene in the light of Laplanche's "general theory of seduction," we can suggest that the patent lack of love between Dombey and Fanny operates as an "enigmatic signifier" or compromised message in the psychical development of their children (and in the novel's own symbolic processes). The scene reveals Dickens's brilliance at rendering minutiae:

every gesture and act is encoded and points towards the fundamental problem. Each of the parents claims ownership of a different child; Florence is aligned with their mother, Paul with their father. The opening sentence finds Dombey sitting at the hearthside, toasting his son like a muffin (1); calling his wife "My—my dear," as her face flushes with embarrassment and surprise (1). Her eyes close at the mention of her son's proposed name (2), and open only as a response to her daughter's gaze (3). She clasps her daughter to her, but cannot rouse herself to look at her son (9). At the sound of her daughter's voice a final "shadow" of a smile appears on her face (10). Fanny's motherhood is idealized through her relationship with Florence, rather than through Paul, and Mrs. Chick chastises the dying woman for having spent little time with her son. It is the lurking pathos of the love between mother and daughter which provides any kind of sentimental ideal, but even so, this is presented quite distantly by Dickens: the small six-year-old girl is described (perhaps ironically, but no less coldly) as clinging to her mother "with a desperate affection very much at variance with her years" (3). Fanny's death appears to be hurried along by the inexorable march of her husband's watch, which seems to assume a faster and faster pace as she fades away:

> "Fanny! Fanny!"
>   There was no sound in answer but the loud ticking of Mr. Dombey's watch and Doctor Parker Peps's watch, which seemed in the silence to be running a race.
>   (10)

The watch takes the place of her heartbeat. Through this eloquent displacement we can imagine a quickening of her pulse followed by nothing: "The race in the ensuing pause was fierce and furious. The watches seemed to jostle and trip each other up" (10). The disjunctive correlation implied between heart and watch establishes the fundamental schism found in the novel between feminized and masculinized forms of both time and value—cyclical physical time, opposed to regimented watch-time: love opposed to materialism. The feminine image is submerged under the male: there is a sense of symbolic oppression suggested by Dickens's narrative technique. We cannot hear Fanny's heartbeat directly.

Rather than the children intruding upon the parents' intimate goodbyes, it is Fanny and Florence who are the unwelcome intruders in Dombey's eyes. Dickens's narrative technique means that there is a clear disjunction created between the tragic event and its narration. The question of exclusion is inverted when Dombey later cannot forget that he was excluded from this scene; he remembers the "two figures clasped in each other's arms, while he stood on the bank above them, looking down a mere spectator—not a sharer in them—quite shut out" (31; ch. 3). These patterns of inclusion and exclusion resonate with Ikonen and Reichardt's interpretation of the "primal scene of fantasy": as we can see, Fanny's death is a shared traumatic event, but the event is crossed over by conflicting desires. Even in Freud's own rather literalistic theory of the "primal scene of fantasy" as the scene of parental sex, the notion of exclusion is also key: children are forced to situate themselves in relation to a parental desire to which they are refused access, as Florence does later when Dombey marries Edith. Dickens consistently implies the traumatic affect bound up with familial exclusion; as we can see this is not only relevant to Florence, but also (in mutated form) to Dombey himself.

Dombey feels the loss of his first wife solely as the loss of Paul's natural nurse, and the consequent socio-sexual anxiety that follows upon this. He pities himself through the child (20; ch. 2). Following Fanny's death, Dickens reveals the potent social and psychological implications of Paul's having a wet-nurse rather than being nursed by his mother, a woman of his own class, in chapter 2, "In which Timely Provision is Made for an Emergency that will Sometimes Arise in the Best Regulated Families" (11). The obsessive concern shown regarding the Toodles family's respectability blurs naturally into comedy. Mrs. Chick checks Polly's "marriage certificate, testimonials and so forth," and Miss Tox ascertains that the blister on the nose of little Biler is "accidental," rather than "constitutional" (16; ch. 2). As Margaret Wiley reminds us, this remark about a "constitutional" blister probably refers to a secondary syphilitic lesion (220). While Dickens undoubtedly intends the Toodles family to represent a positive familial ideal, its members are also caricatured and undifferentiated: each is "apple-cheeked" and identical to the next. Polly Toodles is (to appropriate Shakespeare's term) the thing itself: a soft, round, cushioned representation of motherhood. This operates through synecdoche; as an abstract vision of "wholesome" motherhood, Polly actually seems more like a personified, disembodied, breast. Dombey represents the transaction between the two families as a whoring of motherhood, in which, tellingly, no memory traces will be left of the bond between nurse and child: "the child will cease to remember you; and you will cease, if you please, to remember the child" (18; ch. 2). It is interesting that in his ponderings Dombey perceives a symbolic sexual relation between himself and the wet nurse, for she will be neither more nor less than a stand-in for Fanny Dombey. Dombey's enjoyment in rejecting the maternal candidates displaces the punishment he feels his dead wife deserves for deserting their son; through her very absence, Fanny Dombey is a potentially dangerous force. Dombey attempts to abnegate his own anxiety by removing Polly's womanhood at one fell, and unknowingly comic, stroke by renaming her "Richards." This strong decisive name, with its connotations of male leadership, could not be further away from the round and comfortable sound of "Polly Toodles," and Dombey undoubtedly intends to emphasize his own centripetal power with the name. However, this renaming, while removing Polly's femininity, potentially posits *her* as a source of power in Paul's life, a supposition that is supported by the fact that the little boy calls for her upon his death-bed, much to Dombey's chagrin.

Despite the life-giving nourishment provided by Polly, Paul's infancy takes on an overtly funereal character. Although the traumatic affect engendered by the mother's death has not yet been reinforced by the loss of Polly, the Dombey house seems to be transformed into a dead space, "ghosted by the . . . mother" (Schor 50). The affect is displaced from the subjective to the material: the whole house seems consumed with melancholy, as the "shadow of the lost object" falls upon it (Freud, "Mourning" 249). Freud, of course, famously defined melancholia in opposition to mourning as the inability to work through grief. An "object loss" becomes an "ego loss" as the ego identifies with the lost object. Fanny's death is not openly mourned. Her portrait is shrouded in bandages, as if she is an Egyptian mummy, waiting for her chance to return and wreak violence upon the family: "Odours, as from vaults and damp places, came out of the chimneys. The dead and buried lady was awful in a picture-frame of ghastly bandages" (24; ch. 3). As this passage suggests, no fresh influence can enter, not even from the sky above the house: it is as if the chimneys reach down into the ground, rather than rise up to the sky. Dickens relentlessly emphasizes the air of melancholia through the house's physical presence:

> Every gust of wind that rose, brought eddying round the corner from the neighbouring mews, some fragments of the straw that had been strewn before the house when she was ill, mildewed remains of which were still cleaving to the neighbourhood: and these, being always drawn by some invisible attraction to the threshold of the dirty house to let immediately opposite, addressed a dismal eloquence to Mr. Dombey's windows.
>
> (24; ch. 3)

This image of the straw returning magnetically to the street echoes the sea imagery used by Dickens throughout the novel: a gentle flow, a passing and return, which becomes suggestive of the lost mother. The returning fragments "address" a rebuke towards the Dombey house. The fact that this dirty straw stands in for the mother's absence is suggestive; these mouldering remnants returning on the wind are indicative of the fragmentary (and compromised) nature of maternity in the novel. Mrs. Skewton emerges as the embodied reality of this when Dombey travels to Leamington Spa with Major Bagstock. Dickens's narrative treatment of her death is one of the most effective elements in *Dombey and Son*, but the ghastly disintegration of the mother is foreshadowed from the beginning of the novel.

Paul's second maternal trauma occurs when Polly is dismissed and he is hastily weaned, an event described as "Paul's second deprivation" in Dickens's plan for the novel (Dickens, "Number Plans" 836). Dickens clearly underlines this as a key moment. Chapter 6 concludes with Paul's "crying lustily": "for he had lost his second mother—his first, so far as he knew—by a stroke as sudden as that natural affliction which had darkened the beginning of his life" (84). This is a crucial moment in the development of Dickens's traumatic model. Tellingly, like Freud's, it is characterized by belatedness, by a relationship between two temporal moments: Fanny's death and Polly's loss. Dombey wonders uneasily what consequences this loss had for his young son, the narrator referring much later to the fact that Paul had not been "weaned by degrees" (141). Crucially, as in Emma's case history (Freud "Project"), there is a series of symbolic correlatives between the two moments. The question of maternal blame is again placed at the forefront of the narrative: Polly's dismissal follows upon her visit to the Toodles family in Staggs's Gardens, a visit that, in Dombey's eyes, could potentially contaminate Paul. He is much more concerned with this possibility than the very real fact that Florence has been kidnapped by Good Mother Brown (the maternal pimp). In the wake of his mother's death, and the loss of Polly, Paul grows up into a fragile, thoughtful, little boy. The narrator places the responsibility for Paul's ill health onto the second maternal loss: "Naturally delicate, perhaps, he pined and wasted after the dismissal of his nurse" (91; ch. 8). The problem is not now one of maternal pollution (as with the Good Mother Brown episode), but of glaring maternal absence. Mrs. Chick notes with anxiety that "His soul is a great deal too big for his frame" (96; ch. 8): it is as if his father's soul has been forced upon him, and Paul is physically crushed by the weight of being the "Son."

This second traumatic loss reinscribes (even to a great extent *creates* in subjective terms) the emotional potency of the first, while subtly re-presenting the notion of maternal culpability, which was ironically commented upon by Mrs. Chick in the first scene. Significantly, the repetition dispenses with the irony; Dickens augments the question of maternal responsibility through Florence's childhood episode. Although Dombey's insistence that Polly must abstain from contact with her own family is undoubtedly brutal, her decision to ignore his prohibition leads directly to Florence's falling into the hands of Good Mother Brown. The narrative colludes with Dombey's prohibition through this course of events. Motherhood is not only disrupted but dangerously fragmented by not having a domestic center. As Alice Marwood remarks about Good Mother Brown later in the novel, "she's as much a mother as her dwelling is a home" (464; ch. 33).

Arrested Development

The traumatic structuring of *Dombey* is by no means linear or straightforward. As in Freud's own case histories, the identification of a stable "origin" is inherently problematic. In "Miss Lucy R's" history (*Studies on Hysteria* 106–24) the key traumatic scenes constantly refer back to an earlier moment: there is an unnerving proliferation of scenes that undermines Freud's attempt to limit the trauma to only three of them. In this history, an English governess, "Lucy," initially presents to Freud with a strange hysterical symptom: the perpetual smell of burnt pudding in her nose. Through analysis Freud restricts the functional operation of this symptom to the unrequited desire Lucy has for her widowed male employer, thus creating two obvious problems. The first involves Freud's simplistic temporal model: his contention that the first scene happens in the nursery when Lucy first smells the pudding simply cannot be substantiated, since this scene can only make sense in the context of the earlier deathbed request from the mother for Lucy to take charge of her children. This temporal problem points towards the fundamental duality within Lucy's desire that is ignored by Freud: an identification with the dead mother is offset by (but may also create) the desire for the father. Her hysterical symptom relies on her identification with the mother, and the desire for the father, and the varying messages she receives from both of them. While the origin of the trauma may seem evident, it duplicates itself even in the process of identification. This "problem" in the theory does, in fact, effectively illuminate Lucy's position and the identificatory processes that determine her.

While in *Dombey*'s traumatic structure the two maternal losses are undoubtedly central, Paul's christening is also a key moment, referring back to his birth, as well as looking forward with a gloomy premonition to his sentimental demise and subsequent interment: two very private moments, flanked neatly by their social performances. Although we are told that Paul "pined and wasted after the loss of his nurse," the atmosphere of the christening is also retrospectively interpreted as a negative influence, the narrator speculating that "the chill of Paul's christening had struck home, perhaps to some sensitive part of his nature" (91; ch. 8). Dickens juxtaposes the private (maternal) losses, with the public (paternal) ceremonies, reinforcing the tension between maternal and paternal culpability in Paul's demise. Dickens reminds us in this christening scene that the crisis set in motion by the opening scene was not only one of maternal loss, but also of intrusive paternal fantasy. Paul is born into death: his mother's and his own. The christening is a freezing affair: as the narrator notes, the "chief difference between the christening party and a party in a mourning coach, consisted in the colours of the carriage and horses" (58; ch. 5): "It happened to be an iron-grey autumnal day, with a shrewd east wind blowing—a day in keeping with the proceedings" (54). Paul is welcomed into a deathly world: "dusty urn[s]" adorning the drawing room, as if "dug up from an ancient tomb" (54; ch. 5). Melancholy details abound, even the leaves fall "blighted" (54; ch. 5) as autumn passes into winter. The "chimney glass" bears witness to Dombey and his portrait and "seemed fraught with melancholy meditations" (54; ch. 5). With this image Dickens subtly implies the function that Paul (as well as the christening) serves in Dombey's narcissistic conception of self. Dickens constructs the scene with a moralizing and sustained symbolism. In the church, Mr. Chick accidentally reads out "the reference to Mrs. Dombey's tomb in full, before he could stop himself" (59; ch. 5). Maternal loss, melancholia, and premature death: all are invoked. Dombey's emotional frigidity is extended to his surroundings, and, with a typical Dickensian flourish, affect permeates even the food:

> "This," returned Mr. Dombey, "is some cold preparation of calf's head, I think. I see cold fowls—hams—patties—salad—lobster. Miss Tox will do me the honour of taking some wine? Champagne to Miss Tox."
>   There was toothache in everything.
>
> (60–61; ch. 5)

Dombey's paternal influence is overwhelming and his "cold and distant nature" refuses to share ownership of his son (49; ch. 5), while he is happy to concede the role of godmother to Miss Tox "in virtue of her insignificance" (49; ch. 5), he does not recognize the need for the traditional role of godfather. This narrowing of male influence is clearly intended to alert the reader to the danger that Paul will be crushed by the concentration of his father's love. The dialectical relation between maternal and paternal influence is firmly reinforced; Dombey symbolically forces an icy particle into his son's heart. While, as we saw in the previous section, maternal influence was a dubious flux, a stream that bore the risk of contamination and fragmentation, Dombey's influence is hard and inflexible: the rigid application of a preexisting set of values. In an eloquent passage, the narrator describes how Dombey incorporates the birth of his son into his worldview:

> And now when that nature concentrated its whole force so strongly on a partial scheme of parental interest and ambition, it seemed as if its icy current, instead of being released by this influence, and running clear and free, had thawed for but an instant to admit its burden, and then frozen with it into one unyielding block.
>
> (49; ch. 5)

Dickens does not allow us to soften towards Dombey's obsession. The word "partial" in the passage is telling, since Dombey's fatherhood not only excludes Florence, but also excludes Paul's own childhood. Dombey's manner is impatient and irritable. Paul's infancy is a matter of acute indifference to him: "So that Paul's infancy and childhood pass away well, and I see him become qualified without waste of time for the career on which he is destined to enter I am satisfied" (48–49; ch. 5). The irony is, of course, that Paul's childhood "passes away" far more literally than Dombey could possibly foresee. Dickens's use of this phrase subtly creates a link between Dombey's fantasy and Paul's premature death: without realizing it, Dombey wishes away his son's childhood and consequently, his life. He destroys both the symbolic and physical vitality of childhood, a criminal act in the eyes of the author who showed a passionate concern for educational standards and reform throughout his writing career.

Like the Medusa's head, Dombey has the magical ability to turn those around him into stone; he is "not only a constraint upon [Florence's] mind, but even upon the natural grace and freedom of her actions" (32–33; ch. 3). When she first meets him again after her mother's death, "The tears that stood in her eyes as she raised them quickly to his face, were frozen by the expression it wore" (32; ch. 3). He petrifies his children.

Paul himself becomes increasingly otherworldly as the novel progresses. The death into which he is born surrounds him. The narrator presents us with the pathetic figuration of a dying child, struggling to come to terms with the world around him; but Paul is also ageless, deathless, evading time itself. In Brighton he avoids the company of other children aside from Florence, picking out "a weazen, old crab-faced man, in a suit of battered oilskin" to pull his carriage (110; ch. 8). Paul instinctively feels that he has more in common with those close to death, those who can hear the seductive call of the sea. He reminds us of those changelings in fairy tales who cannot grow older, but who have an aged quality nevertheless; Dickens self-consciously uses fairy-tale imagery to codify a dark reality. Paul's decline and death are presented as an answer to a seductive call encoded in the sea's murmurs. He senses that only those closer to death can hear the call: "And though old Glubb don't know why the sea should make me think of my Mama that's dead, or what it is that it is always saying—always saying!—he knows a great deal about it" (151; ch. 12). Paul struggles to make sense of the loss of his mother, even while the sea itself becomes the location for her uncanny reappearance. As we saw in the opening scene, the sea is feminized through its symbolic relation to Fanny Dombey and its later association with Florence's feminine influence. Although Claire Senior interprets it as representing a shared "community of feminine feeling" (108), this description does not adequately take account of the ambiguous feminine presence that haunts the periphery of *Dombey and Son*.

In the wake of Polly's departure, Paul is plunged into a liminal state where maternal love is correlated with a kind of erotic seduction. The sea's call is not simply the maternal voice crying to the young boy—it is also a call to death. The sea is a symbol of eternal maternal love, a love that returns as inevitably as the waves breaking on the beach. In this context, Lynn Cain interprets the sea as not only maternal, but "amniotic," drawing upon Julia Kristeva's idea of the maternal "chora." In this schema, Paul's return to the sea is a regressive return to the womb (70). While the symbolic connection between the mother and the sea is irrefutable, Cain's interpretation of the sea as choric (and therefore relating to primal bodily drives), rather than symbolic, means that the mother necessarily emerges as an "archaic" archetype (78) rather than the seductive presence I interpret her to be.[2] Crucially, maternity in *Dombey* is not represented by one cohesive image, but is represented through a proliferation of bodies: the novel is wary of mothers, but it is erroneous to perceive this wariness as solely emerging from the idea of a "regression" to the womb. In fact, this wariness indicates Dickens's deep awareness of maternity's relentless symbolic permutations, its differential quality: its undying ability to reproduce itself. Even the sterile Edith has a dangerous double, her cousin Alice. The traumatic loss of the mother(s) provokes the reemergence of an enigmatic maternal presence that possesses Florence, while haunting Paul. The uncanny maternal presence in *Dombey* can be provocatively linked back to Laplanche's concept of the compromised parental message. Through the narrative's convoluted symbolic processes (which crucially also take in Edith, Mrs. Skewton, Good Mother Brown and Alice), Dickens poses an underlying and unanswerable question: what is it that mothers want from their children? What constitutes the maternal demand? The sexualization of this demand is apparent in Mrs. Skewton and Good Mother Brown. These maternal pimps simply wish to sell their daughters to the highest bidder, both old women, however, also desire their daughters' love and absolute loyalty. This impossible dichotomy underpins the representation of maternity in *Dombey and Son*, and Fanny Dombey's haunting presence seems to stand in for this paradox: this parental fault line.

Fanny beckons Paul, and it is only Florence, the living maternal substitute, who can keep him alive in the buildup to the annual school dance at Blimber's. Both Moynahan and Cain argue that Florence is essentially a murderer, drowning others with her oceanic, regressive maternal love (Moynahan 125–26; Cain 68): however, these readings entirely gloss over the novel's traumatic echoing. Paul is plunged into a perpetual dreamlike state: he cannot fully access the source of his trauma, and therefore his mourning is circular and impotent. As LaCapra argues, "when absence, approximate to loss, becomes the object of mourning, the mourning may (perhaps must) become impossible and continually turn back into endless melancholy" (*Writing History* 68). Florence's own subjectivity, as in Freud's model of the melancholic ego, is obscured by the shadow of what she has lost (Freud, "Mourning" 249). In a key passage, Paul describes the night-time sea by the "lonely shore":

> "Not blowing at least," said Paul, "but sounding in the air like the sea sounds in the shells. It was a beautiful night. When I had listened to the water a long time, I got up and looked out. There was a boat over there, in the full light of the moon: a boat with a sail . . . in the full light of the moon. The sail like an arm, all silver. It went away into the distance, and what do you think it seemed to do as it moved with the waves? . . . it seemed to beckon," said the child, "to beckon me to come!—There she is!—There she is!"
>
> Toots was almost beside himself with dismay at this sudden exclamation, after what had gone before, and cried "Who?"
>
> "My sister Florence!" cried Paul, "looking up here, and waving her hand. She sees me— she sees me!"
>
> (169; ch. 12)

A summoning spell is woven about Paul, a magical call that he cannot resist. The traditional symbolic connection between the moon and femininity, found from the Greeks onwards, is invoked here to hint at the potency of the mother's absent presence: the Greek goddess, Artemis, and her Roman equivalent, Diana, were not only moon goddesses, but goddesses of the hunt, of entrapment. The slippage between Fanny and Florence in Paul's speech—a slippage that terrifies the simple Toots—means that Florence also briefly emerges as an uncanny emanation: a maternal revenant. By sending Paul to school, Dombey has undoubtedly hoped to "wean" Paul from his sister, but in fact, he opens the way for the more insistent call of the dead mother. Despite this, it is not Florence's actions, but Paul's entry into the school that signals his demise. As Claire Senior notes, Florence nurtures and educates her brother in Brighton before he enters Doctor Blimber's establishment (107). Dickens constructs the prosaic dance at the school at which Florence will appear as a potent fantasy, which (as his Doctor observes) has the capacity to keep Paul alive for a number of days (204; ch. 14). Florence is both the nurturing sister *and* a seductive maternal revenant. Dickens does not choose, but neither does one aspect negate the other. As Freud demonstrates throughout his writings, each family member assumes multiple positions, actual and symbolic, which become determinant for familial fantasy and the development of the individual subject. At the end-of-term dance, Florence's presence is connected over and over again to the dead mother's call, emanating from the sea: "The same murmur he had wondered at, when lying on his couch upon the beach, he thought he still heard sounding through his sister's song" (200). The tie between Florence and the dead mother is created persistently throughout these final scenes: the mother is correlated with the call of the sea, which is, in its turn, correlated with Florence's song. Reading across Dickens's use of imagery, we find that the dance at Doctor Blimber's represents Paul's passing from his sister's hands into his mother's: the collapsing in of past and present, described by the narrator, signals the uncanny reemergence of the mother and Paul's inevitable death.

Paul's deathbed becomes a magical site, translating, as the title of the chapter says, "What the Waves Were Always Saying." Before meeting Polly for the first time since infancy he asks, "Is she dead too, Floy, are we *all* dead except from you?" (223; ch. 16). Lynn Cain quotes this question in order to reinforce her argument that "Florence thrives and prospers at the expense of those she loves; as Paul foresaw" (73), but the logic of this critical position is unclear: if, as Paul's uncanny question suggests, Florence is the only person left living, this clearly does not put her in a privileged position. She is consistently defined in relation to what she has lost, or what she lacks. Lying waiting, the boy calmly watches the golden light playing on his bedroom wall. He experiences death as a journey down a river, passing to the sea, where his mother waits for him, the river "running very fast, and confusing his mind" (223; ch. 16); he boards the boat which he had earlier described to Toots:

Now the boat was out at sea, but gliding smoothly on. And now there was a shore before him. Who stood on the bank!—

"Mama is like you, Floy. I know her by the face! But tell them that the print upon the stairs at school, is not Divine enough. The light about the head is shining on me as I go!"

(225)

As in the earlier scenes at Doctor Blimber's, Florence and Fanny Dombey merge into one welcoming, or seductive, presence. The repeated mantra that Paul is "old-fashioned" is finally explained, with heavy emphasis: "The old, old, fashion! The fashion that came in with our first garments, and will last unchanged until our race has run its course, and the wide firmament is rolled up like a scroll. The old, old fashion—Death!" (225) The call from the mother welcomes Paul to death, and implicitly (but only implicitly) to God. As we have seen, this can also be read as a dangerous maternal seduction, urging Paul away from Dombey and life itself. The maternal call is destabilizing: ultimately, Paul must renounce life and remain ever a child in his mother's arms. The maternal embrace, never realized in the first scene (9; ch. 1), is finally imminent. But the effectiveness of the call is undoubtedly not only compounded, but also *created* by Dombey's interest, or investment, not in Paul as a child, but speculatively as a future adult companion and business partner. Dickens is doing something quite complicated with the parental dialectics here: motherhood is an atemporal force, while fatherhood is cold and "forcing" (the term applied to Doctor Blimber's educational techniques). Crucially, both are equally compromised through the density of Dickens's writing. While Paul Dombey's death may seemingly stand out within Dickens's fiction because of its sentimental portrayal of a child's innocent bravery in the face of tragedy, it is in fact much more notable for its depiction of a child caught, even crushed, between two parental powers over which he has no control: the father—a "tall shadow on the wall" (204), the mother—a powerful, but whispering voice.

Echoes

Paul's death functions in relation to the maternal loss; as the narrator's repeated mantras reveal, it is the "destiny" that Dombey unconsciously foresaw for his son in the first chapter (3). Further, however, Paul's death reconfigures the structures of fantasy and desire at stake in the novel: it replaces the mother's death as the key trauma although remaining inseparable from it. Again, Dickens creates a sense of belatedness, or delayed affect: Paul's death leads to the inevitable crisis in Florence and Dombey's relationship (prefigured in the first scene), a crisis that becomes even more pronounced following Edith's entrance into the household. It is ultimately *only* through Paul's posthumous influence that the father and daughter can begin to be healed, potentially enabling a process of working through.

For both children, the sibling relationship had filled the void left by the mother's death, and so, with the traumatic loss of Paul, Florence is truly bereft for the first time. Absence is figured as a glaring void, free of the parental whispers and shadows that passed through Paul's childhood. Following Auerhahn and Laub, we can interpret this deathly silence as a potent message in its own right, and one that precipitates Florence's obsessive (and uncomfortable) desire to make her father love her. It is at this point in the novel that Florence is reconfigured as an Echo, desperately trying to articulate what has passed. Following Paul's death, when confronted with the horrific absence of both mother and brother, Florence appears to reaffirm her relation to her dead mother, which had been such a central aspect of her relationship with her brother:

> It was not long, before, in the midst of the dismal house so wide and dreary, her low voice in the twilight, slowly and stopping sometimes touched the old air to which he had so often listened, with his drooping head upon her arm. And after that, and when it was quite dark, a little strain of music trembled in the room: so softly played and sung, that it was more like the mournful recollection of what she had done at his request on that last night, than the reality repeated. But it was repeated, often—very often, in the shadowy solitude; and the broken murmurs of the strain still trembled on the keys, when the voice was hushed in tears.
>
> (242; ch. 18)

A refashioned Echo, Florence's broken voice covers over the dead mother's silence, but she has no words of her own. Fanny Dombey summoned Paul, but Florence has been left behind: she simply represents the resonance of the lost call. In symbolic terms, Dickens portrays Florence as a kind of maternal remainder, a redundant household presence. Denied her role as daughter, unable to be a sister, Florence is meaningless: her singing is a "broken" fragmented collection of dead utterances. As Judith Greenberg suggests, echoes can effectively correspond to the disrupted articulations created by a traumatic stress disorder, and Dickens uses Florence's echoing voice to this effect. Whether he did so knowingly or not, Dickens undoubtedly translates the metamorphic logic of Echo and Narcissus into the Dombey family. Florence cannot express her desire for her father's love and is condemned to reiterate the whispers of her dead mother; Dombey is, like Narcissus, captivated by his own reflected greatness—previously passed onto Paul. Greenberg argues that the story of Echo and Narcissus acts as a "didactic parable," which "emphasises the need to confront one's own echoes to avoid falling into the pool of one's own reflection, death" (339); Dickens likewise highlights the danger of not attending to echoes: the narrator's portentous call "Let him remember" (used when referring to Dombey and Florence) clearly underscores this. Directly after Paul's death the daughter is caught obsessively reproducing familial loss, while the father cannot tear himself away from his own representation. The two forms of frustrated love are inextricably connected. Just like Echo, Florence compounds her father's narcissism by feebly echoing the primary enigma: his inability to love her. When Florence enters his study after Paul's death, she cries out "speak to me, dear papa!" (252; ch. 18): her speech constitutes a demand for his words, rather than operating as an effective articulation in its own right. Like Narcissus, Dombey already knows that he is an object of desire; the tragedy is that he does not care. Florence's realization of this leads to her "prolonged low cry" (252). Following Paul's death, Florence can only exist through others, dead or alive; Dombey will perish from himself. As Jacqueline Rose explains in relation to Sylvia Plath's *Daddy*, the father demands an identification that he then refuses to accept (230): the double bind of daughterhood is revealed. Florence's obsessive desire to love Dombey in the wake of Paul's death is a proportionate mirroring of Dombey's own self-love, which is likewise dealt an irretrievable blow by this same event.

While the figure of the daughter is undoubtedly problematized throughout the novel, this becomes increasingly anxiety-ridden following Dombey's second marriage, when Florence's presence in the house is, as Lynda Zwinger has argued, positively perverse (41). The entry of Edith into the family provides Florence with the "Mama" she has always craved, and, as a result of the crisis that follows, the primal conflict between the "mother" and "father" that was established symbolically by Fanny Dombey's death is fully realized in the plot. Dombey's second marriage testifies to a crisis in the family's conflicting desires: Florence's association with her own neglected mother and the despised Edith engenders her as a dangerous sexual object in the household: this culminates in Dombey striking Florence across her breast after Edith has fled with Carker. The negative relation between Dombey and Florence is revealed in all of its interpretative violence here: owing to the identification between Florence and Edith (itself a differential repetition of Florence's identification with Fanny in the primal scene), Florence is also rendered guilty in her father's eyes. The irony being that the identification Florence felt for Edith (described as the "old association" by the narrator [621; ch. 47]) was based upon her voyeuristic desire to gain her father's love. The blow destroys the identification Florence has tentatively felt for Dombey himself, the desire she had cherished that he would love her:

> But she looked at him, and a cry of desolation issued from her heart. For as she looked, she saw him murdering that fond idea to which she had held in spite of him. She saw his cruelty, neglect, hatred, dominant above it, and stamping it down. She saw she had no father on earth, and ran out, orphaned from the house.
>
> (637; ch. 47)

The dangerous circling of identification and desire is presented at its most extreme here: nowhere else in Dickens's fiction do we see quite so painfully the way in which self and other become locked into ambivalent processes of self-constitution and destruction. In an extraordinary passage, standing in front of the mirror at the Midshipman, Florence remembers her feeling that she had witnessed a murder:

> In the last lingering natural aspect in which she had cherished him through so much, he had been torn out of her heart, defaced and slain . . . if her fond heart could have held his image after that, it must be broken; but it could not and the void was filled with a wild dread that fled from confronting its shattered fragments—with such a dread as could have risen out of nothing but the depths of such a love, so wronged.
>
> She dared not look into the glass; for the sight of the darkening mark upon her bosom made her afraid of herself, as if she bore about herself something wicked.
>
> (655–56; ch. 49)

There is a slippage here; no one has destroyed the image of Dombey but Dombey himself, but the gaping void left behind testifies to Florence's inability and her unwillingness to recreate his image in the wake of the blow. Much like the speaker of *Daddy*, Florence therefore sees herself as implicated in the murder. It is significant that Dickens uses the metaphor of glass-like "shattered fragments" to describe Florence's picture of her father: it is as if the "mirror" itself (as the abstract guarantor of identity) is shattered, the mirrored image of ourselves that we find in the other, and which assures our identity. The key point to note here is not that Florence bears the murderous mark of Cain (Cain 72), but that identification necessitates desire—a desire that is brutally repudiated by Dombey himself. The violence is engendered by Dombey alone: as we have seen, the obsessiveness of Florence's desire for his love is a mirror image of his desire for himself, as well as being the foundation for her sense of self after Paul's death.

The supposed irony of *Dombey and Son*, hinted at by Dickens himself in his notes to John Forster, is that rightly it should be named *Dombey and Daughter* (Dickens *Dombey* xv). Considering that Paul dies only a quarter of the way through the novel (at the end of the fifth number), this can be seen as a literal truth, without being an accurate textual analysis. As we may expect from the opening birth scene, the "Son" is an overarching schema. The material presence of the "Son" is replaced with Paul's magical, talismanic non-presence, without which the father and daughter would remain locked in their torturous processes of identification and repudiation: the "Son" allows the trauma to be partly worked through. Without Paul's blessing, the union between Walter and Florence would be meaningless. Florence describes the relationship between herself and Walter to Edith after her father's marriage:

> He was my brother, Mama. After dear Paul died, we said we would be brother and sister. I had known him for a long time—from a little child. He knew Paul, who liked him very much; Paul said, almost at the last, 'Take care of Walter, dear Papa! I was fond of him!'
>
> (485; ch. 35)

Walter's character is almost irrelevant; structurally he is destined to rescue Florence because he takes the place of Paul—her only stable (if curtailed) family bond. His survival from the sinking of the ship *The Son and Heir* reinforces the sense that, Lazarus-like, he has the power to take Paul's privileged place. Dickens was clearly aware of the difficulty of maneuvering Walter from the position of surrogate brother to lover. In chapter 50, in a protracted dialogue between the two young people, Walter explains to Florence that he must renounce the brotherly closeness he had with her, saying "I left a child, I find a woman" (678; ch. 50). The right to "protect" the woman is seen as either a (biologically) fraternal or a husbandly concern. This scene constitutes a moment of sexual recognition for Florence, as "The colour overspread her face" (678). With her "bosom swelling with its sobs" (679), she proposes Walter's transition from brother to husband herself: "If you will take me for your wife, Walter, I will love you dearly. If you will let me go with you, Walter, I will go to the world's end without fear" (679). Florence's recognition is key to creating the union as a reciprocal exchange between two adults, although Dickens could not resist a final flourish at the end of the scene, with Florence falling asleep "like a hushed child" on Walter's bosom (679).

The role of the "son" as a center of gravitation is clear, and it is probable that Dickens had the son/sun pun in mind throughout his writing of the novel. Paul's posthumous influence does not end with his blessing of Walter Gay. His symbolic reincarnation in Florence's own son provokes the former's return to her father as a married woman in chapter 50: having been neglected, and then physically abused by her father, Florence returns to him in continuing self-abasement to beg for his forgiveness for abandoning him. This disturbing scene can only make sense if we take into account the way in which Paul's influence reverberates through the book after his death. Paul's talismanic role in the text is clear, even before Florence enters the scene. Dombey, pondering his family life, realizes that he should have conceived of his children as one being: "Oh, how much better than this that he had loved her as had his boy, and lost her as he had his boy, and laid them in their early grave together!" (796; ch. 59). Dombey reformulates the question of familial exclusion (so key to the novel's primal scene) by situating Florence in relation to Paul, rather than to the dead mother, or indeed to Edith. Dickens demonstrates the potency of psychical reality here. As in Freud's case histories, it is the subject's *phantasmatic* investment that determines the trauma, and their relation to the originary "event." It is only through Paul's mediating (non-)presence that Dombey is able to conceive of Florence as his daughter and a potential recipient of his love. As a consequence, he continues to wish her dead, as he has done since Paul's demise, Florence is a ghostly presence who has "never changed" (796; ch. 59). Dombey thinks of his children in terms of a "double childhood" and a "double loss" (797). Florence is meaningless without Paul: "It was one child no more. He reunited them in his thoughts, and they were never asunder" (798). Dombey's mirror image is again seen, just as it was at the christening party, but now it appears as a "picture": a "spectral" "It," which imagines the blood of a "wounded man" wending a path into the hallway (801). Dombey's suicidal alienation is beautifully rendered here; it is the mirror image who thinks, the mirror image whose hand looks "wicked and murderous" (801). As Cain argues, the absolute collapse of Dombey's narcissistic conception of self is at hand prior to Florence's return, "which re-establishes Dombey as subject" (66). As Florence enters, Dombey looks to the glass and "only saw *his own* reflection . . . and at his knees, his daughter!" ([my emphasis] 802). However, something must be added to this analysis. Just as Florence enters, a "gleam of light" finds its way into the darkened room, "a ray of sun" (801). The slippage between sun/son is used to indicate Paul's necessary presence in this encounter between father and daughter: the text's symbolism colludes with Dombey's earlier idea of the children as one being. Further, Florence's identification with her son, Paul Gay, "teaches her" to return to her father: "'We will teach our little child to love and honour you; and we will tell him, when he can understand, that you had a son of that name once, and that he died, and you were very sorry'" (802). This child is a new talisman, a living point of emotional orientation, correlated with "glorious sun [son] shine" (802). The rebirth of "Paul" means that Florence's internal image of her father coalesces, and she feels retrospectively guilty that she was not able or willing to achieve this previously. If, as Mary Armstrong and Lynn Cain persuasively argue, *Dombey and Son* is a novel about perception (Armstrong 281; Cain 62), then the internal images held by the characters are clearly central to the novel's functioning. The continuing tragedy for the reader is that Florence can only situate herself in the "expectation" of her father's desire if she is the keeper of a boy: little Paul Gay becomes the conduit for a "heterosexual" father-daughter romance. Later, in the Midshipman, while Dombey lies on his sickbed, "Florence, having her baby in her arms, began in a low voice to sing to the little fellow, and sang the old tune she had so often sung to the dead child" (819; ch. 61). Florence reappropriates her old maternal role with this echo of the tune and, through the baby, assumes her daughterly place for the first time. The birth of Paul Gay legitimizes Florence's association with maternity, drawing it out of the shadows of the old house into the light, and into life in the Midshipman under the auspices of the appropriately named Uncle *Sol*.

In the deleted passage with which Dickens initially planned to conclude the novel, Dombey is haunted by the whispering waves for the first time:

> They speak to him of Florence and of his altered heart; of Florence and their ceaseless murmuring to her of the love, inimitable, extending still, beyond the sea, beyond the sky, to the invisible country far away.

Never from the mighty sea may voices rise too late, to come between us and the unseen region on the other shore. Better, far better, that they whispered of that region in our childish ears, and the swift river hurried us away!

(833n)

He hears a maternal call; a call that urges him to remember: to perform a reparative mourning which simultaneously acknowledges that he too must die. In Greenberg's terms, Dombey allows himself to hear the traumatic echoes, thus enabling the trauma to be worked through. In his analysis of the intimate, sociologist Jeffrey Weeks argues that "the need for equal freedom and equal chances for all is in the end dependent on our willingness to recognize an 'equality of vulnerability' . . . : our equal fallibility of negotiating the conditions of our intimate life; . . . the equal likelihood that one day we will fall ill, and the certainty that eventually we will all die" (654). I argue that we see a similar argument being put forwards in *Dombey*; the need to "live in death" is an ethical one, and in Dickens's final schema the maternal voices terrifyingly, but inescapably, negotiate our journeys between life and death.

Despite this ethical exhortation the parental problematic remains unresolved, and symbolically irresolvable. The published ending to the novel yet again complicates the familial dynamics: "But no-one, save Florence, knows the measure of the white-haired gentleman's affection for the little girl. That story never goes about. The child herself almost wonders at a certain secrecy he keeps in it. He hoards her in his heart. . . . He is fondest of her and most loving to her, when there is no creature by" (833; ch. 62). While Dombey's celebrated love for his grandson is a straightforward reformulation of his love for his dead son, the love for the granddaughter is an entirely new phenomenon. Dickens undoubtedly intended this love to represent a displaced reparation towards Florence herself, and yet it is kept secret. Without being mediated through the male figure, whether the son or the grandson, there is still something potentially dangerous about love for the (grand)daughter. Considering the centrality of the firm "Dombey and *Son*" in his worldview, Dombey's untold desire for another son must logically have been the motive for his second marriage, and yet the novel never refers to this, perhaps because it would make it all too clear that symbolically it is his own daughter who finally gives birth to the longed-for second son. The love that Dombey develops for Florence is primarily displaced onto her daughter, and remains hidden from the world, if not from Florence herself. This is a highly compromised resolution of the maternal and paternal conflicts established in the novel's primary trauma; the father-son narrative is still openly embraced and celebrated, a "story" to be told to the world (833); the father-daughter story is private, a love happening behind closed doors. Further, while at the beginning of the novel, the daughter was a "base coin" who could not be traded, by the end of the novel, the (grand)daughter emerges as a coin who will be miserly and possessively "hoarded." A sense of thwarted possession underlies both images. As we may expect based upon our reading of the novel's primal scene, the circulation of desire between father and daughter is dependent on the emotional potency of the son and the tacit blessing of the mother,[3] but despite all of Dickens's maneuvers, this working-through remains, provocatively, only a "partial" scheme.

NOTES

1. Some of the earlier bibliographies had claimed, fairly unproblematically, that Dickens had entered the factory on 9 February 1824 (see Johnson 31 and Ackroyd 45).

2. In this context it is appropriate to note that the sea is the site of mercantile activity and the source of capitalist profit in *Dombey*: by implication both profit and death are explicitly feminized concerns. The "wholesome" (or regressive) image of maternal love is undercut by the lurking idea of prostitution. In "Riddling the Family Firm: The Sexual Economy of *Dombey and Son*," Robert Clark cites the 1858 preface to the novel in which Dickens relates "what the waves were always saying" to his wanderings round the vice-ridden streets of Paris, Clark argues therefore that Dickens's sea symbolism is inescapably bound up with an idea of sexual danger (69). Ella Westland has likewise emphasized the plurality of the sea symbolism in her article, "Dickens's Dombey and the Storied Sea," in which she examines Walter Gay in the context of the sea stories that constitute him and the world of the Midshipman (87). The sea is relentlessly symbolic, representing eternity, the mother, trade, whoredom, excitement, death, and danger (and all of these things in amalgam), but not a simple return to a pre-symbolic state.

3. Edith gives this blessing when Florence visits her in the care of Uncle Feenix at the end of the novel: "When he loves his Florence most, he will hate me least. When he is most proud and happy in her and her children, he will be most repentant of his own part in the dark vision of our married life. At that time I will be repentant too—let him know it then" (827; ch. 61).

WORKS CITED

Ackroyd, Peter. *Dickens.* Abridged Edition. London: Mandarin, 1994.

Armstrong, Mary. "Pursuing Perfection: Dombey and Son, Homoerotic Desire and the Sentimental Heroine." *Studies in the Novel* 28.3 (Fall 1996): 281–302.

Auerbach, Nina. "Dickens and Dombey: A Daughter After All." *Charles Dickens: Dombey and Son and Little Dorrit: A Casebook.* Ed. Alan Shelston. Houndsmills: Macmillan, 1985. 97–107.

Auerhahn, Nanette and Dori Laub. "The Primal Scene of Atrocity: The Dynamic Interplay between Knowledge and Fantasy of the Holocaust in the Children of Survivors." *Psychoanalytic Psychology* 15.3 (1998): 360–77.

Berry, Laura. *The Child, the State and the Victorian Novel.* Charlottesville: UP of Virginia, 1999.

Cain, Lynn. *Dickens, Family, Authorship: Psychoanalytic Perspectives on Kinship and Creativity.* Hampshire: Ashgate, 2008.

Caruth, Cathy. *Unclaimed Experience: Trauma, Narrative, History.* Baltimore: Johns Hopkins UP, 1996.

Clark, Robert. "Riddling the Family Firm: The Sexual Economy in *Dombey and Son.*" *ELH* 51.1 (Spring 1984): 69–84.

Dickens, Charles. *A Christmas Carol and Other Christmas Books.* Ed. Robert Douglas-Fairhurst. Oxford: Oxford UP, 2008.

———. *David Copperfield.* Ed. Nina Burgis. Oxford: Clarendon, 1981.

———. *Dombey and Son.* Ed. Alan Horsman. Oxford: Clarendon, 1974.

———. *Great Expectations.* Ed. Margaret Cardwell. Oxford: Clarendon, 1993.

———. *Little Dorrit.* Ed. Harvey Peter Sucksmith. Oxford: Clarendon, 1979.

———. "The Number Plans." *Dombey and Son.* Ed. Alan Horsman. Oxford: Clarendon, 1974. 835–55.

Donoghue, Denis. "The English Dickens and *Dombey and Son.*" *Nineteenth-Century Fiction* 24.4 (1970): 343–403.

Douglas-Fairhurst, Robert. *Becoming Dickens.* Cambridge, MA: Belknap Press of Harvard UP, 2011

Dever, Carolyn. *Death and the Mother from Dickens to Freud: Victorian Fictions and the Anxiety of Origins.* Cambridge: Cambridge UP, 1998.

Fletcher, John. "Introduction: Psychoanalysis and the Question of the Other." *Essays on Otherness.* Routledge: London, 1999. 1–51.

Forster, John. *The Life of Charles Dickens. Volumes 1–3.* London: Chapman and Hall, 1874. Vol. 1.

Freud, Sigmund. "A Case of Paranoia Running Counter to the Theory of the Disease." *The Standard Edition: The Complete Psychological Writings of Sigmund Freud.* Vols. 1–24. Ed. and trans. James Strachey. London: Vintage, 2001. 18: 146–58.

———. *The Interpretation of Dreams.* Ed. and trans. James Strachey. London: Penguin, 1991.

———. "Letter 52." *The Standard Edition.* Ed. and trans. James Strachey. London: Vintage, 2001. 1: 233–239.

———. "Mourning and Melancholia." *The Standard Edition.* Ed. and trans. James Strachey. London: Vintage, 2001. 14: 239–58.

———. "A Project for a Scientific Pathology." *The Standard Edition.* Ed. and trans. James Strachey. London: Vintage, 2001. 1: 283–411.

———. "Remembering, Repeating, Working Through." Ed. and trans. James Strachey. *The Standard Edition.* London: Vintage, 2001. 12: 146–56.

————. "Screen Memories." *The Standard Edition.* Ed. and trans. James Strachey. London: Vintage, 2001. 3: 189–224.

————. *Studies on Hysteria. The Standard Edition.* Ed. and trans. James Strachey. London: Vintage, 2001. Vol. 2.

————. "Three Essays on Sexuality." *The Standard Edition.* Ed. and trans. James Strachey. London: Vintage, 2001. 7: 125–248.

Greenberg, Judith. "The Echo of Trauma and The Trauma of Echo." *American Imago.* 55.3 (1998): 319–47.

Ikonen, P., and E. Reichardt. "On the Universal Nature of Primal Scene Fantasies." *International Journal of Psychoanalysis* 65.1 (1984): 63–72.

Johnson, Edgar. *Charles Dickens: His Tragedy and Triumph.* London: Penguin, 1986 [1971].

Klimaszewski, Melisa. "The Contested Site of Maternity in Charles Dickens's *Dombey and Son." The Literary Mother: Essays on Representation, Maternity and Childcare.* Ed. Susan Staub. Jefferson, NC: London: McFarland, 2006. 138–58.

LaCapra, Dominick. *History and Psychoanalysis.* Minnesota: U of Minnesota P, 1985.

————*Writing History, Writing Trauma.* Baltimore and London: Johns Hopkins UP, 2001.

Laplanche, Jean. "Notes on Afterwardsness." *Essays on Otherness.* Ed. and trans. John Fletcher. London: Routledge, 1999. 260–65.

Laplanche, Jean and Jean Bertrand Pontalis. *The Language of Psychoanalysis.* Trans. Donald Nicholson Smith. London: Karnac, 1988.

Leys, Ruth. *From Guilt to Shame: Auschwitz and After.* Princeton: Princeton UP, 2007.

Moynahan, Julian. "Dealings with the Firm of Dombey and Son: Firmness vs. Wetness." *Dickens and the Twentieth Century.* Ed. John Gross and Gabriel Pearson. London: Routledge and Kegan Paul, 1962. 121–31.

Ovid. *Metamorphoses.* Ed. E. J. Kenney. Trans. A. D. Melville. Oxford: Oxford UP, 2008.

Rose, Jacqueline. *The Haunting of Sylvia Plath.* London: Virago, 1991.

Sadrin, Anny. *Parentage and Inheritance in the Novels of Dickens.* Cambridge: Cambridge UP, 1994.

Schor, Hilary. *Dickens and the Daughter of the House.* Cambridge: Cambridge UP, 1999.

Senior, Claire. "What the Waves Were Always Saying: Submerging Masculinity in *Dombey and Son." Dickens Studies Annual* 32 (2003): 107–25.

Slater, Michael. *Charles Dickens.* New Haven: Yale UP, 2009

Tomalin, Claire. *Charles Dickens: A Life.* London: Viking, 2011.

Weeks, Jeffrey. "The Sphere of the Intimate and the Values of Everyday Life." *Modern Criticism and Theory.* Eds. David Lodge and Nigel Wood. Edinburgh: Pearson, 2008. 641–64.

Westland, Ella. "Dickens's Dombey and the Storied Sea." *Dickens Studies Annual* 35 (2005): 87–108.

Wiley, Margaret. "Mother's Milk and Dombey's Son." *Dickens Quarterly* 13.4 (1996): 217–28.

Zwinger, Linda. *Daughters, Fathers and the Novel: The Sentimental Romance of Heterosexuality.* Madison: U of Wisconsin P, 1991.

"Shall memory be the only thing to die?": Fictions of Childhood in Dickens and Jerome K. Jerome

Carolyn W. de la L. Oulton

This article focuses on Dickens's David Copperfield *(1849–50) and Jerome K. Jerome's* Paul Kelver *(1902) in order to question how these autobiographical novels should be read against the manuscript or nonfiction accounts written by their respective authors on the same subject. The two works are connected by their concern with victimized children who become successful writers. Throughout their autobiographical writings, whether novels or professedly accurate accounts of their lives, Dickens and Jerome repeatedly use mythologizing practices to create a type of the ideal writer (although in Jerome's case this ideal may never be attained by the protagonist either in fiction or in life). A similarly self-conscious anxiety about reader-response informs the narrative strategies of both novels, manifested through their embedding of, and coded gesturing towards, a personal history which paradoxically remains concealed. The dilemma faced by both authors is that their accounts gain conviction and the lives of their characters become important, only by being edited or fictionalized.*

In 1902 when Jerome K. Jerome published his partly autobiographical novel *Paul Kelver*, about the rise to fame of a lower-middle-class boy from the

Dickens Studies Annual, Volume 43, Copyright © 2012 by AMS Press, Inc. All rights reserved.

east end of London, critics inevitably framed it in the context of Dickens's *David Copperfield*, written more than fifty years earlier, although *The New York Times* quickly qualified the comparison with the observation that "Perhaps Dickens accomplished a little more than [an account of the struggles of a young man in London]" (18 Oct. 1902, Book Reviews 1). A lifelong admirer of *David Copperfield*, Jerome's challenge was precisely to reference Dickens's account of the writer's struggles while also defining his own work against it. Jerome was eleven at the time of Dickens's death in 1870, and strongly influenced by the myth Dickens himself had largely created, of the special intimacy existing between him and his readers. As Jerome grew older, he would also have become aware of the enduring myth (likewise created by Dickens) of the suffering child led to success by his own earnestness of purpose. In *Paul Kelver* Jerome revises both ideas, as his writer protagonist struggles, and fails, to live up to this iconic figure.

The thematic connection is not the sole reason for considering these two texts together. What this article seeks to explore is the vexed question of how these autobiographical novels should be read against the manuscript or non-fiction accounts written by their respective authors on the same subject. In each case the first person narrator is a famous, "self-made" writer, strategically equipped to project a particular version of himself onto the page. As Donna Loftus has commented in the context of real autobiographies by middle-class Victorian men, "the narrative of self-help was not always stable: there were occasions when the narrative of self-making broke down to reveal the fractured status of class and gender identities and the role of narrative in constructing agency" (71). In this case the reader of either novel is not so much eavesdropping as engaging with a carefully orchestrated presentation of a life. In other words, the very plot of each novel makes it impossible to take the narrator as an ingenuous presenter of an unrehearsed story. But in each case the framing by a fictional editor invites the reader to consent to precisely this proposition, that the narrators are unaware of the presence of a reader. In his recent *Self-Impression: Life-Writing, Autobiografiction, and the Forms of Modern Literature*, Max Saunders argues that, in contradistinction to fin de siècle and modernist writers, "Though nineteenth-century fiction drew deeply on auto/biographical material, such material is usually lent to characters who, though they might be writing their experience down for our benefit, are not presented [as] creative artists, but artless recounters and transcribers of their experience" (11). Significantly, he goes on to note *David Copperfield* as a rare exception. While *David Copperfield* predates the period of Saunders's study, the less-known *Paul Kelver* stands between late Victorian and early modernist writing and, as I will suggest, deploys many of the autobiografictional strategies that Saunders identifies in other works of the time. Notably the novel prefigures the "modernist challenge to such Victorian biographical concepts as 'personality,'" (23) as Paul (in contradistinction to David Copperfield) repeatedly fails to "act out" the romantic traits on which he bases his fantasies about himself. Again, through the metafictional deployment of chapter headings, Paul draws attention to the fictional nature of what is ostensibly his own autobiography, and in so doing encourages the reader to question its reliability.

While Jerome seems not to have made any explicit connection between the two books himself, he referred to *David Copperfield* in articles of 1898 and 1912[1] and confirmed his belief in it as "[Dickens's] greatest book" ("Jerome K. Jerome"). To a modern reader, the parallels are clear enough. Both novels are concerned with the difficult early years and final success of the writer-protagonist, and there is a further, internal link in the encounter between a young Paul and an older writer, whom the reader is driven to recognize as none other than Dickens himself. One evening the young Paul confides to this man his own ambition to be a famous writer when he grows older, and discusses his current favorite reading. On being questioned about the work of Dickens, he admits that his mother finds the author "a trifle vulgar" in places, while confiding his own predilection for *The Pickwick Papers*. The scene ends with the author pointing out that Paul has not asked him his name, and teasingly withholding it as they say goodbye (156).

This is a pivotal moment in the novel and is in fact, as Jerome would make clear in his 1926 autobiography *My Life and Times*, recorded "fairly truthfully" (26). He particularly remembers that the man he met in Victoria Park certainly did say, "oh, damn Mr Pickwick!" as he is made to do in the novel. In fairy-tale mode, the child apparently took to haunting the park where he had talked to the stranger at twilight—he never saw him again, but "the fancy would persist" that it was Dickens he had met ("Charles Dickens: The Fellowship of Love"). Certainly the news of Dickens's death in 1870 seems to have had a profound effect on the eleven-year-old Jerome, who later recalled how

> I slipped quietly from the room. I do not think that anyone noticed my going. Reaching my attic, I closed the door and softly turned the key. I hoped they would forget me. Then pushing aside the low chest of drawers, I opened the window, and putting my elbows on the sill, stared out across the maze of chimney-pots to where the light still lingered beyond the dark mass of the city; and after a while tears came to my relief.
>
> ("Charles Dickens: The Fellowship of Love")

Jerome's open admiration for Dickens's work (despite some reservations about his tendency to "gush"), as much as the striking similarities between their personal histories, may well inform the structure of the later novel. In each case the early trials of the writer are followed by a period of youthful folly redeemed by intense work, before the story closes on the success of both literary career and romance plot. In *Paul Kelver* one of the characters goes so far as to say that David Copperfield "reminds me of you, Paul, a little" (377; ch. 9).

Both Dickens and Jerome had been exposed to the difficulties of life in the East End of London at a young age, Dickens through the imprisonment of his father for debt in 1824 and Jerome through the removal of his family from Walsall to Poplar in 1862, after the failure of his father's mining venture. Both writers specifically cite class consciousness as an important factor in their distress. Dickens remembered his work at Warren's blacking warehouse more for the social dislocation and the disruption of his education than for the physical conditions. In the autobiographical fragment entrusted to John Forster, he emphasizes how he "felt my early hopes of growing up to be a learned and distinguished man, crushed in my breast" (*David Copperfield* [Appendix A] 60). Nonetheless, he derived solace from the memory that his young companions treated him as a gentleman despite his outward condition. Meanwhile Jerome remembered "being persecuted by the street boys. There would go up a savage shout if, by ill luck, I happened to be sighted. It was not so much the blows as the jeers and taunts I fled from, spurred by mad terror. My mother explained to me that it was because I was a gentleman" (*My Life and Times* 11).

Both boys then clung to the idea of their superior status as a means both of comfort and of distancing themselves from their tormentors or associates. In the published fictional texts, *David Copperfield* and *Paul Kelver*, this sense of specialness is crucial to determining the status of the hero/writer, and both work hard to establish this special status in the mind of the reader without obviously compromising the limited perspective (or modesty) of the character-narrators. Most notably, David Copperfield puts in his claim in the famous opening line of the book, "Whether I shall turn out to be the hero of my own life, or whether that station will be held by anybody else, these pages must show" (*David Copperfield* 1; ch. 1). Perhaps partly with this question of status in mind, both authors allow their characters the double authority of a first-person account backed up by the supposedly impersonal ordering of a third-person narrator or editor; after its numerous and complicated draft titles Dickens's novel is generally known simply as *David Copperfield*, but even in the final published title David's narrative is conceived as both unique and official, "The Personal History and Experience of David Copperfield." As Gareth Cordery points out, all but one of the preliminary ideas for a title included the phrase "personal history" (369).

The two works are also connected in their embedding of, and coded gesturing towards, a personal history that paradoxically remains concealed. Jerome would have known from Forster's biography that Dickens had refigured his father as the hapless Micawber, whose confidence in the likelihood of something "turning up" is miraculously justified at the end of the novel. Luke Kelver, whose ill-fated optimism results in the loss of the family fortunes, is characterized far more soberly and dies (as Jerome's father had done in 1871) without recovering his position. Both authors are clearly subject to the same impulse, to present a version of their own childhood, but without revealing their partial identification with their fictional characters. For this reason both are at pains to authenticize their fictional lives through the figure of a shadowy editor or witness, even as they conceal the historic basis of their accounts. Several of Dickens's draft titles for *David Copperfield* included the enigmatic phrase "which he never meant to be published on any account." Michael Slater has recently noted Dickens's enjoyment of private jokes as semi-revelation throughout his fiction, and this unused subtitle invokes the author's own ambivalence about publishing the story of his life. As David puts it with no apparent consciousness of being in a false position, "I feel as if it were not for me to record, even though this manuscript is for no eyes but mine, how hard I worked at that tremendous short-hand" (590; ch. 42).

David's frequent references to the invocation of memory can be seen in this sense as a double bluff, his memories by definition being derived from his creator. Jerome, meanwhile, is at pains to provide Paul with a detached commentator, who may or may not be his older self, and who comments on the confessions of the ostensible, first-person narrator through satirical chapter titles such as "Prologue: In which the author seeks to cast the responsibility of this story upon another." In each case the main narrators incorporate personal and written memory in their texts—Dickens famously redeployed his 1847 autobiographical fragment in the writing of David's Murdstone and Grimsby experience; Jerome's personal memories of his childhood in Poplar may well be reinforced by his mother's journal from the same period.[2] At least one reviewer felt tempted to speculate on the biographical context of the book, writing somewhat provocatively, "One might fancy that the author presents his own biographical experiences" ("The Cheerful Paul"). Certainly, Jerome makes little attempt to conceal place and personal names, locating Paul's London home in Poplar, where he himself grew up, and even bestowing the name of his own maternal aunt, Frances Jones, on Paul's "Aunt Fan."

If Jerome's novel is clearly based on his own experience, passages taken almost unchanged from the original leave no doubt as to the influence of Dickens's fragment on his most famous novel. But the status of Dickens's fragment is highly problematic, not least in its self-conscious use of emotive language in the presentation of himself as hapless victim of both family circumstances and his mother's ostensible lack of maternal feeling at this period. Rosemarie Bodenheimer has perceptively cited "the fictionality of Dickens's self-creation" (54) in his autobiographical accounts and correspondence, as in his novels, as a major source of his fascination. Certainly the fragment deploys a number of fictional strategies, including its offer to the reader of limited intimacy (while the tone is overtly emotional, the episode related is incomplete and not fully contextualized), and the sense of an ultimate order that explains and shapes his early experience. As Nicola Bradbury notes, "Together with the intimacy of indignation is a kind of analytical poise, and a pride in the detail and flourish of recall" (20). Saunders's comment on aesthetic autobiography that "The autobiographical needed to be poetized or fictionalized, turned into *art*, before it could provide an adequate representation of the artist's subjectivity" (74) is equally applicable here. Again anticipating the practice of later writers, the fragment also invites the reader's participation, the narrator insisting that the narrator's suffering as a boy is "utterly beyond my power to tell. No man's imagination can overstep the reality" (*David Copperfield* [Appendix A] 862). In a discussion of *David Copperfield*, Cordery notes that "David's hypersensitivity triggers memories so intensely that past becomes present" (372). In the context of the fragment itself, Bodenheimer similarly suggests that the presentation of the child's suffering erases the temporal gap between the event itself and the moment of retelling it, in order to give the writer power over the past:

> The outraged narrator of the fragment seems to be trying hopelessly to be making up to the abandoned child for that failure of parental feeling and appreciation during and after the period of his father's imprisonment for debt. If they would not provide the appropriate protection or the necessary remorse and horror, he would, in retrospect, do it for them.
>
> (52)

The fragment's adaptation (in parts, a simple transfer of passages) in the pages of *David Copperfield* further complicates its status and raises questions about the authority of the fictional voice in the novel. For instance, while both David and the narrator of the fragment accord their memories of working in London the power to intrude unexpectedly on their adult selves for no known reason, David strongly suggests that the events he describes have never before been written down: "No one has ever raised that curtain since. I have lifted it for a moment, even in this narrative, with a reluctant hand, and dropped it gladly" (210; ch. 14). In fact, the immediacy of David's voice both echoes and is undermined by Dickens's fragment. Despite David's evident trustworthiness, this is not as he claims the first time these events have been written down, in that beyond the world of the novel a version of them already exists. The fragment even uses the same image to describe the act of voluntary recall, "I have never, until I impart it to this paper, in any burst of confidence with anyone, my own wife not excepted, raised the curtain I then dropped, thank God" (*David Copperfield* [Appendix A] 869). By contrast it now seemed to Forster, as he later expressed it, that Dickens was taking the world into his confidence (*David Copperfield* [Appendix A] 858.)

For anyone who has first read the novel with no awareness of its personal elements, the experience of then reading the autobiographical account framed in Forster's *Life of Dickens* is (as it would have been for its first readers) necessarily colored by an existing sympathy with the fictional David. Adding to the uncertainty about how it should be read, Forster implied the accuracy of Dickens's account not through the corroborating evidence of written sources or reliable witnesses, but by offering his own memory of unspecified and undated conversations with the writer himself: "There is another blank, which it is however not difficult to supply from letters *and recollections* of my own" (*David Copperfield* [Appendix A] 863; my italics).

As readers have noted, Dickens makes little effort to understand his mother's position in blaming her for his suffering in Warren's. But regardless of the justice of Dickens's account, or its framing first in the novel and later in Forster's *Life*, the authority of the fragment is *already* compromised by its very mode of composition. Unlike Marguerite Jerome's diary, this is a document written by and about a public figure, with a known audience. Inevitably, Dickens's childhood experience is filtered through his later consciousness of his own position as a famous writer. It is the very existence of this audience that enables the writer's autobiography to be written in the first place, so that paradoxically the present status of the writer, rather than the convincing presentation of his memory, legitimizes and gives authority to his account of the past. It is in this context that the Warren's Blacking episode can be best understood. As in the overtly fictional account, the personal experience of the narrator, what he terms "the secret agony of my soul" (*David Copperfield* [Appendix A] 860), is of considerably greater significance than the condition of the working boys who have no hope of education and therefore escape. It is precisely such an identification with the laboring boys of his own age that Dickens dreads decades later and depicts himself as having managed to avoid even at the time. Throughout this account he remains determinedly the young gentleman. Notably, while his fiction goes to great lengths to comprehend the sufferings of the urban poor, his earliest eponymous heroes, such as Oliver Twist and Nicholas Nickleby, share their plight only for a time and often with the same sense of being in a false position on display in the unpublished fragment. In the arguably skewed focus of the narrative, the young Dickens is made to occupy a central position rather than appearing as one of a number of boys; while the fictional David is one of "three or four" boys, such is the narrator's self-focus in the fragment that it is never made clear how many other children of either gender Warren's employed. This situation resurfaces in the self-scrutiny of David Copperfield.

The self-consciousness of the fragment initially makes Marguerite Jerome's diary appear more reliable in its account of urban poverty. Written day by day, this diary was the work of a lower-middle-class woman with no literary aspirations, and its very brevity (many entries consist of a single line or even phrase) might suggest that there is no tendentious purpose or eye on future readership. The longest entry is a deeply moving account of the death of her son Milton Jerome in January 1862 (shortly before the family's removal to Poplar), in which Marguerite details his last illness day by day, vividly capturing the voice of the child as he asks questions about heaven and where his blood will go after his death. Otherwise, further knowledge is required even to make sense of most of the entries, with their uncontextualized allusions to particular streets or acquaintances. At various points, God is appealed to, as a listener rather than a reader of what she has written. But an occasional interpolated entry is the only obvious attempt to edit what she has written, and these interpolations are most often used to record significant details such as the coming and going of family members shortly after the original entry. This lack of awareness of a potential audience—her son's fame was many years in the future, after her own death in 1875—might at one level seem to enhance the diary's credibility as a source of information about Jerome's early life. But, ironically, Marguerite's diary loses authority through its very failure or refusal to engage with the craft of writing, as she is unable to shape her personal experience as convincing narrative.

This lack is redressed in *Paul Kelver*, as Jerome expands on the narrative of the diary, adding further detail and emotional color to the events it describes. Where Marguerite's absorption into the life of the poor appears in disheartened entries accurately charting the cost of new boots or the difficulties of paying back-rent, the fictional narrator in *Paul Kelver* sets emotional trauma against the realization that he is one unit in a crowd. Like Jerome, Paul loses his father at a young age and vividly describes his own sensations as he takes in the inevitability of his parent's approaching death: "The bus on which I was riding became entangled in a block at the corner of Snow Hill, and for ten minutes we had been merely crawling, one joint of a long, sinuous serpent moving by short, painful jerks. It came to me while I was sitting there with a sharp spasm of physical pain" (136; bk. 1, ch. 8). In this formulation, the character narrator is both part of the long serpent (itself an image of corruption or death) and the one feeling element, who feels a spasm of pain and runs from the bus to find his father.

In the case of *Paul Kelver* the authority of the fictional work would actually be reinforced twenty-four years after its first publication, by the appearance of Jerome's autobiography *My Life and Times* in 1926. As noted above, the autobiography directly references the earlier novel, as well as commenting on the inclusion of an actual encounter between Jerome himself and a man he believed to have been Dickens. Again, while *Paul Kelver* may or may not be drawing on Marguerite Jerome's diary for a supplement of small details, the later autobiography openly does so, excerpting a number of entries from the period of Jerome's childhood. Here again, the diary is insufficient as testimony, and Jerome works it into a larger narrative of his own memories, which in turn it apparently supports. Through these means the fictional account from 1902 is given a greater credibility, deriving a retrospective authority through the genres of allegedly truthful autobiography and published diary.

However, this endorsement becomes problematic in itself when the excerpted entries are compared with the original manuscript. Jerome's admission that he has been "reasonably truthful" points to the potential unreliability of the narrative voice in *My Life and Times*, the ostensibly nonfictional version of *Paul Kelver*. In his excerpts from his mother's diary, he is notably careless about dates, but, more importantly, he strategically embellishes her rather uninspiring comments in order to supply a more rounded narrative than the original ever attempts. For instance, "So time rolls on," on 1 January 1866, becomes the more grandiloquent "So time rolls on with its sorrows, conflicts, its unrealised hopes. But these will pass away and be followed by the full, unmeasured bliss of Eternity" (*My Life and Times* 15). Whether such minor emendations add much to the literary quality of the manuscript is open to question. What they do show is both an awareness of the textual status of diaries as "integral to the authentic presentation of a Victorian life" (Hewitt 27) and a deep preoccupation with the status of this one family's suffering, a concern shared with Dickens in both versions of his own early life. Martin Hewitt has suggested that even rereading their own diaries could be alienating for Victorian autobiographers:

> Diaries challenged autobiographers with an authenticity which magnified the treacheries of hindsight. They undercut those processes of mapping a coherent narrative and constructing a unified subject which were at the heart of the autobiographical project. They could create a powerful sense of alienation and lack of comprehension between the autobiographer and their former selves.
>
> (34)

Reading his mother's diary is doubly difficult for Jerome, in that he is presented with her perspective on events from his remembered past, but his absorption and redeployment of this account is further threatened by her failure fully to articulate her experience. The relationship between archive and published fiction then is a complex one, and is subject to revision even after the publication of the novel itself.

* * *

A similarly self-conscious anxiety about reader-response informs the narrative strategies of both novels. Notably, in *David Copperfield*, David, quoting Dickens, assures the reader that "no words can express the secret agony of my soul" as he is forced into a drudgery to which he sees no likely end. Tellingly, words may be inadequate to express his feeling, but they are the narrator's sole resource in pointing the reader to a state beyond the power of language to demonstrate. Elsewhere, he gestures towards the extraordinary power of words, as if they might almost be able to alter the events they describe. As the story moves towards Emily's elopement with Steerforth, a reluctant David writes:

> A dread falls on me here. A cloud is lowering on the distant town, towards which I retrace my solitary steps. I fear to approach it. I cannot bear to think of what did come, upon that memorable night; of what must come again, if I go on.
> It is no worse, because I write of it. It would be no better, if I stopped my most unwilling hand. It is done. Nothing can undo it; nothing can make it otherwise than as it was.
>
> (436; ch. 31)

In both novels the very self-doubt expressed by the narrators creates a sense of intimacy with the reader, increasing trust—or suspension of distrust—in the speaking voice. In *Paul Kelver* the child-hero is questioned and some-times taken to task by his older self, as when he has pathetically failed to seize his one chance of impressing his schoolmates by his prowess at running and returns home in tears. The adult narrator attempts self-reassurance as he abjures him: "Your poor, pitiful little brat! Popularity? It is a shadow. Turn your eyes towards it, and it shall ever run before you, escaping you. Turn your back upon it, walk joyously towards the living sun, and it shall follow you. Am I not right? Why, then, do you look at me, your little face twisted into that quizzical grin?" (145; bk. 1, ch. 11). But such strategies remind the reader of a writer behind the moment described even as they appeal to that reader's sensibilities (373; bk. 2; ch. 9). Elsewhere, both Dickens and Jerome avail themselves of the privileges of realist fiction, such as accurate recall and close observation, conventions which form part of the contract between the writer and reader of novels but are not normally available to the autobiogra-pher. In the tradition of *Jane Eyre*, the child narrators are offered a sustained viewpoint, underpinned in each case by a more articulate adult self, who repre-sents, in both senses of the word, the child protagonist. The partial identifica-tion of character and author in the reader's mind (almost inevitable given that both stories are about the development of literary talent) further reinforces the authority of the fictional narrators.

Through these fictional first-person narrators, Dickens and Jerome are able to control reader-response both by selective use of detail and by character-izing their speakers in particular ways. Despite the different possibilities or constraints associated with the authors' own reputations, both novels employ foreshadowing and flashback as mirrored strategies in asserting the status of their narrator protagonists. The adult David, in particular, constantly reminds the reader of the significance of his experience when narrating the trials of his childhood, and later in the novel he periodically recalls this time even as he drives the story onwards to the time of his literary fame. The persistent invo-cation of the Dover Road obviously recalls the story of Dick Whittington, the poor boy who returns to London in triumph after unspecified tribulations, and this insistent focus on the road as a visible symbol of David's progress allows the reader a greater prescience than the child himself is allowed. The reader is asked to engage with both perspectives, sometimes simultaneously. As Kerry McSweeney notes:

> For David Copperfield the industrious professional writer with a blank page before him, recollection is one of the tools of the trade, a voluntary, willed activity that oils the machinery of the narrative and provides important rhetorical opportunities. For David Copperfield the explorer of past time, memory is less conscious recollection than a felt contact between past and present and a vital part of the life experience.
>
> (106–07)

While the reassuring presence of the adult voice alerts the reader to the final triumph of the hero, the text nonetheless emphasizes the end of childhood as deeply distressing. This is no less significant in the novel than in the fragment, with its "knot of history, confession, record, and performance . . . psychological currents of anger and pride, utterance struggling with concealment" (Bradbury 24). Even while the adult David accepts that, as Dickens put it in the fragment, "I know how all these things have worked together to make me what I am" (*David Copperfield* [Appendix A] 869), he posits a traumatic division between his adult and child selves, using the death of his mother and the ensuing Murdstone and Grimsby interlude to create a rupture in the narrative.

This abrupt shift is all the more powerful for its concentration on a single child. In the later novel, Jerome likewise makes Paul an only child (the author himself was the youngest of four). Notably, Robert E. Lougy has drawn attention to the displacement of David's infant brother by David himself in the scene where he imagines being buried with his mother as an infant himself. Crucially, in this context this scene also allows David to posit two versions of himself at once, the innocent but doomed infant and the suffering child whose precocious knowledge will form the basis of the successful writer. The comic scenes with the Micawber family are notably predicated on the assumption that David should be treated as an adult rather than a small boy in need of protection: "A curious equality of friendship, originating, I suppose, in our respective circumstances, sprung up between me and these people" (158; ch. 11). This shift in David's consciousness, as he moves from uncomprehending witness of his own suffering to a sensitive perception that he must not accept the impoverished Mrs. Micawber's offers of hospitality, signals a brutally inflicted move towards adult responsibility. But, as in the fragment, these moments of rupture nonetheless form part of an overall design, signaled by David's circular travels between Suffolk, Dover/Canterbury, and London. Such strategies involve the reader in a kind of doublethink, in which the events presented are both cruelly random and ultimately significant.

But if the author's special status is in each case provisional and subject to the ratification of a reading public, the first-person narrators at least partly escape this dilemma, as the reader is induced to accept their own accounts of their success. Dickens, having resolutely shaken off the Pickwick label by this point in his career, feels no scruple in endowing David with all the weight of mid-Victorian moral purpose as he reports Agnes's message: "As the endurance of my childish days had done its part to make me what I was, so greater calamities would nerve me on, to be yet better than I was; and so, as they had taught me, would I teach others" (795; ch. 58). Later Agnes confirms that if she could spare him, "perhaps the time could not" (821; ch. 60).

Jerome is more modest in his reflections, casting his child self as a disappointed ghost at the opening night of his first play. Recalling the young

Paul's excitement at his own first visit to the theater, the narrator confides, "it happened to be before that very same curtain that I took my own first bow as a playwright [and saw] a dreamy-looking lad, but he appeared disappointed, having expected better work from me" (*Paul Kelver* 134; bk. 1, ch. 8). Nonetheless, in the significance Jerome accords to Paul's meeting with the unnamed author, he implicitly places himself in a tradition of literary men, just as Wordsworth had done in *The Prelude* (first published in 1850, the same year that *David Copperfield* appeared in volume form). It was inevitable that Jerome, like other male writers of the fin de siècle, would be judged by the yardstick of Dickens's achievement, and this was especially true of *Paul Kelver*, given the parallels with *David Copperfield*. In the novel Paul accepts that he will never attain the same iconic status, but he is nonetheless "a bit" like David, and in implicitly defining himself against Dickens's work he is able to create a metafictional space for his own talent as being equally necessary.

This assurance of a literary vocation is upheld, albeit comically, by Paul's school friend Dan. Inevitably, given Jerome's own position as a would-be serious writer renowned predominantly for his comic masterpiece *Three Men in a Boat* (1889), Paul Kelver finds his niche as a humorous author despite his own inclination towards tragedy. As Dan puts it:

> Aren't there ten thousand penny-a-liners, poets, tragedians, tub-thumpers, long-eared philosophers, boring [the world] to death? Who are you to turn your nose up at your work and tell the Almighty His own business? You are here to make us laugh. Get on with your work, you confounded young idiot!
>
> (*Paul Kelver* 335; bk. 2, ch. 7)

As Norah, Paul's future wife, more poetically puts it at the end of the novel, "This fortress of laughter that a few of you have been set apart to guard—this rallying-point for all the forces of joy and gladness! How do you know it may not be the key to the whole battle?" (398; bk. 2, ch. 10).

Throughout their autobiographical writings, whether novels or professedly accurate accounts of their lives, Dickens and Jerome repeatedly use mythologizing practices to create a type of the ideal writer (although in Jerome's case this ideal may never be attained in either fiction or life). Specifically, they set up a complex relationship between memory and personal history that goes far beyond the reproduction of individual experience as fiction. While a knowledge of Dickens's work in Warren's blacking factory or Jerome's early life in Poplar brings particular scenes in *David Copperfield* and *Paul Kelver* into sharp relief, this one-way focus occludes important issues such as the possibly fictional quality of Dickens's original fragment and the interplay between Marguerite Jerome's diary, *Paul Kelver* and *My Life and Times*. For Jerome, in particular, it seems that no one version of his life was adequate, although like Dickens he was wary of open disclosure—even in his published autobiography several of his "clues" turn out to be misleading. Paradoxically, both writers were clearly impelled to record their experience, even as they attempted to retreat from the reader behind a series of constructed narrative voices.

As the mother of Paul Kelver demands, "Shall memory be the only thing to die?" (167; bk. 1, ch. 10). The context of her rhetorical question is religious, but it has a further significance in that for memory to be culturally transmitted, it must be recorded in some way. Despite the difference in provenance, both Dickens's fragment and Marguerite Jerome's diary need to be edited or reworked in order to convey a shaped experience and to emphasize the importance of the lives they convey. In each case, placing them in the context of a novel or autobiography powerfully suggests to the reader not the disingenuousness of fictional narrators, but the limitations of the diary or personal memoir as a form in which to capture lived experience. The dilemma faced by both Dickens and later Jerome is that their accounts gain conviction and the lives of their characters become important only by being edited or fictionalized (in the case of *My Life and Times*, the case is doubly complicated as the reader has no way of knowing that the diary has been embellished). What *David Copperfield*, *Paul Kelver*, and the supposedly authoritative *My Life and Times* all demonstrate is that if language conveys experience most convincingly by moving beyond the moment itself to provide its context and significance, it is necessarily dependent on shaping strategies such as perfect recall and a command of polished prose not usually associated with child figures. In other words, both Dickens and Jerome self-consciously achieve their most moving accounts of their own lives in the terms of fiction.

NOTES

1. "My Favorite Novelist and His Best Book." *Munsey's Magazine* 19 (Apr. 1898): 28–32. "Jerome K. Jerome Thinks He Once Met Dickens." *The Bookman* (16 Feb. 1912): 252.
2. It is not possible to trace any of the details in *Paul Kelver* to this source with any certainty, but Paul's confident recollection that he slept on the floor on his first night in London may well be determined by Marguerite Jerome's comment "Came to our empty house" on 3 October 1862, followed by the line "Furniture arrived" on 6 October. As Jerome was three at the time, it is unlikely that he could be certain about the lack of furniture on his first night without reference to this source.

WORKS CITED

Amigoni, David. *Life Writing and Victorian Culture*. Aldershot: Ashgate, 2006.

Bodenheimer, Rosemarie. "Dickens and the Writing of a Life." *Charles Dickens Studies*. Ed. Bowen, John, and Robert L. Patten. *A Companion to Charles Dickens*. Basingstoke: Palgrave Macmillan, 2006. 48–68.

Bradbury, Nicola. "Dickens's Use of the Autobiographical Fragment." Paroissien 18–32.

"The Cheerful Paul." *New York Times* (10 Apr. 1902): Book. Reviews 11.

Cordery, Gareth. "*David Copperfield*." Paroissien 369–79.

Dickens, Charles. *David Copperfield*. Oxford: World's Classics, 1999.

Hewitt, Martin. "Diary, Autobiography and the Practice of Life History." Amigoni 21–39.

Jerome, Jerome K. "Charles Dickens: The Fellowship of Love." *Youth's Companion* 86 (4 Jan. 1912): 3.

———. "Jerome K. Jerome Thinks He Once Met Dickens." *The Bookman* (16 Feb. 1912): 252.

———. "My Favorite Novelist and His Best Book." *Munsey's Magazine* 19 (Apr. 1898): 28–32.

———. *My Life and Times*. London: Folio Society, 1992.

———. *Paul Kelver*. London: Hutchinson, 1902.

Jerome, Marguerite. Manuscript diary. Private collection.

Loftus, Donna. "The Self in Society: Middle-Class Men and Autobiography." Amigoni 67–85.

Lougy, Robert E. "Dickens and the Wolf Man: Childhood Memory and Fantasy in *David Copperfield*." *PMLA* 124 (2009): 406–20.

McSweeney, Kerry. "*David Copperfield* and the Music of Memory." *Dickens Studies Annual* 23 (1994): 93–119.

New York Times. Untitled, unattributed review of *Paul Kelver*. 18 Oct. 1902: Book Reviews 1.

Paroissien, David, ed. *A Companion to Charles Dickens*. Oxford: Blackwell, 2008.

Saunders, Max. *Self-Impression: Life-Writing, Autobiografiction, and the Forms of Modern Literature*. Oxford: Oxford UP, 2010.

"'Make Her Pay'":
Fanny Dorrit's Disruption in
Charles Dickens's *Little Dorrit*

Katie R. Peel

This essay considers the significance of the relationship between Fanny Dorrit and her mother-in-law, Mrs. Merdle. I argue that these women form a homosocial bond via Edmund Sparkler, Fanny's husband and Mrs. Merdle's son, that is much like the relationship formed between men via a woman in common, as examined by Eve Kosofky Sedgwick. Fanny sets a socioeconomic goal for herself, to best Mrs. Merdle, and enacts her own class warfare. Her rhetoric is specifically economic, and her goal forces Mrs. Merdle to pay first literally, with material bribes, and later figuratively, with wounded pride. Fanny achieves her goal in this relationship through her manipulation of performance. Dickens thus offers a portrait of how women arrange such relationships and work within cultural and narrative constraints to exert power, and does so using a conventionally male-empowering Sedgwickian triangle. Little Dorrit suggests a way to consider relationships among women that are not nurturing, but are a matter of business, as well as a way to read destabilizing forces within ostensibly conventional narratives.

In her landmark work *Between Men: English Literature and Male Homosocial Desire*, Eve Kosofsky Sedgwick outlines the use of relationships between men in eighteenth- and nineteenth-century literature, examining how male-bonding

Dickens Studies Annual, Volume 43, Copyright © 2012 by AMS Press, Inc. All rights reserved.

often functions via a relationship with a woman in common. She finds, as René Girard and Gayle Rubin have, that heterosexual marriages can be read as a means for two men to form a relationship, and that this relationship is the primary one among the three participants.[1] Instead, however, of two men forming a relationship via an intermediary woman, in *Little Dorrit* (1855–57) Charles Dickens offers a gender reversal: Fanny Dorrit, the older sister of Amy ("Little") Dorrit, uses her husband in order to form a relationship with his mother. The novel tells the story of the Dorrit family, and follows them from their confinement in the Marshalsea, a debtor's prison, to their freedom upon a discovered inheritance. While Fanny is poor, and a dancer in a local theater, Edmund Sparkler falls in love with her. Mrs. Merdle, Edmund's mother and a woman of "Society" (capitalized by Dickens), disapproves of the attachment, and bribes Fanny to keep her distance from Edmund. Fanny, whose pride is hurt by Mrs. Merdle's condescension, uses her position to extort material goods from Mrs. Merdle. Later, after the Dorrits have come into their money and are recognized as members of Society, Fanny marries Edmund with the express intent of antagonizing his mother. In doing so, Fanny manipulates a relationship conventionally used by men to her own advantage, and empowers herself in a role that usually disempowers women.[2]

One cannot, however, make a simple transference of Sedgwick's triangle. In the case of this Dickensian triangle, Edmund Sparkler, while in the position of the object trafficked, still enjoys as a white male the privileges conferred upon him by Victorian patriarchal and heterosexual institutions of power. For him to be trafficked via marriage does not have the same implications or consequences that it would for a woman in the same position, as illustrated by Rubin. Although they occupy the two power positions of the triangle, Fanny and Mrs. Merdle are still otherwise subjugated as Victorian women, while Edmund is not. For example, when Mr. Merdle loses the Merdle and Dorrit fortunes, both Fanny and Mrs. Merdle are left dependent upon Edmund. Any agency that the women find in their relationship must still be read in the context of their limited power in the rest of their world.

That said, I choose to plot Fanny and Mrs. Merdle on Sedgwick's triangle, and not Adrienne Rich's lesbian continuum, because it is distinctly this historically male relationship (as articulated by Girard, Rubin, and Sedgwick) with business implications that Fanny engages in with Mrs. Merdle. Not only does Fanny's relationship with Mrs. Merdle take priority over her romantic relationship with Edmund, but Edmund is used as a conduit for the relationship between the two women. Additionally, Rich posits that women share a kinship of the oppressed; Fanny and Mrs. Merdle, while both oppressed, however, remain closer to Girard's male rivals than women enjoying a mutually beneficial relationship.[3] Built on baubles and pride, the business that Fanny and Mrs. Merdle engage in is markedly feminine, in that they otherwise have little power. Dickens underscores this by constantly reminding readers of Mrs. Merdle's femininity, referring to her synecdochally as "the Bosom." These two women operate within the constraints that their culture places upon females, and locate this conventionally male relationship both within their domestic realm, in their intimate relationships, and their public realm, in their interactions with other members of Society. The rivalry between Fanny and Mrs. Merdle is neither a nurturing nor a survival relationship of Rich's continuum; referred to by Dickens as Fanny's "demolition of the Bosom," it cannot be (724; bk. 2, ch. 24). The only thing nurtured in this triangle is a desire for vengeance.

Fanny sets a socioeconomic goal for herself, and enacts her own class warfare. In the first half of the novel, Fanny and her family are inhabitants of the Marshalsea Prison for debtors. Feeling the direness of her situation as a poor girl, and believing "the miserably ragged old fiction of the family gentility" (230; bk. 1, ch. 18), Fanny works the very class system that others use to judge her. She feels the insult of Mrs. Merdle's condescension, and vows to "make her pay" (262; bk. 1, ch. 20). Her own rhetoric here is specifically economic, and her goal forces Mrs. Merdle to pay first literally, with material bribes, and later figuratively, with wounded pride. Fanny's methods have a material dimension invested with social significance; while plotting, she tells Amy, "'I'll go on improving that woman's acquaintance until I have given her maid, before her eyes, things from my dressmaker's ten times as handsome and expensive as she once gave me from hers!'" (521; bk. 2, ch. 6). Her ultimate goal in life is not only to best Mrs. Merdle socioeconomically, but also to remind her of it. All of her actions are aimed at attacking Mrs. Merdle in this manner. Fanny muses to her sister, "'I know that I wish to have a more defined and distinct position, in which I can assert myself with greater effect against that insolent woman,'" and it is her marriage to Edmund that ensures this position (618; bk. 2, ch. 14). Fanny specifically uses the rhetoric of business in her calculated approach: "'But, perhaps she little thinks how I would retort upon her if I married her son. I would oppose her in everything, and compete with her. I would make it the business of my life'" (619; bk. 2, ch. 14). It is just this, marrying Edmund to make her relationship with his mother the "business of [her] life," that makes Fanny's a Sedgwickian triangle. Fanny thus places herself in the role historically and literarily occupied by a male, in which he would benefit from the business arrangement that is heterosexual marriage.[4] Aware of the power of the heterosexual marriage, Fanny manipulates it to further her own goals.

Although Fanny initially engages in her relationship with Mrs. Merdle for material gain, she later modifies this arrangement. Fanny does not marry Edmund until after her family has inherited their fortune, and thus she does not need to gain financially through her marriage. By marrying, she instead extorts emotionally. While critic Kathleen Woodward does discuss Fanny as "a Dickensian Becky Sharp" who "uses her sex appeal to maneuver Edmund

Sparkler into position," she simplifies Fanny's "primary motivation for wealth and social respectability," overlooking Fanny's relationship with Mrs. Merdle (147). Already wealthy, Fanny does not marry up: she marries *closer*. The significant bond in Fanny's marriage is that between her mother-in-law and herself. Sedgwick's triangular relationship of marriage as a strengthening of bonds between men through the bride's body is now inverted: in Fanny's case, the groom's body strengthens the bonds between the women. Fanny empha- sizes Edmund's role as the trafficked body when she tells her sister, "'I'll make a slave of him. . . . I shall make him fetch and carry, my dear, and I shall make him subject to me. And if I don't make his mother subject to me, too, it shall not be my fault'" (522; bk. 2, ch. 6). Edmund barely figures into Fanny's concerns, other than as a means to an end, and is usually depicted as stammer- ing and submitting to these two strong women; at the wedding, the event that legalizes Fanny's relationship with Mrs. Merdle, "Nobody noticed the Bride- groom" (636; bk. 2, ch. 15).[5] Fanny's primary relationship in this text, then, is a homosocial bond with Mrs. Merdle, and the business (indeed with a socio- economic dimension) occurs between these two women.

To maneuver in her relationship with Mrs. Merdle, Fanny makes deliber- ate use of performance. She is a master of artifice, and this ability to perform empowers her as she postures for control with her nemesis. Fanny's interac- tions with Mrs. Merdle consist of a series of roles that she deliberately deploys in order to elicit certain responses, and to do so she draws on her expertise gained from her own employment as a performer in a theater. Fanny exag- gerates and makes visible the performance that Erving Goffman argues hap- pens in the presentation of self in everyday interactions. Fanny also does what Joseph Litvak argues many nineteenth-century novels do in that she normal- izes theatricality by locating it in the domestic sphere (x). She does so by per- forming in her relationships, particularly the ones that are ostensibly the most intimate, such as those with her husband and mother-in-law. Fanny's theatri- cality presents an unpredictable energy that, in its difficulty to be contained, Litvak argues, presents a destabilizing effect to nineteenth-century narrative.

Furthermore, Litvak writes, "[t]he trope of 'theatricality' enables us both to unpack subjectivity as performance and to denaturalize—to read as *scene*—the whole encompassing space in which that subjectivity gets constituted" (xii). Thus Fanny's performance affects our reading of larger systems at work in the text, including those of gender, class, and narrative. Fanny's performance with Mrs. Merdle not only takes advantage of a conventional patriarchal relation- ship structure, but her theatricality also destabilizes this patriarchal authority. Fanny does more than irk Mrs. Merdle: in underscoring the artifice of their behaviors, her performance also exposes the very ideologies that govern them, supposedly rooted in things "natural," as constructs.

* * *

The fact that Fanny is a performer not only inspires Mrs. Merdle's condescension and their consequent triangular relationship, but performance is the very method that Fanny uses against her. As a dancer, a professional performer, Fanny is quite conscious of acting in everyday life. She is quite open with her sister Amy about her need for what Goffman, in his work using dramaturgical rhetoric to discuss the presentation of self, refers to as "impression management," or the presentation of a particular role in order to determine a given situation (Goffman 238). Fanny finds agency in her performance as a woman who poses a threat to Mrs. Merdle's social reputation, which is a role in that she has no romantic inclinations towards Edmund. Upon learning that her son is in love with a dancer at a second-rate theater, Mrs. Merdle seeks out Fanny with the intent of bribing her to discourage Edmund's attentions. What follows is the establishment of a relationship in which the two women elicit performance from each other. While both Fanny and Mrs. Merdle perform, however, Fanny is the one who actively manipulates this relationship in order to pursue and disempower Mrs. Merdle.

The two women perform their respective roles: Mrs. Merdle acts the part of the woman who would not care that her son is in love with a dancer, except that Society requires her to ("'I wish Society was not so arbitrary, I wish it was not so exacting'" [258; bk. 1, ch. 20]), and Fanny acts the part of the woman who has an understanding with Mrs. Merdle, and accepts gifts as tokens of Mrs. Merdle's acknowledgement and approval of their similar sensibilities (that is, the agreement that Fanny cannot possibly marry Edmund). Mrs. Merdle's protests are lain bare as performance by the fact that she intentionally buys and wears cheap jewelry to offer Fanny as bribes (260; bk. 1, ch. 20), and she is otherwise described as false: Dickens writes, "Mrs. Merdle concurred with all her heart—or with all her art, which was exactly the same thing" (626; bk. 2, ch. 15). Mrs. Merdle is also given to hyperbole, indicating an insincerity: she claims "'If a few thousand persons moving in Society, could only go and be Indians, I would put my name down directly'" (261; bk. 1, ch. 20).

While enhancing her role with a deliberate formality and mock deference to Mrs. Merdle, Fanny's performance hiccups (and thus exposes itself as performance) when her pride is hurt: she asserts that she is of a better class than her fellow dancers, and that she had already discouraged Edmund before Mrs. Merdle made her request (258–61; bk. 1, ch. 20). Fanny's role is further exposed as performance to the reader when she tells her sister Amy what her intentions are with respect to Mrs. Merdle, though given Fanny's tendencies toward melodrama, readers would have likely suspected performance without this admission. When Amy expresses her dismay at this performance, Fanny replies, "'Would you let a woman like this, whom you could see if you had any experience of anything to be as false and insolent as a woman can be—would you let her put her foot upon your family, and thank her for it?'" (262; bk. 1, ch. 20). Fanny continues, explaining her modus operandi to Amy: "'Then make her pay for it, you mean little thing. What else can you make her do? Make her pay for it, you stupid child; and do your family some credit with the money!'" (262; bk. 1, ch. 20). Fanny refuses to let Mrs. Merdle insult her without consequence, and extorts material compensation, including dresses at Mrs. Merdle's dressmaker's, and a token of appreciation placed in her hand by Mrs. Merdle upon their exit (261; bk. 1, ch. 20). Fanny justifies this, of course, in her role as the guardian of her family's reputation: "'And while you have been thinking of the dinner or the clothes, I may have been thinking, you know, of the family'" (264; bk. 1, ch. 20). Part of Fanny's performance, then, is alleging a noble justification for acting the part of dancing temptress, when she really is acting only from her wounded pride.

A dancer by trade, Fanny is literally a performer, and she uses conscious performance in her vengeful encounters with Mrs. Merdle. Fanny earns "a few weekly shillings" as a dancer in a small theater (89; bk. 1, ch. 7). Dancing onstage was at midcentury still a relatively dubious profession.[6] Fanny's virtue and reputation are kept "safe" by the fact that her uncle, who plays the clarionet in the orchestra, acts as her chaperon. Fanny, however, is not favored by the narrator, and is depicted as possessing some qualities of the dancer stereotype. She is initially described as "wayward" (84; bk. 1, ch. 7), and is usually paired in both the novel and criticism with Tip, the ne'er-do-well Dorrit brother. Amy asks for dancing lessons for her sister because Fanny "seemed to have a taste that way" (87; bk. 1, ch. 7), which, to the middle class at midcentury, is not likely a compliment. Fanny loves dress and finery: her new bonnet is notably "more gauzy than serviceable" (256; bk. 1, ch. 20). These tastes not only conflate her with the stereotype of the morally negligent female performer, but also indicate the lack of feeling that ultimately contrasts her with the novel's heroine, Amy. Fanny preoccupies herself with appearance, and Amy with work. Dickens underscores Fanny's truly "common" qualities in a comical passage in which she yells, "'Don't, stupid!'" at her bumbling uncle, and Arthur Clennam, the genteel guest, catches a glimpse of Fanny as "an appearance of loose stocking and flannel," indicating "that the young lady was in an undress" (108; bk. 1, ch. 9). This disrespect of her uncle, as well as the unbecoming exposure of her undergarments, indicate that any gentility of Fanny's behavior is a sham. Amy, the moral center of the book, is certainly not depicted in any state of undress.[7] A professional dancer is convenient shorthand for a woman of questionable character; while not suspicious sexually, Fanny is indeed suspicious morally, and this is evident in her manipulation of others.

Fanny is aware of contemporary perceptions of dancers, knows that Mrs. Merdle thinks less of her "'because [she is] a dancer!'" (263; bk. 1, ch. 20), and ironically shares these perceptions about her fellow performers. Fanny tells Amy: "'If I am ever a little provoking, I am sure you'll consider what a thing it is to occupy my position and feel a consciousness of being superior to it. I shouldn't care . . . if the others were not so common. None of them have come down in the world as we have. They are all on their own level. Common'" (256; bk. 1, ch. 20). These stereotypes of female performers actually justify Fanny's own perception of being wronged due to her family's fallen class status, and help her perpetuate this particular myth. Fanny's work, then, liberates her from the debtor's prison, commits her to an entire set of dubious Victorian associations, and encourages her performance of a myth by which she defines herself. Her obsession with her socioeconomic status, while indicating that she is herself imprisoned by ideas of class, is also the motivation for her agency. Fanny tells Amy: "'I am impatient of our situation, I don't like our situation, and very little would induce me to change it. Other girls, differently reared and differently circumstanced altogether, might wonder at what I say or may do. Let them. They are driven by their lives and characters; I am driven by mine'" (618; bk. 2, ch. 14). Fanny's essentialist ideas of her own gentility conflict with her work as a dancer. This not only helps her to understand how Mrs. Merdle thinks of her, but also her work in the theater arms her with the skills she uses to combat Mrs. Merdle's active prejudice.

Regardless of dubious connotation, Fanny's work as a professional performer underscores her expertise in performing both on and off stage. Furthermore, the passage in which Amy visits Fanny at the theater during a rehearsal, "coming behind," exposes the performative nature of Fanny's work and interactions throughout the novel. In this passage Amy encounters all that happens literally behind the scenes, from the seedy entrance and dark passageways, to the dancers gossiping and looking for an audience as they wait for their cues (251–52; bk. 1, ch. 20). Life behind the curtain is fast-paced, and the performers breathless, countering the fluid beauty of a stage performance, and dismantling the fantasy of the performance for both Amy and the reader. For the dancers the performance is work, and they leave their job immediately afterwards: "they all came back again, more or less out of breath, folding themselves in their shawls, and making ready for the streets" (254; bk. 1, ch. 20). Unlike her fellow dancers, Fanny brings her performance beyond her workplace, and the associated taint of performance follows her.

Additionally, there are certain Victorian stereotypes about women who have access to backstage. The space itself is considered taboo for genteel women. Fanny exclaims, "'But the idea, Amy, of *you* coming behind! I never did!'" (252; bk. 1, ch. 20). Fanny means this as a backhanded compliment, illustrating that she, a woman of worldly experience, is quite at home both on and behind stage, whereas Amy, the domestic homebody, is clearly uncomfortable, perpetuating yet another family myth (252; bk. 1, ch. 20). This self-aggrandizement also claims the backstage as a special place, and off-limits to certain women. Fanny says to Amy, "'The notion of you among professionals, Amy, is really the last thing I could have conceived! . . . Why, how ever did you get here?'" (252; bk. 1, ch. 20). Fanny, of course, uses the word "professional" in the sense of referring to acting as "the profession" ("Profession" *OED*). This term also doubles conveniently as a euphemism for prostitution ("Profession," "Professional," "Amateur" *OED*). Later, Mrs. Merdle perpetuates this conflation, referring to Amy as the "non-professional" (261; bk. 1, ch. 20). Fanny's disparagement of her sister contrasts her own employment of artifice and sexual connotations with Amy's sincerity and innocence. Amy cannot perform (she is berated for not acting "upper-class" enough once the Dorrit family is rich), and this is an indicator of her moral character. Even Mr. Dorrit can see that "'There is adaptability of character in Fanny'" (498; bk. 2, ch. 5), but not in Amy. In Dickens's schema, the sincerity embodied by Amy is the trait that gains the approval of the narrator, and is privileged by the narrative. This passage in which the performance is exposed as a stage act also emphasizes the performative nature of Fanny's other roles, which, while subversive, is not favored by the narrative.

In a novel so much about the performance of roles, Fanny is a star actress. Not only does she literally work on stage, but Fanny performs in nearly every aspect of her daily life. Fanny and Amy must not allow their father to know that they work, and so both maintain the illusion of having to leave the prison for various errands. Together they perpetuate "the genteel fiction that they were all idle beggars together" (89; bk. 1, ch. 7). Fanny's affection, too, is performed, as she alternately blames and then gushes over Amy, and deliberately leads on Edmund. Fanny is adept at performing on a practical level in her daily life: she "pretended to prepare [the meal] for herself, though her sister did all that in quiet reality" (262; bk. 1, ch. 20). Once the family becomes wealthy, Fanny's transition appears effortless, and she excels in her new role as a woman of leisure. Mr. Dorrit hires Mrs. General, ostensibly for the education of his daughters, but really to teach them how to "form a surface" (501; bk. 2, ch. 5). What Mr. Dorrit and Mrs. General mean by this is the "graceful equanimity of surface which is so expressive of good breeding," (501; bk. 2, ch. 5) or, in other words, upper-class drag. Already well-varnished, Fanny resists Mrs. General's recommendation, though "she always stored it up in her mind, and adopted it at another time" (505; bk. 2, ch. 5). Fanny, an expert in artifice, has been rehearsing for this role for most of her life.

When the Dorrit family's wealth is established, Fanny's social relationship with Mrs. Merdle changes. At the beginning of the second half of the novel, the Dorrits encounter Mrs. Merdle on the Continent, and this time as social equals. Despite recognizing Fanny, Mrs. Merdle pretends that it is their first acquaintance (486–87; bk. 2, ch. 3). For Fanny, this is a triumph, as she explains Mrs. Merdle's performance to Amy: "'Don't you see that I may have become a rather desirable match for a noodle [Edmund Sparkler]? And don't you see that she puts the deception upon us, and makes a pretence, while she shifts it from her own shoulders . . . of considering our feelings?'" (521; bk. 2, ch. 6). When Amy suggests, "'But we can go back to the plain truth,'" or, in other words, stop performing, Fanny responds, "'Yes, but if you please we won't. . . . No; I am not going to have that done, Amy. The pretext is none of mine; it's hers, and she shall have enough of it'" (521; bk. 2, ch. 6). Fanny thus recognizes and participates in Mrs. Merdle's pretense that they have never met, and the two women continue their mutual performances. Goffman writes, "together the participants contribute a single over-all definition of the situation which involves not so much a real agreement as to what exists but rather a real agreement as to whose claims concerning what issues will be temporarily honored" (9–10). Fanny accepts Mrs. Merdle's version of the situation, but uses her own performance to remind her of "what exists." Their private interactions, then, consist of their shared awareness that they are both performing, and this falsity recalls their prior acquaintance. Fanny knows that not only will her suitability as a marriage partner bother Mrs. Merdle, but also that her very presence will uncomfortably remind Mrs. Merdle of the dancer she once was, as well as of Mrs. Merdle's own artifice: "'And the dancer, Amy, that she has quite forgotten—the dancer who bore no sort of resemblance to me, and of whom I never remind her, oh dear no!—should dance through her life, and dance in her way, to such a tune as would disturb her insolent placidity a little. Just a little, my dear Amy, just a little!'" (619–20; bk. 2, ch. 14). Fanny's presence, as a reminder of her former status as a dancer, will act in tandem with Mrs. Merdle's pet bird, which squawks every time she says something insincere.

Fanny chooses to marry Edmund, and not only does she use her mere existence as Edmund's wife to pique Mrs. Merdle, but she also draws upon one other advantage she has over her mother-in-law: youth. When planning how she will avenge Mrs. Merdle's condescension, Fanny settles upon the method she will use in public, when moving in Society:

> "One thing I could certainly do, my child: I could make her older. And I would! . . . I would talk of her as an old woman. I would pretend to know—if I didn't, but I should from her son—all about her age. And she should hear me say, Amy: affectionately, quite dutiful and affectionately: how well she looked, considering her time of life. I could make her seem older, at once, by being myself so much younger. I may not be as handsome as she is; I am not a fair judge of that question, I suppose; but, I know I am handsome enough to be a thorn in her side. And I would be!"
>
> (619; bk. 2, ch. 14)

The reader already knows that Mrs. Merdle cares about appearing youthful, as Dickens initially writes that she "was not young and fresh from the hand of Nature, but was young and fresh from the hand of her maid" (257; bk. 1, ch. 20), and when telling Amy that she has an adult son, she inserts "'(I was first married extremely young)'" (258; bk. 1, ch. 20). Fanny uses patriarchal standards of beauty (largely invested in youth) against Mrs. Merdle, knowing that given these

Victorian values, age can be devastating to a woman. Fanny thus wages her public war against Mrs. Merdle, using methods of devaluing women implemented by their patriarchal culture. Indeed, Fanny flourishes upon her engagement to Edmund, and her only setbacks are when she feels Mrs. Merdle's condescension, and when "Mrs. Merdle looked particularly young and well" (631; bk. 2, ch. 15).

Fanny does triumph: "Mrs. Sparkler, installed in the rooms of state—the innermost sanctuary of down, silk, chintz, and fine linen—felt that so far her triumph was good, and her way made, step by step" (640; bk. 2, ch. 16). She achieves her material goals, presenting luxurious gifts to Mrs. Merdle's own maid, and her position in becoming Mrs. Merdle's daughter-in-law: "[Fanny] saw the fair bosom that beat in unison with the exultation of her thoughts, competing with the bosom that had been famous so long, outshining it, and deposing it. Happy? Fanny must have been happy. No more wishing one's self dead now" (640–41; bk. 2, ch. 16). While the narrator suggests that this is merely an empty happiness, as her own bosom competes to surpass and ultimately replace Mrs. Merdle's, Fanny commits to it. When Amy asks if Fanny would "condemn [her]self to an unhappy life for this,'" Fanny replies, "'It wouldn't be an unhappy life, Amy. It would be the life I am fitted for. Whether by disposition, or whether by circumstances, is no matter; I am better fitted for such a life than for almost any other'" (619; bk. 2, ch. 14). Indeed, Fanny has made her relationship with Mrs. Merdle the business of her life, and continues satisfying her goals indefinitely. Fanny's relationship with Mrs. Merdle consumes not only her everyday life but also her life's landmark events. She makes her own wedding plans based on Mrs. Merdle's travel plans (632–33; bk. 2, ch. 15), and after reacting emotionally to the deaths of her father and uncle, takes "every precaution that could ensure [her mourning wear] being as becoming as Mrs. Merdle's" (724; bk. 2, ch. 24), again demonstrating her placement of performance over sincerity. While Fanny at times seems miserable in her life as Mrs. Sparkler, this is directly due to the fact that she is unable to go out into Society while pregnant (she is unwilling to show herself in less than peak form) and continue her war against Mrs. Merdle (726; bk. 2, ch. 24). This makes her resentful and impatient. Fanny, however, otherwise thrives in her performance:

> And Mr. Dorrit's daughter that day began, in earnest, her competition with that woman not present; and began it so well, that Mr. Dorrit could all but have taken his affidavit, if required, that Mrs. Sparkler had all her life been lying at full length in the lap of luxury, and had never heard of such a rough word in the English tongue as Marshalsea.
>
> (646; bk. 2, ch. 17)

No longer a dancer, Fanny makes her performance with Mrs. Merdle her lifework, and the novel leaves her at work, "going into Society for ever and a day" (859; bk. 2, ch. 34).

Surprisingly, given Dickens's condemnation of her, Fanny does betray one moment of emotional vulnerability. This one glimpse humanizes her, and makes her less a caricature than a true character. Upon announcing her engagement to Edmund to Amy,

> Fanny laughed at first; but soon laid her face against her sister's and cried too—a little. It was the last time Fanny ever showed that there was any hidden, suppressed, or conquered feeling in her on that matter. From that hour, the way she had chosen lay before her, and she trod it with her own imperious self-willed step.
>
> (623; bk. 2, ch. 15)

This passage indicates that there is more than mere surface to Fanny, since she, as Sedgwick argues that Scarlett O'Hara does, "learns to manipulate" sexuality, male power domination, and her traditional gender role, and this "is the numbing but effective lesson of her life" (8). Just before deciding to accept Edmund's proposal, Fanny feels the pressure of her situation, of having not discouraged his attentions. Hemmed in by social implication, Fanny resolves to take control of the situation and use it to her advantage against Mrs. Merdle (614; bk. 2, ch. 14). While Fanny would never admit it, this moment with her sister indicates an awareness of the limitations of her choices. Like any sincerity expressed by Fanny, however, this moment is fleeting, and she wholeheartedly maintains her combative relationship with Mrs. Merdle, much to the dismay of her sister: "the skilful manner in which [Mrs. Merdle] and Fanny fenced with one another on the occasion, almost made her quiet sister wink, like the glittering of small-swords" (537; bk. 2, ch. 7).

Fanny thus uses her relationship with Mrs. Merdle and Edmund in the way that men conventionally do, according to studies by Girard, Rubin, and Sedgwick. In fact, the character Henry Gowan does just this in the same novel. He marries Pet Meagles in order for her father to assume his debts. Henry's mother tells Mrs. Merdle as much, and furthermore, that Mr. Meagles will provide an income upon which the new couple will live, offering evidence of the financial relationship between the two men as a result of Henry's marriage to Pet (415; bk. 1, ch. 33). Both Fanny and Henry Gowan, then, use marriage to their own advantages; neither marries for love. Whereas Henry Gowan is motivated by financial need, Fanny Dorrit is motivated by pride. Victorian (and earlier) literature is rife with stories of men using marriage to increase financial security, as a business relationship, and to pay off debts. While not entirely noble, these uses of marriage are barely remarkable when employed by a Victorian man.[8] In fact, as Dickens, tongue-in-cheek, has Mrs. Merdle explain to Henry Gowan's mother, it is even expected behavior: "'As to marriage on the part of a man, my dear, Society requires that he should retrieve his fortunes by marriage. Society requires that he should gain by marriage. Society requires that he should found a handsome establishment by marriage. Society does not see, otherwise, what he has to do with marriage'" (412; bk. 1, ch. 33). Fanny's move is subversive because she comes from a position of (female) disempowerment to a position of (male) empowerment. For a female to occupy a conventionally male position is alone a form of performance; for her to use this position to her own benefit in a patriarchal culture is downright radical.

There are other female characters in *Little Dorrit* who, like Fanny, seek material compensation for their suffering. In addition to Mrs. Clennam, whose drive for vengeance frames the plot, Miss Rugg is a minor character whose given identifier is that she has sued her fiancé for breaking off their engagement. This particular acquisition of material compensation is a novelty, and imparts upon Miss Rugg "distinction in the neighborhood" (316; bk. 1, ch. 25). While mocked by Dickens, this piece of legislation offered women a matter of legal recourse in a relationship that offered them few legal rights independent of their male providers.[9] Miss Rugg's act, at least in part, allows her to resist conventional gender ideology regarding marriage. Fanny takes legal action, as Miss Rugg does, but hers is in the masculine manner of Henry Gowan: marriage.

* * *

Fanny attains the conventional narrative closure offered female characters— marriage—and while she does not get the happy romance that Amy does, for Fanny marriage was never about love, but rather, the fulfillment of her socioeconomic goals. Fanny's trajectory is anything but conventional, as she sets out to form and maintain a relationship in a way not usually afforded to women, and does so using her performing talents. That said, Dickens does not depict Fanny's relationships with Mrs. Merdle and Edmund Sparkler in a positive light. In fact, all three triangular relationships discussed here, Fanny and Edmund's, Henry and Pet Gowan's, and Mr. Dorrit and Mr. Merdle's, are unhappy at best, and destructive at worst. While Fanny and Mrs. Merdle continue to battle both at home and in the lists of Society, and Mr. Meagles pays off Henry's debts, the marriages that facilitate both relationships are relatively miserable. The relationship that Mr. Dorrit looks forward to with Mr. Merdle, as a result of Fanny's marriage to Edmund Sparkler, devastates both families, and Fanny and Mrs. Merdle are scandalized by Mr. Merdle's financial improprieties. At the end of the novel, the reader leaves Fanny and Mrs. Merdle embroiled in battle both in the home that they share and in Society, cramped by men's business actions, and literally dependent upon poor Edmund Sparkler for their support (849; bk. 2, ch. 34). Fanny can expose the performative nature of social standards and practices, but she cannot escape them, and in this manner is contained by Dickens. His moral condemnation of her is in accord with social and narrative standards; the narrator is not fooled by Fanny, and Dickens depicts her as someone who will never have the true feeling that Amy does, and therefore, will never have true gentility.

This reading offers a way to think about women's relationships with women in a society that disprivileges them. Adrienne Rich offers a positive model for thinking about women's relationships (239). Fanny's "demolition of the Bosom," however, does not fit into this schema, and in fact, places one woman against another woman in an adversarial relationship. Dickens offers a portrait of how women arrange such relationships and work within constraints to exert power, and does so using a conventionally male-empowering Sedgwickian triangle. Fanny performs within this triangular relationship, but while performance is subversive, it necessarily makes the performer insincere. Fanny's lack of sincerity and her use of traditionally male standards of beauty against another woman keep her relationship with Mrs. Merdle from being one in Rich's lesbian continuum, and keep Fanny from attaining the position of narrative privilege enjoyed by her sister, Amy.

Not only does Fanny's performance contribute to the significances revealed by performance as theorized by Judith Butler (33) and other social constructionists, but Fanny also enacts what Litvak describes as the destabilization of authority via theatricality. Performance is integral to Fanny's manipulation of the triangle. Performance exposes; in this case, class and gender are exposed as not natural. The unhinging of these identity categories from any fixed definitions challenges the patriarchal, heterosexual authorities that perpetuate their fixedness. Furthermore, the awareness that Fanny and Mrs. Merdle share of their own and each others' performances not only exposes class as a construct, but also their deep investment in class as ridiculous. Society in *Little Dorrit* turns out to be a group of elite people arbitrarily assigning standards out of their own self-interest: upon the news of Mr. Merdle's financial improprieties and suicide, "many important persons had been unable to determine whether they should cut Mrs. Merdle, or comfort her. As it seemed, however, essential to the strength of their own case that they should admit her to have been cruelly deceived, they graciously made the admission and continued to know her" (838; bk. 2, ch. 33). Here Dickens makes blatant the social construction of Society. The ultimate irony, of course, is that while Fanny demonstrates the performative natures of some governing ideologies, she does so in order to assert what she believes to be her natural claim to an upper-class identity.

Ultimately, Litvak writes that theatricality "cause[s] further embarrassment for those forces in the novels . . . that would seem to uphold traditional family values" (xii). Indeed, despite the conventional ending to the novel, Amy Dorrit's marriage to Arthur Clennam, Fanny's theatrical energies pose a challenge to this narrative normativity. Her own marriage is not one that adheres to formulas of either romance or male privilege. The destabilization offered by her theatricality, combined with her relationship with Mrs. Merdle, counters patriarchal norms that otherwise determine the narrative. Dickens thus creates a narrative structure and order that adheres to Victorian social standards, and yet allows for the exposure of these social standards as constructs.[10]

NOTES

1. Sedgwick draws upon René Girard's work on the primacy of relationships of male rivals over heterosexual love attachments, and Gayle Rubin's work on the traffic in women in arrangements of kinship. She notes that while Girard does allow for the existence of female rivals in such a relationship, his work uncovers mostly male rivals (21).

2. Rubin writes that this relationship "does imply a distinction between gift and giver. If women are the gifts, then it is men who are the exchange partners And it is the partners, not the presents, upon whom reciprocal exchange confers its quasi-mystical power of social linkage" (174).

3. For more discussion on the distinction between the lesbian continuum and male homosocial desire, see Sedgwick's "Introduction" in *Between Men*.

4. Indeed, this is what Sedgwick refers to as "men promoting men's interests" (3), and Rubin details as often having an economic and/or political component. Fanny's own father, for example, treats her marriage to Edmund Sparkler as a vehicle for his relationship with Mr. Merdle, Edmund's stepfather. Mr. Dorrit says of Fanny's marriage that she "has contracted—ha hum—a marriage, eminently calculated to extend the basis of our—ha—connection, and to—hum—consolidate our social relations" (638; bk. 2, ch. 15).

5. This is also what makes Fanny's relationship with Mrs. Merdle different from those of mother-in-law narratives of comic cliché. Usually, the bride's relationship with her mother-in-law is secondary to her romantic, heterosexual relationship.

6. In his essay "Image and Reality: The Actress and Society," Christopher Kent traces the increase in the gentility of the profession, especially for women, in the latter half of the nineteenth century.

7. In fact, in the passage in which Amy has left her family in order to change her dress, Arthur Clennam finds her, passed out, still in her original dress (452; bk. 1, ch. 36).

8. Of course, women had long relied on marriage for financial and social security, a kind of business relationship as well. Their primary relationships and objects, however, were not usually their mothers-in-law.

9. In her study of the breach of promise legislation, Ginger S. Frost finds that the law was remarkable in that it made women agent with respect to matters of engagement, but also underscored what little agency they did have in that it relied on the ideology of female dependency. Many read Dickens as exploiting this legislation for its

comic potential both in *Little Dorrit* and *The Pickwick Papers*, in which Samuel Pickwick's landlady, Martha Bardell, believes (due to a miscommunication) that they are engaged, and consequently sues.

10. I am grateful for the suggestions given me by my *Dickens Studies Annual* readers, as well as the advice and support of Margaret Breen, Margaret Higonnet, Jean Marsden, Thomas Recchio, Sarah Winter, and Amy Schlag, all of whom have read various versions of this essay.

WORKS CITED

"Amateur." *Oxford English Dictionary Online*. Oxford: Oxford UP, 2007. Web. 30 Aug. 2010.

Butler, Judith. *Gender Trouble*. 2nd ed. New York: Routledge, 1999.

Dickens, Charles. *Little Dorrit*. Ed. Stephen Wall and Helen Small. London: Penguin, 2003.

Frost, Ginger S. *Promises Broken: Courtship, Class, and Gender in Victorian England*. Charlottesville: UP of Virginia, 1995.

Girard, René. *Deceit, Desire, and the Novel: Self and Other in Literary Structure*. Baltimore: Johns Hopkins UP, 1965.

Goffman, Erving. *The Presentation of Self in Everyday Life*. Garden City, New York: Doubleday, 1959.

Kent, Christopher. "Image and Reality: The Actress and Society." *A Widening Sphere*. Ed. Martha Vicinus. Bloomington: Indiana UP, 1977. 94–116.

Litvak, Joseph. *Caught in the Act: Theatricality in the Nineteenth-Century English Novel*. Berkeley: UP of California, 1992.

"Profession." *Oxford English Dictionary Online*. Oxford: Oxford UP, 2007. Web. 30 Aug. 2010.

"Professional." *Oxford English Dictionary Online*. Oxford: Oxford UP, 2007. Web. 30 Aug. 2010.

Rich, Adrienne. "Compulsory Heterosexuality and Lesbian Existence." *The Lesbian and Gay Studies Reader*. Ed. Henry Abelove et al. New York: Routledge, 1993. 227–54.

Rubin, Gayle. "The Traffic in Women: Notes on the 'Political Economy' of Sex." *Toward an Anthropology of Women*. Ed. Rayna R. Reiter. New York: Monthly Review, 1975.

Sedgwick, Eve Kosofsky. *Between Men: English Literature and Male Homosocial Desire*. New York: Columbia UP, 1985.

Woodward, Kathleen. "Passivity and Passion in Little Dorrit." *The Dickensian* 71 (1975): 140–48.

Epitaphic Representation in Dickens's
Our Mutual Friend

Jolene Zigarovich

*Working with a novel that has dust mounds looming over its action, this
essay addresses Charles Dickens's preoccupation with the tombstone
and pseudo-epitaph in* Our Mutual Friend. *Symbolic and absent tombstones can give us a particular lesson in reading death, resurrection, and
inscription: the novel's central themes. In exposing real and imagined
gravesites, as well as various other forms of signifying death, we can
assess the fetishized idea of the headstone and epitaph in terms of not
only existential affirmation and epistemological insight, but as a dialogic
construct for inscribing death and representation in the novel. This essay
thereby unpacks various forms of epitaphic rhetoric as it sheds new light
on the dialogue* Our Mutual Friend *has with the dead.*

Centered on the death-in-life topos—drowning, resurrection, "articulation,"
and its towering dust mounds—*Our Mutual Friend* has historically engendered critical readings of death and preservation, such as in works by Andrew
Sanders and Albert D. Hutter, and more recently, political, economic, and
queer readings, among others, that examine the novel's death-like economies, the deathly results of homosocial desire, and posthumous agency.[1]
While many of these approaches contribute, in particular, to a better understanding of the deployment of the novel's death-in-life theme, this essay
will address what I have discovered to be a largely neglected preoccupation
of Dickens's later novels: the tombstone. As we will see, the tombstone's

main function—to mark the corpse and memorialize the deceased—becomes secondary for Dickens. Instead, the primary function of the epitaph is to identify and instruct the living. At once articulating presence (the location of the dead as well as the presence of the epitaph's reader) and absence (the deceased), the tombstone becomes a particularly relevant signifier deployed by an aging author struggling with his declining health.[2] *Our Mutual Friend*, I will argue, takes up this unique symbol of articulation and disarticulation, and modifies it: the tombstone itself becomes personified; there are numerous unmarked and erroneously marked graves; and, most importantly, there are pseudo-epitaphs, forms of writing that stand in the place of and mimic the tombstone. Thus symbolic tombstones give us a particular lesson in reading death, resurrection, and inscription: the novel's central themes.

Graves are common sites for Victorian melodrama, from Emily Brontë's *Wuthering Heights*, to Wilkie Collins's *The Woman in White*, to Thomas Hardy's *Tess of the d'Urbervilles*. The fictional Victorian cemetery is no longer only relegated to the dead and their mourners: it is a meeting place for lovers; the setting for violent confrontation; or the inspiration for imaginative fantasy and introspection. Reflecting the grim realities of the poor, many novels depict characters not fortunate enough to be buried in a properly marked grave who are left in anonymous churchyard oblivion. In sensation plots, some novels dramatize characters who find themselves in the strange position of being alive yet pronounced dead by the tombstone and thus by society. Therefore, tombstones emerge in the Victorian novel as emblems of lost identity and decipherment. It isn't surprising, then, to find them erected throughout Charles Dickens's oeuvre.[3] Influenced by eighteenth-century Graveyard and Romantic poetry, Dickens resurrects and reassembles the tombstone trope in an urban, modern manner. Critics have traced his ongoing fascination with churchyards and tombstones, memorable in such early fiction as *The Old Curiosity Shop* (1840–41) and *Martin Chuzzlewit* (1843–44), mid-career fiction such as *David Copperfield* (1849–50) and *Bleak House* (1851–53), which illustrates the terrors of the pauper's graveyard, and especially pertinent later in *Little Dorrit* (1855–57), where literal and figurative epitaphs become modes of humor and satire, and also in *Great Expectations* (1860–61), which depicts prosopopeiac mirroring. And while there have been decisive readings of particular epitaphs and tombstone scenes in Dickens's other works, epitaphic representation in *Our Mutual Friend* has yet to be examined.[4] Therefore, I wish to consider actual tombstones, imagined gravesites, and various forms of signifying death as figured in a novel constructed around the image of dust. By this, we can assess the fetishized idea of epitaph and tombstone in terms not only of existential affirmation and epistemological insight but also as a dialogic construct for inscribing death and representation in the novel. In turn, unpacking various forms of epitaphic rhetoric will shed new light on the dialogue *Our Mutual Friend* has with the dead.

Before we uncover the workings of the epitaph in *Our Mutual Friend*, it is important to frame the epitaph as a unique rhetorical text, which embodies inscription, voice, and symbol. In "Essay upon Epitaphs—I" (1810), Wordsworth critically evaluates epitaphs and poetic practice. He asserts that the first requisite of an epitaph is that it should "speak" the "general language of humanity as connected with the subject of Death—the source from which an Epitaph proceeds, of death and of life" (100). The tombstone, Wordsworth explains, stands at the origin of writing, crossing linguistic boundaries. It is a monument to a presence it does not contain but whose absence it commemorates. In its "speech," the epitaph vocalizes language, embodying the act of inscribing reality into structure. This speech can address the deceased, address the reader/visitor, or refer to the deceased in the third-person. As an uncanny form of writing, a phantom-narrative, the epitaph is an inscription haunted by a presence that it has created itself. Visually symbolizing the gap between writing and speech and at times providing a voice for the absent body, inversely the epitaph hinders access to the dead. As a poetic genre, epitaphs symbolize physical absence but promise immortality because they often evoke the lost voice. Yet the presence implied by this voice is, indeed, a fiction, a specter. The imperative "Halt, Traveller" instructs readers to reanimate briefly the deceased who, through inscription, demands attention. The silent voice of the tombstone is heard when it is read; the deceased speaks through the living readers (and inadvertently readers recite their own deaths). This process of proleptic imagining of one's own death is made possible, argues Paul de Man, only through language. In *The Rhetoric of Romanticism*, de Man compares the epitaph to "the latent threat that inhabits prosopopeia." He notes, "By making death speak, the symmetrical structure of the trope implies, by the same token, that the living are struck dumb, frozen in their own death" (78). Agency is diminished when part of their own power of speech is given over to the dead. This "dead" communication to the living has what de Man terms a "sinister connotation that is not only the prefiguration of one's own mortality but our actual entry into the frozen world of the dead" (78). Of course, by no means does de Man's position assert the possibility of speaking to the dead, even though some epitaphs do exactly this—for example, "Rest in Peace." Prosopopeia is the fiction that something or someone other than ourselves can speak; if we succumb to this, we give a voice to the fear within ourselves that ensures that we are also deprived of voice. Essentially, living agency deteriorates as the power of speech shifts to the dead. This is a dangerous prospect, one which the epitaph particularly dramatizes.

The epitaph—as narrative on the brink of silence—can therefore be seen as part of the process of figurative representation: it is both metaphor and pictorial analogy. In Wordsworth's recognition, a mossy stone, dirt mound, or inscribed name are all considered representations of the dead. And like a representation, a text, or a figure, the epitaph is *already dead*. For this discussion, symbolic markers, remnants of writing (a decayed name, or simply dates) should be considered an epitaphic performance. We can then recognize that the act of writing itself is related to the act of inscribing a gravestone. In fact, writing is inherently haunting: it represents the proof of existence and the acknowledgement of mortality, for the complicity of writing and death is rooted in the mortality of the speaking subject. Karen Mills Campbell remarks: "The epitaph is not just one *kind* of language, a literary genre, but a functional metaphor for, almost a visual representation of, the workings of language itself" (658). Every linguistic gesture can be seen as a kind of "speaking monument." In Geoffrey Hartman's terms, any inscription might become "epitaphic" because "the corpse is in the poet himself, his consciousness of inner decay, and the history he meditates is of nature's relation to the mind" (402). As we will later see, this consciousness of the decaying self fittingly describes Dickens's own mediation of history and mortality.

In the "Essay," Wordsworth praises churchyards for fostering "the community of the living and dead" (56). I would argue that this intercourse finds itself blurred in the Victorian novel, where often the world of the dead and living are confusingly depicted. And this "community" is quite evident in *Our Mutual Friend*, which, we could say, takes the epitaph for its thematic condition: it at once articulates and disarticulates, is about ends and the suspension of ends, about death and the preservation of life. And similar to the locus of the grave, the novel's dust mounds combine decomposition (of things, not human bodies) and inscription, the organic and inorganic.[5] Dickens sets up *Our Mutual Friend* to be seen as an encryption, as embodying the silence of the tomb (or tome). This is seen on the dedicatory page of volume 1 of the first two-volume edition (1865) of the novel, inscribed by Dickens as a gift to Sir James Emerson Tennent, Irish MP, former colonial secretary of Ceylon, and at the time of the novel's dedication, permanent secretary to the Board of Trade. Tennent was an early friend of Dickens when both were fellow law clerks and, in the 1830s, members of the Macready circle. (In fact, both had many "mutual friends"). Dickens often corresponded with Tennent, even meeting him in Europe while Dickens toured with Augustus Egg and Wilkie Collins. The Chapman and Hall dedication copy includes two letters from Dickens to Tennent, expressing the significance of the Tennent dedication for Dickens, as well as his motivation to complete the novel. In the letter dated 26 August 1864 Dickens writes, "I am heartily pleased that you set so much store by the dedication. You may be sure that it does not make me the less anxious to take pains, and to work out well what I have in my mind" (Pilgrim *Letters* 10: 422). In the second letter, dated 24 January 1865, he writes:

Trade requirements necessitate the publication at this time of the first 10 N^{os} of Our Mutual Friend, as the first volume of that story. That first volume necessarily includes the Dedication to you: otherwise some 30,000 and odd buyers would not have it in their copies. But as the book is not complete, I don't send it to you now. I don't want you to have it from me, until the Dedication is the culmination of a finished whole. Then please God the inscribing of it to you will mean much more, and will better express my love.

(Pilgrim *Letters* 11: 9)

As Dickens states, when the first volume of the novel was published (which included the first ten numbers), Chapman and Hall included the dedication.[6] When the novel was complete, the dedication copy also included (among the necessary title page, table of contents, and so on) Dickens's personal letters to Tennent (a unique move on Chapman and Hall's part), which contribute to the theme of friendship and also to the "memorial" tone of the volume.

In particular ways, the Tennent dedication performs epitaphically: it invokes a live reader, gives voice to the absent (Dickens), and consists of a few short lines with "Sir James Emerson Tennent" prominent (see fig. 1). Of interest is the shape of the dedication: it graphically resembles an epitaph with its brief, centered text, traditional font-style, and enlarged name. The content of the dedication further aligns itself with an epitaph: it is "inscribed" by Dickens as a "memorial of friendship." Though Tennent lived until 1869, it is as if Dickens anticipates his friend's impending death. Peculiar is Dickens's aligning of the narrative with a "memorial." If a memorial is something designed to keep remembrance alive, the novel itself can be seen as a lengthy epitaph. But while the dedication points to the future death of Tennent or of Dickens himself, we can also read our own epitaph among the novel's pages. And, as Dickens's last completed novel, *Our Mutual Friend* is in many ways his own self-inscription. In the end, the novel leaves us with the impression that "our mutual friend" is not Sir James Tennent, or even John Harmon/Rokesmith, the character associated with the title, but that which any epitaph ultimately points to: Death.[7] This universal familiarity with death, the core of the novel, is poignantly expressed by Jenny Wren. With her communal invitation "Come up and be dead! Come up and be dead!," Jenny invites Riah, Lizzie Hexam, Fledgeby, and others to forget their troubles through the imagination of death. In being temporarily "dead," they communally experience the absence of physical pain and poverty, the absence of "life." Beyond the confines of the novel, where for many death is a happy escape from life's cruel realities, Dickens's title satirically points to the fact that all of us share the same fate. The title's phantasmagoric "our" encrypts us all, buries us alive, irretrievably.

Wordsworth's poetry and his three essays on epitaphs confirm his interest in the grave and offer a critique of burial reform, as well as consider the epitaph the primal form of language and poetics. Karen Sanchez-Eppler has observed that Wordsworth's poetics and essays rely on the decomposing corpse and the monument it inspires. While Wordsworth regards the finest epitaph to be a moss-

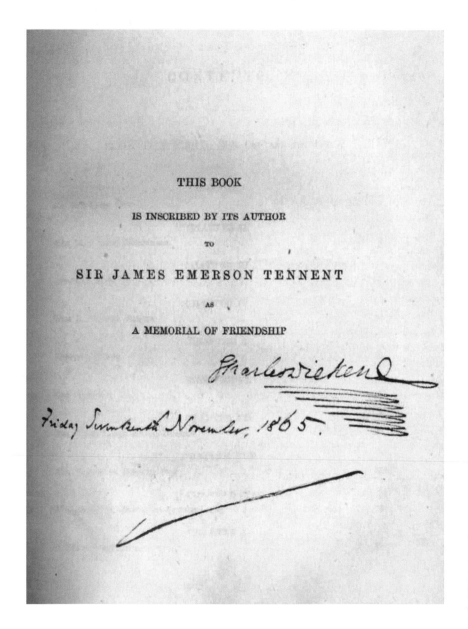

Fig. 1. Dedication in volume 1 from the Chapman and Hall two-volume edition of *Our Mutual Friend* (1865). Signed by Dickens and presented as a gift to Tennent. Courtesy of Special Collections, Honnold/Mudd Library of The Claremont Colleges.

covered stone that invites imagination, sympathy, and sorrow, reformers sought to maintain proper commemoration, which would include the designing of an ideal place for the meditations of the living. The decrepit and wild churchyards where Wordsworth found inspiration would be replaced with the rural, manicured memorial park. With this, we can naturally connect these ideas to *Our Mutual Friend*, a novel centered on a giant graveyard of decomposing objects, dust, and buried texts. As a novel of death, *Our Mutual Friend* repeatedly associates writing and language with mortality. For instance, Gaffer Hexam's cottage is wall-papered with grisly handbills advertising the rewards for the bodies of the missing and murdered. References to these haunt the novel, from the first number where there is a passing mention of a poster on the wall of the Hexam dwelling, about the drowning of a "drunken old chap, in a pair of list slippers and a nightcap" (65; bk. 1, ch. 3). (We discover in book 2, chapter 1 that the man is actually Jenny Wren's grandfather.) Subsequently, the placard announcing Gaffer Hexam's retrieval of George Radfoot's corpse reads: "BODY FOUND" (64; bk. 1, ch. 3).[8] Later, John Harmon (under the alias "John Rokesmith") has the handbill varnished and framed, preserving his own premature obituary. Bella Wilfer discovers the veneered curiosity when secretly inspecting John Rokemith's office: "Carefully backed with canvas, varnished, mounted, and rolled like a map, was the placard descriptive of the murdered man who had come from afar to be her husband. She shrank from this ghostly surprise" (511; bk. 3, ch. 4). In a curious manner, Harmon's preservation of his anonymous "epitaph" ("BODY FOUND") reflects the preservation of his dead sister's signature, penciled beside his own on the wall of a neglected staircase in the Harmon estate. "We must take care of the names," Mr. Boffin says quietly, twice.

But in some cases writing is absent, creating a blank space symbolic of death. Gaffer Hexam's boat—which is used to fish nameless corpses from the Thames—appropriately has "no inscription." Like Krook in *Bleak House*, Gaffer is illiterate and unable to read the handbills of death. And similar to Krook, he has developed a system to be a "scholar":

> "I can't read, nor I don't want to it, for I know 'em by their places on the wall. This one was a sailor, with two anchors and a flag and G.F.T. on his arm . . . This one was the young woman in grey boots, and her linen marked with a cross . . . This is him as had a nasty cut over the eye. This is them two young sisters what tied themselves together with a handkecher."
> (64–65; bk. 1, ch. 3)

The walls of the cottage mock the walls of a church, advertising the corpses Gaffer has fished from the Thames for profit. Even the city's warehouse signs become visible emblems of the pervasive *thanatos*, appropriately linking the imagery of writing and death. Eugene Wrayburn notices that their lettering looked "like inscriptions over graves of dead businesses" (219; bk. 1, ch. 14). And those unfortunate characters doomed to be buried without a tombstone—

without a sign to mark their life and death—are left with a nameless grave representing not only death's ambiguity, but the anonymity (even in death) of the modern social condition. This is a theme experimented with in early Dickens. In "The Story of the Convict's Return" in *Pickwick Papers* (1836–37), the convict is reunited with the unmarked grave of his mother. In *Oliver Twist* (1837–39), the location of the corpse of Oliver's mother Agnes Fleming is unknown, and Oliver kindly erects "Agnes" on a plate in "the old village church," though the tomb it marks lies empty. In *Bleak House* (1852–53), the corpses of poor Jo and the infamous Nemo lie in unconsecrated heaps, never to be "marked" or properly identified in death. Dickens amplifies this problem of the improper burial or unmarked grave in *Our Mutual Friend*.

If the quantity of deaths in the novel is not enough, many of the dead may perhaps lie in mortal oblivion: Little Johnny, Rogue Riderhood, Bradley Headstone, Gaffer Hexam, Mr. Dolls, and Betty Higden all may lie in anonymous graves. With these posthumously "blank" characters Dickens reminds us that death is the ultimate equalizer; that inscription only signifies for the living. For *Our Mutual Friend*, the blank epitaph signifies the inevitable horrors of death, especially of the impoverished and disenfranchised. Little Johnny, John Harmon's double who also has anonymous origins, has a proper funeral, but the narrator only mentions a "small grave." We never see the tombstone or read the epitaph. Perhaps that is why Mrs. Boffin, his adoptive mother, makes this announcement following the funeral: "I have grown timid of reviving John Harmon's name. It's an unfortunate name, and I fancy I should reproach myself if I gave it to another dear child, and it proved again unlucky" (388; bk. 2, ch. 10). She then states, "We agree not to revive John Harmon's name, but to let it rest in the grave" (389; bk. 2, ch. 10). Mr. and Mrs. Boffin have associated Little Johnny with the "supposed dead" John Harmon, as if they share an identity.

Riderhood and Headstone both die in a deadly embrace, their bodies submitted to a watery grave. Though the narrator informs us that their corpses are "found," we never know if funerals have been performed or tombstones have been erected. Jesse "Gaffer" Hexam, a dredger himself, ironically drowns and must be towed to shore, his corpse tangled with his own lines for scavenging corpses. He is buried off-scene, and his daughter Lizzie is perhaps forced to work to pay for the burial fees.[9] And Mr. Dolls, Jenny Wren's perpetually drunk "child"-father, receives the most haunting pseudo-epitaph of the novel: "A ghastly light shining upon him that he didn't need, the beast so furious but a few minutes gone, was quiet enough now, with a strange mysterious writing on his face, reflected from one of the great bottles, as if Death had marked him: 'Mine'" (800; bk. 4, ch. 9). With the line "as if Death had marked him: 'Mine'" Dickens may have had in mind Thomas Gray's "Elegy Written in a Country Churchyard," specifically, the last line from the first stanza of "The Epitaph":

Here rests his head upon the lap of Earth
A Youth to Fortune and to Fame unknown,
Fair Science frown'd not on his humble birth,
And melancholy mark'd him for her own.
                                   (my emphasis; lines 117–20)[10]

And with the reading of "our mutual friend" as "death," the possessive "mine" reinforces the idea of some form of familial relationship or entitlement. Overseen by a clergyman, the funeral and burial take place, but we are uncertain if Mr. Dolls receives a tombstone or inscription. Dickens intends the "ghastly light" and "strange mysterious writing" to be the true epitaph, and alluding to Gray's "Elegy" reinforces this reading.

To be buried in a nameless necropolis, to have one's identity erased, to embody a virtually empty tomb are horrifying prospects. And in many ways the "ghastly light" and nameless "grass-mounds" resemble the dust mounds of the novel that are filled with decaying remnants. In the end, Betty Higden, along with the other inhabitants of the novel's nameless tombs, is literally no more than dust when she is interred. Betty, who carried coins for her funeral, is buried "in a corner of a churchyard . . . so obscure that there was nothing in it but grass-mounds, not so much as one single tombstone" (577; bk. 3, ch. 9). Few mourners attend the funeral, overseen by Reverend Frank Milvey, and witness her "lowly grave." The narrator remarks, "Not a penny had been added to the money sewn in her dress: what her honest spirit had so long projected, was fulfilled" (577; bk. 3, ch. 9). Dickens's belief in sanitary and burial reform is voiced in the narrator's lengthy soliloquy:

> It might not be to do an unreasonably great deal for the diggers and hewers, in a registering age, if we ticketed their graves at the common charge; so that a new generation might know which was which: so that the soldier, sailor, emigrant, coming home, should be able to identify the resting-place of father, mother, playmate, or betrothed. For, we turn up our eyes and say that we are all alike in death, and we might turn them down and work the saying out in this world, so far. It would be sentimental, perhaps? But how say ye, my lords and gentleman and honourable boards, shall we not find good standing-room left for a little sentiment, if we look into our crowds?
>
> (577–78; bk. 3, ch. 9)

Yet Betty's nameless grave is not visited without sentiment. Her devoted apprentice Sloppy, in defending Betty's goodness, inadvertently inscribes the nameless grave with this poetic speech: "She went through whatever duty she had to. She went through with me, she went through with the Minders, she went through with herself, she went through with everythink. O Mrs Higden, Mrs Higden, you was a woman and a mother and a mangler in a million million!" (578; bk. 3, ch. 9).[11] Consistently obsessed with his characters' peculiar body parts, Dickens oddly has Sloppy rhetorically perform his own beheading. Questioning his treatment of Betty, he says, "I've took it into my wretched head that I might have sometimes turned a little harder for her, and it cuts me deep to think so now." The cutting is indeed deep: Sloppy lays his head "inconsolable, against the church door," later removes it from the door, and "took it back to the grave in the corner, and laid it down there, and wept alone" (578; bk. 3, ch. 9).[12] Sloppy's figural beheading is a form of repentance; his wretchedness inspires this odd sacrifice or offering. Observing Sloppy's utter despair for the loss of Betty inspires the Reverend to remark, "Not a very poor grave . . . when it has that homely figure on it. Richer, I think, than it could be made by most of the sculpture in Westminster Abbey!" (578; bk. 3, ch. 9). The head and body of the grieving Sloppy merge with the grass-mound, momentarily creating a grave sculpture worthy of Betty's good spirit. Without a proper tombstone to not only mark the location of the dead, but to memorialize a life, Betty's grave will become overgrown, destined to obscurity. Yet John Rokesmith, Bella Wilfer, Lizzie Hexam, and the Reverend Frank Milvey and his wife witness Sloppy's verbal epitaph and tombstone sculpture: both momentary forms of commemoration, but deeply meaningful nonetheless.

The "grass-mounds" signify death without recourse to letters or inscription. Yet Betty's unmarked grave, as well as the novel's towering dust mounds, carries meaning across cultural and linguistic boundaries. The mound or blank marker gestures to an anonymous dead body beneath it; it represents the anonymity we all will find in death. Wordsworth explains that the tombstone stands at the origin of signification; it is the primal "inscription":

> It need scarcely be said, that an Epitaph presupposes a Monument, upon which it is to be engraven. Almost all Nations have wished that certain external signs should point out the places where their dead are interred. Among the savage tribes unacquainted with letters this has mostly been done either by rude stones placed near the graves, or by mounds of earth raised over them.
>
> (49)

The custom of marking the site of interment derives, according to Wordsworth, "from a twofold desire" to arrest "violation" and to facilitate "memory" (49). The monument thus hinders yet announces access to the dead. An epitaph, he writes, preserves memory, and it must be "accomplished in *close connection with the bodily remains of the deceased*" (Essay 1, 96; Wordsworth's emphasis). In this sense, words incarnate; they give and signify the spirit. Yet that is the irony of the epitaph: it protects a corpse and monumentalizes the memory of the deceased, but it is relegated to stone which is unprotected, exposed to the elements, and susceptible to decay. Though in its decomposition an epitaph may be unreadable, the stone or mossy lozenge still marks the corpse, still speaks for the deceased. The symbolic stone or mound is the primitive memorial. The unmarked thereby marks. Without the epitaph to perform this unique function, we are left with a type of symbolic ruin: the markerless grave signifies lost meaning as well as the residue of meaning. All of the unnamed dead are denied the inscribed word and identity; they are rhetorically and literally decomposed. But, simultaneously, the primitive marker still has the power to signify perhaps not the identity of the dead, but, maybe just as significantly, the location of the dead and the remnant of a life.

The decrepit corner of the churchyard that the deceased Betty is so unfortunate to inhabit, with markerless graves and only primitive grass-mounds to signify the dead, is certainly an improvement from the unconsecrated heap to which the corpses of Nemo and, we assume, Jo are relegated in *Bleak House*, and it brings to mind the churchyard in which Pip's deceased parents and brothers are buried.

> The shape of the letters on my father's, gave me an odd idea that he was a square, stout, dark man, with curly black hair. From the character and turn of the inscription, '*Also Georgiana Wife of the Above*,' I drew a childish conclusion that my mother was freckled and sickly. To five little stone lozenges, each about a foot and a half long, which were arranged in a near row beside their grave, and were sacred to the memory of five little brothers of mine—who gave up trying to get a living, exceedingly early in that universal struggle—I am indebted for a belief I religiously entertained that they had all been born on their backs with their hands in their trousers-pockets, and had never taken them out in this state of existence.
>
> (1; ch. 1)

While his parents' grave is properly inscribed, the graveyard holds the bodies of "Alexander, Bartholomew, Abraham, Tobias, and Roger, infant children of the aforesaid, [who] were also dead and buried." Pip is the sole surviving son; the "five little stone lozenges" are slabs signifying his survivorship. (Dickens repeats this enormous fraternal loss in *Edwin Drood*, where Septimus Crisparkle is supposedly named "because six little brother Crisparkles before him went out, one by one, as they were born, like six weak little rushlights, as they were lighted.")[13] Yet even from these small stone markers, without epitaph, Pip conjures their five names and bodies, picturing their clothes, hands, and how they were born (as dead, "born on their backs," which is how they are laid to rest). The stone lozenges are a comfort to Pip, and aid him in imagining some connection to the brothers he never had the fortune to know. Though the lozenges are primitive markers (we can infer the Pirrip family was too poor to pay for five inscribed headstones; six, if we include Georgiana), they still signify the "close connection with the bodily remains" that Wordsworth determines is necessary for the epitaph. The lozenges are nonetheless inscribed by Pip's imagination, just as Sloppy "inscribes" Betty Higden's grave. In *Our Mutual Friend*, the grass and dust mounds are signifiers of anonymity and lack of sanctification. Primitive remainders, they eternally await inscription.

While Betty and numerous others of the novel's victims decompose in unidentified obscurity, Dickens brings his interest in graveyards and epitaphs to the forefront by blatantly naming one of his most sinister and disturbed characters after memorial sculpture. Noted in the novel's manuscript as "Bradley Deadstone," "Amos Deadstone," and "Amos Headstone" (Amos being one of the twelve minor prophets in the Hebrew Bible), Bradley Headstone's surname appropriately reflects, as earlier noted, the beheading rhetoric associated with him and also his cold, rigid demeanor. This becomes more ironic when he steps into a churchyard—he embodies the speaking yet lifeless pieces of stone that surround him.[14] In some morbid form of courtship, appropriate to a man named "Headstone," Bradley conveys Lizzie Hexam to a decrepit churchyard to profess his love to her. Angered by Lizzie's rejection of him, he commits an act of self-flagellation, beating a piece of the coping of the burial-ground enclosure "with a force that laid the knuckles raw and bleeding" (454; bk. 2, ch. 15). It is as if the body and epitaph are joined prematurely (Headstone the man merges with burial stone). In fact, Bradley seems to embody his surname. His white face is described often as "ashy," "as if it were being overspread with ashes" until it resembles a "decaying statue," and "the powdered mortar from under the stone at which he wrenched, rattled on the pavement to confirm his own words." The headstones and erect coping align with Headstone's rigidity and sexual frustration (he wildly beats the coping until he bleeds). Marcus Stone's eerie illustration of Riah "saving" Lizzie from this attack leaves out Headstone, who has already left the scene, yet he is represented by the dark, looming shadows and stone coping ("he wrenched at it"), as well as by the graveyard in the background (fig. 2). In this way, "Headstone" is restrained, contained, and trapped behind the iron fencing while his object of violent desire stands safely outside its perimeter.

Baptized by Dickens as the embodiment of the novel's central theme, Headstone, too, is susceptible to posthumous oblivion. While placing Headstone adjacent to an actual burial stone is a macabre form of humor for Dickens, the irony of the word "Headstone" is also prominent in the school scene with Rogue Riderhood, who confronts the teacher in his classroom, threatening to expose him as Eugene's attacker. After Headstone "placed his usual signature, enlarged, upon the board," Riderhood asks the children to "read the name off, from the writing" (865; bk. 4, ch. 15). The children's voices reply, "'Bradley Headstone!' 'No?' cried Riderhood. 'You don't mean it? Headstone! Why, that's in a churchyard'" (865; bk. 4, ch. 15). Riderhood foreshadows the death of Bradley Headstone, pointing out that the inscription of his name on the blackboard ironically doubles his impending resting place. As if to defeat Riderhood's game with his name, Headstone then commits a virtual suicide by slowly wiping his name from the board (867; bk. 4, ch. 15), leaving a blank space.[15] This moment appropriately foreshadows his death, which is bound with confused identities and predictably suspended with anonymity. And his death by drowning perhaps results in another unmarked grave in this novel. The narrator informs us that "the two were found, lying under the

Fig. 2. Marcus Stone, "A Friend in Need." Original illustration for *Our Mutual Friend* (1865).

ooze and scum behind one of the rotting gates," still "girdled" together with Bradley's "iron ring" and its rivets (874; bk. 4, ch. 15). "Ooze," "scum," and "rot" imply some kind of primordial ooze, as if through violent death Bradley and Riderhood have degenerated, or are have been pickled and displayed as one of Venus's "bottled" specimens. The narrator relating to us that Bradley's corpse has evidently been found and identified, we can only speculate that Miss Peecher arranged a funeral (a Headstone family is not mentioned in the novel). Even if we do assume that Bradley received a proper burial, the lack of a funeral and tombstone in the narrative suggests the novel's river and dust mounds must represent the mortality of all.

Our Mutual Friend not only portrays the horrors of watery or unmarked graves; its sensational plot is centered on a wrongly marked grave. This fascination is not surprising: Dickens had published the serialized version of Wilkie Collins's *The Woman in White* (Nov 1859–Aug 1860) in *All the Year Round* and was greatly influenced by its dead-alive plot. *The Woman in White* dramatizes the mortal predicament of Laura Fairlie, legally pronounced "dead" yet physically alive, who works to have the legal pronouncements of her death overturned and her "life" reinstated. In order to do this, she must prove her identity and reveal the true identity of the corpse the grave erroneously marked "Laura, Lady Glyde" holds, which we later find is that of her half-sister, Anne Catherick. At the end of the novel, when the villainous actions of Sir Percival Glyde and Count Fosco are fully exposed, Laura's name is erased from the lying tombstone by the textual excavator Walter Hartright, and "Anne Catherick" is rightly inscribed. The sensational erasing of the false epitaph legally and rhetorically resurrects Laura and kills Anne Catherick.[16]

Collins's burial plot is uncannily mirrored by Dickens in *Our Mutual Friend*. First, Dickens acknowledges that epitaphs lie, as evidenced by the narrator's description of the churchyard where Bradley Headstone confronts Lizzie Hexam: "Here, conveniently and healthfully elevated above the level of the living, were the dead, and the tombstones; some of the latter droopingly inclined from the perpendicular, as if they were ashamed of the lies they told" (451; bk. 2, ch. 15). Always intertwining humor with the macabre, Dickens pokes fun at the "lies" the epitaphs tell about the deceased (assuming many of the dead aren't lovingly regarded or deeply missed). Dickens's simile also cleverly personifies the tombstone ("droopingly inclined") and invokes the dead speaker and living reader ("ashamed of the lies they told"). Indeed, all epitaphs embody a contradiction as they often ventriloquize for the dead; their words pronounce an identity or address a visitor. In this way, epitaphs simulate a life as they mark a death. In *The Rhetoric of Romanticism*, de Man terms this prosopopeiac exchange with the dead the "madness of words," the "endless prosopopeia by which the dead are made to have a face and a voice which tells the allegory of their demise and allows us to apostrophize them in our turn" (122). The personification and apostrophe Dickens conjures resemble a mutual intelligibility between us and the "healthfully elevated" dead, and by succumbing to this transaction and belief, we disfigure, deface, and deprive our own voice. This is the linguistic and rhetorical mystification underlying *Our Mutual Friend*.

There is no doubt that the notion of living on (or deferring the "now"), of playing dead, is most obvious in the case of John Harmon, a pseudo-Laura Fairlie of sorts. Dickens's description of Harmon's character in a letter to John Forster in 1861 as he developed the plot for the novel is particularly interesting: "I think a man, young and perhaps eccentric, feigning to be dead and *being dead*" (*Life* 338; bk. 3). Through this character—in his liminal existence—Dickens attempted to push the limits of fictional mortality and death's signification. The Harmon story is intimately bound up with articulation, narration, and death. Returning to England to claim an inherited fortune, Harmon, like Eugene Wrayburn, is involved in a murderous plot. Having switched clothes with George Radfoot, a sailor, he is robbed and left to drown. His account of his own attempted murder is carefully set apart from the rest of the novel by the device of double-spacing at its beginning and end. Similar to Eugene, who is separated from his identity as he nearly drowns, Harmon describes his death-like experience with curious detachment. After being drugged, robbed, and beaten, Harmon seems to lose his sense of self: "I could not have said that my name was John Harmon—I could not have thought it—I didn't know it." His nearly lifeless body is then thrown into the Thames, causing a shift in consciousness (and narration from first person to third person) as he seems to observe himself drowning: "'This is John Harmon drowning! John Harmon struggle for your life. John Harmon, call on Heaven and save yourself!' I think I cried it out aloud in a great agony, and then a heavy horrid unintelligible something vanished, and it was I who was struggling alone in the water" (426; bk. 2, ch. 13). Here John attempts to narrate his own story (within Dickens's story), himself. It is as if we (and the novel's narrator) are strolling by the epitaph of "John Harmon" on which is inscribed "Pause, Traveller!" as the "dead" is given voice. Stone's original illustration "More Dead than Alive" (fig. 3) dramatizes Harmon's liminal situation as he hovers between life and death, drowning and resuscitation. With his face obscured, Harmon is thus Everyman, the figure symbolizing the novel's central themes. The virtually unidentifiable Harmon is soaked, bent over, and in the act of reviving himself; as if he is taking his "first breath." This baptism and rebirth is known only to us; Harmon invites the reader to keep the mystery of his identity a secret, to hold the key to the novel's dead-alive scenario.

As in the case of *The Woman in White*, the Harmon plot then takes us through a series of aliases, unsolved mysteries, and false stories. First is the remarkable multiplicity of names and identities that Harmon is associated with: George Radfoot (the dead sailor who attempted to rob Harmon), Little Johnny (the orphan that Mr. and Mrs. Boffin attempt to adopt to replace the memory of the young

John Harmon), Julius Handford (the first and most short-lived of Harmon's aliases), and John Rokesmith (the second alias under which Harmon marries Bella Wilfer). Harmon in fact commits a verbal murder-suicide with: "So John Harmon died, and Julius Handford disappeared, and John Rokesmith was born" (428; bk. 2, ch. 13). Mrs. Veneering calls him "The Man from Tumwhere," the

Fig. 3. Marcus Stone, "More Dead than Alive." Original illustration for *Our Mutual Friend* (1865).

Buffers call him "The Man from Nowhere" (55; bk. 1, ch. 2), the narrator, Lady Tippins, Lightwood and others refer to him as "The Man from Somewhere," and Lightwood calls him "Chokesmith" (472; bk. 2, ch. 16), which is further degenerated to "Artichokc" (472; bk. 2, ch. 16). And as Stone's illustration depicts, he is no one and everyone (fig. 3). Harmon is quite literally dispersed (or dismembered) throughout the text. Harmon's name is also resurrected by the Boffins, who adopt the orphan already named "Johnny" and in Harmon's honor, name him John Harmon. Perhaps to avoid any future name confusion, Dickens summarily kills the boy off in the second book.

In *The Rhetoric of Romanticism*, de Man suggests that language is a source of inevitable mystification: "Death is a displaced name for a linguistic predicament, and the restoration of mortality by autobiography (the prosopopeia of the voice and the name) deprives and disfigures to the precise extent that it restores" (81). While in *Little Dorrit* John Chivery's epitaphs are imaginary, but made real through speech and mock-inscription, John Harmon's tombstone is real, yet (like Chivery's) prematurely announces his death. This unnatural position of reading the announcement of one's death before it occurs is also similar to *A Christmas Carol* (1843), where Scrooge reads "upon the stone of the neglected grave his own name" (70). John Harmon—who is living under the alias "John Rokesmith"—speaks of this mortal, linguistic predicament when he visits a churchyard at Limehouse Church and recites a Hamletesque soliloquy:

> "It is a sensation not experienced by many mortals," said he, "to be looking into a churchyard on a wild windy night, and to feel that I no more hold a place among the living than these dead do, and even to know that I lie buried somewhere else, as they lie buried here. Nothing uses me to it. A spirit that was once a man could hardly feel stranger or lonelier, going unrecognized among mankind, than I feel."
>
> (422; bk. 2, ch. 13)

In a way Dickens has returned us to the Pirrip gravesite in *Great Expectations*, where Pip's epistemological enlightenment occurs (and his parents' tombstone becomes a scene of identification). Harmon experiences a moment of posthumous contemplation that only a "textual" death can provide, the proleptic imagining that de Man recognized Wordsworth enacting in the poem "Boy of Winander" (73). Scrooge's confrontation with his own tombstone is also rewritten here—Harmon is reminded of his own death and character through the contemplation of the "sign" of death. "Lie buried," repeated twice in the same sentence, not only refers to Harmon-Radfoot and his fellow dead, but the play on "lie" reminds us of the false epitaph and the "lying" epitaphs discussed earlier. In *Demeure*, Jacques Derrida observes, "I certainly cannot testify to my death—by definition. I cannot say, according to common sense, I should not be able to say: I died or I am dead."[17] But Harmon has strangely testified to his own textual "death." He has miraculously survived his "articulation" and embodied Mr.

Venus's postmortem fantasy of "customers" witnessing his arrangement of their own skeletons.[18]

Harmon even ponders delaying the "resurrection" of his true identity until he has tested Bella Wilfer's ideals. "John Harmon is dead. Should John Harmon come to life? If yes, why? If no, why?" he asks himself (428). Delaying his virtual exhumation, Harmon decides to remain buried:

> He went down to his room, and buried John Harmon many additional fathoms deep . . . heaped mounds upon mounds of earth over John Harmon's grave. His walking did not bring him home until the dawn of the day. And so busy had he been all night, piling and piling weights upon weights of earth above John Harmon's grave, that by that time John Harmon lay buried under a whole Alpine range; and still the Sexton Rokesmith accumulated mountains over him, lightening his labour with the dirge, "Cover him, crush him, keep him down!"
>
> (435; bk. 2, ch. 13)

His words "heaped mounds upon mounds of earth" evidently evoke the real dust mounds that Harmon will inherit, but also signify the mounds that eventually all of us will inherit: the dusty origins and destinations of man. What makes this speech remarkable is the invocation of the image and representation of both the real and imagined tombstone. Contemplating the existence of his own false epitaph (which incidentally, Dickens never shows us), Harmon chooses to bide his marginal position between life and death for his own purposes. This is a unique form of prosopopeia, what Barbara Johnson describes in *Persons and Things* as an epitaphic moment when "the voice from beyond the grave, speaks *from* the grave" (13).[19] It appears as if he could sever his identity merely through the employment of a figure of speech that metaphorically entombs its speaker. Traditionally, the tombstone, the "speaking site," warns the traveler of the approach of death; the epitaph animates the dead, who speaks of the grave. Harmon's relationship with the speaking dead is reversed: he speaks of resurrection and murder. The narrator's satiric naming of Harmon as "Sexton Rokesmith" reflects the burial rites performed by Harmon himself, further associating the scene (and much of the novel) with the biblical sources of man, dust, burial, and death. With this comes to mind Krook from *Bleak House*, who spontaneously combusts and leaves only some soot and a little puddle. Through Harmon, Dickens reminds us, "For dust thou art, and unto dust shalt thou return" (Gen. 3:19).

As with Collins's Laura Fairlie, Harmon-Rokesmith's liminal position as "more dead than alive" gives him a unique point of view; for much of the novel he embodies Jenny's emphatic "Come up and be dead!" Though one's death is never known and must always be imminent, Harmon is given such paradoxical (and impossible) lines as "I have no clue to the scene of my death" (422; bk. 2, ch. 13) and "Dead, I have found the true friends of my lifetime" (429; bk. 2, ch. 13). Nicholas Royle terms this a "spectrality of experience" that "is everywhere in *Our Mutual Friend*" (49). The necrophilic aspect to "pretending to be dead" is made more apparent when in Harmon's embrace Bella describes that his arms are her "last resting-place," as if she entered a gravebed. This impossibility of language (or de Man's "madness of words") is made apparent when Harmon is literally declared dead after Radfoot's corpse is found by Gaffer Hexam weeks later and is mistakenly marked "John Harmon." Harmon visits the police station to see if he recognizes the body. Reminiscent of Mr. Venus's fantasy of Silas Wegg witnessing the articulation of his own skeleton, the traumatized Harmon is in the strange position of staring at his own corpse: "It's a horrible sight. O! a horrible, a horrible sight!" (68; bk. 1, ch. 3). Here he experiences the *horror vacui* of his own mortality as he confronts the corpse of his double.[20] In an epitaphic mode, Harmon both articulates and disarticulates language as he describes his dead-alive position. And while the close resemblance of Laura and Anne (they are half-sisters) explains why Anne's corpse could be substituted for Laura's in *The Woman in White*, George and John's doubling occurs through the exchange of clothes (a doubling later recycled by Dickens in the Bradley-Riderhood plot).

The Woman in White centers on properly burying the real victim, exposing the villains, and exhuming Laura Fairlie's "dead" name. Collins fetishizes the gravesite and erroneous epitaph, having numerous characters visit, read, clean, erase, and inscribe the tombstone. By the novel's close, the mysteries are solved and Anne Catherick rests in a properly marked grave. Despite the prevalent borrowing from Collins's novel, Dickens never shows us the false epitaph, leaves the Harmon-Radfoot grave unvisited, the tombstone improperly marked, George Radfoot's corpse misidentified, and his murder unsolved.[21] Even with the efficiency of the police in the novel, no one is ever apprehended for this crime. There seems to be little interest in the real victim or the murderer. Dickens isn't invested in the sensational plot and the importance of rightly writing death. Though the gravesite is never shown, we can assume that the deceased son of a man, not only of substantial wealth, but who is obsessed with controlling his own burial and afterlife, would be properly buried and commemorated. Thereby, we are forced to realize that somewhere within the novel a tombstone is inscribed with "John Harmon" and the grave holds the body of George Radfoot. With this, Dickens leaves the reader grasping for truth, but what remains is the fraudulent headstone, a floating signifier for the arbitrary nature of writing death and identity.

While Dickens seems to be approaching an ending in the last chapter "The Voice of Society," this movement proves to tease and delay conclusion, and once again the eternal image of dust is evoked. At the close of the novel we learn that Old Harmon himself wished to prolong his last will and testament: a third will was discovered by Mr. Boffin and preserved in a gin bottle and buried in his own little dust mound—much like a corpse. Old Harmon's fear of being buried alive is countered by his reluctance to write his final words and wishes. In fact, the novel demonstrates how Old Harmon—despite all his eccentric "precautions against coming to life"—lives beyond the grave through the power of his writing (58; bk. 1, ch. 2). It is this persistence of living through writing (here a writing of death), of speaking from beyond the grave, that is of significance. Royle remarks: "*Our Mutual Friend* invites us into the dark, into other scenes of reading, leading us along strange waterways, into the desiccation of headstones and crypts, the silence of the tome" (40). As his father's earlier will requested, John Harmon indeed marries Bella and inherits the mounds. And it is the will, and Harmon's claiming of his inheritance, that commences the novel. So have we in fact made full circle in the end? Has the plot been a monstrous detour leading us back to the beginning? Without concluding the chapter with "The End," the novel unnervingly suspends its own conclusion. Indeed, Dickens answers Bella's question, "But *is* the Story done?" with a definitive "Not yet" (845; bk. 4, ch. 13). The ghostliness of reading and of the implacable, unending demands it makes, is reiterated (Royle 39).

If we read the Tennent dedication as the Preface or "beginning" of the first-volume edition of *Our Mutual Friend*, then the narrator's curious "POST-SCRIPT: IN LIEU OF PREFACE" is the true "ending." These epitaphic tributes appropriately bookend a novel that literally self-buries. The Dedication and Postscript involve "real" moments outside of the fiction, and in their own way serve as visual and rhetorical tombstones. The Postscript serves as the narrator's defense of the novel's dead-alive and buried will plot, including the fact that well before the novel's characters, the reader is aware that Harmon is not dead and indeed has reinvented himself as Rokesmith. Betty Higden's fear of the workhouse and "death from destitution" are also defended as accurate portrayals of the effects of the "ill-supervised" Poor Law. And for this conversation, the last paragraph is eerily relevant. The well-known Postscript exposes the omnipotent narrator in his description of a train accident. Veiled by this ironic voice, Dickens reveals and disguises his identity, making us witnesses to his trauma:

> On Friday the Ninth of June in the present year, Mr. and Mrs. Boffin (in their manuscript dress of receiving Mr. and Mrs. Lammle at breakfast) were on the South Eastern Railway with me, in a terribly destructive accident. When I had done what I could to help others, I climbed back into my carriage—nearly turned over a viaduct, and caught aslant upon the turn—to extricate the worthy couple. They were much soiled, but otherwise unhurt. The same happy result attended Miss Bella Wilfer on her wedding day, and Mr. Riderhood inspecting Bradley Headstone's red neckerchief as he lay asleep.
>
> (894)

This account is based upon Dickens's real brush with death on the date that he specifies when he and his mistress Ellen Ternan (along with her mother) were involved in an actual train wreck at Staplehurst. The phrase describing the Boffins "in their manuscript dress" is coyly apt: he carried with him the completed sixteenth monthly number for August 1865, which contained book

4, chapters 1–4. While in France, he had worked on the second chapter of the sixteenth number, having by June completed more than three-fourths of the novel. He brought this portion of the manuscript back with him "in the pocket of his overcoat," remembering to retrieve it from the derailed train car after assisting the numerous injured (Ackroyd 960). As Michael Slater observes, "The phrase working 'for hours among the dead and dying' recurs again and again" in brief notes Dickens sent to various friends from the *All the Year Round* office the following day" (536).[22] The mixture of the fictional with the real isn't unique for Dickens, but using the traumatic accident to close the narrative is an uncanny foreshadowing of Dickens's own death five years later: amazingly on 9 June, 1870.[23] In a disturbing manner, authoring and mortality are here intertwined. The notion that the author "saves" his fictional characters from death reflects the God-like power inherited by all authors: they can choose to "kill off" a character or not. Dickens's self-conscious narration anticipates "modernization," and this scene becomes a touchstone for modern authors such as T. S. Eliot and such postmodern authors as John Fowles (who also meets his characters on a train in *The French Lieutenant's Woman*, one of whom is named Charles). Dickens's usual method of closing all his novels with the fictional terminus "THE END" is delayed until this retrospective close of the Postscript: "I remember with devout thankfulness that I can never be much nearer parting company with my readers for ever, than I was then, until there shall be written against my life, the two words with which I have this day closed this book:—THE END" (894). Dickens admits that the train accident and the subsequent trauma are signs of the recognition of his mortality, of his own impending epitaph that reads "THE END." Yet he has used the powers of authoring to deflect the signs of his own mortality, to "write against" a life. It can be understood that inscription opens an alternative to oblivion, insuring the remembrance of the one who writes. Through writing, the word ostensibly preserves the soul, the trace, of the writer. Each word, each sentence, is a deferral of the ending, a deferral of death. With the close of Dickens's last completed novel, he inscribes that very attempt at deferral.

In *The Rhetoric of Romanticism*, de Man maintains that "To read is to understand, to question, to know, to forget, to erase, to deface, to repeat—that is to say, the endless prosopopeia by which the dead are made to have a face and a voice which tells the allegory of their demise and allows us to apostrophize them in our turn" (122). This intricate process reflects Dickens's motive to delay, deface, and forget *mortalitas*. It must be remembered that he *and* a portion of the manuscript for *Our Mutual Friend*—a novel with a theme that had already transported Dickens into the world of death—narrowly escaped destruction on the South Eastern Railway. Both survive and the novel signifies this near-death experience. In her reading of apparent death and the John Harmon plot, Catherine Gallagher observes that "the value of Life itself . . . is only discoverable from some vantage point outside the body" (95). I would add that the Postscript, written after the accident, depicts this recognition for the author: Dickens's life—along with the novel's corpus—is revitalized and revalued by this near-death experience. With the Postscript, Dickens memorializes (or immortalizes) the reluctance to "kill" his authorial self and put down his pen. As de Man suggests, once the reading (or in this case, the writing) ends, the life disappears. Like the novel's dust mounds, river, and effigies, the possibility of any kind of "end" is withheld, and we are again submitted to the uncanny experiment of suspended animation, the "spectral elusiveness of living on" (Royle 49).

At the end of *Our Mutual Friend*, Dickens fictionalizes the trauma of a brush with death, but at the same time demonstrates his own attempt to write against that very death. Blatantly acknowledging the complicity between death and writing, Dickens gestures towards the necrotized immortality of the written word. Recent deaths of loved ones and close friends such as John Leech, the Staplehurst accident, Dickens's letters and acknowledgement of the trauma that the accident produced, his declining health during the period of the novel's production, coupled with the novel's Postscript—all attest to Dickens's concern about his literary legacy and mortality. With this in mind, when he writes during this period he may be imagining his own paradoxical future as a corpse and a textual presence. In the first of his "Essays upon Epitaphs," Wordsworth proposes that the desire to remember others, and be remembered oneself, is due to "the consciousness of a principle of immortality in the human soul" (50). For the author, this desire is especially poignant, and for Dickens this anxiety manifests in a literary monument. Angus Collins observes that "*Our Mutual Friend* is both a *memento mori* and a means of coping" with the recognition that death is defeated, in part by the power of the word (259).[24] And as both a reminder of death and memorial of life, the novel epitaphically performs, simultaneously composing and decomposing, giving voice to the deceased and living alike. *Our Mutual Friend* dramatizes Dickens's belief in a prosopopeiac dialogue, and by postponing the close of the novel, and thereby the end of his own life, Dickens reasserts his voice and living agency.

NOTES

I wish to thank Edgar Rosenberg and Talia Schaffer for reading earlier versions of this essay.

1. For recent discussions of mortality and *Our Mutual Friend* see Černý, Scoggin, Rothenberg, and Cregan-Reid. Levine reads the state of suspended animation as necessary for epistemological insight. See Sedgwick for a reading of the novel's homosocial (and phobic) underpinnings. Gallagher's essay is an especially insightful reading of posthumous agency. It was reprinted in *The Body Economic: Life, Death, and Sensation in Political Economy and the Victorian Novel* (Princeton: Princeton UP, 2008).

2. Dickens's contract with Chapman and Hall included a provision for what should happen in the event of the author's death during *Our Mutual Friend*'s serialization. See Pilgrim Edition of the *Letters* 10: 477 for this contract. After completion of the first two monthly numbers, Dickens was also called upon to write an obituary of Thackeray for *The Cornhill*. Thackeray had been working on *Denis Duval*, a serialized novel that he didn't live to finish. Five years later Dickens would also die during the serialization of an incomplete last novel. See Slater 521–22.

3. In *The Night Side of Dickens*, Stone lists the many books Dickens had in his library related to death, including *Report on a General Scheme for Extramural Sepulture, 1850* and G. Walker's *Lectures on the Conditions of the Metropolitan Graveyards, 1864–69*, showing his interest in burial reform, tombstones and epitaphs (569–70). The General Board of Health's *Report on a General Scheme* . . . recommended that, for reasons of health, no further burials be permitted in towns and cities and that the government provide new cemeteries outside built-up areas. Originally proposed by Edwin Chadwick in 1843, the recommendation became law on 5 August. Dickens received the report from his brother-in-law Henry Austin, and in a letter to Austin dated 27 February 1850 he writes, "Many thanks for the Report, which is extraordinarily interesting. I began to read it last night, in bed—and dreamed of putrefaction generally" (Pilgrim *Letters* 6: 47).

4. For seminal readings of the epitaph in Dickens's fiction, see Brooks, Dever, Franklin Fisher IV, Walbank, Hill, Wheeler, Stewart, Hennelly, Jr., and Carey illuminate the tombstone and coffin motifs respectively.

5. The heaps did not ordinarily contain human corpses, though I am emphasizing their symbolic role as exposed burial sites. See Poole's notes to the Penguin edition for commentary on the contents of the dust mounds. As Eve Sedgwick, J. Hillis Miller, and others have pointed out, there has been an ongoing controversy over the actual contents of the "dust heaps." (See Miller 294–96.) For Sedgwick, as well as for many others, human excrement (and its relation as a commodity) becomes a critical component of the heaps in terms of symbolic value and waste (170).

6. In the 29 October, 1864 letter to Tennent, Dickens remarks, "I am heartily vexed that you go this set of my books, because I had hoped to send you one when your own book should be finished. For the present I stand committed to a white lie, in the inscription I have written; but means must be devised for making it a piece of truth" (Pilgrim *Letters* 10: 446). Storey et al. note that "On hearing from Mamie Dickens that her father intended to dedicate it to him Tennent wrote to Forster on 30 July: '*I cannot tell you how* this has charmed me. It seems like attaining the *garter* of literature, to have such an honor paid me by Dickens'" (MS Morgan; quoted in Pilgrim *Letters* 10: 446n). As Dickens explained in a letter of 24 January 1865, he was compelled to publish the dedication after ten numbers of *Our Mutual Friend* had been issued.

7. An insert in the first monthly part of *Our Mutual Friend* explains, "The Reader will understand the use of the popular phrase OUR MUTUAL FRIEND, as the title of this book, on arriving at the Ninth Chapter." There Boffin identifies Rokesmith as "Our Mutual Friend." See Poole 801–02, n. 1, for other examples of the phrase in

Dickens. I agree with Poole that "perhaps it is death that makes the world go round. And death who is our mutual friend" (xix).

8. All quotations from *Our Mutual Friend* will refer to the 1971 Penguin edition.

9. I read Lizzie's statement to her brother Charley as evidence of her working to repay expenses incurred by her father's burial. With "The child's father is employed by the house that employs me; that's how I came to know it" (277), Lizzie admits that she is indebted to Jenny Wren and her father for her employment. When Charley remarks to his sister, "I don't see what you have to do with [Jenny Wren]," Lizzie replies, "Any compensation—restitution—never mind the word, you know my meaning. Father's grave" (277). The first portion of this comment could indicate that she is helping Jenny as some form of "restitution" or appreciation for Jenny having assisted her in finding employment. It could also indicate her desire to help Jenny Wren is an attempt to make restitution for Gaffer's theft of money from the corpse of the "terrible drunken old man" who was Jenny's grandfather (277). The fragment "Father's grave" oddly and awkwardly completes Lizzie's response. This directly refers to Lizzie's father's grave, and connects it with monetary repayment (Gaffer having stolen from Jenny's grandfather's corpse). Thereby, we can infer that Lizzie is working not only to support herself, but that her compensation is going towards some sort of fees incurred by Gaffer's burial. I am grateful to John O. Jordan for his input on my interpretation of this scene.

10. Cotsell also notes the similarity (267).

11. I wish to thank an anonymous *DSA* reader of this essay for the suggestion that Sloppy's heartfelt words can be read as epitaphic.

12. Emphasizing his change in the surname from *Dead*stone to *Head*stone, Dickens later revisits the beheading theme in bk. 3, ch. 10 at the end of the chase scene when Mortimer and Lightwood, pursued by Bradley Headstone, reverse the chase and surprise the baffled Bradley: "[Bradley] went by them in the dark, like a haggard head suspended in the air: so completely did the force of his expression cancel his figure" (608; bk. 3, ch. 10). Fixated on this metaphorical decapitation, Dickens repeats the trope of the "headless Headstone" several times in the following chapter as well. One example: "So, the haggard head suspended in the air flitted across the road, like the spectre of one of the many heads erst hoisted upon neighboring Temple Bar" (610; bk. 3, ch. 11).

13. I can't help but be reminded of the magnitude of the Brontë familial loss figured on the tombstone for Maria Brontë in Haworth Church, which lists five deceased children below their mother's name. In her *Life of Charlotte Brontë*, Elizabeth Gaskell emphasizes this loss in the graphic reproduction of the family tombstone, and refers to the Brontë children as "six little motherless children" (9).

14. See Brattin (147–48) and Stone ("What's in a Name" 198–99) for a discussion of Headstone's naming in the manuscript.

15. The marking with and erasing of chalk (thereby dust) in terms of signification and mortality emerges in *Bleak House* (with Krook specifically), and later in *Edwin Drood*, where the concluding lines tell of Datchery's adding one thick line of chalk to the score in his cupboard.

16. See Zigarovich, "Wilkie Collins, Narrativity, and Epitaph" for further discussion of Collins's deployment of the dead-alive plot (229–64).

17. Derrida 46. Derrida continues, "I cannot, I should not be able to, testify to my own death, only to the imminence of my death, to its *instance* as *deferred imminence*. I can testify to the imminence of my death."

18. In bk. 1, ch. 7, Venus threatens a boy whom he mistakenly accuses of stealing a tooth with, "You've no idea how small you'd come out, if I had the articulating of you" (126), and in the same chapter he impresses Mr. Wegg with, "If you was brought here loose in a bag to be articulated, I'd name your smallest bones blindfold equally with your largest, as fast as I'd pick 'em out, and I'd sort 'em all, and sort your wertebræ, in a manner that would equally surprise and charm you" (128).

19. I must note the particular coincidence between Johnson's title and that of ch. 16 from the final book of *Our Mutual Friend*: "Persons and Things in General."

20. For a discussion of the interchangeability of characters in the novel, see Bodenheimer (170–73). I am surprised that Dickens did not suggest that Marcus Stone illustrate this scene which is a direct replication of Scrooge's confrontation with his own grave and epitaph in *A Christmas Carol*. It is known that Dickens discussed some of the illustrations with Stone in detail, but some have argued that Dickens was largely uninterested in the illustrations for *Our Mutual Friend*, which may indeed be the reason this significant scene was not drawn. Ackroyd notes that his deferral to Stone "suggests that Dickens himself was less interested in the illustrations to his work, perhaps because he realized that they were no longer as necessary to his design as once they had been. In fact, the story of his collaboration with Stone over these months indicates a certain decline of enthusiasm and concern" (942–43). Slater writes, "Generally, Dickens seems to not have been very closely engaged with the illustrations, often leaving Stone to choose his own subjects and mostly just expressing general approval of his efforts" (524). Cohen, who denies the general claim of a decline in interest, admits that "Dickens was soon prevented by the demands on his time and dwindling energies from continuing to exercise such close supervision" of Stone (205). Stone produced 40 illustrations for the original serial publication.

21. Molly Anne Rothenberg's claim that the drugged Harmon kills Radfoot in self-defense is inaccurate. (Harmon later explains that Radfoot is "murdered for money" by "unknown hands"). The sensational mystery of who murdered George Radfoot is never solved. It is one of the loose threads of the novel, obviously of little importance to Dickens.

22. "No imagination," wrote Dickens to Thomas Mitton on 13 June, "can conceive the ruin of the carriages, or the extraordinary weights under which the people were lying, or the complications into which they were twisted up among iron and wood, and mud and water." (Pilgrim *Letters* 3: 425–26).

23. Newsom observes, "It is hard for me to accept this as mere coincidence. I rather suspect that Dickens, always the great stage manager, timed his own sudden demise with some probably-not-quite-conscious care" (197).

24. Collins goes on to state: "Death is defeated (in a strategy both classic and intensely local) by means of a defiant act of will and an accomodatory insistence on the power of
the word." I certainly agree with Collins's contention that this "power of the word" finds
support in the motif of "the preservation or possible cancellation of the name" (259).

WORKS CITED

Ackroyd, Peter. *Dickens*. New York: Harper Collins, 1990.

Bodenheimer, Rosemarie. "Dickens and the Identical Man: Our Mutual Friend
Doubled." *Dickens Studies Annual* 31 (2002): 159–74.

Brattin, Joel J. "The Creation of Bradley Headstone." *Dickens Studies Annual* 14
(1985): 147–65.

Brooks, Peter. *Reading for the Plot: Design and Intention in Narrative*. New York:
Knopf, 1981.

Campbell, Karen Mills. "Poetry as Epitaph" *Journal of Popular Culture* 14.4 (1981):
657–80.

Carey, John. The *Violent Effigy: A Study of Dickens' Imagination*. London: Faber, 1973.

Černý, Lothar. "'Life in Death': Art in Dickens's *Our Mutual Friend*." *Dickens
Quarterly* 17.1 (2000): 21–35.

Cohen, Jane R. *Charles Dickens and His Original Illustrators*. Ohio State UP, 1980.

Collins, Angus P. "Dickens and *Our Mutual Friend*: Fancy as Self-Preservation."
Études Anglaises 38, 3 (1985): 257–65.

Cotsell, Michael. *The Companion to "Our Mutual Friend*." London: Allen & Unwin, 1986.

Cregan-Reid, Vybarr. "Bodies, Boundaries and Queer Waters: Drowning and
Prosopopeia in Later Dickens." *Critical Survey* 17.2 Summer (2005): 20–33.

De Man, Paul. *The Rhetoric of Romanticism*. New York: Columbia UP, 1984.

Derrida, Jacques. *Demeure: Fiction and Testimony*. Stanford: Stanford UP, 1998.

Dever, Carolyn. *Death and the Mother from Dickens to Freud: Victorian Fiction and
the Anxiety of Origins*. Cambridge: Cambridge UP, 1998.

Dickens, Charles. *A Christmas Carol. Oxford Illustrated Christmas Books*. Oxford:
Oxford UP, 1989. 1–77.

———. *Great Expectations*. Ed. Edgar Rosenberg. Norton Critical Edition. New York:
Norton, 1999.

———. *The Letters of Charles Dickens*. The Nonesuch Edition. Ed. Walter Dexter. 3
vols. London: Nonesuch, 1938.

———. *The Letters of Charles Dickens*. The Pilgrim Edition. Ed. Madeline House,
Graham Storey, Kathleen Tillotson. 12 vols. Oxford: Clarendon UP, 1965–2002.

———. *Our Mutual Friend*. Ed. Stephen Gill. London: Penguin, 1971.

Forster, John. *The Life of Charles Dickens*. 3 vols. London: Chapman and Hall, 1872–74.

Fisher IV, Benjamin Franklin. "Graveyards, Water and Dickensian Darkness." *Essays
in Arts and Sciences* 15 (1987): 37–53.

Gallagher, Catherine. "The Bio-Economics of *Our Mutual Friend.*" *Zone 5: Fragments for a History of the Human Body.* Ed. Michel Feher. New York: Zone, 1989.

Gaskell, Elizabeth. *Life of Charlotte Brontë.* Vol. 1. London: Smith Elder, 1857.

Gray, Thomas. "Elegy Written in a Country Churchyard." *Eighteenth-Century Poetry: An Annotated Anthology.* Ed. David Fairer and Christine Gerrard. Oxford: Blackwell Publishers, 1999. 329–33.

Hartman, Geoffrey H. "Wordsworth, Inscriptions, and Romantic Nature Poetry." In *From Sensibility to Romanticism: Essays presented to Frederick A. Pottle.* Ed. Frederick W. Hilles and Harold Bloom. Oxford: Oxford UP, 1965. 389–415.

Hennelly, Jr., Mark M. "'Playing at Leap Frog with the Tombstones': The Danse Macabre Motif in Dickens." *Essays in Literature* 22 (1995): 227–43.

Hill, Nancy K. *A Reformer's Art: Dickens' Picturesque and Grotesque Imagery.* Athens: Ohio UP, 1981.

Johnson, Barbara. *Persons and Things.* Cambridge: Harvard UP, 2008.

Levine, George. *Dying to Know: Scientific Epistemology and Narrative in Victorian England.* Chicago: U of Chicago P, 2002.

Miller, J. Hillis. *Charles Dickens: The World of His Novels.* Cambridge: Harvard UP, 1958.

Newsom, Robert. *Charles Dickens Revisited.* New York: Twayne, 2000.

Rothenberg, Molly Anne. "Articulating Social Agency in *Our Mutual Friend*: Problems with Performance, Practices, and Political Efficacy." *ELH* 71.3 (2004): 719–40.

Royle, Nicholas. "*Our Mutual Friend.*" *Dickens Refigured: Bodies, Desires, and Other Histories.* Ed. John Schad. Manchester: Manchester UP, 1996. 39–54.

Sanchez-Eppler, Karen. "Decomposing: Wordsworth's Poetry of Epitaph and English Burial Reform." *Nineteenth-Century Literature* 42.4 (1988): 415–31.

Scoggin, Daniel P. "A Speculative Resurrection: Death, Money, and the Vampiric Economy of *Our Mutual Friend.*" *Victorian Literature and Culture* 30.1 (2002): 99–125.

Sedgwick, Eve Kosofsky. *Between Men: English Literature and Male Homosocial Desire.* New York: Columbia UP, 1985.

Slater, Michael. *Charles Dickens.* New Haven: Yale UP, 2009.

Stewart, Garrett. "The Secret Life of Death in Dickens." *Dickens Studies Annual* 11 (1983): 177–207.

Stone, Harry. *The Night Side of Dickens: Cannibalism, Passion, Necessity.* Columbus: Ohio State UP, 1994.

———. "What's in a Name: Fantasy and Calculation in Dickens." *Dickens Studies Annual* 14 (1985): 191–204.

Walbank, Alan. "With a Blush Retire." *Dickensian* 57 (1961): 166–73.

Wheeler, Michael. *Death and the Future Life in Victorian Literature and Theology.* Cambridge: Cambridge UP, 1990.

Wordsworth, William. "Essay upon Epitaphs–I," *Literary Criticism of William Wordsworth.* Ed. Paul M. Zall. Lincoln: U of Nebraska P, 1966. 90–106.

Zigarovich, Jolene. "Wilkie Collins, Narrativity, and Epitaph." *Dickens Studies Annual* 36 (2005): 229–64.

On Honor and Consequences:
The Duel in Trollope's
The Small House at Allington

Jennifer Preston Wilson

Anthony Trollope's novels of the 1860s examine jiltings and rivalries that would have instigated duels only a generation earlier. As his characters agonize over what course of private justice remains in lieu of the notoriety of public legal recourse, Trollope adds to the mid-century debate over the "New Man." The Small House at Allington *brings these preoccupations together as it engages in an ironic deflation of the role of the hero, yet stages a series of pseudo-duels that exemplify the human need to know firsthand that wrongdoing has been addressed. Although dueling has a negligible effect upon the outcome of the romance plots in his fiction, Trollope shows that in cases of jilting the drive for retribution and closure is too overwhelming to abjure violence altogether.*

Despite the fact that dueling was illegal in England during the latter half of the nineteenth century, the custom is referenced repeatedly in Anthony Trollope's fiction, channeling conflicts over broken engagements, masculine aggression, rites of passage, and social class distinctions. Trollope is most likely to refer to the duel, or reflections about its prohibition, in his mid-career works; beginning with *Doctor Thorne* (1858) and continuing through *Phineas Finn* (1869), he engages in a serious consideration of its code and significance in a world that can remember, but not legally practice, its mode of justice.[1] During these years, Trollope examines the duel in many contexts, including a brother's duty to a jilted sister, the rivalry between suitors, and the revenge fantasies of a spurned lover. His novel that deals with all of these issues in dialogue at once is *The Small House at Allington* (1864). This work complicates the very idea of a hero, and at the same time that it thwarts romance idealism, it deplores an unmoored future where men may do ill and seemingly get away with it. *The Small House at Allington* has received substantial critical attention for its interrogation of the "Woman Question," but through its debate over dueling it thoroughly examines the role of the "New Man" as well.

The 1860s can be distinguished as a separate phase of Anthony Trollope's career, one in which he gained security in his identity as writer and moved beyond disappointments at the Post Office to initiate new professional ventures. As we consider his thematic preoccupations during this range of years, we can see a greater ability to stand apart from his youth and incorporate its painful episodes into his fictional portrayals. Besides the sheer effect of the distance of time, Trollope was abetted in this retrospective view by a newfound sense of his arrival as a writer. He felt that he had achieved what he had set out to do with his life, and in his *Autobiography* he reflects that by 1862 he had "gained [his] object" of literary success and a comfortable income (167–68). To his delight, he was elected into the Garrick Club, an event of momentous importance to him. He comments, "I have ever had a wish to be liked by those around me,—a wish that during the first half of my life was never gratified." "The Garrick Club was the first assemblage of men at which I felt myself to be popular" (159). Even though he enjoyed a new confidence in his midlife, Trollope by no means read his accomplishments as inevitable. At the beginning of *The Bertrams* (1858), he meditates upon success and how easily those who struggle to find their way are cast off by Victorian society. It is from his own vantage point of precarious preservation that Trollope is able to survey the problems of masculine honor and self-assertion, including the complicated demands of standing up for oneself in a modern, legalistic world. During his works of the 1860s, Trollope revisits the haunts, occupations, and grievances of his younger self as he considers his precipitous journey to adulthood.

Besides being an apt time for Trollope's personal reflection on coming of age, the 1860s also brought the gender debate to the forefront of public notice. The Matrimonial Causes Act of 1857 changed divorce from an ecclesiastical to a civil law proceeding, allowed a wife who had separated from her husband to claim legal protection, and permitted a woman to petition for divorce for aggravated adultery. Although these reforms brought divorce into the realm of possibility for women, there was still nothing like parity between husbands and wives before the law. Along with the attention given to the fate of married women, the status of single women emerged as a subject of national concern, with the 1851 census reporting that "42 percent of the women between the ages of twenty and forty were unmarried and that two million out of Britain's six million women were self-supporting" (Poovey 4). As Mark W. Turner has argued, readers of Trollope's serialized fiction would simultaneously encounter articles such as W. R. Greg's "Why Are Women Redundant?" and Francis Power Cobbe's "What Shall We Do with our Old Maids?" in the magazines, thus magnifying their anxieties about this sensitive social issue ("Intertextuality" 231–32).

While the woman debate was closely tied to the institution of marriage and its insufficiency for many both inside and outside of its purview, the "man question" renegotiated gender ideals in response to the spiritual and social crises between the two reform bills of 1832 and 1867. The publication of *Tracts for the Times* and growth of the High Church movement occurred at the same time as scientific discoveries made religious faith increasingly tenuous. The rise of Tractarianism and awareness of labor inequities also fueled a darkened world view. The imperative to seek a "vigorous, socially aware Christianity" in response to these developments emerged in the midcentury (Vance 2–3). From *Tom Brown's Schooldays*'s appearance in 1857, the ensuing decades featured dispute over the qualities of "manliness," drawing on the muscular Christianity of Thomas Hughes and Charles Kingsley, as well as upon the spiritual definitions of manliness inculcated by Samuel Taylor Coleridge and Thomas Arnold (Newsome 197).

Even though they differ in describing the nature of the change, today's critics agree that the mid-nineteenth century marked a significant shift in gender expectations for men. John Tosh discusses how a new "manly" ideal arose to usurp the idea of the gentleman. Although linked to the muscular Christianity movement and its cult of physical vigor, "manliness," in his formulation, also denoted qualities of character including "energy, assertiveness, independence, directness and simplicity" (88–89). Peter Gay likewise traces the rise of the "manly" standard of behavior, but portrays its development as a problematic alibi for aggression (115). Other critics contend that "the gentleman" survived, but took on new meaning. Arthur Pollard argues for an increasingly moral definition of the gentleman, citing W. R. Browne in the *National Review*: "the gentleman is 'one to whom discourtesy is a sin and falsehood a crime'" (87). Similarly, Robin Gilmour describes the "root virtue" of the new gentleman as the ability to transcend selfishness (156), and James Eli Adams shows how the ideal was increasingly determined by personal qualities rather than birthright, noting that the title of "gentleman" might be achieved by a regimen of civility (195).

Trollope explores both the extrinsic and intrinsic dimensions of the manliness debate as he constructs the duel to represent a crisis of Victorian masculinities. When we survey Trollope's young men in the 1860s fiction, we find that they often share a romanticism and sensitivity to social class dynamics that animated Trollope himself as a boy. He writes in the *Autobiography* of his time as a spurned day-boarder at Harrow and can only find solace in the memory of a "great fight" in which he emerged victorious: "From the first to the last there was nothing satisfactory in my school career," he comments, "—except the way in which I licked the boy who had to be taken home to be cured" (13, 19). Trollope's young heroes typically feel that circumstances call upon them to take action. Lord Chiltern and George Vavasor are defined by their class standings and their ruthless behavior. Both bear signs of a violent temper; Chiltern is a "red man" whose identity is associated with the aristocratic, yet also primitive, patterns of the hunt (*Phineas Finn* 77; ch. 4), and Vavasor bears a "cicatrice," a "black ravine running through his cheek" which in a fit of anger, reddens and makes him look like the devil himself (*Can You Forgive Her?* 41; ch. 4). Vavasor is characteristically brutal and mercenary. Each of these men already has blood on his hands from committing manslaughter in self-defense, and so his propensity to duel is not surprising. In contrast to these characters' fierceness, Phineas Finn and Will Belton are both portrayed as honest and promising young men, and each in turn either unquestioningly accepts or longingly wishes for the opportunity to duel when losing in rivalry with another suitor. Their bravery and yearning for exertion can be linked to the mid-century trend of muscular Christianity.[2]

The novels where the duel is contemplated as a response to romantic betrayal are infused with frustration. Frank Gresham and Theodore Burton are cast in the role of brother to a young woman in danger of being jilted. Gresham, accompanied by a Cambridge friend, leaves school, traps the offender, one Mr. Moffat, outside his club, and horsewhips him repeatedly for breaking an engagement with his sister, Augusta. The punishment is not a formal duel, and although it serves as a substitute, its lack of ritual is a problem. Afterwards, Gresham "thought, almost with despair, that he had not yet at all succeeded as became a man and a brother" (*Doctor Thorne* 261; ch. 21). The suddenness of the attack and quick intervention of bystanders has so blurred Gresham's memory that he faults himself for not doing enough. In a parallel incident, Theodore Burton, faced with the likelihood that Harry Clavering will jilt his sister Florence, cannot find an honorable alternative to the duel: "But what can he do now? A thoughtful, prudent, painstaking man . . . feels that it is not given to him to attack another with his fists, to fly at his enemy's throat, and carry out his purpose after the manner of dogs . . . But any aid that the law can give him is altogether distasteful to him" (*Claverings* 290; ch. 28). Burton's dilemma in this passage comes through in a series of negatives: "it is not given to him to attack another" without the formal guidelines of the duel, and yet the law is "distasteful." The idea of Christian forgiveness in this case "becomes broken to pieces and falls to the ground" (290–91; ch. 28). Burton ends his interior monologue with no resolution to his problem. We see him gnashing his teeth as he turns on his heel to go (291; ch. 28).

Nostalgia for the clear, if imperfect, system of the duel and a consequent darkness of tone also infuses *The Small House at Allington*, Trollope's fourteenth novel and fifth installment of the Barsetshire series. In this work, Trollope engages in an extended meditation on the hero, setting up the conflict of his plot as the Allington residents meet and attempt to understand the new-comer, Adolphus Crosbie. An urbane and eligible clerk, Crosbie travels with his friend Bernard Dale to the latter's family estate at Allington, where, in an unguarded moment, he finds himself affianced to Bernard's cousin, a country girl, Lily Dale. Crosbie learns too late that Lily expects no dowry and finds himself trapped between remaining true to his word and acting in accord with self-advancement. He then breaks the engagement to make a seemingly more advantageous match (and what will prove to be a miserable marriage) with Lady Alexandrina De Courcy. Lady Julia De Guest, a neighbor and relation of the Allington set, confronts Crosbie at Courcy Castle and reproaches him for his ungentlemanly behavior. Lily Dale, her father long dead, has only her uncle Christopher, a squire, and her cousin Bernard, an officer in the Corps of Engineers, to play the traditional roles of patriarchal protectors of her virtue and honor, but they falter between the outmoded duel and the modern court of law. When the Squire and Bernard fail to act, Johnny Eames, an old friend and admirer of Lily, punches Crosbie in a railway station to punish his wrongdo-ing. Even after her jilting, however, Lily continues to reject Eames, the suitor who still pursues her. Trollope uses the conflict in *Allington* to ask how honor can be defined in an age where you cannot openly duel to prove it. Without the accountability of the duel, what is to prevent scoundrels from acting in self-interest and what is to satisfy those wronged that their pain is not meaningless?

The Hollow Hero

Trollope begins his novel from the point of view of the "two pearls of Alling-ton," Lily and Bell Dale, as they analyze London newcomer, Adolphus Cros-bie. The first sentence registers an objection, initiating a conflict over male identity that will continue to complicate the plot: "But Mr. Crosbie is only a mere clerk" (12; ch. 2). As the Dale sisters discuss their new acquaintance, they acknowledge that Crosbie's cosmopolitan persona does not fit his pedes-trian job title. They eventually solve the dilemma by comparison. If their child-hood friend, Johnny Eames, has also taken a clerkship in London at a mere eighty pounds a year rather than Crosbie's seven hundred, perhaps the title does not stretch far enough to describe their potential suitor. Their grasping at measures to evaluate this young man is indicative of a larger cultural difficulty of assessing masculine worth. What matters more? Job title or income? Family name or fortune? Character or social network?

Lily finally hits upon it: "I'll tell you what he is, Bell; Mr. Crosbie is a swell" (13; ch. 2). Her choice of this word fits precisely because it encompasses a leap of logic. According to the *OED*, a "swell" is: "A fashionably or stylishly dressed person; hence, a person of good social position, a highly distinguished person."

Mr. Crosbie dresses, speaks, and comports himself as a somebody, and therefore he cannot be pinned down by the title "clerk." The beginning of the novel emphasizes Crosbie's self-made status and the power he exudes by controlling his image. He has "picked the locks [of society] and let himself in" (15; ch. 2). "He was handsome, graceful, clever, self-confident, and always cheerful when [Lily] asked him to be cheerful. But he had also his more serious moments . . . . His voice, too, was pleasant, and well under command" (57; ch. 6). This passage listing Crosbie's social assets focuses on his management of his image, regulating his voice and responding cheerfully or seriously when called upon to do so. His control of his persona carries a sinister overtone, however. With his ambition and self-centeredness, Crosbie represents a type unfamiliar in Allington; in this setting, he is "the first really powerful invader from London, and the Pastoral world seems to collapse before him" (Kincaid 126).

Lily nicknames him "Apollo," acknowledging his power, but also foreshadowing that this false god will eventually fall. Crosbie is a golden boy whom Lily and Bell both find of interest. He is contrasted with Johnny Eames, the hobbledehoy, caught between boyhood and manhood, who awkwardly struggles with his transformation into an adult. The first section of the novel is built upon this bifurcation: Crosbie and Eames are technically both "clerks," but they are completely opposite as well. "Apollo" Crosbie works in Whitehall at the prestigious "General Committee Office" and frequents both Sebright's and the Beaufort (the imagery of brightness and beauty in these club names surely is not accidental). Eames works in Somerset House at the Income Tax Office and only gets so far as imagining that he might join a club. Trollope's narrator comments, "When I compare the hobbledehoy of one or two and twenty to some finished Apollo of the same age, I regard the former as unripe fruit, and the latter as fruit that is ripe" (35; ch. 4). As he continues the metaphor, the narrator decides in favor of the naturalness of Eames's slow ripening, although he concedes the world's overwhelming preference for the early, "forced" development of Crosbie (36; ch. 4).

Even though Crosbie may be "ripe," and an "Apollo," he fails to be "manly," a mid-century watchword for "someone who performs her or his duty and who has learned to control the baser animal passions" (Hilton 65). He has reached the appearance of manhood before Eames, and yet there is an element missing in his moral character that makes it clear that the hobbledehoy may win out in the end. The word "manly" does appear frequently, but it occurs in free indirect discourse conveying Crosbie's self-flattery; the narrator never calls him such, excepting one favorable comment that his character had too much "manliness" in it to commit suicide (304; ch. 28). Every other usage shows how Crosbie lies to himself about his behavior and amplifies his own sense of worth. He prides himself when bringing up the subject of Lily's dowry that he is speaking in a manly way, when he is really quite mercenary (61, 75; ch. 6, 7). Later, he makes up his mind "in a manly way" to endure poverty for Lily's sake (75, 162; ch. 7, 15), which, we later see, he does not do. Trollope shows that despite his attendance to his external appearance, Crosbie has neglected his internal worthiness. Besides his wavering on the issue of dowry, Crosbie, it appears, has kept a mistress in London; as Trollope's narrator hedges around the subject, we are told that Crosbie "spoke of entanglements, meaning, as he did so, to explain more fully what were their nature,—but not daring to do so when he found that Lily was altogether in the dark as to what he meant" (154–55; ch. 15). His "forced" development has meant a hastening of adulthood with its lies and entanglements, not necessarily a more composed maturity.

The word "forced" sets character into the realm of cultivation or art, reminding the reader of Trollope's presence as creator of the fictional personages in his novels, but also suggesting that one might author one's own character. Crosbie is "finished" in the sense of a high polish carefully acquired through his own efforts; his advancement over Eames comes from his future-sightedness as he pushes himself ahead of his peers. In this sense, Lily's nickname of Apollo fits him well; Apollo's connections with the arts and prophecy coincide with Crosbie's prescient self-refinement. Trollope easily topples the idea that one can make oneself into a hero, however, when Crosbie miscalculates, assuming that a girl connected to the Dale family will bring a respectable dowry. Crosbie can only prognosticate based on custom, on expectation based on others' success in the marriage market. Jane Nardin argues that the extreme conventionality of Lily Dale's gender script causes the social tragedy of *The Small House at Allington*, yet Crosbie is complicit in this conventionality as well (105). His investment in the myth he has built around himself both forbids him from abandoning Lily and makes him detest her limitation of his future. James R. Kincaid observes the irony inherent in the plot when Lily's ruminations on how much Crosbie is sacrificing in order to marry her are echoed just a few pages later by Crosbie himself (132).

The change in Crosbie's prospects is as dramatic as his initial, high-soaring expectations. Once he proposes to Lily, the world quits smiling upon him so universally, and his manliness is repeatedly questioned as the future narrows in on him. Instead of figuring as an Apollo, the London man of fashion, Crosbie now suffers "cold" fits of melancholy where he retreats away from social contact instead of shining forth in conversation (68–69, 74–75; ch. 7). The language of the text represents his powerlessness. He is "fallen," "vanquished," and "like a calf at the altar, ready for the knife, with blue ribbons round his horns and neck" (69; ch. 7). These images of defeat and humiliation convey the catastrophe that has decimated Crosbie's self-image. Over and over again, he questions who he will be once he has moved to prudently priced lodgings and finds himself surrounded by a needy brood of children. Rather than the god who receives offerings, he now sees himself as the sacrificial victim. As he contemplates the life before him, Crosbie repeatedly thinks in terms of his own "ruin," nursing a sense of injustice at his approaching doom (155, 158–59; ch. 15). Clearly, Crosbie has acted the "hero" because he needs to think of himself that way. When it appears he will no longer fulfill that role in the public realm, he flails miserably.

As his brooding turns into rationalization of the injustice he will soon inflict upon Lily, Crosbie repeatedly thinks of himself in the third-person, trying to reinstate his place as young Apollo. He questions whether, "he, Crosbie of Sebright's, Crosbie of the General Committee Office, Crosbie who would allow no one to bore him between Charing Cross and the far end of Bayswater," "Could it be that he, Adolphus Crosbie, would settle down on the north side of the New Road, as a married man, with eight hundred a year?" (69, 62; ch. 7, 6). Why would someone with so strong of an image of himself as "Crosbie of Sebright's" even bother with a country girl named Lily Dale? Trollope is reticent with direct explanations, and the text moves swiftly from Crosbie's first acquaintance at Allington, where he expresses an initial interest in the prettiest daughter, Bell, to his return visit. The reader knows nothing of Crosbie's transferred affections until jolted into awareness of the engagement when it is announced to Johnny Eames upon arrival home. As Mrs. Dale delivers the news to Eames, the reader is likewise surprised. However, as the narrative progresses, it becomes clear that Lily's appeal to Crosbie ties in to his habit of figuring himself as hero. His best resolves all occur in her presence. Her avowals cause him to feel "awed by her great love, and exalted to a certain solemnity of feeling which for the time made him rejoice in his late decision. For a few hours he was minded to throw the world behind him, and wear this woman, as such a woman should be worn—as a comforter to him in all things, and a strong shield against great troubles" (160; ch. 15). Lily's effect on Crosbie is quasi-religious; he feels awe, solemnity, and rejoicing in her presence and radiates his new sense of purpose, albeit only for a few hours. Without Lily's faith in him, Crosbie turns back into the urban "hollow man," dependent on the exterior markers of neighborhood, job title, and club affiliation to anchor his sense of self.

Leaving Allington devastates Crosbie's better intentions toward Lily. While by her side, Crosbie bolsters himself with flattering thoughts of the sacrifice he will make for her sake. Once away from her influence, though, Crosbie passively dallies through the city of Barchester[3] only to arrive at his destination, the infectious "atmosphere of Courcy Castle . . . [where] every word that he had heard, and every word that he had spoken, had tended to destroy all that was good and true within him, and to foster all that was selfish and false" (244; ch. 23). Trollope situates Crosbie on the periphery of evil. He is capable of good and yet is corrupted by environment. However, he is the one who has chosen to visit Courcy Castle, and the deciding factor seems to be his own cowardice. He is afraid of poverty, hesitant to speak out to Squire Dale, unable to accept Lily's offer of release from the engagement, and apprehensive of offending Lady Alexandrina and her "noble" family. Had his story occurred earlier in the nineteenth century, another fear would have outweighed these other ones—the certainty of the duel.

Forced Developments

A generation earlier, Crosbie's offense against Lily would not have been branded as merely shameful; it surely would have provoked a challenge. However, during the first half of the nineteenth century, dueling faded out in England and, indeed, in most of the western European countries. In 1821 the English Chief Justice Abbott ruled that since dueling was premeditated, it must be prosecuted as murder. There was, nevertheless, a substantial gap between this law and its enforcement. Duels continued to occur frequently and were often not prosecuted; when they were prosecuted, juries often failed to convict (Kiernan 204). In July of 1843, scandal began to change what law could not. Two army officers, who were also brothers-in-law, dueled, and one was killed; the press reacted indignantly to this instance of killing one's own relation. *The Times* proclaimed that dueling was ridiculous and hateful and should be ended by "authority." *The Pictorial Times* observed that if the participants had been lower class, the survivor would have been charged with murder (Richardson 266). In the aftermath of this event, the Anti-Dueling Association came into being, and the Articles of War received amendment to ban dueling in the army. What has been called the last duel in England was fought in 1852, but, of course, it was still possible to fight duels abroad (Kiernan 218). Until the nineteenth century, dueling had largely been confined to the upper classes and had been associated with the nebulous concept of gentility. Dueling's function in large part was to preserve a gentleman's sense of honor, and its decline and abolition raised the question of how that sense of honor could henceforth be maintained.

Trollope highlights this dilemma facing his male characters by framing their inaction against the instant reaction of Lily's neighbor, Lady Julia. While Lady Alexandrina De Courcy is still trying to manipulate Crosbie into an offer of marriage and he is still trying to rationalize his way out of his previous engagement to Lily, Lady Julia "nearly every day [had] repeated stiffly to the countess some incident of Crosbie's courtship and engagement to Miss Dale—speaking of it as with absolute knowledge, as a thing settled at all points" (247; ch. 23). Lady Julia's anger at Crosbie's behavior stems as much from personal dislike and offended principle as from any affection for Lily Dale; yet her sense of honor demands that she act on those principles as much as she can, and she does so with considerably more forthrightness than any of the men in the novel.

When Crosbie passes by her in a doorway, making to her some "indifferent remark," Lady Julia "gives the lie" to him:

"Mr. Crosbie," she said, "have you heard lately from our dear friend, Lily Dale?" And she looked him full in the face, in a manner more significant, probably, than even she had intended it to be.

Crosbie instantly made an effort to bear the attack gallantly, but he felt that he could not quite
command his color, or prevent a sudden drop of perspiration from showing itself upon his brow.

(248; ch. 23)

In this passage, the language of combat stands in place of an actual duel, with
Crosbie clearly presented as the weaker side. Lady Julia doggedly pursues her
opponent and stands up for her right to do so:

"Yes, sir, you do know; you know very well. That poor young lady who has no father and
no brother, is my neighbor, and her friends are my friends. She is a friend of my own, and
being an old woman, I have a right to speak for her. If [the report of a new engagement] is
true, Mr. Crosbie, you are treating her like a villain."

(264; ch. 24)

Lady Julia acts out of a sense of responsibility, given Lily's place in "her"
neighborhood and her network of mutual friends. She further believes that
she has an obligation to act, "being an old woman," and thus above concerns
about her own honor. Even as an old woman, however, her action is still a
transgressive one: as Pat Jalland notes, "the belief in the natural separation of
the spheres between the sexes [meant that] the unmarried middle- and upper-
class woman was restricted to the domestic sphere just as rigidly as her married sister" (257–58). Despite this limitation, Lady Julia is depicted as acting
in a thoroughly competent, although stereotypically masculine way, thinking
tactically, staging her ambush, and forcing her opponent into abject retreat. If,
as Shirley Robin Letwin argues, by the strict tenets of the code of gentlemen
"the most perfect gentleman in Trollope's novels is Madame Max Goesler"
in *Phineas Finn* (74), then *Allington*'s Lady Julia can be said to have accomplished her own "dueling" victory here.[4]

Lady Julia's fierce response to Crosbie only highlights the failure of what
should have been Lily Dale's traditional protection, her uncle, Squire Dale, and
cousin, Captain Bernard Dale. Lily's jilting is the sort of social transgression that
would have clearly called for a male-on-male duel only a few decades earlier
in England. If anything, the only problem would have been figuring out which
man had the greater right to fight on her behalf. In an otherwise very perceptive
chapter on Victorian dueling, John R. Reed has argued that in *Allington*, "Trollope lightly dismissed the idea of duelling altogether" (150), but this, I think,
misinterprets the complexity of Trollope's exploration of the idea, particularly
through his male characters' anxiety. The desire for the duel remains hotly alive
in all these men, but, unfortunately, the law has now eliminated such a relatively
straightforward course of action, and law-abiding Englishmen to the core, the
Dale men cannot bring themselves to violate it. The Squire is convinced that
times have changed much for the worse. When he meets with those who suggest that perhaps Lily is better off and will recover from her loss, he replies

that "when I was a young man, I would sooner have burnt out my tongue than have spoken in such a way on such a subject" (276; ch. 25). The Squire does respond to Crosbie's offense, but he lets circumstances dictate his actions. He tells Bernard that he "had tracked Crosbie to his club, and had there learned the whole truth from Crosbie's friend, Fowler Pratt. . . . [Meanwhile,] 'The coward escaped me while I was talking to the man he sent down'" (295; ch. 27). Thus thwarted from even meeting face to face with the "rat," Squire Dale is even more convinced that violence would have been preferred: "I should have brained him in the hall of the club" (298, 295; ch. 27).

Trollope's depiction of the drive to fight in *The Small House at Allington* came after traveling for half a year throughout the warring United States, gathering observations for his travel account, *North America*. In that volume—published in May 1864, the same month he began writing *Allington*—he portrays the Civil War as an unavoidable combat between two fundamentally opposed sides.[5] As Trollope imagines what responses the North might have made to the South's rebellion, he considers the two armies as individuals obliged to uphold their reputations. If the Union failed to react with force,

She would have been twitted with cowardice, and told that she was no match for Southern energy . . . But having struck that one blow, and having found that it did not suffice, could she then withdraw, give way, and own herself beaten? Has it been so usually with Anglo-Saxon pluck? In such a case as that would there have been no mention of those two dogs, Brag and Holdfast?

(186; ch. 13)[6]

As Trollope sees it, the North has no option but to fight or be abused by other nations. Even though his pronouns follow the conventional characterization of nations as feminine, his argument adheres to the codes of masculine valor. The insistent questions of this passage prod its readers into response—urging us to agree that once a cause is started it must be seen through. The idea of continuity with the past, of maintaining a reputation of national honor, of one's actions keeping apace with one's words, all of the expectations of these sentences demand stoic determination.

Revaluation of the meaning of honor was not just Trollope's hobbyhorse, but a point of great cultural interest in the 1860s. At least one contemporary reviewer of the novel shared Squire Dale's opinion that Crosbie's affront was almost inconceivable in an English gentleman. According to an anonymous notice in *Reader*,

The Crosbie described by Mr. Trollope is not the Crosbie who describes himself by the unspeakable folly and shabbiness of his acts. The former would not have broken his promise to Lily under the circumstances detailed to us. It is scarcely probable that he would have contracted the engagement at all; having once done so, the necessity of adhering to it would have been as evident to him as to Fowler Pratt.

(Smalley 196)

Other contemporaries were more convinced. The *Saturday Review* considered Crosbie "one of Mr. Trollope's masterpieces—he behaves with such admirable consistency, and is so exactly the sort of man who would court and deserve the fate that overtakes him" (Smalley 205). Just as he did with the Dales, Crosbie left no *Allington* reader unmoved, and there was such debate over the nature of Crosbie's characterization that one writer noted in the April 2, 1864 *Reader*, "for the last year Adolphus Crosbie had been as much a public character as Lord Palmerston" (Smalley 10). This level of controversy implies that Trollope's readers were themselves uncertain as to whether or not traditional gender roles and expectations could still function in a socially viable way.

Like those readers, Cousin Bernard is equally confused and anxious, although characteristically more concerned with his own image than Lily's or anyone else's, as he ponders his response:

> What would it become him to do in this emergency if Crosbie had truly been guilty of the villainy with which Lady Julia had charged him? Thirty years ago he would have called the man out, and shot at him till one of them was hit. Nowadays it was hardly possible for a man to do that; and yet what would the world say of him if he allowed such an injury as this to pass without vengeance?
>
> (294–95; ch. 27)

Whatever the world might say of him, his uncle is explicit; he accuses Bernard of bringing the scoundrel Crosbie into the family without first determining his character (295; ch. 27). As Eleanor Gordon and Gwyneth Nair note, "the family friendship network was fertile territory for meeting potential suitors, as it was usually a guarantee of suitability" (77). When Bernard plaintively inquires of his uncle, "What are we to do to him?," however, Squire Dale offers Bernard a retreat from those older obligations to avenge Lily's honor:

> "Treat him as you would a rat. Throw your stick at him, if he comes under your feet; but beware, above all things, that he does not get into your house. That is too late for us now."
>
> "There must be more than that, uncle."
>
> "I don't know what more. There are deeds for committing which a man is doubly damned, because he has screened himself from overt punishment by the nature of his own villainy. We have to remember Lily's name, and do what may best tend to her comfort. Poor girl! Poor girl!"
>
> (297–98; ch. 27)

The potential dishonor created by further bandying Lily's name in the public, for Squire Dale here outweighs the loss of honor to himself and Bernard for failing to punish Crosbie. This assessment implies that the question of honor has become one rather more liable to public, not private, definition.[7] Paradoxically, the changing role of masculine protector here means that, the initial transgression over, Squire Dale can only protect Lily by letting her continue to be a silent victim, rather than a vocal one who calls attention to her victimization. Bernard, less concerned with protecting Lily than protecting himself from public chastisement, concurs, since this serves his own desires as well.

If the first "duel" in the novel, and not coincidentally its first marked transgression of gender roles, may be said to be Lady Julia's confrontation with Crosbie at Courcy Castle, the second "duel" occurs when Johnny Eames punches Crosbie in the railway station, in a chapter titled "The Combat." Johnny has himself been dallying in a less than wise or honorable fashion with Amelia Roper, who is past thirty and ready to be married, but whose active role in seeking marriage drops her—despite the narrator's sympathy—from the rank of more innocent girls like Lily Dale. Johnny has become a favorite of the childless earl, Lord De Guest, the neighbor of the Dales, after saving the earl from a bull, and the earl's anger at Crosbie seems to empower Johnny to even more anger himself. Both men feel a nagging sense that Crosbie has not been adequately punished for his jilting of Lily Dale:

> "He is a damned blackguard," said the earl. . . .
>
> "He ought to have his neck broken," said Johnny.
>
> "I don't know about that," said the earl. "The present times have become so pretty behaved that corporal punishment seems to have gone out of fashion. I shouldn't care so much about that, if any other punishment had taken its place. But it seems to me that a blackguard such as Crosbie can escape now altogether unscathed."
>
> "He hasn't escaped yet," said Johnny.
>
> "Don't you go and put your finger in the pie and make a fool of yourself," said the earl. If it had behoved anyone to resent in any violent fashion the evil done by Crosbie, Bernard Dale, the earl's nephew, should have been the avenger. This the earl felt, but under these circumstances he was disposed to think that there should be no such violent vengeance. "Things were different when I was young," he said to himself. But Eames gathered from the earl's tone that the earl's words were not strictly in accordance with his thoughts, and he declared to himself over and over again that Crosbie had not yet escaped.
>
> (367–68; ch. 34)

When Johnny Eames returns to London from visiting Allington, he finds himself sitting directly across from Adolphus Crosbie in the rail carriage. Crosbie knows Johnny Eames, knows of his unrequited love for Lily Dale, and during their engagement had chided her for continuing a friendship with Johnny, yet he dismisses Johnny's unblinking stare: "among all his many troubles, the enmity of John Eames did not go for much" (371; ch. 34). Johnny, sweating, furious, and uncertain what to do, nonetheless feels that "it was a great occasion—great in its imminent trouble, and great in its opportunity for action" (369; ch. 34). He cannot bring himself to attack Crosbie in the presence of the old woman sharing their car, however, fearing that "the world and the police would be against him" (370; ch. 34). Johnny follows Crosbie to the platform when they arrive, seizes him by the throat as soon as he turns to face him, and manages to get one blow to Crosbie's eye before being dragged away by the police.

Trollope thus divides the gendered historical concept of the duel into two elements: Lady Julia's "duel" contains the formal elements of a challenge to character and honor, but notably violates its traditions of gender, and Johnny Eames's "duel" retains some milder form of its masculine violence, but then subverts its notions of honor with farcical elements like having the combatants fall into a W. H. Smith bookstall filled with "yellow shilling-novels" (371; ch. 34). While Crosbie's black eye does cause him much grief among supervisors at work and future in-laws at home, Trollope's mock-chivalric treatment of the fight scene leaves the question of gentlemanly honor still on the table. Johnny's status as hero is complicated by the fact that fist-fighting was seen as an adolescent pursuit: "As Thomas Hughes declared in his best-selling 1857 novel *Tom Brown's School Days*, 'Fighting with fists is the natural and English way for English boys to settle their quarrels'. . . . Though Hughes expected boys to grow out of settling quarrels with their fists when they became men" (Wiener 51). Also detracting from Eames's glory is the fact that he has hated Crosbie from the beginning, wishing to punish him long before any crime actually occurred; thus the fracas at the train station seems to be more about Eames's frustrated romantic daydreaming than protection of Lily's honor. In this way, Eames approaches a Quixote figure, questing in service to a lady without her sanction.

Trollope treats Eames with sympathy, insofar as he is suffering and conscious of having played the fool, but also with rigor. The ending of *Allington* thwarts the expected comic resolution of Lily's marriage plot by refusing to transform Eames's character suddenly. Michael Sadleir contends that Eames could never be a satisfactory partner for Lily, and the reason Trollope refuses to let him win her hand by the end of the Barsetshire series is precisely because Eames is not a gentleman. Although Sadleir acknowledges him "a manly youth" (118), he argues that Eames strongly resembles the awkward, young Trollope portrayed in the *Autobiography* who had been tormented at school for not being a gentleman's son. As he characterizes Eames, Trollope resists the urge to reconstruct a valorous version of his past. He even offers an apology for spending so much time on Eames, whose "life hitherto, as recorded in these pages, had afforded him no brilliant success" (653–54; ch. 59). Trollope's plot resolution, devoid as it is of success, does, however, nudge us toward a revised estimation of honor. Gentleman or no, Eames finally behaves with courage, acting with what Lord De Guest calls "that other kind of pluck"—carrying himself with the appearance of equanimity, even though it feels like he has "some wolf to gnaw [him] somewhere" (640–41; ch. 58). Even though he is defeated in his strategy to win Lily, Eames is victorious over himself as he acknowledges the earl's critique and attempts to bear himself without complaint.

Trollope experimented with a similar pattern of comic deflation, where the hero is let down in spite of his romantic view of himself, in the short story "The Journey to Panama" of 1861. Ralph Forrest, the male lead, befriends a woman traveling to carry out an arranged marriage in South America; he becomes her confidant and protector, in spite of the warnings of the other travelers and the narrator who calls the liaison "The dangerous alliance" (210). Forrest and his new acquaintance, Miss Viner, teeter on the brink of propriety as they ignore appearances and spend much time in each other's company. As in *Allington*, Trollope treats this theme in mock-chivalric fashion, and we overhear Miss Viner smoothing over her qualms with the motto of the Order of the Garter: "'*Honi soit qui mal y pense*,' she said to herself, as she took his arm" (207). Trollope makes it clear that only the sea-voyage context facilitates this degree of recklessness between the two strangers. Miss Viner takes advantage of their circumscribed relationship to confess her calculated reasons for entering a marriage she, quite frankly, dreads. Forrest acts heedlessly, too, in spite of being advised not to "interfere with the rights of that gentleman in Peru, or he might run a knife into you" (211).

Once the ship arrives in Panama and news comes in that Miss Viner's husband-to-be has died, she assumes a conventional coldness toward Forrest who bewilderedly wonders what happened to their intimate relationship. She ignores their time together as she announces with priggish authority, "now that it is my duty to mourn for [my fiancé], could I do so heartily if you were with me?" (218). Like Eames, Forrest has undertaken a risk to serve a woman who is more interested in cleaving to her own past than accepting a forward-looking, if qualified, bond with a new mate. These men are rejected so the women can preserve an illusion of widowhood, one that occurs without official marriage and even without reciprocated love.

Thus, Trollope's view on the duel seems to be split in this intense 1860s retrospective on its ban. Dueling between rivals, as it turns out, has surprisingly little effect upon romance in Trollope's fiction. Phineas Finn is shocked that life goes on just as usual after dueling with Lord Chiltern. Johnny Eames's punch to Crosbie's eye transpires unknown to Lily Dale, and Ralph Forrest's "protection" of Miss Viner at the risk of his own life wins him no extra consideration. Women control the field of love in Trollope's novels, often motivated by a fixed idea that cannot be shaken from their minds; Violet Effingham, Alice Vavasor, Lily Dale, and Emily Viner all fixate on an earlier love or prior commitment and have trouble moving on.

Dueling is of central concern, however, in the jilting plots. The law is portrayed as a completely unacceptable option for this sort of offense, yet some action is needed to counteract the socially debilitating skepticism that would follow from no response at all. In the *Allington* plot, readers are made aware of Crosbie's punishment, but the Dales and their supporters hear nothing of it, assuming that he has abused their trust and prospered. Thus, we have the irony of two sets of people, each assuming the superior fortune of the other. As he is constantly reminded of how happy he might have been with Lily, Crosbie emblematizes David Castronovo's contention that "Honor becomes the 'absence of self-reproach'" in the Victorian era (26). Likewise, the Allington set are held in perpetual opposition to Crosbie. Trollope's narrator comments: "Those who offend us are generally punished for the offense they give; but we so frequently miss the satisfaction of knowing that we are avenged! It is arranged, apparently, that the injurer shall be punished, but that the person injured shall not gratify his desire for vengeance" (547; ch. 50). For these reasons, Trollope's own answer to the question of honor seems clear. Since dueling is out of bounds, some form of physical punishment is necessary. Scoundrels may suffer some adversity as a result of their wrongdoing, but that is not enough, because that adversity may not be known by those wronged. Significantly, Johnny Eames remembers with pleasure "the sensation of his fist as it went into Crosbie's eye" (389; ch. 36). Toward the end of the novel, Eames becomes a favorite of Lady Julia's, as the two "manly" duelists commiserate. Neither is socially adept, but together they represent Trollope's response to the problem of social accountability; even with the erosion of the duel and the category of "the gentleman," people will fight privately rather than resort to the public court of law over issues of private honor. The move toward confrontation and violence is a gratifying one, not because it is always the best method of seeking amends, but because it satisfies the human urge to feel in control of events. Action is easier than the cold skepticism of letting the rules be bent and trusting to "apparent" justice.

NOTES

1. This 1860s phase that concentrates on dueling as an ethical dilemma stands apart from the rest of Trollope's career. His first novel, *The Macdermots of Ballycloran*, features a duel, but the insult that instigates it actually happens to be a true observation, and the altercation itself is described with farcical humor. In his later career, from the 1870s onwards, Trollope's treatment of the duel and connected issues of honor becomes much more peripheral and non-thematic. In a number of works (*The Eustace Diamonds*, *Lady Anna*, *The Amerian Senator*) the impugned woman is portrayed as a calculating risk-taker rather than a victim. When an innocent woman is egregiously wronged in the later novels, an outraged parent-figure is apt to take impulsive, violent action, rather than initiating a formal duel (*Is He Popenjoy?*, *An Eye for an Eye*). In several works as well (*Ayala's Angel*, *Mr. Scarborough's Family*), dueling is considered, but ruled out as inappropriate.

2. For further analysis of the Chiltern-Finn duel "as integral to a process of maturation," see Turner (*Magazines* 168). Turner connects Finn's version of masculinity, "middle-class, urban (perhaps even metropolitan), and upwardly mobile" to the masculinity projected by *St. Pauls Magazine* (153).

3. A. O. J. Cockshut's analysis of Crosbie's layover in Barchester places his betrayal of Lily in the "passive centre" of the book. Cockshut writes, "In this sunny, quiet

interlude when he is thinking of other things, the most important decision of Crosbie's life is being taken for him by his unconscious mind, and will only emerge into daylight some days later" (153).

4. Markku Peltonen analyzes the greater freedom of speech given to women and clergymen by virtue of their exemption from the duel (199).

5. For more on Trollope's attitude toward the Civil War, see Halperin and Ross.

6. The two dogs, Brag and Holdfast, allude to William Shakespeare's *Henry V* (2.3.52) where Pistol counsels wariness against those who would trick with lies or exaggeration: "And holdfast is the only dog, my duck."

7. The opposition of the code of honor to the rule of law lay at the heart of the debate over dueling. Donna T. Andrew discusses this tension, asking, "When men of fashion were permitted to kill each other on the field of honour, and go unpunished, what convincing reason could be given for the execution of the highwayman or pickpocket[?]" (421).

WORKS CITED

Adams, James Eli. *Dandies and Desert Saints: Styles of Victorian Masculinity*. Ithaca, NY: Cornell UP, 1995.

Andrew, Donna T. "The Code of Honour and Its Critics: The Opposition to Duelling in England, 1700–1850." *Social History* 5.3 (1980): 409–34.

Castronovo, David. *The English Gentleman: Images and Ideals in Literature and Society*. New York: Ungar, 1987.

Cockshut, A. O. J. *Anthony Trollope: A Critical Study*. New York: New York UP, 1968.

Gay, Peter. *The Cultivation of Hatred*. New York: Norton, 1993.

Gilmour, Robin. *The Idea of the Gentleman in the Victorian Novel*. London: Allen and Unwin, 1981.

Gordon, Eleanor, and Gwyneth Nair. *Public Lives: Women, Family and Society in Victorian Britain*. New Haven: Yale UP, 2003.

Halperin, John. "Trollope and the American Civil War." *Clio* 13.2 (1984): 149–55.

Hilton, Boyd. "Manliness, Masculinity, and the Mid-Victorian Temperament." *The Blind Victorian: Henry Fawcett and British Liberalism*. Cambridge: Cambridge UP, 1989. 60–70.

Jalland, Pat. *Women, Marriage and Politics: 1860–1914*. Oxford: Clarendon, 1986.

Kiernan, V. G. *The Duel in European History*. Oxford: Oxford UP, 1988.

Kincaid, James R. *The Novels of Anthony Trollope*. Oxford: Clarendon, 1977.

Letwin, Shirley Robin. *The Gentleman in Trollope: Individuality and Moral Conduct*. Cambridge: Harvard UP, 1982.

Nardin, Jane. *He Knew She Was Right: The Independent Woman in the Novels of Anthony Trollope*. Carbondale: Southern Illinois UP, 1989.

Newsome, David. *Godliness and Good Learning: Four Studies on a Victorian Ideal.* London: John Murray, 1961.

Peltonen, Markku. *Duelling and the English Gentleman.* Cambridge: Cambridge UP, 2003.

Pollard, Arthur. "Trollope's Idea of the Gentleman." *Trollope Centenary Essays.* Ed. John Halperin. New York: St. Martin's, 1982. 86–94.

Poovey, Mary. *Uneven Developments: The Ideological Work of Gender in Mid-Victorian England.* Chicago: U of Chicago P, 1988.

Reed, John R. *Victorian Conventions.* Athens: Ohio UP, 1975.

Richardson, John. *The Annals of London.* Berkeley: U of California P, 2000.

Ross, Ann Marie. "Ploughshares Into Swords: The Civil War Landscape of Trollope's *North America.*" *Nineteenth-Century Literature* 45.1 (June 1990): 59–72.

Sadleir, Michael. *Anthony Trollope, a Commentary.* New York: Farrar, Straus, 1927.

Smalley, Donald, ed. *Trollope: The Critical Heritage.* London: Routledge and Kegan Paul, 1969.

"Swell." Def. 9. *Oxford English Dictionary.* 2nd ed. Oxford: Oxford UP, 1989.

Tosh, John. *Manliness and Masculinities in Nineteenth-Century Britain.* New York: Pearson/Longman, 2005.

Trollope, Anthony. *An Autobiography.* Ed. Michael Sadleir and Frederick Page. Oxford: Oxford UP, 1980.

———. *The Belton Estate.* Ed. John Halperin. Oxford: Oxford UP, 1986.

———. *The Bertrams.* New York: Dover, 1986.

———. *Can You Forgive Her?* Ed. Andrew Swarbrick. Oxford: Oxford UP, 1991.

———. *The Claverings.* Ed. David Skilton. Oxford: Oxford UP, 1998.

———. *Doctor Thorne.* London: Oxford UP, 1963.

———. "A Journey to Panama." *The Complete Short Stories.* Vol. 5. Ed. Betty Jane Breyer. Fort Worth: Texas Christian UP, 1983. 199–219.

———. *North America.* Ed. Donald Smalley and Bradford Allen Booth. New York: Knopf, 1951.

———. *Phineas Finn.* Ed. John Sutherland. New York: Penguin, 1985.

———. *The Small House at Allington.* Ed. Julian Thompson. New York: Penguin, 1991.

Turner, Mark W. "Gendered Issues: Intertextuality and *The Small House at Allington* in 'Cornhill Magazine.'" *Victorian Periodicals Review* 26.4 (Winter 1993): 228–34.

———. *Trollope and the Magazines: Gendered Issues in Mid-Victorian Britain.* New York: St. Martin's, 2002.

Vance, Norman. *The Sinews of the Spirit: The Ideal of Christian Manliness in Victorian Literature and Religious Thought.* Cambridge: Cambridge UP, 1985.

Wiener, Martin. *Men of Blood: Violence, Manliness, and Criminal Justice in Victorian England.* Cambridge: Cambridge UP, 2004.

Interpretation, Genre, Revaluation: The Conventions of Romance and the Romance of Religion in Benjamin Disraeli's *Lothair*

Nils Clausson

By offering a rereading and revaluation of Disraeli's Lothair, *this essay attempts to account for the unjustified neglect of Disraeli's novels and proposes a way of reading them that will reveal their artistic merit. Lo-thair should be read not as a realist novel in the tradition of Jane Austen and Anthony Trollope but as a romance in the tradition of Sir Walter Scott's* Waverley *and* Old Mortality. *Drawing on Northrop Frye's influential account of romance in* The Secular Scripture, *the article offers a generic perspective from which* Lothair *can be interpreted as Disraeli's adaptation to contemporary society of Scott's groundbreaking historical romances, which explored Scotland's transformation into a modern society. Using similar narrative conventions and character types, Disraeli explores the contemporary struggle between the forces of tradition, represented by the Anglican and Catholic churches and their representatives, and the modern forces of revolutionary nationalism represented by Garibaldi's struggle to unify Italy by wresting secular power from the Papacy. Lothair thus resembles a typical Scott hero, a "man in the middle" between the forces of tradition and change.*

Romance is the structural core of all fiction.

—Northrop Frye

You have to submit to the huge power of the genre you are in. Genre really does determine outcomes.

—Martin Amis

If [the reader] ignores or despises genre, or gets it wrong, misreading results.

—Alastair Fowler

I

"The novelist who has not been revived is Disraeli," remarked F. R. Leavis more than sixty years ago in *The Great Tradition*:

> Yet, though he is not one of the great novelists, he is so alive and intelligent as to deserve permanent currency, at any rate in the trilogy *Coningsby*, *Sybil*, and *Tancred*: his own interests as expressed in these books—the interests of a supremely intelligent politician who has a sociologist's understanding of civilization and its movement in his time—are so mature.
>
> (1)

Leavis's call for "permanent currency" came when the New Critics, who did not appreciate novelists with a "sociologist's understanding" of society, were in the ascendancy, and their successors—new historicists, neo-Marxists, post-colonialists and poststructuralists—are no more sympathetic to a Tory politician who wrote novels with a political purpose. Not surprisingly, then, few have agreed with Leavis's evaluation, and today Disraeli's novels are read only by a few scholars and a select coterie of devotees.

The orthodox view of Disraeli's Young England trilogy (on which his modest reputation rests) is that it was written to espouse the political ideals of Young England, a splinter group of young aristocratic Tories who opposed Sir Robert Peel, and since most critics cannot take seriously a cause that advocated neo-feudal ideals, they cannot take the novels seriously either. Patrick Brantlinger, for example, believes that "there has been no revival of interest" in Disraeli's novels because the "three most important novels, *Coningsby*, *Sybil*, and *Tancred*, espoused a cause [Young England] that was more laughed at than respected even in the 1840s" (13). The limited criticism the novels have received has focused on what they supposedly can tell us about Disraeli's political ideas, his enigmatic personality, and his oddball beliefs about Jews and race. Indeed, his novels have been read not as novels at all, but as historical documents or psychological clues. Consequently, historians and biographers have shown more interest in them than have literary critics, who find little or no value in them as novels. This puzzling anomaly—treating the novels as valuable historical documents but evaluating them as failed novels—provides an opportunity for reopening the question of Disraeli's longstanding neglect. The main obstacle to revaluing the novels is not, in my view, that critics cannot take Disraeli's reactionary ideas seriously, but that on the few occasions when critics do read the novels they persistently *mis*-read them. To illustrate this claim and to suggest an alternative way of reading Disraeli's novels, leading to a revaluation of them, I propose to offer a rereading of *Lothair* (1870). Such a rereading will, I hope, not only reorient criticism of the novels to their status *as novels*, but also illustrate the crucial role that genre plays in both the interpretation and evaluation of literary texts, and thus have broader implications for literary theory.

To reassess *Lothair* we must abandon the two approaches that have dominated the little attention it has attracted and read it afresh. First, we must ignore (or at least diminish the importance of) the contemporary political and religious events in late 1868—Cardinal Manning's betrayal of Disraeli over the question of establishing a Catholic university in Dublin, and the conversion of the 3rd Marquess of Bute to Roman Catholicism—that titillated contemporary readers and reviewers and has continued to distract later commentators on the novel.[1] Second, and more importantly, we must recognize that *Lothair* should not be judged as a realist novel in the tradition of Jane Austen, Anthony Trollope, and George Eliot, but as a romance closely modeled on the historical novels (or, more accurately, *romances*) of Sir Walter Scott, especially *Waverley* (1814) and *Old Mortality* (1816). (Significantly, *Ivanhoe*, *The Monastery*, and *Kenilworth* are each subtitled *A Romance*.) Although both historians and literary critics have long acknowledged what Donald Stone calls "the romantic impulse" in Disraeli's fiction,[2] and his novels have often been criticized for their theatrical and romantic extravagance, their relation to the literary conventions of romance have not been given sufficient attention. Robert O'Kell, in three important articles, has explored the romance elements in Disraeli's early novels and in *Coningsby* and *Sybil*.[3] However, he uses the term "romance" not in its traditional literary sense but as a way of characterizing what he calls "the fantasy structure upon which his [early] novels rest" (O'Kell "Autobiographical Nature" 253). Reading the early novels as instances of what he calls "the autobiographical mode of fiction," O'Kell concludes,

As both the structure of the fantasies within the characterizations of the heroes and the fantasy structure of the plots themselves show, in embodying the ambivalences of his senses of his own identity in these novels, Disraeli was able to explore imaginatively the possibilities of various roles and to some extent make the fiction serve the function of self-realization.

(284)

Granted, fantasy is likely to be more compatible with the conventions of the romance genre than with realism; however, O'Kell's approach to the early novels is biographical, and thus his use of the term "romance" denotes more of a psychological rather than a literary concept. He similarly reads *Coningsby* not as the political manifesto of Young England it is widely taken to be, but as a "psychological romance," which was the subtitle of *Contarini Fleming* (1832), concluding that *Coningsby*,

> very much like Disraeli's earlier fiction, is chiefly concerned with his conflicts of identity; that politics, while an integral part of the work, is essentially a motif within the genre of the "psychological romance"; and, that "romance," however quixotic the struggles of Young England, was to be a shaping force in Victorian politics.
>
> (O'Kell "Disraeli's 'Coningsby'" 76)

Thus the dynamics and conflicts of Disraeli's personal psychological romance, rather than the conventions of literary romance as a genre, provide the context for O'Kell's reading of *Coningsby*. His essay on *Sybil*, however, does confirm the belief that the way we interpret a text depends on the generic lens through which we read it, for in *Sybil* the literary conventions of romance are, in O'Kell view, at odds with the attempt to portray realistically the political and social condition of post-Reform Bill England: "Whiggish assumptions about what the work as a realistic social novel ought to be arguing" (O'Kell "Two Nations" 215), he remarks, have led to a misreading of the novel, which in O'Kell's revisionist view ought to be read as an "allegorical romance" in which Disraeli "blend[s] the conventions of realism and romance" (231).

Although, in contrast to O'Kell, I use romance in the sense that Northrop Frye, particularly in *The Secular Scripture*, uses it, O'Kell's concept of generic blending is a fruitful one. As I hope to show, a similar blending of genres— romance and realism—is present in *Lothair*, and the failure to recognize the determining role played by romance conventions in that novel has meant that it has suffered from the misjudgments of both those who have praised it and those who have condemned it. Its few admirers have persistently praised it for the wrong reason, or at least for a reason that will certainly not give it "permanent currency." From James Anthony Froude's biography of Disraeli, published in 1890, to Vernon Bogdanor's introduction to the Oxford English Novels edition in 1975 and Sarah Bradford's 1982 biography of Disraeli, *Lothair* has been repeatedly valued for painting a truthful, and hence historically valuable, portrait of the Indian summer of the Victorian aristocracy. "The true value of the book," wrote Froude, "is the perfect representation of patrician society in England in the year which was then passing over; the full appreciation of all that was good and noble in it; yet the recognition, also, that it was a society without a purpose, and with no claim to endurance. It was then at its most brilliant period, like the full bloom of a flower which opens fully only to fade"

(231). Just how, one wonders, can a society be "good and noble" and yet lack a sense of purpose?

In his discussion of *Lothair* in his biography of Disraeli, Robert Blake quotes this passage to support his assertion that the English "aristocracy, having lost much of their political power but having preserved all their prestige and multiplied their wealth, were in danger of losing the sense of duty which alone prevented them from degenerating into a useless caste" (518–19). Four years earlier, Sir Llewellyn Woodward expressed a similar view:

> *Lothair* . . . described the last chapter in the reign of the English territorial magnates. The book was written shortly after the appearance of the first volume of Marx's *Capital*; this conjunction of two worlds, the older, and more familiar world of caste, and the distant yet more brightly burning vision of a classless society, may be taken as a significant date in the political history of England.
>
> (191)

Over a century after Froude, Bogdanor echoed his assessment, calling the novel "the best picture that we have of the Victorian aristocracy's Indian summer before the agricultural depression was to destroy the supremacy of the land in English life, and render unattainable Disraeli's conception of British society" (xvi). And a decade later, Bradford (406) followed Blake in quoting Froude's nostalgic evocation of an effete and fading aristocracy. Critics of *Lothair*, it seems, have a penchant for recycling one another's dubious judgments, and as a result criticism of the novel remains stuck where it was a decade after Disraeli's death. The language used by these critics to praise the novel—"perfect representation," "best picture"—reveals their unstated belief that good novels are realistic and mimetic: they hold a mirror up to the world and give us an accurate representation of an historical society that exists independently of the conventions of fiction. It is perhaps not surprising that such a view would be held by historians and biographers, but it is disappointing to find that literary critics share it.

While praising *Lothair* as a realistic picture of late-Victorian patrician society, critics are disappointed to find that its realism does not extend to it plot and characters. There is almost unanimous agreement about what is considered the novel's artistic faults: its passive, characterless hero and its absurd, improbable plot. Criticism of the hero of *Lothair* dates back at least to Leslie Stephen, who complained that he "reduces himself so completely to a mere 'passive bucket' to be pumped into by every variety of teacher, that he is unpleasantly like a fool" (2: 295). Believing that Disraeli "seems incapable of creating a real human being," Bogdanor insists that "Lothair is not for a moment believable; he is curiously characterless" (xi), and he then quotes Stephen's criticism of Lothair as confirmation. Bradford repeats this view: "It is difficult for a modern reader," she says, "to take a deep interest in the spiritual pilgrimage of the dull and priggish Lothair" (405). Critics find the plot as unbelievable as the hero. Bogdanor dismisses it as "preposterous," "careless and implausible," "absurd and theatrical." "The course of events," he says, "depends almost entirely upon chance, and hardly at all upon the psychology of the characters" (xi). These adverse judgments are all based on the standards used to evaluate the realist novel. But *Lothair*, like *Waverley*, is a romance, and in a romance events conventionally depend on chance and rarely, if at all, on the psychology of the characters. "In displaced or realistic fiction," observes Northrop Frye in *The Secular Scripture*, "the author tries to avoid coincidence. That is, he tries to conceal his design, pretending that things are happening out of inherent probability" (47). But in romance, which operates on different principles, improbabilities are readily accepted, as in *Jane Eyre*, where "the heroine, in flight from Rochester's proposal to make her his mistress, wanders into the world at random, and is eventually taken in by the only family in England with which she has a previous connection unknown to herself" (Frye 47). Both Stephen and Bogdanor fail to perceive that the passivity of its hero and the implausibility of its plot would be faults only if *Lothair* were a realist novel. Although it does contain realist elements (a point to which I will return), its shaping generic conventions are primarily those of the romance in the tradition of Scott's historical romances, which provide both the generic pattern for understanding *Lothair* and the proper grounds for judging its artistic merit.[4]

II

Frye's description of the characterization and plot structure typical of the romance is helpful in illuminating the kind of story Disraeli is telling in *Lothair*:

> The characterization of romance is really a feature of its mental landscape. Its heroes and villains exist primarily to symbolize a contrast between two worlds, one above the level of ordinary experience, the other below it. There is, first, a world associated with happiness, security, and peace; the emphasis is often thrown on childhood or on an "innocent" or pre-genital period of youth, and the images are those of spring and summer, flowers and sunshine. I shall call this world idyllic. The other is a world of exciting adventures, but adventures which involve separation, loneliness, humiliation, pain, and the threat of more pain. I shall call this world the demonic or night world.
>
> (*Secular Scripture* 53)

Most, if not all, of the elements that Frye finds in the "mental landscape" of romance appear in *Lothair*. Frye's idyllic world of happiness, security, and peace is represented in *Lothair* by the summer world of Brentham. Romance, states Frye, is the mythos of summer. The symbolic function of Brentham is revealed by this description of it, emphatically placed at the end of the first chapter:

It would be difficult to find a fairer scene than Brentham offered, especially in the lustrous effulgence of a glorious English summer. It was an Italian palace of Freestone; vast, ornate, and in scrupulous condition; its spacious and graceful chambers filled with treasures of art, and rising itself from statued and stately terraces. At their foot spread a gardened domain of considerable extent, bright with flowers, dim with coverts of rare shrubs, and musical with fountains. Its limit reached a park, with timber such as the midland counties only can produce. The fallow deer trooped among its ferny solitudes and gigantic oaks; but beyond the waters of the broad and winding lake the scene became more savage, and the eye caught the dark form of the red deer on some jutting mount, shrinking with scorn from communion with his gentler brethren.

(4–5; ch. 1)

Such a passage is not one that, as Henry James sniped in his review of *Lothair*, "could have emanated only from a mind thoroughly under the dominion of an almost awful sense of the value and glory of dukes and ducal possessions" (304). Rather, it emanates from the requirements imposed by the romance genre on Disraeli to imagine a symbolic world typical of romance rather than to mirror a real one. Words and phrases such as "fairer scene," "lustrous effulgence," "glorious summer," "spacious," "graceful," and "bright," and those with similar connotations evince the qualities and values that Brentham stands for.

Significantly, the focus of the description moves from the house itself to the garden adjacent to it—gardens abound in romance—and thence to the more remote park, and finally to the distant and wholly natural world of the red deer. The implication is that Brentham is a locus of culture and civilization, but a culture that, even as it represents the triumph of culture over the nature symbolized by the "dark form of the red deer," is nevertheless still firmly rooted in the natural world, taking its fundamental character from it. Brentham was supposedly modeled on Trentham, the country house of the second duke of Sutherland, and Disraeli's description of it may very well be accurate, as the duke's son claimed, but its *literary* value does not lie in such historical verisimilitude. Such a description is not imitating an actual world; it is creating the symbolic one found in romance.

In *Lothair* Frye's demonic or night world is represented by the hero's "exciting adventures" in Italy, which involve his separation from England, the threat of death as a result of his participation in Garibaldi's political movement to unify Italy, and his humiliation and pain at the hands of Cardinal Grandison and his cohorts. Within the conventions of the romance genre, the devious, if not demonic, political campaign to revive Catholicism in England, in which Lothair becomes entangled, similarly stands in symbolic opposition to the idyllic world of Brentham from which he is separated but to which he will be reunited, through marriage to Lady Corisande, at the end of the novel. And just as Brentham symbolizes Frye's idyllic world, Cardinal Grandison's town house in London, Hexam House, symbolizes the dark, demonic world:

A considerable portion of the North side of [Hexam] square is occupied by one house standing in a courtyard, with iron gates to the thoroughfare. This is Hexam House, and where Lord Hexam lived in the days of the first Georges. It is reduced in size since his time, two considerable wings having been pulled down about sixty years ago, and their material employed in building some residences of less pretension. But the body of the dwelling-house remains, and the courtyard, though reduced in size, has been retained.

(16; ch. 6)

In the romance structure of the novel, Grandison plays the role of the villain, and his house reflects his role. Hexam House, in contrast to Brentham, is a dark, solemn and confining residence—urban rather than rural. It is certainly not a place where pleasure and joy, the hallmarks of Brentham, predominate. Even the changed seasons emphasize the contrast: Brentham is associated with summer, Hexam House with winter. (It is worth noting parenthetically that Lytton Strachey, in *Eminent Victorians*, describes Manning's palace in Westminster as "that gaunt and gloomy building—more like a barracks than an Episcopal palace" [104].)

The romance conventions of *Lothair* stand out all the more clearly when its plot structure and characters are compared to those in Scott's historical romances. Particularly noticeable are the structural similarities between the roles played by the heroines in *Waverley* and *Lothair*. In romance, notes Frye, we often get two heroines, "one associated with virginity, and the other with love and marriage" (*Secular Scripture* 83). Like Waverley, Lothair goes through a series of adventures, each associated with a woman, until he finally knows which one he ought to marry. In *Waverley* there are two heroines, Rose Bradwardine and Flora MacIvor. The equivalent of Rose in *Lothair* is Lady Corisande, daughter of the duke. The role played by Flora in *Waverley* is split into two characters in *Lothair*: Theodora Campian, a devotee of Italian nationalism, and Claire Arundel, the Roman Catholic niece of Lord and Lady St. Jerome. At first, Waverley is more attracted to Flora (as Lothair is to Clare and then Theodora), but she refuses him outright (as Theodora refuses Lothair's gift of the pearl necklace), for she is wholly committed to the Jacobite cause and realizes that Waverley has only blundered into his tepid Jacobitism, just as Theodora is passionately committed to Italian nationalism and soon realizes that the quixotic Lothair is no revolutionary. Theodora, an uncompromising idealist, dies fighting in Garibaldi's army. At the end of *Waverley*, when the Jacobite cause collapses, Flora retires to a convent; at the end of *Lothair*, Clare enters a convent, as she had intended to do before being persuaded it was her religious duty to win Lothair's soul for her Church by winning his heart for herself. *Lothair* ends, as its romance conventions dictate, with the anticipated nuptials of Lothair and Lady Corisande.

As all these parallels with *Waverley* indicate, *Lothair* is much closer to Scott's romances than to mid-Victorian realist novels. Disraeli has appropriated the characters and plot structure of Scott's historical romances and used them to tell a story that, set in the present, examines the political and religious forces shaping Victorian society. Thus *Lothair*, like the Young England Trilogy, is a kind of "contemporary" historical romance. If Disraeli is indebted mainly to *Waverley* for the romance structure of *Lothair*, it is likely to Scott's *Old Mortality* that he is indebted for its politico-religious themes. Both novels explore the tangled relations between politics and religion. *Old Mortality* is set in Scotland in 1679 against the backdrop of the political and religious conflicts between Covenanters and Episcopalians near the end of the reign of Charles II. The Covenanters, who had refused to take an oath of allegiance to the crown and to submit themselves to bishops, rebelled against Charles's reintroduction of Episcopalian church government. The struggle between the establishment Episcopalians and the rebelling Covenanters is replaced in *Lothair* with the less violent religious struggle between the Anglican and Roman Catholic churches for religious power in England. (The actual rebellion of the Covenanters finds its structural counterpart in Garibaldi's military campaign.) Lothair, like Henry Morton, resembles Scott's typical hero, the so-called "man in the middle"; his religious loyalties are divided between two guardians, his Scots Presbyterian uncle and Cardinal Grandison. In both Scott and Disraeli, religious and political enthusiasms—for Disraeli, Roman Catholicism and Italian nationalism—are seen as a threat to political stability and order, their threat magnified by their inherent romantic attractiveness.

The similarities between Scott's and Disraeli's heroines are mirrored by the parallels between their heroes. Disraeli's much-maligned protagonist owes a good deal to the characterization of Scott's heroes. According to George Goodin, what often happens in a Scott novel "is that the hero suffers at the hands of established political power and as a result commits himself to those who are opposing it, after which he suffers at their hands also" (17). In *Old Mortality*, for example, Henry Morton is imprisoned for harboring a Covenanting friend of his father, Burley, who (unknown to Morton) has participated in the murder of Archbishop Sharpe, a man hated by the Covenanters for abandoning them and supporting the restoration of Episcopalianism. When the Covenanters are defeated at the battle of Bothwell Bridge, Morton is saved from execution only by the intervention of the Royalist Lord Evandale (his rival for Edith Bellenden). A similar, though not identical, pattern is clearly evident in *Lothair*. Although Lothair obviously does not suffer at the hands of established political power (this is where Disraeli modifies Scott's pattern), he does rebel against the influence of his dour Scottish Presbyterian guardian, Lord Culloden, and commits himself first to the Catholic cause in England, represented by the St. Jeromes and their beautiful niece, and then to the cause of Italian nationalism, a movement associated with European secret societies and hence perceived as a threat to England. He is nearly killed fighting in the battle of Mentana. When Clare implausibly discovers the wounded Lothair on the battlefield (as one expects in a romance, she is conveniently in Rome at the same time he is), the chance discovery is exploited by Cardinal Grandison, who misrepresents it in a Roman newspaper as the direct result of the miraculous intervention of the Virgin Mary. Lothair, like Morton, naturally feels exploited and betrayed.

The parallels between *Old Mortality* and *Lothair* are not limited to their similar romance structure and religious themes. The criticisms that have been made of Scott's novel are remarkably similar to those directed at Disraeli's. When *Old Mortality* was first published, it drew the fire of the Reverend Thomas McCrie, who charged that the hero, the moderate Presbyterian Henry Morton, was so weak and indecisive as to be hardly capable of political or religious motivation, that the Presbyterians were all depicted as irrational fanatics, that the uprising of the Covenanters was portrayed as politically futile, and that the novel could be used to justify the political repressions of the post-Waterloo period (Goodin 15–16). The same criticisms have been made by later critics, whose attacks on *Old Mortality* resemble those directed at *Lothair* by its critics, who charge that its hero is weak and indecisive, that both the Catholics and the Italian nationalists are irrational extremists (or ideologues), that the Italian nationalist movement is portrayed as misguided and futile (even though Italy had become unified shortly after the novel was written), and that nationalist movements like the one Theodora is devoted to are linked to secret societies fomenting revolution and thus, as a threat to established order, justify political repression.

In his reply to McCrie, Scott, anticipating Northrop Frye, defended his novel on literary rather than political grounds. *Old Mortality*, Scott insisted, is not history but a romance. Moreover, he argued that there is a "dramatic principle upon which the author frames his plots," thereby placing the reader "in some measure, in the situation of the audience at a theatre who are compelled to gather the meaning of the scene from what the *dramatis personae* say to each other, and not from any explanation addressed immediately to themselves"; this dramatic form, Scott continues, "compel[s] the reader to think of the personages of the novel and not of the writer" (Williams 239, 240). The reason readers do not think of the writer is that he, like the dramatist, controls his point of view so as to remove himself from his work. As Goodin points out, ideas expressed in *Old Mortality* appear to proceed not from the author but from the characters themselves, and are almost always addressed to another character rather than directly to the reader. Like the description in the novel, they are used in what Scott calls a "reflective" manner: that is, they reflect the character of the speaker and the auditor(s), and the first criterion for judging these ideas is not their historical truth but their appropriateness to the character expressing them (Goodin 16). It is by appealing to this dramatic principle that Scott defends the characterization of his hero, whose fate, he says, is "uniformly determined by the agency of the subordinate persons," who pull him in conflicting directions (Williams 239). Writing to Lady Louisa Stuart about

Old Mortality, Scott noted that "there are noble subjects for narrative during that period full of the strongest light & shadow, all human passions stirr'd up and stimulated by the most powerful motives, & the controlling parties [are] as distinctly contrasted in manners & in modes of thinking as [they arc] in political principles" (*Letters* 4: 293). "What results," observes Goodin, "is that the hero is relatively uncommitted, yet it is through him that we see those who are strongly committed" (17). The same is true of Lothair, through whose eyes we see the enthusiasms of those much more "strongly committed" than he.

Scott's defense of *Old Mortality* from McCrie's attack parallels my defense of *Lothair*. Lothair's fate, like Henry Morton's and Waverley's, is largely determined by the agency of the other characters in the novel, and Disraeli, like Scott, is more interested in the strong dramatic contrasts he can develop among the subordinate characters—Scott's "strongest light & shadow"—than he is in creating a fully rounded, psychologically complex hero, or reflecting contemporary events. And in order to develop these contrasts, Disraeli, like Scott, sacriifices characterization to dramatic design and to the conventions of romance.

III

A benefit of reading *Lothair* as a romance modeled on Scott's historical novels is that doing so not only explains the novel's hero and its plot structure but also accounts for the apparent inconsistency between the characters under whose influence Lothair comes and the causes they embody. What is particularly striking about characters like Clare Arundel and Theodora Campian is that they are represented positively while the movements they belong to are portrayed as threats and are ultimately defeated. However, as Frye, as well as numerous other critics, has pointed out, the same paradox appears in Scott's novels: the representatives of the forces that are defeated at the end—Jacobites, Saxons, Roman Catholics, Covenanters—are always more energetic and attractive to the reader than the passive hero and the forces that defeat them. "The Waverley novels were written by a Tory," states Frye, "yet the defeated insurgent forces, the Jacobite Highlanders in *Waverley*, the supporters of Queen Mary in *The Abbot*, the Saxons in *Ivanhoe*, express the greatest social passion and power in these novels" (*Secular Scripture* 164). In *Waverley*, Frye comments, "Flora is much the more memorable of the two heroines: in fact, she and her brother, with his tragic fate, upstage the whole cast" (84). Similarly, in *Lothair* both Clare Arundel and Theodora, who dies operatically on the battlefield, are much more memorable than the faultless but mild Corisande and the passive Lothair. But, despite the attacks of critics, this is not an artistic flaw in either novel. And if it is considered a fault, it is the inevitable result of the romance conventions within which both writers are working, conventions that are much stronger than the individual voice of the author. "With romance," remarks Frye, "it is much harder [than with the realist novel] to avoid the feeling of convention, that the story is one of a family of similar stories. Hence in the criticism of romance we are led very quickly from what the individual work says to what the entire convention it belongs to is saying through the work" (60). Changing the generic lens through we read *Lothair* can help us see that it is not the unique expression of the unique personality of Disraeli, but one of a family of similar stories.

If we ignore what historians and biographers have said about the novel, and instead read *Lothair* as a mid-Victorian romance in the tradition of Scott's historical romances, then we will we be able to distinguish between what Disraeli the man may have been trying to say and what the entire convention *Lothair* belongs to—romance—is saying through this particular work. For example, a historical critic is likely to view Disraeli's representation of the Italian nationalist movement led by Garibaldi as historically inaccurate and as an expression of an unprogressive, if not downright reactionary, view of Italian nationalism. It is certainly true that Disraeli, for all his talk of race, had little sympathy with what today is regarded as legitimate nationalism. But his representation *in the novel* of Garibaldi's nationalist movement is complicated by the fact that, within the literary conventions created by Scott's historical romances, Italian nationalism is analogous to the rebellions of the Covenanters in *Old Mortality* and the Jacobites in *Waverley*, or the struggles of the Saxons in *Ivanhoe*, or the intrigues of the Catholic supporters of Queen Mary in *The Abbot*—all of which are losing causes. But we should not interpret these defeats as expressing Scott's private views of Saxons, Roman Catholics, or Jacobites; after all, he confessed to "having a very strong prejudice in favor of the Stuart family, which I had originally imbibed from the songs and tales of the Jacobites" (qtd. in P. H. Scott 208). All these groups, however, are associated with the demonic or night world that, as Frye explains, the romance hero must travel through before returning to the idyllic world from which, at the beginning of the novel, he becomes separated but into which he is reintegrated, a changed man, at the end. Whatever political merit Garibaldi's movement to unify Italy may have when judged historically, within the romance conventions of *Lothair* it must stand, along with Grandison's Catholic party, in symbolic opposition to the idyllic world of Brentham. Within the romance plot structure Disraeli has taken over from Scott, the Italian nationalists are required to function in the same way that the Covenanters do in *Old Mortality* and the Highland Jacobites in *Waverley*: they all lose. Even though Garibaldi's movement succeeded historically, within the romance that is *Lothair*, his army must lose, whatever Disraeli's private views of Garibaldi's politics might have been.

My point is that the structural conventions of romance are more helpful in explaining what is going on in *Lothair* than an appeal to the historical events happening at home and abroad in the late 1860s. This claim might seem only to confirm Frye's observation that, in so far as romance has any political commitment at all, it is on the side of the *status quo*:

> In every age the ruling social or intellectual class tends to project its ideals in some form of romance, where the virtuous heroes and beautiful heroines represent the ideals and the villains the threats to their ascendancy. This is the general character of the chivalric romance in the Middle Ages, aristocratic romance in the Renaissance, [and] bourgeois romance since the eighteenth century.
>
> (*Anatomy* 186)

And although I would certainly not want to attribute Disraeli's conservatism, as Mark Twain did that of the American antebellum South, to reading too many of Scott's romances, it is likely that the (conservative) historical romances of the Tory Scott appealed to Disraeli, perhaps in part unconsciously, because they confirmed his own conservative political allegiances and beliefs. But I would also stress that no writer, even one as idiosyncratic as Disraeli, stands entirely outside of generic conventions and their force.

The inherent conservatism of the romance conventions shaping *Lothair* is also qualified by the fact that the work is not a pure romance. Perhaps the most obvious reason that *Lothair* has been read and judged as a realist novel, albeit a flawed one, rather than as a romance, is that parts of it do read like one. For *Lothair*, as well as being a romance, also participates in one of the dominant traditions of the novel from Cervantes to Henry James: the parody-romance. Once again, Frye's analysis is indispensable:

> When the novel was established in the eighteenth century, it came to a reading public familiar with the formulas of prose romance. It is clear that the novel was a realistic displacement of romance, and had few structural features to itself. *Robinson Crusoe, Pamela, Tom Jones*, use much the same general structure as romance, but adapt that structure to a demand for greater conformity to ordinary experience. This displacement gave the novel's relation to romance . . . a strong element of parody. It would hardly be too much to say that realistic fiction from Defoe to Henry James, is, when we look at it as a form of narrative technique, essentially parody-romance. Characters confused by romantic assumptions about reality, who emphasize the same kind of parody, are central to the novel: random examples include Emma Bovary, Anna Karenina, Lord Jim, and Isabel Archer.
>
> (*Secular Scripture* 39)

Frye then goes on to point out that "the tradition of parody can be traced through the history of the novel . . . and extends to many novelists who have been thought to be still too close to romance. Thus Fielding's *Joseph Andrews* began as parody of *Pamela*, and Jane Austen's *Northanger Abbey* is a parody of Gothic romance" (39). James could have added Lothair to his list of characters "confused by romantic assumptions about reality."

The presence of both romance and anti-romance conventions in *Lothair* complicates—and, I would also argue, enriches—our response to it. Frye emphasizes the "polarized characterization" typically found in romance, "its tendency to split into heroes and villains. Romance avoids the ambiguities of ordinary life, where everything is a mixture of good and bad, and where it is difficult to take sides or believe that people are consistent patterns of virtue or vice. The popularity of romance, it is obvious, has much to do with its simplifying of moral facts" (50). But *Lothair*, like the realist novel and unlike most romances, presents us with the ambiguities of life. Lothair is an idealistic and inexperienced young man (the type of the hero Disraeli borrowed from Scott), and it is part of Disraeli's purpose in the novel to show that idealists—especially religious idealists—are easily victimized and made fools of by worldly, pragmatically minded men precisely because the former idealize people and then proceed to act on the assumption, which will be proved false by their adventures, that their idealized image of the world is the real world. What Frye observes about Waverley can also be said of Lothair: "Waverley is a romantic hero . . . but, like a small-scale Don Quixote, his romantic attitude is one that confirms the supremacy of real life. He is over-impressionable, and his loves and loyalties are alike immature" (40). Lothair is "like a fool" because in a very real sense he is a fool—his quixotic idealism makes him one.

The quixotic hero derived from parody-romance is essential to Disraeli's serious moral concern in *Lothair*: the role that religion should play both in the lives of individuals in a society and in the society as a whole. For the novel takes for granted the assumption—admittedly an unpalatable one to liberals and radicals alike today—that there ought to be a connection between religious institutions and the State. In a speech at Aylesbury in 1861, Disraeli said: "A wise government, allying itself with religion would, as it were, consecrate society and sanctify the State. But how is this to be done? It is the problem of modern politics which has always most embarrassed statesmen" (Monypenny and Buckle, 4: 362). As a conservative, Disraeli believed that a "wise government" would recognize that the progressive, liberal doctrine of an absolute separation of Church and State, religion and politics, is not in the best interests of a civil society—a principle that Christian neoconservatives have recently revived and Islamic fundamentalists never abandoned. The delicate and difficult question, of course, as the conservative *and* politically pragmatic Disraeli recognized, is exactly how a wise government can successfully ally itself with religion so as to "sanctify society and consecrate the State" without sacrificing its secular power and authority to a rival institution (such as the Roman Catholic Church).

For Disraeli this question was closely allied to another issue that many of his novels—especially the Young England Trilogy—address: the relationship between the real and the ideal. Religions propose an ideal for humans to aspire to, but this ideal must be striven for and realized in a world that is far from ideal. Thus implementing the ideal in the world always requires some kind of compromise between what the ideal demands and what, realistically, can be attained. Disraeli explores this perplexing question in his serio-comic story of a young religious idealist who, like the hero of many parody-romances, finally has to come to terms with and live in a world that does not—*cannot*—live up to his idealized expectation of it. This theme is explicitly announced at the opening of chapter 22: "Although Lothair was not in the slightest degree shaken in his conviction that life should be entirely religious, he was perplexed by the inevitable obstacles which seemed perpetually to oppose themselves to the practice of his opinions" (72). At the beginning of the novel, Lothair "wonder[s] how any man who is religious can think of anything but religion" (55; ch. 17), only to learn that there is much more to think about in life than religion.

In keeping with this theme, the novel is structured so that it consists of a number of contrasting characters, or groups of characters, who represent varying embodiments of the ideal and the real—a schematic approach to characterization typical of romance and parody-romance.[5] The St. Jeromes and their niece Clare Arundel, for example, are idealized representatives of the Roman Catholic Church, whereas Cardinal Grandison (usually taken to be modeled on Cardinal Manning) represents the practical, politically expedient side of the Church as a secular institution. The ideal political aspirations of the Italian nationalist movement are represented by Theodora Campian; its pragmatism, by Captain Bruges, who, after the nationalists are defeated at the Battle of Mentana, sells his military expertise to the oppressive Ottoman Empire. Similarly, the idealized Paraclete, a Christian who carries on the traditions established by his Jewish ancestors, is contrasted to the Greek-inspired artist, Mr. Phoebus, who expediently forgets his Aryan principles of art when he is invited by the Court of St. Petersburg to paint sentimental scenes of the Holy Land. The impossibility of implementing the religious ideal in its pure, unmediated form is illustrated by the complete unworldliness of the idealized religious characters: Clare Arundel can live the ideal Christian life only by withdrawing at the end of the novel into a convent on Mt. Athos. Similarly, Paraclete can remain true to the original precepts of Christ only by remaining outside of *any* established church, thereby avoiding that compromise with the world which is unavoidably attendant upon the institutionalization of ideals in actual historical churches.

The complexity and ambiguity that Frye says is typically absent from romance is certainly evident in Disraeli's satirical representation of the duke's country estate of Brentham, which is less than perfect. It is simply as close to perfect as we are likely to get in this imperfect world. When Lothair experiences the religious fervor of Vauxe, Brentham, which had seemed perfect, now appears unsatisfying, parochial and just a little frivolous. At Vauxe, the St. Jeromes are passionately devoted to a religious cause, re-establishing the universal Church in England; at Brentham, the object of near universal enthusiasm is—croquet! Chapter 5 opens with an example of Disraeli's satirical wit at its most brilliant:

Lord Montairy was passionately devoted to croquêt. He flattered himself that he was the most accomplished male performer existing. He would have thought absolutely the most accomplished, were it not for the unrivalled feats of Lady Montairy. She was the queen of croquêt. Her sisters also used the mallet with admirable skill, but not like Victoria. Lord Montairy always looked forward to his summer croquêt at Brentham. It was a great croquêt family, the Brentham family; even listless Lord St. Aldegonde would sometimes play, with a cigar never out of his mouth. They did not object to his smoking in the air. On the contrary, "they rather liked it." Captain Mildmay, too, was a brilliant hand, and had written a treatise on croquêt, the best going.

(11; ch. 1)

Placed at the opening of the chapter describing Lothair's visit to Brentham, this passage provides a satirical perspective from which to view the hero's first encounter with the English aristocracy: whereas Theodora is passionately devoted to Italian nationalism and Clare to the Catholic cause in England, Lord Montairy is passionately devoted to croquet. Disraeli's novels have sometimes been attacked for what his critics see as his uncritical acceptance, even envy, of aristocratic life. But Disraeli the novelist's attitude to the aristocracy as represented by Brentham and its owner is anything but uncritical, and it is certainly not, as Henry James claimed, "infantine" (304). The satire is most obviously conveyed through the choice of names: Montairy and Mildmay suggest the airiness and insubstantiality of life at Brentham, notwithstanding its undeniable charm and beauty. His criticism goes beyond the ironic description of the devotion to croquet at Brentham to include the Duke himself: "Every day when he looked into the glass, and gave the last touch to his consummate toilette, he offered his grateful thanks to Providence that his family was not unworthy of him" (4; ch. 1). In *Lothair*, observes Blake, "Disraeli depicts with a touch of satire, so subtle that its objects did not recognize it, the grand social world in which he had been a familiar though slightly mocking traveler for over thirty years" (518).

But there is more than "a touch of satire" in *Lothair*. The Duke's family clearly does not understand the major political issues of the time; indeed, they try to ignore them. Controversies of any kind—and especially the political and religious ones that figure so prominently in the novel—are deliberately avoided at Brentham. For example, Corisande's brother Bertram, who is a Conservative MP, is indifferent to the Irish Church question—the very issue that brought down Disraeli's government in late 1868. Although Corisande affirms that she has "every confidence in Bertram, in his ability and his principles" (63; ch. 19), when her brother is called upon to make a principled choice during the debate on the disestablishment of the Irish Church, he conveniently travels to the East with St. Aldegonde to avoid the vote: "They had left England about the same time as Lothair [had left for Rome], and had paired together on the Irish Church till Easter, with a sort of hope on the part of St. Aldegonde that they might neither of them reappear in the House of Commons again until the Irish Church was either saved or subverted" (309; ch. 76).

It is an interesting fact of literary history that while Disraeli was composing *Lothair* in 1869, Matthew Arnold's *Culture and Anarchy* was published in book form. Disraeli criticizes the aristocracy for the same deficiencies Arnold finds in them: their lack of ideas. As well as instinctively avoiding controversy, the Duke's family members, like Arnold's barbarians, are insular and unreceptive to ideas, and so they are unable to understand why everyone does not think and believe as they do. Corisande, for example, cannot understand why young men are leaving the Church of England for Rome; all she can do is irrationally attribute the defections to some weakness in their characters— a lack of masculinity—rather than the real cause: the inherent attractiveness of the religion they have adopted. "And if all did their duty like papa," she naively exclaims, "there might be less, or no cause . . . to be alarmed. But when I hear of young nobles, the natural leaders of the land, going over to the Roman Catholic Church, I confess I lose heart and patience. It seems so unpatriotic, so effeminate" (41; ch. 12). For the parochial Corisande, converting to Roman Catholicism is simply un-English. Disraeli's choice of the word *confess* is a brilliant stroke: genuine religious confession is something unfamiliar to a family almost as devoted to croquet as to the Established Church. At Brentham, the mention of religious controversy is an occasion for the expression either of incomprehension (Lady Corisande) or of the hope that its political inconveniences can be avoided (St. Aldegonde and Bertram.) The contrast between the intense Catholicism at Vauxe and the rather tepid Anglicanism of Brentham is nicely caught in one of Disraeli's many brilliant, Wilde-like aphorisms in the novel: "In a truly religious family," observes the narrator, "there would always be a Father Coleman or a Monsignore Catesby to guide and to instruct. But a Protestant, if he wants aid or advice on any matter, can only go to his solicitor" (59; ch. 18). Everyone at Brentham is, in Cardinal Grandison's choice phrase, "a Parliamentary Christian" (57; ch. 17), and such a compromised, tepid faith is not likely to satisfy the religious longings of the earnest Lothair.

It is within the conventions of romance, particularly those of Scott's historical romances, that the religious themes of the novel, along with the Lothair's marriage to Lady Corisande, need to be viewed. Roman Catholicism and Roman Catholic protagonists figure prominently in Disraeli's novels from *The Young Duke* (1831), whose hero, after making a speech in the House of Lords in support of Catholic Emancipation, marries at the end of the novel the Catholic May Dacre, to *Sybil*, whose eponymous heroine is Roman Catholic and heir to lands where an abbey once stood. In these novels, however, the protagonist does not face a choice between Roman Catholicism and Protestantism. Roman Catholicism in them is associated not with the protagonist's choice of faith but with England's pre-Reformation, medieval past, when the Church was an institution that discharged its social responsibility of caring for the poor and ameliorating the suffering of the people. The Church then had a *social* mission, a mission that is carried out in the present by Sybil, and by the factory owner Trafford, who is also, significantly, Roman Catholic, and who, like the monks of Marney Abbey, discharges his social responsibilities to his workers. What is significant about the Catholic faction in *Lothair* is that (with the exception of Lord St. Jerome) they are converts to Rome and loyal not to an indigenous, pre-Reformation English tradition of Catholicism but to a foreign church that shows no signs of interest in the welfare of the people and is devoted entirely to strengthening its political power and influence. In contrast to the Catholicism of recent converts like his own wife and Cardinal Grandison, Lord St. Jerome's is a native, thoroughly English Catholicism, as evinced by the description of his country seat, Vauxe:

> Vauxe, the seat of the St. Jeromes, was the finest specimen of the old English residence extant. It was the perfection of the style, which had gradually arisen after the wars of the Roses had alike destroyed all the castles and the purpose of the stern erections. People said Vauxe looked like a college: the truth is, colleges looked like Vauxe, for when those fair and civil buildings rose, the wise and liberal spirits who endowed them, intended that they should resemble as much as possible the residence of a great noble.
>
> (44; ch. 13)

At the end of the novel that English tradition is symbolically represented by the garden Corisande is restoring, and in marrying her Lothair is not so much rejecting Catholicism in favor of Anglicanism as committing himself to reviving and perpetuating an English tradition of social responsibility. The ruins of the garden, which Corisande is restoring to its original condition, are similar to the ruins of Marney Abbey in *Sybil*, and thus Lothair's marriage to Corisande symbolizes his dedication to renewal through restoration, by returning to his ancient roots rather than flirting with foreign beliefs and institutions.[6]

The ending of the novel—Lothair's return to England and marriage to Lady Corisande—conforms to the conventions of romance but also subtly modifies those conventions. In terms of the romance structure of the novel, Lothair's return to Brentham and his marriage represent his integration into a society in which religion is not the only thing one should think about. And his marriage to Corisande stands for his final accommodation to reality that we expect in both a romance and a parody-romance. But it is not so much the marriage that symbolizes that accommodation as Lady Corisande's obviously symbolic garden, which becomes a metaphor for the proper relationship of the individual to society and of innovation and change within it. Whereas Vauxe, representing the static, unchanging Catholic Church, has remained unchanged for centuries, and Theodora's thoroughly modern house has no connection at all with the past, Lady Corisande's garden represents the ideal realized, or the closest thing we have to the ideal in an imperfect world. Lord St. Aldegonde has just been criticizing modern, geometrical gardens: "How I hate modern gardens," he remarks. "What a horrid thing this is! One might as well have a mosaic pavement there" (369; ch. 89). So the party, including Lothair and Corisande, decides to visit her "very old-fashioned" garden:

> In the pleasure-grounds of Brentham were the remains of an ancient garden of the ancient house that had long ago been pulled down. When the modern pleasure-grounds were planned and created, notwithstanding the protests of the artists in landscape, the father of the present Duke would not allow this ancient garden to be entirely destroyed, and you came upon its quaint appearance in the dissimilar world in which it was placed, as you might some festival of romantic costume upon a person habited in the courtly dress of the last century. It was formed upon a gentle southern slope, with turfen terraces walled in on three sides, the fourth consisting of arches of golden yew. The Duke had given this garden to Lady Corisande, in order that she might practice her theory, that flower-gardens should be sweet and luxuriant, and not hard and scentless imitations of works of art.
>
> (369–70; ch. 89)

In realizing her idea of what a garden ought to be, Corisande does not begin with an abstract conception or with wholly new materials. Rather, in true Burkean fashion, she builds upon the foundations of "an ancient garden," which is an inheritance from her grandfather. The implication is clear: those who wish to build a better society—whether religious enthusiasts or political revolutionaries—must imitate Corisande rather than Theodora, who cares more for the present and the future than for the past, or Clare, who lives only in the past.

As well as exemplifying the balance between past and present, Corisande's garden also exemplifies the creative imagination at work in society at large, including religion, politics, and art. The garden is, of course, Corisande's, but it is not her creation alone, an expression of only her individuality, for she is creating something new out of old materials not of her own making. The remnants of the garden built by Corisande's grandfather—it is partly *his* garden, too—contain within them the lineaments of an ideal garden, just as the remains of Marney Abbey in *Sybil* suggest to the imagination of Egremont the lineaments of an ideal, or at least a better, more natural society. The restoration of the garden is the result of the interplay of tradition and the individual talent, resulting in a creation that, like Disraeli's novel, is at once new and traditional.

IV

My experiment in genre criticism has, I believe, two implications: one concerns interpretation and the other evaluation. The two are related since, as E. D. Hirsch points out, "Any accurate description of literary works must . . . have reference to values that make them literature and not another thing" (97). Moreover, we cannot innocently read a text in a wholly unmediated way and then interpret it; we must perforce read it *as* an instance of a particular *kind* of text. As Peter Rabinowitz observes in his instructive book *Before Reading*:

> We often think of genre designation as one of the last acts a reader performs—and to some extent it is true that a work's *precise* generic placement is often unclear until we have finished reading it. But some preliminary generic judgment is always required even before we begin the process of reading. We can never interpret entirely outside generic structures: "reading"—even the reading of a first paragraph—is always "reading as."

(176; italics in original)

Rabinowitz's observation that "some preliminary generic judgment is always required even before we begin the process of reading" points to the paradox of genre: whilst we can never interpret a text entirely outside of generic structures, the same structures that are necessary for us to interpret it at all can also blind us to other generic perspectives by, in effect, "pre-interpreting" the text for us. Novelist Martin Amis is right: "You have to submit to the huge power of the genre you are in. Genre really does determine outcomes" (qtd. in Duff 1). And how we classify a text in order to interpret it also determines our evaluation of it. If *Gulliver's Travels* is read as a novel, it will appear to lack unity and its hero will seem flat and inconsistent. But if we read Swift's masterpiece as a Menippean satire, those "faults" will never appear since we are not expecting round and consistent characters. What genre we place a work in determines both our interpretation and our evaluation of it. Reading *Lothair* primarily as a realist novel has led us both to misread and to misjudge it. Rereading it as a romance and as a parody-romance can not only correct this misreading but also provide the basis for a revaluation of its merits. A rediscovery and revival of this witty and insightful novel on the complex relations between religion and politics, and on the pitfalls of religious enthusiasms, would be especially timely today, when the global emergence of a militant form of Islam and the resurgence of Christian fundamentalism in America and Orthodox Judaism in Israel are transforming our world and affecting our daily lives. And, finally, if we agree that *Lothair* has been undervalued because it has been misread, then is it not possible, even likely, that the same fate has befallen at least some of Disraeli's other novels?

NOTES

1. On Christmas Eve, 1868, the third Marquess of Bute, heir to an immense fortune, was received into the Roman Catholic Church. The conversion was the topic of considerable gossip and speculation. "It was," writes Vernon Bogdanor, "this episode that

provided the inspiration for *Lothair*" (xiii). Bogdanor also summarizes the political events that led up to the defeat of Disraeli's Conservatives in November 1868:

> Disraeli, as Prime Minister, had attempted to solve the vexed problem of the 'alien church'—the Anglican establishment in Ireland—by setting up a Catholic University in Dublin, to be subject to lay control. Manning hinted to Disraeli that such a proposal would be found acceptable by the hierarchy in Ireland. But after complex negotiations, it became clear that the Irish bishops would be satisfied with nothing less than complete Episcopal control. . . .
>
> (viii–ix)

Most commentators on the novel, including Bogdanor, regard Cardinal Grandison as Disraeli's vengeful portrait of Manning. But none of the backroom political maneuvers that led to Disraeli's defeat, it should be noted, appear in the novel.

2. See Stone 74–98; ch. 3. According to Stone, "Disraeli viewed a political career as a Romantic mission, as a vehicle for his Romantic artistry: in public service a Shelleyan devotion to the welfare of others could be united to a Byronic display of will and a Keatsian display of imagination" (74).

3. See O'Kell, "The Autobiographical Nature"; "Disraeli's 'Coningsby'"; and "Two Nations, or One?"

4. For readers unfamiliar with the plot of *Lothair*, Robert Blake's masterful summary of it, which I cannot improve upon, may be helpful (see *Disraeli*, pp. 517–18).

5. This pattern in the parody-romance derives ultimately from *Don Quixote*. "Perhaps the simplest and yet the most adequate idea which will help up to enter understandingly into [*Don Quixote*]," observes Dorothy Van Ghent, "is the idea of a structure based upon a system of contrasts" (9).

6. For a fuller discussion of Roman Catholicism in Disraeli's novels and specifically in *Lothair*, see my "English Catholics," 454–74.

WORKS CITED

Blake, Robert. *Disraeli*. London: Eyre & Spottiswode, 1966.

Bogdanor, Vernon. "Introduction" to *Lothair*. Oxford: Oxford UP, 1975.

Bradford, Susan. *Disraeli*. London: Grafton, 1985.

Brantlinger, Patrick. "Tory Radicalism and 'The Two Nations' in Disraeli's *Sybil*." *The Victorian Newsletter* 41 (1972): 13–17.

Clausson, Nils. "English Catholics and Roman Catholicism in Disraeli's Novels." *Nineteenth-Century Fiction* 33 (Mar. 1979): 454–74.

Disraeli, Benjamin. *Lothair*. Ed. Vernon Bogdanor. Oxford: Oxford UP, 1975.

Duff, David. Introduction. *Modern Genre Theory*. Harlow: Longman, 2000.

Froude, James A. *Lord Beaconsfield*. 1890. Freeport, NY: Books for Libraries, 1971.

Frye, Northrop. *Anatomy of Criticism*. Princeton: Princeton UP, 1957.

————. *The Secular Scripture: A Study of the Structure of Romance*. Cambridge, Harvard UP, 1975.

Goodin, George. "Walter Scott and the Traditions of the Political Novel." *The English Novel in the Nineteenth Century: Essays on the Literary Mediation of Human Values*. Ed. George Goodin. Urbana: U of Illinois P, 1972. 14–24.

Hirsch, E. D., Jr. *The Aims of Interpretation*. Chicago: U of Chicago P, 1976.

James, Henry. *Literary Reviews and Essays: On American, English, and French Literature*. Ed. Albert Mordell. New York: Twayne, 1957.

Leavis, F. R. *The Great Tradition*. London: Chatto & Windus, 1948.

Monypenny, W. F., and G. E. Buckle. *The Life of Benjamin Disraeli*. 6 vols. London: John Murray, 1910–20.

O'Kell, Robert. "The Autobiographical Nature of Disraeli's Early Fiction." *Nineteenth-Century Fiction* 31.3 (Dec. 1976): 253–85.

————. "Disraeli's 'Coningsby': Political Manifesto or Psychological Romance?" *Victorian Studies* 23.1 (Autumn 1979): 57–78.

————. "Two Nations, or One?: Disraeli's Allegorical Romance." *Victorian Studies* 30.2 (Winter 1987): 211–334.

Rabinowitz, Peter J. *Before Reading: Narrative Conventions and the Politics of Interpretation*. Ithaca: Cornell UP, 1987.

Scott, P. H. "The Politics of Sir Walter Scott." *Scott and His Influence*, J. H. Alexander and David Hewit. Eds. Aberdeen: Association for Scottish Literary Studies, 1983. 208–17.

Scott, Sir Walter. *The Letters of Sir Walter Scott*. 12 vols. Ed. H. J. C. Grierson. London: Constable, 1932–37.

Stephen, Leslie. *Hours in a Library*. New Edition. 4 vols. New York: Putnam's, 1904.

Stone, Donald D. *The Romantic Impulse in Victorian Fiction*. Cambridge: Harvard UP, 1980.

Strachey, Lytton. *Eminent Victorians*. Harmondsworth: Penguin, 1971.

Van Ghent, Dorothy. *The English Novel: Form and Function*. New York: Harper & Row, 1961.

Williams, Ioan, ed. *Sir Walter Scott on Novelists and Fiction*. London: Routledge & Kegan Paul, 1968.

Woodward, Sir Llewelling. *The Age of Reform: 1815–1870*. 2nd ed. Oxford: Oxford UP, 1971.

A Kindred Writer:
Dickens in Russia, 1840–1990

Julia Palievsky and Dmitry Urnov

This essay examines the extraordinary popularity of Dickens in Russia. It covers translations, literary criticism, and theater productions from the 1840s to the end of the Soviet era. The major focus is on the interest in Dickens by Russia's foremost writers: Gogol, Turgenev, Tolstoy, Dostoevsky, Chekhov, Gorky, and Bulgakov. None of them was immune to Dickens, and their reading of his works manifested itself in such Russian classics as Dead Souls, Sportsman's Sketches, The Insulted and Injured, The Idiot, The Resurrection, *and* The Lower Depths.

> For a long time, on anything going "contrary" in the public or private direction with him, he would tell me he had ordered his portmanteau to be packed for the more sympathizing and congenial climate of "the remotest parts of Siberia."
> —John Forster, *The Life of Charles Dickens*

It was a letter from a Russian translator that initially prompted this kind of response by Dickens. In that letter, one of the first interpreters of Dickens in Russia wrote about his fame spreading "from the banks of the Neva to the remotest parts of Siberia," whereby the mere name Dickens "enjoyed a wide celebrity" (Forster 77). The letter was written in 1848 after the first translations of the complete texts of *The Posthumous Papers of the Pickwick Club* and *Dombey and Son* were made. Starting in the late 1840s and throughout the following hundred and fifty years, in spite of the variable ideological and literary climate in the country, Dickens's status as the greatest English novelist was unequivocally recognized. With the sole exception of Shakespeare, no other English author ever received as much attention on the part of critics, writers, and the broad reading public.

What follows is a brief survey of only a few major aspects of the broad and multifaceted subject "Dickens in Russia." The essay is based, first and foremost, on the work done by two Russian scholars: Academician Mikhail P. Alekseev (1896–1981) and Dr. Igor M. Katarsky (1919–1971.) Their comprehensive and thorough research covered the history of translations and critical interpretations of Charles Dickens in Russia from the late 1830s through the early 1960s and Dickens's influence on Russian writers, as well as Russian readers' responses to Dickens's work. In this essay we have also attempted to give credit to other Russian scholars who have worked in the field.

Dickens came to be known in Russia early enough. In the late 1830s, after the writer's name was mentioned several times in the press, an abridged version of *The Posthumous Papers of the Pickwick Club* was published by the journal *Sin Otechestva*. Soon after, two other periodicals, *Otechestvennie Zapiski* and *Biblioteka dlya Chteniya*, serialized *Nicholas Nickleby*, *Oliver Twist*, *Barnaby Rudge*, *The Old Curiosity Shop*, and *Martin Chuzzlewit*. Abridged and stylistically inadequate as these translations were, they familiarized Russian readers with the work of their great contemporary. Within two or three months of the publication of any new Dickens novel in his homeland, its translation into Russian appeared. Moreover, for those readers who knew English the original text of some of these novels was run concurrently with their Russian translation.

The popularity of Dickens in Russia increased dramatically with the translation in 1847 of *Dombey and Son* and, somewhat later, of *Nicholas Nickleby*. The translator was Irinarkh Vvedensky (1813–1855), whose letter to Charles Dickens is quoted above. Probably because John Forster did not know the Russian language, he inadvertently made a symbolic spelling mistake by referring to the man as "the good Vredensky," thus linking the name to the Russian word "vred" that is, "harm." Although one can hardly question Vvedensky's role in promoting Dickens's fame in Russia, some harm was also done. In an attempt to make the English writer more accessible to his Russian readers, the translator needlessly russified the originals by inserting uniquely Russian phenomena and even adding passages of his own creation. Mistakes, cuts, and interpolations occur on every other page, and yet the Russian reading public accepted these translations as "the true Dickens." They laughed and cried over Dickens as presented to them by Vvedensky—the outstanding proof of the effectiveness of these free translations. In a sense, Vvedensky's achievement can be compared to that of Constance Garnett. Notwithstanding the cuts and the liberties that she took with the texts, Garnett created the "English" Tolstoy, Turgenev, Dostoevsky, and

Chekhov; similarly, the most fastidious critics of Vvedensky's translations had to admit that he managed to make Dickens part of an indispensable and enjoyable reading experience for every educated Russian.

The singular emotional appeal that Dickens evoked in Russians since his first works were published in the country never showed any signs of decline. "A kindred writer"—Russian authors, scholars, and critics with divergent philosophical and political views use these words over and over again whenever they mention the unflagging popularity of the writer. At the beginning of the twentieth century, during the so-called "Russian craze," D. P. Mirsky, while lecturing in England, said, "People are not good or bad; they are only more or less unhappy and deserving sympathy—this may be taken as the formula of all the Russian novelists" (179). To this, one could add that in the eyes of Russian readers the "formula" definitely held true for Dickens. Ivan Shmelyov (1873–1950), when asked what it was that he loved about Dickens, spoke for all Russians when he said "compassion" (Sorokina 336). The utterly emotional sympathy for "the insulted and injured," to use Dostoevsky's title, which Russians treasured in their own literature was what attracted them to Dickens and turned him into "a kindred writer," in many ways closer to them than any other English novelist, past or present.

The perception of an artist or writer in Russia had always had at its core the view that literature and the arts in general are nothing less than vehicles for approaching the Truth itself. Inherited from German Idealism of the first decades of the nineteenth century, it became a widespread idea among Russian intellectuals and has retained its viability till now. "Works of art should not entertain or moralize but display the Truth," wrote the acknowledged intellectual leader of his time, Vissarion Belinsky (9: 434).[1] By no means did he try to diminish the role of the entertaining or the didactic elements in literature. What he meant was that, for literature to provide a unique, superior understanding of life, all narrative means must be subordinated to one goal: the comprehension of the Truth.

It should be noted that, in Russia, an additional factor came into play whenever a work of literature was being discussed. Because of the pervasive political control and limited public discourse, the role of literature as a social medium came into prominence and acquired immense significance. "The reason why literature exercises such an influence in Russia is self-evident. There is no open political life, and with the exception of a few years at the time of the abolition of serfdom, the Russian people have never been called upon to take an active part in the framing of their country's institutions," Prince Pyotr Kropotkin stated in 1905 while addressing an American audience (vi). Long before that, Alexander Pushkin, in his poem "The Prophet," couched in a succinct and powerful way the writer's mission in the world: "On sea and land thy task fulfill/to burn men's hearts with Heaven's word" (106, lines 29–30).

Disagreements among Russian literary critics emerged when a question was bound to arise as to what kind of truth "Heaven's word" should reveal. An answer to this question shaped, to a large extent, the opinion of Russian critics about Charles Dickens. The proponent of antiliberalism Appolon A. Grigoriev (1822–1864) welcomed Dickens's world—"a happy, poetic idyll, filled with whimsical fantasy, down-to-earth look at things, and humor which brings tears to your eyes" (Katarsky 140). This down-to-earth look, according to Grigoriev, levels out life's glaring contradictions. A position like that was unacceptable to Russian progressives, who rejected Dickens's benevolent outlook toward, or his sentimental portrayal of, the "respectable bourgeoisie." Belinsky, with all his appreciation of the novel *Dombey and Son*, nonetheless expressed regret that Dickens was closer to Sir Walter Scott than to Byron. In other words, instead of protest, or *Sturm und Drang*, Dickens, as Belinsky saw him, was inclined to reconcile himself to the philistine prose of life. But herein lies a paradox, which Belinsky could not miss seeing in Dickens: no one else but this English novelist, with his unsurpassed mastery, portrayed social evils which devastate and maim human lives, and Belinsky had to acknowledge that.

This particular train of thought was followed by Belinsky's contemporary, the first prominent Russian political émigré, Alexander Herzen (1812–1870). His life in Dickensian London provided him with first-hand experience of the writer's grotesque characters, or "caricatures," as Herzen called them. There he discerned a frustrating outcome of social progress that brought about dehumanization, noticeably present in Dickens's "caricatures." Herzen wrote, "There is a stumbling block that no bow or brush or chisel could ever overcome, and art, in order to camouflage its failure, mocks at it by creating caricatures. This stumbling block is philistinism" (136). In other words, Dickens idealizes something that by definition cannot be idealized. The opinion was formulated early enough by radical Russian critics and political thinkers, and it remained in the center of polemics surrounding Dickens's work well into the twentieth century. The argument acquired ultimate topical significance with the establishment in Russia of "the first state of workers and peasants" and the subsequent rejection of all that was related to the bourgeois ideology of the past.

Irrespective of any divergences in ideological standpoints of Russian scholars, there was one more aspect of Dickens's work that appealed to practically all of them. It went back to Johann Herder's *Der Volkische Geist*, and in Russian was rendered by the term *narodnost'*—a derivative of the word *narod* (people)—a distinctive national quality intrinsically present in art and specifically in literature. "In the 1840s both Slavophiles and Westernizers demanded *narodnost'* of Russian literature, but defined it differently, the former seeing it in Russia's Orthodox heritage and communal spirit (sobornost'), the latter believing that the Russian national spirit, having embraced Western civilization, was now in the process of creating its own national version of that civilization" (*Handbook of Russian Literature* 293). But whatever was the case, *narodnost'* served as one of the basic criteria in the evaluation of any work of literary art.

Of all Western writers, it was Dickens who served as an example of true *narodnost'* to Alexander Ostrovsky, often referred to as "The Russian Shakespeare." While trying to avoid the extremes of both approaches to the concept of *narodnost'*, Ostrovsky wrote, in connection with the novel *Dombey and Son*, "All Dickens's works show clearly that he knows his native land and that he has thoroughly and painstakingly scrutinized every detail of it. In order to be a people's writer, it is not enough to love one's land since love can give energy and feeling, but it cannot provide content. Therefore, it is necessary to have a proficient knowledge of the people, understand their concerns, become really close to them" (137). Perusal and comprehension, plus feeling, become a precondition of creating fictional characters who, like Mr. Dombey or Ostrovsky's own Mr. Dombeys—Russian merchants and entrepreneurs—are lifelike figures who eventually reach, in both countries, the status of household names.

Not a single Russian writer, from Gogol to Chekhov, remained immune to Dickens. The reading of Dickens manifests itself in major Russian classics such as *Dead Souls*, *Sportsman's Sketches*, *The Insulted and Injured*, *Crime and Punishment*, *The Idiot*, *The Resurrection*, and *The Lower Depths*.

* * *

In Russia Dickens emerged as a foremost Western writer at the start of a new literary trend that came to be known as Gogolian or Gogolesque. It was named after Nicholai Gogol (1809–1852), the author of *Dead Souls*, *The Inspector General*, and the novella *The Overcoat*. "We all come from Gogol's *Overcoat*," Dostoevsky said, meaning the concern of literature with the country's social reality and the fate of its injured and deprived.

It is impossible to ascertain which of Dickens's works Gogol read and in what language. There is, however, an eyewitness account of *how* he read Dickens. The account was left by the philologist Fyodor Buslaev (1818–1898), who, as a young man, accidentally found himself sitting next to Gogol in Rome, at the café Greco. (Since that time, the café has become a tourist attraction, and the names of its famous visitors, including Gogol and Dickens, were engraved on memorial plaques. In actual fact, the writers could have met at the café, and if they did not, it was by mere chance.) In a remote corner, amid all the noise, writes Buslaev, "hunched over a book, there sat a gentleman who was a stranger to me, and over half an hour, while I was waiting for Panov [Buslaev's friend who knew Gogol], he was so immersed in reading that he did not utter a single word, did not pay the slightest attention to anyone around as if petrified in his own unperturbed concentration. It turned out that I had spent an entire half-hour sitting at the same table with Gogol himself. He was reading something by Dickens" (Katarsky 28). This occurred sometime between 1841 and early 1842, and by that time *The Pickwick Papers*, *Nicholas Nickleby*, and a few of Dickens's stories had been translated into Russian. A year later, the second, final version of *Dead Souls* appeared. It exhibited visible traits of Gogol's reading of Charles Dickens.

The striking similarities between the two writers' narrative techniques and, more generally, between their visions of life, instantly caught the attention of critics and of the reading public in Russia. Some even mistook Dickens's translated texts for back translations of Gogol's unknown works. Compare the following passages from *Sketches by Boz* and *The Overcoat*, dealing with the theme of "loneliness in a crowd" or "lonely crowds," as it is sometimes called. In Dickens's "Thoughts about People" we see:

> 'Tis strange with how little notice, good, bad, or indifferent, a man may live and die in London. He awakens no sympathy in the breast of any single person; his existence is a matter of interest to no one save himself; he cannot be said to be forgotten when he dies, for no one remembered him when he was alive. There is a numerous class of people in this great metropolis who seems not to possess a single friend, and whom nobody appears to care for.
>
> (229)

Now, in Gogol:

> And Petersburg was left without Akakii Akakyevich, as if he had never been therein. There vanished and disappeared a being protected by none, endeared to no one, of no interest to anyone. . . .
>
> (*The Overcoat* 227)

There is a remote possibility that Gogol may have read *Sketches by Boz* in the original when it was published in 1839, but because of his early death in 1852, he never read *The Mystery of Edwin Drood*. Nonetheless, there are in Gogol's *Dead Souls* and in Dickens's last work some passages that seem like almost verbatim restatements of one another. Here is, for instance, how Gogol in *Dead Souls* describes Sobakevich's looks:

> We know there are many such faces in the world to whose symmetry nature has paid little heed, disdaining the use of any such fine tools as files or gimlets, and the like, having simply gone about it straight from the shoulder: one swing of the axe and the nose would appear, another and the lips, one turn of the drill and the eyes would emerge, and so, without any finish, nature will cast this product out into the world: "He lives!"
>
> (96–97; ch. 5)

And here is a description of Mr. Grewgious in *The Mystery of Edwin Drood*:

The little play of feature that his face presented, was cut deep into it, in a few hard curves that made it more like work; and he had certain notches in his forehead, which looked as though Nature had been about to touch them into sensibility or refinement, when she had impatiently thrown away the chisel and said: "I really cannot be worried to finish off this man; let him go as he is."

(109–10; ch. 9)

No reverse influence could be considered here, since an abridged and free translation of *Dead Souls*, published in England in 1854 under the title *Home Life in Russia*, did not include a description of Sobakevich's looks. Therefore, it seems a tenable proposition to interpret this and some stylistically similar passages, like the ones quoted above, in terms of what Victor Vinogradov called "similar points of stylistic orientation" (10).

The second version of *Dead Souls*, which exhibits notable traits of Dickensian influence, showed that Gogol with greater determination was now moving in the direction that initially was at the core of his artistic identity. It looked as if Dickens made Gogol seek even greater expressivity of every narrative detail, whether it was a description of a human face, any object, or a character's state of mind. The narrative was filled with realistic details, which, naturally, caused the utmost indignation in conservative critics, who branded them as "dirty trifles" and "disgusting particulars." This harsh and hostile criticism proved that Gogol had indeed achieved his goal of creating a world in which the meaning of every detail and every object, as if put under a magnifying glass, reached enormous proportions, transcending its appearance.

"Let us point, as an example, to Chichikov's servant, who brings with him his disgusting stink wherever he goes," one resentful critic wrote. He was appalled at Gogol's describing a drop falling from a boy's nose into his soup, the fleas in a puppy's coat, a slit below the waist on a woman's dress, Plushkin's old tooth-pick, Chichikov sleeping naked and plucking hairs from his nostrils, a baker . . . , but here the critic stopped, as if unable to continue, suffocated by his indignation (qtd. in *Polnoe sobranie sochineny* Gogol 5: 172). If that wrathful critic had read as closely any work by Dickens, he would have easily produced an equally long list of offensive "dirty details" and "disgusting particulars." For example:

The filthy and miserable appearance of this part of London can hardly be imagined by those (and there are many such) who have not witnessed it. Wretched houses with broken windows patched with rags and paper: every room let out to a different family, and in many instances to two or even three; fruit and 'sweet-stuff' manufacturers in the cellars, barbers and red-herring vendors in the front parlors, cobblers in the back; a bird-fancier in the first floor, three families on the second, starvation in the attics, Irishmen in the passage; a 'musician' in the front kitchen, and a charwoman and five hungry children in the back one—filth everywhere—a gutter before the houses and a drain behind them—clothes drying and slops emptying, from the windows; girls of fourteen or fifteen, with matted hair, walking about barefooted, and in white great-coats, almost their only covering; boys all ages, in coats of all sizes and no coats at all; men and women, in every variety of scanty and dirty apparel, lounging, scolding, drinking, smoking, squabbling, fighting, and swearing.

(*Sketches by Boz* 196)

"Dickens breathes life even into inanimate things," Leo Tolstoy said (Mako-vitsky 143). With no reservations the same could be said about Nicholai Gogol. In the Dickensian-Gogolian world, anything and everything turns into an object worthy of representation, and because it appeals to all our senses, we are beguiled with an illusion that we are not just reading *about* life, but are in the midst of a tangible reality.

* * *

Turgenev's *A Sportsman's Sketches* was published sixteen years after *The Posthumous Papers of the Pickwick Club*. In Russian the titles of the two books sounded similar, since in both of them the first key word was "zapiski" that is, notes, sketches, or papers. The similarity of the titles reflected the underlying likeness of genre of these two works.

There is no doubt that Turgenev was familiar with various English *Papers*, *Notes* and *Sketches*, including *Notes of a Hunter*. But Dickens's *Pickwick Papers*, as well as his *Sketches by Boz*, made the genre of pseudo-notes and loose sketches really famous. Just as *The Tragedy of Hamlet*, *The Adventures of Robinson Crusoe*, and *Gulliver's Travels* became the quintessential representatives of their respective genres, *Pickwick Papers*, emerging on top of the wave of works created in the same vein, remains the unique work representing its genre.

The success of *Pickwick* gave Turgenev an idea of a narrative held together by, but not dealing with, the characters' occupations. We learn next to nothing about the findings or "investigations" of the members of the Pickwick Club, and Turgenev's *A Sportsman's Sketches*, sometimes translated as *Notes of a Hunter*, is not about hunting.

The Pickwickians' love of knowledge brings them to experience adventures somewhat incompatible with the position of respectable English gentlemen and to face sides of life they could hardly imagine existed. Similarly, the narrator in *A Sportsman's Sketches*, enjoying a pursuit typical of a Russian nobleman with little initial knowledge of his serfs' lives, gradually and consistently acquaints the reader with the plight of the Russian peasantry.

The structural principle of both books enabled Dickens, and Turgenev after him, to portray whatever got into the focus of their attention and to approach social issues in a natural, unobtrusive way. The seeming casualness of narrative made it all the more impressive.

Mr. Pickwick's very first adventure puzzles him and ends almost in disaster. "What!" exclaims Mr. Pickwick when he learns that the cabman keeps his horse harnessed for two or three weeks: otherwise the cabman's horse would fall down "on account of his veekness" (29; ch. 2). Dickens's humor in the episode does not mitigate the power of the implication. Mr. Pickwick had certainly hired a cab before, but it seems that he was totally unaware of the fact that not only horses, but some people toil long hours with yokes on their necks. Before his incarceration in Fleet prison did he have any idea of what human misery and suffering really are?

A Sportsman's Sketches, notwithstanding the Russian names, from the start sets a familiar Dickensian note:

> Anyone who has chanced to pass from the Bolhovsky district into the Zhizdrinsky district, must have been impressed by the striking difference between the race of people in the province of Orel and the population of the province of Kaluga. The peasant of Orel is not tall, is bent in figure, sullen and suspicious in his looks; he lives in wretched little hovels of aspen-wood, labors as a serf in the fields, and engages in no kind of trading, is miserably fed, and wears slippers of bast: the rent-paying peasant of Kaluga lives in roomy cottages of pine-wood; he is tall, bold, and cheerful in his looks, neat and clean of countenance; he carries on a trade in butter and tar, and on holidays he wears boots. The village of the Orel province (we are speaking now of the eastern part of the province) is usually situated in the midst of ploughed fields, near a water-course which has been converted into a filthy pool. Except for a few of the ever-accommodating willows, and two or three gaunt birch-trees, you do not see a tree for a mile round; hut is huddled up against hut, their roofs covered with rotting thatch.
>
> (1–2)

In his preface to the 1847 edition of *Pickwick Papers*—the year of the publication of the first story from *A Sportsman's Sketches*—Dickens, without attributing to himself the role of a social reformer, nonetheless seemed to establish some sort of an indirect connection between social changes that occurred after the publication of *Pickwick*, such as pulling down the notorious Fleet prison, and the book itself. Because of censorship, Turgenev could not give reasons for the striking difference in the lives of the peasants in two neighboring districts, while in fact it was the difference in the position of a serf who had to work for his landlord three, four, and, during the harvest, six days a week, and the peasant, who only paid *obrok*, a rent in kind or money. Turgenev owned 450 serfs in the Zhizdrinsky district of the province of Kaluga, and with serfdom being a universal law in the country, he let his peasants pay *obrok* of less than half the norm. As a young student Turgenev had sworn "Hannibal's Oath" to conquer his enemy—the lawfulness of serfdom in Russia; his *Sketches* did contribute to the abolition of this social evil.

Turgenev was reading Dickens, novel after novel. The proof is his extensive correspondence, which does not contain a detailed analysis of Dickens's works but suggests this writer's supreme position among all foreign authors (4: 303, 392, and *passim*). Not only was Turgenev an enthusiastic reader of Dickens; he was a rapt listener, too. He attended several of Dickens's readings, and they filled him, in his own words, with "childlike glee." When finding fault with any other writer, Turgenev would add that *even* in Dickens himself it would not have been acceptable. Thus, the English master was held as a *metre etalon*, and no minor weakness—in Turgenev's view, not even Dickens's excessive sentimentality—could overshadow the significance of Charles Dickens (Katarsky 12, 285, 289).

"The English writer (of our day) of whom I remember to have heard him [Turgenev] speak with most admiration was Dickens, of whose faults he was conscious, but whose power of presenting to the eye a vivid, salient figure he rated very high," Henry James wrote in 1903 in his long and laudatory essay about Turgenev (136–37). Turgenev's contemporaries made many similar remarks.

Of all the major Russian writers, Ivan Turgenev was the only one who personally knew Dickens; in 1855 Dickens included in his *Household Words* translations of three stories from Turgenev's *A Sportsman's Sketches*. It remains unknown how many times they saw each other, but the relationship must have been close enough for Dickens to share with the Russian writer some circumstances of his family drama. Turgenev's friend recorded his story of seeing Dickens in London in the spring of 1858 or 1859:

> Well, indeed, I saw him, but I found him utterly distraught. As I could conclude from his words, a grief had struck his family. Can you imagine that this wonderful man, who was also a rare husband, is divorcing his wife? It's incomprehensible to me what on earth could happen after so many long and happy years of their married life; we both were so terrified that I hastily left him.
>
> (Katarsky 323)

The memoir is remarkable in the apparent ambiguity of the situation: Turgenev's lack of knowledge of the circumstances of the family drama and Dickens's readiness to share them openly with his Russian friend.

Turgenev welcomed the development in Russia of both the Dickensian novel and also the George Sand type of novel. Yet again, out of censorship considerations, he could not expand on this theme, though it was clear that he meant novels dealing with momentous social issues of the time. On one occasion, Turgenev had to defend Dickens against the attacks of Russian men of letters who were planning to set up a Literary Organization similar to England's Royal Literary Fund. A rumor was spread that Dickens was against the English Fund because it allegedly charged too much money for financial support to writers in need. Turgenev, who had been present at the meeting, clarified the issue. Yes, Dickens was critical of the activities of the Fund, but from an altogether different standpoint. The Fund provided little help to needy writers, while wasting its ample means on supporting its own bureaucracy.

Turgenev did not have to defend Dickens against Leo Tolstoy, whose attitude towards Dickens was that of profound reverence, but when Tolstoy after his short trip to England made some critical remarks about the English, Turgenev wrote to him, "It seems to me that you probably did not have a chance or time enough to reach to that warm current which manifests itself in so many characters of Dickens's novels and which is flowing deeply down there, in people's soil and in every Englishman" (*Polnoe sobranie pisem* 4: 303).

* * *

"There he is, sitting in my room, waiting for me. How good it is!" (Makovitsky 25). Tolstoy was referring to Dickens's portrait in his study, the only portrait of a writer among many family photographs that were there, in Tolstoy's estate, Yasnaya Polyana. The room with Dickens's portrait served as Tolstoy's study from 1856 through 1862, after the publication of *Childhood*, *Boyhood*, and *Youth*, the works which carry the imprint of reading Dickens, and again in his last years, from 1902 till 1910. At that time, while citing the books that produced the strongest impression on him, out of all his reading experiences, Tolstoy named *David Copperfield*.

Like most nineteenth-century Russian authors, Tolstoy was a lifelong, indefatigable reader. Russian writers were assimilating great traditions of Western literature, and Tolstoy, who read with educational and professional aims in mind, was in this sense an unequaled model. It did not take much time for his reading of Western masters to affect his own writing, but Tolstoy did not fear any accusations of imitation. Nor did his critics or readers, including the English reading public, ever accuse him of such practice. Even when, in a few instances, Tolstoy's text seemed to follow too closely that of Dickens, such as the opening lines of *The Resurrection* and of *Bleak House*, with Tolstoy the same words acquired his own, Tolstoyan sense and significance.

"He influenced me greatly, he was my favorite writer, I reread him several times," Tolstoy said about Dickens (Elpatievsky 30). Tolstoy was reading and rereading Dickens in translation and in the original throughout his entire life. He revered Dickens as a young man, not yet confident of his own writing talent, and in his later years, as a world-renowned literary and moral authority. In Dickens, Tolstoy sought and found the realization of the artistic goals that he himself was striving for. He called Truth his sole hero, and he found that Truth in Dickens. For Tolstoy, Dickens embodied a maximum approximation to the ideal that Tolstoy expected of literature: a unity of the aesthetic and the moral, the secular and the religious, the means and meaning of art.

An incomplete list of Dickens's works that Tolstoy read includes *The Pickwick Papers*, *The Mudfog Papers*, *David Copperfield*, *A Tale of Two Cities*, *The Old Curiosity Shop*, *Oliver Twist*, *Dombey and Son*, *Bleak House*, *Little Dorrit*, *Our Mutual Friend*, *Great Expectations*, *The Mystery of Edwin Drood*, *The Chimes*, and *A Child's History of England* (Apostolov 71–84). In the early 1900s, summarizing his life's reading experiences, he said, "If you sift the world's prose literature, Dickens will remain, sift Dickens, *David Copperfield* will remain, sift *David Copperfield*, the description of the storm at sea will remain" (Maude 125). For Tolstoy there was obviously something absolutely unique about that fifteen-page-long chapter which made him not just quote it at the end of his life, but single it out of all world prose literature.

David Copperfield, in Vvedensky's translation, was published in 1853. At the time, Tolstoy was in the Caucasus, in the army. In November of the same year he writes to his brother, "Send me Dickens—*David Copperfield*—in English." It seems he may have already read the translation. Early the next year, Tolstoy is heading towards his new destination, the Danube army. On this journey, he visits his Yasnaya Polyana estate and then leaves for Bucharest. All this time he is thinking over the conception of his new novella, *The Snowstorm*. At the same time, he is probing and thinking over some other ideas, each of which could determine his further development as a writer. He makes the following entry in his diary, "At present an interest in particulars of feeling is replaced by the interest in particulars of the events themselves" (*Sobranie sochineny* 65: 329).

In *The Snowstorm* the storyline is in fact the story of the narrator's concern with, anxiety about, and awe of the power of nature, until finally his hallucinations, with an ever-increasing speed, flood his imagination. Thus, every change in the flow of events is presented through a description of the narrator's feelings, just as in David Copperfield's story of the storm in chapter 55, which Tolstoy regarded as the greatest scene in world literature:

> For years after it [the storm] occurred, I dreamed of it often. I have started up so vividly impressed by it, that its fury has yet seemed raging in my quiet room, in the still night. I dream of it sometimes, though at lengthened and uncertain intervals, to this hour. I have an association between it and a stormy wind, or the lightest mention of a sea-shore, as strong as any of which my mind is conscious. As plainly as I behold what happened, I will try to write it down. I do not recall it, but see it done; for it happens again before me.
>
> (380)

According to his own words, Tolstoy wrote "from the heart," whether it was describing an emotional experience of the young Nicholenka Irteniev in his autobiographical trilogy, the thoughts of the wounded Prince Bolkonsky on the field of Austerlitz, "the inward work" by Pierre Bezukhov during his captivity in *War and Peace*, or Dmitry Nechludov's pangs of guilty conscience in the court trial scene from *The Resurrection*. Gogol, as if putting every object under a magnifying glass, was creating, not without Dickensian influence, grotesque images, whereas Tolstoy, while holding Dickens as his ideal of a writer, remained within the limits of natural verisimilitude.

Using Tolstoy's method of "sifting," one could single out chapter 12 from the novel *Dombey and Son*. It describes the pernicious effects of forced "education" and the miraculous results of teaching "by that most wonderful of masters, love" (165). Tolstoy read *Dombey and Son* and was familiar with chapter 12. Not only did he read it, but he most likely heard it read by Dickens himself.

It seems, therefore, somewhat surprising that, according to one memoir, he did not like Dickens's "lecture on education." (The following discussion of Tolstoy's response to Dickens's reading is partially based on the project of James Epstein, Dmitry Urnov's graduate student at Adelphi University.)

"Tolstoy was present at Dickens's lecture on education" (Tolstoy, *Sobranie sochineny* 48: 451), but for a while it remained unclear what exactly Tolstoy had heard during his brief stay in England, because Dickens did not give any lectures during that time. Comparing the dates of Dickens's readings with the time of Tolstoy's sojourn made it possible to come to the conclusion that on March 22, 1861, at St. James Hall, Piccadilly, Tolstoy heard Dickens reading his "story of Little Dombey" (Lucas 34–36). Some biographers argue that Dickens was reading from *A Christmas Carol* (Wilson 160–61), but the dates and the topic indicate that in all probability Dickens's "lecture" was about the schooling of Dombey's son.

As is known, Tolstoy was a strong opponent of coercive education, whereby teaching is forced upon the student, weans him from the beliefs and habits of his parents' culture, and transforms him into the image of his instructor. Tolstoy cited boarding schools in particular as examples of institutions that alienate the child from his culture, which alone can provide a solid base for a child's development into a worthy human being: "A child who is compelled to sit motionless at his book for the period of six hours, studying the whole day that which he ought to learn in half an hour, is artificially trained in the most complete and most baneful idleness" (*Sobranie sochineny* 10: 525).

Tolstoy's criticism of the stifling atmosphere with which he associates "education" could very well serve as a description of Dr. Blimber's educational institution. The boarding school for "young gentlemen" is an establishment where there is nothing but learning going on from morning to night. "In fact, Doctor Blimber's establishment was a great hothouse in which there was a forcing apparatus at work. All the boys blew before their time," Dickens writes, in *Dombey and Son*, and further on, "Nature was of no consequence at all" (141; ch. 11).

Dickens inherited from Rousseau the concept of original innocence, and Tolstoy's indebtedness to Rousseau is equally known. "Man is born perfect" and "For the most part educators forget that the child's age is the prototype of harmony" (Tolstoy, *Sobranie sochineny* 10: 526). To preserve this harmony and enhance one's ability to comprehend truth, beauty, and goodness, a child's development must not be artificially accelerated. It seems that in respect to this issue both writers were in fundamental agreement and voiced similar concerns.

When young Paul is introduced to Dr. Blimber, the latter rhetorically asks Mr. Dombey, "Shall we make a man of him?" Paul's response to Dr. Blimber's query concisely captures the essence of Tolstoy's pedagogical beliefs: "I had rather be a child" (*Dombey and Son* 145; ch. 11). Dickens's Mr. Toots, the most senior of Dr. Blimber's charges, is the fictional counterpart to Tolstoy's hypothetical child. Years of relentless routine and drilling have driven him into a state resembling premature senility. He registers surprise when Paul claims to "think about a great many things" (167; ch. 12), since Toots himself is no longer capable of independent thought and wiles away the hours indulging in writing pointless letters to himself.

Although Dickens presents a thorough, well-realized portrait of the system of forced education, it is probable that from Tolstoy's point of view he did not pay enough attention to moral coercion or the influence of Dr. Blimber's school education on Paul Dombey's character. At the time the boy enters the school, he is described as a delicate, quiet, and dreamy child. In the course of the so-called education, he "retained all that was strange, and old, and thoughtful in his character: under circumstances so favorable to the development of those tendencies, became even more strange, and old, and thoughtful, than before" (184–85; ch. 14). Continuing in this vein, Cornelia's "character analysis" laments his "singularity" because his nature is resistant to change (her influence).

In spite of all those minor differences in the writers' thinking about what can be right and wrong in a child's education, there is still that basic similarity between Dickens's and Tolstoy's views. A careful comparative reading of the relevant passages from *Dombey and Son* and Tolstoy's pedagogical writings offers compelling evidence that Tolstoy was indeed engaging in and reacting to the ideas that underlay Dickens's reading.

Given the lofty status Tolstoy accorded Dickens, it is possible to assume that Tolstoy's initial response to Dickens's reading was affected by his insufficient knowledge of the English language: "At the time I could hardly understand spoken English, my knowledge of the language was just theoretical." This is how Tolstoy accounted for his first impression (Makovitsky 134). Nonetheless, in contrast to Tolstoy's alleged early disappointment with Dickens's "lecture," there exist reliable recorded accounts of how he, in later years, remembered Dickens's "excellent reading," and "what a powerful impression the writer produced by his fit and strong figure" (*Tolstoy v vospominaniyakh sovremennikov* 2: 126–27). The interlocutor who left the memoir pinpoints Tolstoy's detailed knowledge of Dickens's texts, as well as his fascination with Dickens's magnificent graphic descriptions and with the writer's ability to arouse compassion for the weak and the poor.

During the same conversation Tolstoy said that he kept rereading Dickens in the original; therefore his words about Dickens's "excellent reading" reflect an opinion of a writer who was well acquainted with Dickens's works and not his possible spontaneous impression of "the lecture" in London. "Dickens is the kind of genius that is born once in a hundred years" (*Tolstoy v vospominaniyakh sovremennikov* 2: 126–27). These words, which Tolstoy uttered close to the end of his life, may be taken as the summation of his opinion about Dickens.

* * *

"When I get tired and feel dissatisfied with myself, nobody can set my mind at rest and gladden my heart better than this world writer," Dostoevsky said about Charles Dickens (Belov 299–300). He read Dickens in Russian and French translations. Torn away from literary life by his imprisonment in Siberia, he managed to read Dickens even in exile.

In his country Fyodor Dostoevsky was sometimes called "the Russian Dickens" (*Letopis'* 3: 162). Similarities between the two writers were defined as common themes of a city with its poorest population, recurrent images of those wronged by life, the weak, the unhappy, and the oppressed, a special love of children, a detailed treatment of emotions, and the tendency to create engaging plots. Russian scholars drew parallels between *Dombey and Son* and *Netochka Nezvanova*, *The Old Curiosity Shop* and *The Insulted and Injured*, and *Great Expectations* and *Crime and Punishment*. They also discerned Dickensian motifs in the novel *The Idiot*.

Dostoevsky never met Dickens, though an account of an alleged meeting got into the pages of a respectable literary journal and understandably attracted scholarly attention. However, not a single biography of the writer, published in Russia or abroad, or the Russian *Letopis' Zhizni i Tvorchestva* (*Annals of Life and Works*) mentions the meeting, and the letter, in which Dostoevsky describes the encounter, has not yet been found. Michael Slater, when referring to the letter in the first edition of his authoritative biography, wrote, "[I]t is fascinating to read Dostoevsky's account of his interview with Dickens at the *All the Year Round* Office in the summer of 1862, with Dickens surely speaking far more freely about himself to a visitor from the non-English speaking world than he would have done to a British or American one" (502). But this reference to the "interview" was later removed by Slater from the paperbound edition of *Charles Dickens*, with the explanation that "the letter purportedly written by Dostoevsky in 1862 describing an interview with Dickens . . . cannot be satisfactorily authenticated" (xvii).

Nevertheless, this literary myth deserves to be analyzed, since it accentuates some real aspects of Dostoevsky's mindset as revealed through his supposed opinion about the English writer. Here is the most revealing passage:

> He [Dickens] told me that all the good simple people in his novels, Little Nell, even the holy simpletons like Barnaby Rudge, are what he wanted to have been, and his villains were what he was (or rather, what he found in himself), his cruelty, his attacks of causeless enmity towards those who were helpless and looked to him for comfort, his shrinking from those whom he ought to love, being used up in what he wrote. There were two people in him, he told me: one who feels as he ought to feel and one who feels the opposite. From the one who feels the opposite I make my evil characters, from the one who feels as a man ought to feel I try to live my life. Only two people? I asked.
>
> (Harvey 233)

In this "letter" Dickens's train of thought is strongly suggestive of Dostoevsky: as is known, the cohabitation of good and evil within the same human being was one of the pervasive themes of his entire work. To what extent it was based on the writer's own personality and life is a different issue and not an easy question to answer. For this reason, the treatment of the subject in the letter attributed to Dostoevsky seems oversimplified. What is known, however, is that Dostoevsky inherited the theme from Gogol, and that in the twentieth century it was further explored by Robert Louis Stevenson, Joseph Conrad, and Graham Greene, to name just a few.

Dickens's three-dimensional figures, who were both good and bad, like Mr. Micawber in *David Copperfield*, were particularly appealing to Dostoevsky. While he regarded *Don Quixote* as the greatest work of literature ever written, the book which mankind could put on the scales of history to justify its very existence, *The Posthumous Papers of the Pickwick Club* belonged to same class of books and was a runner-up, so to speak. "If the virtuous Don Quixote and Mr. Pickwick are appealing to readers as credible characters, this is only because they are comic figures," Dostoevsky wrote (*Sobranie Sochineny* 9: 239–40). He borrowed the principle of chiaroscuro, of light and shade, from Cervantes and Dickens, in order to create his own positive character, a Christ-like figure in the novel *The Idiot*. Prince Myshkin is not a comic figure, but a sick man and therefore a credible character.

Dostoevsky "digested" Dickens to such an extent that he was able to claim, "I am sure that in the Russian language we understand Dickens almost as well as the English do, probably even with all the nuances" (*Sobranie Sochineny* 11: 71) This consummate understanding of Dickens "with all the nuances" helped Dostoevsky create his own characters of the disadvantaged and the poor. "Remember The Bleeding Heart Yard [in *Little Dorrit*, London's poorest place of habitation]?" Vasiliy V. Rozanov inquired in his essay *Dickens*. "It seems to me that Dostoevsky copied all his 'insulted,' 'injured,' and 'poor folk' from here" (335). Dostoevsky "copied" from life, being familiar with the existence of the poor better than most nineteenth-century writers. On the other hand, there can be no denying that when introducing those characters he fell under the spell of Charles Dickens, and this manifested itself in the disturbing realism of graphic details and in sheer sentimentality.

* * *

For Chekhov's and Gorky's generation, Dickens was not a contemporary, but a classic writer, standing on a par with Shakespeare, Byron, and Sir Walter Scott. "This man has mastered profoundly the hardest of loves—love of people," Gorky once said about Dickens (214); his own play *The Lower*

Depths was a variation on the motifs found in Dickens's portrayal of Bleeding Heart Yard. Turgenev, Tolstoy, and Dostoevsky, who had professed their admiration for Dickens's expressive imagery, spoke about his ability to describe the feeling of love in a remarkably convincing way, no matter for what or for whom that love was revealed. But their admiration of Dickens ceased to be unreserved when his treatment of love was reduced to tearful sentimentality. In the last analysis, however, the Russian writers held the same opinion: Dickens was an incomparable genius.

In the years preceding Dickens's centennial celebrations and in 1912, a significant number of articles appeared in the Russian press commemorating the occasion. Written by critics of differing ideological trends, these essays had one thing in common: an immensely high assessment of Dickens's works combined with carefully formulated reservations. Typical in this sense was an article by the conservative philosopher and publicist whom we have quoted above, Vasiliy V. Rozanov (D. H. Lawrence's source of apocalyptic visions). Having mentioned a few writers who were then in vogue, Rozanov wrote, "And I am reading and reading . . . Dickens" (Rozanov 334). The ellipsis reveals his wonder at his own willingness to read Dickens in preference to popular novelists of the time. What follows is Rozanov's point-counter-point personal account of what he finds great and not so great in Dickens, as a man and as a writer. Here is a characteristic excerpt from Rozanov's thought-provoking essay that seems to capture the bewildering contradictions of Dickens's literary vision:

> I am reading now for the first time *The Old Curiosity Shop*, and last summer I reread *Little Dorrit*. There is no way I could ever render, no, not my infatuation, but the happy feeling at the bottom of my heart that this summer reading has given and is giving me. The novel is long-winded and has huge flaws. One could hardly stand Flora's two or three ridiculous talks, and there are about eighty of them here. This is simply outrageous! Out of all the characters, only Gowan is a full-fledged figure: an egotistic aristocrat and an amateur artist who finds fault with aristocracy but would probably die if he was not an aristocrat himself. The character, with his ambivalence, is a wonderful, remarkable creation . . .
> When you finish reading, it occurs to you that perhaps all that is somewhat "contrived," and in general the entire story is "contrived." No charming girls like that Little Dorrit, the heroine of the book who gave her name to the novel, exist. But while you are reading, you succumb to the illusion: who knows? Perhaps they do exist? Who could reach the inexhaustible depth of life?
>
> (335)

And further down, "I was thinking about Dickens: poor, poor angel of Europe, her true angel who said such wonderful words to the heart of mankind" (335).

Out of the many articles about Dickens that appeared in Russia in the jubilee year of 1912, two deserve special mention: one by the future People's Commissar of Education, A. V. Lunacharsky (1875–1933), and the other by V. D. Nabokov, the father of Vladimir Nabokov. Both authors developed the familiar theme that had been noticeably present in nineteenth-century Russian criticism of Dickens: his ability to create a host of life-like figures and arouse readers' compassion for the unhappy and the poor. A. V. Lunacharsky wrote: "His [Dickens's] love for all people, especially for those who were ill-treated in some way, is revealed most strongly and forcefully not in his moralizing or proving something, but in his immortal characters whom we love as if they were eccentric relatives from our own childhood whose memories bring a gentle smile to our lips" (5: 198).

The year 1917 saw the publication of a four-volume *History of Western Literature* that contained a lengthy chapter on Dickens in which V. D. Nabokov wrote about "the writer's unique ability to combine thousands of miniscule attributes of life in a viable artistic synthesis and thus enrich the world by creating immortal human characters" (*Istoriya* 4: 241). That was the last word about Dickens to be pronounced on the eve of the birth of the newly formed Soviet Russia.

* * *

Vladimir Lenin did not stay until the end of the Moscow Arts Theater First Studio's production of *The Cricket on the Hearth*. He "was turned off by its philistine sentimentality" (Lenin 295). This typical characteristic of Dickens's writing had "turned off" his critics since the first translations of his works appeared in Russia, but after the revolution "the harmless" *Cricket on the Hearth* was perceived as a work carrying a political statement. The production was originally arranged by Tolstoy's follower Leopold Sulerzhitsky. In the atmosphere of postrevolutionary red terror and the civil war, this stage version of Dickens's novella, with Mikhail Chekhov (the writer's nephew, 1891–1955), as Caleb, radiated kindness and gentle love. In response to this political demonstration, Lenin left, bringing it home to the producer and the actors that their message was not lost on him. In the sphere of arts, however, the leader of the Russian revolution trusted the People's Commissar of Education A. V. Lunacharsky, and the play not only remained in the repertoire, but was even performed for children. In 1922 the theater celebrated the five hundredth performance of *The Cricket on the Hearth*, and it ran until Mikhail Chekhov's emigration in 1928.

In 1934, the Moscow Arts Theater produced *The Pickwick Club* with Mikhail Bulgakov, the coauthor of the stage version, acting in the play. The main roles in the production were performed by the theater's leading actors: Ktorov, Massalsky, Toporkov, Zueva, and others. The production was revived in 1955, and, in keeping with the government policy of bringing classical art to broad masses, it was broadcast all over the country. In 1949, the Moscow Arts Theater staged *Dombey and Son*. The authors of this essay saw the play and remember it as one of their strongest theater experiences.

Speaking about the publication of Dickens's works in the Soviet Union, we must take into account two factors: the existence of the centralized system of the publishing business, which was controlled from above, and the problems of translation. In the 1920s, *Oliver Twist, Nicholas Nickleby*, and *Dombey and Son*, works with more explicit social content, were the first to be published. The old translations of Dickens's novels were regarded as unacceptable, and when Irinarkh Vvedensky's translation of *The Posthumous Papers of the Pickwick Club* was reissued in 1929, it was justifiably criticized. Because there were few publishing houses, and they were state-run, there was competition among translators for the right to translate Dickens, and this inevitably slowed down the entire process. Still, according to M. P. Alekseev's 1946 Bibliographical List, the overall number of copies of Dickens's works issued in Soviet Russia from 1917 to 1936 exceeded 1,100,000 (*Charlz Dikkens* XXIV). By 1941, it was more than two million.

In the 1920s, the philosopher and literary scholar Mikhail Bakhtin, studying Dostoevsky's narrative poetics, conducted a survey of the use of semidirect speech in literature, including the works of Dickens. Bakhtin knew Walter Dibelius's *Englische Romankunst* (1910) and his *Charles Dickens* (1910). The influence of Dibelius's "morphology of the novel" is strongly felt in what Bakhtin was saying about Dostoevsky, although Bakhtin excluded that chapter from his *Problems of Dostoevsky's Poetics* (1929). It was published much later as "From the Prehistory of Novelistic Discourse" and "Discourse in the Novel" in Bakhtin's collection of essays *The Dialogic Imagination*. Bakhtin wrote, "What is present in the novel is an artistic system of languages, or more accurately a system of images of languages, and the real task of stylistic analysis consists in uncovering all the available orchestrating languages in the composition of the novel" (416).

Victor Shklovsky's influential *On the Theory of Prose* (1929), with its detailed analysis of various devices of plot construction, contained numerous references to Charles Dickens.

In 1940, the publishing house Detskaya Literatura, the major Soviet publisher of children's literature, initiated the publication of Dickens's collected works, but only the first four volumes came out before the war began, and the entire project had to be abandoned.

Evgeny Lann's historical novel *Dickens* (1946) was the work of a specialist in English literature whose major aim was to depict the complex relationship between Dickens's life and his writing. Also noteworthy were V. Ivasheva's *Tvorchestvo Dickensa* (*Dickens's Creative Work*, 1954) and T. E. Sylman's *Dickens. Ocherki Tvorchestva* (*Dickens. Essays on His Creative Work*, 1958), two comprehensive monographs by scholars with fundamental academic training.

In 1957–63, the leading state publishing house Goslitizdat issued a thirty-volume edition of Dickens's works (ed. A. A. Anikst, V. Ivasheva, E. Lann) that included the writer's essays and letters. The print run for each volume was 500,000.

Charlz Dikkens. Bibliografiya (*Charles Dickens. Bibliography*), issued in 1962 (ed. M. P. Alekseev), contained hundreds of titles of books, theses, articles about the writer, theater productions and films based on Dickens, and Dickens's works in Russian translations.

One of the major studies of Dickens's work during the Soviet era was Igor Katarsky's *Dickens in Russia: The Middle of the Nineteenth Century* (1966), a monograph which is extensively quoted above. The scholar devoted his entire life to the study of Charles Dickens. The second volume of his research, for which he had collected an enormous amount of material, was never published: he had neither time nor energy to complete it. The effects of a head wound that he received in World War II brought about his untimely death. When Katarsky was hospitalized and his friends and colleagues, Dmitry Urnov among them, came to visit him, Katarsky said, with a kind of Dickensian humor, "They removed parts of my brain, so now I can claim that at least I used to have brains, while some people could hardly say that." In less than a month Katarsky was gone, and Dr. A. A. Elistratova, the Grand Dame of Russian English studies, paid tribute to him in a eulogy, "An endearing crank to accompany Mr. Pickwick."

In 1982–87, Gosltizdat, now called Khudozhestvennaya Literatura, issued a ten-volume collection of works by Dickens. It included his major novels, and the number of copies of each was 200,000. The 1984 print run of *The Posthumous Papers of the Pickwick Club* (1984, trans. A. Krivtzova and E. Lann, intro. Mikhail Urnov) was 1,500,000.

It is worth mentioning that in the 1980s not only were Dickens's works published in hundreds of thousands of copies but he remained the most widely admired English novelist. In 1980 the publisher Moskovskiy Rabochiy issued an autobiographical novel, inspired by Dickens. It was Nelly Morozova's *My Passion for Dickens: Family Chronicle. Twentieth Century*, a story covering the 1930s to the 1950s. The girl's first powerful reading experience is *Great Expectations*: the gloomy atmosphere of the opening pages is similar to her own environment. Dickens accompanies the heroine throughout her entire life. "When I meet a stranger," writes Morozova, "I can always tell whether he has read Dickens or not" (111). Everything that happens to her is related in one way or another to Charles Dickens.

A special mention should be made here of a survey of Russian Dickens studies between the 1970s and 1990s, published in *Dickens Quarterly*. It was compiled by Nina Diakonova (Diakonova 181–86) and contained brief analyses of many important contributions to Dickens's Soviet studies of the 1980s. Among them, Anna Eslistratova's Dickensian chapter in her *Gogol i problemi zapadnoevropeiskogo romana* (*Gogol and Problems of the West-European Novel*, 1972), books by M. P. Tugusheva, N. P. Mikhal'skaya, and others. The author of the survey singles out the book *Taina Charlza Dikkensa* (*The Mystery of Charles*

Dickens, 1990), by E. Yu. Genieva, as a particularly significant publication. Abundantly illustrated, the book, besides giving a full list of Russian translations of Dickens's works issued between 1960 and 1980, includes a list of all Russian publications about Dickens, which was compiled by B. M. Parchevskaya. In addition to that, the book offers a list of Russian works of fiction, tales, and poems in which Dickens is mentioned or presented in one way or another.

In 1990 the publisher Kniga (Book) issued a monograph by Mikhail Urnov (father of one of the current authors), *Nepodrajaemiy. Dickens Redaktor i Izsatel'* (*The Inimitable: Dickens, Editor and Publisher*). The book tells the story of *Household Words* and *All the Year Round* and analyzes Dickens's work in connection with his activities as editor, teacher, and critic. The book abounds in facts little known to Russian readers, such as, for instance, the publication in Dickens's *Houshold Words* of stories from Turgenev's *A Sportsman's Sketches* (Diakonova 184).

Mikhail Urnov's monograph was one of the last, if not *the* last, book on Dickens issued during Soviet times. Soon after, the publishing house ceased to exist, and the USSR itself was transformed into a very different country.

NOTE

1. Here, and *passim*, when no translator's name is indicated, the translation is by the authors of this essay.

WORKS CITED

Apostolov, Nikolay. "Tolstoy and Dickens." *Family Views of Tolstoy*. Ed. Aylmer Maude. Trans. Louise and Aylmer Maude. London: George Allen and Unwin Ltd. 1926, 71–84.

Bakhtin, M[ikhail] M [ikhailovich]. *The Dialogic Imagination. Four Essays*. Ed. Michael Holquist. Trans. Caryl Emerson and Michael Holquist. Austin: U of Texas P, 1990.

Belinsky, V[issarion] G[rigorievich]. *Polnoye sobranie sochineniy*. Tom 9, 12. Moskva: Izdatel'stvo Akademii Nauk SSSR, 1956. (Belinsky V. G. *Complete Works*. Moscow: Soviet Academy of Sciences. Vols. 9, 12, 1956.)

Belov, S[ergey] V[ladimirovich]. *Entsiklopedicheskiy slovar'. F. M. Dostoevsky i ego okrujenie*. Tom 2. SPB: Aleteiya, 2001. (*Encyclopedic Dictionary. F. M. Dostoevsky and his Surroundings*. Vol. 2. Saint Petersburg: Aleteiya, 2001.)

Charlz Dikkens. Ukazatel' vajneishei literatury na russkom yazyke (1838–1945). Sostavila Y. V. Friedlender. Pod redaktsiey i s predisloviem M. P. Alekseeva.

Leningrad: Gosudarstvennaya Publichnaya Biblioteka imeni Satlykova-Shchedrina, 1946. (*Charles Dickens. The List of Major Publications in Russian. 1838–1945.* Comp. by Y. V. Friedlender. Ed. M. P Alekseev. Leningrad: The State Saltykov-Szhedrin Public Library, 1946.)

Charlz Dikkens. Bibliografiya. Sostavili Y. V. Fiedlender i I. M. Katarski. Redaktor I. M. Levidova. Otvetstvenniy redaktor M. P. Alekseev. Moskva: Izdatel'stvo Vsesoyuznoi Knijnoi Palaty, 1962. (*Charles Dickens. Bibliography.* Compiled by Y. V. Friedlender and I. M. Katarsky. Editor I. M. Levidova. General Ed. M. P. Alekseev. Moscow: Book Chamber, 1962.)

Diakonova, Nina. "Russian Dickens Studies, 1970–1995." *Dickens Quarterly* 12 (Dec. 1995): 181–86.

Dickens, Charles. *David Copperfield.* Garden City: Literary Guild of America, 1948.

———. *Dombey and Son.* Oxford: Oxford UP, 1989.

———. *The Mystery of Edwin Drood.* Harmondsworth: Penguin, 1974.

———. *The Pickwick Papers.* New York: Penguin, 1980.

———. *Sketches by Boz.* London: Chapman and Hall, 1889.

Dostoevsky, F[yodor] M[ikhailovich]. *Pis'ma.* Red. A. S. Dolinin Tom 2. Leningrad: Gosudarstvennoe izdatel'stvo, 1928. (*F. M. Dostoevsky. Letters.* Ed. A. C. Dolinin. Vol. 2. State Publishing House: Leningrad, 1928.)

———. *Sobranie Sochineny.* Tom 9, 11. Gosudarstvennoe izdatel'stvo: Moskva-Leningrad. 1929. (Dostoevsky, F. M. *Collected Works.* Moscow-Leningrad. Vols. 9, 11: State Publishing House, 1929.)

Elpatievsky, S[ergei] Ya[kovlevich]. *Literaturnye vospominaniya.* Moskva, 1916. (Elpatievsky, S. Y. *Literary Reminiscences.* Moscow, 1916.)

Epstein, Charles. *Tolstoy at Dickens's Lecture.* Adelphi University (1993) Manuscript.

Forster, John. *The Life of Charles Dickens.* Vol. 2. New York: Scribners, 1900.

Gertzen, A[leksandr]. *Sobranie sochineny v tridtzati tomakh.* Tom 16. Moskva: Akademiya Nauk SSSR. 1959. (A. Herzen, *Collected Works in Thirty Volumes.* Vol. 16. Moscow: Academy of Sciences of the USSR, 1959.)

Gogol, Nikolay. *Dead Souls.* Trans. George Reavey. New York: Norton, 1985.

———. *The Overcoat.* Trans. Bernard Guilbert Guerney. *The Portable Nineteenth Century Russian Reader.* Ed. George Gibian. New York: Penguin, 1993. 202–32.

———. *Polnoe sobranie sochineny v pyati tomakh.* Red. E. Lyatsky. Tom 5. Saint Petersburg: Narodnaya pol'za. 1902. (N. Gogol. *Complete Works in Five Volumes.* Ed. E. Lyatsky. Vol. 5. Saint-Petersburg: Popular Use. 1902.)

Gorky, Maxim. *Sobranie sochineniy. 2-e izd.* Tom 27. Moskva: Gosudarstvennoe izdatelstvo, 1933. (M. Gorky, *Collected Works.* 2nd ed. Vol. 27. Moscow: State Publishing House, 1933.)

Handbook of Russian Literature. Ed. Victor Terras. New Haven: Yale UP, 1984.

Harvey, Stephanie."Dickens's Villans: A Confession and a Suggestion." *The Dickensian.* Spring 2002. No. 456. Vol. 98. 233–35.

Istoriya zapadnoi literatury pod redaktsiey F. D. Batyushkova. Tom 4. Moskva: Mir, 1917. (*A History of Western Literature.* Ed. F. D. Batyushkov. Vol. 4. Moscow: Mir, 1917.)

James, Henry. "Ivan Turgenev." *The Art of Criticism. Henry James on the Theory and the Practice of Fiction.* Eds. William Veeder and Susan M. Griffin. Chicago: Chicago UP, 1986.

Katarsky, I[gor]. *Dikkens v Rossii. Seredina XIX veka.* Moskva: Izdatel'stvo Nauka, 1966. (Katarsky, Igor. *Dickens in Russia. The Middle of the Nineteenth Century.* Moscow: Nauka, 1966.)

Kropotkin, Peter. *Ideals and Realities in Russian Literature.* New York: Knopf, 1915.

Lenin, Vladimir. *Lenin o kulture i iskusstve.* Moskva: Izogiz, 1938. (*Lenin on Culture and Arts.* Moscow: Izogiz, 1938.)

Letopis' jizni i tvorchestva F. M. Dostoevskogo. Sost. S. V. Belov. Tom 3. Sankt -Peterburg: Pushkinsky Dom, 1995. (*Chronicle of Dostoevsky's Life and Work.* Comp. S. V. Belov. Vol. 3. St. Petersburg: Pushkin House, 1995.)

Lucas, Victor. *Tolstoy in London.* London: Evans Brothers, 1979.

Lunacharsky, A[natoliy] V[asilievich]. *Sobranie sochineny v vos'mi tomakh.* Tom 5. Moskva: Khudojestvennaya Literatura, 1965. (A. V. Lunacharsky. *Collected Works in 8 vols.* Moscow: Khudojestvennaya Liteteratura, 1965.)

Makovitsky, Dushan. *Yasnopolyanskie zapiski. 1904–1910.* Redaktor N. Gusev. Vypusk 2. Moskva: Zadruga, 1923. (Makovitsky, Dushan. *Yasnaya Polyana Notes. 1904–1910.* Ed. N. N. Gusev. Issue 2. Moscow: Zadruga, 1923.)

Maude, Aylmer, ed. *Family Views of Tolstoy.* Trans. Aylmer and Louise Maude. London: Allen and Unwin, 1926.

Mirsky, D[mitry P [etrovich]. *A History of Russian Literature from its Beginnings to 1900.* Ed. Francis E. Whitfield. Hammondsworth: Penguin Books, 1958.

Morozova, Nelly. *Moe pristrastie k Dikkensu. Semeynaya khronika.* Moskva: Moskovskiy Rabochiy, 1980. (N. Morozova, *My Passion for Dickens. A Family Chronicle.* Moscow: Moskow Worker P., 1980.)

Ostrovsky A[lexander] N[ikolaevich]. "O romane Dikkensa *Dombi I sin.*" *Polnoe Sobranie Sochineniy.* Tom 13. Moskva: Goslitizdat, 1952. ("On Dickens's novel *Dombey and Son.*" *Complete Works.* Vol. 13. Moscow: Goslitizdat 1952.)

Pushkin, Alexander. *Selected Lyric Poetry.* Trans. and ann. James A. Falen. Evanston, IL: Northwestern UP, 2009.

Rozanov, Vassiliy. "Dikkens." *Rozanovskaya encyclopedia.* Sost. i red. A. N. Nikolyukin. Moskva: ROSSPEN, 2008. ("Dickens." *Rozanov Encyclopedia.* Comp. and ed. A. N. Nikolyukin. Moscow: ROSSPEN, 2008.)

Slater, Michael. *Charles Dickens.* New Haven: Yale UP, 2009.

———. *Charles Dickens.* New Haven: Yale UP, 2011. Paperbound.

Sorokina, Olga. *Moskoviana.* Moskva: Moskovskiy Rabochiy, 1994. (O. Sorokina. *Moscoviana.* Moscow: Moscow Worker P., 1994.)

Tolstoy, Lev. *Pedagigical Articles. Linen-Measurer.* Trans. Leo Wiener. London: J. M. Dent, 1904.

———. *Sobranie sochineny v devyanosta tomakh.* Kommentrarii E. V. Molostova i N. R. Rodionov. Moskva: Goslitizdat, 1952. (Leo Tolstoy. *Collected Works in Ninety Volumes.* Comm. E. V. Molostova and N. R. Rodionov. Moscow: Goslitizdat, 1952.)

Tolstoy v vospominaniyakh sovremennikov. Sost. K. N. Lomunov. Moskva: Goslitizdat. Tom 2. 1960. (*Tolstoy as Remembered by His Contemporaries.* Comp. K. Lomunov. Moscow: Goslitizdat. Vol. 2. 1960.)

Turgenev, Ivan "A Sportsman's Sketches." *The Novels of Ivan Turgenev.* Vol. 1, Trans. Constance Garnet. London: Heinemann, 1906.

———. *Polnoe sobranie pisem.* Tom 4. Moskva: Nauka, 1987. (*Complete Letters.* Vol. 4. Moscow: Nauka, 1987.)

Urnov, Mikhail. *Nepodrajaemiy. Dickens Redaktor i Izsatel'.* Moskva: Kniga, 1990. (Mikhail Urnov, *The Inimitable: Dickens, Editor and Publisher.* Moscow: Kniga, 1990.)

Vinogradov, Victor. *Etyudi o stile Gogolya.* Leningrad: Academia, 1926. (Vinogradov, Victor. *Essays on Gogol's Style.* Leningrad: Academia, 1926.)

Wilson, A. N. *Tolstoy.* New York: Norton, 1988.

Dickens in Post-Soviet Russia

Tatiana A. Boborykina

This essay considers the extent to which Dickens is still needed and still read in post-Soviet Russia—a country with a relatively new kind of government, a new ideology, and new literary standards. In fact, my survey opens with a question: what happens to Dickens now on the big stage of post-Soviet Russia? To answer it, I first briefly consider (1) several outstanding editions in translation of Dickens's works, then examine (2) significant recent scholarly studies, and then review (3) a few doctoral dissertations, before describing (4) some noteworthy adaptations into film, audiobooks or CDs, and theater performances. The many different kinds of editions of Dickens's works now available in Russia indicate a demand, at least in the book market. In addition, during the last two decades there have appeared important scholarly books, essays, and dissertations that explore new aspects of the world of Dickens. Finally, the large number of adaptations of his fiction into other media gives grounds for hope that he is just entering the post-Soviet scene and that the play, of which this inimitable writer is the author, editor, theater director, and principal actor, is only beginning.

> . . . and The Play begins!
>
> —Dickens, "A Christmas Tree"

What happens to Dickens now on the big stage of post-Soviet Russia? To help me answer this question, I decided to reread Igor Katarsky's book *Dickens in Russia*, published in 1960.[1] Within the opening twelve pages, Katarsky gives

Dickens Studies Annual, Volume 43, Copyright © 2012 by AMS Press, Inc. All rights reserved.

brief analyses of Dickens's interpretation by different Russian and Western critics, accurately dividing them into two opposite "camps": (1) progressive— Marxist, antibourgeois, democratic, revolutionary, and (2) anti-progressive— bourgeois, retrograde, shortsighted. The rest of this book offers just the author's own interpretation of Dickens's novels in their chronological order, seen through the prism of Marxist orientation. Throughout his book, Katarsky advances the idea that Dickens stood for the poor and for the workers, who are sometimes called "proletarians," and that he advocated for reforms, for the Chartist movement, and against capitalism.

In a certain sense, the book undoubtedly presents Dickens in the light of 1960s Russia, when ideology ruled over art. It draws a portrait of "The Soviet Dickens." With the political changes in Russia, which ironically started in 1984, the image and the interpretations of Dickens began changing, too. With the fall of the "Iron Curtain," the burden of ideological censorship was thrown away. This metaphorically happens in a dream in George Orwell's *1984*: "What overwhelmed him in that instant was admiration for the gesture with which she had thrown her clothes aside. With its grace and carelessness it seemed to annihilate . . . a whole system of thought, as though . . . the Party and the Thought Police could all be swept into nothingness by a single splendid movement of the arm" (29; ch. 3).

Spiritual freedom could not but influence literary criticism. Dickens in today's Russia seems to be a different writer, not because anything has changed about him, but because a lot has changed in the eyes of those who read and those who analyze. It is like the situation in *Gulliver's Travels* in which Gulliver himself remains the same, but the tiny Lilliputians and the gigantic Brobdingnagians see him quite differently. Not that in Soviet times there were no critics that were independent and talented enough to regard Dickens primarily in the context of art, scholars such as Anna Romm, Eugeny Lann, Mikhail and Dmitry Urnov, Tamara Silman, and others, but the mainstream was the one described in Katarsky's book.

So, how do we in Russia see Dickens today? In other words, by what standards, or rather by what values, should we measure Dickens now? Or to put it even more straightforwardly—is Dickens still relevant in Russia?

As one may find out from the following brief and incomplete survey, Dickens's works have been published, printed, and reprinted in large numbers during the last two decades, beginning with *The Collected Works* in twenty volumes in 2000 and including separate exclusive, expensive coffee-table editions, like a gilt-edged *Oliver Twist*, in 2009, or cheap editions like *Classics in Rendition* (books for school children and older students). There are also available many bilingual audiobooks and CDs of various Dickens novels and stories, the most popular among them being *Oliver Twist*, *Pickwick Papers*, and the Christmas books.

Unlike the situation in Soviet times, when getting hold of each book of Dickens, not to say a complete collection, was a piece of luck and an event, nowadays it is not a problem: one can buy editions in Russian, English, or both languages in most bookstores or easily order them on the internet. Besides, practically all of Dickens's works are available free online. There is, however, another problem: the reading of these books. To my astonishment, most of the freshman students and sophomores that I recently surveyed at a few Russian universities have not read Dickens at all. Only about twenty out of a hundred students indicated that they had read (or listened to) *Oliver Twist*, or had just started reading *David Copperfield* for university assignments. The rest stated (some confessing "to their shame") that they only knew that Dickens was a nineteenth-century English writer. Some added that they had watched one or two film adaptations, mainly *Oliver Twist* by Roman Polanski (2005) or the 3-D film of *A Christmas Carol* by Robert Lee Zemeckis (2009). Some expressed the hope that they would learn more about Dickens that might stimulate their desire to read his works. There was one common theme in all of the students' responses: the absence of Dickens from their earlier school programs.

During the Soviet period, Dickens was included in the school curriculum, mainly at the so-called specialized "English schools," with extensive (advanced) study of the English language and literature. In these schools, in the classes in English and American literature that were (and still are) conducted in English, extracts from Dickens's novels were (and in some of such schools still are) read in the original. In regular schools, however, Dickens now appears only in either the seventh or the tenth grade. Out of 100 to 105 academic hours of literature, instructors usually dedicate ten to twelve hours to foreign literature, and, as a rule, to ten to twelve foreign writers. This means that in regular schools today, throughout all the tenth and eleventh years, students have only one to two hours for Dickens. And even that seems to be not always true.

This distressing situation brought back to mind what Joseph Brodsky, a poet who was imprisoned in Soviet Russia as a dissident and later immigrated to America, had to say in his Nobel Prize Lecture, on December 8, 1987: "Regardless of whose image we are created in . . . for a human being there is no other future save that outlined by art. . . . I believe that, for someone who has read a lot of Dickens, to shoot his like in the name of some idea is more problematic than for someone who has read no Dickens."

Brodsky's idea, that a man who has read Dickens would be reluctant to kill, seems to be worth considering. Every day we learn in domestic and world news about terrible, inhuman crimes "in the name of some idea" or for no idea at all. In all these cases there is something lacking in those who commit these acts—the absence of "something" that may be called "the soul"—that which is given to everyone, but often remains tragically unwanted, undeveloped, and undiscovered. Is there any way—as there was with the soulless Scrooge—to discover and to find a thin, invisible thread of people's better and pure selves and pull it from their Past into the Present? Dickens does this with the help of the Spirits.

For a modern person, however, such a spiritual teacher could be Dickens himself. The power of his art is capable of working miracles similar to those that happen in his Christmas books. It is literature and Dickens's work, in particular, that may touch the sleeping soul and teach it how to laugh and to cry, and how to be a human being. I think this is what Joseph Brodsky meant to say when he referred to Dickens in his Nobel speech.

But reading Dickens is not an easy task. The speed of twenty-first-century life is much faster than that of nineteenth-century literature, for their inner rhythms do not concur. Dickens requires close and slow reading, whereas life today evidently requires constant acceleration. Regarding this, we could fully apply Mark Twain's ironic definition of a classic to Dickens: "A classic is something that everybody wants to have read, and nobody wants to read." But various attempts are now being made to remedy this situation, and I will discuss some of these later in my survey. Indeed, I find most of the scholarly studies described below to be interesting and inspiring.

There is a sense of novelty—considering the Russian historical context—in a recent dissertation entitled "Christian Motifs in Charles Dickens's Works," by T. Sheveleva (2004). "Christian Motifs"—this theme is a sign of the new times, as well as the publication of Russian translations of Dickens's *The Life of Our Lord* by several publishing houses, one of which is Sretensky Stauropegial Monastery in Moscow. Looking back to 1990, when I was trying to publish my book on Dickens in Russian, I recollect that the word *Christmas* was taken away from the title for ideological reasons. For those were still the atheistic days, when former churches kept on functioning as swimming pools or skating rings, while others had been blown up and razed to the ground, and some just remained closed and cross-less.

But although the times have changed and many churches have been restored and reopened, we still often see unkindness, the absence of high aspirations, and the kind of education that may seem to freeze people, as it metaphorically freezes young Scrooge in the school he attended, where "the maps upon the wall, and the celestial and terrestrial globes in the windows, were waxy with cold." In this context, another recent dissertation, D. Tchudin's "Pedagogical Conception of 'A New Education' by Charles Dickens" (2008), seems quite timely. It gives hope that through pedagogical theory Dickens, who seldom appears now in regular school programs, will come back to the schools.

In the following survey, I first briefly consider (1) a few outstanding editions and translations of Dickens's works, then examine (2) significant recent scholarly books and essays, and then review (3) a few dissertations, before proceeding to describe some noteworthy (4) adaptations into film, audiobooks, and theater performances. Finally, my conclusion seeks to assess the future of Dickens in Russia, and I suggest an approach that seems valuable.

Editions

As I observed in my introduction, during the last twenty years many new editions and translations of Dickens have been published and are available in bookstores or libraries. I will comment on just a few examples. These recent volumes of Dickens, however, very often lack the names of editors, perhaps because these new publications are reprints of earlier editions. Sometimes, the recent editions will include new but brief introductions.

Basically, most of the publications of the last decades, be it *The Collected Works of Charles Dickens* or separate editions, utilize the translations presented in *The Complete Works of Charles Dickens* in thirty volumes, published by Moscow State Publishing House of Fiction, 1957–63, which remains the most complete edition of Dickens in Russian to date.

The Collected Works, in twenty volumes published in Moscow by Terra-Knizny Club in 2000, is no exception. With the new editor, E. Subbotina, and the compiler, Boris Gribanov, the translators are the same. This collection contains most of Dickens's novels, but, unlike *The Complete Works* in thirty volumes, it includes neither minor prose nor letters. It also omits *Barnaby Rudge*, the Christmas books, *Hard Times*, and *A Tale of Two Cities*. The compiler of the collection, Gribanov, a well-known translator, critic, and writer, famous for his books on Faulkner, Hemingway, Elizabeth I of England, and others, is the author of introductions to practically every novel in the collection.

This twenty-volume incomplete edition does not surpass its predecessor and its main resource either in number of copies sold or in popularity. Published in the years of crises, it did not do well in sales and consequently went up in price. Nowadays it costs about $300 and is mainly available on the internet or in used bookstores, whereas the original complete thirty-volume edition may still be bought for $100 to $200. Yet both editions are also being offered in reprinted deluxe copies, designed as "antique" leather-covered, gilt-edged books. The price of such editions varies from $5,000 to about $7,500. And again, the more reliable and "less expensive" choice seems to be the time-tested thirty-volume *Complete Works*.

Apart from the above-mentioned collected works, there have been dozens of other Dickens editions issued by various publishing houses during the last decades. First of all we should notice the Azbuka-Classica publishing house, which was founded in St. Petersburg in 1995. Azbuka-Classica books appeared as another sign of the Westernization of post-Soviet culture, for they were (and still are) artistically designed with colorful covers and in a comfortable pocket-book format. Azbuka-Classica is growing rapidly: it now has a publishing house in Moscow, and is today considered one of the leading publishers in Russia. Several of Dickens's books have been issued by this company, including *Great Expectations*, *A Tale of Two Cities*, and a collection of the Christmas books, each selling for about $3 to $5. In addition, this publisher has produced, for only about $5, a compact but elaborate edition of *The Mystery of Edwin Drood*, an edition with commentaries and a bibliography that are informative and quite helpful to those readers who want to know more about Dickens's unfinished final novel.

As mentioned above, there are editions of Dickens's works in Russia today that vary in quality, design, and price. Alongside Dickens's books published by Azbuka-Classica—with their pocketbook size, light weight, and popular prices—there appear exclusive, expensive editions, like *Oliver Twist*, issued in 2009 by the Moscow publishing house Pan Press that specializes in richly designed and well-illustrated "gift" books.

The Pan Press *Oliver Twist* in 423 pages with gilt edges and stamping is illustrated by the well-known artist and illustrator Anatoly Itkin, who is famous for his keen artistic sense of humor and his capacity to grasp and convey the style of the writer he illustrates. This edition of *Oliver Twist* costs about $100 to $150.

Another publishing house, Eksmo, which was founded in Moscow in 1991, also specializes in gift editions. For example, Eksmo has issued several of Dickens's books: (1) *David Copperfield*, illustrated by H. K. Browne, bound in cloth and gilt-edged, which costs about $50; (2) an edition of *The Posthumous Papers of the Pickwick Club*, published in 2010, that is a similar clothbound volume, with illustrations by both Browne and Robert Seymour; (3) another edition, published in 2008, is quite exclusive—a volume of 560 pages, bound in leather with metallic stamping and gilt edges, with illustrations by Robert Seymour and Browne, costing about $300.

Moscow Mesheryakov Publishing House is building a series called Books with History. In 2010 this company published Dickens's *Stories for Children*. This edition, stylized as antique, with colored illustrations by Copping Harold, includes stories by Dickens about children from such works as *The Holly-Tree—Three Branches*, *Oliver Twist*, *Our Mutual Friend*, *A Christmas Carol*, *David Copperfield*, *The Cricket on the Hearth*, *The Old Curiosity Shop*, and *The Chimes*—all translated by Vera Dorofeeva. This antique-looking book of 160 pages costs about $50.

Still another Moscow publishing house, Anatolya, founded in 2003, which also specializes in exclusive editions and produces limited numbers of copies, has issued Dickens's *Oliver Twist*, translated by Alexandra Krivtsova in 2009, an exclusive limited edition of 250 copies, each costing over $1,000, and, in 2005, a collection of the Christmas books illustrated with engravings of the first Dickens editions and including colored pictures by the English book illustrator Arthur Rackham (1867–1939). This beautiful red-leather covered book is a real work of art. The edition is truly exclusive and limited—each of the hundred numbered copies costs about $1,100.

Amidst this variety of Dickens's publications in post-Soviet Russia, there are some that are exclusive and rich not only in form, but also in their unusual contents. Such, for example, is the 2003 edition of *The Posthumous Papers of the Pickwick Club*, by Bely Gorod publishing house in Moscow. Bely Gorod, founded in 1996, specializes mainly in highly artistic and socially significant publications. Dickens's novel was published in Big Illustrated Classics Library, a series with the motto: "A new insight into familiar books." This beautifully designed hardcover and unusually large, thick book of 640 pages offers a lot of useful information apart from the text of the novel itself. The book contains commentaries by Evgeny Lann; a great number of photographs as well as illustrations by various artists; the list of calendar dates of the novel; a description of the political divisions of Great Britain; the scheme of Mr. Pickwick's itinerary; a directory of characters; a directory of geographic and other names; an essay on Dickens; a chronicle of Dickens's life and literary activity; and a bibliography. Paradoxically, this invaluable book is comparatively inexpensive—about $25. The same edition is also offered in a gift format, leather-bound, for $250 to $400.

Finally, I want to comment on the outstanding edition of Dickens's *The Life of Our Lord* published in 2008 by Sretensky Stauropegial Monastery Publishing House. This beautiful illustrated book of 125 pages, edited by Hieromonk Simeon (Tomachinsky) and translated by Nina Demurova, contains a foreword to a 1969 English version indicating that the work was written by Dickens for his children and was not supposed to be published. In a second foreword, Nina Demurova, famous for her versions of Lewis Carroll's *Alice* books, discusses the difficulties she faced while translating this work. Since the English version of the Gospels that Dickens relied on and quoted sounds more modern and more colloquial that the traditional canonical Russian translation, Demurova felt a need to make some changes in Dickens's text. But she states that she attempted to stay "faithful to the simplicity of Dickens's style and his personal heartfelt intonation" (7).

The artist Olga Ionytis, another famous contributor to this book, is known for her illustrations of various fairy tales and particularly for her decorative design of a 2009 edition of Nicolai Gogol's *The Night before Christmas*. Her colorful and fairy tale–like illustrations appear on practically every page. This big hardcover volume, which has large print and a beautiful red-lacquer binding with gilt lettering, is, despite all its merits, quite inexpensive, selling for about $8. Available on the internet and in bookstores, it is loved by many Russian readers: devout Christians, parents and children, lovers of Dickens, and connoisseurs of art.

Various publishers have recently published many new editions of a number of Dickens's individual books, including *Pickwick Papers*, *Oliver Twist* (in a dozen additional versions), *A Child's History of England*, *Dombey and Son*, *David Copperfield*, *Bleak House*, *Little Dorrit*, *A Tale of Two Cities* (in four different translations), *Great Expectations*, and *The Mystery of Edwin Drood*, in addition to collections of the Christmas books. The vast range of different editions of books by Dickens gives hope that he remains *our mutual friend*, the writer whom nearly everyone wants to read.

Scholarly Works

Mikhail V. Urnov's *The Inimitable: Dickens, Editor and Publisher* (in Russian, illustrated and with photos) examines Dickens's creative personality in his relations with the epoch and environment, especially with various literary circles. Urnov is interested in Dickens's fiction as a social and cultural phenomenon, the work of a writer and of an editor.

In this study, consisting of nine informative, vivid chapters, Urnov engages in a vibrant, highly intellectual "dialogue" with the reader. Referring to the book's title, *The Inimitable*, Urnov on the very opening page explains:

> Charles Dickens was a great novelist. And he was the inimitable and famous reader of his novels, and the creator of a one-man show theater, in which he was everybody: the author, the director, and the actor. And he was the inimitable editor: the master-mind, the manager, the supervisor, and the soul of the two celebrated journals which were being issued one after another for twenty years. . . . "Inimitable" is the name which the friend and the biographer of Dickens, John Forster, had given him. In this country the inimitable novelist is known to everybody who can read. No one anymore can know the inimitable actor, the reciter of his compositions.
>
> (5–6)

The chapter "Charles Dickens Reviews" offers an extremely interesting interpretation of Dickens's critical essay "Old Lamps for New Ones" (1850). This article's negative response to the Pre-Raphaelite movement is explained by referring to Dickens's skepticism towards "progress" in general. Urnov, however, points out similarities, unnoticed by Dickens himself, between the principles of the Brotherhood and his own literary art. For Urnov, Dickens's views on the arts and on the work of the Pre-Raphaelites are more complicated than we may at first think. Finally, a supplement at the end of Urnov's study seems especially fascinating: it discusses Dickens's interpretation in his letters of his own dreams and then considers how these views are connected to some of the dreams described in his fiction—for example, the dreams of Scrooge, Toby Veck, and John Jasper. Mikhail Urnov's book seems a great achievement, a work that I believe deserves to be translated into English and reissued.

The Mystery of Charles Dickens, edited by Ekaterina Genieva, is no doubt one of the most complete collections in Russian of various essays, comments, pictures, poems, and passages from fiction and drama referring to Dickens or to subjects connected with Dickens. Richly illustrated, it contains a wide variety of materials, many of which had never appeared in Russian publications before. However, this book is at points perhaps a little too crowded and unfortunately lacks essential information about the sources, which often makes it hard with the translated texts to identify the original titles and the authors. Among the numerous writers included are G. K. Chesterton, C. P. Snow, John

Wain, Oscar Wilde, Virginia Woolf, T. S. Eliot, Henry James, Bernard Shaw, George Orwell, Franz Kafka, James Joyce, Evelyn Waugh, and Graham Greene.

My book *The Artistic World of Charles Dickens's Tales*, in Russian, consists of an introduction; five chapters, each dedicated to one of Dickens's Christmas books in their chronological order; an afterword; and a selected bibliography. The basic motif of this book is understanding that, in Dickens's writing, much lies below the surface. By consistently paying attention to small, seemingly unnecessary details, we are enabled to see that these stories have not one, but several layers of plots, often not a happy ending, but an endless Dostoevskian chaos of incompleteness. The Christmas books, as I try to illustrate, reveal a certain cinematic nature in which the plot serves as the background and what may initially have seemed the background plays a leading part (as happens in *The Battle of Life*). In these stories metaphors become visible facts, as in Fellini's films or in Dali's paintings, and plastic images, almost choreographically, replace words. As I remarked in my introduction, a Moscow publisher, considering my book in 1990, asked me not to use the word *Christmas* in the title, as it was ideologically "disloyal." Later in 1990, when the book was published elsewhere, the abbreviated title was retained. A version of my book in English, *The Artistic World of Charles Dickens's Christmas Books: The Dramatic Principle in Prose*, is discussed by Ruth Glancy in her "Dickens's Christmas Books, Christmas Stories, and Other Short Fiction: An Annotated Bibliography, Supplement I: 1985–2006," in *Dickens Studies Annual* 38 (2007): 314–15, 411–12 (no. 2644).

In E. G. Khaitchenko's *The Great Romantic Shows*, the fifth chapter, "Charles Dickens's Theater Which William Thackeray Has the Honor to Open," is entirely dedicated to Dickens and explores the following aspects: actor and spectator, reciter, playwright, novelist, sets, costumes, makeup, props, characters, and performers. The chapter opens with a quotation from the prologue to Thackeray's *Vanity Fair*, in which the author calls himself the puppeteer, the "Manager of the Performance." Khaitchenko dwells on the idea that most of the writers of that time had been strongly influenced by the theater. As Khaitchenko states, the integral part of theater, illusion, which was so typical of Thackeray, adds elements of Romantic irony to his realistic narration.

Intentional theatricality—a typical feature of the nineteenth-century novel—found its reflection in book illustrations of the time. Thus, Charles Allston Collins, the cover illustrator of the first edition of *The Mystery of Edwin Drood*, painted a curtain, as well as Melpomene and Thalia, "who seem to watch the characters of the strange novel of which the title with its first word *Mystery* echoes the medieval performing genre."

According to Khaitchenko there are many reasons to call Dickens not just the greatest writer, but also the most theatrical writer of nineteenth-century England. All the nuances of masks and pretense appear on the pages of his books, which often include theater as a theme. Of course, there was much theater in Dickens's own life, since he was also a great performer. Exploring the development and evolution of Dickens as an actor, Khaitchenko comes to the conclusion that he was moving from the visual to the inward, to a deep psychological portraying of characters. If in the beginning he depended on makeup, wigs, and costume, there gradually came the time when he could change appearance through other, inner means.

When Dickens became a reciter and performer, he was able to fill a practically empty stage with many different characters using only changes of tone, rhythm, eloquent gesture, and mimicry. His readings were truly a theater of one actor, a one-man show. He was not just reading or speaking: he was acting on stage, using a whole score of expressive means, which created an atmosphere of scenic reality.

Examining the evolution of Dickens as a stage reader, Khaitchenko points out the changes in the nature of his performances—from comedy and sentimental prose to truly dramatic and even tragic pieces that required a new manner of presentation. She stresses that scenes of cruelty—like the "written in blood" murder of Nancy—were the specific means that Dickens used in trying to move society away from cruelty. And this was, perhaps, one of the major moral issues of Dickens's late readings. "But—as we all know—raising his hand upon Nancy, Sikes injured Dickens himself," asserts Khaitchenko. Each reading of this passage would become a stunning spectacle. The writer was burning himself out on the stage, as great tragic actors often do.

Further, Khaitchenko discusses Dickens as a playwright. She begins with a statement that his fame as a playwright is much less than that he gained as a writer and actor-performer. His first plays, written at the ages of eight and sixteen, are lost, but the later plays *The Strange Gentleman* (a comic burletta in two acts) and *The Village Coquettes* (a comic opera), were performed in 1836 at St. James's Theater. In 1837 another Dickens's play, the burletta *Is She His Wife? (Or, Something Singular!)*, was shown in the same theater. Khaitchenko observes that Dickens himself did not have a high opinion of his dramatic works and once even said that he wished they had been forgotten. His subsequent attempts at playwriting were in collaboration with other authors.

For Khaitchenko, "The Theater of Charles Dickens" includes at least two topics. First, we should consider the episodes from Dickens's novels devoted to the contemporary theatrical scene, such as the puppeteers in *The Old Curiosity Shop*, the theater performances in *Nicholas Nickleby*, David Copperfield's attendance at a play at Covent Garden, theater scenes in *Great Expectations*, and the description of the circus in *Hard Times*. Secondly, and—as Khaitchenko stresses—most importantly, we should be aware of the influence of the popular Victorian theater upon the architectonics, style, and imagery of Dickens's novels. For Dickens, as Khaitchenko notes, "popular Victorian theater not only mirrored reality, but was also a cheerful form of bridging over the daily routine." Furthermore, Khaitchenko comments, "It is well known that not the plays, but the novels by Dickens, came to the stage in dozens and hundreds of adaptations, although not all of the stage versions won Dickens's approval."

Most of Dickens's characters are in keeping with the types in melodramatic theater where virtue triumphs over evil, which is punished. However, Khaitchenko remarks, Dickens's novels are not melodramas. Highly esteeming melodrama for its emotional action and modernity compared to classical drama, Dickens nevertheless did not admire all of the qualities of the genre. The striking demonstrations of this are the numerous parodies of melodramas in his novels and essays. Melodrama, concludes Khaitchenko, "constitutes only one part of Dickens's view of reality; the other part was burlesque and satirical parody."

Dickens's burlesques differ in themes, which may involve genre, artistry, or politics. The target for ridicule in artistic burlesques is usually theater, including melodrama, and Khaitchenko gives an example from the *Great Expectations*. But Dickens's political parodies deal with performances larger in scale, where the spectators are the whole nation. One of these brilliant parodies, Khaitchenko states, is *Bleak House*.

For many commentators, the brightness of the outward existence of Dickens's heroes is not supported by the equally vivid expression of their inner passions. But Khaitchenko disputes this view and maintains that Dickens's psychological insight is simply different in nature. According to her, Dickens often seeks not to describe the emotional process but to find its visual outward expression. She further argues, "The psychological dimension is also reached through the environment, which is never indifferent to the character. . . . It is surprising how by means of creating an atmosphere Dickens skillfully speaks about the inner state of his characters, whereas directly he doesn't say a word about it." In my opinion, this is one of the most outstanding features of Dickens's style, the characteristic that makes his art so cinematic in nature.

After comparing this psychologically powerful method of Dickens to theatrical and cinematic techniques, Khaitchenko concludes, "In his novels, Dickens not only utilizes the generic features and stylistic devices of melodrama, but he also ridicules them, as if foreshadowing the birth of a new theatricality that is imprinted in his later works."

A subsequent book by Elena Khaitchenko also contains considerations of Dickens's relation to the art of his time. In *Victorian [England] in the Mirror of the Music Hall* (or *Victorianism in the Mirror of the Music Hall*), she explores the history of the British music hall, starting from ballads and street shows in the Renaissance. Khaitchenko focuses her attention, however, on the Victorian music hall in the context of the social and cultural life of the time and traces the connection of the music hall to various figures in literature—Dickens, Thackeray, Kipling, and T. S. Eliot.

Dickens is considered quite often in the book. Here and there one comes across quotations from *Sketches by Boz* and other works in which Dickens refers to the street shows and circus performances. Khaitchenko notes that

Dickens liked to insert street musicians and all kinds of musical instruments in his writings. Basically, there is always a significant musical element in his novels and stories "where not only the kettles sing"—as in *The Cricket on the Hearth*—but also the pans, plates, and cups create music and dancing, as they do in the family of young Tetterby in *The Haunted Man*.

In the chapter "The Stars of the Music Hall," Khaitchenko discusses Gilbert MacDermott (1845–1901), the most popular star of the Victorian English music hall, and mentions that he wrote a dramatic adaptation of *The Mystery of Edwin Drood* in which he himself played the part of Grewgious. He also played the part of Mr. Peggotty in a dramatized version of *David Copperfield*.

When writing about Gus Elen, a music hall singer who achieved success from 1891 on, performing cockney songs and sketches as a comedian, Khaitchenko calls him "the kid brother" of Samuel Weller. The way he used to dress, his manner of walking, and his style of speaking—all reminded the audiences of the not-so-distant times of Dickens.

The following chapter examines Dan Leno, a Victorian English music hall comedian of the 1880s. Khaitchenko compares him to the Ghost of Christmas Past in *A Christmas Carol*: "It was a strange figure—like a child; yet not so like a child as like an old man, viewed through some supernatural medium, which gave him the appearance of having receded from the view, and being diminished to a child's proportions." And here the author refers to Max Beerbohm's *Around Theatres*, in which he compares Dan Leno to a Spirit and refers also to *Pillars of Drury Lane* by Walter James MacQueen-Pope, who calls Leno "[t]he Charles Dickens of music hall and pantomime." Elena Khaitchenko adds that Leno "had much in common with many of Dickens's characters not only in appearance, but also as a person—he could have appeared on the pages of Dickens's books as one of his eccentric characters. However, as an actor he—like Dickens himself—drew his humor from everyday life, be it a store, a pawnshop, or a railway station. All the habitual revealed its hidden phantasmagoric gist in his shows."

In the last chapter, "The Decline of the Music Hall," the author tells about late Victorian comedians, among them George Robey, who, like Dan Leno, had also been considered "the Dickens of the Music Hall" for his talent of depicting everyday life in its grotesque, comic, and utterly theatrical manifestations. It is not by chance, Elena Khaitchenko states, that at the age of eighty-two he played Tony Weller in a dramatization of *The Pickwick Papers* produced, directed, and adapted by Noel Langley in 1952.

Summing up her book, the author reconstructs the image of Laurence Olivier in John Osborne's *The Entertainer*, in which he plays a washed-up stage comedian. "Both the Royal Court play and the 1960 film version of it by Tony Richardson, with the hunched up figure of the comedian in an empty playhouse, seem like the last farewell to the music hall." However, music hall techniques, "which may be rooted in Dickens, are still required in the modern theater. It was none other than Tom Stoppard who stated that his *Rosencrantz and Guildenstern* had been written in a manner of a slightly elevated music hall."

Elena Khaitchenko, in whose book the name of Dickens seems to be omnipresent, concludes that

> the music hall, which in a sense has come to its end, still carries on living as a form-building device in modern performing arts. This proves one of Sergei Eisenstein's statements, that to produce a good performance of a play means to build up a strong music hall-circus program. And this perhaps also means, as a Dickensian reader of Dickens might find out, that some of Dickens's typical artistic devices proved essential in the formation of the Victorian music hall, while, on the other hand, after its decline, its innate devices, artistic methods, and styles are being used by other theater genres today.

Mikhail B. Iampolski, who teaches Russian and Slavic studies at New York University, has published *The Memory of Tiresias* in Russian and also in an English edition entitled *Memory of Tiresias: Intertextuality and Film.* In this book, divided into four parts, chapter 3 in part 2, "Intertextuality and the Evolution of Cinematic Language: Griffith and the Poetic Tradition," considers Dickens.

Speaking of cinematographic intertextuality, Iampolski suggests that "every new figure in cinematic language is essentially a quote." Further, he states that Sergei Eisenstein's study *Dickens, Griffith and Film Today* "brilliantly demonstrates how Griffith's use of close-ups, as well as certain figures related to montage, can be clarified by referring to the works of Charles Dickens." In fact, in his own article "What I Demand of Movie Stars" (1917), Griffith made such a comment: "I borrowed the 'cutback' from Charles Dickens." According to Iampolski, "That Griffith was interested in Dickens is beyond question. . . . It is Dickens, who embodies the principles of narrative development in prose, whose adaptation for cinema has been ascribed to Griffith."

Victoria Levitova's essay "On Dickens's Visuality, Proust, Eisenstein and Next to Nothing on Griffith" proposes that the language of some writers is so visual and cinematic that it is very hard to move their heroes to the screen. The author begins by stating that she once took up a copy of *David Copperfield* just for the pleasure of reading it, not for analyzing. But associations came in spite of her wish, and she had to respond to Eisenstein's invitation to explore Dickens, though this time in the context not of cinematography, but, instead, of literary study. It is exactly in *Copperfield*—partly a biography of Dickens himself, but no less a chronicle of great expectations and hard times—that one can catch this visuality, this optics and refraction. There also is a certain distance, timely distance. The attempt of Copperfield, a mature writer, to return to his own past merges with Dickens's own attempt to embrace his emotional experience. It's interesting, observes Levitova, that both authors—Dickens and Copperfield—try to hold and comprehend the running flow of their consciousness. Some of the chapters in this novel are about "looking back into the past," but it's a strange flashback, an unusual relationship with time, since all the novel is in the past. Or is it the past within the past, the layers of time? And to separate these layers is next to impossible. There are optics or refractions of memory to consider.

This essay then compares this approach to the problem of time in Proust. But Dickens's images seem in a kind of bas-relief, like embossed printing. Levitova maintains that this made it especially hard for the illustrators of Dickens, who were under the hypnotic spell of his visuality, his optics.

Further on, Levitova asks whether Dickens was indeed the motivating power of cinematography. In her opinion, most of the film directors of adaptations try not so much to reflect Dickens's vision and optics, as they seek to consider the genre in which they are working. Thus, *Oliver!* (1968), Lionel Bart's work directed by Carol Reed, is an impressive musical and a good movie, but, asserts Levitova, a bad version of Dickens: "the movie is beautiful and full of godsends, but all this has nothing to do with Dickens." Levitova argues that finding the visual equivalent of Dickens's stylistics is difficult, since we see his characters through their own souls.

Dissertations

During the last decade, Dickens has attracted the interest of graduate students at Russian universities and has therefore been studied in a number of doctoral dissertations. The kinds of topics considered include his use of fairy-tale methods throughout a long career; the functioning of leitmotifs and symbols in novels like *Bleak House, Little Dorrit,* and *Our Mutual Friend*; Dickens's Christian motifs and Christmas philosophy in the context of nineteenth-century English life; the relations between his Christmas books and Russian Christmas stories written from the 1840s to the 1890s; the typology of child characters in Dickens's works; and the interaction in his fiction between two contrasting literary traditions—the Gothic and the realistic. I'll briefly consider just three recent dissertations that can serve as examples of current interests.

Irina Kondarina's *The Reception of Dickens in Russia from 1850 to 1950* states that the interest of Russian readers in Dickens arose in the beginning of the 1840s. In 1838 there appeared translated fragments of *Pickwick Papers*, and a little later several stories from *Sketches by Boz* were translated. Still later, the Christmas books appeared in various translations, which were warmly accepted by Russian readers and by famous critics of the time—Belinsky, Grigoriev, and others. Of course, I must add that not all of Dickens's Christmas books were warmly received by one of the Russian critics mentioned above. In a letter to Bodkin, Vissarion Belinsky wrote about one of Dickens's short novels that he evidently had not understood, missing important symbolic parallels to profoundly metaphoric pictures of the battlefield: "Please, read Dickens's *The Battle of Life.* In it you will clearly see all the narrow-mindedness, and all the limitations of this hidebound and block-headed Englishman, when he appears to be not a talent, but a man." (In my own study of Dickens's Christmas books, I try to prove that *The Battle of Life* is one of the most outstanding works written by Dickens, the man and the artist.)

Nevertheless, Kondarina seems basically correct in stating that nearly all writings of Dickens were liked and admired by Russian readers. Of course, we must agree with Kondarina that "the study of Dickens's reception by Russian culture is inseparable from the quality of the translations." Therefore, she explores differences in the quality of translations that illustrate the evolution of the principles of translation. To analyze the relations between the original Russian literature and literature in translation, particularly that of Dickens, Kondarina refers to early investigations by a number of Russian scholars. She then affirms that "the main issue in the sphere of reception and understanding of translated literature is the vivid, sensory perception of the word and the representation of the original as a true work of art."

In *The Poetics of Landscape in Charles Dickens's Novels*, O. Y. Bogdanova observes that since Dickens is considered an urban writer, his use of landscape is often considered insignificant and frequently ignored by scholars. But, she argues, nature descriptions are an essential part of his artistry. These descriptions, moreover, have a certain peculiar feature: nature symbols based on Christian beliefs enter into complicated relations with the tradition of mythological poetics. Dickens's landscapes, asserts Bogdanova, "demonstrate the search for harmony in the relations between the man and the world, which becomes particularly important in literature written in the second half of nineteenth to the beginning of twentieth century, as shown, for example, in the works of Thomas Hardy, John Galsworthy, and D. H. Lawrence." Bogdanova examines her subject by giving careful attention to five of Dickens's novels: *Pickwick Papers*, *Martin Chuzzlewit*, *David Copperfield*, *Great Expectations*, and *The Mystery of Edwin Drood*.

Dmitry Tchudin's "Pedagogical Conception of 'A New Education' by Charles Dickens" examines basic elements in Dickens's pedagogical conception that endorse new tendencies in the development of educational theory and practice: humanitarian ideals of scholarship and culture. Dickens, states the author, may be considered as one of the founders of humanistic pedagogy in the nineteenth century; his New Education concept, however, has never been an object of special interest in Russian educational studies. Until now (2008), Tchudin continues, there has not been a single investigation dedicated to Dickens's contribution to the field of education. One of the reasons is that Western systems of humanitarian education were not popular in Soviet pedagogical historiography. Thus, the main goal of this dissertation is defining the theoretical and methodological essence of Dickens's New Education concept.

For this, different groups of Dickens's works are to be explored: (1) essays, such as "Our School" and "Infant Gardens"; (2) novels and stories that reflect

Dickens's educational views: for example, *Pickwick Papers*, *Oliver Twist*, *Nicholas Nickleby*, *The Old Curiosity Shop*, *Dombey and Son*, *David Copperfield*, *Hard Times*, and *Little Dorrit*; (3) Dickens's speeches to different audiences on various problems of education; (4) journalistic sketches and notes on the problems of education in *The Mirror of Parliament*, "Doctors' Commons," from *Sketches by Boz*, the *Daily News*, and his journals *Household Words* and *All the Year Round*, and elsewhere; (5) Dickens's books: *A Child's History of England* (1853) and *The Life of Our Lord* (1846); (6) Dickens's letters concerning the problems of education, especially—in the context of this investigation—his correspondence with the Minister of Education; (7) the works of Western Dickens scholars on the topic—for example, Philip Collins's *Dickens and Education*, William T. Harris's *Dickens as an Educator*, and John Manning's *Dickens on Education*; and (8) the general works on Dickens of such Russian scholars as T. Silman, I. Katarsky, V. Ivasheva, and A. Annenskaya. Tchudin believes that considering this comprehensive list of Dickens's publications on education for the first time in the context of scientific pedagogical research in Russia will provide a more objective analytical indication of Dickens's contribution to education.

Adaptations

One indication of Dickens's popularity in post-Soviet Russia can be found in the various adaptations of his fiction into other media. Although the cost of preparing original Russian film or video adaptations makes such productions rare, at times Russian movies not directly using Dickens's writings include a number of Dickensian motifs, and in many cases foreign adaptations of Dickens's narratives and foreign videos and films based on Dickens's life have been modified for Russian audiences by the addition of subtitles or by dubbing and voice-over effects. Moreover, there have been many audio versions in Russian, as well as numerous stage adaptations. I will discuss some film adaptations, then consider audio versions, and then examine several theater adaptations.

Leonid Netchaev's musical *The Cricket on the Hearth* (2001), an example of a recent original Russian film adaptation, is not entirely successful. One weak point is that the actor portraying the Cricket, who sings and accompanies himself on a violin, is unfortunately rather monstrous-looking, since he is always shown in an allegedly "mysterious" deadly-blue light. Moreover, the entire plan for the film seems rather simple. The movie focuses on the love story of John Peerybingle and his wife, Mary (or Dot), and provides a mysterious intrigue of "secret relations" between Mary and Edward, disguised as an old man. It is the Cricket who saves the home hearth—talking to John in the night of his bitter doubts, and dancing with Mary in her dream. In the movie the story of another home, where the toymaker Caleb Plummer and his blind daughter Bertha live, is extremely subordinate to the main theme. This inevitably makes the movie differ from the original story's genre of a psychological drama and deprives the film of Dickens's complexity and subtlety.

The subtitle of Dickens's story is "A Fairy Tale of Home," but, strictly speaking, there are two homes and two fairy tales, one of which ends happily, while the other does not. And the title encodes these two different—illusory and dramatic—meanings of the expression *fairy tale*. In the standard Russian translation, based on the most authoritative collection of Dickens's works in Russian, the thirty-volume edition, the subtitle is rendered as "Skazka o semeinim schastje," meaning "A Fairy Tale of Family Happiness," thus leaving no doubts about the happy ending and about the particular home, that of John and Mary. Netchaev's interpretation is evidently derived from this Russian subtitle, whereas in Dickens's original story things are not so one-dimensional. The second home—of a poor toymaker—is no less important in Dickens's text, for just as Caleb wishes to improve his toys within the limit of their prices, so he seeks to improve, "at a price," the situation of his blind daughter by means of a fairy tale and fantasy. Netchaev's film omits many of the symbolic details used by Dickens to suggest the vulnerability of the illusory world and to metaphorically reevaluate his own position and role as a story-teller.

An interesting example of a movie that includes significant references to Dickens is *Come Look at Me* (*Prikhodi Na Menya Posmotret*), written by Nadezda Ptushkina (the author of the original play, staged in several Russian theaters under different titles). This movie begins with an off-screen woman's voice reading: "They walked in to dinner arm-in-arm, and sat down side by side. Never was such a dinner as that, since the world began"—a passage from chapter 63 of *Nicholas Nickleby*, lines that will be heard several times as a leitmotif throughout the entire film. A spinster daughter is reading Dickens to her old disabled mother, with whom she lives in a big old-fashioned apartment. The mother desperately wants her daughter to marry, and the daughter, driven by the supposedly imminent death of her mother, invites into their home a total stranger, who by mistake has knocked at their door, and introduces him as her boyfriend. Everything happens at Christmastide. The man, who had some plans for a love affair with a young woman whose door he missed in the darkness when the electricity was turned off, eventually starts liking his prospective mother-in-law and makes every effort to be liked by the daughter.

The mother "blesses" the couple with a portrait of Dickens, which the daughter hands her instead of an icon. Having an impression (probably the right one) that her daughter's "fiancé" is fond of Dickens, the mother presents him as a Christmas gift a thirty-volume set of the *Complete Works* of her favorite writer. The movie is full of wit, warmth, music, beauty, and love, all of which help miracles to happen. All this, alongside snowflakes falling beyond the window, old-fashioned toys on a Christmas tree, candles, and a beautiful romance, makes the movie *Come Look at Me* (a line from a poem by Anna Akhmatova) a true Christmas story over which the spirit of a smiling Dickens seems to hover. The movie has been broadcast on TV many times, especially on New Year's Eve, and is available on DVD.

Another film that includes references to Dickens and conveys his motifs is *Melody for a Street Organ* (*Melodiya dlya sharmanki*, 2009), directed by the famous Kira Muratova. The film was an official selection at the 2009 Toronto International Film Festival, was shown on the Ninth Russian Film Week in New York City in 2009, and received a Nika award for the best film of the countries in the Commonwealth of Independent States and the Baltics.

The movie tells of events that take place at Christmastide, and among other characters there appears one dressed as a fairy. *Melody* thus immediately calls up associations with Christmas stories, Dickens's in particular. But Muratova's story of two children—a young boy and his sister who are suddenly left to fend for themselves after the death of their mother—ends tragically, which seemingly deconstructs the tradition of Christmas fairy tales. The cruel realism of the movie does not, however, produce an impression of an anti-Dickensian philosophy, for in Dickens's own Christmas books there is always the dark side of a fairy-tale reality, in which there are no miracles and no happy endings. Dickens shows it not openly, and not so much in the text, but rather in the deep undercurrent that flows sometimes in the opposite direction from that of the visible plot. This Dickensian concept reflects in Muratova's movie as in a mirror: quite the reverse, it depicts brutal Russian reality in the visible foreground, and the fairy tale–like illusionary dream goes deep into an encoded subtext. This happens in the final episode, when the leading character, the orphan boy, eventually dies of hunger and cold on Christmas night. The thread of a balloon with the word *Love* imprinted on it is clutched in his dead little hand, symbolizing a fragile, airy dream of love that the child had not experienced on earth but maybe will encounter in heaven. This key image of *Melody for a Street Organ* is very Dickensian, not only in its method of visualizing the invisible, but also in a deep social, psychological, and philosophic sense. And it is not by chance that the name of Dickens is mentioned in this movie, and not by chance that many of those who watched it recall Dickens. In 2010 in a review in the Russian journal *Seans* the supporting characters of the movie were compared to Dickens's "inexhaustible gallery of great comical, eccentric, weird, inimitable picturesque types." After the presentation in New York City the movie received several reviews on the internet, one titled "A Christmas Carol: *Melody for a Street Organ*," thus pointing out the tragic tune of a modern Russian Christmas story. After the Toronto film festival, the film was referred to in one of the reviews as "a Dickensian glance at the modern soul."

Before I consider foreign video or film adaptations, I wish to explain that these movies are provided with dubbing, subtitles, voice-over, or much-voice-over. In Soviet times, foreign movies were usually dubbed by professional actors at central government studios. Nowadays, films are normally subtitled or include translations into Russian in voice-over or much-voice-over: *voice-over* means that the original soundtrack plays very softly and over it we clearly hear the voice of one translator; *much-voice-over* means that we hear the voices of various actors (men, women, and perhaps children) speaking the dialogue in Russian, while once again still hearing, more softly, the original actors' voices. One advantage of voice- or much-voice-over over dubbing (where the original voice tracks are not heard at all) is that the viewers of the movie can hear the voices and intonations of the film's original actors, which are sometimes a large part of their performances. The audience is also able to grasp some words, since the two soundtracks are not exactly simultaneous: usually, the Russian translation is audible just a very little time after the original. This slight delay can produce the effect of allowing viewers to think that they understand what the actors are saying in English (or any other language). Moreover, on DVDs there are often several choices of format: (1) only the original soundtrack; (2) the original soundtrack at low volume with voice-over or much-voice-over; (3) the original soundtrack with Russian subtitles; and (4) the original soundtrack with French or German subtitles. When watching a Western film at home, viewers can therefore choose the format they prefer.

Of the many Russian versions of recent foreign video or film adaptations, nearly all are made from British and American originals. Although films of *Oliver Twist*, *A Christmas Carol*, and *David Copperfield* have been especially popular, almost all the other major works are represented. I will consider a small number of recent examples.

There are eight films of *Oliver Twist*, all available on DVDs in Russian translations. Roman Polanski's 2005 interpretation, though inferior to both David Lean's version (UK, 1948) and Carol Reed's musical film (UK, 1968), is much better known by Russian young people. Unfortunately, this later version of one of the best Dickens novels lacks Dickensian subtlety and humor and may produce a wrong and unfavorable impression of the writer as dull and gloomy.

A Christmas Carol is presented in Russia in several different versions, beginning with a 1935 British movie *Scrooge* (Russian title: *Mister Scrooge*), by Henry Edwards, with Seymour Hicks as Ebenezer Scrooge, which was issued on DVD in Moscow in 2009. A much more popular version, one beloved by Russian audiences, is *A Christmas Carol* (*Duhi Rozdestva*), a 1999 British TV film, by David Hugh Jones, with Patrick Stewart as Scrooge, given in a much-voice-over Russian translation. This has been broadcast on TV many times and is available on DVD. Perhaps less known is an unusual adaptation offering a combination of live action and animation: *A Christmas Carol* (*Rozdestvenskaya istoria/skazka*), a 2001 British film directed by Jimmy T. Murakami and featuring the voices of Simon Callow, Kate Winslet, and Nicholas Cage. The music and songs were written, composed, and performed by Julian Nott. A Russian translation using much-voice-over is available on DVD and also for free computer download.

Yet another version of this story, Robert Lee Zemeckis's *A Christmas Carol* (*Rozdestvenskaya istoriya*), is a 3-D adaptation that had its world premiere on November 3, 2009 and was first shown in Russia just about two weeks later on November 19 (Russian translation in much-voice-over; another version is dubbed entirely in Russian). This adaptation is very popular among young schoolchildren, high school and college students, and other age groups.

Martin Chuzzlewit, a six-part 1994 British version by Pedr James (Russian translation in voice-over), has been broadcast on TV and is available on DVD. A number of Russian viewers, many of whom confessed they had not read the novel, expressed gratitude to the TV channel that broadcast this movie.

David Copperfield is available in Russia in four versions: (1) George Cukor's 1935 American production (Russian in much-voice-over, or with English or French subtitles), now available on DVD; (2) a 1999 BBC film by Simon Curtis (Russian in much-voice-over), broadcast on TV several times and available on DVD; (3) an American version by Peter Medak, 2000 (Russian in much-voice-over), available on DVD; and (4) finally, a 2009 Italian TV film by Ambrogio Lo Giudice, 2009 (Russian in much-voice-over), shown on TV several times, the last time in August 2011. Each of the three later films is good in its own way, but I would recommend Simon Curtis's interpretation, with an absolutely superb cast and great directing. This film, which reveals a keen sense of humor and deep understanding of characters and their drama, seems the most moving and most faithful to Dickens.

Dombais et fils (after *Dombey and Son*), a 2007 French film by Laurent Jaoui, with a screenplay based on Dickens's novel by the Russian film drama- turge Aleksandr Adabshyan (Russian in much-voice-over), was broadcast on TV several times, most recently in 2011. In this movie version everything is "translated" into French, including the spelling of names and places. Often, an off-screen voice is reading Dickens's text on behalf of the author. The acting is extremely impressive.

One of the three versions of *The Old Curiosity Shop*, the 1995 American film by Kevin Connor, with Peter Ustinov as Nell's grandfather, is especially loved by Russian audiences (Russian translation in much-voice-over). It was broadcast on TV several times and is available on DVD.

Great Expectations, a 1998 Hollywood production by Alfonso Cuarón, with Robert De Niro as Magwitch, was released in the United States and Russia in 1998 (Russian translation in much-voice-over). It has been broadcast on TV several times and is available on DVD. The movie, although seeking to present a modernized version of Dickens's plot, translates his ideas into postmodern metaphorical language. Shari Hodges Holt discusses this production in volume 38 of *Dickens Studies Annual*.

Some appealing films dealing with Dickens's life have also gained attention in Russia. *Dickens*, a 2002 BBC docudrama in three hour-long episodes writ- ten and presented by Peter Ackroyd, with Anton Lesser as Dickens, directed by Mary Dawnes and Chris Granlund (Russian translation in voice-over), was broadcast on TV in 2005. This brilliant work is unfortunately hard to obtain on DVD and difficult to find on the internet. The movie begins with the idea that every man is a mystery and proceeds to show that Charles Dickens—above all people—is still a mystery to us. We see the crash of a train on which Dickens was traveling secretly with his mistress and her mother. This real episode would later echo in one of Dickens's ghost stories—"The Signalman." Ackroyd, the author of a lengthy biography of Dickens, is not just the narrator, but also a character who walks along the streets of old and modern London passing by or meeting face to face with Charles Dickens himself. The leitmotif image of the film is three women in mourning with long black veils, who silently move together as if flowing in the misty air like dark shadows or like the Weird Sisters or Fates. They are Dickens's mother, wife, and lover. This, in my view, is one of the most impressive images of the entire movie and makes this docudrama a real piece of art.

Dickens' Secret Lover, a 2008 British docudrama (included in the four-part TV cycle *Victorian Passions*) by Sarah Aspinall, is presented by Charles Dance (Russian in voice-over) and was broadcast on TV. Another movie, *Charles Dickens's England*, a 120-minute 2011 British documentary by Julian Richards, starring Derek Jacobi (Russian translation in voice-over), was shown on TV in 2011 and is available on DVD. This film received very positive responses from Russian viewers.

All in all, if we consider works produced prior to the end of the Soviet era in addition to those created afterwards, there are over ninety movies based on Dickens's works or his life that are available in Russia today, beginning with a ten-minute version of *Bleak House* made by Lee De Forest in 1926 and *The Mystery of Edwin Drood* by Stuart Walker in 1935.

DVDs of Dickens-related films may be obtained in specialized video shops or ordered online. Usually, the price of each DVD ranges from $10 to $35, depending on the quality and on the store. Because of the increase in online ordering, many video shops are closing. Recently, however, I asked the owners of some surviving shops about the interest of customers in works related to Dickens. Always, the answer was that DVDs with Dickens's movies stay on the shelves no longer than one or two days. All kinds of people—schoolchildren, students, their parents or grandparents, anybody—immediately choose these films. But this does not yet prove the fact that Dickens is much read in Russia. It is well known that television and movies have made Charles Dickens "the most important unread novelist in English." Nevertheless, one cannot deny that Dickens on screen is not only a great pleasure for moviegoers and TV viewers, and not only an essential resource for students and scholars, but also proof of a never-dying interest to this writer. In fact, some people have told me that they first started reading Dickens only after watching movies based on his novels.

In recent years there have been many audiobooks and CDs presenting works by Dickens, including at least six adaptations of *Oliver Twist*. Among various Dickens audiobooks is one—*Little Dorrit*—published by the Novospassky Monastery in Moscow. This fact once again confirms Dostoevsky's notion (in his *Diary of a Writer*) that Dickens was a "great Christian," and, as we can see, it's not surprising that in the last decades the Russian Orthodox Church and the monasteries refer to Dickens.

In addition, there are several bilingual versions of Dickens's novels and stories, performed by English and Russian actors, like *A Christmas Carol* and "The Signalman," presented on one CD by Moscow studio Ardis; or *Great Expectations*, *David Copperfield*, and *Oliver Twist*, issued one after another by CDCOM in the last several years. These bilingual CDs have an additional value for those who study English and do it not only by textbooks, but mastering the vivid, witty, multicolored language of Dickens. One 2010 audiobook that has attracted extremely favorable reviews on the internet is *The Posthumous Papers of the Pickwick Club* (in Russian), produced by Media-Kniga. This four-part book is read by Ivan Litvinov, who masterfully performs each character. One correspondent wrote that someone who claimed not to have liked Dickens listened to this CD and was charmed by both the actor and the author.

There have been a number of theater adaptations, including several that have appeared in the last four years. *The Cricket on the Hearth*, first performed in April 2008 at the St. Petersburg State Theater of Young Spectators, was directed by Georgy Tshilava. The determining feature of this serious and moving production was the stage design by one of the most prominent theater artists in Russia today, Emil Kapelush. According to his and the director's interpretation, Dickens's image of the mock Noah's Ark (which Caleb, the toymaker, tries to improve) plays an important role in the story. Unlike the musical film adaptation by Leonid Netchaev (discussed above), in which the drama of Caleb and his blind daughter is placed on the periphery, giving way to the family "detective melodrama" of John and Mary, Emil Kapelush covers the whole of the stage with the interior of the "Noah's Ark," and the action of the story unfolds within this metaphorical space.

Another big success of the production involved the Honored Artist of the Russian Federation Liana Zhvania starring as Mrs. Fielding. This supporting role, played by a superbly sensitive actress, becomes central towards the final scenes of the performance. Liana Zhvania is so faithful to Dickens's humor that the audience roars with laughter, or at times literally laughs to tears, whenever she utters a word or makes a gesture. This wonderful performance is one of the rare little chefs d'oeuvre in Russian theater today, not only concerning Dickens adaptations, but in general.

Lionel Bart's two-act musical play *Oliver!* (a version of *Oliver Twist*) was produced for the first time in St. Petersburg on December 18, 2010 at the St. Petersburg Musical Comedy Theater. Although all of the actors were from the St. Petersburg Musical Comedy Theater, the company invited a Hungarian creative group to stage the performance, which was directed by Attila Ratly, with set design by Robet Mensel, and costumes by Rita Velikh, all from Hungary. (The musical conductor, Yuri Krylov, and the choreographer, Sergey Gritsay, however, are both Russian.) This play is mainly shown at Christmastide and is warmly received by audiences, especially by the young, since children from the age of seven are allowed to attend.

The Battle of Life: *A Love Story* was first produced by the Moscow Studio of Theater Arts in May 2008, with Sergey Zhenovach as director. This performance, which fulfills the promise of Dickens's subtitle, *A Love Story*, won a Golden Mask award for best small-scale production. This involvement with Dickens is the first in the theatrical and pedagogical career of the director. As Zhenovach confesses, he was trying to discover the nature of Dickens's thought. To begin with, the director and the actors, students at the Studio, went to London and visited Dickens's places there. They also bought some old objects in a flea market—to use for the props and costumes. Because the director was looking for new expressiveness in the language, he decided, following Dickens's own tradition, to "read" this Christmas book like some kind of Dickensian home reading, at a fireside before a narrow circle of family and friends. The actors, sitting in cozy armchairs in their old English clothes, are holding papers with the text, someone is eating an apple, and someone is making notes with a pencil. Dickens's text flows, as music, and the striking of a clock is heard.

Less successful were two more plays: (1) a two-act modern interpretation of *The Pickwick Club* in Chekhov Moscow Arts Theater with Beatles music, first performed in May 2009, and (2) a musical *A Christmas Story with Ghosts* (after Dickens's *Christmas Carol*) in St. Petersburg Theater on Liteiny, first performed in December 1997.

Conclusion

Although the discussions above testify to the continuing Russian interest in Dickens, I now want to consider the future. My introduction expressed the hope that he would again be included in the curriculum of Russian schools. Of course, when school graduates enter universities to study the humanities or the arts, they will most certainly encounter Dickens—be it in literature, theater, journalism, or cinema courses. My own experience as a teacher of Dickens makes me optimistic.

In 2008, in the Department of Liberal Arts and Sciences of St. Petersburg State University, I dedicated my Literature and Theater course, which always covers two semesters, totally to Dickens. The students who enrolled were more interested in theater than in literature, and almost none of them had read Dick-

ens. Besides, they were all prejudiced against him as dull, too long, old-fashioned, and boring. We started reading *Sketches by Boz* and dwelt on chapter
21 ("Brokers' and Marine-Store Shops"). As we were reading a passage in
which only the old articles of clothing were described, but through which "the
misery and destruction of those whom they once adorned" was showing, my
students became evidently more involved. Then we moved to chapter 23 ("The
Pawnbroker's Shop"), to a passage describing a meeting of a young, delicate
girl and a female "whose attire miserably poor, but extremely gaudy, plainly
spoke of her situation." The young women caught sight of each other, and we
understand, by Dickens's specific "close-ups," that one saw in the delicate
girl her own past, whereas the other saw in the impoverished woman her own
inevitable, horrific future. I especially noticed the eyes of my students when
they thus faced the art of Dickens. Something happened: they were surprised,
enchanted, inspired. By the next class they had to elaborate these scenes and
perform them, which they did perfectly. Then we read *Oliver Twist*, and we
paid attention to "The Flight of Sikes," the episode describing a "reflection of
the pool of gore that quivered and danced in the sunlight of the ceiling" and
the episode with the blood spot-remover. In *The Cricket on the Hearth* I drew
their attention to a most striking detail that spoke volumes about Dickens's
philosophy—the "broken toy" in the end of the story. After that, the students
were totally converted and convinced. Since then, Dickens for them has been
the most modern, modernist, existentialist, surrealist, great, real, vivid, cool,
awesome writer.

By the middle of the spring semester, we finally created our own scenario
based mainly on the Christmas books, and we then made the costumes and dec-
orations. At the end of the course, the students wrote in their final papers that
they could not imagine how it had been possible that they had not known Dickens. And they came to know him not only by reading, but with their senses,
with their hearts—by acting, they passed his characters through themselves.
We performed our play at our university, then at a Dickens pub at a Christmas
dinner for orphans, and finally, in Holland, at a Dickens festival in Deventer.

The quickest way to gain students' interest in Dickens is through attention to details, through exploring and discovering Dickens's unique artistic
methods that foreshadow various modern trends in visual arts: for example,
in cinematography, theater, painting, and choreography. When the students
detected Dickens's skillful cinematic way of showing the invisible through the
visible, when they got the keys to decipher materialized metaphors, or ran into
scattered verbal close-ups, they were won over. During the two semesters, in
addition to reading Dickens's writings and studies by various critics, we also
watched theater and film adaptations.

Having said all this, I come to the conclusion that Dickens is required in
Russia. He is needed by young, inexperienced readers, even if they don't know
it yet; he is needed by those who take time to reread and enjoy; and by those

who stage him and by those who come to theaters to watch; by those who make movies, even if Dickens appears there just as a motif, as in *Melody for a Street Organ* or *Come Look at Me*. This means that his works are vital and vibrating; time has no power over them, and they keep inspiring new emotions, ideas, and creations. I personally am convinced that the story of Dickens in post-Soviet Russia is only beginning: as he writes in the 1850 *Household Words* sketch "A Chrismas Tree," "the magic bell commands the music to cease, and the great green curtain rolls itself up majestically, and The Play begins!"

NOTE

1. Translations of titles and other materials from Russian are my own.

WORKS CITED

Books, Dissertations, and Essays
Boborykina, T[atiana] A. *The Artistic World of Charles Dickens's Tales*. In Russian. St. Petersburg: Hippocrat, 1996.
———. *The Artistic World of Charles Dickens's Christmas Books: The Dramatic Principle in Prose*. In English. St. Petersburg: Hippocrat, 1997.
Bogdanova, O. Y. *The Poetics of Landscape in Charles Dickens's Novels*. In Russian. Tambov: Derzavin State University Publishing House, 2006.
Dickens, Charles. *Christmas Books*. In Russian. St. Petersburg: Azbuka-Classica, 2010.
———. *Christmas Books*. Ed. unknown. Trans. T. Ozerskaya. Illus. Arthur Rackham. Moscow: Anatolya, 2005.
———. *Collected Works*. Copy of twenty-volume edition (Moscow: Terra Publishing House, 2000). Moscow: Anatolya, 2005.
———. *Complete Works*. Copy of the thirty-volume Complete Collection (Moscow: Moscow State Publishing House of Fiction, 1957–63). Anatolya, 2005.
———. *David Copperfield*. Copy from the thirty-volume Complete Collection (Moscow: Moscow State Publishing House of Fiction, 1957–63). Moscow: Anatolya, 2005.
———. *Great Expectations*. Ed. I. Tarasenko. Trans. M. Lorie. St. Petersburg: Azbuka-Classica, 2011.
———. *The Life of Our Lord*. Ed. Hieromonk Simeon (Tomachinsky). Trans. N. Demurova. Illus. O. Ionaytis. Moscow: Sretensky Stauropegial Monastery Publishing House, 2008.
———. *The Mystery of Edwin Drood*. Ed. S. Antonov. Trans. O. Holmskaya. Commentaries: E. Desnitskaya. Afterword: A. Efremov. St. Petersburg: Azbuka-Classica, 2006; Moscow: Azbuka-Classica, 2011.

————. *Oliver Twist*. Trans. Alexandra Krivtsova, Moscow: Pan Press, 2009.

————. *Oliver Twist*. Trans. Alexandra Krivtsova. Illus. George Cruikshank and Gustave Doré. Moscow: Moscow Anatolya, 1996.

————. *Oliver Twist*. Trans. Alexandra Krivtsova. St. Petersburg: AST, 2010.

————. *The Posthumous Papers of the Pickwick Club*. Trans. Alexandra Krivtsova and Eugeny Lann. Moscow: Eksmo, 2003.

————. *The Posthumous Papers of the Pickwick Club*. Trans. Alexandra Krivtsova and Eugeny Lann. Illus. Vladimir Milashevsky, S. Aldin, Hablot Knight Browne, and Robert Seymour. Moscow: Eksmo, 2008.

————. *The Posthumous Papers of the Pickwick Club*. Ed. V. P. Butromeev, V. V. Butromeev, and N. V. Butromeeva. Trans. Alexandra Krivtsova and Eugeny Lann. Illus. S. Aldin, Hablot Knight Browne, Robert Seymour, Daniel Maclise, Ernest Nister, et al. Series: Big Illustrated Classics Library. Moscow: Bely Gorod, 2003.

————. *Stories for Children*. Trans. Vera Dorofeeva. Illus. Harold Copping. Series: Books with History. Moscow: Mesheryakov Publishing House, 2010.

————. *A Tale of Two Cities*. Trans. E. Beketova. St. Petersburg: Azbuka-Classica, 2010.

Genieva, E[katerina] Y., ed. *The Mystery of Charles Dickens*. In Russian. Moscow: Kniznaya palata, 1990.

Iampolski, Mikhail B. *The Memory of Tiresias*. In Russian. Moscow: Kultura, 1993.

————. *Memory of Tiresias: Intertextuality and Film*. In English. Berkeley: U of California P, 1998.

Katarsky, Igor. *Dickens in Russia*. Moscow: Nauka, 1960.

Khaitchenko, E[lena] G. *The Great Romantic Shows*. In Russian. Moscow: Gitis, 1996.

————. *Victorianism in the Mirror of the Music Hall*. In Russian. Moscow: Gitis, 2009.

Kondarina, Irina. *The Reception of Dickens in Russia from 1850 to 1950*. In Russian. Moscow: RGB, 2004.

Levitova, V[ictoria]. "On Dickens's Visuality, Proust, Eisenstein and Next to Nothing on Griffith." *Kinovedcheskie zapiski* no. 67 (2004): 230–38.

Orwell, George. *1984*. New York: New American Library, 1983.

Sheveleva, T. "Christian Motifs in Charles Dickens's Works." In Russian. Diss. Nizni Novgorod, 2004.

Tchudin, Dmitry. "Pedagogical Conception of 'A New Education' by Charles Dickens." In Russian. Diss. Volgograd State Pedagogical University, 2008

Urnov, M[ikhail] V. *The Inimitable: Dickens, Editor and Publisher*. In Russian. Moscow: Kniga, 1990.

Films, Television Presentations, and Videos

Charles Dickens's England. Documentary. Dir. Julian Richards, with Derek Jacobi. UK, 2009.

A Christmas Carol. (*Duhi Rozdestva*.) Dir. David Hugh Jones, with Patrick Stewart as Scrooge. UK, 1999.

————. (*Rozdestvenskaya istoria/skazka*.) Live action/animated film. Dir. Jimmy T. Murakami. UK, 2001.

———. (*Rozdestvenskaya istoriya.*) 3-D film. Dir. Robert Lee Zemeckis. USA, 2009.

Come Look at Me (*Prikhodi Na Menya Posmotret*). Dir. Oleg Yankovsky and Mikhail Agranovich. Screenplay by Nadezda Ptushkina. Musical score by V. Bibergan. Starring Oleg Yankovsky, Irina Kupchenko, and Ekaterina Vasiljeva. Russia, 2001.

The Cricket on the Hearth. Musical film. Dir. Leonid Netchaev. Screenplay by Galina Arbuzova. Musical score by E. Krylatov. Song lyrics by Y. Entin. Available on DVD with English subtitles. Russia, 2001.

David Copperfield. Dir. George Cukor. USA, 1935.

———. BBC film. Dir. Simon Curtis. UK, 1999.

———. Dir. Peter Medak. USA, 2000.

———. Italian TV film. Dir. Ambrogio Lo Giudice, 2009.

Dickens. BBC docudrama. Dir. Mary Dawnes and Chris Granlund. Written and presented by Peter Ackroyd, with Anton Lesser as Dickens. UK, 2002.

Dickens' Secret Lover. Docudrama. (In the miniseries *Victorian Passions.*) Dir. Sarah Aspinall. Presented by Charles Dance. UK, 2008.

Dombais et fils (after *Dombey and Son*). Dir. Laurent Jaoui. Screenplay by Aleksandr Adabashyan. France, 2007.

Great Expectations. Dir. Alfonso Cuarón, with Robert De Niro. USA, 1998.

Martin Chuzzlewit. Six-part miniseries. Dir. Pedr James. UK, 1994.

Melody for a Street Organ (*Melodiya dlya sharmanki*). Dir. Kira Muratova. Screenplay by Vladimir Zuev and Kira Muratova. Music by Zemfira. Featuring Lena Kostyuk, Roma Burlaka, Renata Litvinova, and Oleg Tabakov. Russia, 2009.

The Old Curiosity Shop. Dir. Kevin Connor, with Peter Ustinov. USA, 1995.

Oliver! Musical film based on Lionel Bart's stage musical. Dir. Carol Reed, with Mark Lester as Oliver. UK, 1968.

Oliver Twist. Dir. David Lean. UK, 1948.

Oliver Twist. Dir. Roman Polanski. UK, France, Italy, Czech Republic, 2005.

Scrooge (Russian title: *Mister Scrooge*). Dir. Henry Edwards. Featuring Seymour Hicks as Ebenezer Scrooge. UK, 1935; DVD issued in Moscow, 2009.

Audiobooks

Dickens, Charles. *A Christmas Carol* and "The Signalman." Series: In Foreign Languages. In Russian. Read by Vladimir Samoilov. English by Cora McDonald. CD. Moscow: Ardis, 2011.

———. *Little Dorrit.* Series: Dickens's Theater. Scenario and direction by N. Agapova. In Russian. Performed by Moscow theater actors. MP3. Moscow: Novospassky Stauropegial Monastery, 2010.

———. *The Posthumous Papers of the Pickwick Club.* Series: Audiobook. In Russian. Performed by Ivan Litvinov. DVD, Moscow: Media-Kniga, 2010.

Theater Productions

The Battle of Life: A Love Story. Dir. Sergey Zhenovach. Design by Alexander Borovsky, Music by Grigory Gobernik. Moscow Studio of Theater Arts. May 2008.

A Christmas Story with Ghosts. Musical intended for children. Dir. Y. Tomashevsky. Music by A. Gorbenko. Choreographer: E. Smirnov. Stage design: B. Kaminsky. Costume design: I. Tcherednikova. St. Petersburg Theater on Liteiny, 1997.

The Cricket on the Hearth. Dir. Georgy Tshilava. Set design by Emil Kapelush. St. Petersburg State Theater of Young Spectators, Malaya scena (small stage). April 2008.

Oliver! Lionel Bart's musical version of *Oliver Twist*. Dir. Attila Ratly. St. Petersburg Musical Comedy Theater. December 18, 2010.

The Pickwick Club. Two-act comedy. Dir. Eugeny Pisarev. Adapted by Natalia Vekstern. Set design by Zinovy Margolin. Costumes by Leonid Alexeev. Chekhov Moscow Arts Theater. 2009.

Recent Dickens Studies: 2010

Nancy Aycock Metz

This review surveys over a hundred articles, book chapters, and books comprising the year's scholarship on Dickens studies published in 2010. In addition, I consider two recent fictionalizations of the Dickens biography—a novel and a play. Where scholarly materials are concerned, I aimed to be comprehensive. I have not, however, attempted to examine the full range of Dickens adaptations and representations in popular culture. Throughout the review, my goal has been to serve readers engaged in their own scholarly projects by suggesting what could prove valuable to them in the methods, insights, and subjects of this impressive and wideranging—but dauntingly voluminous—body of research. The article is organized under the following headings: Biography, History, and Reference; Dickens the Writer/Dickens and His Readers; Sources, Influence, Intertextual Engagements; Language, Structure, Style, and Genre; Gender, Family, Children, Education; Social Class, Economics, Politics, and the Law; Urban and Cosmopolitan Contexts; Science, Technology, and the Arts; Ethical and Philosophical Approaches; Adaptation.

Although the scholarship reviewed here was published in 2010, I write this article on the cusp of the bicentennial year with a consciousness of how strongly this body of research reflects Dickens's soon-to-be-celebrated global impact and significance. International scholars will be found in abundance in the year's bibliography, and the study of Dickens in relationship to other cultures and to a more broadly defined world literature has gained visibly in breadth and momentum. The year's work in Dickens studies is notable in particular for a rich strand of scholarly conversation around the concept of "cosmopolitanism"—Dickens's relation to nation and world and our own relationship as readers to the worlds of his fiction. Recent studies of Dickens and his audiences—most comprehensively, Juliet John's *Dickens and Mass Culture*—offer a window into the bicentennial phenomenon itself, helping us to understand the "portability" of Dickens's appeal across cultures, historical eras, and media and offering insights into the question of why, 200 years after his birth, worldwide communities continue to form and thrive around his potent art.

In addition to the welcome challenge of total-immersion in Dickens scholarship, I faced the challenge of organizing this large and various body of scholarship. Ten (by no means inevitable, and necessarily overlapping) categories eventually made sense to me: Biography, History, and Reference; Dickens the Writer/Dickens and His Readers; Sources, Influence, Intertextual Engagements; Language, Structure, Style, and Genre; Gender, Family, Children, Education; Social Class, Economics, Politics, and the Law; Urban and Cosmopolitan Contexts; Science, Technology, and the Arts; Ethical and Philosophical Approaches; Adaptation.

Biography, History, and Reference

The year's work in Dickens studies includes noteworthy contributions to biography inviting significant reconsideration of the way we view Dickens's formative years and relationships. Scholarly work on Catherine Dickens, Ellen Ternan, and their changing biographical representation speak to a growing interest in the intersection of biography with history, ideology, and culture.

Pursuing contradictions and gaps in the scholarly record pertaining to Dickens's Blacking Factory period, Michael Allen reaches the following conclusions: "Dickens was employed not by Jonathan Warren but by William Edward Wodd." "He began labouring in the blacking warehouse at the age of 11 not 12." "His relationship to the Lamerte family drew him into the world of Jewish families around Whitechapel and Holborn," introducing him to "a very plausible model for Fagin" (5).

Allen's article "New Light on Dickens and the Blacking Factory" provides a first person account of a scholarly quest pursued with great persistence and ingenuity. It takes us through genealogical records, insurance company documents, and Chancery Court briefs—documents that provide insights into the blacking business in the first decades of the nineteenth-century and into the fierce rivalry between Jonathan and Thomas Warren and their families, patriarchs of a thriving enterprise into whose protracted feud the child Dickens was unwittingly drawn. The trail is difficult to follow because the warring parties in competition to corner the blacking market engaged in strategic obfuscation, and because references in Forster's account of the period are difficult to reconcile with the genealogical record, itself subject to gaps and contradictions.

Although many details in the story remain elusive (was it George Lamerte or James Lamerte who was the manager of Warren's Blacking, and was the name spelled with or without a final "e"?), Allen's research prompts reconsideration of the crucial Blacking Factory episode in significant ways. Court papers from the Woodd v. Lamerte case, which make it possible to date more precisely the firm's move from Hungerford Stairs to Chandos Street, suggest that Dickens's ballpark estimate of a year's abandonment to drudgery was not retrospectively exaggerated by the trauma of the experience. Revising the earlier calculations in his groundbreaking study *Charles Dickens's Childhood*, Allen calculates that Dickens "started at Hungerford Stairs in September 1823, that he was moved to Chandos Street in January 1824, when the business was relocated, and that his father removed him from Warren's Blacking in September 1824" (28). Allen speculates that Dickens's cousin George (James?) Lamerte could have taken him to visit his "rather loosely related relatives," the Lamerte and Worms families, of German descent in the Whitechapel area. Such visits may have given Dickens access to Jewish culture in the very neighborhood he would later depict in *Oliver Twist*. In the person of Laurence Worms, a receiver of stolen goods, surrounded by six of his eight children and living "within spitting distance of Field Lane" (25), Dickens may even have found a model for Fagin. While no proof of these hypothetical encounters has been found, Allen notes that family associations would have given Dickens more likely and more intimate access to Worms than to Ikey Solomon, the accepted prototype for Fagin. Allen's resourcefulness, persistence, and close attention to detail make this essay as fascinating on the grounds of its scholarly process as for the rich context it provides on Dickens's early trauma.

In another kind of biographical quest narrative, Steven Jarvis, in "Robert Seymour's Tombstone: A Personal Account of Its Recovery," traces an interest in Pickwick's first illustrator from his first acquaintance with Seymour's work, to the discovery of the artist's abandoned remains in the churchyard of St. Mary Magdelene, Islington, to the removal of the tombstone and its placement in the garden of the Dickens Museum in January 2010.

Although a suicide via gunshot wound to the heart, Seymour was declared a victim of "temporary insanity" and thus eligible for burial in consecrated ground. His tombstone had long been missing, however, when Jarvis found a reference in the Islington archives to its storage in the crypt of St. Mary's Magdalene—a location that on closer inspection proved to be a mere "tombstone dump" (37). Struck by the dishonor of this "filthy, neglected tombstone which had been left to crumble away in total darkness" (38), Jarvis began to plan for its removal to the garden at Doughty Street, a fitting tribute to the prolific artist known as a contemporary Hogarth and as "The Shakespeare of Caricature" (38). In the process of investigating this possibility, Jarvis discovered photographic evidence of an alternative monument once extant in East Finchley, the inscription of which perpetuated Seymour's wife's claim that he was "the originator of Pickwick" (40). The reference on this later tombstone to family members buried in Robert Seymour's Islington grave, together with the absence of inscriptions on the original monument, evidenced "one harsh fact: after Seymour's suicide, the family was reduced to poverty, and were too poor to pay a stonemason's fees. Everyone had benefited from *Pickwick*, except them" (41).

Jarvis notes that final approval for the removal of this original tombstone to the garden of the Dickens House Museum has been granted. A plaque now honors Seymour's achievements, which were formally recognized at an unveiling ceremony this past year.

Lillian Nayder's revisionist biography of Catherine, *The Other Dickens*, though technically copyrighted 2011, came to me before the end of the year. The most ambitious, meticulously researched, and provocative of the year's biographical contributions, it deserves to be recognized here. Nayder proves adept at building up the texture and significance of Catherine's life from an ingenious range of evidence—visual iconography, household inventories, banking records, "conception waits," testamentary bequests.

Avowedly Catherine's champion, Nayder dedicates the biography to Catherine's youngest sister Helen, "her advocate, companion, and chief mourner"; she positions it against the context of previous biographical treatments that "reinforce the logic of coverture" by subsuming Catherine's story within Dickens's own, in the process reducing her to "the helpmeet gone bad" (1). Nayder is interested in exposing the "mythic elements" in this insufficiently questioned narrative and the "unspoken functions they serve" (1). Removing Dickens from the center to the margins, she seeks to recover Catherine, not as an essential self, but in relation to many with whom she shared experiences and affections.

The biography's structure, which pauses from strict chronology to fold in three "interlude" chapters, especially foregrounds Catherine's relationships with Mary, Georgina, and Helen at the stage in Catherine's life when each sister was most important to her; these chapters make substantive and original contributions to our understanding of the family dynamic. Arguing against the traditional view of Mary as a pretty, diminutive, worshipful figure—Catherine's rival for Dickens's affections—Nayder gives us an intelligent and frequently irreverent Mary, offering credible evidence from existing letters of the sisters' camaraderie, companionship, mutual support, and sense of humor.

Nayder cautions against adopting the "standard geometry of Dickens studies," in which "the novelist appears at the apex of a love triangle and the Hogarth sisters below, their own connection notably foreshortened" (194). She cites household accounts, banking records, letters, and the diaries of acquaintances and friends to show that an affectionate sisterly bond marked the relationship between Catherine and Georgina for many years before the marital break-up, and that—so far from filling the void left by Catherine's "incompetence"—through the early 1850s, Georgina deferred to Catherine, who was highly active in the home and "senior partner" in domestic management. That Georgina did ultimately "rise" over Catherine in household authority should not be attributed to the latter's "lassitude," Nayder argues: "the two sisters were set apart . . . by their marital status, a dozen pregnancies, two miscarriages, and the births of ten children" (200).

About Helen, the least well-known and youngest of the Hogarth sisters Nayder provides a helpful, interestingly developed context. "The only Hogarth sister 'unclaimed' by Dickens" (299), Helen became the target of Dickens's wrath when she assertively defended Catherine in the aftermath of the separation. Helen earned her own living as a professional musician, sharing this love of music and the opportunities for community arising from musical performance with her sister, to whom she became increasingly close after the separation—at a time when Catherine felt her dislocation and isolation most sharply. Keenly observant of these extended familial relationships, Nayder testifies to what was strong and affirming in them, ultimately outlasting Dickens's prohibitions and even Catherine's death.

In the Afterword to *The Other Dickens*, entitled "Suttee Business," Nayder remarks that "Since the 1880s, Catherine Dickens has been consigned to her grave prematurely, her death assumed to coincide with her husband's in 1870—or with their separation twelve years earlier" (338). Extending the frame to give due emphasis to the 42 of her 64 years that she lived apart from Dickens (1), Nayder gives us a young Catherine possessed of a strong sense of self-worth, who had been raised in an educated and musical household in an atmosphere that recognized women as reasoning adults and intellectual partners. Most interestingly for me, she provides a wealth of detail about the post-separation and widowhood years—a story that has never been fully told—how Catherine reconstituted her life in Gloucester Crescent, supported her sister's musical career, cultivated social networks and family connections, coped with financial constraints, and in general lived a life that was "much busier and happier than critics acknowledge" (289). Although the terms of Dickens's will left Catherine more constrained financially than she had been after the separation, widowhood (the news of which, it is alleged, she learned from a billboard before Georgina's dispatch could reach her) imbued her with a kind of perverse dignity since "it was considerably more prestigious to be Dickens's widow than to be his jilted wife" (323). The queen telegraphed her condolences.

Nayder's analysis of the marriage years resists the narrative, scripted by Dickens and perpetuated by many of his biographers, that Catherine's incapacities and the couple's fundamental incompatibility doomed the union from the start. Emphasizing how their reciprocal affection and mutual attachment were strengthened in the early years by the experience of parenthood, Nayder identifies her own warning signs in Dickens's micromanaging of household affairs and in his constant evocation of an "ideal" (compliant, selfless) Catherine to whom the "real" (femininely flawed) Catherine should aspire. Dickens's powers as a mesmerist, and Catherine's pattern of alternately succumbing to and resisting his considerable hypnotic prowess, figure significantly in the biography—not only in the analysis of Dickens's relationship with Madame De La Rue and its aftermath, but more generally: "In fact the mesmeric state might be seen as a fitting emblem for Catherine's experience of coverture during that period, as Browning suggests it could be for Victorian wives generally" (90).

An early review by D. J. Taylor of *The Other Dickens* in *The Wall Street Journal* (Dec. 7, 2010), credits Nayder for her painstaking research but wonders about its larger significance: "It is difficult to see what wider point she is trying to prove. Hardly anything in her study seriously illuminates Dickens's work, which, after all, is the only reason anyone cares about him 140 years after his death." The comment seems to me to miss the point, for it is manifestly Catherine herself—her human story disentangled from that of Dickens and his loyal biographers—that Nayder cares about. Justice for Catherine. And although I am not convinced that a "wider significance" is necessary to authorize Nayder's impressive biographical research, the study's multidisciplinary contextualizing of nineteenth-century gender issues does, in fact, give it an interest and significance beyond Catherine's individual experiences or her relationship with her famous husband. Particularly fascinating are Nayder's discussions of women's bodies in relationship to medical practice—the psychological impact of lengthy confinements, the physical consequences associated with "great grand multiparity," the rewards in terms of "worth, purpose, and community" of even such seemingly excessive childbearing, the vulnerability to blame and misrepresentation of the female body itself (160). In the same way, the patiently detailed background Nayder provides about marriage and custody laws, wills, and property rights, which function as essential background to our understanding of Catherine's status as wife, abandoned spouse, and widow, also serves to illuminate the broader context of the law's restrictive powers over the lives of ordinary women in their pursuit of happiness, self-realization, and agency.

Ewa Kujawska-Lis shares Nayder's interest in the historical and cultural context of biography and in the process by which biographical interpretation is shaped by ideology and culture. In her essay "Dickens and Ternan in Polish Criticism," she considers Polish representation of the Ellen Ternan relationship, framing her discussion in terms of more general historical and cultural trends in the reception of Dickens's work.

Kujawska-Lis notes that nineteenth-century readers of Dickens's novels regarded his fiction as exemplary on the basis of its humor, humanity, and treatment of social issues, but consigned him to the category of "popular" novelist when modernism ushered in a new appreciation for concision and psychological depth. In the socialist People's Republic of Poland created after World War II, Dickens served propaganda purposes in exposing the capitalist system, but some felt that he did not go far enough, showed no real understanding of class struggle, and shied away from revolutionary solutions. In democratic Poland, with its free-market economy, publishers seized on the commercial value of Dickens's works, and literary critics explored overlooked dimensions of his artistry and literary technique.

In similar ways, the representation of Dickens's marriage and relationship to Ellen Ternan was shaped by available knowledge and by shifting ideological trends. Nineteenth-century critics knew of the separation but not of Ellen Ternan's role in it—no surprise since facts were slow in coming to light even in England. The first Polish monograph on Dickens was published in 1936 after the scandal was public knowledge in England and America, but no mention is made of the Dickens/Ternan relationship, and the dissolution of the marriage is attributed to Catherine's inability to respond to the needs of her genius husband. In the 1940s the subject was considered taboo: "A paragon of virtue, Dickens could not be presented as leading a secret life with a lover" (50). Rather, the failure of the marriage was attributed to flaws in the social system that encouraged marriages of convenience over more meaningful partnerships. For nearly a century, Dickens was seen as the victim of an abandonment so cruel that it cast its gloom over the later novels. The translation in 1953 of Thomas A. Jackson's *Charles Dickens: The Progress of a Radical* (1937) opened the door to an interpretation of Dickens's marriage based on class-based incompatibilities. In one interpretation, Dickens was seen as ending the marriage in an effort to break out of the constraints of the bourgeois family.

In 1955, the facts of the Ellen Ternan relationship were accurately disclosed, but misinformation and interpretation grounded in stereotypes persisted. Kujawska-Lis notes that in the 1970s, Irena Dobrzycka's comprehensive study of Dickens and Stefan Majchrowski's fictionalized biography made significant inroads against earlier moralizing and mythologizing treatments. Her article provides a solid contribution to the burgeoning scholarly interest in Dickens's global circulation and reception.

Reference works published in 2010 include Bernard A. Drew's *Literary Afterlife: The Posthumous Continuations of 325 Authors' Fictional Characters* and John Mee's *The Cambridge Introduction to Charles Dickens*.[1] The first of these, an encyclopaedia of sequels, continuations, and other forms of literary pastiche has the potential to be useful to scholars, but alarming errors of fact, including the claim that Dickens married Maria Beadnell and "after that marriage ended, he wed Catherine Hogarth" (40) do not inspire confidence in the results. Drew provides six entries for *A Christmas Carol* between 1998 and 2003 and fifteen *Drood* "collaborations and pastiches" from 1871 to 1993.

John Mee's *The Cambridge Introduction to Charles Dickens* is structured around five topics selected to "open up the richness of the Dickens world" (ix). In chapters on "Dickens the Entertainer," "Dickens and Language," "Dickens and the City," "Dickens, Gender, and Domesticity, and "Adapting Dickens," Mee addresses students and other general readers of Dickens in an accessible overview designed to be read in its entirety rather than strip-mined for research paper purposes. Whether students are likely to read in the way Mee intends is perhaps an open question, but those who do will find engaging discussions of familiar themes. Tracing Dickens's commitment to popular entertainment to the childhood plays he directed in the family kitchen and the songs he sang in the local pub, Mee touches on the expansion of literacy that created new audiences for fiction and the serialized form that Dickens exploited so brilliantly. He describes the radical, sentimental, and sensational elements in Dickens's popular fiction.

The chapter on language pays specific attention to Dickens's acts of naming, his use of zeugma or syllepsis, and his deployment of presiding metaphors to provide linguistic structure in the later novels. Mee emphasizes the heteroglossia of Dickens's narrative voice, the way "tone and register are continually changing to provide a shimmering sea of different kinds of speech that plays across their surface" (34). In the chapter on "Dickens and the City," Mee introduces his readers to cinematic dimensions of Dickens's urban descriptions, to Benjamin's concept of the flâneur, and to the "forensic desire" that led Dickens to penetrate London's darkest neighborhoods for the benefit of his middle-class readership.

Mee identifies *Dombey and Son* as the novel that "marks the beginning of a more detailed exploration of the dark mysteries that haunt family relationships" (75). His discussion of gender and domesticity focuses on the "little" women of Dickens's novels, their angry and resentful counterparts in his later fiction, and the surrogate families that "resolve themselves into quasi-familial groups" in response to the forces of alienation and fragmentation (82). A final chapter on adaptation begins with the plagiarisms of Dickens's own time, goes on to explore the original illustrations to the novel within the context of Victorian visual culture, and considers briefly the contributions to cinematic adaptation of Sergei Eisenstein, David Lean, Alphonso Cuarón, and Christine Edzard. A helpful chronology and list of further readings is provided.

The final entry in the "Biography, History, and Reference" section of my review fills a gap in the documentary record by offering the beginnings of an institutional history—a timely intervention given the tendency of memories to fade. David Paroissien's "The Dickens Society: A Retrospect" offers a fascinating narrative of the forty-year history of the Society, from the events leading to its founding in 1970 to its flourishing state of affairs in 2010.

In December 1969 at the MLA convention in Denver, interest in the formation of a Dickens society based in the United States was first proposed.

Though the first proposal was defeated, an ad hoc planning committee pursued a set of related goals, including the publication of *Dickens Studies Newsletter*, which first appeared in 1970 as an add-on to the first edition of *Dickens Studies Annual*. In December 1970 the Dickens Society was officially constituted at the MLA convention in New York "with eight Articles of Incorporation and twenty-seven By-Laws." The society still honors many of the original goals— an annual MLA seminar, transatlantic scholarly exchanges, prizes and stipends to support the work of young professionals.

What started out as *Dickens Studies Newsletter* has matured into *Dickens Quarterly*, "a serious critical journal offering special issues, a forum for the discussion of particular topics, substantial book reviews, and the quarterly Checklist" (70). Paroissien notes that grander goals born of the availability of large grants in the humanities in the 1960s have required adjusting. The society never did garner the funds necessary to underwrite large editorial projects like the proposed Dickens concordance. But modest assistance to young scholars is offered in the form of the Robert B. Partlow Prize, now awarded as travel support to the annual conference. In 1997 the first of the annual symposia was held at Worcester Polytechnic Institute, an addition to the MLA special sessions. The Symposium now meets alternatively on each side of the Atlantic.

The article outlines these changes in the organization and the influential role played by scholars and advocates in the years between 1970 and the present. [A not-to-be-missed sequel to Paroissien's narrative is Jerome Meckier's long, entertainingly anecdotal letter to the editor in the June 2011 issue of *Dickens Quarterly*, which fills in details and, in a cheerfully contentious way, corrects the record. Because of its publication date, the piece is not covered by this review but it is worth noting in the context of Paroissien's pioneering efforts to establish an archival record.]

Dickens the Writer/Dickens and His Readers

Two ambitious studies of Dickens in relationship to his audience appeared in 2010, Juliet John's *Dickens and Mass Culture* and Robert McParland's *Charles Dickens's American Audience*.

Juliet John's *Dickens and Mass Culture* offers an astute, wide-ranging commentary on the productive tensions and contradictions underlying Dickens's distinctive role as a popular artist of unprecedented power and reach. John's book is divided into two parts—"Dickens in His Day" and "Afterlives"—with individual chapters addressing the development of the Dickens "brand," the impact of the first American journey on Dickens's conception of mass culture, Dickens's journalistic method and message, his strategic deployment of changes in methods of mass communication and mechanical reproduction, the public readings, Dickens and the evolution of film, heritage Dickens, and the Dickens World controversy. A close and insightful reader of these widely varying literary and cultural phenomena, John weaves together their significance in probing, thoughtful ways. Dickens's ambivalence about mass culture (whose markets he brilliantly tapped) and his continuing "vexed relationship" with academic criticism (whose categories and binaries his work provocatively blurs) are placed in an illuminating, richly contextualized context.

John notes that Dickens promoted key elements of a narrative about his own popularity—that, for example, his work "united readers of all social classes," creating a worldwide community with himself at the center (7). She identifies three characteristics that, combined, make Dickens's popularity unique—his conscious engineering of the Dickens brand through strategic exploitation of the new possibilities inherent in the dawning age of mechanical reproduction, his high degree of seriousness about his art, and his lasting impact on popular culture. Dickens's "portability," the facility with which his texts can be translated into various media, continuing to circulate through a global marketplace into contemporary times, constitutes a feature of his work with significant implications for John.

John's discussion of Dickens's popular aesthetic emphasizes his view of culture as a flexible bridge, a "linking, mobile, transformative sphere and idea" whose "value to individuals and societies lies in its ability to evade categorization, to grow, to change, to be itself and not itself" (40). Dickens conceived of literary texts as porous and elastic, open to popular influences and translatable into different genres and formats for different audiences. He believed that through the shared medium of culture, class divisions could be minimized and community affirmed.

John offers a carefully modulated and context-sensitive analysis of Dickens's politics, finally settling on "the oxymoronic idea of paternalistic populism" to describe Dickens's political stance (62). In Dickens's case, she argues, paternalism did not signal an affirmation of the status quo so much as a recognition that in a class-based society, "those with cultural capital [must] help, nurture, or educate those below them in the social hierarchy in order to erase inequalities" (62). The culture shock of his visit to America, however, challenged in important ways Dickens's sense of himself as a populist, highlighting the difference between "cultural inclusivity" and "cultural democracy"—the latter leading dangerously to a fading away of intellectual and cultural leadership and its replacement by the lowest common denominator (84). John believes that Dickens's American experience left him with "a repressed, subterranean rage against the kind of mass culture [he] perceived there, and a yearning for a culture that somehow transcends the market" (87).

In a fascinating chapter on Dickens's journalism, John shows how Dickens worked through some of the contradictions and paradoxes of this yearning through his editorial work for *Household Words* and *All the Year Round*.

Wanting to compete successfully for market share—and also to transform the market into an imagined community transcending commercial interests, wanting to exert political power, but from a position outside politics, Dickens's logic was "that of intimate publicity," the development of a personal mode with a universal mass appeal. The public readings physically enact this complex relationship. Dickens establishes intimate relationships with his audience and through the sheer power of his performance builds them up as a community of shared feeling. At the same time, his success becomes manifest and meaningful to him in the currency of head counts and ticket sales.

John argues that Dickens occupies a "threshold position in cultural history, his works and philosophies informed by both a mechanical *and* an organicist conception of art" (158). Dickens, she says, "is clearly not opposed to mechanism per se, but to the use of mechanism without a larger commitment or emotional investment in community and human relationships: he envisages ideally a 'halfway house' or creative fusion between people and things, the personal and the wholesale" (172).

For John, no machine has been more influential in Dickens's contemporary re-invention than the camera. Two substantial chapters in the "Afterlives" section of the book are devoted to Dickens's "portability" in the cinematic medium. In the first, she explores some of the reasons that filmmakers so often turn to Dickens's novels, noting the marketability of the Dickens "brand," but also the aesthetic dimensions of Dickens's novels that translate well into film—the emphasis on the visual and the scenic, the representation of ideas or psychological states through things, the use of montage, the fusion of realist and anti-realist techniques. In the next chapter, she offers an absorbing case study of "*Oliver Twist* on Screen," situating film and television adaptations of the novel in the context of their historical moments and their relationships both to the original text and to each other. In so doing, John helpfully complicates the "fidelity" issue, noting that "it is not just adapters that adapt texts. History adapts texts; contexts frame them; texts are never simply themselves" (220).

The closing chapters of the study address "Heritage Dickens" and "Dickens Worlds Past, Present, and to Come." In the first of these, John demonstrates the ways in which Dickens's own writing embodies a "heritage aesthetic," especially in his descriptions of inns or homes imbued with a nostalgic celebration of pre-industrial objects or in his "picture postcard" representations of his own homes in letters from afar. She points to the paradoxical place of *A Christmas Carol* in this regard: "[its] ability . . . to appear to elevate morality over money whilst simultaneously generating wealth, to rise above a historical moment whilst remaining steeped in it, captures in miniature the story of heritage Dickens" (272).

As the most recent focal point of the controversy over Dickens in relationship to mass culture, the Dickens World theme park in Kent provides a fitting point of reference for the conclusion of John's study. John's measured, thoughtful response to the Dickens World phenomenon addresses the question of its "educational value," interestingly taking into account the closely observed reactions of her own children, their degree of engagement and choice of entertainments. Ultimately, though, she is less interested in what they and other visitors to the theme park learn about Dickens than in the larger question the park raises about mass culture: "whether commercial popular culture can ever be 'good' in the sense that Dickens intended—that is, in its ability to empower 'the People governed'" (283–84).

A new edition of *Balzac, Dickens, Dostoevsky: Three Masters*, volume 1 of the *Master Builders of the Spirit* series makes available once more an eloquent tribute to Dickens, the writer, by the early twentieth-century Austrian novelist, playwright, journalist, and cosmopolitan, Stefan Zweig. Originally published in 1930, the three-volume work represents Zweig at the height of his powers and international literary reputation. In his portrait of Dickens (one of nine in the series), Zweig acknowledges "the almost incomprehensible phenomenon" of a "man of genius" perfectly merging with the spirit of his age (55). In Dickens's fiction, Zweig argues, "the apotheosis of the commonplace" achieves the status of art (67). Dickens's imagination "created the idyll of England," "his finest achievement" (94). Zweig predicts: "he will always be a present refuge in time of trouble, when the human heart craves for joyfulness, and . . . turns to the quiet things of life in order to catch the strains of the poet's minstrelsy" (95).

Robert McParland's *Charles Dickens's American Audience* offers the first extended study of Dickens's American audience between 1837 and 1912, arguing that the reading of Dickens's fiction "contributed significantly to the making of American culture" (1). McParland focuses on ordinary readers rather than on professional reviewers or literary figures; he recovers the voices of these readers from a rich variety of primary and often ephemeral sources, including memoirs, autobiographies, letters, marginalia, the minutes of nineteenth-century reading circles, public library circulation records, letters to the editor, newspaper accounts of Dickens's public readings, and publishers' archives.

McParland aligns his work most closely with Benedict Anderson's concept of "imagined communities" and with the work of Ronald J. Zboray on Americans as a "fictive people." Zboray's arguments about the relation between fiction-reading and national identity in antebellum America inform McParland's focus, which is at once more restricted (limited to *one* novelist's impact on the national identity) and more sweeping (embracing a seventy-five-year period of American history).

McParland contends that reading Dickens was a "social and participatory act" that "crossed class, gender, racial, occupational, and national boundaries," "contributed to the development of the American character," and (though not in a political sense) fostered coherence and community (11). Reading Dickens helped Americans to see themselves *as* American in opposition to the British scenes and characters his novels so vividly epitomized, and references in diaries or letters to specific Dickens characters suggest that Dickens's language gave American readers a common shorthand—"ways of coding strangers, ways to cast their fleeting impressions of people, their appearance and mannerisms" (15). As a "shared source of sentiment" providing a "vision of connection among fragmentation" (33), Dickens's novels offered "a home-like point of stability in a rapidly changing society" (1).

McParland draws on Meredith L. McGill and others to position Dickens's texts within a periodical "culture of reprinting" "saturated with an emerging literary nationalism" (52). Remarking that his novels appeared in newspapers adjacent to news, fashion notes, politics, and even "scandalous texts," he observes that Dickens's fiction "intersected with public and private life" (52). Press opposition to Dickens in the wake of his 1842 visit, though temporarily damaging his reputation, did not diminish his readership in the long term, according to McParland, whose analysis of library records shows Dickens's continuing popularity across categories of gender, age, and social class. At midcentury, his novels shared with those of Walter Scott and James Fenimore Cooper the honor of most-circulated texts.

McParland believes that during the Civil War years, when division threatened families, regions, and political constituencies, reading Dickens's texts became "a socially unifying practice," suggesting "a convergence of home-space and public space, the mediation of which presented a challenge for his readers" (122). He notes the circulation of Dickens's serialized novels North and South among civilians, soldiers, and public officials.

McParland views Dickens's theatricality as another element in the novelist's democratic appeal. He notes that theatrical productions of Dickens's novels were numerous during and after Dickens's American reading tour, but in domestic settings as well, Dickens was read aloud in participatory and performative ways or even staged (as in the "Pickwick Club" productions of *Little Women*) in the form of private theatricals (159, 165).

The strength of McParland's study lies in the careful and respectful attention accorded to the voices of ordinary readers—voices reclaimed through patient and resourceful archival research. The book would have benefited, however, from a more disciplined and analytic deployment of these voices. McParland sometimes strings quotes together loosely, using half a dozen instances where one or two would make the point. McParland also assumes that readers will need extensive quoted passages in order to recall famous set-pieces from Dickens—the death of Little Nell, Oliver asking for more, Squeers's spelling lesson at Dotheboys Hall. In general, the book could have been tightened and edited with no loss to its interesting content.

In his essay, "*Pendennis, Copperfield*, and the Debate on the Dignity of Literature," Michael Flynn offers a fresh look at the quarrel waged over several decades between Thackeray, Dickens, and their allies over the professional status of the writer. Readers will remember that the first round of this fight occurred in 1847 when Thackeray published *Novels by Eminent Hands*, parodying contemporary authors and implying that most current fiction was the work of social-climbing Grub Street hacks. At the time Dickens and Forster were sponsoring projects intended to raise the social status of the writing profession.

When the tenth and eleventh numbers of *Pendennis* introduce the hero to London's sleazy literary scene, Forster publically chastised Thackeray, setting off a longstanding division between "self-professed gentlemanly writers who identified with Thackeray" and "proud bohemian journalists who followed Dickens" (154). Flynn's article looks at three dimensions of the feud that have not previously been addressed: (1) how the rift allowed Thackeray to extend the attack on literary snobbery he had started in *Novels by Eminent Hands*; (2) how Forster's rhetoric confirmed Thackeray's belief that proponents of "The Dignity of Literature" were really just clamoring after a social status to which their birth did not entitle them; and (3) how *David Copperfield* picked up and responded to this conversation about literary snobbery.

Starting with the 13th number of *Pendennis*, the novel's shabby literary types either disappear or reform, and critics have traditionally seen this change as a victory for the Forster/Dickens party. But Flynn notes that the rhetoric of class anxiety implicit in the argument Forster made is reproduced in the behavior of these characters. And, in the meantime, the controversy led Thackeray to experiment with a different kind of novel, one that would eschew the incident-driven plots he had come to associate with lower class tastes—but which he himself had written and profited from—in favor of a more realistic treatment of gentlemanly life.

The controversy confronted both authors with contradictions and double-binds, and Flynn is particularly adept in making these underlying tensions visible. Dickens saw snobbery as inherent in the literary marketplace rather than as a character flaw of the writers themselves. But in raising money for the Provident Union of Literature, Science, & Art, the Guild of Literature and Art, and the Royal Literary Society beginning in 1847, he found himself caught up in this system, currying favor with aristocrats in various ways and validating the very patronage he opposed.

Though he could not break through the patronage system as an activist, in *David Copperfield*, Flynn argues persuasively, Dickens did create "exactly that portrait of the unsnobbish professional writer which Forster had failed to provide" (170). The timing and thematic significance of David's decision to become a writer suggest that Dickens had *Pendennis* in mind. David must get beyond his class-based worship of Steerforth and their patronage-based relationship to adopt a middle-class work ethic characterized by effort, persistence, and respect for one's profession.

Glimpses of that work ethic are discernible in the article by John Drew and Michael Slater, "What's in *The Daily News*? A Re-evaluation—Part 1." Since 1900 Dickens's contributions to *The Daily News* have been considered relatively modest—two poems on Corn Law themes, eight Italian "Travelling Letters," a lead article on the Ragged School movement, and five lead articles on capital punishment. Noting Dickens's statement to Bradbury and Evans on assuming the editorship that he intended "frequently writing for the Paper, from day to day," Drew and Slater embark on a more thorough inventory of his contributions (197).

In this first of a two-part article (the second part falls outside the period covered by this 2010 review), the authors weigh the evidence for three heretofore unacknowledged contributions by Dickens, all published in January 1846: a review of Macready's performance of *King Lear* and a pair of satirical letters to the editor engaging timely political issues. With respect to the theater review, they note that though Dickens hired his father-in-law George Hogarth as Theatrical and Music Editor, it is unlikely that Hogarth would have composed *both* the theater review (more likely to have required Hogarth's expertise) and the article adjacent to it, a well-informed piece on "English Glees and Madrigals." Moreover, Dickens was experienced as a theater-reviewer and clearly enjoyed this kind of writing. A comparison of the *Daily News* review to Dickens's 1849 notice in the *Examiner* of Macready's performance at the Haymarket reveals a similar emphasis in each on the role of the Fool as well as "semantically and lexically similar sequences" (200). Moreover, Dickens's magisterial use of "we" in the *Daily News* piece conveys a *gravitas* incompatible with Hogarth's more modest use of the editorial pronoun.

The paired letters to the editor enact a satirical form Dickens perhaps inherited from eighteenth-century essayists—one that he had employed previously in *Master Humphrey's Clock*. The appearance of the letters, one above the other at the top of a page set off with generous leading invests this minor, apparently improvisational contribution with an importance it might not otherwise be thought to warrant. The first letter strikes at a target Dickens had attacked before in his *Examiner* piece of 1843, "Report of the Commissioners Appointed to Enquire into the Condition of the Persons Variously Engaged in the University of Oxford." In the letter, Dickens makes similarly characteristic jabs at Peel's reputation for timid vacillation.

The second letter, lampooning Young England with its reactionary penchant for "the rare old times" adopts a persona and stylistic features Dickens had previously used in his "Threatening Letter to Thomas Hood from an Ancient Gentleman." Cancelled passages from *The Chimes* rehearse many of the same themes and reference some of the same details. "Young England" and the "Bull" family were to reappear in Dickens's 1850 *Household Words* leader, "A Crisis in the Affairs of Mr. John Bull." The signatures to the two letters ("Cocker" and "A Grazier") evoke joking allusions Dickens used elsewhere.

Drew and Slater conclude that the three items attributed to Dickens in this first installment of the article constitute "a relatively minor addition to the canon of Dickens's known journalism" (204). The second part of the essay will consider a much longer piece parodically addressing "the great political issue of the day, and raison d'etre of *The Daily News*—the Repeal of the Corn Laws" (205).

Paying similarly close attention to Dickens's working habits and style, Arthur J. Cox offers the provocative argument that Dickens composed the number plans for *The Mystery of Edwin Drood*—in their entirety—after the fact, "with at least one eye cocked in the direction of . . . readers" (148). In his two-part article, "The *Drood* Remains Revisited: The Monthly Plans," Cox observes a certain playfulness in the style of these notes, evidence of an effort to make them amusing, cryptic, or suggestive for an audience beyond the author's private study. Dickens's allusions in a letter to Wilkie Collins to a brainstorming stage of composition, involving an "immense number of little bits of paper" suggest that Dickens's writing process may have included a primitive, gestational stage of planning anterior to the number plans. Moreover, there is a possible precedent for the order of composition in *Drood*; it has previously been demonstrated that Dickens sometimes wrote the notes to individual serial installments after he composed the chapters themselves.

Such a hypothesis, Cox believes, might explain the notable lack of expository detail in Dickens's notes to *Drood*. Unlike the number plans to earlier novels, where mysteries and plot developments can be deduced from the planning notes and where Dickens records adjustments and transfers of material from number to number, the working plans for *Drood* are notably silent both about narrative outcomes and about Dickens's own composing process. Cox speculates that with respect to *Drood*, Dickens was operating on a different set of assumptions about the likely readers of his plans. Dickens's deteriorating health gave him reason to suspect that he would not live to see the completion of this final novel; indeed, he admitted this fear to his daughter Kate when she visited Gad's Hill in June 1870.

Did the *Drood* plans constitute Dickens's final playful engagement with readers beyond the grave? Cox's ingenious argument does not offer positive proof, but the article does demonstrate convincingly that the notes were staged and timed to preserve the mystery of the novel—indeed to contribute to its teasing suspense—and it is certainly consistent with what we know of Dickens's personality and editorial practices that he would seek to exercise maximum control over literary effects that might fall into the hands of readers at his anticipated death.

In "Reading, Sympathy, and the Bodies of *Bleak House*," Katherine Montwieler focuses on the activity of reading, offering *Bleak House* as a kind of primer on how Dickens models ideal reading for his audience of actual readers. Reading ideally conceived "involves both the body and the mind, or, perception, and apprehension" (238). By paying attention to embodied experience—especially to the profound experiences of birth and death—*Bleak House* seems to say—we learn to appreciate connections and recognize that differences often prove fictive, constructed by language itself. In its capacity to prompt physical reactions, "to cause hearts to flutter or pulses to race" (239), literature helps us to return "to our own physicality—albeit a physicality that is always mediated by language—to better listen to, see, and hear others" (239) and thus to respond to the suffering in the world. In this regard, literature may serve a higher purpose than other kinds of texts sponsored by institutions ostensibly promoting social welfare.

Bleak House, Montwieler asserts, offers "lessons in reading—disastrous examples and pattern models" (241). Mrs. Jellyby, Sir Leicester Dedlock, and Esther Summerson exemplify various forms of myopia—Mrs. Jellyby through her "telescopic philanthropy" and Sir Leicester through his fascination with his aristocratic family history. Esther is literally blinded by her disease, but this blindness functions to move her "from struggling to comprehend the world around her and the historical mysteries created by its institutions to an acceptance of its uncertainties, sufferings, and injustice" (243). Mrs. Snagsby's misreading stems from her blind acceptance of the culture's preoccupation with "naming and codifying of sexual relations" (246). Jo is able to read physical detail but lacks the intellect for genuine understanding. Krook knows instinctively that secrets lie concealed in trash but cannot process the significance of his finds. Krook's undescribed death and Esther's unnamed disease underscore "the limits of language and rationality" (249) while affirming the importance of bearing witness to suffering.

Sources, Influences, Intertextual Engagements

Scholarship in 2010 positions Dickens within a variety of illuminating contexts, identifying possible sources for his characters, textual influences on his work, and negotiations of his language, motifs, and ideas by later writers.

Shane McCorristine's *Spectres of the Self: Thinking about Ghosts and Ghost-Seeing in England, 1750–1920* shows how Dickens inherited a rich and influential tradition of spectral literature, which he absorbed, made his own, and in turn marketed in his periodicals and Christmas books, in the process playing an influential role in stimulating the burgeoning nineteenth-century appetite for accounts of ghostly visitations. McCorristine has done his homework, and one of the pleasures of his study is the proferred wealth of fascinating detail culled from primary sources ranging from fictional works to the case reports of the Society for Psychical Research. Casting a wide net, McCorristine considers such phenomena as telepathy, ghost-hunting, wakeful dreaming, phantasmagoria, and hallucinations. He connects this fascination with ghostly phenomena—a fascination that flourished despite the rationalizing influence of scientific and secular thinking—with "the new conception of the mind as a haunted entity" leading ultimately to "a 'ghostifying' of mental space" (35).

McCorristine considers *A Christmas Carol*, together with Hawthorne's "The Haunted Mind," as poetic treatments of hallucination that point the way toward a modern psychologizing of spectral phenomena. He notes that even before Scrooge receives his ghostly visitors he has identified himself as a "possessed man," occupying chambers once belonging to Marley and answering to his name. Scrooge's initial reactions echo the contemporary spectral illusions theory of hallucinations; like Nicolai, the subject of a famous case study, he is certain that his experiences can be traced to a physiological origin. But "the appearance of so many apparitions bombards and literally frightens Scrooge into a belief in the reality of the spiritual world" (963). McCorristine interestingly explores the gradual "normalization of the idea of hallucinations in the sane in experimental psychology" of the period, noting how Dickens's own creativity came to be connected in literary criticism and in artistic representation (for example, in Robert W. Buss's "Dickens's Dream") to his cultivation of wakeful dream states and to his hallucinatory powers of evocation.

In "Savage and Skimpole," Chris Louttit proposes an overlooked influence on the conception of *Bleak House*'s famous freeloader. From Dickens's own immediate contemporaries down to recent biographers, the identification of Leigh Hunt as the prototype for Harold Skimpole has been universally acknowledged. Dickens himself admitted as much to Forster, at the same time publicly denying that he ever intended Skimpole's vices to be laid at the door of the man who merely served as a model for a character in a work of fiction. Chris Louttit argues that both the admission and the denial can be read as truthful representations if we consider another model for Skimpole—one who explicitly embodies the vices of *Bleak House*'s charismatic sponge.

Louttit proposes as a likely candidate the minor eighteenth-century poet Richard Savage, citing firm evidence in the *Letters* that Dickens knew both Samuel Johnson's *Account of the Life of Mr. Savage* (1744) and Charles Whitehead's fictional biography published in 1842. He notes that Dickens was just beginning to compose *Bleak House* when he received a letter from the literary critic Peter Cunningham proposing that a memorial to Savage be sponsored by the Guild of Literature and Art. The request prompted an angry outburst from Dickens who railed against Savage as a "flagrantly impracticable" vagabond unworthy to represent the Guild.

While Johnson's account of Savage is marked by balance and a "generous relativism" (34), the traits on which Dickens based his more judgmental portrait of Skimpole are very much in evidence. Johnson notes Savage's skill as a conversationalist, his graceful, easy manner, and his lively ability to engage the company on a variety of subjects. Johnson also testifies to Savage's irresponsibility and to his child-like abandonment of any settled purpose or plan, characteristics which provide a gentle moral lesson to Johnson's readers that knowledge, wit, and even genius will in the end fail to compensate where prudence and self-discipline are found wanting.

"Rather than straightforwardly attacking a writer and contemporary that he says he 'admired', Dickens created a composite character, one that combines some of the more positive qualities of Hunt with the deficiencies of Savage" (3–34), Louttit argues. That Dickens read Savage through a harsher and more unforgiving lens than Johnson can be attributed to the changing ideals of the artist as professional in which Dickens was so deeply invested: "As a believer in the need for authors to be self-reliant and hard working professionals, it is hardly surprising that Dickens attacks 'Vagabond[s]' like Savage and Skimpole in so withering a fashion" (34).

In a parallel line of inquiry, Rodney Stenning Edgecombe proposes "A Source for Rigaud in *Little Dorrit*" that expands the range of candidates heretofore considered likely. Scholars have identified several historical personages on whom Dickens based his portrayal of Rigaud in *Little Dorrit* (Napoleon III, according to Edgar Johnson; Thomas Griffiths Wainewright and Pierre-Francois Laçnaire, English and French criminals respectively, according to Trey Philpotts).

To these candidates, Edgecombe adds a possible literary prototype, the foreign count who marries and kills the heroine in Thomas Hood's famous comic poem "Miss Kilmanssegg and Her Precious Leg," which Dickens had likely already referenced in *The Old Curiosity Shop* in scenes depicting Quilp's domestic persecutions. Edgecombe sees a "darker reworking" (235) of the "Miss Kilmansegg" material in Dickens's later portrayal of Rigaud. Like Hood's foreign count, Rigaud possesses a "Mephistophelian nose," black eyes that conceal their depths, and a predatory affect. In Rigaud, Dickens slightly moderates the anti-Semitic features of Hood's villain. Just as Hood's count is not finally prosecuted for murdering his wife ("they brought it in as Felo de Se,/'Because her own Leg had killed her!'"), so Rigaud, who claims his wife leapt to her death on the rocks, ultimately escapes justice.

Stewart Justman's "Oriental Tales and *Great Expectations*" provides a useful corrective to the popular view of *The Arabian Nights* as synonymous with the fabulous—a view given authority by generations of eighteenth- and nineteenth-century readers enraptured by Galland's translation. The tales often mock enchantment rather than romanticize it, frequently valorizing common sense and exposing the self-delusion and "enslavement to fantasy" (40) of the fool. Justman demonstrates this anti-romantic bent of the tales through close analysis of the "Barmecide Feast" story—a story so popular among early readers that the phrase itself entered the English language in 1713.

Justman reads *Great Expectations* as a "significant twist" on the Barmecide feast story: "Pip's romantic hopes turn out to be as empty as that rich, attractive, brilliantly pictured Arabian supper . . . [except that] in this case no one really designs the deception that entraps him; it is the work of his own imagination" (43). Pip, thus, bears "a trace resemblance to fool figures of . . . premodern stories—stories all the more brilliant for their renunciation of the fabulous and their concentration on the workings of delusion" (45).

Viewed in this light, Dickens's apparent romanticizing of Pip's fate in the famous allusion to Misnar's pavilion just before the return of Magwitch is both curious and paradoxical. In a dramatic piece of scene-setting, Pip compares the impending revelation of his benefactor to the "Eastern story" (actually attributable to the eighteenth-century *Tales of the Genii*) where a massive slab suspended from the ceiling by patient cunning is suddenly released on the unwitting victims below. By such means, the text seems to construe Pip's story as an "operatic tale of death from above" rather than as the "fool-story" it really is (46). A nearer analogy to Pip's situation would seem to be the *Arabian Nights* fable of the would-be glass merchant so lost in an escalating and ultimately violent chain of fantasies about his capital investments that he kicks over the basket of glass on which his fortune was to have been made.

Dickens's use of the Misnar story is thus a puzzle, explained in part by his childhood love for the tale, on which he had based an early dramatic composition. Justman speculates that "the portentous 'Eastern' allusion at the exact turning-point of Great Expectations" may also have been intended to "warn of the fate that hangs over the crystal palace of Victorian complacency" (46).

In "Hawthorne's 'Ethan Brand' and *Great Expectations*," Shifra Hochberg offers a possible subliminal influence on Dickens's classic novel. Noting Dickens's enthusiasm for Hawthorne's early tales following the first American journey, Hochberg proposes that "Ethan Brand," published eleven years before *Great Expectations*, may have figured into Dickens's representation of Estella and may have provided the original inspiration for the limekiln episode.

Esther's name (Persian for "star") parallels and phonetically echoes Estella's name (Latin for "star"). Hochberg notes that Esther's victimization as "the subject of destructive experimentation by others" (119) may be echoed in Miss Havisham's experimental attempt to make Estella into an instrument of her own revenge. But while Hawthorne's Esther is destroyed by Brand's soul-destroying experiments, Estella's suffering (in Dickens's original ending) ultimately makes her stronger.

Observing that *Great Expectations* is the only Dickens novel to feature a limekiln, Hochberg speculates that Dickens may have been influenced by Hawthorne's allegorization of the limekiln in "Ethan Brand" as "an emblem for hell fire" (120). In Hawthorne's short story, the kiln is the site of Brand's suicide, prompted by his realization that the Unpardonable Sin of intellectual hubris resides within himself. Dickens's rendering of the setting transforms Hawthorne's vision into "a far more complex exploration of the intricacies of the human heart" (121), bifurcating the landscape into the hearth-like fires of Joe Gargery's forge and the terror-inducing "fire baptism" of the limekiln (120).

In "The Revolution Is Dead! Long Live Sensation!: The Political History of *The Woman in White*," Lanya Lamouria demonstrates how Collins "repurposes" the narrative structures and themes of *A Tale of Two Cities* in order to serve "the new fiction of domestic terror" (312). *A Tale of Two Cities* completed its serial publication in the issue that launched *The Woman in White*. Lamouria notes parallels in the cast of characters of the two novels, with, for example, Dr. Manette, the prisoner of the *ancien régime* set in counterpoint to Professor Pesca, an exile of the Risorgimento. Doubled characters feature in both novels. As with *A Tale of Two Cities*, *The Woman in White* "moves between the poles of incarceration and death, on the one hand, and freedom and resurrection, on the other" (312–13); both explore the relationship between incarceration and insanity.

Collins's use of Dickens's materials, however, serves fundamentally different ends. "Moving terror out of the public realm and into the private domestic spaces of the home and psyche," Collins implicitly challenges Dickens's continued belief in a revolutionary narrative "that, in his view, came to an end at midcentury, a full decade before Dickens attempted to recall it to life" (313). Deflating Dickens's "prophetic mode" and idealism—his association of revolutionary violence with themes of Christian redemption—Collins adopts a materialist stance. No "resurrectionist" working in the artistic sphere to restore the past and imbue life with meaning, Collins sees himself as at best "preservationist"—"a post-'48 writer who can simply maintain the past in lifeless form" (315). "*The Woman in White* does not celebrate the end of the revolutionary era but, instead, feels its loss. Collins's fiction of the post-'48 world is a fiction in which meaning is liquidated" (316).

Lamouria's essay speaks to what she views as a blind spot in critical approaches to Victorian literature: "we do not think of Victorians as Europeans, and as a result, are wary of reading Victorian texts in terms of nineteenth-century European history" (316). She argues: "This analysis of Collins should begin to show that, for many Victorian writers, political events on the Continent were powerful forces shaping the way they experienced and imagined modern Victorian life" (316).

Dickens's influence on the Polish writer Henryk Sienkiewicz is traced in Aleksandra Budrewicz-Beratan's "American Travel Books of Charles Dickens and Henryk Sienkiewicz." Sienkiewicz had read *American Notes* in Polish translation and acknowledged Dickens as his favorite British author prior to his 1867 journey. In his thirties and gaining fame as a writer, just as Dickens was at the time of his first trip to America, Sienkiewicz also shared Dickens's "strong, authentic belief in the inborn goodness of people . . . and their deep humanitarian sympathies" (90). Extensive verbal imitation—for example, in the description of New York, suggests that Sienkiewicz carried *American Notes* with him as his guidebook and referred to it specifically while traveling.

Budrewicz-Beratan argues that crucial differences in the attitudes, interests, and perspectives of the two travelers can also be inferred. Dickens "behaved like an inspector, or controller" (94). His intense English sympathies led him to set up a series of unflattering Anglo-American comparisons, whereas Sienkiewicz carried with him a broader European perspective: "He saw the British, Belgian, Irish, and German people as one big family" embracing "the traditions and customs derived from different nations over the centuries" (96). Sienkiewicz's rich classical background informed a more genuinely historical perspective that provided a rich context for understanding America. Nature was "an integral part of history" for Sienkiewicz, and he found in the American prairie a landscape echo of the Ukrainian steppes with their history of graves and burial mounds. Sienkiewicz was inclined to be more open-minded than Dickens. His trip, which lasted over two years, was a form of self-exploration that yielded, in addition to the travel book comprised of his letters, several short stories that have since been incorporated into the Polish canon.

In "'How Many Women Is Power': Dickens's Sarah Gamp and Fitzgerald's Resentful Care-Taking in *Tender Is the Night*," Chris Messenger explores the resonance of Dick Diver's allusion to Sairy Gamp at the end of *Tender Is The Night*, an allusion ultimately cut from the published novel. Drunkenly taking his leave from Mary North, Diver was to have mumbled: "Final message of Sairy Gamp, the drunken nurse: power measured in women. How many women is power. Women are the real gold standard" (qtd. in Messenger 160). Messenger argues that though ultimately cut from the novel the Sarah Gamp allusion "allows a significant look at Fitzgerald's imaginary as he mused on gender, class, and power in the material that became *Tender Is the Night*" (161). Messenger notes that "*Tender* is replete with images of nurses and nursing situations from beginning to end" (164), and that Dick's role in particular is often defined in feminized ways as "mother-caretaker-nurse" to the wealthy for whom he provides care but by whom he is also bought and constrained.

Mary Clarke's "'Not in charge of the story': The Presence of Rapunzel in Charles Dickens' *Great Expectations* and Margaret Mahy's *The Other Side of Silence*" identifies affinities between Mahy's contemporary young adult novel and Dickens's *Great Expectations*, especially with regard to the two texts' engagement with the "Rapunzel" triad of witch, captive, and rescuer. Both Dickens and Mahy acknowledge the serious value of the fairy tale in nurturing the imagination from which adult identity is shaped, but both also recognize that storytelling can take a pathological turn, generating harmful narratives that turn inward, entrapping the listener into plots divorced from healthy reality.

Pip's naïve belief that he has been called to fulfill the hero/prince's role in the witch-like Miss Havisham's version of "Sleeping Beauty" fits this pattern, and references to Estella's long hair evoke the "Rapunzel" plot. As in the original fairy tale, the beautiful hair functions as an ambivalent symbol—"both the conduit for the prince to his object of desire . . . and also the means by which he is entrapped by the witch" (66). Estella's long hair links her to the two women similarly described—her adoptive mother Miss Havisham and her birth mother, Molly.

Clarke sees a final parallel with the plot of "Rapunzel" in the reunion of Pip and Estella in the blighted garden of Satis House. Margaret Mahy's *The Other Side of Silence* likely references both the original fairy tale and Dickens's use of it in *Great Expectations*. Mahy employs symbolic naming practices evocative of Dickens and creates a similar witch-like figure of Miss Credence, whose flattering and seductive ways come near to entrapping Hero.

In "Mary Russell's *Bleak House*: Reforming Victorian Ideology in Detective Fiction," Mary O'Donnell explores parallels in character, plot, and theme between Dickens's *Bleak House* and Laurie King's *A Monstrous Regiment of Women* (2005), the second novel in a series featuring the protagonist Mary Russell as Sherlock Holmes's fictional protégé.

Orphans foisted upon their cold and abusive aunts, Dickens's Esther and King's Mary both suffer from scarring and disfigurement, and each performs detective work to solve the mysteries thrust upon her. O'Donnell scripts Mary as in most respects a counterpart to the Victorian ideal of the modest and docile woman. Mary's relationship to Holmes mirrors in some ways Esther's relationship to Jaryndyce. May–December relationships, they position the woman as mentee to a man of greater experience.

In a conclusion that calls for a bit more qualification and development, O'Donnell asserts that the ending of *Bleak House* implies that the world "would have been better off without meddling" (20), thus indirectly affirming the status quo with its divisions among social classes. By contrast, she views the resolution of King's novel as "a great leveler of classes" illustrating the "horrible consequences in murder, theft, and corruption of otherwise good charity work" (21). She sees a counterpart to *Bleak House*'s forceful denigration of women's work in King's largely positive portrayal of a charity that trains women for professional work. O'Connell holds up King's *A Regiment of Women* as "a systematic and effective dismantling of some Victorian philosophies by the contemporary historical detective story," one that addresses "issues of women's identity and place in the public sphere, charity, class, and ultimately the meaning of justice in detective fiction" (24).

The most ambitious and complex of the year's works on Dickens in relationship to other texts is Lauren Watson's *Contingencies and Masterly Fictions: Countertextuality in Dickens, Contemporary Fiction and Theory*. Watson takes her prompt from the Dickensian model of decomposition and regeneration as it applies to the "recycled" texts that comprise the novel—"the discourses of fairy tale, scripture, theatre and the popular press are broken down and rearticulated" (2). Noting "the propensity of composite textual bodies to break down and generate new products, and the ability of those products not only to reflect the instability of their progenitor but also reflect *upon* their own fragile composition" (2), Watson puts into play a series of textual triangulations that generate deconstructive dialogues. In each of four chapters, she positions one of Dickens's later novels in relationship to a contemporary text (often a novel that in some way speaks to or adapts Dickensian themes or characters) and in relation to an essay by a contemporary literary theorist (unrelated to Dickens and generically alien). In a final chapter, Watson reflects on the limitations of her own method and its inevitable implication in the status and value systems of the academy.

The subtitle of Watson's book, naming "countertextuality" rather than "intertextuality" as its subject, signals the author's debt to Derrida's concept of the *contre*—"a work . . . which places itself against a hegemonic structure, opposing that body yet simultaneously emulating its desires and deficiencies" (3). Watson's approach recognizes each text in the triangle as *contre*, "both deconstructing the machinations of its counterpart and resisting interrogation" (4). Strange bedfellows inhabit the chapters where these countertextual readings are staged—one chapter, for example, positions *Little Dorrit* against Peter Ackroyd's *The Great Fire of London* and Roland Barthes's *Image, Music, Text*; another looks at *A Tale of Two Cities* in relationship to Graham Swift's *Waterland* and Julia Kristeva's *Revolution in Poetic Language.*

These choices have the effect of foregrounding instabilities and ruptures within Dickens's texts. In a memorable discussion near the end of the book, Watson analyzes the etymological relationship between "text" and "textile," with respect to Dickens's composition of *Hard Times*: "his writing weaves a dogmatic adherence to fact with hyperbolic flights of fancy into a 'coarse' yet fragile literary material; immensely authoritative and compelling, Dickens's later novels are also peculiarly liable to split and unravel under scrutiny" (238). A close and respectful reader of Dickens, Watson declares him "profoundly metafictional—a proto Magic-Realist, rather than a failed Realist" (12). "The excessive length, generic instability and narrative unpredictability which were once considered by critics to be signs of an 'ill-disciplined' mind are, in the context of this work, melodramatic demonstrations of the uncontrollable and dialogic nature of literary productivity" (11).

Language, Style, Narrative, Genre

The year's work in Dickens studies is notable for its contributions to linguistic and narratological perspectives on Dickens's fiction, its attention to significant structural dimensions of his novels, including the relationship between text and paratext, and its engagement with questions of genre and generic influence.

In his note, "The Four Bottle Man in *Dombey and Son*," Tapan Kumar Mukerjee revisits a phrase that has puzzled modern editors of the novel. Conversation Brown is described as a "four bottle man," an expression that does not appear in the *OED*. Rodney Stenning Edgecombe has proposed, in the absence of a documented definition, the possible meaning, "super-arch Tory," but Mukerjee notes that the *OED* does define "three-bottle" as "one who can drink three bottles of wine at a sitting." Dickens, Mukerjee believes, likely riffs on this accepted sense of the phrase.

News of a comprehensive project to define and classify the idiomatic expressions appearing in Dickens's novels comes to us by way of Osamu Imahayashi, whose article "Dr Tadao Yamamoto and The *Dickens Lexicon* Project" provides an interim report on the progress of a searchable website compiled from the handwritten cards of Dr. Tadao Yamamoto, whose death in 1991 prevented the completion of a lifetime's research into the development of Dickens's style, idiom, and language. With the 1997 bequest of his library by family members, scholars from Hiroshima University and Kumamoto University have undertaken the task of compiling electronic entries from Yamamoto's cards. The Dickens Lexicon online, together with the Dickens Textbank and the 18th and 19th Century Textbank, are planned for release during the 2012 bicentennial.

In a related essay, Miyuki Nishio's article, "Definition of Idioms in the *Dickens Lexicon*" provides details about how the project defines and classifies these idioms. In Dickens's novels idioms appear in the form of verbs, adverbs, nouns, adjectives, and occasionally sentences. They may be "frozen," resisting syntactical manipulation, or they may exhibit considerable variation. "Steam," for example, can be "gotten up," "put on," or "disposed of" in combinations that consistently suggest uncommon energy or special effort (175).

In a subtle, carefully elaborated, and original analysis of one characteristic Dickensian figure of speech—syllepsis—Garrett Stewart explores the far-reaching ethical and philosophical dimensions of a trope generally recognized for its mildly comic effects. "Ethical Tempo of Narrative Syntax: Sylleptic Recognitions in *Our Mutual Friend*" takes a close look at the "twinned temporal prongs" of syllepsis—by which "a predicate is understood in two different senses with separate objects, whether indirect or direct" (119). Thus, in *Pickwick* (35): "Miss Bolo went . . . home, in a flood of tears and a sedan-chair"—an example that appears, loosely quoted, in Fowler's *English Usage* and other handbooks.

The humor evoked by syllepsis derives from the "category-mistake" of linking events that are incommensurable or mutually unavailable. Rather than viewing syllepsis as illogical though, Stewart associates this kind of figure with poetic language that invokes an "anti-Cartesian wordplay" in the splits it enacts between body and mind, the material and the affective. The time it takes readers to negotiate a sylleptic split is a time "of unfixity if not indecision, of openness, of leap, with consequences ethical as well as linguistic" (126). Readers negotiating the sylleptic fork "along the conveyor belt of syntax" frequently must engage with issues of moral, ethical, social, or poetic jus-tice (127). Dickens's description of the hypocritical colonial project in *Bleak House*, launched "with a view to the general cultivation of the coffee berry— *and* the natives," is but one example of the productive rifts that syllepsis can open up and the hypocrisies it can efficiently expose. More than its local satiri-cal impact, though, Stewart wants us to see syllepsis as installing "a program of openness: alertness *per se* before the critique it facilitiates" (127).

Turning his attention to the use of syllepsis in *Our Mutual Friend*, Stew-art notes that the syllepsis "stands watch" in this late novel over a systemic erasure between material forms and inner life: "Its shaky syntactic yokings mark an imploded cultural dialectic between outer and inner, object and sub-ject, fortune and worth, class and person" (137). More than simple mockery is thus involved in Dickens's description of Podsnap "with his temper and his shirt-collar about equally rumpled." Noting that "syntax is what keeps meaning from happening all at once" (128), Stewart focuses attention on the temporal dimension of syllepsis and its "latent ethical energy" (127). Link-ing language use to philosophy and metaphysics in ways both erudite and witty, he evokes in his own performative and playful style the complex lin-guistic effects that are the subject of this sustained and challenging analysis: "Never over till it's over, syllepsis opens minds as well as grammar, keeps things going and up for grabs" (144).

Eventfulness in British Fiction, a collection of essays edited by Peter Hühn, analyzes fifteen British novels and stories from late medieval times through the twentieth century, mapping them onto a narratological framework in which the central construct is the "event." In the specialized sense employed here, an "event" is "a departure or deviation from the norm" or "the violation of an established order" (7). Events, which are context-sensitive, genre-specific, and historically-variable, make up the story's "tellability," account for readers' motivations, and serve a vital function in the organization and meaning of the narrative. Hühn, together with his contributors, Markus Kempf, Katrin Kroll, and Jette K. Wulf, seeks to demonstrate the method, vocabulary, and interpre-tive power of the concept by applying it to a broad range of texts representing historically contingent understandings of "eventfulness."

Great Expectations, with its large number of characters, many of them with individual storylines mediated through Pip's subjectivity, makes for an inter-esting illustration of the method. Hühn begins by establishing the initial story of Pip's ascent marked by "eventful turning points in Pip's development"—hap-penings that take place within a more general expectation in society that some degree of social mobility can be taken for granted. Tracking Pip's choices and progress through Dickens's complex narrative, Hühn demonstrates the extent to which the "eventful turns" in his plot are strongly determined by storylines that play out in the background before Pip was even born. He shows how networks of possible alternative plot lines weave through the narrative, and he notes how reversals and regressions redefine the valence of initially positive turns. Hühn's highly detailed analysis of *Great Expectation*'s structure underscores the remarkable subtlety and complexity of Dickens's plot, which is woven from events that mean differently as contexts are redefined within a shifting narrative—a narrative that engages deeply with the culture's permeable and mobile attitudes to work, social class, and hierarchy.

As his title suggest, Mario Ortiz Robles, in *The Novel As Event*, reads "eventfulness" in a different way; Robles considers "the extent to which the novel can itself be considered an event" (xi). Focusing on the linguistic performativity of novels, on their power to "intervene materially in the reality they describe," Robles pays close attention to the functioning of plot, character, realism, voice and affect, analyzing each of these mechanisms in turn, in chapters devoted to individual Victorian novels. Five such novels are considered—*Jane Eyre, Our Mutual Friend, Vanity Fair, Middlemarch*, and *The Woman in White*. Robles draws on the concepts and applies the theories of Jacques Derrida, Paul de Man, Pierre Bourdieu, Judith Butler, and J. L. Austin. He sees himself extending the work of traditional Cultural Studies approaches, which have long recognized the role British fiction played in nation- and empire-building and in the construction of "gendered, racialized, and otherwise minoritized subjects" (x). Robles wishes to demonstrate how novels achieved this kind of agency through "discursive instruments whose performative force" rivaled physical power (xiv).

Robles's discussion of *Our Mutual Friend* turns to the question of characterization and focuses on Dickens's deployment of what is for him a signature literary device, the secret. Secrets, he notes, recur as thematic issues in Dickens's late works, and also play a defining role in their complex narrative structure. Robles demonstrates "how the many disguises, impersonations, frauds, and pretenses through which characters negotiate their identity become the very means of acquiring it" (xvi). Keying in on "impersonation" as the central motif of secrecy in *Our Mutual Friend*, Robles emphasizes the ease with which one character can pass for another almost as a form of theatrical or linguistic performance. He concludes that "impersonation thus becomes the staging ground for ethical struggles. . . . For if impersonation gives rise to an instability of reference productive of social and ideological effects, the performative speech acts give rise to an instability of *meaning* productive of acts of justice and responsibility" (106).

In "Alfred Jingle and the Pleasures of Incompleteness," Galia Benziman explores the loose and disconnected structure of *Pickwick Papers* as part of a larger pattern of "flirtation," "a pleasurable play of inconsistency that makes it possible to renounce commitment not only to others but to one's own self, one's own moral consistency, social identity, or even authorial control" (292). In terms borrowed from Mrs. Gradgrind, she christens this structural and thematic principle, "never hearing the last of it," posing the following questions: "How and why do Dickens's characters fail to bring their love affairs, sentences and narratives to completion? What are the ethical and aesthetic implications of this avoidance? And how is the pattern of incompletion manifested aesthetically, as one of the characteristics of Dickens's early narrative technique?" (292).

As the character who most embodies this lack of commitment, Jingle mirrors in his "syntactically deficient sentences" (292) a creative and energetic volubility lacking agency, grounding, or responsibility. His fragmentary clauses connected by signature dashes thwart coherence; he is all interruption, digression. Avoiding first-person pronouns, Jingle obscures agency, especially his own agency for dodgy ethical behaviors. At the same time, his "tense-less temporality" frames actions as hypothetical rather than as completed deeds for which he could be called to account.

Benziman argues that the linguistic features characterizing Jingle as a character have parallels in the structure of the novel. Dickens's loose handling of dates mirrors Jingle's slippery tenses, while dashes within chapter titles create "paratactic fragments" opening up a space for spontaneous invention. The structure of the novel follows the picaro's pursuit of the pleasure principle from adventure to adventure. Once past the Bardell vs. Pickwick episode, however, "the narrative opens up to wider horizons, to greater complexity and to the need for a character . . . who . . . lives in more than one dimension and not just for the pleasurable moment" (297).

Not delay or incompletion but deliberate abdication on the part of the storyteller is the theme of Robin Warhol-Down's essay "What Might Have Been Is Not What Is: Dickens's Narrative Refusals." Warhol-Down defines "narrative refusals" as "narratorial references to some of the specifics of *what might have been and yet is not*" (46). Looking at "narrative refusals," she asserts, has the value of "'allowing us to see differently what is there by turning our attention to what is marked as explicitly *not-there*" (47). Warhol-Down's essay provides a detailed taxonomy of narrative refusals, outlines the prominence of this technique in such novels as *Dombey and Son*, *Great Expectations*, and *Our Mutual Friend*, and then offers a glimpse of Dickens's experimental and exploratory "refusals" in *Nicholas Nickleby*.

Warhol-Down helpfully distinguishes between that which is simply absent from the narrative and the "vividly *present absence*" of the unnarrated and the disnarrated. (In "unnarration," the narrator says that he or she "can't or won't tell what happened"; in "disnarration" the narrator "tells something that did not happen, in place of saying what did") (48). Disnarration became a dominant mode of narrative discourse for Dickens in the late and middle novels, Warhol-Downs claims. A classic example is the ending of *Great Expectations*, where "Dickens puts Pip through a paroxysm of disnarration, unbinding the novel's closure by negating and then double-negating the final action, rather than simply telling it" (49). Like the disnarrations of *Great Expectations*, those of *Our*

Mutual Friend "heighten a sense of absence," creating a "shadow world, an alternate story that is not quite not-there" (51–52). We can see Dickens working through techniques of narrative refusal in an early novel like *Nicholas Nickleby*, where unnarration adds "depth-effects" to characters and contributes to the prevailing comic mode (56).

Warhol-Down's taxonomy of narrative refusals (which I have greatly simplified for this brief summary), together with the supple distinctions she makes among her examples, helpfully illuminates Dickens's progressively more sophisticated use of a technique he likely inherited in a simpler parodic form from Pope and Fielding. I found provocative and useful her conclusion that unnarration and disnarration mark "something like the unconscious of a text" representing "a collection of specific possibilities and details the text presents in order to leave out, while not altogether forgetting" (58).

Arguing for the central importance of focalisation in fiction, particularly in novels where the narrator is also the protagonist, David Paroissien, in " 'If you knew all my story . . .': The Rhetoric of Pip's Tale," examines the power of Pip's story to "teach us something about the human condition and the complexity of life" (227). Paroissien identifies "mobility and dexterity" as the distinguishing features of Pip's narration, noting how past and present, in constant collision, provide a panoramic canvass for the "re-evaluations and self-censuring re-perceptions" that are "seamlessly interwoven" throughout Pip's story (228). In contrast to the announced and self-contained "retrospective" chapters in *David Copperfield*, in *Great Expectations* Dickens achieves the effect of "a retrospective cast to almost every paragraph in the novel" (228).

Paroissien demonstrates how even in the early scenes readers are made aware that the teller is educated, well-read, and distanced from the events he is describing. But this wise narrator, who has learned to create meaning out of past suffering, moves flexibly in and out of the foreground, his voice punctuated by other voices who bring the unmediated past explosively into the present. In a series of close readings, Paroissien offers a nuanced analysis of the varied linguistic means by which these effects are created, paying attention especially to the play of resonant metaphors ("chains") and the structure and flow of extended passages (Pip as "self-swindler"). Good stories, Paroissien concludes, overcome the self-protective refusal to engage embodied in Jaggers's professional stance: "They seek to enlarge our knowledge rather than to contain it, to show events from all sides, rather than confine our perspective to a single, forensic objective" (234).

Dickens's craftsmanship—the sheer bravura of his narrative method—is similarly the concern of John R. Reed, whose *Dickens's Hyperrealism* proposes a maestro in full control of the orchestration, directing readers' interpretations in highly self-conscious ways through an array of sophisticated strategies. Reed uses the term "hyperrealism" in an "honorific" sense to name "Dickens's ability to convey a sense of the everyday world while at the same time almost magically transforming it" (4). Dickens, Reed argues, "did not want to be a mere realist, master though he was of many of its techniques. He wanted rather to be something closer to a magus" (84).

In chapters devoted to "Description," "Present Tense," "Naming," "Metonymy," "Personification," and "Redundancy," Reed focuses on the methods he considers most distinctive to Dickens's art and on the deployment of these methods to subvert or move beyond the goals of realism. For example, he argues that Dickens's descriptions of real places within fictional works deliberately undermine transparency. In describing Jacob's Island in *Oliver Twist*, Dickens's "brief and not very particularized" (15) account relies "on what is not there" rather than on conventional topographical detail. "By not elaborating his description in the way Mayhew did, or a realist novel might do," Dickens gave it a wider and more intense resonance. In the same way, naming in Dickens invariably signals "Dickens's own ultimate authority as the source of all such naming" (44); naming is performative rather than naturalized.

Reed adeptly illustrates Dickens's increasing linguistic virtuosity over time. The chapter on metonymy, for example, with its close reading of the Man in the White Waistcoat, Pip's Avenger, and the Analytical Chemist, demonstrates how Dickens's style ultimately prefigures "the leitmotif technique of Richard Wagner in music or Thomas Mann's application of that technique to fiction" (58). Similarly, in his analysis of Dickens's "redundancy," Reed distinguishes between the more or less randomly gratuitous details of the early novels and the more purposefully clustering (but still excessive) detail provided in *Our Mutual Friend*, most of which relates to interlocking motifs of water, mud, and dust.

Reed gives us a Dickens increasingly self-aware with respect to his craft, and increasingly "crafty" about concealing his "tricks." Whereas in the early novels, Dickens may reveal his authorial control directly to readers, in the later novels he is more likely to imitate the ways of providence, becoming the "power that creates the design, makes his subjects follow it, and discloses its form when it has been fulfilled" (106). "Not only did [Dickens] not believe the author was dead," Reed strenuously avers, "he believed that the true author never died. And he believed that the true author had genuine intentions to carry out and should control his narratives in such a way that they had their intended effect" (13).

Four of the 2010 essays address the relationship between plotting and narrative structure in Dickens's fiction: Rebecca Lane's "'The sin, most gross, most palpable, which Dickens everywhere commits . . .': In Defence of Dickens's Use of Coincidence," John McBratney's "'What Connexion Can There Be?': Secrecy and Detection in Dickens's *Bleak House*," Lorri Nandrea's "Desiring-Production and the Novel," and Michal Peled Ginsburg's "Sentimentality and Survival: The Double Narrative of *The Old Curiosity Shop*."

The subject of Lane's article is coincidence, defined as a meaningful concurrence of events or circumstances carrying with it an element of surprise that comes from the absence or invisibility of causal connection. As used by Dickens, the word "coincidence" conveyed pejorative connotations; Dickens employs the term only in comically deflating contexts. Nevertheless, his fiction is rife with surprising connections that invite speculation about causality. Finding Dickens's coincidences implausible and the author silent on their underlying cause, critics have accused Dickens of violating the literary realism he steadfastly claimed for his fiction.

Lane argues that Dickens was silent about agency because he could not himself explain it in any unitary or stable way. Rather, Dickens used coincidence as "a device that serves to blend 'governing agencies': specifically the traditionally non-compatible agencies of fate, providence, and chance" (125). She observes a shift in the novels "from fate dominating his fictional world, to the near-collapse of the providential model and its subsequent usurpation by chance" (125), noting that a similar pattern can be traced in Dickens's understanding of causation in the coincidences that he observed in his own life.

Whereas in *Pickwick Papers* readers align with the benign agency of the author, enjoying a privileged perspective on the unexpected connections that drive the comic plot, in *Oliver Twist* Dickens invokes the agency of chance, which in retrospect is revealed as fate. Though Oliver's implausible rescue has been described as fairy tale, Dickens might just as easily have seen it as realistic; his own rescue and improbably meteoric rise would have confirmed that such things happen.

No passive, fate-driven character like Oliver, Nicholas Nickleby exercises free will, and in the exercise of free will, chance encounters come his way. Chance and providence operate independently in *Nicholas Nickleby*, as evidenced by Nicholas's unplanned meeting with the Cheeryble brothers, who play a providential role. Beginning with Bray's premonition of his death in *Nicholas Nickleby*, Dickens pairs the dream world with coincidences, reflecting his own belief in dreams "as an unexplainable perceptive agency" (129). The pattern is also notably evident in *David Copperfield* and *Little Dorrit*."

Lane remarks that Dickens's consciousness of a "guiding agency behind his personal life and career" was shaken in the years after his marital break-up, the death of his mother, and the Staplehurst crash. The coincidences in *Bleak House* and *Hard Times*, Lane believes, "mark the start of the collapse of the providential model" (133). With *Our Mutual Friend*, Dickens introduces "a world at the mercy of chance" where coincidences are relatively rare, death ubiquitous, and both suffering and happiness "apportioned at random" (133).

In "'What Connexion Can There Be?': Secrecy and Detection in Dickens's *Bleak House*," John McBratney similarly acknowledges limits to the providential model in Dickens's later fiction. He links the preoccupation with the detection of secrets in *Bleak House* to the invisible processes by which social narratives are themselves constructed. *Bleak House*, McBratney notes, is the novel that most memorably attests to the difficulty of detection, whether criminal, social, or narrational. He shows how all three dimensions are embedded in the famous "What connexion can there be" passage—a passage that raises questions about the solution to a criminal investigation, about the surprising links between "many people . . . from opposite sides of great gulfs," and about the issue of a providential order that may (or may not) be reflected in the plot. Crucial to a consideration of all three kinds of detection, Bucket occupies a "wide-ranging and central role" (61). McBratney focuses on Bucket as "a potential nexus of social connection and as an analogue of the novelist himself" (61).

McBratney notes that Bucket has a "mixed record" of success as a detective, solving Tulkinghorn's murder with impressive finesse, but inexplicably failing to penetrate Lady Dedlock's disguise and thus failing to save her life. Bucket's lapse proves that he is "vulnerable to the contingent," thus calling into doubt his role as "the epitome of a new administrative disciplinarity" (64). By cold-heartedly bullying the ill and impoverished Jo, Bucket is also responsible for setting in motion the contagion that spreads from city to country. His significant lapses as a detective can be traced to his insensibility to "the unexpected and the random that is beyond his surveillance and control" (67).

Viewing Bucket as "a stand-in for the third-person narrator and, implicitly, for Dickens himself," McBratney notes the importance of the detective's "book of fate," his record of notes about his cases (68). Though apparently "guided by a god-like intelligence" (69), Bucket will find the integrity of his book disrupted by the "very element of chance that novelistic narrative is supposed to domesticate into intrinsic design" (71). In the same way the novel calls into question the supposed omniscience of the third-person narrator by signaling in various ways that this viewpoint is limited and can be only part of the story. McBratney believes that "while holding both to the idea of a Christian Providence and to its artistic corollary in the image of the artist as god-like, [Dickens] nonetheless opened his later works to the idea of a destabilizing contingency in ways that anticipate late Victorian and modernist experiments in realistic fiction" (71–72).

Lorri Nandrea's essay employs Deleuze and Guattari's conception of "desiring-production" (entirely focused on the production process rather than its ends) in order to analyze novels where plot is subordinated to process. Nandrea cites *Tristram Shandy* as a good example of a work of fiction that undermines all assumptions that the productive process is meaningful in relation to its ends or products. Openly declaring itself a "cock-and-bull story," *Tristram* "sides with the joy and madness of desiring-production" (20). In the same way, Mr. Dick's memorial partakes of the kind of "pointless production" that fits the Deleuze and Guattari model. Eventually, Mr. Dick's mad scribbling is brought under control and harnessed to useful tasks of transcription. But the novel evinces "a nostalgic attraction to [the] less disciplined, less oedipal mode of writing and desiring" that Mr. Dick seems to represent. "His presence,"

Nandrea concludes, constitutes . . . a schizophrenic alternative to the patterns of writing, subjectivity, desire, relationships, and temporality embraced by the other characters and by the novel as a whole" (22).

Michal Ginsburg's argument about the narrative structure of *The Old Curiosity Shop* calls on readers to see beneath the seeming inevitability of the novel's sentimental conclusion to its dominant, but less visible counter-narrative—a survival plot foregrounding the never-ending process of overcoming obstacles in order simply to move forward in time and space. Whereas the sentimental plot is typically goal-governed and recursive (a "progress" or journey of discovery toward rest, achievement, acquisition, or home), the survival plot follows a linear path more reminiscent of the *picaro*'s existential story—"the story of life, of everyday beginning anew the labor of living from which there is no rest, a story of the survival of the weak in an uncongenial world." The "end" of this kind of story "can only be death, understood as the eventual defeat of body and/or spirit in the struggle with the world and time" (89).

What happens in *The Old Curiosity Shop*, Ginsburg contends, is that a journey prompted by no motive more concrete than a directionless impulse to leave the past behind—a journey whose continuous forward motion through most of the novel frames rest as an interruption that must be perpetually overcome—morphs into the more conventional and sentimental narrative in which death is figured as "homecoming." In death, Nell reaches the ultimate point of rest where all signs of struggle are entirely erased. But the "consolation [the novel] attempts to offer . . . is belied by the story that precedes it" (98). Nell is no Oliver preserved as a perpetual child, protected by a badge of innocence against a corrupt and hostile world and destined to connect with a future that is also an idealized point of origin. Until the novel's hijacked conclusion, she has been conspicuously *disconnected* from nostalgic memories of home and family; her daily struggles enact the more mundane and repetitive plot of "reproduction and maintenance . . . of the labor necessary for material, social, affective survival" (99). *The Old Curiosity Shop* Ginsburg, argues, offers an opportunity both "of reading a plot that as become all but invisible and seeing the process by which it has been made so" (99).

The co-presence of mixed plots and genres in Dickens's fiction, and the tensions and paradoxes arising from these sometimes competing discourses, is also addressed by David Chandler in "'Above all natural affections': Sacrifice, Sentiment and Farce in *The Battle of Life*," and Nils Clausson in "Dickens's *Genera Mixta*: What Kind of a Novel is *Hard Times*?"

Chandler analyzes the "interesting failure" of *The Battle of Life*, arguing that the plot "fails, morally and artistically, to reconcile means with ends. The end is noble (arguably), the means essentially farcical, and the different elements in the story, far from fusing into a convincing whole, actually work against each other" (140). He compares Dickens's rendering of this love-triangle plot to Scott's *Ivanhoe* (1819), Boccaccio's story of Titus and Gisippus (c. 1350), and Carlo Goldoni's *Il Vero Amico* (1751, rev. 1764).

As in the story of *Ivanhoe*, duty triumphs over love, but Dickens ratchets up the moral idealism of Scott's formula and the nobility of the sacrifice by reducing the claims of the rival on the affections of the hero to a "childish fancy" (143). But having scripted a noble sacrifice, Dickens fails in contriving a plot mechanism of parallel nobility. Marion's out-of-character absconding makes her look "morally culpable" and positions Alfred as an absent, passive figure for much of the story.

In using Alfred as an instrument through which the sisters show their love for each other, Dickens draws on an earlier tradition of (male) friendship literature dating back to Boccaccio and given a nineteenth-century interpretation in Gerald Griffin's play *Gisippus: or The Forgotten Friend* (produced by Macready in 1842). Griffin's play develops some of the same themes, but in his version the sacrifice is made openly, without resorting to trickery. Sophronia is simply handed over to her former lover. In Goldoni's play *Il Vero Amico*, Rosaura is reluctant to be simply transferred to the man she loves, and stratagems must be deployed. In introducing trickery, Goldoni draws on the farcical traditions of the commedia dell'arte tradition, traditions that contrast with the eighteenth-century opera seria conventions of the selfless hero. He uses these contrasting traditions boldly and with "calculated theatrical effect" (148).

Dickens, Chandler argues, is unsuccessful in his parallel attempt to "graft a sentimental drama onto a farcical apparatus" (149). "Rather than enriching that story (as, say, the farce enriches *Nicholas Nickleby*), the farce seems to dilute the sentiment, just as, to an even greater extent, the sentiment clogs the farce" (150).

"What kind of a novel is *Hard Times*?" For Nils Clausson, this question, originally posed by David Lodge in *Working With Structuralism* (1981), has never been adequately addressed. Viewed as it typically is—as an "industrial novel," a "social-problem novel" or a "condition-of-England novel," *Hard Times* has been criticized for employing mutually incompatible genres and for failing to imagine satisfactory solutions for the social problems it exposes. Clausson proposes that the condition-of-England novel itself is a *Genera Mixta* best understood in the context of the culture's wider struggle to "find a narrative form commensurate with the new social realities" and to incorporate these realities within traditional fictional conventions, "conventions that were never designed to do the work of social analysis" (175).

Clausson frames his argument in the context of *Hard Times*'s shifting critical reputation. Debate over the genre of *Hard Times* began with F. R. Leavis's designation of it as a "moral fable." Framing the novel this way, Leavis was led to emphasize the education theme and the opposition between Utilitarianism and life. Slackbridge, the trade unions, and the role of Parliament were hardly noticed. Clausson points out that the decisive shift in the critical reevaluation of the novel came with Raymond Williams and Arnold Kettle who grouped

Hard Times with Gaskell's *Mary Barton* and *North and South*, Disraeli's *Sybil*, and Kingsley's *Alton Locke* as social-problem novels. Read through this lens, Dickens was faulted for his failure to see class divisions as a root cause of social problems and for his insufficient political understanding.

When *Hard Times* came to be viewed as a condition-of-England novel, two results followed. Critics now expected that the novel would "not only represent the historical facts accurately but also offer a solution to the problems it has raised" (163). Second, their assumption of generic uniformity caused them to overlook the novel's roots in Jonsonian comedy of humors and Menippean satire, genres that presuppose different assumptions about the individual's relationship to society than realist narratives concerned with institutional progress and reform. "The generic label social-problem novel or condition-of-England novel has imposed on texts like *Hard Times* a generic unity that they do not in fact possess," Clausson concludes. "And once this fact is recognized we should be able to understand what Dickens and his fellow condition-of-England novelists were trying to do rather than interpret and judge their works as failed attempts at realism" (178).

Melissa Valiska Gregory, in "Dickens's Collaborative Genres," also praises the "attractive fusion dishes" Dickens brings to the table, seeing in them notable and underappreciated forms of creative experimentation (216). Recalling Dickens's love of working "in company" and his interest in "composite" writing, Gregory proposes a generic approach to Dickens's collaborative writing; the Christmas numbers and "excursion articles" published in *Household Words* and *All the Year Round* serve as case studies in a broader discussion of these collaborative methods and relationships.

Gregory demonstrates how Dickens's Christmas numbers draw on familiar genres like the medley, the miscellany, and the keepsake but aspire to a higher degree of formal coherence. They allowed Dickens to accept other writers' contributions while retaining control over the unifying context. Dickens exercised a high degree of control over the whole process, but in certain ways the resulting product resists that control, revealing "a vertiginous textual energetics of friction, dissonance, and rupture" (218). Dissonance is created by the wide variety of subjects, themes, and literary forms accommodated under one umbrella and by the minor characters who claim center stage, "running amuck" among weak protagonists (219).

Dickens provides an overarching framework for each Christmas number, but the framework itself (e.g., stories as castaways from a shipwreck) frequently emphasizes "the violent energy required to force texts from multiple authors together into one space" (220). In his editorial practices, Dickens emphasizes a comradeship in which hierarchy was nevertheless clear, yet he performs "sporadic acts of self-effacement" by contributing stories that do not reveal his authorship (220). Gregory notes that eventually Dickens made the Christmas numbers more recognizably and exclusively his, reprinting his own contributions apart from the collections and using his frame narrators as subjects for public readings. In the process, he dismantled the original text to create new forms, obscuring the original genre's strangeness and creative energy—an energy based on friction, difference, and competition among genres and voices.

More spontaneous than the annual Christmas numbers, excursion articles were based on shared experience, composed in conditions of greater intimacy involving the sharing of drafts, and published as single-authored, often first-person pieces. A "complex representation of male partnership" (225), they represent collaboration as an "evolving process, one where internal tensions fuel progress, and the transitions between the writers become catalysts for movement" (226).

Gregory sees "The Lazy Tour of Two Idle Apprentices" as the "apotheosis of the excursion article" (228), giving "much fuller expression to the kinds of energies derived from male collaboration" (229). From the playful "mutual harassment" of the two protagonists, creative benefits accrue, including "emotional and creative balance" as each plays off of the other's temperamental differences (229). The relationship resembles that of a married couple on honeymoon, but neither author "adopts the stance of the traditional patriarch" (231), and the end of the relationship is assumed from the beginning. Collaborations are figured as "holidays away from the traditional authorial masculine self" (234) rather than as a sustainable alternative. Gregory contends that "the Christmas numbers and excursion articles constitute an important counterpoint to more dominant forms of Victorian fiction, an experiment with literary forms, processes, and gender relations that converse with rather than merely service the novel" (235).

In *The American Slave Narrative and the Victorian Novel*, Julia Sun-Joo Lee explores the shaping influence of the slave narrative on nineteenth-century fiction, paying special attention to the way Charlotte Brontë, Thackeray, Gaskell, and Dickens integrate generic features of the narrative into novels set on British soil. Lee identifies three features of the genre that spoke powerfully to Victorian novelists: its "emancipatory plot," its "emphasis on literacy as a tool of liberation," and its concern with "the ethical implications of resistance and rebellion" (9). Reversing "the traditional vector of influence from Britain to America," and situating the slave narrative within the broad and disparate networks through which it circulated, Lee shows how the figure of the fugitive slave came to operate as a Bakhtinian "chronotope"—"the embodied intersection of time and space, geography and history, . . . circulat[ing] within a literary, as well as a social contact zone" (18). A study in "genre tectonics," Lee's work imagines a "textual Atlantic," "a dynamic system characterized by the metonymics, as well as metaphorics, of slavery and its cultural productions" (22) within which the novel occupies a contested space.

Lee's chapter on "Fugitive Plots in *Great Expectations*" makes a convincing case that this "steadfastly national text," steeped in English provincial life and committed to social reform, "is radically informed by the genre of American slave narrative" (115). She shows how the fugitive slave chronotope impels the narrative forward, from Pip's initial collision with Magwitch to the hero's own progress from indentured apprentice to gentleman. Noting the novel's organization around "scenes of incarceration, clandestine reading, violence, and illicit escape," Lee demonstrates how the generic themes of the American slave narrative are adapted and reconstituted to address "issues of class mobility, freedom, colonialism, and self-fashioning" (115).

Noting that *Great Expectations* was written on the eve of the American Civil War at a time when Dickens was deeply suspicious of the North's intentions with respect to abolition, Lee finds ambivalence and anxiety in Dickens's appropriation of the slave narrative. That Joe chooses "accommodation over blatant 'opposition'" (127), subscribing "to gradual, peaceable change" over outright rebellion—even acquiring literacy "off the page, away from Pip's gaze," fits Dickens's cautious skepticism with regard to the slavery issue in 1860.

Three recent articles look at the relationship between text and paratext in Dickens's fiction. Robert Allen's "Perpetually Beginning Until the End of the Fair: The Paratextual Poetics of Serialized Novels" proposes a revised theoretical understanding of how paratext functions, particularly within temporal frameworks. Allen seeks to move beyond Gerard Genette's synchronic and taxonomic approach with its "neat border between what we can classify as text and the elements we can group together under the heading of paratext" (182). Expanding the range of elements that can be considered paratext to a "potentially limitless number" including "illustrations, covers, prefaces, chapter titles, pictorial initials and footnotes," (182), Allen wants also to recognize a diachronic dimension as the text engages with different audiences at different times and as it is repackaged in successive editions intended for different markets. Accordingly, he advocates moving away from spatial metaphors of paratext ("zone," "vestibule," "threshold"), instead focusing on key moments in the production and reception of the text.

Allen turns to serial fiction, "a form of the novel preoccupied with the temporal framework of its own production," as the site for an extended analysis of the relationship between text and paratext (182). His discussion is informed by Frank Kermode's work on duration, particularly Kermode's deployment of the concepts of *kairos* and *chronos* to define "tick-tock units." "Each installment of a serial narrative," Allen asserts, "is like the tick to the tock of the subsequent installment." *Chronos* (mere succession) is transformed into *kairos* (a moment charged with significance by virtue of its relationship to the end) through the structure of the serial, with duration "dictated by the vicissitudes of industrial print capitalism" functioning as the paratext (184). Thus, serial fiction "provides the perpetually deferred narrative and the promise of a final resolution that we typically associate with mystery and sensation plots" (184).

Noting how date-stamped part-issue wrappers, published apologies for delays, and "janus-faced" prefaces perpetually call attention to the effect of time on the production of part-issue fiction, Allen describes the serial as "a novel being written publicly" (185). Dickens's address to his readers halfway through *Pickwick Papers* captures the idea of "perpetual progress" central to Allen's argument about the diachronic dimension of the paratext: "we will keep perpetually going on beginning again, regularly, until the end of the fair."

In "Advertising and Fiction in *The Pickwick Papers*," Andy Williams focuses on a specific paratextual supplement to Dickens's first novel, "The Pickwick Advertiser," a roughly ten-page compendium of ads stitched into the binding of each installment after the last chapter. He notes that nearly a third of the material text of *Pickwick* is taken up with these advertisements. Williams is interested in how the "seemingly discrete cultural forms" of fiction and advertising "continually blend and clash," arguing that "while advertising (fiction's 'other') continually invades the novel, fiction (its ideological struc-tures, vocabulary, and lexicon) also importantly contributes to the existence of advertising as a cultural form" (319).

A hallmark of Williams's essay is the serious attention it pays to textual artifacts generally considered marginal or inconsequential. "The Pickwick Advertiser" contains many ads that blend poetry with commercial appeal, and Williams closely analyzes several such poems, including "Reform your tailor's bills!!," a poetic ad that engages in a "complex blend of irony, word-play, and intertextuality," mingling multiple discursive registers to create "comedic textual anarchy" (323), and an ad for Rowland's cosmetics that publishes a "missing stanza" from *Don Juan* written in Byron's characteris-tic *ottava rima*.

Did Dickens's text engage (consciously or unconsciously) in "product placement"? Williams speculates that allusions in *Pickwick* to commodities overtly marketed in the advertising supplement (optics, pocket maps) may plausibly suggest an advertising function. Regardless, he wants us to see that the borderline between the novel proper and its advertisements is more fluid and permeable than has been generally recognized and that, as a result, "the Dickensian serial is thoroughly entangled with the commodity culture of Vic-torian Britain" (332).

Like Williams and Allen, Caroline Reitz asks us to look at Dickens's serial fiction within a broader context that includes not just "what lies ahead but also . . . what lies to the side" (72). Focusing on the magazine fiction, she argues that Dickens "makes his journals both the novel's and the nation's mobile home" (72). Recurring characters like "the roving Englishman" and the "Uncommer-cial Traveller" emphasize the value Dickens placed on mobility, but the idea of home is at least as important: "A driving force behind Dickens's work, and arguably the Victorian novel, is a tension between mobility and home, dyna-mism and limits. The seemingly fixed place of home becomes, like the form of the journal issue, the serialized novel, or the idea of the nation, a structure through which to imagine motion" (73).

Reitz's "The Novel's Mobile Home" forms part of a larger project that treats the Victorian periodical as a "technology of public space" (73). With respect to *Household Words*, she is particularly interested in Dickens's twin goals for the journal—his desire that it represent "the diversity and mobility of modern culture" and his equally strong conviction that a coherent structure and editorial viewpoint are needed to provide a stable foundation. While critics have often viewed Dickens's journals as temporary resting places for fiction "before their permanent residence as complete, separate entities" (76), Reitz wants us to see the original context as creating meaning by providing productive tension and dialogue.

Gender, Domesticity, Children, and Education

Important new work in the area of Dickens, gender, and the domestic ideal appeared in 2010, most notably and substantially Kelly Hager's *Dickens and the Rise of Divorce: The Failed-Marriage Plot and the Novel Tradition* and Charles Hatten's *The End of Domesticity: Alienation from the Family in Dickens, Eliot, and James*.

Hager's study argues that marital dysfunction is such a consistent feature of the Victorian novel that "it constitutes a plot in and of itself," complementing and competing with the courtship plot (6). She sets out explicitly to question theories of the novel that overlook or minimize the failed marriage plot. Hager wants, in particular, to break the "lock" Ian Watt's thesis has had on novel criticism, noting that his influence can be seen even in the views of "more self-consciously historicist and more skeptical critics" like Carolyn Heilbrun, D. A. Miller, Alexander Welsh, and Mary Poovey, who see marriage as, in one way or another, "nonnarratable" (15). As the novelist who "best embodies stereotypical notions of the age," Dickens is the test case for Hager's hypothesis; "if we can find instances of the failed-marriage plot in his fictions, then . . . we have fairly conclusive evidence that the failed-marriage plot is one of the Victorian novel's favorite stories" (23).

Hager finds it significant that the rise of the novel took place against a backdrop of legal codification focused on stabilizing and defining marriage and divorce. Her study maps matrimonial legislation in England between 1670 and 1923, illustrating the importance of landmark reforms like Lord Hardwicke's Marriage Act and the Divorce Act of 1857 in supplying plot lines and narrative conventions to the novel. At the same time, she demonstrates the presence of domestic estrangement themes in eighteenth- and nineteenth-century fiction, in some cases well before the issues they address became topical. Turning to Dickens specifically, she highlights his interest in "the disintegration of marriage, the far-reaching and disastrous effects of the doctrine of coverture, and the comic, spectacular, and monstrous possibilities afforded by the failed-marriage plot" (43).

"Monstrous" marriages, a feature of Dickens's early novels according to Hager, are characterized by their mismatch of parts, by their shameful secrecy or marginality, or by their function as a warning to other characters. Hager develops illuminating linkages among the marriages of Ralph Nickleby, Quilp, Monks's parents, and even Jasper Packlemerton, the "serial killer and serial husband" of Jarley's waxworks. Often in the early novels, failed marriages— later revealed to be central to the plot—lie deeply buried within the narrative or appear as disturbing, uncanny images.

Hager shows Dickens working within the traditions of the melodrama in *Dombey and Son*; Dombey plays the role of "Patriarchal Villain" and Edith that of "Victimized Wife" in an energetic and spectacular enactment of "the evils of coverture" (103). Hager reads *David Coperfield* as explicitly a novel of divorce, "almost obscenely interested in the phenomenon of wives who leave their husbands" (135). *Hard Times*, she argues, "does not so much plot the failure of marriage as it takes that failure for granted as the condition that generates the plot" (161).

Hager's readings of Dickens, spanning six novels from the beginning of his career to its midpoint, hew closely to these complex texts, offering nuanced and original interpretations. Neither a feminist nor a believer in patriarchy, Hager's Dickens is shown to possess conflicting viewpoints and to have approached the failed marriage plot from significantly different vantage points over the course of a long career. In doing so, he participated in a much wider discourse that Hager brings insightfully into play. Among the notable strengths of *Dickens and the Rise of Divorce* is its rich contextualization of Dickens's novels and the sometimes surprising but always interesting connections Hager makes to the broader culture—to the voices of John Stuart Mill, Caroline Norton, Eliza Lynn Linton, and Sarah Stickney Ellis, among others.

Disenchantment with marriage and the domestic ideal is similarly the subject of Charles Hatten's *The End of Domesticity: Alienation from the Family in Dickens, Eliot, and James*. The fiction of Dickens, George Eliot, and Henry James anticipates the modernist preoccupation with family dysfunction and alienation, Hatten argues, and this growing "anti-familialism" is, in turn, "a complex product of a long historical development that has produced our contemporary world" (32). Hatten's study recognizes many factors in this cultural shift, including religious skepticism and the rise of mass culture, but he is particularly interested in the intersections between gender roles and marketplace anxieties.

Beginning with "the nineteenth century's greatest writer in the domestic tradition," Hatten examines familial relationships in *Barnaby Rudge*, *Dombey and Son*, and *David Copperfield* (34). Even in the early fiction, at the point of greatest cultural capital for the domestic narrative, Hatten argues, Dickens found in it "an apparatus that serves contradictory functions" (34), allowing him both to enhance his status as a writer and to align himself with "an alternative, historically emergent, pattern of familial and social discipline" (43). In *Barnaby Rudge*, Dickens affirms the middle class domestic life of his own era as against the aristocratic cruelties and authoritarianism of the *ancien régime*.

Hatten sees *Dombey and Son* as "at once celebratory of and hostile to the social changes linked to industrial capitalism" (74). On the one hand, the novel was "the most thoroughly and completely domestic of Dickens's novels" (58–59), framing domestic ideals as the antidote to laissez-faire capitalism. On the other hand, its anxieties about failed mothering and transgressive female agency invoke a woman-blaming rhetoric that distracts the narrative from deeper levels of awareness. With *David Copperfield*, Dickens creates an apotheosis of domestic harmony in which family discipline and idealized gender norms are wrapped around the triumphant portrait of the novelist's rise from lowly origins to fame, but Hatten sees "a subtle countertext that suggests ambivalence about and even resistance to major aspects of Victorian familial and gender ideology" (87).

David Copperfield's occluded narratives of sexuality and its silences about gender conflicts point to a fundamental rupture in Dickens's portrayal of the domestic ideal. For Dickens, Hatten believes, domesticity was ultimately "a house of cards" (127). Though he "accepts the bourgeois ideological norms of the centrality of family and women to individual happiness," he remains skeptical about feminine capacity in general and about domesticity's power "to insulate men from the corrosive energies of class ressentiment and economic competition" (127).

Lina L. Geriguis offers a brief explication of the marriage proposal scene in chapter 50 of *Dombey and Son*, suggesting that it functions to illustrate Florence's liberation from the restrictive Victorian paradigm of the prearranged marriage. In this scene, "Florence emerges as a perceptive and intuitive observer," reading the signs of a coming estrangement in Walter's words and looks (106). Resolved to speak to Walter, she intervenes assertively to redefine their relationship, in effect projecting the kind of marriage the two will likely share. In so doing, Geriguis argues, Florence demonstrates that she is no longer dependent on her father.

"Is *David Copperfield* a domestic novel?" inquires Emily Rena-Dozier in her thought-provoking article, "Re-gendering the Domestic Novel in *David Copperfield*." The answer to the question, she believes, will get us closer to understanding Dickens's relationship to this novel and its place in literary history. It also will call into question prevailing assumptions about "masculine" and "feminine" forms of writing.

Rena-Dozier notes that nineteenth-century critics considered the domestic novel a female genre, and since domestic fiction was considered the "basal form," they came to think of novel-writing in general as a feminine pursuit

(813). In *David Copperfield*, Dickens addresses the problematic question of whether a man can write domestic fiction by "writing a novel about a man who does just that" (813). David works from home and his activities are described in terms that evoke "the idealized vision of domestic labor epitomized in Agnes" (814): "Like a good housekeeper, the good writer works invisibly, quietly, without calling attention to his labor; both master dirt and misery by putting things in their proper places; both create a sphere to which one can retreat" (814).

But this equation of novel-writing with woman's work could be a problem for male writers, and Dickens's fiction in particular was often criticized for its lack of a masculine tenor of mind. Rena-Dozier sees *David Copperfield* responding to cultural assumptions about the domestic novel in two ways. First, Dickens describes "an androgynous domestic space," where masculine concentration and a disciplined work ethic "infuse the domestic sphere with rigor and purpose" (814). Second, Dickens recasts the domestic novel so as to evoke the paradigmatic masculine novel of the eighteenth century, *Tom Jones*—but without the impropriety for which Fielding's novel was criticized. In effect, Rena-Dozier argues, he "attempted to rewrite the history of the novel entirely, placing himself at its origin" (815). In so doing, he also put forth a tacit claim that "a male novelist can do the domestic as well as a female novelist—that, in fact, he can do it better" (821).

Maia McAleavey takes the Victorian marriage plot beyond the grave in her fascinating essay "Soul-mates: *David Copperfield*'s Angelic Bigamy." Because nineteenth-century religious literature popularized the idea of "a familial heavenly reunion" (192), remarriage posed a dicey theological problem. After all, Jesus's response to the Sadducees who questioned him about how heaven would be configured for a woman who had married seven brothers sequentially had been troubling: "in the resurrection they neither marry, nor are given in marriage, but are as the angels of god in heaven." MacAleavey explores a range of literary responses to "the vexed problem of a conjugal heaven" (195), including those of Coleridge, Rossetti, and Kingsley. *David Copperfield*, she believes, occupies a unique position in this cultural discourse: it is "not only the only Victorian text that explores simultaneous remarriage in light of heaven, but its insistent descriptions of Agnes as an angel, its multiple suggestions of possible afterlives, and the unusual solution it proposes to the Sadducees' riddle make it an important test case for the possibility of spiritual bigamy" (201).

McAleavey notes that *David Copperfield* skirts cultural anxieties about bigamy frequently treated in Victorian sensational and pornographic literature, using the metaphor of woman as angel—one of the culture's most conservative tropes—"in order to suggest a plural vision of multiple loves" (214). In doing so, the novel gives classic expression to the Victorian marriage plot as "an arc beginning on earth but continuing after death" (214).

In "'She brings everything to a grindstone': Sympathy and the Paid Female Companion's Critical Work in *David Copperfield*," Lauren N. Hoffer insightfully explores the cultural status and narrative function of the paid companion in *David Copperfield* and other Victorian novels. A "redundant" woman like the governess, the companion frequently occupied a social class position at or slightly below that of her employer, but was nevertheless expected to be subservient to the household and to endure routine slights. She was "a 'friend' who was always at her employer's disposal as a sympathetic receptacle for blame and frustration," and a monitor who protected her mistress's reputation and circumscribed her independence (193). Her presence allowed a Victorian lady "the opportunity to *receive* sympathy, without the necessity of reciprocation" (193), but such purchased sympathy had a darker side; it could be manipulatively employed in order to gain power, social mobility, or romantic attachment.

Rosa functions in these ways in *David Copperfield*. Revealing more about other characters than David can know or tell, she acts as an "agent of the narrative" (194), a precursor to the Jamesian *ficelle*, who models for readers the work of criticism. She "emerges as the more adept, and dangerous storyteller" (199) in several key scenes. When David tells Rosa the news of Steerforth's death, she reveals what David could not otherwise have known, the full story of her relationship with Steerforth, the "origin story of the family's current dynamics and dysfunction" (206). But she also reveals the limits of her interpretive ability—"she cannot fully see beyond her love" (207).

"Sharpening and bringing into focus obscured histories and deeper meanings beneath the surface of the text" (208), Rosa functions like a grindstone. But Dickens does not reward her for this critical work because "he cannot condone her problematic behavior on the level of the plot" (208): "Thus, Dickens acknowledges, explores, and even seems to identify with the darker side of sympathy in *David Copperfield* but ultimately refuses to align himself with it" (208).

Food, drink, merry-making, and the ceremonies of hearth and home play an important role in Dickens's depiction of domestic scenes. Three recent offerings explore this dimension of his fiction. In "Space of Celebration in Dickens's *A Christmas Carol*," Aleksandra Kedzierska focuses on the opening and closing staves of *A Christmas Carol* demonstrating how, as a result of Scrooge's conversion, the world of spiritual hollowness, represented by his counting house and his private quarters, eventually gives way to "the space of celebration of life" (123). She notes that the characteristics of Scrooge's counting house and Spartan living quarters—their gloom, freezing temperatures, paucity of possessions, and coffin-like enclosure—emblematize both his inner spiritual state and his demeanor to others. When forced out of this space and "made to explore the vast domain of Christmas," Scrooge proves capable of expanding his world and infusing it with the spirit of play and community. Through Scrooge's transformation, she argues, Dickens "almost makes us believe that life and celebration are one" (130).

David Paroissien, in "Dyspepsia or Digestion: The Pleasures of the Board in *Martin Chuzzlewit*," sketches in the culture and context of consumption as it plays out across Dickens's novels, with particular attention to *Martin Chuzzlewit*. Paroissien notes that though food was an important element of celebration to Dickens, and though he features food prominently in the novels, Dickens himself was "abstemious" (223). He points out that *Martin Chuzzlewit* features a number of characters whose eating practices define their values and personalities. Mr. Pecksniff's hypocrisy is revealed at its worst through the gourmandizing in which he indulges while lecturing on the necessity of contentment among the poor. Less pretentious and more matter-of-fact, Mrs. Gamp is clear about her nutritive and spirituous requirements, which take precedence over the needs of her clients, living or dead.

Dickens describes dining in American boarding houses as a form of combat in which speed, silence, animalistic aggression, and solitary gorging supplant the social rituals of English dining characterized by formal seating plans, service in courses, and conversational interludes. Sunday dinner at Todgers's, while more of a communal event than boarding house commons, was a strictly commercial affair, with the profit motive determining how much water got added to the beer, the gravy, and the soup. Ruth's cooking, however, and the fare served at the Dragon, receive a sentimental and nostalgic treatment—the latter contrasting mightily to the experience of eating at the new railway termini, which were beginning to alter the experience of travel. Witty and wide-ranging, Paroissien's essay offers a useful reminder of Dickens's extensive Bill of Fare and of its value to critics of the novels and the culture.

Annette Cozzi's *The Discourses of Food in Nineteenth-Century British Fiction* looks at the role of food in the construction of British identity, relating consumption to anxieties about industrialism and imperialism. Her study examines a variety of sources, including pamphlets, cookbooks, and literary texts by Dickens, Emily Brontë and Thomas Hardy. Devoting an entire chapter to "Men and Menus: Dickens and the Rise of the 'Ordinary' English Gentleman," Cozzi frames her discussion of Dickens in terms of larger questions about what, where, when, and how much Victorians ate and how class and gender differentiation, nationalism, and imperialism shaped their food choices. Cozzi provides a helpful general context for understanding the representation of food in Dickens's novels, touching on, for example, the way ever more discriminating tastes functioned to safeguard social boundaries and to consolidate national solidarity and class allegiance.

Cozzi helpfully teases out the social implications of dining in an "ordinary" ("hearty food, free of Frenchified over-refinement"), a restaurant ("suspiciously French!"), an inn ("staunchly English" but "allowed for the undesirable mingling of classes"), a coffee house ("haunt of the aspiring professional"), a club ("exclusive" but could also occasionally provide "a home to the transplanted Other"), and on the street (where the omnipresence of filth and excrement encouraged an association between the poor and the bestial) (43–59). She offers extended readings of the discourse of food in *The Old Curiosity Shop*, *David Copperfield*, *Great Expectations*, and *Oliver Twist*, especially as dining choices, customs, and attitudes intersect with concerns about "gentility, the ascendancy of the working class, and the corrosive presence of the Irish and the Jew in the metropolis" (48).

Child-rearing and education were treated in three significant pieces of scholarship during 2010: Sarah Gates's "'Let me see if Philip can/ Be a little gentleman': Parenting and Class in *Struwwelpeter* and *Great Expectations*," Clotilde De Stasio's "*Starving vs Cramming*: Children's Education and Upbringing in Charles Dickens and Herbert Spencer," and Sally Shutleworth's *The Mind of the Child: Child Development in Literature, Science and Medicine, 1840–1900*.

When Herbert Pocket objects to the name "Philip" as sounding too much like "a moral boy out of the spelling-book, who was so lazy that he fell into a pond," editors have linked the allusion to William F. Mavor's *The English Spelling Book Accompanied by a Progressive Series of Easy and Familiar Lessons* (1801). Sarah Gates proposes that "The Story of Fidgety Philip" in Heinrich Hoffman's *Struwwelpeter* (1845) should also be considered a source. "The Story of Fidgety Philip" sounds the central theme of *Great Expectations*: "Let me see if Philip can/ Be a little gentleman" (284).

Gates notes that *Struwwelpeter* and *Great Expectations* are ambivalent texts "in that the desired result in each—of becoming a gentleman, of civilizing children—seems hollowed out or undermined by the portrait of parenting that emerges in them" (284). Frequently the tales "capture perfectly a sort of entrapment or temptation of the child with his or her own impulsiveness that is set up by the adults' absent-mindedness or stupidity, an incompetence that deepens into a sadistic 'I told you so' when the child inevitably succumbs to the trap" (287). Thus "foolish Harriet" burns herself up with matches when her neglectful parents leave her alone with them.

Gates speculates that Herbert's renaming of Pip may stem from his dislike of these kinds of stories—a dislike that is a product of his own dysfunctional upbringing. When Herbert takes Pip to visit his family, Pip witnesses many instances of maternal neglect. At the root of this neglect is Mrs. Pocket's social-climbing. "The very social desires that fuel the Pocket parents guarantee their inability to socialize their children, who must 'tumble up' and raise themselves" (289).

Although Herbert's instruction of Pip models a civilizing form of impulse-control tempered with imagination (a way of relating to children practiced by Hoffman himself in his medical rounds), the novel's ambiguous conclusion seems to evidence an ambivalent attitude about parenthood. Certainly, the writing of *Great Expectations* called up for Dickens memories about his own haphazard upbringing. And his own domestic situation "was in turmoil" at that time (294). Indeed, Gates sees something of Matthew Pocket in Dickens himself, citing the novelist's comment to George Dolby a few years after the writing of *Great Expectations*: "I can't get my hat on in consequence of the extent to which my hair stands on end at the costs and charges of these boys. Why was I ever a father!" (294).

Focusing specifically on Herbert Spencer's views, Clotilde De Stasio looks at the educational theories embodied in Dickens's fiction in relation to those current at the time. Spencer's *Essays on Education* appeared in respected magazines like the *North British Review* before book publication in 1861.

Especially in *Hard Times*, Dickens exposed deficiencies in the "cramming" or "forcing" approach to childhood education—a method that subjected students to forcible consumption of disconnected and decontextualized facts. Public outcry over the cramming system, and Spencer's *Essays on Education* in particular, frequently linked attitudes toward the feeding of children with approaches to their education, noting "the great paradox in the teaching of children in Britain at the time . . . that the more their brains were stuffed with information, the less food went into their stomachs" (300).

In *Dombey and Son*, Dickens offers "a paradigmatic illustration of the disasters of the 'forcing system'" (302). Dr. Blimber's ambition to "gorge" the minds of his hapless pupils plays on the original association of the word with unhealthy eating. Dickens connects this form of education with Paul's wasting death and with his schoolmate Toots's mental disability. These same destructive pairings of "deficiency and excess—starving and cramming" (304) show up in "A Schoolboy's Story" (1853) and later in "Mrs. Lirriper's Lodgings" (1863), where, in the character of the Major, "a sort of Montessori before his time" (304), Dickens shows the power of an alternative pedagogy based on playful exploration of ordinary objects. Though different in many respects, Dickens and Spenser shared "a strong anti-Utilitarian creed and an aversion to the evangelical stern attitude to childhood"; both "warned against coercion and particularly against cruelty to children" (306).

In a similar vein, Sally Shuttleworth devotes a chapter of *The Mind of the Child* to "The Forcing Apparatus: *Dombey and Son*," placing Dickens's novel in the context of the culture's more general concerns about "forced education, overpressure on the young, and the dangers of precocity" (11). Shuttleworth notes that the story of Paul Dombey played an important role in contemporary debates about the optimal pace for children's mental development. Indeed, it "passed rapidly into psychiatric literature as a defining case study" (107). Pairing *Dombey and Son* with *The Ordeal of Richard Feverel* as novels propelled by an authoritarian father's drive to control a child's schooling, Shuttleworth offers illuminating and deeply contextualized close readings of these texts. Particularly compelling is her demonstration of how Paul Dombey's education relates to "new models of time and space generated in the emerging railway economy of the era" (108).

Although Shuttleworth focuses on Dickens most specifically in the chapter on *Dombey and Son*, the book as a whole provides an essential window into changing constructions of childhood that will be of great interest to readers of Dickens's fiction. Impeccably and thoroughly researched, it casts a wide net, examining medical texts, scientific journals, autobiographies, literary representations, and photographs. Shuttleworth traces the disciplines of child psychology and psychiatry from their earliest manifestations to the growth of the Child Study Movement in the 1890s, paying special attention to the impact of post-Darwinian conceptions of inheritance and child sexuality. Along the way, she considers a rich array of themes—lying and fantasy, night terrors, precocity, child suicide, even the first baby shows, and the phenomenon of monkey-keeping. Throughout the book, Shuttleworth affirms the impact of literary representation, demonstrating how fiction entered the discourse of medicine, science, and educational theory, providing examples that were appropriated by experts and disseminated widely in the culture.

Social Class, Economics, Politics, and the Law

In "'What do you play, boy?': Card Games in *Great Expectations*," Kirsten L. Parkinson examines references to card games in *Great Expectations* with special attention to how these games intersect with issues of class and social mobility. She argues that as Pip gains experience and sophistication in game-playing, he aligns himself with the superficial and morally suspect values associated with older notions of gentility connected with birth and wealth. In both literal and figurative senses he must give up "playing games" in order to become the kind of gentleman increasingly valued by the Victorian age—honest, hardworking, manly, and kind.

Parkinson's well-crafted argument locates game-playing within the ongoing cultural conversation about the nature of gentility. In particular, competing definitions of the gentleman created mixed messages about the value of work. On the one hand, conspicuous leisure signaled cultivation and prestige; on the other hand, the "gospel of work" articulated by Carlyle and others elevated labor to a kind of spiritual discipline.

Pip, who knew only one simple game at the beginning of the novel, plays a variety of games by the end, including French games with Estella and whist with Miss Havisham, Estella, and Jaggers. That Pip is never successful in any of these games may suggest a fundamental goodness and capacity for redemption innate in him. His turning away from game-playing, his recognition of Magwitch's sacrifice, Joe's faithfulness, and Herbert's cheerful, steady effort and friendship help him "finally begin to play his cards right" (137).

The year 2010 saw important, original contributions to the study of Dickens in relation to economic theories and issues, notably: Audrey Jaffe, *The Affective Life of the Average Man: The Victorian Novel and the Stock-Market Graph*; Tamara S. Wagner, *Financial Speculation in Victorian Fiction: Plotting Money and the Novel Genre, 1815–1902*; Georges Letissier, "'The wiles of insolvency': Gain and Loss in *Little Dorrit*"; Ruth Livesey, "Money, Manhood and Suffrage in *Our Mutual Friend*"; Andrew Burke, "'Purloined Pleasures': Dickens, Currency, and Copyright"; Matthew Rowlinson, *Real Money and Romanticism*; and Andrew Smith, *The Ghost Story, 1840–1920: A Cultural History*.

I turn first to Audrey Jaffe's fascinating study of modern subjectivity as constructed by stock market rhetoric and its visual representation. Jaffe is interested in the stock market as a register of collective emotion and character dependent on the concept of the average man. Noting that fluctuations in the prices of stocks and shares were closely tracked and reported from the 1840s on, Jaffe demonstrates how "economic journalism created an imagined community of readers who saw in these figures a reflection of their collective material and emotional condition" (15). The market itself came to be thought of as a "mass character, the imagined embodiment of an average man" (15); individuals, meanwhile, were described as "speculators" and "investors" beyond and outside of narrowly economic contexts. Jaffe suggests that these changes in the larger culture contributed to a paradigm shift in the way identity and interiority were constructed. Individuals could now be seen as "fungible, possessing characteristics interchangeable with those of the larger society" (13), and the self took on a vicarious quality, defined and differentiated in relation to internalized synthetic representations of the social whole.

Jaffe's fine reading of *Little Dorrit* brings into focus the "mutually-reinforcing discourses of the novel and the stock exchange" (46). The novel is framed around the emotional values of self-mastery, restraint, and patience—qualities traditionally linked to successful investment practices. Meanwhile, frauds, bubbles, and financial crises provide "grist for the novelistic mill precisely because their strategies of representation . . . were already novelistic" (46). Projecting the market as a character mediated by the novel, *Little Dorrit* makes speculators or investors of all its personae and potentially of its readers as well. Each is tested against the ideal of self-restraint, and nearly all give way to impulse at some point, in the process falling prey to the Merdle scheme. Jaffe notes: "In *Little Dorrit*'s character system—the system twentieth- and twenty-first-century market culture has inherited from the Victorians—investment and speculation are the terms of a psychic drama: that same drama from which the stock market draws its emotional power" (58)

The concept of "happiness" is central to Jaffe's discussion of *David Copperfield*. As "a summary or averaging term" that is "money's symbolic equivalent," happiness is aligned with various objects of desire and is itself the object of competition (16, 21). Jaffe notes that economists in the eighties began supplementing annual statistics on wealth and production with national measures of happiness derived from large surveys. In so doing, they defined happiness as "a translation . . . of complex social interactions into a readable trajectory and an assimilation of diverse affects into a collective emotional identity" (84).

In Jaffe's view, the "drumbeat repetition of the term 'happy'" sets *David Copperfield* apart from Dickens's other novels. In a form of emotional hoarding, David files away happiness moments as "emotional touchstones" (81) constituting a library of images to which he can later refer. But Jaffe notes how the very question "are you happy?" evokes "a mental roster of comparisons" (85). "A rhetoric of measurement" enters David's relationship with other characters. Indeed, the novel can be described as a "happiness competition, in which David's only true rivals are those who want what he wants" (98). The novel's conclusion, thus, "has about it a feeling not just of ending, but of winning" (98, 99).

Jaffe's argument, which draws on the work of nineteenth- and twentieth-century economic and political theorists, as well as on the scholarship of Nancy Armstrong, Mary Poovey, and Catherine Gallagher, is far more subtle than can be represented in this brief review. In addition to her contributions to Dickens studies, she offers strong readings of Trollope's *The Prime Minister* and George Eliot's *Middlemarch*. The book makes original contributions to the study of emotion and subjectivity as well as to Victorian studies and economic criticism. In tracing continuities between twentieth- and twenty-first-century representations of the market and Victorian accounts, Jaffe offers timely insight about our own relation to the graphs, tickers, and price lists that continue to structure collective feeling.

Like Jaffe, Tamara S. Wagner is interested in the way financial fluctuations "function as an expression of concerns with indeterminacy and inscrutability" extending into emotional as well as epistemological domains (2). Taking a formalist approach to the plotting of financial speculation and considering nearly a century's worth of novels both minor and canonical, Wagner wants to show fiction's substantial investment in the themes and motifs of the market. The trajectory she traces follows a chronological model that emphasizes literary influences, the emergence of new subgenres, and intertextual engagements with influential pre-texts. It can also be imagined spatially as a series of Venn diagrams describing points of intersection and overlapping domains—Ouida's *The Massarenes* talking back to Trollope's *The Way We Live Now*, Charlotte Riddell's *The Uninhabited House* engaging the suburban themes of *The Three Clerks*. Wagner is sensitive to the way recurring figures, extended metaphors, and thematic motifs related to the credit economy morph through texts often considered generically dissimilar—silver-fork novels, detective fiction, the domestic novel, the Gothic. She references an impressive number and range of these novels.

The first two chapters of Wagner's book map the development of the stock-market speculator as a recurring figure in fiction and explore the plot-structures associated with speculation motifs. Wagner begins by considering Jane Austen's *Sanditon*, revisits representative silver-fork novels from the perspective of their engagement with the "magicality" of speculative enterprises, and considers the watershed sensation novels of the 1860s with their misers, white-collar criminals, and clever villains. In general, she discovers a development from the "cardboard characters" of early-nineteenth century narratives to the "psychologically complex victims of risk taking" found in later fiction (26). Wagner's discussion of sensation fiction emphasizes its self-reflexive preoccupation with "the power as well as the exchangeability of various forms of paper" (65). The plots of these novels, she argues, play out the "potential of paper's intrinsic fragility," linking social instability to "fluctuations in the book market and the stock market" (64).

In the final chapters of the book, Wagner considers "Speculators Abroad" and "Speculators at Home," departing from a chronological sequence in order to emphasize intertextual interchanges between novels across various subgenres. In an interesting pairing of *Little Dorrit* with Thackeray's *The Newcomes*, Wagner examines Dickens's and Thackeray's depiction of "the guilt-stricken returnee from an essentially amorphous 'east'" (27). She shows how China functions in *Little Dorrit* as "the nodal point of interlinked metaphors of foreign 'infections'" (106), foreshadowing the "idolization of magic Merdle and the spread of speculative fever as an exotic disease" (107). A final chapter examines fictional portrayals of suburbia as the object of speculation and colonization. Wagner's extended reading of *Little Dorrit*, her incidental treatment of Dickens throughout the book, and her careful and thorough research into the genres and contexts that inform Dickens's treatment of financial themes make this book a useful contribution to Dickens studies.

Georges Letissier, following Barbara Hardy, argues that Dickens's resistance to Victorian ideology in *Little Dorrit* was more Kafkaesque than Marxist, leading him to emphasize the essential unknowability of the economic system to the human beings entrapped in its wiles. He argues that although the overplotting of the novel has been criticized, its intricacies serve a thematic function, replicating the financial labyrinth—particularly the "wiles of insolvency"—within which and through which characters are bound.

The apparent teleology of its division into "Poverty" and "Riches" notwithstanding, the structure of *Little Dorrit* runs counter to the narrative either of moral progress or of providential intervention. Gains and losses operate as random occurrences, with the plotlessness of the novel reflecting "the contingencies of Victorian economy" (262). Dickens shows through the labyrinthine pattern of the plot that "the circulation of money has become abstruse" (267). The "real world of goods and services" no longer bears a clear relationship to the economy. The entropic Circumlocution Office "generates loss without the compensation of work"; meanwhile Clennam and Company's book-keeping, like Doyce's invention and the engine of the plot, is exposed as mere "machinery in motion." Through Merdle, Dickens "shows how a delusive commercial scheme can lead whole segments of the population to loss and perdition" (269).

Little Dorrit's apparent plotlessness is thus, according to Letissier, a "ramification of plots" through which Dickens probes economic issues on a variety of levels. The novel ultimately suggests that natural laws, not human will, govern the operation of economies. It is "nobody's fault" that individuals are helpless to understand the transactions that result in gain or loss: "All lost, and all gained, in whatever order, could very well be *Little Dorrit*'s epilogue" (272).

Placing *Our Mutual Friend* in the context of contemporary debate about franchise extension, Ruth Livesey examines the novel's play with issues of money, credit, and representation. In the mid-nineteenth century, arguments about extending the vote took several forms and increasingly identified financial investment with political representation. Dickens remained skeptical about franchise reform in general, believing that the right kind of education was needed to lift up the working classes and that entrenched middle-class "toadyism" threatened representative government. But in various ways, he takes up the issues raised by the national debate about representation.

Livesey identifies two narrative strands in *Our Mutual Friend*—the "realist" river plot following Eugene Wrayburn and Bradley Headstone in their pursuit of Lizzie, and the "sentimental" plot revolving around wealth and dust, in which Bella is domesticated out of her desire for money. These plots, Livesey believes, reflect the competing systems of representation articulated in Parliamentary debates about suffrage. In the former plot, Bradley Headstone, whose profession would have guaranteed him suffrage under one of the proposals before Parliament, attains respectability at a cost; it becomes "the forcing-house that brings out his violence against the gentleman he can never be" (94). In the latter narrative, Bella must learn to trust "the liminal figure of the lodger" (93) whose values oppose "the mercenary world of credit" (93): "Where national government has succumbed, household government remains a site in which manhood, rather than money, legislates on behalf of others" (93).

Andrew Burke's "'Purloined Pleasures': Dickens, Currency, and Copyright," analyzes the metaphors of circulation and exchange Dickens employed in his letters and later in *American Notes* in response to the pirating of his texts by American publishers. Dickens creates an analogy between pirated texts and counterfeit notes. Notes in the form of royalties returning to the author complete a circuit of exchange that begins with the pages originating from the creative act. Fraudulent papers of both kinds lack the "issuing authority" that would give them legitimacy; their circulation thus undermines the healthy functioning of the marketplace. Copyright prevents both the corruption of the text itself—its diffusion in error-filled editions—and the infection of the reader who participates in the moral corruption of the theft.

In his letters, Dickens expresses "extreme resentment" over the violation of his own rights as an author—a resentment that Burke explains in terms of Slavoj Žižek's theory that national identity is "bound to the ways in which enjoyment is organized, sanctioned, and protected" (64). Dickens "takes exception to the very pleasure that American readers derive from reading pirated copies of his work," believing that "pleasure . . . is made wholesome through the mechanisms of the market as governed by the rules of copyright" (64). He depicts the pleasure of reading purloined texts as "both inauthentic and unwholesome, a matter of bestial indulgence" (70), contrasting in highly idealized ways the "illicit enjoyment of the pirated text in America to the legitimate reading pleasure of the English reading public" (70). Linking "the nation, its authors, and its national literature," Dickens frames his personal loss as "an assault on the integrity of the nation itself" (69). But his disgust with the American reader's pleasure may displace an underlying anxiety about the respectability of the novelist's profession in his own country and context.

Matthew Rowlinson's *Real Money and Romanticism* looks at British literature of the late-eighteenth and early-nineteenth centuries in relation to changes in the literary marketplace and conceptions of intellectual property. In a chapter on "Reading Capital with Little Nell," he looks at the period leading up to the composition of *The Old Curiosity Shop* as marked by a decisive turn in Dickens's relationship to his texts. In negotiating for the purchase of the copyright to *Sketches By Boz*, Dickens, Rowlinson states, was "abruptly confronted with the speculative rise in value that his texts had undergone because of his own success" (184). These "revenants from the past, overlooked a few years ago as used-up by-products of the productive process, now came back to haunt him bearing a vastly and outrageously increased value" (184). From this point on, Dickens intervened aggressively to own the products of his own labor. He set about to re-purchase the copyrights of earlier work, negotiated to share in the profits of *Master Humphrey's Clock*, and ensured that the texts he produced in the future would remain in his own possession.

Employing a Marxist analysis of Dickens's texts in relationship to the changing economics of publishing, Rowlinson argues that "by the date of *Master Humphrey's Clock* it was as capital that Dickens' text was owned and exchanged, and that it was as capital that it confronted Dickens as a writer" (163). Noting that in the case of *Pickwick Papers* and *The Old Curiosity Shop*, Dickens sold texts that had not yet even defined themselves as novels, texts that would be marketed and repackaged in multiple formats, he concludes: "The fact that Dickens's texts existed as abstractions, and in consequence circulated as exchange-values and were owned as capital, before they were written, was perhaps the most important single circumstance of his work in the 1830s and 1840s" (163). The production, sale, and marketing of Dickens's fiction during this period, Rowlinson believes, aligns well with Marx's definition of capital: "an accumulation of exchange-value that is unattached to any specific object and throws itself without reserve into whatever form promises at any moment to maximize its capacity of absorbing surplus value from labor" (157).

In an extended reading of *The Old Curiosity Shop* that draws on the work of Slavoj Žižek and Alfred Sohn-Rethel as well as on classical Marxist and psychoanalytical theory, Rowlinson analyzes the novel as a sustained "meditation on the nature of property"—a meditation continued in *American Notes*, *Martin Chuzzlewit*, and *Dombey and Son* and reaching its final articulation in Paul Dombey's question to his father: "What is money?" (185). Rowlinson sees Nell as "the central allegorization of the impossible materiality of money" (188) and demonstrates how in *The Old Curiosity Shop*, the "misrecognition of money functions as a general principle of narrative organization" (185).

Andrew Smith's *The Ghost Story, 1840–1920: A Cultural History* argues that Dickens's most significant contribution to the genre's development is his use of allegory "to encode wider issues relating to history, money, and identity" (33). Smith looks specifically at Dickens's use of ghosts in *A Christmas Carol*, "A December Vision," and "The Signalman." The first two works, he asserts, deal more or less explicitly with economic issues framed in allegorical terms. "The Signalman" addresses the industrial economy more obliquely. But while allegory breaks down, the story's use of the spectral raises important questions about identity and interpretation. Smith believes that Dickens's contributions to the ghost story genre have "not always received due acknowledgment" for their "considerable innovations" (33).

Although ghost stories appear in Dickens's fiction as early as *The Pickwick Papers*, and although these interpolated tales address serious issues such as insanity and moral conduct, Dickens invokes the spectral with a comedic touch in his early fiction. He "cannot quite take the ghost story too seriously" (34). Smith considers *A Christmas Carol* the point at which a darkening mood begins to infuse Dickens's ghost stories. In *A Christmas Carol* and afterwards, Dickens explores "how consciousness is formed in a money-based economy" (34). In his Marxist reading of the narrative, Smith shows how the encounter with Marley's ghost "makes visible what capitalism tries to render invisible, namely the labour which is inherent to, and so sublimated within, the process of commodity production" (36). In a similar way, he argues, "A December Vision" invokes allegory to make visible the apocalypse industrial capitalism is bringing about. While the meaning of the spectral is cloaked in ambiguity in "The Signalman," the story foregrounds, along with Dickens's other ghostly texts, the imperative to ask difficult questions and "to see the world differently" (45).

Smith's analysis of the ghostly in Dickens takes place within the context of a much broader cultural history. Impressively researched and wide-ranging in its implications, the study looks at the spectral in relation to gender, colonialism, creativity, and economics, considering along the way works by Wilkie Collins, Charlotte Riddell, Vernon Lee, May Sinclair, George Eliot, Robert Browning, Sheridan Le Fanu, and many others. It makes important contributions to Dickens studies, to the study of the Gothic, spectral, and uncanny, and to economic criticism.

Johathan Arac's *Impure Worlds: The Institution of Literature in the Age of the Novel* considers broadly political dimensions of Dickens's work. Its subject is literature in relation to "the condition of people's lives—that is politics," and its specific focus is on "impure" literature and the "politically charged arguments about value" that surround its reception and circulation (ix). Arac reminds us that neither Shakespeare's plays nor Victorian novels were highly valued as literature at the time they were published and that the Gothic mode so brilliantly deployed in Dickens's later novels is still associated with trashy novels and commercial fright movies. Drawn to the "power and the striking effects" of "impure" forms, Arac offers a series of close readings ranging widely across the chronological spectrum—Shakespeare, Dickens, Baudelaire, Twain, Flaubert. Each essay is self-contained, but the readings share a common view of literature as a social institution and of texts as permeable constructions drawing their subjects, styles, genres, and forms from other texts, past and present.

Arac's fine chapter on "*Hamlet*, *Little Dorrit*, and the History of Character" traces the construction of Arthur Clennam as a character to a series of discursive strands found in *Hamlet*. Like Hamlet, Clennam is "caught between his dead father and his morally compromised mother"; like Hamlet, he lacks will and becomes "inmeshed in a problem of inheritance." Moreover, the initials on the watch-paper, D. N. F. (Do Not Forget), specifically evoke the Ghost's challenge. *Little Dorrit* also derives its Gothic elements—its claustral spaces, ghostly presence, its portrait, and theme of usurpation—from *Hamlet*. And like Shakespeare's tragic figure, Clennam lives in the aftermath of others' actions; lacking a "heroic preexistence," he must "forge his own identity" (43). Dickens was "saturated in the Shakespearean milieu of the 1830s," Arac notes; his Shakespeare would have been mediated by Romantic criticism and stagecraft. Thus the novel "stands at a triple intersection: *Hamlet* as theatricalized, as novelized by Goethe, and as theorized by Coleridge" (46).

In his chapter on "The Struggle for the Cultural Heritage: Christina Stead Refunctions Charles Dickens and Mark Twain," Arac takes a close look at Christina Stead's 1940 novel, *The Man Who Loved Children*, as it evokes and redeploys two "cultural treasures," Dickens and Twain. Stead's revisionist stance on these two novelists forces the question, "What are they good for now?" (54). Arac shows how Stead operates as much on the images of Dickens and Twain—their "magnetic personal power . . . over those who knew and loved them"—as on their fiction (57). In doing so, she redeploys their "masculine comic philistine humanist genius," making it into "a woman's weapon against them" (60). Following Benjamin's assertion that "there is no document of civilization which is not at the same time a document of barbarism," Arac wants us to abandon narrow conceptions of literature as autonomous and aesthetically complete in order to open up productive possibilities for studying the mediating function of texts in a variety of cultural transactions.

In the chapter on "Narrative Form and Social Sense in *Bleak House* and *The French Revolution*," Arac considers Carlyle's role in instituting a new form of literature that became dominant in the nineteenth-century—a mode of writing shared by *Bleak House*. He notes a number of formal and structural similarities between these two works. For Arac, the parallels between the two works go beyond technique and structure to include "the articulation and interweaving of specific 'cultural codes'"—the Gothic, the scientific, and the apocalyptic (84). Finally, he argues, *Bleak House* and *The French Revolution* convey an ambivalence about the future born of frustration: "Both books share a mood of hope and apprehension, and both teach the patience needed when there is no end" (91).

Francesco Marroni's *Victorian Disharmonies: A Reconsideration of Nineteenth-Century English Fiction* proposes that "the struggle against disharmony is . . . the unifying theme of Victorian culture." Marroni traces the perception of disharmony to poor sanitary conditions and other socioeconomic ills, believing that it was felt most keenly in the phenomenon of threatening crowds, especially the violent crowds that gathered in support of Chartist reforms. The emergence of evolutionary thinking, he emphasizes, heightened awareness of the brutality, impulsiveness, and cruelty native to the human animal. Marroni's study, which is strongly influenced by semiotic analysis, rereads the canon of Victorian novelists in the light of the culture's central preoccupation with disharmony. Chapters on Dickens, Collins, Gaskell, Gissing, and Hardy grapple with the forces of tension, unrest, and disintegration as they engage with a culture tirelessly in pursuit of order. For Marroni, "the crowd and the gentleman represent the two poles around which much Victorian fiction revolves," and the "search for a middle ground implies . . . the fabrication of a hero that can be dialogically placed between two apparently irreconcilable worlds" (29).

The chapter devoted to "*A Tale of Two Cities*: Dickens and the Guillotine," seeks to dislodge the novel from the category of historical fiction. Not a novel *about* the French Revolution, it is instead a novel that uses that historical event "as a symbolic model for the Victorian age" (52). *A Tale of Two Cities* thematizes "Evil" and makes it relevant to middle-class city-dwellers anxious about crowds and apt to see in them analogues of the French Revolution's bloodthirsty mobs. Marroni is interested in the Christian narrative of *A Tale of Two Cities* and in the centrality of the resurrection theme to its various plots and subplots. He sees the novel as "constructed around two interrelated meaning-generating poles—London and Paris" and two sets of characters, those linked by "the golden thread" of Lucie Manette's blond hair to the redemptive values of the domestic sphere and those caught up in the swirling vortex of history. In Sydney Carton, he sees the suggestion of "a better world to come . . . in which all conflicts are resolved and the sacred serenity of domestic life becomes the triumphant representation of harmony" (78).

Four interesting studies shed light on Dickens's novels in relation to legal issues. The first I will consider is Cathrine O. Frank's *Law, Literature, and the Transmission of Culture in England, 1837–1925*. Frank's ambitious project looks at the concept of the will and its changing representation in law and literature between the passing of the Wills Act of 1837 and the Administration of Estates Act in 1925. The first piece of legislation greatly expanded the testator's power, which was now vested in a single, authenticated document directing the orderly transmission of assets—"a permanent, visible record of the writer's worldly goods, and of the writer" (3). The 1925 Act, by legislating more uniform and consistent ways of distributing property among heirs, reduced the testator's power and shifted the emphasis from the will as an expression of individual character to the will as a utilitarian tool of social identity. Frank proposes a parallel trajectory in the novel's movement from realism to modernism—a move that entailed a shift away from representational language and belief in essential character. She is interested in how both law and literature engage with issues of character and subjectivity—both as rhetorically constructed in documents and as acted on (or acted upon) in the world.

Focusing first on the testator in the context of Victorian legal culture, Frank examines the nineteenth century's fascination with "curious" wills as reflected in the periodical literature. She looks at the push and pull between the will's status as a private document and as a bureaucratic instrument, and she offers close readings of actual wills and their representation in fiction. In the second part of her study, Frank turns her attention to the implementation of wills, paying close attention to the inheritance laws affecting women and their gradual reform. These issues are closely studied in analyses of Victorian novels that imagine liberating alternatives to the standard inheritance plot for their female characters. In parallel fashion, Frank then turns to a series of Edwardian novels that frame the male inheritance plot as an exercise of will on the part of sons who must struggle to define themselves in relation to their Victorian fathers. In the final section of the book, Frank looks at the conflict between legality and justice raised by contested wills in selected Victorian and Edwardian novels, and she offers a final perspective on modernism as a movement with intertwined literary, cultural, and legal dimensions.

Interesting in itself, Frank's archival research—which takes her into case law, journalism, legal manuals, and actual wills, "curious" and otherwise— will prove a useful context for Dickens scholars. When she turns to Dickens specifically, Frank offers valuable insights. She notes Dickens's stalwart objection to the ecclesiastical oversight of wills, citing the *Household Words* exposé, "The Doom of English Wills," that Dickens wrote with W. H. Wills. She frames Dickens's own will perceptively in terms of the telling tonal dissonance it embodies. On the one hand, Dickens rather reluctantly adopts the public, legal language necessary to the achievement of his financial ends; on the other, he lays claim to a private "testamentary persona" through which he asserts control over the narrative of his own life, passes judgment, articulates lessons in morality and conduct, and makes claims upon his heirs.

Frank offers extended readings of the legal plots in *Little Dorrit* and *Our Mutual Friend*. Drawing on Hilary Schor's work in *Dickens and the Daughter of the House*, she reads Amy's destruction of the will as a "form of dissent from her father's narrative," "a revision of Mr. Dorrit's inheritance plot in which she was a passive, or at most a resistant, reader," and the means by which she assumes "active management of her own marriage plot" (122). In her discussion of *Our Mutual Friend*, Frank helpfully illuminates the function of Old Harmon's three wills in creating a series of roles that John Harmon must engage in his own quest for identity. Surprisingly, *Bleak House*, the novel that deals with the most contested will in the Dickens canon, appears only in a footnote.

Saskia Lettmaier's *Broken Engagements: The Action for Breach of Promise of Marriage and the Feminine Ideal, 1800–1914*, offers broad historical coverage of a legal concept that was first articulated in the mid-seventeenth century, rose to prominence in the nineteenth century, and became defunct by 1940. "What accounts for this dramatic rise and fall?" Lettmaier wants to know. Interweaving legal history, social history, and literary analysis, and referencing several hundred actual breach of promise cases, Lettmaier looks at literary and cinematic representations of this idiosyncratic kind of lawsuit. She concludes that the breach-of-promise action, by codifying a sentimentalized ideal of true womanhood fatally at odds with the whole idea of women going to law, doomed itself to vulgarization and ultimately extinction. Dickens scholars will find interesting Lettmaier's brief comments on breach-of-promise in Dickens's early novels, in particular his use of the established comic types of "the ridiculous strong woman or the lusty widow" (116). Laughter at the expense of such characters, she argues, "is invoked to signal a warning, to all women, against falling out of the patriarchal system"; such laughter functions to exorcise "the twin threats of female dominance and female sexual deviance" (116).

Deborah Wynne's *Women and Personal Property in the Victorian Novel* offers an interesting corrective lens for understanding the representation of women's objects in fictional settings of the period. Wynne's study pivots on the often-overlooked fact that women attained fully property rights only with the passing of the 1882 Married Women's Property Act. Thus, to view women's relationship with material goods as merely or primarily consumerist may obscure more passionate and more complex attachments. Examining representations of women and material culture in the novels of Dickens, George Eliot, and Henry James, Wynne offers a new perspective on Victorian "clutter." Her work, while drawing on recent "thing theory" scholarship, resists its emphasis on the value objects acquire at the moment of exchange. Wynne sees possession, rather, as performative, associated with acts of identity formation and assertion. Possession of property, in her view, implies relationship; it is "a site of affect, sentiment, dreams and passions which focuses on objects" (16).

Wynne argues that Dickens's fiction displays a deep anxiety and ambivalence with regard to female ownership of property. She shows how *Bleak House* and *Great Expectations* represent contrasting models for female property ownership, each nontraditional, each an alternative to primogeniture.

While the male characters in *Bleak House* exemplify a range of irresponsible behaviors, female characters tend to take care of and pass along property. Both Esther and Ada pay off the debts of others, and Caddy manages Prince's business efficiently. As a collective, Esther, Ada, and Caddy comprise a community possessing more power than they would each have as isolated, unprotected females—a principle illustrated as well by the negative examples of Miss Flite and Lady Dedlock.

Examining the possession and circulation of property in the novel, Wynne focuses on Esther's complex relationship to her doll and on the significance of the handkerchief, "an object with a particularly complex biography" "exchanged within a circle of women who find it consoling" (71–72). As the handkerchief's narrative trajectory shows, "Dickens gives serious attention to the issue of women's property, demonstrating its ability to circulate in unregulated and unconventional ways" (72). This "utopian vision" offers "an idealized female communal alternative to patrilineal forms of property transmission and possessive individualism" (72).

Wynne contrasts the communal circulation of property among women in *Bleak House* to the "museal worlds" Mrs. Clennam and Miss Havisham create in *Little Dorrit* and *Great Expectations*, "the apparent deadness of which is belied by the violent energy which is emitted from their carefully presented display of objects" (73). She compares the domestic still lives Miss Havisham and Mrs. Clennam each compose to the *vanitas* scenes created by seventeenth-century Dutch painters, "a genre which . . . points toward transient pleasures and the forces of time and decay upon the material world" (80).

Wynne notes that Miss Havisham's refusal to circulate her property in the conventional way is roundly punished at the conclusion of the novel when we learn that Satis House is to be dismantled and sold as building materials. But Estella's statement that "the ground belongs to me" offers "an unusual moment in Victorian fiction, a suggestion of the heroine's renunciation of renunciation by means of a projected future based on the ownership of real estate" (85). Although Dickens is traditionally seen as emphasizing Estella's broken submissiveness at the end of the novel, this significant detail shows that she is not entirely defeated; in her relationship to inherited property, she is "free to transcend women's usual lot" (85).

In her essay, "On Settling and Being Unsettled: Legitimacy and Settlement around 1850," Josephine McDonagh explores the 1850s controversy over the laws of settlement, which codified the grounds on which paupers were entitled to relief and on which local taxes were assessed. Established as part of the English Poor Laws in the sixteenth century, these laws were considered anachronisms by the 1850s, "trapping people in locations that were no longer appropriate to the needs of a modern economy" (50). McDonagh points out that this legal context has not been a part of the critical conversation about issues of nation and identity in the Victorian novel. She demonstrates that reformers were beginning to see that these settlement laws had outlived their original purpose and in their present form posed absolute restrictions on liberty, permitting the eviction of paupers on the mere "expectation that they might become a burden on the parish" (54). Such laws were perceived as costly, profiting only the legal profession, and creating "totalizing systems that distort people's sense of normality and even their rationality" (56). To this "stranglehold of the past on the present identity of the English nation" could be attributed many modern ills—the dense population of paupers in towns, the spread of disease, forced emigration (55). In *Bleak House*, Dickens supports the claims of those who believed in a national space within which all citizens should be permitted to move freely. The novel thus engages profoundly with a constellation of concerns about place, identity, and belonging, then under violent pressure from changing political and economic conditions.

Satyendra Prasad Singh's *Institutional Satire in Dickens's Fiction* surveys Dickens's critique of Victorian institutions in an overview of the subject intended primarily for students at Indian universities. Singh's analysis draws on Althusser's concept of interpellation; individuals willingly become accomplices to their own subordination at the hands of the ideological state apparatus. She sees this process at work in Dickens's satirical depictions of schools, law courts, churches, government bureaucracies, and other institutions. Singh notes that these institutions serve as instruments of the ruling class, affirming "unequal relationships which are paraded as common sense and labeled as normal or natural" (265). In chapters devoted to the "Social Matrix of Victorian England," "Administration and Judiciary," "Religion and Its Practitioners, "Politics, Commerce, and Utilitarianism," and "Education," Singh places examples from the novels alongside historical documents to demonstrate the "rare blend of horror and irreverent comedy" that constitutes Dickens's satire (ix). She relates Dickens's satirical style to the visual tradition of caricature. Among the specific objects of satire covered in Singh's book are the incompetencies of the police, the failures of the New Poor Law, delays in the administration of justice, and intolerant, exclusive, or bigoted religious practices. Dickens's satire, Singh concludes, "primarily heightens human worth and leaves the social muddle 'unpurged'" (279).

Urban and Cosmopolitan Contexts

In this section, I consider work that offers new ways of thinking about the urban experience—how it is perceived, experienced, and represented in

Dickens's fiction. I consider here, as well, the impact of London on Dickens's travels, paying particular attention the concept of "cosmopolitanism"—a theoretical construct around which a particularly rich strand of scholarly conversation has developed.

Andrew Sanders's *Charles Dickens's London* takes a comprehensive look at the city that brought out Dickens's unique powers as a novelist and that he, in turn, memorably recreated for generations of readers. Noting that Dickens was an adopted Londoner, Sanders analyzes various ways in which the city operated on Dickens's imagination—as a "spur to his creativity," as a "crucible in which ideas and sensations, faces and voices were compounded," as a "a place of assimilation and experimentation" (7). London, Sanders argues, made Dickens articulate: "Given the natural bent of his art, he could really have chosen no other city and no other subject" (12).

Sanders traces Dickens's textual and iconographic encounters with the city through Ben Jonson's London comedies, George Lillo's *History of George Barnwell*, Hogarth's paintings, and the novels of Smollett and Fielding. He notes that in Dickens's fiction, London became more than a setting or backdrop, instead functioning more fundamentally and dynamically as "part of the essence of the action" (16). Its very discordances comprised "the raw material with which [Dickens] could most happily and inventively work" (17). Revisiting Franco Moretti's influential work on London and Paris in his *Atlas of the European Novel 1800–1900*, Sanders emphasizes features of the English metropolis overlooked in Moretti's study—the importance of the suburbs as Dickens's "vital social and fictional middle ground," the English hankering after a nostalgic rural culture, the permeability of London's boundaries, and the chaos of its government (23). Sprawling, tangled, difficult to grasp whole, London, Sanders concludes, mirrored uncannily the shape and structure of Dickens's own novels.

Beyond its illuminating, helpfully contextualized introduction, Sanders offers chapters on pedestrian London, legal London, and suburban London. Three itineraries follow: "Mostly *Little Dorrit*," "Mostly *Bleak House*," and "Mostly *Oliver Twist*." Engaging and generous with topographical detail, Sanders proves an exceptionally knowledgeable tour guide both to the London that has been lost and to the streets and buildings from Dickens's fiction that remain in altered circumstances to evoke his topographically resonant novels. Sanders's layered knowledge of Dickens's London brings to vivid life its rich variety and history. A wonderful archive of photographs adds value to the text, helping readers to visualize, for example, the fog-dimmed view from the Monument in 1857 or the difficulty of stuffing a crinoline into an omnibus in 1860.

Pete Orford's *Charles Dickens on London*, a handy little anthology of pieces Dickens first published in *The Evening Chronicle*, *The Morning Chronicle*, *Bell's Life in London*, *Master Humphrey's Clock*, *Household Words*, and *All the Year Round* collects into one slim volume many of the primary texts to which Sanders alludes. Here readers will find Dickens's journalistic musings on the great, gritty metropolis—from his 1835 essay on "Gin Shops" to the evocative "Night Walks" and "City of the Absent" from the 1860s *Uncommercial Traveller* series. Inexpensively priced, this paperback could usefully supplement the novels in a course devoted to Dickens and the urban experience.

Michael Hollington's "Dickens, The City, and The Five Senses" explores Dickens's engagement with the full-on sensory overload of the Victorian city, an engagement he entered into fully, apprehending the urban experience not only visually, but through hearing, smell, taste, and touch. Hollington offers an overview of contemporary thinking about the role of the senses, paying particular attention to George Wilson's *The Five Senses, or Gateways to Knowledge* (1860), a book that Dickens read and enjoyed at the time he was finishing *Little Dorrit*. Wilson's book recapitulates the concept, familiar in Western tradition, of the body as a "divinely created citadel open to the world through the five portals of the senses" (30). Through these portals, the wonders of the phenomenal world could pass, but these same apertures were also vulnerable to toxic and sinful stimuli. Hollington notes that Wilson's book subscribed to the traditional hierarchy of the senses supposed to be inscribed in the structure of the body—with sight and hearing coming first, and smell, taste, and touch associated with lower functioning. He looks at alternative ways of thinking about the senses, beginning with Lucretius and Epicurus and continuing into recent scholarly work on synaesthesia.

Hollington argues that when Dickens took on the role of "urban detective" in the *Uncommercial Traveller* pieces, he self-consciously set out to read the city with his full sensory arsenal, including the sense of touch and "a refined olfactory apparatus able to detect complex blended city smells" (34). He believes we should be especially attentive to the ways that non-visual stimuli often evoked, in these city ramblings, a trance-like state in which Dickens's unconscious mind played a charged and significant role in perception. Hollington recalls John Picker's discussion of Charles Babbage in *Victorian Soundscapes*. Babbage had an odd theory that all sounds ever made were retained in the atmosphere in a vast library of utterances. Dickens, Hollington argues, "applies this principle of limitless proliferation and contagion to other senses besides sound . . . often mingling and confusing them in the process and thus proposing a defamiliarised nightmare version of the taken-for-granted 'realities' of modernity" (37).

Edyta Świerczyńska's "The Double Face of London: Crime and Space in *Oliver Twist* by Charles Dickens" examines contrasting spatial representations used to sophisticated effect in this early urban novel. The novel, Świerczyńska demonstrates, sharply demarcates "respectable" West End London from the "underworld" in East London, with "bridges serving as intransgressible borders separating the two" (176). On the vertical level the city's boundaries set up an opposition between the underworld, a labyrinth of narrow courts and unexpected turnings, and the daylight London above street level. The horizon-less sky, together with the vast and indecipherable landscape, confuses and disorients Oliver; to the criminals, however, the city offers the illusion of a safe hiding place.

Against this landscape, Świerczyńska reads Nancy as a Persephone figure: "she has already eaten the seeds of Hades's pomegranate by voluntarily taking part in criminal proceedings, and thus has been chained to the underworld, both literally and metaphorically" (180). London Bridge functions in this mytholo-gical reading of the scene as "an extended border . . . on which the two worlds can meet but never mix" (180). No innocent, Nancy cannot participate in the novel's final chapter devoted to blissful escape from the underground into a life of respectability. "This symbolic exclusion," Świerczyńska concludes, articulates the novel's firm division between upper and lower regions, "more striking and deeper than the delineation of borders symbolized by any other spatial representations" (182).

In "Mad Bulls and Dead Meat: Smithfield Market as Reality and Symbol," Trey Philpotts examines with great care and attention to context the richly symbolic space of London's Smithfield Market, often referred to as the "heart" or "center" of the metropolis. He focuses first on mad bull episodes, which made visible and concrete a range of problems associated with "the Smithfield nuisance"—cruelty to animals, danger to passersby, crowding, and inadequate regulation from the Corporation of London. Dickens alludes to the mad bull controversy in *Dombey and Son*, both in the scene where Florence loses her way and in the symbolic details of Browne's illustration, "Another Wedding," which liken the situation of the ensnared Bunsby to the plight of cattle goaded to market and slaughter. In *Bleak House*, the condition of maddened bulls is compared to Jo's condition in an extended meditation on the disappearing dis-tinction between the bestial and the human.

Beyond the specific issue of the maddened bulls, Smithfield was important for what it represented. A "transitional space" beyond the ancient boundary of the City but administratively a part of it, Smithfield was an "obstruction in the way of arterial flow," "a major 'aneurism' undermining London's image of itself as modern and improving" (35). It came to stand for infection arising from slaugh-terhouse effluvia. Constantly driven cattle were thought to be prone to fever, their "pain and terror" affecting the wholesomeness of the meat. Tainted meat was causally associated with cholera, cancer, and other diseases. Smithfield was also associated with its long and shameful record of public executions.

Philpotts shows how Smithfield functions as a transitional space in Dick-ens's novels. In *Dombey and Son*, Florence gets lost here and is "effectively 'rendered' for her byproducts" (37). In *Oliver Twist* and *Great Expectations*, Smithfield "marks the protagonist's first real encounter with London, his entrance into 'unfamiliar space'" (39). Smithfield's close proximity to hospi-tals, courts, and prisons made it highly suggestive and representative. It was for

Dickens "a highly evocative place" bringing close "the reality of London, in all its multiplicity and complexity" (41). Philpotts's thorough research exposes the "animating quality of resistance" embodied by Smithfield—a quality "that called forth Dickens's keenest observational powers" (41).

In "Dickens's 'Supernumeraries' and the Biopolitical Imagination of Victorian Fiction," Emily Steinlight highlights Dickens's preoccupation in *Bleak House* with a dense, uncountable, and discounted urban population—human "remainders" in excess of society's ability either to "provide for" or to "dispose of" (229). In an interesting and productive approach to the representation of urban issues, she examines the way Dickens's novels operate at the level of population and participate in an "emergent biopolitics" focused on the tension between "the category of population and the mass that resists incorporation" (234).

One way the concept of the "supernumerary" takes human shape in *Bleak House* is through the figure of Jo, the "tough subject." Lacking subjectivity and nearly indistinguishable from thousands like him with whom he can be easily confused, Jo is "less an individual than a walking synechdoche for 'the crowd [that] flows round'" (236). In Steinlight's view, he represents more than a "social problem," and the issues raised by his presence in the novel are not fixable by social means. He is "the avatar of a more general condition that no house or nation can hold at bay" (239).

Steinlight examines Jo's role as a vector of contagion, noting that Esther's humanitarian attempts to contain and care for him within the domestic sphere prove ineffectual and even harmful. Through Jo the novel projects a "transpersonal field of power—an epidemiology of power, we might almost say—that does not recognize an individuated subject" (241).

Steinlight argues that prevailing theoretical approaches to Victorian fiction do not address "the political questions raised by this notion of an excess of human life" (230). For example, New Historicist accounts, which read *Bleak House* as "a case study in surveillance and 'preventive policing,'" overlook the fact that the mass, as represented in this novel, remains resistant both to control and detection. "Everywhere immanent," they form "a surplus of ungovernable life that exceeds and threatens the survival of the social body" (246–47).

Igor Webb considers the impact of Dickens's first American journey within the context of a volume of essays that model "old criticism"—a form of close reading that "moves outward as the text demands and as reflection or imagination or learning or the occasion or the times or just idiosyncrasy directs" (1). Such a reading practice acknowledges and seeks to bridge discontinuities between the writer's time and our own and in the process "to find new routes of entry" for modern readers estranged from the novel's original contexts. In addition to *Martin Chuzzlewit* and *American Notes*, *Rereading the Nineteenth Century: Studies in the Old Criticism from Austen to Lawrence* offers fresh readings of *Mary Barton*, *Pride and Prejudice*, *Frankenstein*, and *Lady Chatterley's Lover*.

Webb compares Dickens's rapid disenchantment with America to the experiences of American leftists traveling to Russia in the 1920s. He believes that in Dickens's case, the disenchantment was productive of a new creative period, and that, in particular, *Martin Chuzzlewit* "can be seen as a kind of laboratory in which the paramount formal and thematic dilemmas confronting the major nineteenth-century novelists are defined and an initial effort to 'solve' them is made" (7). Webb's wide-ranging discussion considers Dickens in relation to international copyright, celebrity culture, and the literature of travel. Webb is interested in the initial protective recoil Dickens expresses in *American Notes* and the accommodation made by *Martin Chuzzlewit* and later novels to the tragic dimensions of human life that the American experience made newly visible. What Dickens discovered in the process of composing *Martin Chuzzlewit*, Webb concludes, is that the "improvisations of literature" alone "can salve the naked and aggressive existence of Dickens's world" (98).

In "Charles 'Carlo' Dickens In and Out of Italy in 1844: *The Chimes*," Philip V. Allingham focuses on the relationship between Dickens's London persona and his Italian travels during the period he was composing *The Chimes*. Dickens's letters during the period "reflect his yearning for home and his sense of London as his defining context as a writer" (127). But his stay in Genoa also helped him to see and represent with greater clarity than previously the "condition of England" question.

Allingham's essay notes a series of parallels and connections between Dickens's second residence in Genoa, the Villa Peschiere, and *The Chimes*. The lighthouse beams "flashing five times every four minutes, beating out the time for the writer" (132) evoke the goblin bells that perform the same function for Trotty Veck. The frescoes in the study and bedroom of the Villa Peschiere connect to the plotting and themes of *The Chimes* in previously unrecognized ways. Both "The Fall of Phaeton," the fresco directly above Dickens's bed in the Villa Peschiere, and "Diana Wrestling a Satyr," which was positioned inside and above the entrance to the western bedroom, "exemplify the issue of appropriate and inappropriate uses of power" (139).

Genoa, Allingham argues, gave Dickens the opportunity to observe a different and more benign face of poverty, "without vice or cruelty"—perhaps inspiring the working-class protagonists of *The Chimes*. The New Year's dance at the end of *The Chimes*, an alfresco affair despite the winter weather, "reveals the denizens of these mean streets as connected to their village origins in a communal celebration; in other words, although they are supposedly a realistic facsimile of London's indigent, they behave as if they were Genoa's happy proletariat" (143). But, while Dickens "integrated himself into the social and cultural life of the community" in Genoa, he could imagine no such integration at the conclusion of *The Chimes*. The "disparate social strata in Dickens's most radical fiction remain utterly alienated at the conclusion of *The Chimes*" (145).

Three recent works address the issue of Dickens in relation to cosmopolitanism. I begin with an article by James Buzard, whose work in the field has proved seminal for a number of other scholars.

In "'The Country of the Plague': Anticulture and Autoethnography in Dickens's 1850s," Buzard focuses on the transition from *Bleak House* (1852–53) to *Little Dorrit* (1856–57), a period he considers crucially significant in terms of Dickens's wrestling with "the claims, benefits, and pitfalls of national and wider forms of belonging" (413).

Building on the argument developed in his *Disorienting Fiction: The Autoethnographic Work of Nineteenth-Century British Novels* (2005), Buzard takes *Bleak House*, Dickens's "most restrictively 'national' of novels," as a reference point. If *Bleak House* represents Dickens's response to "the false universalism of the Great Exhibition of 1851," with its "facile internationalism (and self-congratulatory chauvinism)" (413, 415), in *Little Dorrit* Dickens "feels his way toward an understanding of . . . the ecology of local, national and cosmopolitan identities" and toward a recognition of "the interdependence of each category upon the others" (414). In doing so, he engages a series of related questions. To what degree should a novel deeply engaged in issues of national health focus on the nation exclusively? Can "being" national be consistent with "being" "anything else or anything broader" (414)?

In his earlier critical work, Buzard has traced the movements of Dickens's characters "from the deep inside of a particular national community to the wide outside in relation to which that community has its distinctive being" (414). The movement from *Bleak House* to *Little Dorrit*, he argues, pushes that trajectory much further, and widens the perspective: "Where the earlier novel emphasized the definiteness of Britain's place in the world and the impermeability of its boundaries, the later one pushes so far in the opposite direction that the questions of where the national is, and of what separates one place and culture from another, become illuminatingly unanswerable" (414).

Buzard finds in *Little Dorrit* signs that Dickens is re-thinking the "defensive nationalism" of the earlier novel (415). For example, the initial representation of the East as the country of plague and imprisonment is set in a corrective context when Clennam's reentry into London shows unmistakably that the same description could apply to the nation's capital. For *Bleak House*'s fog, *Little Dorrit* substitutes a blazing sun "that bleaches out differences" and "obliterates categories," figuring "a world without any culture at all" (416). Indeed, "the varieties of outsidedness and insidedness on offer in this novel . . . are equally intolerable, each the ruinous travesty of a desired condition—mobility and rootedness, traveling and dwelling" (417). *Little Dorrit* offers on the one hand Rigaud's rootlessness and on the other Clennam's alienation from both nation and world. At the same time, Buzard believes, Dickens seems to be thinking his way through "the false dichotomy of home and world" (418). He proposes that Amy's travels in Italy serve as a kind of apprenticeship in the development of a more cosmopolitan viewpoint, one whose insights she can take with her when she goes down into the "usual uproar" of the national "anticulture" (419).

Drawing on the work of Buzard and other scholars engaged in the rich critical discourse centering on cosmopolitanism, Tanya Agothocieous offers a wide-ranging, and thoroughly illuminating study of *Urban Realism and the Cosmopolitan Imagination in the Nineteenth Century*. In ways that cut across conventional categories of periodization and disciplinary formation, Agothocieous trains her attention on the development and evolution of what she terms "cosmopolitan realism"—a "melding of city and world" entailing shifts in perspective between detailed observations and totalizing views (xvi). She sees the mid-Victorian period, with its burgeoning urban population and broadening empire, as crucial in this development, defining a nexus of conditions that prompted, on the one hand, visions of universal brotherhood and global harmony and on the other dire dystopian predictions. Drawing her evidence broadly from novels, periodicals, and visual art, Agothocieous organizes her study chronologically, beginning with the Great Exhibition of 1851 and the broad range of response elicited by this culturally defining event. She then moves to a chapter on Wordsworth and Dickens, using the touchstone of the sketch and the panorama—two "paradigmatic antithetical modes of cosmopolitan realism" (69), to organize her observations. Finally, she turns to works composed in the late-Victorian and modernist period to examine the breakdown of cosmopolitan realism and the corresponding shift from a spatially conceived city/world to one that relies on expanded notions of time to imagine totality.

Chapter 2, "The Sketch and the Panorama: Wordsworth, Dickens, and the Emergence of Cosmopolitan Realism," examines the impact of these parallel modes of perception on realist writers seeking to represent global space. Agothocieous traces the roots of the sketch form to two sources: the eighteenth-century interest in physiognomy and the popularity of the *Cries of London* series, with its variety of city "types" and its implicit call to bear witness to the suffering of the poor. She establishes the link in the nineteenth century between the sketch form and more scientific and sociological representations of urban types, such as Henry Mayhew's in *London Labour and the London Poor*. Finally, she explores the anthropological dimension of the sketch. Because London was thought to embrace in its diversity all types of human being, sketches of its inhabitants could represent the world in microcosm.

Contrasting the sketch form to the panorama, Agothocieous notes the latter's emergence out of Romantic landscape painting and its promise to provide viewers with a "benevolent clairvoyance" by means of which they might "access encyclopedic levels of knowledge at a glance" (71). The panoramic view "allows the city to blend into the rest of the world or take the form of the world itself" (70). Combined, the two modes allow viewers to access the city's immense variety of life and labor and also to rise above it all—to reanimate its bewildering complexity and to imagine a global human family.

In a persuasive discussion of *The Prelude*, Agothocieous shows how Wordsworth's sketches of urban types, coupled with his "ecstatic urban reverie," prefigure Dickens's cosmopolitan realism and later the radical utopianism of writers like William Morris. She offers a fascinating reading of *Bleak House* in the context of these traditions, focusing on Skimpole's sketches and on the novel's foggy, dystopian panoramas. Noting that *Bleak House* is "chock-full of the urban types associated with the sketches and famously draws attention to the panoramic overview of the omniscient narrator" (108), she demonstrates how the novel reads each form with a jaundiced eye. Skimpole's incomplete sketches and his lack of commitment to anyone but himself associate the sketch form with exploitation and self-indulgence. Meanwhile, *Bleak House*'s famous opening disclaims the legibility of the urban panorama and calls into question any possibility of an urban, much less global, community. Yet Dickens does not completely reject the possibility of collectivity. In an interesting final turning of her argument, Agothocieous imagines *Bleak House* as providing "a kind of time-lapsed panorama wherein the connections between individuals, and an expanded sense of community, emerge from the accumulated knowledge provided by its various parts" (111).

In his fine and thoughtful essay, "Reluctant Cosmopolitanism in Dickens's *Great Expectations*," John McBratney looks at the cosmopolitan figure "as a mediator between native English and colonial subjectivities" (529). In his use of the term "cosmopolitan," McBratney wishes to steer a middle course between Said's emphasis on the center/margin dichotomy and Buzard's more inner-directed "autoethnographic approach" acknowledging differences *within* the imperial nation. McBratney reads the cosmopolitan figure as "Janus-faced, looking both inward toward an insular England and outward toward a 'Greater Britain,' or even the larger world" (529). Focusing on Pip and Magwitch as "reluctant cosmopolitans of indeterminate national identity," McBratney finds ethical gain in the psychological loss each suffers as a result of losing a sense of home. Translating the concept of "Romantic irony" into an international context, McBratney believes that Pip and Magwitch each go through a similarly ironic "oscillating action"; each creates a fiction about his world, and in a moment of shattering insight, each sees that fiction as mere selfish projection (531). In an act of new creation following hard on disillusionment, each moves closer toward an understanding of self and world.

For McBratney, the opening scene of the novel functions as "the primal scene of transnational irony," prefiguring the three important subject positions—native Englishman, colonial, and cosmopolitan—that comprise sites of struggle and becoming (533). Through Joe and Wemmick, Pip will come to associate nativism with "a past frozen in amber," irrelevant to the modern gentleman (536). As colonial space intrudes on native space in the novel's climactic recognition scene, he will realize the falsity of the original dream. But in order to move forward he must re-evaluate his own position in relation to Magwitch in international space. The compassion Pip feels for all the doomed on the occasion of Magwitch's trial represents "an ethical embrace of humankind" emerging from a newly, if partially, cosmopolitan perspective (541). But his enlarged perspective comes at a cost. With Magwitch, though in very unequal ways, Pip will think of home continually from his vantage point as a colonial living abroad. Neither, however, returns to England as "home"; in fact, their lives become "a study in homelessness . . . with no proper origin . . . and no familiar and comfortable resting place" (538). "Both are linked by their reluctant cosmopolitanism, their participation in transnationality as a kind of Hobson's choice" (541). For McBratney the novel's engagement with cosmopolitanism extends beyond its characters or themes to model a practice of writing and reading. Dickens's fluid shifts in perspective and subtle play with moral ironies, he believes, constitute a cosmopolitan form of writing that calls on readers to be alert both to the finely delineated native setting about which Pip and Magwitch feel so ambivalent and to the outer world in which they find themselves unwittingly exiled.

Science, Technology, and the Arts

Studies of Dickens in relation to science and technology range widely over a variety of topics—from Darwinian influence on constructions of class and identity to spontaneous combustion, from the circulation of fluids to the circulation of letters, from medicine in relation to social reform to the relation between case histories and novels.

In his fascinating, carefully researched essay, "Handling the Perceptual Politics of Identity in *Great Expectations*," Peter J. Capuano explores the way in which *Great Expectations* participates in the "surging popular discourse about hands at mid century"—a discourse that engages the connections between "nature" and "culture" central to the concerns of this novel (185). Capuano argues that in *Great Expectations*, where there are more than 450 allusions to the word "hand" alone, "hands" evoke debates about evolution, class, and political economy operating "as starkly visible but barely noticeable features at the core of the novel's identity politics" (187). Seeking to historicize Dickens's seeming obsession with hands in the context of a culture similarly obsessed, Capuano's essay sets out to probe anxieties about class and subjectivity in the years following *The Origin of the Species* (1859).

Capuano notes that with the advent of the Development Hypothesis, culminating in the publication of Darwin's *Origin of the Species*, the hand lost its privileged status as the physiological trait distinguishing humans from the lower animals. The discovery of the gorilla in the 1850s, and the subsequent debate about the species as a possible "missing link" between humans and animals, seemed to lend weight to theories of racial degeneration. Gorillas looked and behaved like humans. Their skeletal features, and particularly the formation of the hands—with its large palms and short fingers—blurred the boundary between higher animal forms and "lower" races, particularly in the case of the "savage" Irish, who seemed built for violence and hard labor. In the scene where Jaggers exposes "the remarkable force of grip" in Molly's hands, these associations converge—Molly's Irish name and gypsy status, her rough labor as a maid-of-all-work, and her characterization as a "wild beast tamed."

Capuano notes that the biological connection between Molly's "wild" hand and Estella's "refined" hand functions as a crucial agent in the plot. Pip's failure to see this connection is premised on his assumption that Estella's scornful superiority and refined manners are "natural" to her social class. But in her capacity for and enjoyment of violence, Estella equally resembles her lower class mother; Pip's gradually dawning realization of their relationship is prompted by repeated observations of a gesture shared by Molly and Estella, "the action of their fingers." Thus, hands convey a "Darwinian truth"—"that criminality and civilization, violence and refinement, wealth and poverty are inextricably linked" (202).

In Pip's mind, Magwitch's large, laboring hands bespeak "animality, labor, and criminality"—qualities that Pip at first elides as he recoils in horror from Magwitch's touch (202). He must learn from the fire that renders his own hands temporarily useless the value of being able to perform physical labor, in this case the physical labor involved in rowing Magwitch to safety. Thus, Capuano, concludes, "Pip's moral development actually becomes manual development; the sensitivity of Pip's character eventually merges with the sensitivity of his hands as he learns to understand . . . the exquisite meaning of the 'slight pressures' of Magwitch's hand while his benefactor lay on his deathbed" (206).

Brooke Taylor's essay on spontaneous combustion, subtitled "When 'Fact' Confirms 'Feeling' in *Bleak House*," helpfully contextualizes the famous exchange between Dickens and Lewes regarding the scientific validity of Krook's spontaneous combustion. Taylor is interested in discovering why it mattered so much to Dickens that readers accept as scientific the evidence he so strenuously proffered in the preface to the novel. Her article probes the relationship between empirical/analytical and imaginative/intuitive forms of cognition, both in Dickens's fiction and in the larger public discourse surrounding it.

Anxieties about the tension between fact and feeling permeated the culture, Taylor demonstrates, beginning her discussion with the value John Keats placed on "negative capability" as a condition of willed openness to uncertainty necessary to creative productivity. While eighteenth-century philosophers saw no necessary opposition between empirical and intuitive ways of

knowing, the professionalization of science in the nineteenth century and the
increasing specialization of its practitioners contributed to a public perception
of the scientific as fact-obsessed and divorced from human values.

With Esther, who represents "the symbiosis of head and heart," at its center, and with a host of minor characters inflecting the theme, *Bleak House*
engages in extended play with the relationship between fact and feeling (172).
Taylor concludes: "Dickens clearly privileges imagination as a mode of cognition, but also recognizes the necessity of its belated confirmation by way of
empirical evidence" (172). Thus Esther knows instinctively that Lady Dedlock
is her mother, long before she hears the confession. And Inspector Bucket,
even as he is arresting George on the basis of empirical evidence, believes
him to be innocent. Facts amassed without human sympathies and instincts to
guide their interpretation produce systems of injustice and spiritual impover-
ishment. But feeling and intuition are never enough in themselves: "Intuition
leaps ahead . . . subordinating 'evidence' to reach the truth. However, without
empirical evidence, without the proof of confessions, circumstances, and facts,
these intuitive insights would have little influence, even in Dickens's fictional
world" (177). Krook's death by spontaneous combustion, born of a flash of
intuitive insight about its metaphorical truth, *must* thus be confirmed as an
empirical possibility.

One of the freshest and most engaging of the voices currently addressing
Dickens in relation to science belongs to Barri J. Gold, whose *ThermoPoetics:
Energy in Victorian Literature and Science* maps the generative and mutually
illuminating interconnections between literature and physics during the nineteenth century. In both domains, writers wrestled to develop new understandings related to energy, work, power, and force. This "widespread word work"
Gold dubs "thermopoetics" (153), finding in it a discourse that vitally engaged
larger Victorian concerns about religion, evolution, race, class, empire, gender, and sexuality.

Gold's book breaks new ground in several ways. Within a field understandably dominated by the impact of evolutionary theory, her project provides the
first book-length study of thermodynamics in relation to Victorian literature. Her
study, moreover, emphasizes the "qualified thermodynamic optimism" that runs
through nineteenth-century literature and science, a departure from the current
focus on entropy—the "bad news" of energy physics (30). Steadfastly avoiding
questions of priority, Gold resists the "'diffusion model' of science and society
manifest in the dominant assumption that science may influence literature, but
not the other way around" (15). She isn't interested in who was "first" or in who
was a "true" genius; it is enough for her that "Tennyson was *a* genius in thermodynamics and that Dickens was a damn good engineer" (14). In terms of her
audience as well, Gold writes at the productive intersection between science and
literature. She sets out to make her writing accessible to scholars on both sides of
that traditional divide—and to general readers as well. Forgoing an excessively

technical vocabulary and a weighty scholarly apparatus, she offers timely explanations with a light touch, unabashedly reveals her own energetic and imaginative engagement with the material, and dares to be funny.

Gold brings an array of influential scientific treatises into conversation with the works of Alfred Tennyson, Herbert Spencer, Bram Stoker, Oscar Wilde, and others. Dickensians will find her interpretations of *A Tale of Two Cities* and *Bleak House* original and insightful. She reads the former novel ("boasting what may be the best equilibrated opening in the history of the novel") as "fraught with thermodynamic instability," preoccupied with "the entropic costs of attempting order," and fearing "the inevitable loss entailed in the exchange" (152). Linking revolution to the dynamic energies of fluid and fire, Gold shows how the novel rapidly destroys the fantasy of social stability and permanence its finely balanced opening seems to promise: "In repeatedly staging the tendency of things to roll downhill, to burn, or to become disorderly, Dickens confronts the problems of universal decay" (156). But though individuals and the larger institutional machines they serve degrade in conformity to the second law of thermodynamics, Dickens also shows how energies can be restored or awakened from dormancy with the aid of external forces. Movement outside the closed system can prompt "counterentropic" change through which "useless energy becomes directed and orderly" (179). Tracing these possibilities through Sydney Carton's energy and work at the level of the individual and the family, Gold finds a message of qualified optimism: "Even in a universe driving to heat death, we may make a little order. It is a modest hope, perhaps, but one that may sustain even the bleakest of houses" (183).

Gold's chapter on *Bleak House* explains *how* "a little order" can be created. Although the novel, with its depiction of Chancery and its prominent allusion to the death of the sun, is perhaps the most explicitly entropic fictional world Dickens created, the massive heat and energy sinks of *Bleak House* are counterbalanced by fictive engines that somehow accomplish genuine work. Esther and Mrs. Bagnet, for example, find ways to store energy, convert it to useful forms, and direct it to practical ends; their local efforts are contrasted to those of Mrs. Jellyby whose energies are dissipated in a sink the size of Africa. Gold's analysis, which takes us deep into James Watt's principles for efficiency in engine design, explains in thermodynamic terms how someone like Bucket could manage to accomplish genuine work "in spite of . . . contact with the novel's biggest heat sinks: the Dedlocks, Chancery, London." (212). *Bleak House* itself, Gold asserts provocatively, "is a particularly complex machine, with hundreds of elements intricately linked and placing checks on one another . . . an apparently self-regulating mechanism, that, like an engine, incorporates its own source and sink" (223).

Louise Penner's book *Victorian Medicine and Social Reform: Florence Nightingale Among the Novelists* traces reciprocal influences between Nightingale's life and work and the novels of Elizabeth Gaskell, George Eliot, Dickens, Wilkie Collins, and Hesba Stretton. Penner establishes Nightingale's early awareness that by using rhetorical strategies and narrative techniques of novels popular at the time she could influence public attitudes and behaviors. She considers Nightingale's Poor Law writings alongside the reform fiction of Dickens and Hesba Stratton, whose books Nightingale read and donated to nurses, soldiers, and charities. Penner shows how Nightingale set out to be the "Indian Dickens," raising sympathy for peasant suffering under colonial rule in the same way Dickens had elicited compassion for workhouse children in *Oliver Twist*. Nightingale was, we learn, "an enormous fan of Dickens," quoting him regularly in her correspondence and benefiting from his philanthropy (65).

Penner speculates that Nightingale would have applauded Dickens's skewering of female philanthropists in *Bleak House*. She held similar views of women "wanting in earnestness" (66). Conversely, she would have applauded Esther's sustained commitment and her patient adaptation to the primitive living conditions of those she visited, values Nightingale incorporated into her training of district nurses. Both Dickens and Nightingale believed strongly in the power of affiliative families to support and mentor those whom poverty, neglect, and abandonment placed at risk. Nightingale, Penner tells us, purchased copies of *Bleak House* for various charities, even though she was pained by the novel's satirical treatment of Caroline Chisholm, Mrs. Jellyby's prototype, and a valued friend.

Meegan Kennedy's *Revising the Clinic: Vision and Representation in Victorian Medical Narrative and the Novel* looks at the relationship between clinical case studies and the novel, examining how and why these genres employ, to very different effects, shared discursive strategies and textual methodologies. Believing that "seeing and stating are crucially linked," Kennedy argues that "change in seeing made new forms of representation necessary, while new theories of representation codified and valorized particular kinds of seeing" (3). Kennedy seeks to trace the trajectory of these changes through three phases. She begins with the value the eighteenth century placed on "curious sights" apprehended through a system of carefully managed observations. She moves on to the technique of distanced observation, developed in Victorian times in association with autopsy investigations and entailing a combination of accurate, dispassionate observation with precise measurement. Finally, she examines the psychoanalytic model of speculative insight combined with clinical observation. Examining "five nodes in the history of the Victorian novel," Kennedy considers the role of literary periodicals in staging clinical medical realism, the sentimental deployment of clinical observations in Dickens and Gaskell, Eliot's revision of mechanical observation in the service of sympathetic realism and speculative insight, and the "scientific mapping of a dark, exotic labyrinth" in Freud and H. Rider Haggard (7).

Kennedy shows how clinical observation and sentimental detail combine in Dickens's two most famous deathbed scenes to represent both the suffering body and "the dramatic emotional energy of grief and regret"—an energy into which readers are drawn to participate through visual and affective means. In the case both of Little Nell and Paul Dombey, physical symptoms of their vague, wasting diseases appear much earlier than the deathbed scene and are even then easily spiritualized. In contrast to the realist depiction of Mrs. Skewton's death, which offers "a real body, with all its human waste and suffering" (104), the representation of Nell's and Paul's deaths is staged to elide clinical detail, providing for readers' visual consumption scenes imbued with pathos and pleasurable regret. In this respect, Kennedy believes, Dickens followed in the tradition of the eighteenth-century medical narrative "that sought to certify the physician's insight by demonstrating his sensibility and sentiment as healing and diagnostic tools" (107). In Dickens's case the sentimental aesthetic served a pragmatic end as well, helping him to "enlist viewers' hearts in his social reformist projects" and thus "marrying idealism to a goal often associated with realism" (107).

In *The Social Life of Fluids: Blood, Milk, and Water in the Victorian Novel*, Jules Law examines the Victorian era's obsession with the circulation of fluids as emblematic of larger anxieties about power, autonomy, and identity and about the body's relationship to social space and social control. Law's cross-disciplinary and thoroughly contextualized study connects these concerns in original and thought-provoking ways to a broad range of technological developments, scientific innovations, and contemporary controversies—the Thames Embankment, the transfusion of human blood, the pasteurization of milk, campaigns against wet nursing, the Canal Boats Act, sanitary reform. If the nineteenth century "gave a distinctive stamp . . . to our privatized sense of the body," it was also the era that demanded "highly unsentimental attitudes toward even the most intimate bodily functions," Law reminds us (x). His study pivots on that paradox—on the body's leaky permeability and on vexed questions about the ownership of fluids related to developments in urban planning and public health administration (x).

Law argues that the question of who owned blood, milk, or water ultimately had less to do with the properties of the fluid in question than with the larger question of how and by whom fluids could be possessed. He shows that the novel engaged this question by imagining "circuits of limited circulation" (5) of which maternal breast milk came to be regarded as an ideal prototype—a "transindividual fluid" designed to pass out of a body and into another, that nevertheless "outlines relatively intimate circuits of sociality" (5). In readings of six novels by Dickens, George Eliot, George Moore, and Bram Stoker, Law works out the implications of these boundary issues as they shape Victorian notions of subjectivity and encode contested understandings about the social body. In each reading he demonstrates how the novel's plot is anchored in "literal problems of fluid management" and then moves beyond the literal to consider larger metaphorical constructions of flow and circulation. Drawing on the discourses of science, economics, politics, and material culture, he offers a window into the Victorian roots of anxieties still very much alive today—anxieties stemming from "the human organism's perilous vulnerability to technological deconstruction" (x).

Law considers *Dombey and Son* "an early and key text in the development of modern attitudes toward the commodification of bodily fluids" (25). He associates the novel with the first phase of sanitary reform marked by Edwin Chadwick's landmark Report in 1842 on *The Sanitary Condition of the Labouring Population*. Chadwick's report portrayed the country as "a chaotic network of fluids linking city with countryside, private households with institutions, and bodies with public space" (28). Chadwick believed that fluids could and should be regulated, and he focused on the individual household as the axis of reform. In linking the wet-nursing plot of *Dombey and Son* to the larger context of public health and in focusing specifically on the domestic scene, Dickens, then, aligns himself with this first decisive phase of a longer conversation about the circulation and management of fluids.

Law shows how anxieties about wet nursing derived both from middle-class fears about exposing infants to lower-class bodies and from more general worries about the family's place in relation to urbanization and industrialization. Thus, Dombey vainly attempts to "insulate his household against the claims of milk kinship" that come to represent the novel's larger pattern of adoptive relationships, but, in the end, the novel "imagines human community . . . as the gradual expansion of kinship ties initiated by the communion of bodily fluids that are themselves inalienable and unalterable essences" (31). In so doing, it affirms households as permeable structures, sites of flow and exchange, all the while holding up the home as "the privileged site of identity-making and identity transformation" (45).

Law sees the shift in focus from breast milk in *Dombey and Son* to the water of the Thames in *Our Mutual Friend* as corresponding to a paradigm shift in the culture's thinking about fluid management—from public health to public works, from the household as the nexus of reform to the urban infrastructure. The ambitious Thames Embankment project, with its profound impact on the river-dwelling population and its dramatic intervention in the city's ecology, exemplifies a whole new way of thinking about bodies in circulation. The issues raised by the project (Who owns the river? When should public welfare trump civil liberties?) focalize a complex set of philosophical, legal, and political questions that inform the plot and characters of *Our Mutual Friend*.

In *Technologies of Power in the Victorian Period*, John C. Murray looks at the impact of capitalism and industrialization on language use during the early to mid-Victorian period. Murray proposes that the rise of print culture, made possible by inventions like the high-speed printing press, diminished the value placed on oratory and speech as instruments for social critique. Closely examining three industrial novels, Dickens's *Hard Times*, Charlotte Brontë's

Shirley, and George Eliot's *Felix Holt*, Murray attends to the ways that voice persists in these novels within the discourse of print culture as a "trace and residue" capable of creating new and powerful forms of speech. In each case, he notes, the printed word turns on itself and imbues with new meaning and relevance an ideal speech community marginalized by the dominant culture or buried in its past—a culture that technical progress has left behind.

In the chapter on *Hard Times*, Murray represents the circus as "an organic counterculture" that "makes critique available for intervention into systems of technical rationality" (18). The first chapter of the novel announces the birth of a highly precise and technical language—one that restricts the capacity to differentiate, imagine alternatives, exercise free will, and make ethical choices. Serving the efficiencies of the industrial economy, such a language disenfranchises workers and paralyzes human agency. The language of the circus characters, on the other hand, freely manipulates speech, extends its range through creative use of gesture and intonation, and defers absolute meaning—in the process disrupting the status quo and allowing for new meaning-making possibilities to emerge. In so doing, it opens a space for critique of hegemony and permanence. In the Bakhtinian sense of the carnivalesque, the circus "becomes a venue for suspending social hierarchies and for disrupting the continuity of logic and factual reasoning" (39). Murray points to the significance of the circus's location: its existence on the periphery of the dominant culture testifies to communicative impulses that cannot finally be purged from the language of technical rationality, but also to its marginality, intermittent subjection to state control, and limited powers of resistance.

In *Posting It: The Victorian Revolution in Letter Writing*, Catherine J. Golden takes a material culture approach to the study of the Victorian revolution in letter-writing brought about by the Penny Post—a technological innovation linked to railway development that had broad economic, social, and cultural impact. She discovers evidence of this impact in literature and history, but also in a wide range of artifacts—from writing desks and manuals to pens and inkwells, from envelopes and valentines to biographies, diaries, book illustrations, and narrative paintings. Such objects function in Asa Briggs's term as "emissaries of culture" and also, following Ann Rosalind Jones and Peter Stallybrass, as "material memories," evoking the culture that produced them and informing understandings about Victorian conceptions of nation, gender, social class, identity, the private and the public spheres. Neither a straightforward history of postal reform nor an analysis of its effectiveness, the book seeks to connect literature, history, politics, and material culture in order to reflect on the affordances, challenges and complications brought on by the Penny Post. Golden also reflects on the links between Victorian reactions to the postal reform and our own culture's obsession with the technological progress made possible by computer-mediated communication. Part 1 of her study examines the need for reform and positions it within the context of rising literacy rates and mass production in the literary marketplace. Part 2 looks at outcomes. Golden shows how the Penny Post brought far-flung lovers and families together, created social networks, and participated in rituals of grief and mourning, and how, on the other hand, it brought about the advent of mass mailings and efficiently served the purposes of blackmailers and slanderers.

Briefly reflecting on Dickens's novels, Golden identifies postal themes and references in *Bleak House*, *David Copperfield*, *Nicholas Nickleby*, and *Oliver Twist*. More than fifty notes and letters play a role in the plot of *Bleak House*, she observes. The Penny Post facilitates Hortense's slander campaign and Jarndyce's marriage proposal. In one of the novel's key scenes, penmanship serves as "the recognizable imprimatur of individual identity" (25). Epistolary habits and style offer a lens into character in the cases of Richard Carstone, Wilkins Micawber, and others. Citing *Household Words*, Golden remarks that Dickens favored postal reform and that 40,000 copies of a pre-reform playlet authored by Henry Cole were bound into part 13 of *Nicholas Nickleby*.

The year's yield in Dickens studies offers interesting new work on Dickens in relation to visual culture, music, dance, and popular theatre. Among the most interesting of these pieces is John O. Jordan's playful, absorbing essay, "The Ghost in *Bleak House*." Jordan asks readers to engage with him in a perceptual conundrum: is the roughly triangular, transparent shape inside the fence of the mausoleum in Browne's final illustration to *Bleak House* meant to represent the ghost of Lady Dedlock? Or is this mysterious shape only another atmospheric shadow in a dark picture? And if the shape *is* meant to represent Lady Dedlock's spirit, whose idea was this ghostly visitor—Browne's or Dickens's?

From these simple questions, Jordan teases out complications that follow many fascinating paths. Even readers looking at the same illustration in the same edition of the novel will disagree about whether the ghost is spirit or shadow. Complicating matters, the text provides no verbal prompts affirming the presence of a ghost.

Jordan reviews the evidence of intent. Dickens did, apparently, send directions for the final illustrations to *Bleak House* to Browne, but the letter containing them has not survived. Browne's intentions can be read indirectly only in the contradictory evidence of two related drawings. In the "working drawing" goblin-like figures in the margins may signal the presence of the supernatural—one figure may even be pointing to the ghost that Sir Leicester can't see. In the second drawing, likely produced after the novel was finished, the ghostly space is "unambiguously vacant" (30). The production process for these illustrations introduces further complexities. The plates tended to wear with use, and the images became less distinct. Lithographic transfers exacerbated this deterioration of images.

In the final analysis, Jordan finds a peculiar appropriateness in the fact that the ghost of the plate appears to some and not to others: "It is often the way of ghosts to come and go mysteriously" (34). In a provocative speculation, he relates the image to the conclusion of *Oliver Twist*: "Is it possible that when he wrote the story of another illegitimate child that yearns for the presence of a mother who dies, a story in which ghosts and ghostly presences abound, Dickens may have reverted to the idea with which his earlier novel ended and instructed his illustrator to suggest the presence of a 'shade' lingering near the site where the mother is buried?" (37).

In "Emblems and Ecphrases in *Dombey and Son*," Rodney Stenning Edge-combe explores pictorial elements in *Dombey and Son*, organizing his well-informed discussion around Dickens's adaptations of conventional pictorial modes. Although the emblem's "naked allegorizing" had fallen into disfavor by the eighteenth century, its mode of signification undercut both by the rise of empirical science and by the Romantic distaste for crude moralizing, Victorians responded positively to Hogarth's domestication of the emblem and to his more flexible and ironic introduction of the pictures-within-pictures that served a choric function. Edgecombe points out that Dickens's own adaptation of the emblematic mode was marked by a strong attraction to the grotesque. Where he does employ emblems, he often does so comically, deflecting sentiment with distance, as in the grotesque image of Flora Finching as a "moral mermaid" (107). In this way, Dickens anticipates the surrealists' fascination with "the unmodulated connection of humans and objects"; numerous "proto-surreal moments in his fiction," are rendered by means of an emblem frame (108).

The content of the fictional pictures in Dickens's novels, Edgecombe argues, offers an implicit critique of contemporary art's failures in imagination, seriousness, and relevance. Dickens deplored pictures that directed the viewer's attention to decorative details, losing the over-arching subject in the process, or that, in sacrificing character to form, encouraged a fetishized objectification of female beauty. His friendships with members of "The Clique," a group of painters who sought to create serious narrative art rooted in present-day concerns, influenced his turn away from the "Grand Style" of Sir Joshua Reynolds and others—a style Dickens mocked in the portrait of Mr. F, the wine merchant, set against "a pillar with a marble pavement and balustrades and a mountain." Not content merely to describe pictures as static assemblages of color, form, and image, or to record the reactions of viewers to the art, Dickens sometimes animates the pictures themselves, reversing the roles of seer and seen. In *Bleak House*, for example, the portraits in Sir Leicester's library "frown" on their dozing owner (116). In these and other adaptations of pictorial modes and representations, Dickens, Edgecombe concludes, played a "maverick" role and imagined a "rich and various . . . latitude" for the fine arts (118).

Jude V. Nixon's "'[Many] jewels set in dirt': Christology, *Pictures from Italy*, and Pre-Raphaelite Art" examines the impact of his Italian travels on Dickens's interest in art beginning in 1844. *Pictures from Italy* and Dickens's letters composed during the period reveal "expansive, insightful, and sustained reflections on art" (83), Nixon observes. The experience Dickens gained in Italy and the critical eye for art he developed during his travels shape his confident repudiation of Pre-Raphaelite Christology in his 1850 article "Old Lamps for New Ones."

Nixon argues that Dickens's outrage against Millais's *Christ in the House of His Parents* can be explained in part by his objections to the Catholic-inspired religious art he had witnessed in Italy. He imposed on Millais's painting the disgust he came to feel for "Italian low art" (95). His senses "immediately traumatized" (98) by a culture so different, Dickens casts Italy in apocalyptic and purgatorial terms. But his experience of Venice as "sublime" helped him to separate "great art from base art, religious art from Catholic art, Italy's jewels from its dirt" (104). Dickens's harangue against the English art of the Pre-Raphaelites, thus, had its roots in Italy, where the employment of professional models came to stand for an excessively imitative naturalism that stifled originality and overlooked the ideal.

Dickens's *Life of Our Lord* (1846–49), written a year before Millais painted *Christ in the House of His Parents*, articulates a reverent view of Christ and the Holy Family consistent with the author's conviction that artistic representations should emphasize their divinity. He objected to the naturalism of Millais's portrayal, the clutter and dirt of the claustrophobic carpenter's shop (associated with disease), the grotesque human forms, and the excessive, overly-crafted details. Moreover, he considered the brotherhood "retrogressive," and lampooned its potential to breed fringe groups that could coalesce into an epidemic subversive of progress and development.

Examining the Millais painting and Dickens's reaction to it in the context of shifts in Christologies and artistic traditions, Nixon offers a well-developed explanation for the apparent hostility of Dickens's attack on Millais and in the process insightfully explores his more general engagement with the pre-Raphaelites—an engagement at once more intimate, more reciprocal, and more complex than has been generally assumed.

In "Theatrical Dance in Dickens," Rodney Stenning Edgecombe looks at the representation of social dance in Dickens's sketches and novels, arguing that its stylized and comically heightened features betray its origins in ballet and pantomime. Dickens compensated for his lack of experience with dance assemblies, Edgecombe argues, by drawing on theatrical representations of dance. Ballet performances and country dances were commonly incorporated into the plays and circus performances Dickens would have attended.

When Dickens describes social dancing, as in the case of Dick Swiveller's participation in the Wackles's quadrilles, he blends in details that would have been out of place and unrealistic in a domestic context. Alcohol-fueled solo flourishes, the coupling of tall and short dancers for comic effect, irregular floor patterns, Dick's "almost superhuman showiness": these features are drawn from the repertoire of popular ballet performances rather than from anything Dickens might have observed in a Victorian parlor (10).

Dickens's "Disneyesque fantasia" of dancing shoes in "Meditations on Monmouth Street" also suggests a "balletic provenance," specifically referenced in the allusion to "a numerous *corps de ballet* of boots and shoes" (12, 13). In addition to the "showy *pas seul* à la Swiveller," the description employs the comic convention of a "grotesquely overweight" dancer (well-wadded to *appear* overweight on the stage) whose hyper-agility strikes a note of absurdity (13). Dickens employs this same comic convention in his depiction of Fezziwig's dance in *A Christmas Carol*.

In "The Last Cab Driver, and the First Omnibus Cad" of *Sketches By Boz*, Dickens makes comic hay out of "the very pretty and graceful process" by which cabmen and passengers express their mutual availability and need—in effect, "quite a little ballet" (18). Edgecombe notes that classical ballet's reliance on allegory conveyed through miming gestures found its way into popular working-class pantomime whose influence on Dickens has been well established.

A rich perspective on the cultural significance of pantomime, and incidentally on Dickens's experience of the genre's imaginative possibilities, can be found in *Victorian Pantomime*, a collection of scholarly articles edited by Jim Davis. The volume reviews the emergence of the Victorian genre from the Regency Harlequinade made famous by Joseph Grimaldi, follows the development of pantomime into its mid-Victorian "golden age," and traces its decline and gradual evolution into the lavish music hall spectacles common at the end of the century. Special attention is given to pantomime's engagement with ideologies of race, class, and gender, to the role of pantomime in the provinces, and to its afterlife in contemporary culture. Dickens scholars will find many of the essays helpful in contextualizing Dickens's deep-rooted and nostalgic attraction to this potent form of popular entertainment. Especially noteworthy are Jeffrey Richards's discussion of fairies and fairy tales (which cites Dickens's *Household Words* article praising the ethical value of these stories in modeling courtesy, consideration, and kind treatment), Janice Norwood's survey of "Sixty Years of the Britannia Pantomime," and Anne Featherstone's analysis of readership and authorship in the theatrical trade journal *The Era*. Dickens, Featherstone reminds us, "regarded himself as a graduate of 'the university of the great theatrical newspaper'" (172).

Ethical, Philosophical, and Religious Approaches

The year's work in Dickens studies explores in interesting ways the ethical value of reading Dickens and offers new interpretations of Dickens's novels viewed through ethical, philosophical, and religious lenses.

Leona Toker's *Towards the Ethics of Form in Fiction: Narratives of Cultural Remission* takes an embracing and methodologically sophisticated approach to the study of fiction in relation to ethical criticism. Toker works on the premise that the aesthetic experience "has an intrinsic ethical effect, irrespective of the presence or absence of 'message'" (3). She is interested in the way that engagement with great works of literature effects a "reprieve" from the pursuit of personal, social, or professional advancement, making it possible for readers to slow down, detour from cultural norms and expectations, and ultimately return to daily life with altered perceptions. Toker proposes to study narrative's role in staging three kinds of cultural remissions: the oppositional, the carnivalesque, and the ludic. Her method involves linking the morphology of these narrative types, the patterns they enact and modes of engagement they prompt, to their moral vision. In semiotician Louis Hjemslev's terms, she sets out to examine "the form of the content." Building on the theoretical work of Bakhtin, de Certeau, and Chambers, Toker's book offers extended readings of canonical texts by Fielding, Sterne, Austen, Hawthorne, Dickens, Conrad, and Joyce.

Toker sees *A Tale of Two Cities* as distinctive in Dickens's work for "the relative prominence of the grimly carnivalesque in its plot and imagery"—a prominence counterbalanced by an emotionally restrained style. (94). In the novel hierarchies are reversed, spectators and participants merge in crowd scenes, architectural and social boundaries are breached, and domestic values profaned, but language mitigates the effect of these events.

Toker divides the characters of the novel into three classifications with respect to these carnivalesque elements: "those swept by the temporarily triumphant sociohistorical forces represented by the crowd, those powerfully attracted by the losing side of the conflict, and those who manage to maintain a psychological distance from both sides in the fray" (99). She considers each in turn.

Dickens represents the crowds who exemplify the first category as "extremely suggestible," a condition exacerbated in the novel by starvation, sleep deprivation, and drunkenness. These somatic conditions lead to vertigo, a recurrent motif in the novel. Toker places Charles Darnay and Sydney Carton in the second category; they are "powerfully attracted to 'the loadstone rock' of their destruction" (104). In this way they participate in another form of "contagious insanity"—"a serial crumbling of the inner boundaries between individuals and their psychological environment" (104). In the third group of characters, Toker places Jerry Cruncher, John Barsad, and Jarvis Lorry—men who through neutrality or a show of conformity seek to evade the forces of history

Throughout the novel, Toker argues, Dickens manipulates style and structure to distance his readers from full emotional involvement with the sweep of these revolutionary events, even mitigating the intensity of the final scaffold scene. Thus the novel plays a role similar to that of the Lord of Misrule, "presiding over limited conditions for emotional release" (112). Toker considers *A Tale of Two Cities* a "landmark in Dickens's narrative reflection on the need for balance between natural impulses . . . and self-restraint." "The pulsations in the reader's distance from the characters and empathy with them," she believes, "form an ethically and aesthetically congruent" pattern (115).

Robert McParland's "Keeping Company With Dickens" explores "the continuing ethical relevance of Dickens's fiction for us" (145), placing this theme within the context of ethical approaches to literature generally. He attributes to Dickens multiple forms of ethical influence: a sympathetic identification with readers that inspires them to pay attention to issues of neglect and injustice, a rhetoric of pathos that effectively moves readers toward enlightenment and action, a successful challenge to individualism and institutional abstraction that emphasizes connection, respect, and support within a web of interrelationships, a gift for embodying multiple voices and perspectives, and an understanding of the historical moment that allowed him to reach readers "caught up in the engine of modernity" (152).

Citing the work of Richard Rorty, Martha Nussbaum, Carol Gilligan, John Rawls, and John Gardiner against those who consider the moral consequences of art "unresearchable," McParland argues that "Charles Dickens's novels help us to map today's ethical turn in fiction. They call us to responsibility and continue to speak to the heart of the humanities, which today is very alive on the margins of a world that is largely absorbed in commercial and techno-scientific activity" (155). McParland asserts that "recently developed methodologies for the empirical study of actual readers can indeed suggest the moral consequences that reading fiction may have had in their lives" (153). "To see how Dickens's novels continue to speak to the inner life of people and to the crisis of modernity," McParland says, "we must look at the reader as well as the text. . . . To listen to [readers] can lend some further support to the view that Dickens's novels perform cultural work, including evoking sympathy and a sense of ethical responsibility" (155).

Wendy Parkins's "Emotions, Ethics and Sociality in Dickens's *Sketches of Young Couples*" rescues these early, ephemeral, anonymously published pieces from critical neglect, arguing for their significance within a larger cultural conversation about "ethical or unethical forms of sociality" (4) prompted by the emerging value being placed on the bourgeois companionate marriage. Parkins uses key dimensions of Levinasian ethics as a means to discriminate among the "multiple and varied representations of couples as archetypes" (20) delineated in the *Sketches*, each pair negotiating in different ways the self-referential inward pull of the romantic dyad as against the ethical response "to a wider world of relationship, obligation, and sociality" (17) characteristic of more authentic forms of intimacy. Thus "The Couple Who Coddle Themselves" expose hypochondria as "the inverse of hospitality," and in their "unrelenting solipsism" (9) remain "trapped in a world of their own projection" (10). By contrast, "The Young Couple" operates as the nearly absent stimulus for the celebratory fantasies of others, creating a more positive structure of feeling, but one that rests precariously on volatile and transient emotions. Dickens finds an ideal balance in "The Nice Little Couple," intimate in their affections for each other but outwardly-focused as well—able to recognize and respond to the singularity of others.

Parkins considers Dickens's Conclusion to the *Sketches*, which focuses on Victoria and Albert as the "final couple," as constituting a retreat from the ethical complexities explored elsewhere. Here Dickens deflects with humor and reassurance an underlying fear that women's voices threaten social harmony and that "sexual difference" ultimately poses an "unbridgeable alterity" (19).

In "Vindication and Vindictiveness: *Oliver Twist*," William Flesch examines the effects of a biologically-determined tendency to altruism on how readers enter narratives (361). Using the scene in which Brownlow is goaded by Grimwig to test Oliver's trustworthiness by sending him with books and a five-pound note to repay a bookseller, Flesch illustrates Dickens's subtle play with the complex drama of human judgment as motivated by unselfishness.

In the scene, Brownlow, who seeks vindication of his trust in Oliver, and Grimwig, who is mildly vindictive—actually hoping that Oliver will betray Brownlow's trust—function as "the audience of Oliver's action" (362). At a further remove, the reader functions as the audience of the whole drama, hoping to see Brownlow vindicated and Grimwig's selfish spite receive its comeuppance. In the meantime, readers see what is invisible to the three characters—that Grimwig's skepticism sets in motion a scenario in which the altruistic impulse misfires. When Nancy and Bill abduct Oliver, claiming that he has run away from his respectable parents, the crowd functions as "mistaken altruistic punishers, cooperating with what they take to be the imperatives of the urchin's family" (364). Flesch classes Oliver with the protagonists of other classic literary vindications of the innocent, including Cordelia in *King Lear* and Hermione in *The Winter's Tale*: "much of the anxiety that we feel is about whether the altruistic punishers—the police or patrons or fathers—will come to see that they have mistrusted wrongly, have punished wrongly. Will they now make it right? Doing so will, in its turn, vindicate them before those they have wronged" (366).

Gail Turley Houston's essay, "'Pretend[ing] a little': The Play of Musement in Dickens's *Little Dorrit*," reads Dickens's novel through the lens of Friederich Schiller's ideas about the value and seriousness of aesthetic play, ideas that influenced Charles Sanders Peirce's work on play and the "generals" (Peirce's term for Platonic abstractions or forms). In *Little Dorrit*, Houston finds a sophisticated working out of these ideas illustrative of the belief that "play is a superlative form of seriousness, leading to the highest levels of knowledge, love, and morality" (266).

Houston explains that Schiller assigned three impulses to human nature: "Stofftrieb," "the material drive toward change and multiplicity" (268), "Formtrieb," resistance to change and need for abstract form, and "Spieltrieb," the ludic impulse that brings the first two into balance and harmony. According to Schiller, love is related to the concept of play. It embodies the ability to negotiate between esteem and attraction, always valuing the freedom of the one loved.

Houston notes that the concept of play is embodied in John Baptist, whose creativity can tease multiple meanings from the single word "ALTRO" and whose imagination transforms a ration of bread into a feast. Mrs. General, on the other hand, with her excessive allegiance to social forms and inability to love, represents "'Formtrieb' gone amok" (274). In this illuminating essay, Houston argues that Little Dorrit herself "enacts complex aesthetic forms of play that allow her a highly ethical compassion and dignity in the face of unrequited love, family dysfunction, and societal breakdown" (269). Her Princess story "represents one of the greatest achievements of the Play of Musement in the novel" (271).

Was Dickens "philosophical" in his novelistic framing of moral and ethical questions? To the extent that he was so, how much was he consciously aware that he was representing issues in this way, and how closely do the philosophical questions raised in his fiction enact conversations with contemporary schools of thought? In "Victorian Moral Philosophy and *Our Mutual Friend*," Dominic Rainsford examines the interplay between Utilitarian and Intuitionist beliefs in Dickens's last completed novel and, more generally, explores what it means to be "philosophical" in Dickens's fiction.

Rainsford notes that although Dickens was not generally considered by his contemporaries to be capable of serious intellectual thought, his characters routinely engage in philosophical questioning, and some of the questions, such as Gaffer Hexam's extended speech on the theme of "Has a dead man any use for money?" resonate with great subtlety and importance throughout the novel. "Dickens," Rainsford concludes, "really is interested in philosophy, or at least in embodied and lived philosophical positions" (282).

One such position relates to Mrs. Boffin's "untaught sense of rightness" (285), an issue that plays into gendered ideas about "women's intuition" at the same time that it represents the value of the conscience-based wisdom beyond "contingent moralities" affirmed by the Intuitionist discourse of Whewell and Maurice (286). Between these Intuitionist beliefs and the Utilitarian outlook there was considerable overlap, however, since Utilitarians acknowledged as valid and useful even faith-based moralities that promoted the social good.

In both Intuitionist and Utilitarian camps, the relationship between truth and expediency, explored in *Our Mutual Friend* through the "pious frauds" committed by John Harmon and Noddy Boffin, remained ambiguous. An Intuitionist belief in the transformative potential of the "human spirit" might be seen to justify Harmon in lying to Bella, who is after all a woman who could be lied to "for her own good." But is the marriage that results even legal? And out of what weak links is the moral structure on which this presumably happy marriage is based ultimately built? Perhaps, Rainsford intriguingly speculates,

Riah's function as a symbol for uncorruptibility is meant to distract readers from such flaws in moral reasoning in a novel where there is otherwise "a lot of quite hard and sophisticated philosophical work going on" (290).

In *Dickens, Drood, and Redemption: Essays about Charles Dickens's Unfinished Novel*, Ray Dubberke gestures toward the religious themes of Dickens's unfinished novel. This collection of twenty brief essays, a number of them reprinted or adapted from earlier versions published in *The Dickensian*, falls under the category of what used to be called *Droodiana*. Dubberke, who produced an earlier volume, *Dickens, Drood, and the Detectives* (1992) revisits and recasts old theories and introduces new arguments and speculations, all the while engaging other "Droodists" in playfully contentious sparring over such questions as: "Does Edwin Drood survive?" "Why the six-month gap in the narrative?" "Who drew the cover illustration?" "Who is Dick Datchery?" "What is the date of the action?" "How do we explain the 'Sapsea Fragment'?"

Dubberke counts himself as of the "Undertaker" (as opposed to the "Ressurectionist") party, offering evidence that Jasper did indeed kill his nephew and that Dickens intended a death's door repentance. He offers textual support to bolster his claim that "the moral of the story, the deep underlying message that the author intended to present in his final chapters, is simply that *God can forgive what man cannot*" (33).

With respect to the minor mysteries of the novel, Dubberke concludes that Drood was buried in the Sapsea vault, that the Princess Puffer is Rosa's maternal grandmother, that Dick Datchery is a detective from Scotland Yard, and that the action of the novel takes place between 1833 and 1855. Dubberke engages in much engergetic speculation and not a little genial mud-throwing as he attacks the claims of others in order to script his own back-stories and plot projections, but he also pays close attention to and sifts carefully many details from letters, illustrations, and manuscript evidence. The book offers witty reflections on the whole industry created by Dickens's unfinished novel, including a chapter quantifying—with elaborate ground rules—solutions and combinations of solutions to the Drood mystery between 1870 and 1999 (the winning combo: Drood is murdered, Datchery is Bazzard).

An explicitly Christian reading of *A Christmas Carol* is offered by Reverend Cheryl Anne Kincaid's *Hearing the Gospel through Charles Dickens's "A Christmas Carol,"* a volume of advent lessons and prayers interweaving character studies and reflections on Dickens's novel with scripture passages and meditations.

Dickens and Adaptation

In this final section of the review, I first consider two creative works that make use of biographical material related to Dickens's life. I also assess the flourishing critical scholarship on the adaptation of Dickens's novels as plays, readings, and films.

Anne-Marie Vukelic's *Far Above Rubies* offers a fictional account of Catherine's life told in journal form and set against a cast of colorful Victorian characters, including Count D'Orsay, Wilkie Collins, and Thackeray's mad wife Isabella. Intending to tell "her story" with empathy and respect, Vukelic emphasizes Catherine's inevitable but frequently self-doubting submission to her husband's will and her doomed competition with her sisters Mary and Georgina for Dickens's love. The novel's appearance in the same year with Lillian Nayder's biography of Catherine makes comparisons unavoidable, even though, of course, Vukelic is entitled to fictional license. The trouble is that in fictionalizing Catherine, Vukelic often makes her cartoonish. Vukelic's Catherine is prone to ventriloquizing views that sound more like what recent commentators have said about her. A virtual newlywed, she is made to muse: "I . . . began to wonder whether he was trying to mould me into a dull, agreeable puppet, someone who would not hinder his growing ambition" (25). Intensely jealous of Mary, Vukelic's Catherine invades her fiancé's lodgings, rifles through his correspondence, and—mistaking letters to Maria Beadnell for letters to Mary—hysterically accuses her sister of being a "deceitful and wicked wretch!" Vukelic's novel, which does give fictional form to the everyday challenges of living with a restless, driven man of genius, often has the unintended effect of reducing Catherine to her small, anxious orbit around Dickens's bright and powerful star.

Sebastian Barry's *Andersen's English*, which premiered at the Theatre Royal, Bury, in February 2010, weaves a compelling drama around the fraught summer of 1857, when Dickens was reviving *The Frozen Deep*, dispatching his reluctant son Walter to India, and presiding over a marriage and household from which he had become increasingly alienated. Enter Hans Christian Andersen, childless, lonely, socially awkward, entranced by Dickens's charisma and by his seemingly idyllic family life at Gad's Hill, and completely incapacitated by his poor English skills from penetrating the façade. The visit, which was to have lasted two weeks, wore on into the fifth week. Afterwards, Dickens famously posted a card on the mirror in the bedroom where Andersen had slept: "Hans Andersen slept in this room for five weeks—which seemed to the family AGES."

Taking our cues from Dickens, most have read this story of "the house guest from hell" for its grim domestic comedy. With his blundering, inappropriate commands and his faltering English, Barry's Andersen enacts the comedy of farcical misunderstanding one might expect (10). But the dominant tone is reflective, melancholy, even elegiac. It's already over at Gad's Hill. What Andersen the outsider cannot see or only dimly sees is somehow rendered more tragic by his need to believe in this "paradise of human hearts" (10). Meanwhile, around the margins of polite conversation, Dickens behaves "like a man on fire—like a sailor in a plunging ship," Katie pursues a course of rebellious desperation, Georgina prepares to abandon her sister, and Catherine discovers an unlikely kinship with the unwelcome guest (30). In this last respect especially, Barry takes some liberties with the biographical facts, but in a way that seems consistent with the empathetic spirit of this interesting play.

Research into adaptations of Dickens's novels has largely focused on theater, film, radio, and television media. Allan Sutcliffe's two-part article on "Dickens in the Music Hall" fills a gap in the historical record by assembling accounts and reviews of music hall entertainments related to Dickens and his novels. Concentrating on the years between Dickens's death and the first World War, Sutcliffe describes the rich variety of these performances and their evolution from simple songs to more elaborate impersonations and sketches.

Sutcliffe explains that in the years preceding Dickens's death, music halls primarily performed his work in the form of songs like "The Artful Dodger," "The Dodger's Return," and "Little Nell." Dramatic sketches and monologues became much more popular in the decades immediately following Dickens's death. Performances of this kind still constituted only a small part of the standard music-hall repertoire, however, until the mid-nineties when Dickensian entertainments proliferated and performers specializing in Dickens material became well-known.

Sutcliffe profiles the most famous of these performers, delving into published reviews and anecdotes of the period and illustrating his discussion with images from playbills and postcards. He notes that Dickens's characters sometimes appeared in the "revues" popular just before World War I. When the war broke out in 1914, however, audiences preferred patriotic subjects, and in the meantime, the development of silent films offered new possibilities for representing Dickens's novels. While performers continued to offer Dickensian monologues and sketches at private entertainments, resorts, and minor variety theatres, Dickens material all but disappeared from the major music halls. During their heyday, however, the music halls served an important role in familiarizing a broad audience with Dickens's characters and stories. "Indeed," Sutcliffe proposes, "for much of the period covered, the music halls and variety theatres did more than the legitimate theatre to develop this familiarity" (224).

In "The Death of Nancy 'Sykes,'" Sue Zemka traces the fascinating story of the *Oliver Twist* murder scene as it was represented in the original serialization and as it was adapted in stage melodrama, public readings, plagiarisms, and silent films. Zemka's essay covers the period 1839–1912; the quotation marks around "Sykes" in her title allude to Victorian reviews and playbills, which euphemistically assigned Nancy a married name. Zemka is interested in the relationship between media and the representation of violence and especially in the "allure of powerful momentary experiences" (32). She notes that Nancy's murder was the subject of over fifty productions in

England and the United States between 1838 and 1850 alone. It was controversial—even at one point banned—because of the "electrifying" impact of the stage violence on its audience.

Dickens's written text, Zemka observes, frames violent action in ways that invite distance and reflection, in the process interrupting and slowing down the breakneck pace. While theatrical productions represented the murder and Bill's flight in a short space of time, positioning the audience as vigilantes screaming for his blood, in the novel the more leisurely pacing and enforced pauses caused by serialization had the effect of building a degree of empathy for Bill as hunted victim. Stage productions invited the audience to behave as mobs behave; the text, on the other hand, positioned readers as observers of the spectacle of mob mentality.

Zemka points out that when Dickens prepared "Sikes and Nancy" as part of his farewell reading tour (the only violent piece in his repertoire), he was reclaiming it from the theaters as his own, in the process sharply curbing the empathy-building pace of the serial version. Counterpoising the mechanical and technological gadgetry then transforming the stage into representations of various catastrophes, Dickens kept the spotlight on "the human body, strung out on emotion, communing with the similarly strung-out emotions of its audience" (41): "Every performance of the murder was an indirect reference to the imminent death of the performer, England's most loved entertainer, here replaying for his audience's delight the first murder he penned, sacrificially pumping it up with his febrile life's blood" (42).

Dickens believed that what he offered his audience would have a humanizing effect—that this "exposure to an unbearable act of cruelty in this controlled environment" would have the transformative power of "a terror that touches the sublime" (42). Zemka contrasts this aesthetic to the numbing effect of violence on contemporary sensibilities.

Zemka offers a suggestive reading of *Oliver Twist* in relation to the development of film technology. For example, she shows how an early plagiarism, Thomas Peckett Prest's *Oliver Twiss, the Workhouse Boy*, stages the murder as a series of climaxes, in the manner of stop-motion photography. Very different in effect, she notes, is D. W. Griffith's allusion to *Oliver Twist* in his 1912 film *Brutality*, where the lingering after-effects of the violence displace the cathartic moment that so transfixed Dickens's original audience.

With Benjamin Poore's "'I have been true to you, upon my guilty soul I have!': Negotiating Nancy, 'Hyperauthenticity' and 'Hyperfidelity' in the 2007 BBC adaptation of *Oliver Twist*," the discussion of Nancy's representation in various media moves forward in time and embraces the wider issue of the "overlapping and contradictory discourses" within which adaptations are inevitably enmeshed (158). Poore argues that "there is no 'true' Nancy to which adaptations can be faithful or otherwise" (158). He notes that Dickens's original text and Cruikshank's illustrations drew on a variety of generic conventions and stereotypes circulating in the 1830s—from the visual style of the comic grotesque, to the coded discourse surrounding the issue of prostitution, to the stage conventions of domestic melodrama. Adaptors, he says, attempt to take these various and mutually inconsistent discourses "and turn them into an individuated, rounded, psychologically realized 'character' called Nancy," who never, in fact, existed in Dickens's original text (160).

The essay examines various ways in which adaptors have represented Nancy's interiority—in part by adapting each other's representations. Poore sees Lionel Bart's 1968 musical as particularly influential, and he takes a close look at its influence on the 2007 BBC serialization of *Oliver Twist*—an adaptation he analyzes both for its "hyperauthenticity" (its grittiness implicitly attacking the cultural hegemony of the musical *Oliver!*) and its "hyperfidelity" (seeking to "trump" the original novel's socially more conservative politics). Thus the filthy children, cockroaches, and putrid gruel of the BBC adaptation conjure by contrast the musical's scrubbed "Dickensian" charm, while the casting of a mixed-race Nancy may be read as "an upbraiding of Dickens for not being more racially inclusive" (166). Poore shows how the BBC adaptation also participates in a much wider range of influences and allusions growing out of its own time and place—adopting, for example, the "dynamic restless camerawork" of the recent BBC *Bleak House* production and the "British soap-opera style of social realism" popularized in the hit show the EastEnders (163). He concludes: "If we are to accept Dickens' novel as a patchwork, a mongrel product of a particular culture, with all its contradictions, theatricality, evasions and implausibilities, then we must do the same for its adaptation, which uses the visual grammar of the soap, the docudrama, the musical and indeed that of the 'classic serial' itself" (168).

In "'Please, Sir, I want Some More': Clive Donner's Marxist Adaptation of *Oliver Twist*," Shari Hodges Holt offers an insightful analysis of the Marxist elements in this 1982 film version of *Oliver Twist*, relating the movie to the economic transformation of the early eighties brought on by the laissez-faire, "supply-side" policies of Margaret Thatcher, to which the film stands in opposition.

In the early scenes of the film, Donner emphasizes the pervasiveness of poverty by depicting Oliver's mother making her way to the workhouse by a well-travelled path (as opposed to Lean's windswept plain). Scenic juxtaposition contrasts the comfortable quarters of parish administrators with the paupers' stark accommodations. Interpolated dialogue between Mrs. Mann and Mr. Bumble highlights their materialism, indifference to suffering, and pretension to middle-class manners. Dick, usually omitted in film treatments of the novel, collapses from starvation at the very moment that Bumble delivers to Mrs. Mann the monthly payment intended for his support.

Donner's film highlights the thin line between the bourgeois and criminal worlds, most dramatically illustrated in the interpretation of Monks, which downplays Gothic elements and emphasizes Monks's aspirations to gentility. It works to build empathy for the criminals, implying that social exclusion has left them with no choice. Sikes's violence is associated with alcohol abuse, his only escape from poverty. George C. Scott's Fagin, from whom all supernatural qualities have been removed, is "a sympathetic victim of circumstance," who defends Nancy against Sikes and becomes himself the victim of an anti-Semitic mob. The final scene of the film, set just outside the workhouse, affirms that while Oliver may have escaped the future represented by the building, the workhouse, together with its conspicuously invisible inmates, remains. Closely reading the visual iconography of the film, Holt demonstrates how "Donner's production reveals the inconsistency inherent in Dickens's text . . . and ultimately acts as a powerful Marxist critique of the novel" (264).

In "From Book to Film: The Semiotics of Jewishness in *Oliver Twist*," Maria Cristina Paganoni compares Dickens's representation of Fagin's Jewishness in the text of *Oliver Twist* to David Lean's and Roman Polanski's film versions of this iconic character. She is interested in how "representational practices can circulate, respond to, and contest discriminatory ideologies" and in how cross-media, trans-historical acts of translation function as a "critical activity that creatively reinvents the past for the modern age" (309).

In Dickens's text, Fagin's status as a receiver and corrupter of children accords with contemporary Victorian attitudes toward the Jewish Other. Cruikshank's original illustrations to the novel reinforce these associations, incorporating stock Jewish traits, such as the hook nose, the matted red hair, and the feminized flannel gown. Fagin's role in the plot demonstrably follows "the ideological strictures of the conventional anti-Semitism of Dickens's time, place, and class" (310). Outsider and scapegoat, he is effectively expelled from the novel's restoration of Christian community in the final pastoral scenes near the village church.

Pagononi shows how David Lean's *Oliver Twist* (1948) reproduces the anti-Semitic features of Cruikshank's illustrations, overlaying them with Jewish caricatures of the kind published in Nazi newspapers during World War II. She notes that the film evoked bitter controversy when it was launched in 1948 in Berlin; in the United States, it was not released until 1951, and only then with heavy cuts prompted by protests from the Anti-Defamation League of B'nai B'rith and the New York Board of Rabbis. In Lean's film, Fagin's strong East-European accent and his role as racketeer and possibly a spy evince an "unstable national identity" and link him to activities associated with Jews during the war. Lean's film seems to reflect a postwar need on the part of the British people to reassert their own national identity by ejecting the Other.

Appearing almost sixty years after Lean's film, Polanski's adaptation of *Oliver Twist* excises the Maylie/Monks subplots, expanding and creating episodes to focus closely on Fagin the Jew. Never explicitly identified as a Jew, Ben

Kingsley's Fagin, while "still capturing his hypocrisy, ambiguity and cynical exploitation of his 'pupils' . . . is a damaged complicated human being who invites a more complex emotional reaction than just contempt and sheer hate" (314). Several years before the launch of the Polanski film, new historical research revealed the Jewish pogrom in Jedwabne to have been the work of Poles rather than Nazis. Paganoni sees allusions to these new findings in the Polanski film, concluding that "it engages with the problematic issue of contemporary Polish identity—refracting it—somewhat paradoxically—through the prism of Fagin" (318).

In *Film Adaptation in the Hollywood Studio Era*, Guerric DeBona contextualizes David O. Selznick's *David Copperfield* (1935) as a "Victorian New Deal," a fantasy of upward mobility perfectly timed to capitalize on its post-Depression cultural moment. The chapter is part of a larger study emphasizing the historical contexts of filmmaking from the 1920s to the 1950s, the political and economic factors that entered into production decisions, and the consequent development of new industry standards after World War II. Along with Dickens, DeBona considers adaptations of canonical novels by Joseph Conrad, Eugene O'Neill, and Stephen Crane, considering each as a culture-text.

DeBona demonstrates that Dickens's "almost folkloric appeal for Americans" was never stronger than during the Great Depression and afterwards (40). Dickens answered a need for escape coupled with the reassurance that hard times could be overcome. Because he advocated moderate reform that did not threaten the social framework, he possessed broad appeal to industrial leaders, intellectuals, the middle class, and the masses. DeBona shows how David Selznick, who could read American culture "as if it were a weather barometer," persuaded studio executives at MGM that Dickens, and the classics more generally, "had strong culture capital for the movie-going public" (43). His "astute assessment of both market forces and American cultural hegemony" took into account the "moral prestige" of adapting the classics during an era where the Legion of Decency and their followers were vociferously protesting sexuality and violence in film (46). The result, De Bona writes, was a new kind of partnership between Hollywood and the educational community. Teacher's manuals and classroom units were developed and sold, and film appreciation texts "valoriz[ed] the film as adaptation" (48). In these texts, Dickens was portrayed as a "mediating influence . . . who healed social divisions, bridged the divide between elite and popular, and promoted concern for others" (50).

The David Selznick/George Cukor collaboration produced a film notable for its incorporation of Victorian narrative conventions and iconography—borrowing images from Phiz's illustrations, adapting the conventions of pantomime in the acting, and creating the concept of the Dickens storyteller who fades into the "screen world" (54). Its message, however, spoke directly to the American moment. The film portrays David as a simple, virtuous man whose fall into poverty is undeserved, and whose recovery positions him to "expose a vulgar financial manipulator" (63). "Such a hero was especially useful in the 1930s, when the gulf between the classes was quite visible, when the more prosperous sectors of the economy needed to develop a sort of bourgeois *noblesse oblige*, and when . . . one of England's greatest novelists became one of Hollywood's most employable talents" (63).

In "Transforming *Great Expectations*: Dickens, Cuarón, and the Bildungsroman," Antje S. Anderson argues that Cuarón's controversial adaptation of *Great Expectations* represents "a postmodern filmmaker's challenge to the idea that the self evolves, that progress and change are the only way to define one's identity" (76).

Alfonso Cuarón's 1998 movie *Great Expectations* has typically been interpreted as an updating of Dickens's novel preserving Dickens's bildungsroman approach. Like Dickens, Cuarón features a protagonist first encountered as a child who becomes an adult in the course of the narrative. Like Dickens's Pip, Cuarón's Finn nourishes personal ambitions vaguely linked to an obsession with an upper-class woman who is beyond his reach.

Anderson argues, however, that these similarities mask a more fundamental difference and that Cuarón's film, especially with respect to the symbolism of its visual elements, is about "stasis and regression" rather than "growth" (72). Unlike Pip's desire to be a gentleman, which can be dated to his initial encounter with Estella, Finn's desires seem already to be in place from the film's opening scene. His drawings (with their representations of the stars and birds associated with Estella) visually allude to her before Finn is even aware of her existence. Finn's ambition to become an artist parallels Pip's longing to be a gentlemen, but in Finn's case drawing seems an innate part of his character associated with the natural world. Images of birds, fish, water, and sky are endlessly repeated in Finn's art as the film unfolds; constancy rather than development structures the narrative.

Whereas Dickens's ending implies that Pip and Estella have undergone transformations as their childhood selves have been tested by experience, Cuarón's ending "challenges the importance, even the possibility of change; it effectively erases the story that has led up to this finale" (77). Cuarón's film visually evokes the opening scenes in its finale, and Finn's words in the final exchange with Estella that "it was as if it had never been" substitutes "erasure or obliteration" for Dickens's emphasis on memory as an agent of growth and transformation. In the last frame of the film, the overexposed light that separates the two main characters—"as if the very sunshine of their love made the lovers vanish along with their own past" (78)—seems to provide a visual counterpoint to Dickens's "rising mists" (79): "If the desire for Estella, the desire to create art, and the desire to be one with nature are all one in the very beginning and do not undergo any change, the ending seems to imply that the only thing that can make these desires go away is not their fulfillment, but the obliteration of all desire in a vast ocean of nothingness" (79).

Conclusion

Pressing the generous page limits afforded me by the editors of *Dickens Studies Annual*, I will be brief in concluding this survey. For me personally, it has been an education for which I am very grateful. My work will have been well rewarded if it helps other scholars enter into some of the fascinating conversations about Dickens that took place in 2010. Although I have been Inter-Library Loan's favorite customer at Virginia Tech this year, I'm certain that I have overlooked someone's work, and I apologize for the inevitable omissions.

Claire Tomalin's new biography of Dickens, an early foretaste of the bicentennial riches, arrived in my mail this past week. "He left a trail like a meteor," Tomalin remarks. "Everyone finds their own version of Charles Dickens" (416). She concludes her biography by cataloging these "versions." One could do the same for the scholarship reviewed in this article. Here Dickens appears as abandoned child, domineering husband, word wizard, popular artist, professional author, editorial journeyman, practical jokester, ethical teacher, powerful magus, master craftsman, generic innovator, collaborative writer, savvy entrepreneur, promoter and underminer of the Victorian domestic ideal, poet of the city, cosmopolitan, intelligent conversant with scientific, philosophical, and political thought, endlessly adaptable "portable property." Still the "brilliance in the room" (Annie Thackeray's words, quoted by Tomalin), he continues to engage our imaginations and critical faculties in remarkably various and productive ways.

NOTE

1. Volume 2 (*Autobiographical Writings, Letters, Obituaries, Reminiscences, Biographies*) of Duane DeVries's ambitious and comprehensive *General Studies of Charles Dickens and His Writings and Collected Editions of His Works: An Annotated Bibliography* (AMS), was officially published at the end of 2010, but was not available in time for a careful review of its contents. It will be duly considered in the survey for works published in 2011.

WORKS CITED

Agathocleous, Tanya. *Urban Realism and the Cosmopolitan Imagination: Visible City, Invisible World.* Cambridge: Cambridge UP, 2010.

Allen, Michael. "New Light on Dickens and the Blacking Factory." *The Dickensian* 106.480 (Spring 2010): 5–30.

Allen, Robert. "Perpetually Beginning Until the End of the Fair: The Paratextual Poetics of Serialized Novels" *Neohelicon: Acta Comparationis Litterarum Universarum* 37 (June 2010): 181–89.

Allingham, Philip V. "Charles 'Carlo' Dickens In and Out of Italy in 1844: *The Chimes*." *Dickens Studies Annual* 41 (2010): 127–49.

Anderson, Antje S. "Transforming *Great Expectations*: Dickens, Cuarón, and the Bildungsroman." *Beyond Adaptation: Essays on Radical Transformations of Original Works*. Ed. Phyllis Frus and Christy Williams. Jefferson, NC: McFarland, 2010. 69–82.

Arac, Jonathan. *Impure Worlds: The Institution of Literature in the Age of the Novel*. New York: Fordham UP, 2010.

Barry, Sebastian. *Andersen's English*. London: Faber and Faber, 2010.

Benziman, Galia. "Alfred Jingle and the Pleasures of Incompleteness." *Dickens Quarterly* 27.4 (Dec. 2010): 292–98.

Budrewicz-Beratan, Aleksandra. "American Travel Books of Charles Dickens and Henryk Sienkiewicz." *Metamorphoses of Travel Writing: Across Theories, Genres, Centuries, and Literary Traditions*. Ed. Grzegorz Moroz and Jolanta Sztachelska. Newcastle upon Tyne, UK: Cambridge Scholars, 2010. 88–103.

Burke, Andrew. "'Purloined Pleasures': Dickens, Currency, and Copyright." *Dickens Studies Annual* 41 (2010): 61–79.

Buzard, James. "'The Country of the Plague': Anticulture and Autoethnography in Dickens's 1850s." *Victorian Literature and Culture* 38.2 (2010): 413–20.

Capuano, Peter. J. "Handling the Perceptual Politics of Identity in *Great Expectations*." *Dickens Quarterly* 27.3 (Sept. 2010): 185–208.

Chandler, David. "'Above all natural affections': Sacrifice, Sentiment and Farce in *The Battle of Life*." *The Dickensian* 106.481 (Summer 2010): 139–51.

Clarke, Mary. "'Not in charge of the story': The Presence of Rapunzel in Charles Dickens' *Great Expectations* and Margaret Mahy's *The Other Side of Silence*." *The Sands of Time: Children's Literature: Culture, Politics and Identity*. Ed. Jenny Plastow and Margot Hillel. Hatfield, UK: U of Hertfordshire P, 2010. 63–74.

Clausson, Nils. "Dickens's *Genera Mixta*: What Kind of a Novel Is *Hard Times*?" *Texas Studies in Literature and Language* 52.2 (Summer 2010): 157–80.

Cox, Arthur J. "The *Drood* Remains Revisited: The Monthly Plans (Part One)." *Dickens Quarterly* 27.2 (June 2010): 139–50.

———. "The *Drood* Remains Revisited: The Monthly Plans (Part Two)." *Dickens Quarterly* 27.3 (Sept. 2010): 209–25.

Cozzi, Annette. *The Discourses of Food in Nineteenth-Century British Fiction*. New York: Palgrave Macmillan, 2010.

Davis, Jim, ed. *Victorian Pantomime*. New York: Palgrave Macmillan, 2010.

DeBona, Guerric. *Film Adaptation in the Hollywood Studio Era*. Urbana: U of Illinois P, 2010.

De Stasio, Clotilde. "Starving vs. Cramming: Children's Education and Upbringing in Charles Dickens and Herbert Spencer." *Dickens Quarterly* 27.4 (Dec. 2010): 299–306.

Drew, Bernard A. *Literary Afterlife: The Posthumous Continuations of 325 Authors' Fictional Characters*. Jefferson, NC: McFarland, 2010.

Drew, John, and Michael Slater. "What's in *The Daily News*? A Re-evaluation—Part 1." *The Dickensian* 106.482 (Winter 2010): 197–206.

Dubberke, Ray. *Dickens, Drood, and Redemption: Essays about Charles Dickens's Unfinished Novel*. New York: Vantage Press, 2010.

Edgecombe, Rodney Stenning. "A Source for Rigaud in *Little Dorrit*." *The Dickensian* 106.482 (Winter 2010): 235–39.

———. "Emblems and Ecphrases in *Dombey and Son*." *Dickens Quarterly* 27.2 (June 2010): 102–18.

———. "Theatrical Dance in Dickens." *Dickens Studies Annual* 41 (2010): 1–23.

Flesch, William. "Vindication and Vindictiveness: *Oliver Twist*." *Evolution, Literature, and Film: A Reader*. Ed. Brian Boyd, Joseph Carroll, and Jonathan Gottschall. New York: Columbia UP, 2010. 360–66.

Flynn, Michael J. "*Pendennis*, *Copperfield*, and the Debate on the 'Dignity of Literature.'" *Dickens Studies Annual* 41 (2010): 151–89.

Frank, Cathrine O. *Law, Literature, and the Transmission of Culture in England, 1837–1925*. Burlington, VT: Ashgate, 2010.

Gates, Sarah. "'Let me see if Philip can/ Be a little gentleman': Parenting and Class in *Struwwelpeter* and *Great Expectations*." *Dickens Studies Annual* 41 (2010): 281–97.

Geriguis, Lina L. "Charles Dickens's DOMBEY AND SON." *The Explicator* 68.2 (Winter 2010): 104–6.

Ginsburg, Michal Peled. "Sentimentality and Survival: The Double Narrative of *The Old Curiosity Shop*." *Dickens Quarterly* 27.2 (June 2010): 85–101.

Gold, Barri J. *ThermoPoetics: Energy in Victorian Literature and Science*. Cambridge, MA: MIT Press, 2010.

Golden, Catherine J. *Posting It: The Victorian Revolution in Letter Writing*. Gainesville: UP of Florida. 2010.

Gregory, Melissa Valiska. "Dickens's Collaborative Genres." *Dickens Studies Annual* 41 (2010): 215–36.

Hager, Kelly. *Dickens and the Rise of Divorce: The Failed-Marriage Plot and the Novel Tradition*. Burlington, VT: Ashgate, 2010.

Hatten, Charles. *The End of Domesticity: Alienation from the Family in Dickens, Eliot, and James*. Newark: U of Delaware P, 2010.

Hochberg, Shifra. "Hawthorne's 'Ethan Brand' and *Great Expectations*." *The Dickensian*. 106.481 (Summer 2010): 118–22.

Hoffer, Lauren N. "'She brings everything to a grindstone': Sympathy and the Paid Female Companion's Critical Work in *David Copperfield*." *Dickens Studies Annual* 41 (2010): 191–213.

Hollington, Michael. "Dickens, The City, and The Five Senses." *Journal of the Australasian Universities Language and Literature Association* 113 (May 2010): 29–38.

Holt, Shari Hodges. "'Please, Sir, I want Some More': Clive Donner's Marxist Adaptation of *Oliver Twist.*" *Literature/Film Quarterly* 38.4 (2010): 254–68.

Houston, Gail Turley. "'Pretend[ing] a little': The Play of Musement in Dickens's *Little Dorrit.*" *Dickens Studies Annual* 41 (2010): 265–80.

Hühn, Peter. With Markus Kempf, Katrin Kroll, and Jette K. Wulf. *Eventfulness in British Fiction: Historical, Cultural and Social Aspects of the Tellability of Stories.* New York: Walter de Gruyter, 2010.

Imahayashi, Osamu. "Dr Tadao Yamamoto and The *Dickens Lexicon* Project." *Aspects of the History of English Language and Literature: Selected Papers Read at SHELL 2009, Hiroshima.* Ed. Osamu Imahayashi, Yoshiyuki Nakao, and Michiko Ogura. New York: Peter Lang, 2010. 159–71.

Jaffe, Audrey. *The Affective Life of the Average Man: The Victorian Novel and the Stock-Market Graph.* Columbus: The Ohio State UP, 2010.

Jarvis, Stephen. "Robert Seymour's Tombstone: A Personal Account of Its Recovery." *The Dickensian* 106.480 (Spring 2010): 36–41.

John, Juliet. *Dickens and Mass Culture.* Oxford: Oxford UP, 2010.

Jordan, John O. "The Ghost in *Bleak House.*" *Dickens Quarterly* 27.1 (Mar. 2010): 23–37.

Justman, Stewart. "Oriental Tales and *Great Expectations.*" *Dickens Quarterly* 27.1 (Mar. 2010): 38–47.

Kedzierska, Aleksandra. "Space of Celebration in Dickens's *A Christmas Carol.*" *Exploring Space: Spatial Notions in Cultural, Literary and Language Studies.* Vol. 1 Ed. Andrzej Ciuk and Katarzyna Molek-Kozakowska. Newcastle upon Tyne, UK: Cambridge Scholars, 2010. 123–30.

Kennedy, Meegan. *Revising the Clinic: Vision and Representation in Victorian Medical Narrative and the Novel.* Columbus, Ohio State UP, 2010.

Kincaid, Reverend Cheryl Anne. *Hearing the Gospel through Charles Dickens's "A Christmas Carol."* Newcastle upon Tyne, UK: Cambridge Scholars, 2010.

Kujawska-Lis, Ewa. "Dickens and Ternan in Polish Criticism." *Dickens Quarterly* 27.1 (Mar. 2010): 48–53.

Lamouria, Lanya. "The Revolution Is Dead! Long Live Sensation!: The Political History of *The Woman in White.*" *Dickens Studies Annual* 41 (2010): 299–321.

Lane, Rebecca. "The sin, most gross, most palpable, which Dickens everywhere commits . . . ": In Defence of Dickens's Use of Coincidence." *The Dickensian* 106.481 (Summer 2010): 123–38.

Law, Jules. *The Social Life of Fluids: Blood, Milk, and Water in the Victorian Novel.* Ithaca: Cornell UP, 2010.

Lee, Julia Sun-Joo. *The American Slave Narrative and the Victorian Novel.* Oxford: Oxford UP, 2010.

Letissier, Georges. "'The wiles of insolvency': Gain and Loss in *Little Dorrit.*" *Dickens Quarterly* 27.4 (Dec. 2010): 257–72.

Lettmaier, Saskia. *Broken Engagements: The Action for Breach of Promise of Marriage and the Feminine Ideal, 1800–1940.* Oxford: Oxford UP, 2010.

Livesey, Ruth. "Money, Manhood and Suffrage in *Our Mutual Friend.*" *Culture, Capital and Representation.* Ed. Robert J. Balfour. New York: Palgrave Macmillan, 2010. 83–99.

Louttit, Chris. "Savage and Skimpole." *The Dickensian* 106.480 (Spring 2010): 31–35.

Marroni, Francesco. *Victorian Disharmonies: A Reconsideration of Nineteenth-Century English Fiction.* Rome: The John Cabot UP, 2010.

McAleavey, Maia. "Soul-mates: *David Copperfield's* Angelic Bigamy." *Victorian Studies* 52 (2010): 191–218.

McBratney, John. "Reluctant Cosmopolitanism in Dickens's *Great Expectations.*" *Victorian Literature and Culture* 38.2 (2010): 529–46.

———. "'What Connexion Can There Be?': Secrecy and Detection in Dickens's *Bleak House.*" *Victorian Secrecy: Economies of Knowledge and Concealment.* Ed. Albert D. Pionke and Denise Tischler Millstein. Burlington, VT: Ashgate, 2010. 59–73.

McCorristine, Shane. *Spectres of the Self: Thinking about Ghosts and Ghost-Seeing in England, 1750–1920.* Cambridge: Cambridge UP, 2010.

McDonagh, Josephine. "On Settling and Being Unsettled: Legitimacy and Settlement around 1850." *Legitimacy and Illegitimacy in Nineteenth-Century Writing and Culture.* Ed. Margot Finn, Michael Lobban, and Jenny Bourne Taylor. Basingstoke, UK: Palgrave Macmillan, 2010. 48–66.

McParland, Robert. *Charles Dickens's American Audience.* Lantham: Lexington Books, 2010.

———. "Keeping Company With Dickens." *Literature and Ethics: From the Green Knight to the Dark Knight.* Ed. Steve Brie and William T. Rossiter. Newcastle upon Tyne, UK: Cambridge Scholars, 2010. 145–58.

John Mee. *The Cambridge Introduction to Charles Dickens.* Cambridge: Cambridge UP, 2010.

Messenger, Chris. "'How Many Women Is Power': Dickens's Sarah Gamp and Fitzgerald's Resentful Care-Taking in *Tender Is the Night.*" *The F. Scott Fitzgerald Review* 8 (Sept. 2010): 160–80.

Montwieler, Katherine. "Reading, Sympathy, and the Bodies of *Bleak House.*" *Dickens Studies Annual* 41 (2010): 237–63.

Mukherjee, Tapan Kumar. "The Four Bottle Man in Dickens's Dombey and Son" *Notes and Queries* 57 (255). 2 (June 2010): 216.

Murray, John C. *Technologies of Power in the Victorian Period.* Amherst: Cambria, 2010.

Nandrea, Lorri. "Desiring-Production and the Novel." *Novel: A Forum on Fiction.* 43 (Spring 2010): 18–22.

Nayder, Lillian. *The Other Dickens: A Life of Catherine Hogarth.* Ithaca: Cornell UP, 2011.

Nishio, Miyuki. "Definition of Idioms in the *Dickens Lexicon.*" *Aspects of the History of English Language and Literature: Selected Papers Read at SHELL 2009, Hiroshima.* Ed. Osamu Imahayashi, Yoshiyuki Nakao, and Michiko Ogura. New York: Peter Lang, 2010. 173–83.

Nixon, Jude V. "'[Many] jewels set in dirt': Christology, *Pictures from Italy*, and Pre-Raphaelite Art." *Dickens Studies Annual* 41 (2010): 81–125.

O'Donnell, Mary. "Mary Russell's *Bleak House*: Reforming Victorian Ideology in Detective Fiction." *Popular Culture Review* 21.2 (Summer 2010): 13–25.

Orford, Pete, Ed. *Charles Dickens On London*. London: Hesperus, 2010.

Paganoni, Maria Cristina. "From Book to Film: The Semiotics of Jewishness in *Oliver Twist*." *Dickens Quarterly* 27.4 (Dec. 2010): 307–20.

Parkins, Wendy. "Emotions, Ethics and Sociality in Dickens's *Sketches of Young Couples*." *Dickens Quarterly* 27.1 (Mar. 2010): 3–22.

Parkinson, Kirsten L. "'What do you play, boy?': Card Games in *Great Expectations*." *Dickens Quarterly* 27.2 (June 2010): 119–38.

Paroissien, David. "The Dickens Society: A Retrospect." *Dickens Quarterly* 27.1 (Mar. 2010): 67–71.

———. "Dyspepsia or Digestion: The Pleasures of the Board in *Martin Chuzzlewit*." *The Pleasures and Horrors of Eating*. Ed. Marion Gymnich and Norbert Lenmartz. Bonn: Bonn UP, 2010. 221–34.

———. "'If you knew all my story . . .': The Rhetoric of Pip's Tale." *The Dickensian* 106.482 (Winter 2010): 227–34.

Penner, Louise. *Victorian Medicine and Social Reform: Florence Nightingale Among the Novelists*. New York: Palgrave Macmillan, 2010.

Philpotts, Trey. "Mad Bulls and Dead Meat: Smithfield Market as Reality and Symbol." *Dickens Studies Annual* 41 (2010): 25–44.

Poore, Benjamin. "'I have been true to you, upon my guilty soul I have!': Negotiating Nancy, 'Hyperauthenticity' and 'Hyperfidelity' in the 2007 BBC adaptation of *Oliver Twist*." *Journal of Adaptation in Film & Performance* 3.2 (Sept. 2010): 157–70.

Rainsford, Dominic. "Victorian Moral Philosophy and *Our Mutual Friend*." *Dickens Quarterly* 27.4 (Dec. 2010): 273–91.

Reed, John R. *Dickens's Hyperrealism*. Columbus: Ohio State UP, 2010.

Reitz, Caroline. "The Novel's Mobile Home." *Novel: A Forum on Fiction* 43.1 (Spring 2010): 72–77.

Rena-Dozer, Emily. "Re-gendering the Domestic Novel in *David Copperfield*." *SEL* 50 (Autumn 2010): 811–29.

Robles, Mario Ortiz. *The Novel As Event*. Ann Arbor: U of Michigan P, 2010.

Rowlinson, Matthew. *Real Money and Romanticism*. Cambridge: Cambridge UP, 2010.

Sanders, Andrew. *Charles Dickens's London*. London: Robert Hale, 2010.

Shuttleworth, Sally. *The Mind of the Child: Child Development in Literature, Science, and Medicine, 1840–1900*. Oxford: Oxford UP, 2010.

Singh, Satyendra Prasad. *Institutional Satire in Dickens's Fiction*. New Delhi: Atlantic, 2010.

Smith, Andrew. *The Ghost Story, 1840–1920: A Cultural History*. Manchester: Manchester UP, 2010.

Steinlight, Emily. "Dickens's 'Supernumeraries' and the Biopolitical Imagination of Victorian Fiction." *Novel: A Forum on Fiction* 43.2 (Summer 2010): 227–50.

Stewart, Garrett. "'Ethical Tempo of Narrative Syntax: Sylleptic Recognitions in *Our Mutual Friend.*" *Partial Answers: Journal of Literature and the History of Ideas* 8 (2010): 119–45.

Sutcliffe, Allan. "Dickens in the Music Hall—Part 1." *The Dickensian* 106.481 (Summer 2010): 101–17.

———. "Dickens in the Music Hall—Part 2." *The Dickensian* 106.482 (Winter 2010): 207–26.

Świerczyńska. Edyta. "The Double Face of London: Crime and Space in *Oliver Twist* by Charles Dickens." *Exploring Space: Spatial Notions in Cultural, Literary, and Language Studies.* Vol. 1. Ed. Andrzej Ciuk and Katarzyna Molek-Kozakowska. Newcastle upon Tyne, UK: Cambridge Scholars, 2010. 175–82.

Taylor, Brooke D. "Spontaneous Combustion: When 'Fact' Confirms 'Feeling' in *Bleak House.*" *Dickens Quarterly* 27.3 (Sept. 2010): 171–84.

Toker, Leona. *Towards the Ethics of Form in Fiction: Narratives of Cultural Remission.* Columbus: Ohio State UP, 2010.

Tomalin, Claire. *Charles Dickens: A Life.* New York: Penguin, 2011.

Vukelic, Anne-Marie. *Far Above Rubies.* London: Robert Hale, 2010.

Wagner, Tamara S. *Financial Speculation in the Victorian Novel: Plotting Money and the Novel Genre, 1815–1901.* Columbus: Ohio State UP, 2010.

Warhol-Down, Robyn. "'What Might Have Been Is Not What Is': Dickens's Narrative Refusals." *Dickens Studies Annual* 41 (2010): 45–59.

Watson, Lauren. *Contingencies and Masterly Fictions: Countertextuality in Dickens, Contemporary Fiction and Theory.* Newcastle upon Tyne, UK: Cambridge Scholars, 2010.

Webb, Igor. *Rereading the Nineteenth Century: Studies in the Old Criticism from Austen to Lawrence.* New York: Palgrave, 2010.

Williams, Andy. "Advertising and Fiction in *The Pickwick Papers.*" *Victorian Literature and Culture* 38.2 (2010): 319–36.

Wynne, Deborah. *Women and Personal Property in the Victorian Novel.* Burlington, VT: Ashgate, 2010.

Zemka, Sue. "The Death of Nancy 'Sykes,' 1838–1912." *Representations* 110.1 (Spring 2010): 29–57.

Zweig, Stefan. *Balzac, Dickens, Dostoevsky: Three Masters.* Volume I of *Master Builders of the Spirit.* 1930. Introd. Laurence Mintz. New Brunswick, NJ: Transaction, 2010.

Recent Studies in Literary Darwinism: 1990–2010

David Garlock

This survey offers a brief summary and appraisal of recent developments in the broad-ranging field of Darwin-based literary criticism. Recent critical analyses based on poststructuralist theory are contrasted with nascent critical movements that depart radically from widely-accepted tenets of late-twentieth-century critics. The trend among literary scholars identifying themselves with "New Literary Darwinism" is toward consilience between traditional approaches to the humanities and empirically-based assessments of works of the literary imagination, an endeavor that seeks to incorporate into literary studies latter-day scientific discoveries in fields such as paleoanthropology, evolutionary psychology, neuroscience, animal ethology, sociobiology, and psycholinguistics. The sometimes unfamiliar landscape traversed in the process of reviewing the critical works surveyed resembled an unpaved road, replete with unexpected dips and jolts, as well as an occasional detour. The terrain can be rocky, at times. (Some of the appraisals of poststructuralist literary theory by science-oriented critics may jostle some passengers.) But the route taken is by no means dull. It is my hope that the reader will not sustain too many bruises, while enjoying the ride.

Compiled at the cusp of a new century, the list of works that comprise this survey chronicles a major shift in the focus of Literary Darwinism—a piv-

Dickens Studies Annual, Volume 43, Copyright © 2012 by AMS Press, Inc. All rights reserved.

otal transition from theory-based explication of Darwinian allusions in Victorian and post-Victorian novels and poetry toward a latter-day reassessment of the role of science in critical analysis. Disparate approaches to Darwinian resonances in literary artifacts attest to the ongoing maelstrom of controversy wrought by "the father of modern biology," whose legacy remains consistently productive of contentious discourse, persisting unabated to the present day.

Darwin among the Critics

In the process of surveying the current state of Literary Darwinism (a newly-minted coinage undergoing its own evolutionary permutations), I have separated critical approaches identifiable as theory-based—those that implicitly co-opt poststructuralist models—from more recent critical points of view lately emerging under the banner of "New Darwinism," a fledgling movement that promotes a closer alliance between scientific study and literary analysis. Segregating this new movement from earlier associations seemed to me a "natural selection," as well as an "intelligent design" (puns intended!), and so I have divided this survey into two major sections. This division recognizes a change in perspective that separates proponents of theory-based criticism from an empirically-oriented cadre of critics that pointedly rejects many of the premises informing the poststructuralist mindset. I have attempted to compare "theory-based" Darwinian analysis of literary texts persistently loyal to the lexicon of late twentieth-century theories with a nascent shift toward linking established literary masterpieces with recent advances in the natural and social sciences. Of necessity, I confronted the inevitable task of winnowing by restricting the survey to a broadly-based cross-section of critical voices in Darwinian criticism, illustrative of varying critical postures and predispositions. The results are, admittedly, more in the nature of a collage than a compendium. As with many collages, the tonal and textural juxtapositions may be jolting, but it is hoped that the overall effect will be invigorating and thought-provoking.

An informative overview of the current state of Darwinian criticism is provided by Harold Fromm's essay "The New Darwinism in the Humanities" (reprinted online: www.hudsonreview.com/frommSpSu03.html). Fromm's analysis encapsulates the mood and tone of some recent critics who have unabashedly abandoned theories that deny, or seem to deny, an empirically measurable universe existing completely outside and independent of the texts under consideration. "New Darwinism" resists intertextual analysis in favor of an approach that relies on nonliterary data, usually scientific and putatively nonsubjective in nature. Alluding to poststructuralist critical templates, Fromm cautions against "forcing a variety of artifacts through a critical grinder," and suggests that much critical theory of recent decades has become shopworn, if not totally effete and divorced from any empirically measurable objective reality: "Though the range of Freudian and Marxian criticism has been great, once certain basic formulae had been applied again and again, there was an increasing tedium and self-parody involved, eliding the most distinctive aspects of art works, while distorting their character" (10). Fromm's assessment of the "New Darwinism" is tightly written and resists simplistic condensation, deserving to be read in its entirety. It comprises a lucid bellwether documentation of what Fromm deems a seismic shift in the humanities away from Platonic mind/body dichotomization—"the view that Mind is more real than Body"(1)—toward the notion that the human longing for spiritual transcendence, facilitated through the mechanisms of artistic endeavor and inventive religious rituals, is merely an example of evolutionary adaptation and perpetuation of the species: ". . . a case could be made for spirituality as another, more genteel, covert form of savagery and control" (1). Portending a movement toward what Fromm and his cohorts refer to as the "modern scientific synthesis," a trend aimed at closer alliances between the sciences and the arts, *Homo aestheticus* (a coinage attributable to Ellen Dissanayake, see below) emerges as a product of evolutionary process, like a bat equipped with sonic radar, or polar hares with protective coloration. Moral codes and the shaping of livable social communities, bound together by religion and the arts, are as much a product of evolution as any other observable phenomena among living beings, according to this viewpoint. Distinctions between popular pulp fiction or hip hop music and "high art" are artificial from the standpoint of sociobiology and group survival strategies. For Fromm, "this human world is not *only* the product of culture and rhetoric, the actions of which no Darwinian would deny, but it is principally driven by the three billion years involved in the making of the human brain and is thus generated from the ground up rather than from the heavens down" (8).

After some rather pointed deflating of recent literary theory, Fromm concludes his essay by summarizing Dissanayake's broadly eclectic amalgamation of aesthetic studies with the disciplinary rigors of the hard sciences: "A Darwinian adaptationist, she connects also with human ethology, sociobiology, evolutionary psychology, psycholinguistics, neuroscience, ethnomusicology, biopoetics, developmental psychology, and much else, and her chief interest, aesthetics, takes account for a wider range of human behavior than the traditional approaches" (11).

New Darwinism notwithstanding, not all contemporary Darwin-based critical studies are devoid of homage to poststructuralist thought and rhetoric. Two recent studies, for example, reflect to some degree poststructuralist influences, highlighting analogical associations between Darwin's major work and literary productions classifiable as "Darwinian." Since the father of modern biology's "one long argument"—comprising both his *Origin of Species* and his subsequent *Descent of Man*—is analogically based, the critics who ground their interpretations on discernible Darwinian analogies are, de facto, employing his methodology—argument by analogy.

Literary Criticism by Analogical Association

In *The Evolutionary Imagination in Late-Victorian Novels*, John Glendening allies himself firmly with earlier critics who explore Darwinian analogues in the works of novelists identifiable as proponents of nineteenth-century empiricism. For close readings of specific examples, he rounds up some "usual suspects," namely, Wells's *Island of Doctor Moreau*, Hardy's *Tess*, Stoker's *Dracula*, and Conrad's early fiction. Glendening's homage to the apostles of indeterminacy (Derrida, et al.) is unmistakable in passages such as the following, which introduces his discussion of *Moreau*: "The novel dramatizes the experience of one caught in the web of indeterminacy constituted by these evolution-based confusions; and it does so especially through its recreation of Darwin's entangled bank" (39). Linguistic and epistemological indeterminacy reflect analogically other kinds of instability—biological, moral, teleological, cognitive. Plasticity is the only constant, as explicated recurrently in Darwin's descriptions of the natural world around us, and in the cultural milieu that produces the fiendish Dr. Moreau and his victims, including the novel's narrator, Edward Prendick.

Glendening's subtitle "An Entangled Bank" derives from Darwin's well-known conclusion to his *Origin*: "It is interesting to contemplate a tangled bank, clothed with many plants of many kinds, with birds singing in the bushes, and various insects . . . and to reflect that these elaborately constructed forms . . . have all been produced by laws acting around us" (373). In his introduction, Glendening recognizes the contributions of Gillian Beer and George Levine, in effect refuting the dismissive appraisal of what Joseph Carroll considers their poststructuralist leanings. The focus of *The Evolutionary Imagination in Late-Victorian Novels* is more reflective of Beer and Levine than Carroll in that it pays implicit homage to such poststructuralist principles as recognizing the metaphoric nature of language itself. Proponents of theory-based analysis, according to Glendening, "have been widely and justifiably influential with their sophisticated demonstrations of how Darwin formulates his arguments in ways consistent with the strategies of creative writers" (8).

Darwin's *Origin* begins with the analogy of animal breeding, which he calls "artificial selection," and exploits its explanatory value as a mirror image of an attenuated "process occurring" all around us, which he calls "natural selection." His argument for the existence of such a process is an analogical argument. Replicable experiments and discoveries in the field of molecular biology that would eventually validate basic principles of Darwin's species development-through-selection hypothesis would come a century later. ("Not only the genetic code but in fact most basic molecular mechanisms are the same in all organizations, from the most primitive prokaryotes up" [Ernst Mayr, *One Long Argument* 150].) With no access to the advances that would inform molecular biology a hundred years later, Darwin had only his keen powers of observation of the world around him, and his genius for inductive reasoning. He also understood the communicative value of metaphoric language and the use of analogy for rendering comprehensible the most profound and far-reaching of hypotheses.

The pervasive significance of the entanglement pictorial evocation in Darwin provides the central metaphoric core of Gendening's book: "The manifestation of evolutionary theory in 1890s Victorian novels is primarily a matter of entanglement, because not only is chaos stressed, but order, when it appears, quickly becomes mixed up within chaotic conditions. The reasons for this are social and epistemological" (27).

It is clear from the novels discussed that the metaphorical significance of evolutionary theory and its underlying principles gave rise to a multitude of analogical comparisons, providing a template that extended far beyond explanations of biological phenomena. Glendening explores the entanglement motif as it relates to the moral, psychological, epistemological, religious, political, social and ethical issues that engage and bedevil human society and culture.

Glendening's chapter titled " 'Green Confusion': Evolution and Entanglement in Wells's *The Island of Doctor Moreau* " explicitly links the postmodernist penchant for relativistic interpretations with Darwin's Malthusian evocation of a teeming, crowded bank: "The novel dramatizes the experience of one caught in the web of indeterminacy constituted by these evolution-based confusions, and it does so especially through its recreation of Darwin's entangled bank" (39). Glendening links the familiar theme of flawed narrative authority, so prevalent among poststructuralist critics, with the Darwinian entanglement motif: "The novel signifies indeterminacy as the ruling element in the universe and in the human condition, even subverting its own textual authority for telling the truth" (40). Even the name of the beleaguered ship *Lady Vain*, which carries Prendick toward his nightmarish encounter with the mad Dr. Moreau, bears a name which suggests the futility of human will and desire in the face of a destiny ruled by chance, "the vainness or futility of believing chance can be denied" (40). Destinies are entangled in a web of circumstances that act independently of human aspirations.

Other analogical associations with Darwinian entanglement that surface are "the novel's treatment of the relationship between humans and animals, another area of uncertainty relevant to evolution" (44). Glendening views the atavism and reversion to type exhibited by the animals with whom Moreau has tampered as "abandonment of Lamarckian optimism" (49) in favor of a kind of Hardyesque ambivalence. Entanglement is as likely to produce examples of devolution, degeneration, and reversion, as it is to foster improvement.

Glendening associates defining vignettes in Hardy's *Tess of the D'Urbervilles* with some of Wells's horrific images of entanglement in *Dr. Moreau*. Though the two novels differ in many exterior features (a rural farm community versus a wild jungle setting; civilized society versus rule by lawless, brute force), both stories seem to reflect a similar dilemma forced upon two quite different protagonists, each doing battle with the inextricable forces that a hostile environment imposes. The levels of chaotic entanglement are complex: "Entangled with her environment, Tess is a site of contestation that defeats any simple characterization of her because of the large number of intertwined variables at work" (90).

The choice of Bram Stoker's *Dracula* as a parable of d/evolution and reversion and its threat to civilization and progress involves the uncovering of more deeply embedded anxieties than the more apparent Darwinian allusions in *Tess* and *Moreau*. The conflict between order and chaos is embodied in the history and perverse nature of the Count, but is also latent in Jonathan Harker's personality and ancestral history. The danger of reversion/perversion is omnipresent: ". . . *Dracula* contains no settings with subversively entangled banks. Nevertheless, it also acknowledges that ideas of order are unable to escape the entanglements of chaos" (107). Atavism and instability threaten at every turn. Transylvania is a pocket of primordial savagery, a horror that suggests Gothic regression, a snare to be eschewed: "The more basic fear, however, is that modernity can never escape the grasp of its own primitive origins" (117). The fear of entanglement of his animal and human nature is part of the horror Harker encounters. But his being lured toward animalism threatens devolution into a sphere of sexual entanglement and ambiguity, as well, through his exposure to the Count's female vampires: "They fill him with desire for a primal sexual experience in which his involvement, by implication, will be oral, anal, and genital as well as both feminine and masculine" (121). The confusion, the vibrant chaos, is Darwinian in the sense that past preys upon the present, as ontogeny recapitulates phylogeny, the angel is embattled by the devil within, and sexual dichotomization and identity are ultimately entangled beyond extrication.

For Glendening, all entangled roads lead to the ultimate entanglement, which is Conrad's heart of darkness, the primordial jungle. The dense fecundity of overgrowth suggests Malthusian gloom and Darwinian struggle, but without Darwin's plea for appreciation of nature's plethora of diversity and grandeur. Darwin's implied allegiance to Victorian notions of ameliorative progressivism surfaces throughout his writing, and particularly toward the conclusion of his *Descent of Man*: "Man may be excused for feeling some pride at having risen, though not through his own [Lamarckian?] exertions, to the very summit of the organic scale; and the fact of his having thus risen, instead of having been aboriginally placed there, may give him hope for a still higher destiny in the distant future" (405). No such "hope of a higher destiny" pervades the evocations of primordial nature in Stoker or Conrad. Civilization cowers in the face of entangled chaos. Like Dracula's lair of iniquity, Conrad's jungle threatens the delicate fabric of social order and decorum: "The tropical forest disturbs because it threatens to spill its lack of meaning back into the modern world, the ultimate source of disquiet" (138). When Glendening frames Conrad's evocations of a menacing natural environment within the context of the ancient evil represented by Dracula's Gothic chambers of horror, the contextualization is analogical.

The threatened unraveling of civilized life conflates to encompass portents inimical to the individual within the society, and inimical to the fragile underpinnings of society itself. For example, looming endangerment of one's civilized identity bears a close resemblance to a loss of manhood in both Conrad's Kurtz and Stoker's Jonathan Harker. Upended geographical identity compromises gender identity. Glendening describes this as a recurring trope: "Becoming unmanned is a common late nineteenth-century trope registering widespread gender anxieties" (144). The Darwinian revolution effectively dismantled firmly entrenched dichotomizations on many levels, blurring distinctions between male and female (emphasizing the androgynous ancestry of all human beings), civilized and primitive societies, masters and slaves. Degradation, reversion to type as in Dr. Moreau's nightmare world, represents a kind of moral entropy requiring unfaltering human vigilance, and, perhaps, ultimately, submission to reclamation by the primordial past.

In his concluding chapter, Glendening allies the Darwinian tropes he has highlighted with poststructuralist concepts of linguistic "interpenetration," calling attention to the intertextual characteristics of the works discussed. In a discussion of several "neo-Victorian" works of fiction, including *Possession: A Romance* by A. S. Byatt (1990), "a 'neo-Victorian' novel that, adopting postmodern orientations, interrelates the late twentieth century with the Victorian era while attending to the nineteenth-century impact of the *Origin of Species*" (185), he describes a contemporary resuscitation of novels that combine earlier Gothic evocations with "some degree of representational stability relative to what exists independent of mind" (197). He explores the homage that these novels pay to their literary predecessors, while pinpointing the ways they depart from earlier Victorian templates: "What they can do, like the Victorian novels in question, is stress the linguistic interpenetration of chaos and order parallel to that which informs all human experience" (197).

In *The Descent of Love: Darwin and the Theory of Sexual Selection in American Fiction*, Bert Bender explores the response of American writers to the Darwinian revolution from the period of Darwin's *Descent of Man* (first published in 1871) onward. Bender compares Darwin's oeuvre to the Bible, and opines that the founder of modern evolutionary theory was the founder of a new literary and scientific ur-text, compendiously fertile and, like the Bible, rich in interpretative possibilities. According to Bender, American authors were quick to capitalize on the widespread awareness of Darwin's challenge to conventional beliefs and cherished dogmas: "They knew that he or she who 'owned' or most effectively interpreted the evolutionary past could claim the greatest right to the literary present. And they showed that the Darwinian book of life could yield as many conflicting and often dogmatic interpretations as the Bible" (xii).

Bender attributes the lack of Darwinian references among literary scholars of the mid-twentieth century to New Criticism's trend-setting tendency to avoid extratextual sources, relegating analogical comparisons as incidental and peripheral. He also provides relevant historical background illustrating the persistent resistance, in America as well as in Europe, to the classification of the human species as one species among many, the Darwinian hypothesis extensively developed in Darwin's *Descent of Man* which contextualizes the development of the human species as a process subject to the same evolutionary forces and exigencies as any other form of life. Comic parodies of Darwin's *Descent* abounded in the late nineteenth century. Bender offers a few representative examples, one of the more extravagant being Richard Grant White's satiric *The Fall of Man; Or, The Loves of the Gorillas: A Popular Scientific Lecture upon the Darwinian Theory of Development by Sexual Selection, By a Learned Gorilla* (8).

Throughout his discussion of sexual selection as a motif in late nineteenth-century fiction and early twentieth-century fiction, Bender explores "the animalistic elements of the courtship drama" (14), a prevailing obsession among a group he classifies as "the courtship novelists." Appropriating the Darwinian linkage of convention-regulated protocols of courtship in human society with observable behaviors among aboriginal populations (or even non-human species) can be viewed as pervading the work of novelists on both sides of the Atlantic: "Competing for their own large audiences as writers who best grasped the 'real' nature of human love, the novelists also participated in a heated social debate over racial and sexual difference and the nature of sex itself" (15).

Chapter 9 of *The Descent of Love* deals with "Harold Frederic and the 'Bio-logico-Literary Interaction' " (230). Frederic, a fin-de-siècle American novelist popular on both sides of the Atlantic, epitomizes an interactive dynamic between biology and literature that was to become vital to understanding recurring plot structures of the roster of American writers Bender discusses, from Howells to Hemingway. His discussion of Frederic's Darwinism emphasizes the downside of hereditary descent, illustrative of degeneracy as the counterpoint to ameliorative evolutionary vigor. A section titled "The Weary English" describes Frederic's view of a society he regards as excessively mannered and effete: "[He] is concerned with the way the English nobility had lost its vigor by having freed itself to some extent from the struggle for existence" (266). The theme of degeneracy or weakening of a noble line of descent is a Darwinian trope appropriated by English novelists—one thinks immediately of Hardy and Lawrence among many others. And, as Bender suggests repeatedly, English aristocracy serves American novelists of the late nineteenth and early twentieth centuries as a metonymic representation of the degenerative process, a quasi-xenophobic distaste for excessively mannered "English" hauteur reinforcing the stereotype of forfeited rigor. Bender ends his discussion of "descent," biological and spiritual, with a summation of the peculiarly end-of-the-line relationship between Jake Barnes and Brett Ashley in Hemingway's *The Sun Also Rises*: "That Jake Barnes's loneliness derives equally from his sexual and spiritual isolation is evident from the way he gravitates to various cathedrals and finally to his hoped-for place of refuge at San Sebastian" (358).

In his concluding summation of *The Descent of Love*, Bert Bender reviews his study of earlier American novelists and their response to the Darwinian revolution within the context of current novelists and the controversies of our own time. Understanding the earlier writers' responses to Darwin's re-positioning human life within the larger context of humanity's biological history requires both an appreciation of the limitations of their knowledge and also an awareness of their imaginative projection of the Darwinian evolutionary model upon the society of their time: "This is not to suggest that they . . . should be regarded as accomplished biologists or, say, evolutionary anthropologists; only that they made the best sense of it they could, and that they were quite intensely and self-consciously engaged in the cultural debate that sought to define and interpret the Darwinian 'reality,' with all its social implications" (366).

The New Literary Darwinism

In the discussion that follows, I review three book-length works of criticism, each by a single author, and one anthology of current Darwin-based criticism by seventeen writers representing a variety of intersecting disciplines. The diverse critical postures of the twenty writers represented lend themselves to a synoptic, if somewhat varying, reading of current trends in the application of evolutionary language and theory to literary studies. It seemed logical to present them in the sequential order of initial publication: *Homo Aestheticus*, by Ellen Dissanayake; *The Literary Mind*, by Mark Turner; *Literary Darwinism*, by Joseph Carroll; and a collection of essays by various authors, *The Literary Animal*, edited by Jonathan Gottschall and David Sloan Wilson. Dissanayake and Turner proceed with less quasi-evangelical fervor than Carroll and are somewhat less strident than some of the collective voices represented in *Literary Animal*, but all of these writers do depart radically from many tenets of their poststructuralist predecessors. Least conciliatory in tone, Carroll's fervor for debunking the dominant trends in literary theory of recent decades calls to mind Nietzsche's cautionary aphorism: "Whoever fights monsters should see to it that in the process he does not himself become a monster" (279). The demolition of deconstruction in *Literary Darwinism* waxes a tad overheated now and then. Here is an example of one of Carroll's acidic assessments: "After the vast groundswell of feminism and the minor tides of post-colonialism and queer theory, no truly new political impulse has animated literary study now for more than three decades, and no essentially intellectual impulse has been felt for something like three decades" (xi).

Having stormed the deconstructionist Bastille, he goes on to query, "How soon will the stale and etiolated rhetoric of postmodernism crumble from within?" (xi). In a less combative style, Dissanayake and Turner are equally committed to an approach to literary and aesthetic study that is putatively more objective, measurable, and scientifically verifiable.

Marshalling the compendious range of her diverse interests and cross-cultural experiences, Ellen Dissanayake embarks on a barrier-transgressing intermingling of art history, anthropology, psychology, sociobiology, and literary criticism in *Homo Aestheticus*. Whether or not one accepts her controlling premise regarding the significance of art production and awareness in the evolutionarily constructed formation of the human brain, the postulated commonalities linking a broad range of extant cultures (Sri Lankan, African, Western European, American) with what is known or surmised from archeological evidence about the quotidian lives of our hominid ancestors is impressive. The inquiry Dissanayake proposes is of no less significance than the primal questions asked by every thoughtful member of our cognition-encumbered species: Who and what are we? How do we define ourselves? Suggesting that the descriptive terminology itself needs to evolve, she places her own definition in etymological context: "Humankind has been called tool-using (*Homo faber*), upright (a hominid precursor *Homo erectus*), playful (*Homo ludens*), and wise (*Homo sapiens*)" (xiii). To this she proposes the addition of a new designation, *Homo aestheticus*. Being of the species *Homo criticus,* I found this wonderfully audacious addendum to the literary and cultural lexicon of our times bracingly relevant, particularly within the context of relating the findings of modern evolutionary biology to the study of drama, the novel, rituals of worship and rites of passage, storytelling, and the arts.

While not as harsh as Carroll in her repudiation of postmodernist analyses of canonically-vetted art, literature and culture, she clearly establishes her distancing stance on the subject of current theory-based critiques in her preface: "Proclaiming that there are a multiplicity of individual realities that are infinitely interpretable . . . many postmodernists forswear the rich, opulent cuisine of high art to offer instead a mess of unsavory, nonnourishing pottage" (xvi). She further describes the kind of criticism she disdains as "brutally impenetrable," characterizing it as "far more arcane and inaccessible to even the well-meaning ordinary reader than anything high art apologists ever composed" (xvi).

According to *Homo Aestheticus*, the role of human biological evolution spanning the last three million years needs to be foregrounded if a more profound understanding of the deep meanings of artistic production and the aesthetic impulse shared by all human beings is to be meaningfully contextualized: "With a Darwinian perspective, one can claim that art is more important—primal and perduring—than has ever before been recognized or demonstrated, insofar as it originated from and played a critical role in human biological adaptation" (xvii). According to this theoretical postulate, the dynamic of "natural selection," combined with the vagaries of "sexual selection," conspires to "select" and preserve over the vast reaches of the geologic time-clock those species-centered individuals whose proclivities toward the aesthetic impulses of their kind not only define their being, but also improve their likelihood of survival and the survival of their genotype and progeny. The theory is community-focused, emphasizing the utility of a kind of primal aesthetic sensibility as a mechanism of survival: "Dionysus coexists with Apollo in the human breast, and individuals who are deprived of socially sanctioned routes of ecstasy and transformation are likely to seek them in asocial 'barbaric' ways" (xviii).

In developing her hypothesis, which emphasizes the primordial antiquity and universality of the impulse toward art creation and preservation, Dissanayake has generated her own lexicon of phrases, suited to the complexity of her conception of the species she designates as " *Homo aestheticus.*" In chapter 3, called "The Core of Art," she defines her use of the phrase "making special": "In my view, the biological core of art, the stain that is deeply dyed in the behavioral marrow of humans everywhere, is something I have elsewhere called 'making special' " (42). She links religious ritual with storytelling, painting, modes of dress, modes of play, and other examples of "customary behaviors" that comprise human ethology, defining characteristics and activities found in all contemporary human societies, and in all discoverable proto-human societies, as well. This evidence is presented to support the conclusion that a core characteristic of *Homo aestheticus* is our species' inherited and self-perpetuating drive to designate particular physical locations to be venerated as "special" and to select specific activities to be designated "special"—set apart from barren ordinariness.

"Making special" as a concept reminds one of the etymological roots of the English word "worship," the core meaning of which harks back to the act of ascribing worth, the designation of a specific person, event, place or object as being somehow "worthy"—set apart, segregated from the ordinary. That which an individual, a tribe, a society, a nation sets aside as deemed "of worth" is "made special." There is nothing new in the realization that this tendency toward lionizing that which is "worthy" comprises a more or less ubiquitous characteristic of our human species. But the startling premise behind the taxonomic designation *Homo aestheticus* is that primordial billions of acts of "making special" comprised "a core behavioral tendency upon which natural selection could act" (42), a proclivity toward seeking to sculpt and reorder the natural—and ultimately the social—milieu that came to reshape and form what we have become. As Dissanayake observes, "Evidence of making special appears as early as 300 thousand years ago, ten times earlier than the cave paintings in France and Spain that (being visual and of grand scale and astonishing quality) are usually considered to mark the beginnings of art" (96). Evidence is cited that earlier hominids were, in fact, collectors of "special" objects: "Wandering Mousterian hominids [Middle Paleolithic], for example, spotted, picked up, and took with them 'curios,' such as unusual fossils or rocks, concretions or pyrites" (96–97). As with any other ecologically reinforced activity recurring along the evolutionary assembly line, the process of "making special" is believed to be ongoing.

In chapter 5 of *Homo Aestheticus*, titled "The Arts as Means of Enhancement," Dissanayake emphasizes the utilitarian nature of art. For example, the art of dramatic performance is closely linked with the human desire to control and manipulate the environment: "Knowing what comes next in a ceremony or dramatic performance may be as moving as not knowing what is going to happen next" (128). This observation will be appreciated by anyone who has ever been importuned by a small child to repeat to the point of absurdity a well-known fairy tale or fable. Knowing the outcome seems to be part of the process of "making special." My own thoughts, upon reading this chapter, also ran to images of the early commedia dell'arte performances, wildly popular with a rustic audience that knew the dénouement before the stock characters walked onstage. One could make a similar assessment of contemporary television dramas, where predictability seems to be part of the fun. The ritual nature of this phenomenon is pointed out by Dissanayake in a reference to Greek drama: "We consider classical Greek drama as an art form, but its origins go back to prehistoric ritual ceremonies of cleansing and atonement" (128). Catharsis, individual experiences of cleansing and resuscitation through drama, storytelling, and community-based rituals are concepts with which everyone is familiar. But it is a bold step to theorize that this means of achieving a temporary sense of euphoria for the individual acolyte extends metonymically to fueling an evolutionary mechanism vital to the actual survival of the species, a bold step that Dissanayake takes: "And what is equally of consequence, insofar as ceremonies inculcate group values and promote agreement, cooperation, cohesiveness, and confidence; they also enhance survival" (129). Transcendence becomes, then, a survival mechanism, a means of evolutionary shaping of the species that inevitably promotes the perpetuating characteristic itself, through "natural selection" (the environment, social as well as physical, tends to nurture and promulgate the characteristics it has favored and to exhibit hostility toward those who lack the defining attributes of the tribe or community) and "sexual selection" (those who inherit the characteristic are the ones most likely to be "chosen" to produce progeny).

In her last chapter, "Does Writing Erase Art," Dissanayake further expresses some of her disillusionment with postmodernist theory, particularly in the area of textual interpretations. She decries the extreme relativism she perceives as a kind of reductio ad absurdum among many contemporary proponents of post-modernist theory, "wedded to the idea that our scientific or physical ideas of space, time and matter are mere mental constructs that rest upon a particular version of the constitution of matter and the origin of the universe" (213). Acknowledging the limitations of the human mind, she offers this rejoinder: "But these limitations make up our reality: the environment's affordances and our senses, cognitions, and emotions that respond to them." And, in a memorable parting shot near the end of her manifesto, she offers this fiery salvo: "Surely soldiers at the front or women in childbirth have the ability to discriminate pretense from reality" (213).

Homo Aestheticus concludes with a reiteration of the defining significance of our human need of "making special," of inventing rituals, of reconfiguring our world, of creating sacred "spaces" in our environment: "We find special ways of saying important things. Ritual and ceremony are occasions during which everyday life is shaped and embellished to become more than ordinary" (223). For the literary critic, Dissanayake seems to be calling for a move toward integrating empirically measurable phenomena into the critical matrix—privileging the perceivable world around us as "real" and viable in our assessment of the values we attach to literary artifacts, canonical and noncanonical: "Making important things special was a fundamental and integral part of human behavior for thousands of years before writing looked at its results and called them 'art' or 'texts'" (223).

Elitist notions of "fine" works of art—pictorial, literary, or otherwise—along with the latter-day patrician snobbery bolstered by absurdly overrated and surreally overpriced artifacts of the "art industry," are pilloried in the final paragraphs of *Homo Aestheticus*. Dissanayake makes an appeal for a return to the primal sources and resources of all artistic endeavor, and the peculiarly human response to an impulse that is endemic to our human nature. "Artistic behavior and response, which Western society treats as an ornamental and dispensable luxury, are really essential parts of our nature" (224).

In a vein similar to Ellen Dissanayake's relating sociobiology and evolutionary theory to art and literature, Mark Turner's *The Literary Mind* explores the significance of storytelling and the generation of "parables," activities he believes to be closely linked with the evolutionary development of human cognition. He commandeers the well-known story of Shahrazad and the vizier as an example and opens his discussion of the literary mind with a definition of the concept "parable," associating Shahrazad's overlapping of one story upon another to the workings of the human mind and the flow of consciousness: " This projection of one story onto another may seem exotic and literary, and it is—but it is also, like story, a fundamental instrument of the mind" (5). Making sense out of the chaos of existence is the essential work of the human brain as a manufacturer of parables: "We understand our experience in this way because we are built evolutionarily to learn to distinguish objects and events and combine them in small spatial stories" (15).

The notion of "making parables" as a vital adaptive mechanism brought about evolutionarily through millions of years of development of the human brain bears a close resemblance to the concept of "making special," a product of evolution described in *Homo Aestheticus*. Turner, like Dissanayake, is engaged in the search for a measurable, scientifically verifiable source of the literary and artistic proclivities that exist throughout, and perhaps define, humankind. Through the fabrication of "small spatial stories" projected parabolically, the evolved human brain attempts to control, or at least manage and make sense of, a chaotic, unstable, and often hostile, environment. "We understand our experience in this way because we are built evolutionarily to learn to distinguish objects and events and combine them in small spatial stories at human scale in a way that is useful for us, given that we have human bodies" (15). According to this theoretical construct, human thought process is directly related to storytelling and parabolic projection of our storytelling capability: "There is a general story to human existence: It is the story of how we use story, projection, and parable to think, beginning at the level of small spatial stories" (15).

Turner's approach is an attempt to link the latest findings of various scientific disciplines, such as neurobiology and cognitive studies related to brain functioning, with human literary and linguistic creativity: "Many cognitive scientists have observed that the human brain is uncommonly sophisticated in its capacity for constructing sequences" (18). According to this hypothesis, the literary genotype characterizing all human beings and the product of evolutionary development passed down to modern humankind from our hominid ancestors is a vital survival mechanism realized in every fully functional individual of our species. Turner comments, "That genotype cannot determine the fine specifics of point-to-point wiring and activity in the individual brain, but it can (and must) contribute to setting up a nervous system that will reach certain target values under experience. That genotype must do this because of Darwinian pressures" (25).

In Turner's third chapter, he begins to demonstrate how the human brain's capacity for parabolic projection can be related to works of literature. He uses imagery from Robert Browning's "Porphyria's Lover" to demonstrate how the literary mind projects one image schema onto another, a basic constituent discernible in most works of literature, whether prose or poetry. "In Browning's poem, a spatial event-story of trees falling before the wind is understood by parabolic projection from a spatial action-story of someone tearing something down intentionally" (31). The wind is personified:

The rain set early in to-night,
The sullen wind was soon awake,
It tore the elm-tops down for spite,
And did its worst to vex the lake.
(Turner 30)

The blending of spatial and temporal "locations" in the human mind is a subject dealt with extensively in Turner's fourth chapter, titled "Figured Tales": "Mental states are physical locations, and a change from one mental state to another is a change of spatial locations" (45). Turner cites Bunyan's *Pilgrim's Progress* as one example of a change in mental state illustrated as a journey from one location to another, a parabolic projection comprehensible to the literary mind, which recognizes and relates to the phenomenon of a cerebral "journey." In the following chapter, "Creative Blends," Turner explores ways in which parabolic projection enhances the process by which the human brain creates meanings that regulate human knowledge and action. "Meanings are not mental objects bounded in conceptual places but rather complex operations of projection, binding, linking, blending, and integration over multiple spaces. Meaning is parabolic and literary" (57).

For Turner, talking animals, familiar to children everywhere and known in the written literature and oral traditions of most countries throughout the world, comprise a conceptual blend and "central parabolic activity of the everyday mind" (58). The blending process in which the mind engages, consciously or unconsciously, extends to "generic spaces" of the mind, as explained in chapter 6 of *The Literary Mind*, called "Many Spaces." Postulating the existence of a "generic space" located somewhere within the cognitive landscape of human thought is related to the human capacity for abstract thinking, allowing, among other functions, the ability to extrapolate data from specific examples and to apply them to general assumptions. In Turner's words, "When we read a proverb in the book of Proverbs, and so have no reason to connect the meaning of the proverb to any specific target, we arrive at a generic reading" (87).

The concluding chapter of Turner's explication of the literary mind deals with the significance of human language and its distinguishing characteristics that separate uniquely human communication systems from forms of communication engaged in by nonhuman species: "The dominant contemporary theory of the origin of language proposes that genetic change produced genetic instructions for building a special module for grammar in the human brain" (140). Turner makes the point that not all communication is grammar-based. A dog or cat learns to communicate with its owner quite effectively, if we are to give credence to what we hear from pet owners. Turner rejects the notion that genetic specialization for grammar was the genesis of language. He proposes that parable precedes grammar: "If we reject the hypothesis that genetic specialization for grammar was the origin of language, what can we propose instead? Let us consider the possibility that parable was the origin of language, that parable preceded grammar" (141).

It is difficult to summarize in a few paragraphs the evidentiary examples offered in support of Turner's central hypothesis as presented in voluminous and well-researched detail in *The Literary Mind*. However, I have attempted to offer enough tantalizing detail to inspire any student of linguistic theory to further investigate his compelling argument, a call for reassessment of storytelling's role in the development of grammar—the bedrock of that most sophisticated of communication tools known as human language. Boldly out of sync with many of his psycholinguistic predecessors, Turner puts forward his primary thesis in the very last sentence of his manifesto: "Parable is the root of the human mind—of thinking, knowing, acting, creating, and plausibly even of speaking" (168). Enough said.

In arranging chronologically by publication date my discussion of major works by Dissanayake, Turner, and Carroll, I had not realized at the outset that I was also presenting their studies in order of escalating iconoclastic fervor. In Part 1 of *Literary Darwinism*, Joseph Carroll reassesses, to the point of evisceration, poststructuralist theory in many of its aspects. He views much of literary criticism of recent decades as persistently nonscientific in its approach, appraising his own literary studies (and that of his fellow Darwinian adaptationists) as more compatible with empirically measurable, scientific standards of inquiry. There is more than a little throwing out of "the baby with the bathwater" in some of his argumentation, but his breadth of interdisciplinary knowledge is impressive. His assessment of the current state of literary criticism and academic study related to the humanities, as currently constructed, will undoubtedly nettle some targets of his barbs.

Carroll views much current literary theory as anti-Darwinian at its core: "The poststructuralist explanation of things cannot be reconciled with the Darwinian paradigm" (25). He elaborates on this position by suggesting that the "liberal reform" politics and policies that are promoted within the academic community (particularly in the humanities) are at odds with an objective study of sociobiology, evolutionary theory, ethological studies, and other scientific modes of investigation. According to Carroll, an emphasis on empirically measurable scientific data has the potential of providing value-added interactive input beneficial to literary studies, but the methodology and premises of science are perceived as inimical to a form of literary study he views as irrevocably divorced from scientific models of objectivity: "For many people, the idea of biological constraints on human nature seems unacceptable because it supposedly limits the range of possible political reform" (25). His chapter on "Biology and Poststructuralism" ends on a positive note, however, expressing hope for the pursuit of "positive knowledge," by which he refers to empirically-based knowledge and its relation to literary analysis informed by scientific methodologies: "Within this pursuit, the opportunites for real and substantial development in our scientific understanding of culture and of literature are now greater than they have ever been before" (27).

In his introduction, Carroll defines the role of adaptationist social scientists in the study of human culture: "Adaptationist literary scholars concur, and they seek to bring literature itself within the field of cognitive and behavioral features susceptible to an adaptationist understanding" (vii). In chapter 6, he offers some concrete examples of adaptationist criticism, with examples from Dickens's *Bleak House* and *Hard Times*. The adaptationist critic approaches literary artifacts from the standpoint of evolutionary biology: "From the adaptationist perspective, psychology is rooted in biology, and all cultural studies, including both the social sciences and the humanities, are rooted in psychology" (63). To illustrate the application of evolutionary biology and psychology to *Bleak House*, Carroll offers his interpretation of the character of the Smallweeds and their role in Dickens's novel: "As a foil for the full humanity and achieved civilization of his protagonists, Dickens depicts a family of misers, the Smallweeds, who are wholly practical in orientation. The family is one of Dickens's most vividly conceived set of grotesques" (66). He compares the Smallweeds with Louisa and Tom Gradgrind in *Hard Times*: "In *Hard Times*, a more schematically didactic presentation of the same theme, there are again, two children who have been deprived of all imaginative cultivation, Tom and Louisa Gradgrind" (67). Carroll goes on to point out that Dickens's intuitive awareness of child psychology is consistent with an adaptationist approach to his protagonists, both those who overcome their milieu, and those who succumb to its deprivations and meanness: "For Dickens, the period of childhood is a highly sensitive and vulnerable stage in which the whole personality can be forever stunted and impoverished by inadequate imaginative stimulus" (67).

Carroll's assessment of David Copperfield's development from an abused childhood to functional adulthood is a lesson in the adaptive power of literary influence upon an individual receptive to its force and sustaining grace. Cloistered reading of some of the great canonical works of fiction from earlier days fortifies David, preparing him to cope with the vicissitudes of the life he will face in adulthood. Admirable fictive models become his tools of adaptation: "What he gets are lively and powerful images of human life suffused with the feeling and understanding of the astonishingly capable and complete human beings who wrote them" (68). David Copperfield is, for Joseph Carroll, an iconic representation of maladaptive heredity and circumstances overcome through the ameliorative adaptive succor provided by nurturing one's inborn literary imagination. The evolutionarily hardwired human proclivity toward cultivation of his inborn literary imaginative nature helps him to rise above his circumstances. He heroically claims his evolutionarily predetermined heritage as a fully-developed human being, possessing a proclivity toward transcendence beyond his circumstances: "By nurturing and cultivating his own individual identity through his literary imagination, he enables himself to adapt successfully to this world. He directly enhances his own fitness as a human being, and in doing so he demonstrates the kind of adaptive advantage that can be conferred by literature" (68).

In a chapter called "Adaptationist Criteria of Literary Value," Carroll explicitly rejects Derrida's consignment of extra textual elements to irrelevancy in the study of literature. The restoration of authorial intentionality and historical contextualization of works may strike one as "déjà vu all over again," but the perception of literary works as "products of an adaptive need to make sense of the world" (164) seems to demand a reversion to earlier interpretations of the literary mind's impetus. Carroll states, "All the elements of the literary situation—the *purposes* [emphasis mine] of authors, the responses of audiences, the behavior, thought and feelings of characters, and the formal properties of literary works—can be assessed and analyzed within the framework of adaptationist theory" (164). Later in this chapter, he further defines the nature and function of literature in sociobiological terms: "For all authors, quality of motive and quality of mind are critical factors in the social exchange between author and reader" (185). Consistent with the approaches proffered by Dissanayake and Turner, Carroll's position connects the impulse that drives both the creation and the appreciation of literary endeavors with the human aspiration to achieve "cognitive order" within the context of a natural environment that seems to offer little more than the slings and arrows of random occurrences and interactive chaos: "We can hypothesize that the need for cognitive order is an adaptive response to 'a world of confusion,' and we can explain how certain works, for us, satisfy that need, or fail to" (185).

Carroll concludes this chapter by illustrating the application of Darwinian adaptationist theory to Jane Austen's *Pride and Prejudice*. In direct opposition to the "social constructionist" approaches that allegedly privilege nurture over nature, the Darwinian adaptationist presupposes "an innate, biologically constrained structure in the human motivational and cognitive system" (214). The literary mind is both the product and the redactor of our primordial history as human beings, according to this perspective on all extant literary heritages, examined and compared cross-culturally. A tabula rasa approach to the social and psychological development of the individual human consciousness—and therefore to fictionally crafted characters in a novel such as Austen's *Pride and Prejudice*—is pure folly to the evolutionarily oriented social scientist.

Carroll's analysis of Austen's novel is presented as a potential paradigm for a form of literary criticism that acknowledges narrative as an evolved adaptational faculty universally extant among all surviving human cultures. For Carroll, narrative form inevitably comprises an accurate cognitive representation of universal norms of human behavior and psychology, and consists of certain primal elements demonstrably ubiquitous, cross-culturally and cross-temporally. Individual characters within a novel (or play, narrative poem, anecdote, comic monologue, or other narrative genre) may deviate substantially from acceptable normative behavior. Individual motives and actions deviate widely in all forms of fiction. However, there exists an array of bedrock templates of normative behavior and taboos that, although transgressed by individuals, are universally recognized as prevailing in all known human cultures, past and present: "The behavior that is depicted in literary texts does not necessarily exemplify universal or species-typical behavioral patterns, but species-typical patterns form an indispensable frame of reference for the communication of meaning in literary representations" (204).

In Carroll's view, certain norms have evolved from the time our proto-human tree-dwelling ancestors descended from the tree tops of Africa and began to inhabit the open savannahs. Australopithecines, an early ancestral relative of *Homo sapiens* who inhabited the African savannahs between two and four million years ago, did not write books. However, as Dissanayake and Turner have hypothesized, their evolving brain developed through natural selection a proclivity toward some prototypical faculty for narrative communication, perhaps as a means of survival against predators on the open plains. A proto-human narrative culture evolving over millennia, and subject to the shaping effect upon the species of environmental conditions adaptationally favorable to some individuals and hostile toward others, would be likely to encode a series of norms that potentially facilitate survival of progeny. Hence, there is the evolution of normative standards embedded in narrative, regarding maternal care of infants, or the prohibition of incest (which seems to prevail cross-culturally among aboriginal peoples as well as industrialized societies). Carroll cites examples from ancient Greek drama: "Medea murders her own children, and Euripides can safely anticipate that the audience will react with instinctive shock and horror to the murder" (204). Likewise, Sophocles can count on the audience's "revulsion of feeling that leads Oedipus to gouge out his own eyes" (204).

Carroll's analysis of *Pride and Prejudice* focuses on certain universal norms of behavior and motivational impulses that he perceives as central to Austen's novel. Eschewing poststructuralist notions of the disappearing or obliterated author, Carroll restores to high standing the authorial "voice," granting Austen a prominent presence in the narrative: "Austen herself grasps with a singular acuity the governing power of the somatic and reproductive foundation of human action, but virtually every character in the novel is assessed also on the basis of the quality of his or her mind" (207). From an adaptationist standpoint, some of Austen's characters are better adapted, and therefore more fitted to produce progeny "selected" for long-term survival in the evolutionary sense of the term. Mr. Darcy and Elizabeth Bennet are supreme models of survivorship, because they are well adapted to the evolutionary principles that govern mate selection and social success within the human community. They are, however, successful as individuals as well, ideal protagonists who conform to the universal normative demands of successful adaptation to the (social and physical) environment, but also possessed of adaptive imaginative flexibility of character, a kind of "style" that is reflective of the author's own compelling grace and elegance, expressed through their facility for appropriate utterances and social aplomb. False and authentic modes of adaptation to acceptable and honorable norms of behavior are illustrated in the characters that do not come up to the high standards Austen sets in her portraiture of Darcy and Elizabeth: "As in many novels, one main plot line involves the long-term discrimination among superficially attractive qualities and the qualities that will wear well—a difference relevant to the basic distinction between short-term and long-term mating strategies" (208). Austen, then, in Carroll's view, exemplifies admirably the values, both literary and philosophically, of a fictional creation that is empirically grounded, which at the same time conforms to venerable norms of narrative structure. Darcy and Elizabeth achieve the highest possible level of success, because they excel as evolutionarily adapted members of their community and their species, but they also prevail as highly individualized contributors to the well-being of their socialized environment: "The successful protagonists fully acknowledge the hard and sometimes harsh logic of the human reproductive economy, but they do so without neglecting the significance of the human mind and individual differences in identity" (210).

Whether one chooses to root for Joseph Carroll's home team of Literary Darwinists or whether one opts for retaining some vestiges of loyalty to the postmodernist critics he takes such pains to discredit, it is hard to resist a bit of ironic commentary. Usurpations and counterusurpations—a common Darwinian theme and post-Darwinian novelistic trope—seem to have dominated the landscape of literary criticism for the last several decades, and probably longer. Beelzebub forever casting out Beelzebub is de rigueur. However, the counterinsurgent posture is somewhat less pointed in a recent compilation of Darwin-focused essays, one in which Joseph Carroll's interpretation of *Pride and Prejudice* is anthologized along with other proponents of evolutionarily-based theory.

Edited by Jonathan Gottschall and David Sloan Wilson, *The Literary Animal* presents a compendium of essays by seventeen scholars representing a wide range of disciplines from academic departments of English, philosophy, comparative literature, sociology, psychology, biology, and anthropology. The focus is on new voices in literary Darwinism. A common thread emphasized by the editors is the desirability of consilience, a search for common goals and common ground shared by the proponents of social constructionism and proponents of evolutionary psychology with its orientation toward theories of adaptationist hard wiring of the human psyche.

In an introductory essay, "Forward from the Scientific Side," two-time Pulitzer Prize winner E. O. Wilson puts forward his take on the impetus of this collection: "Either the great branches of learning—natural science, social sciences, and humanities—can be connected by a web of verifiable causal explanation or they cannot" (vii). He decries what he views as an unsustainable "fault line between two kinds of truth" (vii) that separates the natural sciences from the humanities and humanistic social sciences. Recent advances in comparison of animal ethology with human behavioral psychology seem to indicate that the evolved human brain bears the indelible stamp of our primordial ancestry: "At base we have remained true not only to our origins as primates but as savannah-dwelling African catarrhines" (ix). Now that the catarrhine is out of the bag, knowledge of our close affinities with our hominid forebears promotes inquiry into the adaptational role of the narrative impulse, a proclivity which has been shown by anthropologists to inhere in all known human cultures. This relationship should inform our conception of a more profound understanding of narrative's role in the development and preservation of our species. This story-telling adaptation, a product of natural selection, has evolved to the status of a defining characteristic of "the literary animal." For Wilson, "The mind is a narrative machine, guided unconsciously by the epigenetic rules in creating scenarios and creating options" (ix). Wilson ends his introduction with an acknowledgment of the secondary role of literary criticism, paying homage to creative imaginations unfettered by the ponderous machinery of analytical weights and measures: " We may even hope that authors who generate literature of genuine originality, who use language to transmit images and feeling directly from one mind to the other with aesthetic and emotional power, will remain, as they have ever been, largely unencumbered by theory" (xi).

In a similarly eclectic and broadly tolerant vein, Frederick Crews cautions against merely replacing one potentially restrictive set of literary critical postures (poststructualist, et al.) with an equally monotonous "preoccupation with the survival of Pleistocene psychology in modern works of art" (xiii). His critique of a single-mindedness among proponents of adaptationist interpretation of literary works focuses on its sometimes exclusionary stance: "When I waxed satirical over it in *Postmodern Pooh*, I was merely expressing reserve about the claim that critical Darwinism is *the* answer to the antiempiricism that has reigned over literary theory for the past three decades" (xiii). His call for consilience among all branches of inquiry is spirited, and not without rancor expressed toward some colleagues in the field of literary studies. He endorses a common aim of his colleagues whom he hopes will aspire to "reclaim governance of the field . . . from the fast-talking superstars who have prostituted it to crank theory, political conformism, and cliquishness" (xv). He ends his introductory essay invoking the spirit and legacy of Charles Darwin, the attractively modest and diligent empiricist whose hypothetical constructs, premises, and conclusions were always provisional: "In a word, Darwin conducted himself like a member of a disciplinary community held together by a common regard for truth" (xv). This assessment reminds one of an aspect of Darwin's life and work that seldom gets the attention it deserves, the kind of humility and awe he expresses when describing natural processes occurring all around us. In chapter 3 of his *Origin*, he pauses to reflect on the insignificance of our species' surmises and inquiries: "How fleeting are the wishes and efforts of man! how short his time! and consequently how poor will be his results, compared with those accumulated by Nature during whole geological periods" (66).

Rather than attempting to summarize the content of the thirteen essays that follow two forewords and one introduction, I have listed below what I consider to be five of the most significant recurrent, and often overlapping, threads that run through virtually all of them. The driving force in all of the essays surfaces as the notion that recent developments in the fields of the natural sciences and the social sciences have provided accumulated data that impacts (or should impact) the study of literature. At the risk of oversimplification, I offer the five predominant premises that I observe emerging from these essays: (1) The latest findings in such diverse fields as anthropology, paleoanthropology, neurobiology, animal ethology, and evolutionary psychology, among other empirically oriented disciplines, frequently contradict and generally invalidate many entrenched tenets of the social constructionist theories that have dominated literary study for the last thirty years, or more. (2) Many social mores, customs, gender dichotomies, and other characteristics observable in European and Eurocentric societies are not as culture-specific as has been previously supposed, but are, in fact, being discovered to be intractably cross-cultural. (3) Parallels linking nonhuman and human normative behavior are greater than previously believed. (4) Trepidation about the adverse political and social implications of biological "determinism" is unfounded, or at least exaggerated. (5) Therefore, except for their historical significance, the work of such icons, or progenitors, of social constructivist theory as Margaret Mead, Sigmund Freud, Karl Marx, Simone de Beauvoir, Derrida, Foucault, and their disciples, will be inevitably consigned to the Gehenna of obsolescence in the natural course of further scientific discoveries yet to come. In all of the presentations on the value of interactive dialogue between the humanities and the sciences, there is a clarion call for consilience; however, in many of the essays the tone of the plea is often less than conciliatory, at times reading much like a palliative gloss.

The first and overarching premise I have listed above is developed in the essay "Literature, Science, and Human Nature," by Ian McEwan (distinguished author of the highly popular novel *Atonement*, among other literary accomplishments). McEwan presents evidence regarding universal principles that govern not only the development and use, but also the social significance of language acquisition in all cultures, a cross-cultural characteristic that privileges nature over nurture, suggesting that many traits once deemed acquired are innate: "Extra proficiency in language invariably confers prestige. This surely, at the higher level of mental functioning, is what binds the human family. . . . An instinct for language is a central part of our nature" (17).

Both the first and second premises I have cited above are illustrated in the second essay in the collection, David Sloan Wilson's "Evolutionary Social

Constructivism." He explains, but seeks to modify radically, the social constructivist notion that each human being enters the world as a kind of blank slate (tabula rasa) upon which socialization by the tribe or community may imprint its proclivities and social agenda. His focus on the adaptationist, evolutionarily significant status of storytelling resembles that of Mark Turner: "Constructing stories facilitates a sense of resolution, which results in less rumination and eventually allows disturbing experiences to subside gradually from conscious thought" (31). Viewing the storytelling impetus and function as an adaptational, universally hard-wired characteristic that in many ways defines our species, Wilson attempts to appease social constructivist theorists by wedding an evolved nature to the free will of individuals in a socially fluid culture: "Giving stories genelike status endows them with the potency and centrality that they have always enjoyed within social constructivist perspectives" (35).

The third premise I have mentioned above, highlighting parallels between human and nonhuman, is a central concern of two essays that follow Wilson's, Dylan Evans's "From Lacan to Darwin " and "What Happens in *Hamlet*," by Daniel Nettle. Nettle links human behavior to that of other primates, privileging the love of drama as an adaptationist relic passed on by our anthropoid ancestors: "For monkeys and apes, grooming releases the body's endogenous opiates, which is why they find it so rewarding. In humans, it seems that language may have sequestered this mechanism; we like nothing better than a good conversation" (65). Comparisons between nonhuman primate motivational psychology and that of human beings is consistent with an assertion made in *What Evolution Is* by Ernst Mayr, the generally acknowledged founder of the modern evolutionary synthesis: "There is not justification in the wide-spread assumption that consciousness is a unique human property. . . . it is quite certain that human consciousness did not arise full-fledged with the human species, but is only the most highly-evolved end point of a long evolutionary history" (282). One of Joseph Carroll's chapters in his *Literary Darwinism*, the analysis of *Pride and Prejudice*, is also included in *The Literary Animal*. As in the essays by Evans and Nettle, Carroll asserts that fictional characters reflect hard-wired values and norms that are not culturally-specific, but are, in fact, universal in scope.

Premises 4 and 5 (cited above) are shored up by evidence-based arguments in two essays concerning traditional gender-role assignment in Western literature. The notion that sex-role typologies are culturally-based—and, therefore, socially constructed—is refuted in "The Problem of Romantic Love: Shakespeare and Evolutionary Psychology," by Marcus Nordlund, and in "Male Bonding in the Epics and Romances," by Robin Fox. Nordlund refutes feminist claims that dominant cultural norms in European societies of recent centuries have no basis in nature and are imposed by an arbitrarily imposed patriarchal tradition: "Although early modern English women enjoyed a relative freedom compared with women in other European countries, the nation was also characterized by a rigid sexual double standard that matched the cross-cultural tendency described by evolutionary psychologists" (122). Nordlund recognizes the writer's role as one that defies expectations, but also as one which acknowledges the primordial origins of many conventional prejudices and established norms. Some gender dichotomies have a firmer basis than a superficial overlay generated by localized social norms and customs. In a similar vein, Robin Fox traces the history of male bonding in narrative works from *Gilgamesh* to *Butch Cassidy and the Sundance Kid*. He cites an impressive body of literary and extra-literary evidence to support his premise that the male-bonding proclivity (sometimes with a homosexual component, sometimes without) is primordial, and not a culturally-specific relic of a particular society, but, rather, evolutionarily founded and patently cross-cultural and cross-temporal in scope. Variations and permutations abound, in Fox's assessment, but the ancient bonding impulse is hard-wired. "A good evolutionary prediction would be: while social conditioning may cause the male bond to be muted, they will never extinguish it. As the current saying goes: 'It's a guy thing'" (144).

Brian Boyd's "Evolutionary Theories of Art," anthologized in *The Literary Animal*, is congruent with much that is to be found in Dissanayake's *Homo Aestheticus*, a source he acknowledges in his essay: "My evolutionary theory of art, then, is this: In humans, social attention, which had been developing in importance in the primate line, especially among the apes, became still more important: earlier, more intense, more interactive, more flexible, more precise, more powerful" (152). Boyd's essay is followed by "Reverse-Engineering Narrative: Evidence of Special Design" by Michelle Scalise Sugiyama. She speculates about the crucial role storytelling played in the survival and evolutionary development of the species *Homo sapiens* as hunter-gatherers during the Upper Pleistocene Epoch, when the ancestors of the human species began to move out of the African region about 100,000 years ago: "The antiquity of narrative is significant" (177). Anatomical evidence and the antiquity of language itself are evidentiary supports of the theory that narrative skill played a foundational adaptational role in the development of our species: "Given the prominence of both human life history and cultural transmission in current evolutionary anthropological research, the documentation of hunter-horticulturalist art behavior is both a highly promising and highly pressing task" (192).

In an essay that follows, "Quantitative Literary Study: A Modest Manifesto and Testing the Hypotheses of Feminist Fairy Tale Studies," Jonathan Gottschall presents the results of a survey conducted within "the quantitative framework of scientific methodology" (197). The students chosen to participate in this experiment were given a wide-ranging variety of folk/fairy tales derived from many cultures and culled from a compendious array of historical time periods, and translated into English from several extant languages. Participants of both genders were selected from a diverse array of nationalities and ethnic backgrounds. The results demonstrate an amazing uniformity in gender role expectations within the contextual framework of the stories. The uniformity of responses persisted cross-culturally, and irrespective of the participant's gender. There was a marked consistency in evaluative assessments by participants regarding the norms of mate selection criteria, as well as norms of passivity and heroism in male and female characters. Conclusions may be held in abeyance, but the method of evaluating the universality of gender roles in traditional fables, globally and cross-culturally, opens the door for further debate. Gottschall aims for a middle-of-the-road position: "However, while the folktale patterns are inconsistent with the constructivist notion that individuals are mere products of their sociocultural contexts, they also provide no support for the orientation that is social constructivism's equally incomplete antithesis: biological determinism" (219).

A comparable scientifically-controlled approach informs "Proper Hero Dads and Dark Hero Cads: Alternate Mating Strategies Exemplified in British Romantic Literature," by Daniel J. Kruger, Maryanne Fisher, and Ian Jobling, employing a quantitative approach very similar to that of Gottschall. Engaging an equal number of male and female participants, the purpose of their study was to determine preferences and subjective responses to fictional characters in novels by Ann Radcliffe and Walter Scott. The dad/cad dichotomy (a gentle, loving and nurturing male figure versus an aggressive, emotionally distant, but "sexy" rake) was established to elicit individual reactions of readers, in terms of preference, appeal and suitability as a potential mate, friend, brother-in-law, etc. From the standpoint of adaptationist theory, both evolutionary types have considerable significance, both functioning in differing capacities evolved through the processes of generations upon generations of sexual selection, coupled with the exigencies of natural selection. The authors of this experiment believe they are demonstrating the value of quantitatively evaluating human criteria of preferential selection, which can be evolutionarily significant over time, and from which we can extrapolate proclivities present among our hominid predecessors and among ourselves. "It provides an example of a scientifically grounded approach to literary study by empirically testing a specific literary interpretation that was, itself, derived from evolutionary theory on human sexuality" (226).

Catherine Salmon's "Crossing the Abyss: Erotica and the Intersection of Evolutionary Psychology and Literary Studies, " in a similar vein, explores an evolutionary approach to erotica. She offers data from studies of male-oriented pornography versus female-oriented pornography and erotica, both historical and contemporary. Her hypothesis is based on research that seems to support the notion that female response is geared toward a more romanticized approach to eroticized literature and art, as opposed to a male preference for a genitally-focused, "no frills" approach to graphic depictions, both literary and pictorial, of sexual activity. She allows that this dichotomy of preferences may have some basis in culture, but that the evolutionary basis for the difference must be granted equal weight in our analysis of male versus female responses to erotic stimuli: "Recent research in cross-cultural anthropology and psychology suggests . . . that almost everything that is important about human behavior and psychology always develops through a combination of nature and environment" (244). While the nature/nurture debate continues, neither force predominates to the exclusion of the other.

Coda: The Baby and The Bath Water

In a brief "Afterword" that is appended as a final chapter in *The Literary Animal*, Denis Dutton compares the literary critic's task to the work of a visual artist who strives toward authentic pictorial representation of the phenomenal world around us. He compares the difficulty of accurate portraiture of the human body to the problematic task of accurate analysis of literary artifacts. He draws an analogy between artists who avoid depiction of the human form in favor of still life and landscape painting to the critic who focuses on some facile adherence to one aspect of literary theory, as if to avoid a full confrontation with the complexity of the subject at hand. I found this caveat against excessive academic parochialism uniquely corroborative of my own concluding thoughts at the end of this survey of the current state of Darwin-based literary criticism. Dutton offers this cautionary word: "Anyone who teaches the history of aesthetics is in the business of surveying a long series of exaggerated, partial, one-sided, all-or-nothing claims purporting to explain the nature of art and its creation" (260).

At the end of the day, it seems reasonable that those of us putatively "suckled in a [theory-based] creed outworn" are likely to benefit from exposure to an empirically-based approach to literary study. Darwin's impact on literature and the literary mind has been apparent since Darwinian tropes and themes began to surface in the works of Victorian poets and novelists, from Tennyson and Pater to Eliot and Hardy, and, also, in the writings of a long line of Darwinian apologists, from Edmund Gosse to Thomas Huxley and their successors. However, as the work of innovative interpreters of the Darwinian legacy is superseded by new generations of investigative researchers with access to improved technologies and more accurate research methodologies, it is my hope that at least some of the frequently-trivialized icons of the past will be afforded a niche in the pantheon of innovative pioneering minds that have paved the way for their successors. There is a disturbing vogue among some scholars to speak dismissively of such barrier-transgressive innovators as Sigmund Freud, Karl Marx, Simone de Beauvoir, and Margaret Mead, among others, as if their sometimes misguided, or even brazenly agenda-ridden, predispositions negated every aspect of their benchmark setting achievements. Contextualization, rather than condemnation, seems to me not only a gentler approach, but also one that is more informed and productive. The denigration of an entire career in one or two dismissive sentences sometimes strikes me as unseemly.

With this thought in mind, it is worthwhile to go back occasionally and rediscover some of the original texts that precipitated the Darwinian revolution. It is sometimes refreshing to reflect on the personal attributes exhibited by Charles Darwin throughout his life. Contemporary advocates of so-called Creationism have been known to indulge in fantasies about Darwin's alleged God-defying "arrogance" and his purportedly anti-humanistic world view. No one who has read his autobiography or his *Voyage of the Beagle* could find a shred of evidence to support such an opinion of the mild-mannered, unprepossessing empiricist and collector of specimens.

That Darwin was far from being either arrogant or irreverent in his attitude toward persons of faith is amply evidenced throughout his work. One elegantly expressed example from the second chapter of his *Descent* would deflate puffed up claims that Darwin was in any way cavalierly dismissive of sincere religious belief: "There is no evidence that man was aboriginally endowed with the ennobling belief in the existence of an Omnipotent God. . . . The question is of course wholly distinct from the higher one, whether there exists a Creator and Ruler of the universe; and this has been answered in the affirmative by the highest intellects that have ever lived" (65). Whether or not this passage was merely an attempt (among others) to appease the biblical literalists of his day, the graciousness and generosity of spirit it conveys is still worthy of emulation.

One example of Charles Darwin's essentially humanistic character is provided at the beginning of the second chapter of his *Voyage of the Beagle*. The young explorer's abhorrence of the institution of slavery was well known. In this second chapter, the budding naturalist recalls a visit to the site of a routing of runaway slaves outside of Rio de Janeiro: "This spot is notorious from having been, for a long time, the residence of some runaway slaves . . . At length they were discovered, and a party of soldiers being sent, the whole were seized with the exception of one old woman, who, sooner than again be led into slavery, dashed herself to pieces from the summit of a mountain. In a Roman matron this would have been called the noble love of freedom: in a poor negress it is mere brutal obstinacy" (16).

Humility and a warmth of feeling for humanity are Darwinian legacies that one might hope to see perpetuated, along with his love of intellectual honesty and his unending pursuit of empirical knowledge of our world.

WORKS CITED

Bender, Bert. *The Descent of Love: Darwin and the Theory of Sexual Selection in American Fiction 1871–1926*. Philadelphia: U of Pennsylvania P, 1998.

Carroll, Joseph. *Literary Darwinism: Evolution, Human Nature and Literature*. London: Routledge, 2004.

Darwin, Charles. *The Descent of Man, and Selection in Relation to Sex*. 1871. Princeton: Princeton UP, 1981.

———. *The Origin of Species by Means of Natural Selection, or the Preservation of Favored Races in the Struggle for Life*. 1859. New York: Modern Library, 1977.

———. *The Voyage of the Beagle*. 1839. Walter Sullivan, Ed. New York: Penguin, 1988.

Dissanayake, Ellen. *Homo Aestheticus: Where Art Comes From and Why*. Seattle: U of Washington P, 1992.

Fromm, Harold. "The New Darwinism in the Humanities," Parts 1 and 2. *The Hudson Review* 56 (2003). <http://www.hudsonreview.com/frommSpSu03.html>.

Glendening, John. *The Evolutionary Imagination in Late-Victorian Novels, An Entangled Bank*. Hampshire, UK: Ashgate, 2008.

Gottschall, Jonathan, and David Sloan Wilson, eds. *The Literary Animal: Evolution and the Nature of Narrative*. Evanston: Northwestern UP, 2005.

Mayr, Ernst. *One Long Argument, Charles Darwin and the Genesis of Modern Evolutionary Thought*. Cambridge: Harvard UP, 1991.

———. *What Evolution Is*. New York: Basic Books, 2001,

Nietzsche, Friedrich. *Beyond Good and Evil*. Trans. Walter Kaufmann. New York: Random House, 1966.

Turner, Mark. *The Literary Mind: The Origins of Thought and Language*. New York: Oxford UP, 1996.

Index

(Page numbers in italics represent illustrations)